# Why Do You Need This New Edition?

If you're wondering why you should buy this new edition of *Exploring Language*, here are five good reasons!

- A *new* chapter on **Language and the Brain** explores how language may influence how we think and view the world.

- A *new* cluster of readings on **the future of print media** includes a look at the long-term viability of newspapers.

- In addition, the most popular and frequently-taught chapters from the twelfth edition have been updated with **almost 30 new readings** because fresh voices and diverse viewpoints keep your class relevant and interesting.

- A *new* discussion of **analyzing visuals** with specific advice about advertisements and editorial cartoons.

- Each chapter features **new and updated visuals**, including editorial cartoons in each chapter selected to stimulate class discussion on current issues.

**PEARSON**

# Exploring LANGUAGE

# Exploring **LANGUAGE**

## THIRTEENTH EDITION

*Gary Goshgarian*

NORTHEASTERN UNIVERSITY

Boston  Columbus  Indianapolis  New York  San Francisco  Upper Saddle River
Amsterdam  Cape Town  Dubai  London  Madrid  Milan  Munich  Paris  Montreal  Toronto
Delhi  Mexico City  São Paulo  Sydney  Hong Kong  Seoul  Singapore  Taipei  Tokyo

Executive Editor: Suzanne Phelps Chambers
Development Editor: Anne Leung
Senior Marketing Manager: Sandra McGuire
Production Manager: S.S. Kulig
Project Coordination, Text Design, and Electronic Page Makeup: PreMediaGlobal
Cover Design Manager: Wendy Ann Fredericks
Cover Designer: Kay Petronio
Cover Art: Jasper Johns © VAGA, NY. *False start*, 1959. Photo © Erich Lessing/
    Art Resource, NY
Senior Manufacturing Buyer: Dennis J. Para
Printer/Binder: R.R. Donnelley and Sons
Cover Printer: R.R. Donnelley and Sons

Credits and acknowledgments borrowed from other sources and reproduced, with permission, in this textbook appear on pages 529–533.

**Library of Congress Cataloging-in-Publication Data**

Exploring language / Gary Goshgarian.—13th ed.
    p. cm.
Includes index.
ISBN 978-0-205-17286-3
1. Language and languages.    2. English language—United States.
I. Goshgarian, Gary.
P107.E93 2011
808'.0427—dc23

                                                    2011021281

10 9 8 7 6 5 4 3 2 1—DOC—14 13 12 11

www.pearsonhighered.com

ISBN-13: 978-0-205-17286-3
ISBN-10: 0-205-17286-5

# Contents

speaking less and less like each other? Does Hispanic immigration threaten the English language? Is our exposure to national media wiping out regional differences and causing us all to speak the same? Is the language really in serious decline?"

### Everyone Has an Accent but Me    138
*John Esling*

"The fact is that everyone has an accent. Accent defines and communicates who we are . . . [it is] the map that listeners perceive through their ears rather than their eyes . . . "

### Good English and Bad    143
*Bill Bryson*

"Considerations of what makes for good English or bad English are to an uncomfortably large extent matters of prejudice and conditioning."

### Why Good English Is Good for You    152
*John Simon*

"The person who does not respect words and their proper relationships cannot have much respect for ideas—very possibly cannot have ideas at all."

### Why the U.S. Needs an Official Language    161
*Mauro E. Mujica*

"Parents around the world know that English is the global language and that their children need to learn it to succeed. English is the language of business, higher education, diplomacy, aviation, the Internet, science, popular music, entertainment, and international travel. All signs point to its continued acceptance across the planet."

## ENGLISH AS A GLOBAL LANGUAGE    166

### Why a Global Language?    166
*David Crystal*

" 'English is the global language.' A headline of this kind must have appeared in a thousand newspapers and magazines in recent years. For what does it mean, exactly? Is it saying that everyone in the world speaks English? This is certainly not true. Is it saying, then, that every country in the world recognizes English as an official language? This is not true either. So what does it mean to say that a language is a global language?"

### ▌Exploring the Language of Visuals: English and Globish (cartoon)    177

### What Global Language?    178
*Barbara Wallraff*

"English is not sweeping all before it, not even in the United States. According to the U.S. Bureau of the Census, ten years ago about one in seven people in this country spoke a language other than English at home—and since then the proportion of immigrants in the population has grown and grown."

### English as a Global Language: A Good Thing or a Bad Thing?    189
*Keith Redfern*

"In certain areas of study, English has become accepted as the common language of choice. In all areas of medicine for example, our local doctors, dentists, surgeons and other specialists in France, all understand English and most medical journals are published in English. In the skies, air traffic controllers speak English to each other. In many major international sports, English is the common language of choice. And that is the important phrase to use in this context—*language of choice*."

### Lost in America    191
*Douglas McGray*

"For all the changes globalization has brought to the average American kid's cultural and commercial ecosystem, the average classroom has lagged far behind. As a result, young Americans represent something of a paradox: surrounded by foreign languages, cultures, and goods, they remain hopelessly uninformed, and misinformed, about the world beyond U.S. borders."

## 4  Technology and Language    201

### MAKING CONNECTIONS IN A MODERN WORLD    203

### In the Beginning Was the Word    203
*Christine Rosen*

"Screen technologies such as the cell phone and laptop computer that are supposedly revolutionizing reading also potentially offer us greater control over our time. In practice, however, they have increased our anxiety about having too little of it by making us available anytime and anywhere."

### Is PowerPoint the Devil?    209
*Julia Keller*

"In less than a decade, [PowerPoint] has revolutionized the worlds of business, education, science and communications, swiftly becoming the standard for just about anybody who wants to explain just about anything to just about anybody else."

### ▌Exploring the Language of Visuals: Lincoln's Gettysburg Address— A PowerPoint Presentation    218

### The Making of the *Gettysburg PowerPoint Presentation*    222
*Peter Norvig*

An Internet guru explains how Abe Lincoln might have used PowerPoint when delivering the visionary oratory at Gettysburg.

### Blogging in the Global Lunchroom    225
*Geoffrey Nunberg*

"Taken as a whole, in fact, the blogging world sounds a lot less like a public meeting than the lunchtime chatter in a high-school cafeteria, complete with snarky comments about the kids at the tables across the room. (Bloggers didn't invent the word snarky, but they've had a lot to do with turning it into the metrosexual equivalent of bitchy. On the Web, blogs account for more than three times as large a share of the total occurrences of snarky as of the occurrences of irony.)"

"Despite the widespread belief that women talk more than men, most of the available evidence suggests just the opposite. Why is the reality so different from the myth?"

"More nonsense has been produced on the subject of sex differences than on any linguistic topic, with the possible exception of spelling."

"The idea that men and women 'speak different languages' has itself become a dogma, treated not as a hypothesis to be investigated or as a claim to be adjudicated, but as an unquestioned article of faith. Our faith in it is misplaced."

"It is not that women lack the ability to prioritize informaiton, it is that they don't think life is as simple as men do."

"There is a special intensity to the mother-daughter relationship because talk—particularly talk about personal topics—plays a larger and more complex role in girls' and women's social lives than in boys' and men's. For girls and women, talk is the glue that holds a relationship together—and the explosive that can blow it apart."

"Throughout the world, people use nonverbal cues to facilitate self-expression. To a great extent, however, the culture of a people modifies their use of such cues. Even when different cultures use the same nonverbal cues, their members may not give the cues the same meaning."

"Here is a scene with which we are all familiar: Alex says or does something that Bob interprets as an insult or an attack. Bob retaliates in words or action. Alex, having meant no harm in the first place, now sees Bob's actions or words as an unprovoked attack. The situation can quickly escalate even though there was no real reason for a fight to begin in the first place. What has happened here is not a failure to communicate, but a failure to understand communication."

# 8 Political Wordplay   425

# Preface

I think that instructors who have used earlier editions of *Exploring Language* will agree that the 13th edition is, by far, the best to date. This revision still provides a wide and diverse range of engaging and informative readings connected to language issues. And it still aims to embrace changes in how we approach critical reading and writing in modern college classrooms.

Based on reviewer feedback, we kept the best readings from the previous edition. Yet over a third of the selections here are new, most written since the last edition was published. This revision also features a new section on language and the brain. Other sections have been updated to reflect current events, such as the power of political speech, the influence of technology on the written and spoken word, and the future of print media. We also have new views on advertising and how it influences our consumer desires. The book also continues to explore enduring issues: how men and women still struggle to understand each other; how politicians are blasted for reducing intricate social issues to sound bites; how we still engage in First Amendment debates over freedom of speech.

In spite of the many revisions, the original character and objective of *Exploring Language* remain the same: to bring together exciting and readable pieces that explore the various ways language and American society are interconnected. Once again, the aim is to lead students to a keener understanding of how language works: how it reconstructs the real world for us and how it can be used to lead, mislead, and manipulate us.

Organized around nine major language areas, these selections demonstrate the subtle complexities and richness of English. They also invite students to debate current social and cultural issues that are inseparable from language. And they serve as models for composition, representing a diversity of expository techniques, such as narration, illustration, definition, process analysis, argumentation, persuasion, and comparison and contrast, and a diversity of genres, such as editorial essays, personal narratives, opinion columns, position papers, letters, memoirs, autobiographical musings, personal diaries, academic articles, humorous satires, and interviews.

## New to This Edition

- **New chapters and readings.** Of late, considerable attention in linguistic circles has been given to the connections between the language we speak and how we think and view the world. Reflecting some of the fascinating findings is a new chapter (Chapter 9), "Language and the Brain." Here we explore the fascinating relationships between language and cultural viewpoints as well as the influence of technology on our how we think.

This edition also includes a look at the viability of print media (Chapter 7). When news and information is readily found for free on the Internet, can newspapers survive? In an age of Kindles and Nooks, what is the future of the printed book?

• An expanded "Analyzing Visuals" section aims to help students understand the language of visuals, and how visual information can influence us. Every day, pictures "speak" to us through commercials, billboards, and print ads. Students must be able to critically assess the multiple messages that visually vie for their attention.

## A Wide Variety of Genres

In addition to updating a significant portion of the readings, this edition reflects the wide range of expository modes and genres to which students are exposed. Included here are examples of personal narratives, objective reportage, newspaper opinion columns, position papers, various political arguments, editorials, op-ed essays, letters to the editor, autobiographical musings, descriptive narratives, academic articles, pointed arguments, and even memoirs. This edition also includes several historical pieces and great speeches that influenced our culture and society.

## A Focus on Critical Inquiry and Critical Reading

The premise of *Exploring Language* is that good writing grows out of good thinking, and good thinking grows out of good reading. Therefore, the text includes an introduction, "Thinking and Reading Critically," expanded for this edition, where we discuss what critical thinking and critical reading are, how to do each with step-by-step guidelines, and how each helps readers become better writers. The introduction illustrates the process in a detailed sample analysis of an essay addressing the preservation of linguistic diversity. Besides addressing an issue that should appeal to students, the analysis also gives them the tools to analyze the vast array of other language-based readings that follow.

## Updated "Making Connections" Exercises

At the end of each chapter, "Making Connections" exercises provide several special writing and research questions that ask students to connect essays within chapter subthemes, the entire chapter, or even to other parts of the book. Many questions encourage Web-based research and direct students to additional online resources.

## Apparatus

All of the remaining apparatus in the book has been improved and updated to create penetrating and stimulating assignments. Each selection is preceded by a headnote containing useful thematic and biographical information, as well as clues to writing strategies. Each is followed by a series of review questions, "Thinking Critically," covering both thematic and rhetorical strategies as well as engaging writing assignments and other exercises.

## Visuals

Recognizing the importance of visual communication, the 13th edition of *Exploring Language* includes updated visuals. In addition to the nine photographic chapter openers, we have added cartoons, print ads, comic strips, posters, sign language charts, photographs, and more. Following each visual are "Thinking Critically" questions, directing students to analyze the "language" of the images—the messages and commentary projected from the designs and layouts. Each chapter includes an editorial cartoon designed to connect to a current issue as well as the chapter's theme.

## Instructor's Manual

The *Instructor's Manual,* which is available to adopters, includes suggested responses to selected questions in the text. The *Instructor's Manual* also identifies questions that are particularly good for in-class discussion or collaborative student work and provides recommendations for additional online research.

## Acknowledgments

Many people behind the scenes are, at the very least, deserving of thanks and acknowledgment for their help with this 13th edition. It is impossible to thank all of them, but there are some for whose help I am particularly grateful. I would like, first, to thank those instructors who answered lengthy questionnaires on the effectiveness of the essays and supplied many helpful comments and suggestions: Wendy Crawford, Camden County College; Miriam Gershow, University of Oregon; Philip Hu, Cerritos College; Martin W. Sharp, Rowan University; Judith Stanley, Alverno College; Lori White, Los Angeles Pierce College. To all the instructors and students who have used *Exploring Language* over the past 12 editions, I am very grateful.

A very special thanks to Kathryn Goodfellow for her enormous assistance in locating material, writing the apparatus, and putting together the *Instructor's Manual* under tight deadlines. My thanks also to Amy Trumbull for her help in securing permissions for the text. Finally to the people of Longman publishers, especially my editor Suzanne Phelps Chambers and her assistant Laney Whitt, and my developmental editor Anne Leung, thank you for your continuing support, understanding, and enthusiasm throughout the production process of this edition.

—*Gary Goshgarian*

# Introduction:
# Thinking and Reading Critically

## What Is Critical Thinking?

Whenever you read a magazine article, newspaper editorial, or a piece of advertising and find yourself questioning the claims of the authors, you are exercising the basics of critical thinking. Instead of taking what you read at face value, you look beneath the surface of words and think about their meaning and significance. And you ask the authors questions such as:

- What did you mean by that?
- Can you back up that statement?
- How do you define that term?
- How did you draw that conclusion?
- Do all the experts agree?
- Is this evidence dated?
- So what?
- What is your point?
- Why do we need to know this?

You make statements such as:

- That's not true.
- You're contradicting yourself.
- I see your point, but I don't agree.
- That's not a good choice of words.
- You're jumping to conclusions.
- Good point. I never thought of that.
- That was nicely stated.
- This is an extreme view.

Whether conscious or unconscious, such responses indicate that you are thinking *critically* about what you read. You weigh claims, ask for definitions, evaluate information, look for proof, question assumptions, and make judgments. In short, you process another person's words, instead of just mindlessly scanning them.

## Why Read Critically?

When you read critically, you think critically. And that means instead of simply accepting what is written on a page, you separate yourself from the text and decide for yourself what is or is not important or logical or right. And you do so because you bring to your reading your own perspective, experience, education, and personal values, as well as your powers of comprehension and analysis.

Critical reading is an active process of discovery. You discover an author's view on a subject; you enter a dialogue with the author; you discover the strengths and weaknesses of the author's thesis or argument; and you decide if you agree or disagree with the author's views. The end result is that you have a better understanding of the issue and the author. By asking questions of the author and analyzing where the author stands with respect to other experiences or views on the issue—including your own—you actively enter a dialogue or a debate. You seek out the truth on your own instead of accepting at face value what somebody else says.

In reality, that is how truth and meaning are achieved: through interplay. Experience teaches us that knowledge and truth are not static entities but are the by-products of struggle and dialogue—of asking tough questions. We witness this phenomenon all the time, re-created in the media through dialogue and conflict. We have recognized it over the years as a force of social change. Consider, for example, how our culture has changed its attitudes with regard to race and its concepts of success, kinship, social groups, and class since the 1950s. Perhaps the most obvious example regards gender: were it not for people questioning old rigid conventions, most women would still be bound to the laundry and the kitchen stove.

The point is that critical reading is an active and reactive process—one that sharpens your focus on a subject and your ability to absorb information and ideas while encouraging you to question accepted norms, views, and myths. And that is both healthy and laudable, for it is the basis of social evolution.

Critical reading also helps you become a better writer, because critical reading is the first step to critical writing. Good writers look at another's writing the way a carpenter looks at a house: they study the fine details and how those details connect and create the whole. Likewise, they consider the particular slants and strategies of appeal. Good writers always have a clear sense of their audience— their readers' racial makeup, gender, and educational background; their political and/or religious persuasions; their values, prejudices, and assumptions about life; and so forth. Knowing one's audience helps writers determine nearly every aspect of the writing process: the kind of language to use; the writing style (casual or formal, humorous or serious, technical or philosophical); the particular slant to take (appealing to the readers' reason, emotions, ethics, or a combination of these); what emphasis to give the essay; the type of evidence to offer; and the kinds of authorities to cite.

It is the same with critical reading. The better you become at analyzing and reacting to another's written work, the better you will analyze and react to your own. You will ask yourself: Is my analysis logical? Do my points come across clearly? Are my examples solid enough? Is this the best wording? Is my conclusion persuasive? Do I have a clear sense of my audience? What appeal strategy did I take—to logic, emotions, or ethics? In short, critical reading will help you to evaluate your own writing, thereby making you both a better reader and a better writer.

While you may already employ many strategies of critical reading, here are some techniques to make you an even better critical reader.

## How to Read Critically

To help you read critically, use these six proven basic steps:

- Keep a journal on what you read.
- Annotate what you read.
- Outline what you read.
- Summarize what you read.
- Question what you read.
- Analyze what you read.

To demonstrate just how these techniques work, let us apply them to a sample essay. Reprinted here is the essay "Let Them Die" by Kenan Malik, published in *Prospect* magazine, in November 2000. I chose this piece because, like all selections in this book, it addresses an interesting contemporary language issue, because it is accessible, and because the author raises some provocative questions about current linguistic campaigns to preserve vanishing languages, languages such as Eyak, spoken by only one living human being, rapidly disappearing, because the last speaker herself is dying.

1      There are around 6,000 languages in the world today. Shortly there will be one less. Eighty-one-year-old Marie Smith Jones is the last living speaker of Eyak, an Alaskan language. When she dies, so will her language. Over the past few decades a huge number of languages have died in this fashion. When Ned Madrell died on the Isle of Man in 1974, he also took the ancient Manx language to the grave. The death in 1992 of Tefvic Escenc, a farmer from the Turkish village of Haci Osman, killed off Ubykh, a language once spoken in the northern Caucasus. Laura died in 1990, the last speaker of a Native American tongue, Wappo. Six years later another Native American language, Catawba, passed away with the death of Carlos Westez, more popularly known as Red Thunder.

2      At least half of the world's 6,000 languages are expected to disappear over the next century; some pessimists suggest that by the year 3000 just 600 languages will be left. According to the American Summer Institute of Linguistics, there are 51 languages with only one speaker left—28 of them in Australia alone. A further 500 languages are spoken by fewer than 100 speakers, and another 1,500 by fewer than 1,000 speakers. Most will be lucky to survive the next decade. Such accelerated disappearance has galvanized into action an increasingly vocal campaign to preserve "linguistic diversity." In an obituary to Carlos Westez, the writer Peter Popham warned that "when a language dies" we lose "the possibility of a unique way of perceiving and describing the world." Despairing of the "impact of a homogenizing monoculture upon our way of life," Popham worried about the "spread of English carried by American culture, delivered by Japanese technology and the hegemony of a few great transnational languages: Chinese,

Spanish, Russian, Hindi." The linguist David Crystal echoed these sentiments in a *Prospect* essay last year. "We should care about dying languages," he argued, "for the same reason that we care when a species of animal or plant dies. It reduces the diversity of our planet."

3    Now a new book, *Vanishing Voices,* by the anthropologist Daniel Nettle and linguist Suzanne Romaine, links the campaign to preserve languages to the campaign for fundamental human rights, and for the protection of minority groups, in the face of what they regard as aggressive globalization and cultural imperialism. "Linguistic diversity," they argue, "is a benchmark of cultural diversity." Language death "is symptomatic of cultural death: a way of life disappears with the death of a language." "Every people," Nettle and Romaine conclude, "has a right to their own language, to preserve it as a cultural resource, and to transmit it to their children."

4    Campaigners for linguistic diversity portray themselves as liberal defenders of minority rights, protecting the vulnerable against the nasty forces of global capitalism. Beneath the surface rhetoric, however, their campaign has much more in common with reactionary, backward-looking visions, such as William Hague's campaign to "save the pound" as a unique expression of British identity, or Roger Scruton's paean to a lost Englishness. All seek to preserve the unpreservable, and all are possessed of an impossibly nostalgic view of what constitutes a culture or a "way of life."

5    The whole point of a language is to enable communication. As the renowned Mexican historian and translator Miguel Leon-Portilla has put it, "In order to survive, a language must have a function." A language spoken by one person, or even a few hundred, is not a language at all. It is a private conceit, like a child's secret code. It is, of course, enriching to learn other languages and delve into other cultures. But it is enriching not because different languages and cultures are unique, but because making contact across barriers of language and culture allows us to expand our own horizons and become more universal in our outlook.

6    In bemoaning "cultural homogenization," campaigners for linguistic diversity fail to understand what makes a culture dynamic and responsive. It is not the fracturing of the world with as many different tongues as possible; it is rather the overcoming of barriers to social interaction. The more universally we can communicate, the more dynamic our cultures will be, because the more they will be open to new ways of thinking and doing. It is not being parochial to believe that were more people to speak English—or Chinese, Spanish, Russian, or Hindi—the better it would be. The real chauvinists are surely those who warn darkly of the spread of "American culture" and "Japanese technology."

7    At the core of the preservers' argument is the belief that a particular language is linked to a particular way of life and a particular vision of the world. "Each language has its own window on the world," write Nettle and Romaine. "Every language is a living museum, a monument to every culture it has been vehicle to." It's an idea that derives from nineteenth century Romantic notions of cultural difference. "Each nation speaks in the manner it thinks," wrote the German critic and poet Johann Gottfried von Herder, "and thinks in the manner it speaks." For Herder, the

nature of a people was expressed through its *volksgeist*—the unchanging spirit of a people. Language was particularly crucial to the delineation of a people, because "in it dwell the entire world of tradition, history, religion, principles of existence; its whole heart and soul."

8   The human capacity for language certainly shapes our ways of thinking. But particular languages almost certainly do not. Most linguists have long since given up on the idea that people's perceptions of the world, and the kinds of concepts they hold, is constrained by the particular language they speak. The idea that French speakers view the world differently from English speakers, because they speak French, is clearly absurd. It is even more absurd to imagine that all French speakers have a common view of the world, thanks to a common language.

9   But if the Romantic idea of language has little influence, the Romantic idea of human differences certainly does. The belief that different peoples have unique ways of understanding the world became, in the nineteenth century, the basis of a racial view of the world. Herder's *volksgeist* developed into the notion of racial makeup, an unchanging substance, the foundation of all physical appearance and mental potential, and the basis for division and difference within humankind. Today, biological notions of racial difference have fallen into disfavor, largely as a result of the experience of Nazism and the Holocaust. But while racial science has been discredited, racial thinking has not. It has simply been re-expressed in cultural rather than biological terms. Cultural pluralism has refashioned the idea of race for the post-Holocaust world, with its claim that diversity is good in itself and that humanity can be parceled up into discrete groups, each with its own particular way of life, mode of expression, and unique "window upon the world."

10   The contemporary argument for the preservation of linguistic diversity, liberally framed though it may be, draws on the same philosophy that gave rise to ideas of racial difference. That is why the arguments of Popham, Crystal, Nettle, and Romaine, on this issue if not on anything else, would have found favor with the late Enoch Powell. "Every society, every nation is unique," he wrote. "It has its own past, its own story, its own memories, its own ways, its own languages or ways of speaking, its own—dare I use the word—culture." Language preservers may be acting on the best of intentions, but they are treading on dangerous ground, and they carry with them some unpalatable fellow-travellers.

11   The linguistic campaigners' debt to Romanticism has left them, like most multiculturalists, with a thoroughly confused notion of rights. When Nettle and Romaine suggest, in *Vanishing Voices,* that "the right of people to exist, to practice and produce their own language and culture, should be inalienable," they are conflating two kinds of rights—individual rights and group rights. An individual certainly has the right to speak whatever language he or she wants, and to engage in whatever cultural practices they wish to in private. But it is not incumbent on anyone to listen to them, nor to provide resources for the preservation of either their language or their culture. The reason that Eyak will soon be extinct is not because Marie Smith Jones has been denied her rights, but because no one else wants to, or is capable of, speaking the language. This might be tragic for Marie

Smith Jones—and frustrating for professional linguists—but it is not a question of rights. Neither a culture, nor a way of life, nor yet a language, has a God-given "right to exist."

12      Language campaigners also confuse political oppression and the loss of cultural identity. Some groups—such as Turkish Kurds—are banned from using their language as part of a wider campaign by the Turkish state to deny Kurds their rights. But most languages die out, not because they are suppressed, but because native speakers yearn for a better life. Speaking a language such as English, French, or Spanish, and discarding traditional habits, can open up new worlds and is often a ticket to modernity. But it is modernity itself of which Nettle and Romaine disapprove. They want the peoples of the Third World, and minority groups in the West, to follow "local ways of life" and pursue "traditional knowledge" rather than receive a "Western education." This is tantamount to saying that such people should live a marginal life, excluded from the modern mainstream to which the rest of us belong. There is nothing noble or authentic about local ways of life; they are often simply degrading and backbreaking. "Nobody can suppose that it is not more beneficial for a Breton or a Basque to be a member of the French nationality, admitted on equal terms to all the privileges of French citizenship . . . than to sulk on his own rocks, without participation or interest in the general movement of the world." So wrote John Stuart Mill more than a century ago. It would have astonished him that in the twenty-first century there are those who think that sulking on your own rock is a state worth preserving.

13      What if half the world's languages are on the verge of extinction? Let them die in peace.

## Keep a Journal on What You Read

Unlike writing an essay or a paper, keeping a journal is a personal exploration in which you develop your own ideas without set rules. It is a process of recording impressions and exploring feelings and ideas. It is an opportunity to write without restrictions and without judgment. You do not have to worry about breaking the rules—because in a journal, anything goes.

Reserve a special notebook just for your journal—not one that you use for class notes or homework. Also, date your entries and include the titles of the articles to which you are responding. Eventually, by the end of the semester, you should have a substantial number of pages to review so you can see how your ideas and writing style have developed over time.

What do you include in your journal? Although it may serve as a means to understanding an essay you are assigned, you are not required to write only about the essay itself. Perhaps the piece reminds you of something in your personal experience. Maybe it triggered an opinion you did not know you had. Or perhaps it prompted you to explore a particular phrase or idea presented by the author.

Some students may find keeping a journal difficult because it is so personal. They may feel as if they are exposing their feelings too much. Or they may feel uncomfortable thinking that someone else—a teacher or another student—may read their writing. But such apprehensions shouldn't prevent you, or any other students, from exploring your impressions and feelings. Just do not share anything highly personal with your teachers or classmates. You may even consider keeping two journals—one for class and one for personal use.

Reprinted here is one student's journal entry on our sample essay, "Let Them Die," by Kenan Malik:

> When I read the title of this piece, "Let Them Die," I thought I was about to read an article dealing with euthanasia. Of human beings that is. Of course the piece deals with linguistic rather than human death. The opening paragraph was so dramatic that I was immediately drawn in as I heard of the imminent demise of so many languages. My gut reaction was "Sure, we should protect these languages." It would be such a cultural loss if any ancient language were allowed to simply vanish and along with it the history, lifestyle and values of a people. But Kenan really made me think. He made me see how what he called "the romantic idea of language" could really mask backward thinking. Encouraging certain people of minority cultures whether in the Third World or the West to stick to their old language and traditions in reality might relegate them to a primitive lifestyle and deny them access to modern life through education and new technologies. Is that really fair? Just because linguists think they should continue speaking their dying language? I have to think about this more.

## Annotate What You Read

It is a good idea to underline (or highlight) key passages and make marginal notes when reading an essay. (If you do not own the publication in which the essay appears, or choose not to mark it up, it is a good idea to make a photocopy of the piece and annotate that.) I recommend annotating on the second or third reading, once you have gotten a handle on the essay's general ideas.

There are no specific guidelines for annotation. Use whatever technique suits you best, but keep in mind that in annotating a piece of writing, you are engaging in a dialogue with the author. As in any meaningful dialogue, you may hear things you may not have known, things that may be interesting and exciting to you, things that you may agree or disagree with, or things that give you cause to ponder. The other side of the dialogue, of course, is your response. In annotating a piece of writing, that response takes the form of underlining (or highlighting) key passages and jotting down comments in the margin. Such comments can take the form of full sentences or some shorthand codes. Sometimes "Why?" or "True" or "NO!" will be enough to help you respond to a writer's position or claim. If you come across a word or reference that is unfamiliar to you, underline or circle it. Once you have located the main thesis statement or claim, highlight or underline it and jot down "Claim" or "Thesis" in the margin.

Below is the Malik essay reproduced in its entirety with sample annotations.

1    There are around 6,000 languages in the world today. Shortly there will be one less. Eighty-one-year-old Marie Smith Jones is the last living speaker of Eyak, an Alaskan language. When she dies, so will her language. Over the past few decades a huge number of languages have died in this fashion. When Ned Madrell died on the Isle of Man in 1974, he also took the ancient Manx language to the grave. The death in 1992 of Tefvic Escenc, a farmer from the Turkish village of Haci Osman, killed off Ubykh, a language once spoken in the northern Caucasus. Laura Somersal died in 1990, the last speaker of a Native American tongue, Wappo. Six years later another Native American language, Catawba, passed away with the death of Carlos Westez, more popularly known as Red Thunder.

2    At least half of the world's 6,000 languages are expected to disappear over the next century; some pessimists suggest that by the year 3000 just 600 languages will be left. According to the American Summer Institute of Linguistics, there are 51 languages with only one speaker left—28 of them in Australia alone. A further 500 languages are spoken by fewer than 100 speakers, and another 1,500 by fewer than 1,000 speakers. Most will be lucky to survive the next decade. Such accelerated disappearance has galvanized into action an increasingly vocal campaign to preserve "linguistic diversity." In an obituary to Carlos Westez, the writer Peter Popham warned that "when a language dies" we lose "the possibility of a unique way of perceiving and describing the world." Despairing of the "impact of a homogenizing monoculture upon our way of life," Popham worried about the "spread of English carried by American culture, delivered by Japanese technology and the hegemony of a few great transnational languages: Chinese, Spanish, Russian, Hindi." The linguist David Crystal echoed these sentiments in a *Prospect* essay last year. "We should care about dying languages," he argued, "for the

*Effective use of statistics*

*Labels movement*

same reason that we care when a species of animal or plant dies. It reduces the diversity of our planet."

3     Now a new book, *Vanishing Voices,* by the anthropologist Daniel Nettle and linguist Suzanne Romaine, links the campaign to preserve languages to the campaign for fundamental human rights, and for the protection of minority groups, in the face of what they regard as aggressive globalisation and cultural imperialism. "Linguistic diversity," they argue, "is a benchmark of cultural diversity." <u>Language death "is symptomatic of cultural death: a way of life disappears with the death of a language.</u>" "Every people," Nettle and Romaine conclude, "has a right to their own language, to preserve it as a cultural resource, and to transmit it to their children."

*assume these are experts in field*

*Credible generalization?*

4     Campaigners for linguistic diversity portray themselves as liberal defenders of minority rights, protecting the <u>vulnerable</u> against the <u>nasty forces of global capitalism</u>. Beneath the surface rhetoric, however, their campaign has much more in common with reactionary, backward-looking visions, such as <u>William Hague's campaign to "save the pound"</u> as a unique expression of British identity, or Roger Scruton's paean to a lost Englishness. All seek to preserve the unpreservable, and all are possessed of an impossibly nostalgic view of what constitutes a culture or a "way of life."

*Sarcastic tone*

*Look up these campaigns*

*main idea*

5     <u>The whole point of a language is to enable communication.</u> As the renowned Mexican historian and translator Miguel Leon-Portilla has put it, "In order to survive, a language must have a function." A language spoken by one person, or even a few hundred, is not a language at all. <u>It is a private conceit, like a child's secret code.</u> It is, of course, enriching to learn other languages and delve into other cultures. But it is enriching not because different languages and cultures are unique, but because making contact across barriers of language and culture allows us to expand our own horizons and become more universal in our outlook.

*key claim*

*author's bias?*

6     In bemoaning "cultural homogenization," campaigners for linguistic diversity fail to understand what makes a culture dynamic and responsive. It is not the fracturing of the world with as many different tongues as possible; it is rather the overcoming of barriers to social interaction. The more universally

we can communicate, the more dynamic our cultures will be, because the more they will be open to new ways of thinking and doing. It is not being parochial to believe that were more people to speak English—or Chinese, Spanish, Russian or Hindi—the better it would be. The real chauvinists are surely those who warn darkly of the spread of "American culture" and "Japanese technology."

*Malik's underlying assumption*

7    At the core of the preservers' argument is the belief that a particular language is linked to a particular way of life and a particular vision of the world. "Each language has its own window on the world," write Nettle and Romaine. "Every language is a living museum, a monument to every culture it has been vehicle to." It's an idea that derives from nineteenth century Romantic notions of cultural difference. "Each nation speaks in the manner it thinks," wrote the German critic and poet Johann Gottfried von Herder, "and thinks in the manner it speaks." For Herder, the nature of a people was expressed through its *volksgeist*—the unchanging spirit of a people. Language was particularly crucial to the delineation of a people, because "in it dwell the entire world of tradition, history, religion, principles of existence; its whole heart and soul."

*Again cites those he disagree with*

*Look up von Herder*

8    The human capacity for language certainly shapes our ways of thinking. But particular languages almost certainly do not. Most linguists have long since given up on the idea that people's perceptions of the world, and the kinds of concepts they hold, is constrained by the particular language they speak. The idea that French speakers view the world differently from English speakers, because they speak French, is clearly absurd. It is even more absurd to imagine that all French speakers have a common view of the world, thanks to a common language.

*good distinction*

*Do all linguists agree here?*

9    But if the Romantic idea of language has little influence, the Romantic idea of human differences certainly does. The belief that different peoples have unique ways of understanding the world became, in the nineteenth century, the basis of a racial view of the world. Herder's *volksgeist* developed into the notion of racial makeup, an unchanging substance, the foundation of all physical appearance and mental

potential, and the basis for division and difference within humankind. Today, biological notions of racial difference have fallen into disfavor, largely as a result of the experience of Nazism and the Holocaust. But while racial science has been discredited, racial thinking has not. It has simply been re-expressed in cultural rather than biological terms. Cultural pluralism has refashioned the idea of race for the post-Holocaust world, with its claim that diversity is good in itself and that humanity can be parceled up into discrete groups, each with its own particular way of life, mode of expression, and unique "window upon the world." }

*Main idea*

10      The contemporary argument for the preservation of linguistic diversity, liberally framed though it may be, draws on the same philosophy that gave rise to ideas of racial difference. That is why the arguments of Popham, Crystal, Nettle, and Romaine, on this issue if not on anything else, would have found favor with the late Enoch Powell. "Every society, every nation is unique," he wrote. "It has its own past, its own story, its own memories, its own ways, its own languages or ways of speaking, its own—dare I use the word—culture." Language preservers may be acting on the best of intentions, but they are treading on dangerous ground, and they carry with them some unpalatable fellow-travellers.

*I never made this connection*

11      The linguistic campaigners' debt to Romanticism has left them, like most multiculturalists, with a thoroughly confused notion of rights. When Nettle and Romaine suggest, in *Vanishing Voices,* that "the right of people to exist, to practice and produce their own language and culture, should be inalienable," they are conflating two kinds of rights—individual rights and group rights. An individual certainly has the right to speak whatever language he or she wants, and to engage in whatever cultural practices they wish to in private. But it is not incumbent on anyone to listen to them, nor to provide resources for the preservation of either their language or their culture. The reason that Eyak will soon be extinct is not because Marie Smith Jones has been denied her rights, but because no one else wants to, or is capable of, speaking the language. This might be tragic for Marie Smith Jones—and frustrating for professional linguists—but it is not a question of

*again dismissive tone*

*Good distinction*

rights. <u>Neither a culture, nor a way of life, nor yet a language, has a God-given "right to exist."</u>

*underlying assumption*

12      Language campaigners also confuse political oppression and the loss of cultural identity. Some groups—such as Turkish Kurds—are banned from using their language as part of a wider campaign by the Turkish state to deny Kurds their rights.

*Not clearly explained*

But most languages die out, not because they are suppressed, but because native speakers yearn for a better life. Speaking a language such as English, French, or Spanish, and discarding traditional habits, can open up new worlds and is often a ticket to modernity. But it is modernity itself of which Nettle and Romaine disapprove. They want the peoples of the Third World, and minority groups in the West, to follow "local ways of life" and pursue "traditional knowledge" rather than receive a "Western education." This is tantamount to saying that such people should live a marginal life, excluded from the modern mainstream to which the rest of us belong. There is nothing noble or authentic about local ways of life; they are often simply degrading and backbreaking.

*Very persuasive*

"Nobody can suppose that it is not more beneficial for a Breton or a Basque to be a member of the French nationality, admitted on equal terms to all the privileges of French citizenship . . . than to sulk on his own rocks, without participation or interest in the general movement of the world." So wrote John Stuart Mill more than a century ago. It would have astonished him that in the twenty-first century there are those who think that sulking on your own rock is a state worth preserving.

13      What if half the world's languages are on the verge of extinction? Let them die in peace.

*memorable conclusion*

## Outline What You Read

Briefly outlining an essay is a good way to see how writers structure their ideas. When you physically diagram the thesis statement, claims, and the supporting evidence, you can better assess the quality of the writing and decide how convincing it is. You may already be familiar with detailed, formal essay outlines in which structure is broken down into main ideas and subsections. However, a brief and concise breakdown of an essay's components provides a basic outline. Simply jot down a one-sentence summary of each paragraph. Sometimes brief paragraphs elaborating the same point can be lumped together:

- Point 1
- Point 2
- Point 3
- Point 4
- Point 5
- Point 6, etc.

Even though such outlines may seem rather primitive, they demonstrate at a glance how the various parts of an essay are connected—that is, the organization and sequence of ideas.

Below is a sentence outline of "Let Them Die":

Point 1: Many ancient languages will die as their last living speakers pass on.

Point 2: It is anticipated that over the next century, half of the world's 6,000 languages will disappear and with them the possibilities of understanding the world in a unique way.

Point 3: Some anthropologists argue that to preserve a language is essential to preserving human rights. If a language dies, according to some anthropologists, a culture and the way of life of a people also dies.

Point 4: Supporters of linguistic diversity claim they protect minority groups from cultural imperialism. But Malik claims that, in fact, their vision is backward-looking and seeks to preserve the unpreservable.

Point 5: Since language is meant to enable communication, says Malik, a language spoken by one person or just a few is not really a language. Rather, it is like a private code or child's game.

Point 6: Cultural homogenization by which fewer languages are spoken by greater numbers of people is actually a good thing, Malik thinks, as it enhances communication and thereby produces more dynamic cultures.

Point 7: In paragraphs 7 and 8, Malik rejects the idea that a particular language means that the thinking of the people who speak it is actually shaped by the language. Rather he says language allows us to speak but does not shape the views and values that we hold.

Point 8: Malik points out that romanticizing human differences and claiming
that different groups of people think and feel differently than other groups of
people depending on the language they speak is similar to the notions of racial
differences held by the Nazis. Racial stereotyping is simply being replaced by
cultural stereotyping.

Point 9: Those who argue for the preservation of linguistic diversity have good
intentions but are "treading on dangerous ground."

Point 10: Contrary to linguistic campaigners, Malik argues no culture or
language has a God-given right to exist. Although individuals have the right to
choose to speak a language, no one is obligated to listen to them or is obligated to
see that the language is preserved.

Point 11: Some linguists who argue that peoples of the Third World and
minority groups in the West should follow traditional ways of life are actually
relegating these people to a marginal life, excluded from modern society and its
benefits.

Point 12: Malik says, let those languages on the verge of extinction die.

At this point, you should have a fairly good grasp of the author's stand on the
issue. Now let us analyze Malik's essay in its parts and as a whole.

## Summarize What You Read

Summarizing is perhaps the most important technique to develop for understanding and evaluating what you read. This means boiling the essay down to its main
points. In your journal or notebook, try to write a brief (about 100 words) synopsis
of the reading in your own words. Note the claim or thesis of the discussion (or argument) and the chief supporting points. It is important to write these points down,
rather than to highlight them passively with a pen or pencil, because the act of jotting down a summary helps you absorb the argument.

Now let us return to our sample essay. The following brief paragraph is a student summary of Malik's essay. To avoid plagiarism, the author's words are para-
phrased, not copied. At times, it may be impossible to avoid using the author's own
words in a summary, but if you do, remember to use quotation marks.

Kenan Malik's article addresses the problem of what to do about vanishing

languages. He rejects the arguments of linguistic preservationists. Preservationists

argue that when a language dies, a culture dies and that modern globalization is eradicating ancient traditions and values that have a fundamental right to continue to exist. Malik argues that the loss of language is a natural, irreversible progression. He further argues that, in fact, globalization and with it fewer languages shared by more people actually enhances communication and human well-being. Malik argues that by trying to force minority groups, whether they be in the Third World or in the West, to hang on to ancient languages spoken only by a few, linguistic preservationists are in fact relegating these people to a life devoid of the benefits of mainstream culture and, in a sense, freezing them in an outmoded culture.

Although this paragraph seems to do a fairly good job of summarizing Malik's essay, it is difficult to reduce an essay to a hundred words. So, do not be too discouraged when trying to summarize a reading on your own.

## Question What You Read

Although we break down critical reading into discrete steps, these steps will naturally overlap in the actual process. While reading the essay by Kenan Malik, you were simultaneously summarizing and evaluating Malik's points in your head, perhaps adding your own ideas or even arguing with him. If something strikes you as particularly interesting or insightful, make a mental note. Likewise, if something rubs you the wrong way, argue back. For beginning writers, a good strategy is to convert that automatic mental response into actual note taking.

In your journal (or, as suggested earlier, in the margins of the text), question and challenge the writer. Jot down any points in the essay that do not measure up to your expectations or personal views. Note anything you are skeptical about. Write down any questions you have about the claims, views, or evidence. If some point or conclusion seems forced or unfounded, record it and briefly explain why. The more skeptical and questioning you are, the better a reader you are. Likewise, note what features of the essay impressed you—outstanding points, interesting wording, clever or amusing phrases or allusions, particular references, the general structure of the piece. Record what you learn from the reading and what aspects of the issue you would like to explore.

Of course, you may not feel qualified to pass judgment on an author's views, especially if that author is a professional writer or an expert on a particular subject. Sometimes the issue discussed might be too technical, or you may not feel informed enough to make critical evaluations. Sometimes a personal narrative may focus on experiences completely alien to you. Nonetheless, you are an intelligent person with an instinct to determine if the writing impresses you or if an argument is sound, logical, and convincing. What you can do in such instances—and another good habit to get into—is think of other views on the issue. If you have read or heard of experiences different from the author's or arguments with opposing views, jot them down. Even if you have not, the essay should contain some inference or reference to alternate experiences or opposing views (if it is an argument) from which you could draw a counterposition.

Let us return to Malik's essay, which, technically, is an argument. Although it is theoretically possible to question or comment on every sentence in the piece, let us select a couple of key points that may have struck you as presumptuous, overstated, or inconsistent with your own experience.

Paragraphs 1–4: Malik spent the first four paragraphs of the essay summarizing the impending loss of languages and quoting the reactions of language preservationists, leading the reader to think this would be a pro-preservationist piece. It is a real attention-getter when Malik suddenly states, "All seek to preserve the unpreservable, and all are possessed of an impossibly nostalgic view of what constitutes a culture or a 'way of life.'" I had expected him to be sympathetic about the loss of language.

Paragraph 4: Malik's tone is dismissive when he refers to the attempts of campaigners for linguistic diversity to protect "the vulnerable against the nasty forces of global capitalism" and later compares the campaign with "reactionary, backward-looking visions, such as William Hague's campaign to 'save the pound.'" Will his sarcastic tone work for or against him? Gives him a superior air.

Paragraph 5: Malik makes preserving a disappearing language sound rather silly when he says, "A language spoken by one person, or even a few hundred, is not a language at all. It is a private conceit, like a child's secret code." I do not think I agree with that. Why would it not be a language if it enables communication?

Paragraph 8: Malik makes an interesting point when he says, "The idea that French speakers view the world differently from English speakers, because they speak French, is clearly absurd." But maybe you could argue that they in fact do see the world differently. Malik does not prove or disprove his statement. He just makes it.

Paragraph 10: I would like to hear the response of Popham, Crystal, Nettle, and Romaine to Malik's charge that their attitude to language preservation links them with biological notions of racial difference propagated by the Nazis. Is this not a stretch?

Paragraph 12: Malik seems to gloss over language suppression used as a tool to deny a group their rights as in the case of the Kurds and the Turks. Does this example not prove how powerful language is in terms of conveying a culture and a value system?

Paragraph 12: Hard to deny Malik's point in this paragraph about the benefits of modernization. His charge that Nettle and Romaine's views about language preservation are such that Third World peoples and minority groups in the West would live marginalized lives makes one stop and think. In linguistic preservationists' view, are we asking these people to live in a time capsule and let the 21st century pass them by?

## Analyze What You Read

To analyze something means breaking it down into its components, examining those components closely and evaluating their significance, and determining how they relate as a whole. In part, you already did this by briefly outlining the essay. But there is more, because analyzing what you read involves interpreting and evaluating the points of a discussion or argument as well as its presentation—that is, its language and structure. Ultimately, analyzing an essay after establishing its gist will help you understand what may not be evident at first. A closer examination of the author's words takes you beneath the surface and sharpens your understanding of the issue at hand.

Although there is no set procedure for analyzing a piece of prose, here are some specific questions you should raise when reading an essay, especially one that is trying to sway you to its view:

- What kind of audience is the author addressing?
- What are the author's assumptions about his audience?
- What are the author's purposes and intentions?
- How well does the author accomplish those purposes?
- How convincing is the evidence presented? Is it sufficient and specific? Relevant? Reliable? Current? Slanted?
- How good are the sources of the evidence used? Were they based on personal experience, scientific data, or outside authorities?
- Does the author address opposing views on the issue?
- Is the author persuasive in his or her perspective?

## What Kind of Audience Is Being Addressed?

Before the first word is written, a good writer considers the makeup of his or her audience—that is, its age group, gender, ethnic and racial makeup, educational background, and socioeconomic status. Also considered are the values, prejudices, and assumptions of the readers, as well as their political and religious persuasions. Some writers, including several in this book, write for a *target* audience—readers who share the same interests, opinions, and prejudices. For example, many of the essays in Chapter 9, "Political Wordplay," were written for people familiar with current events and issues. Other writers write for a *general* audience. Although general audiences consist of very different people with diversified backgrounds, expectations, and standards, think of them as the people who read *Time, Newsweek,* and your local newspaper; that is, people whose average age is 35, whose educational level is high school plus two years of college, who make up the vast middle class of America, who politically stand in the middle of the road, and whose racial and ethnic origins span the world. You can assume they are generally informed about what is going on in the country, that they have a good comprehension of language and a sense of humor, and that they are willing to listen to new ideas.

Kenan Malik's essay appeared in *Prospect,* a publication with a reputation as a highly intellectual magazine of current affairs and cultural debate. The publication describes its readership as mature, educated, affluent, and discerning. Many of the readers are professionally accomplished and intellectually curious. A closer look at Malik's essay tells us more:

- The language sounds like the essay is written for an educated audience with, most likely, a college education.

- The tone suggests that he is appealing to a conservative audience—people who might sympathize with Malik's idea that the attempt to preserve minority languages on the verge of extinction is a rather futile and fruitless endeavor.

- Malik makes references to and assumes his reader is, if not familiar with, at least interested in, the writings of linguists such as Suzanne Romaine, anthropologists such as Daniel Nettle, and historians such as Miguel Leon-Portilla. He also makes references to the German critic and poet Johann von Herder and to John Stuart Mill. He makes references to historical events such as the Holocaust, the oppression of Turkish Kurds today, and to the separatist movements past and present of the Bretons and the Basques. He expects his audience to know some world history.

- Malik addresses readers who would be interested in an argument calling for some knowledge of language, philosophy, as well as history.

## What Are the Author's Assumptions?

Having a sense of one's audience leads writers to certain assumptions. If a writer is writing to a general—but highly educated—audience, like Malik's, then he or she can assume a certain level of awareness about language and current events, certain values about education and morality, and certain nuances of an argument. After going through Malik's essay, we can see he makes some assumptions about his audience:

- The examples supporting the thesis assume an audience familiar with and concerned about current language debates, and 20th-century world history.

- When Malik says campaigners for linguistic diversity "portray themselves as liberal defenders of minority rights, protecting the vulnerable against the nasty forces of global capitalism," and when he later describes them as "bemoaning 'cultural homogenization,'" he assumes the audience is conservative and may believe that the push to preserve dying languages is naïve and out of touch with reality. He may also assume the audience shares his sometimes caustic sense of humor.

- The references to the writings of linguists, anthropologists, philosophers, and historic events such as the Holocaust, as well as to 19th-century Romantic notions of cultural differences, show that Malik assumes his audience is widely read and curious.

## What Are the Author's Purpose and Intentions?

A writer writes for a purpose beyond wanting to show up in print. Sometimes it is simply expressing how the writer feels about something; sometimes the intention is to convince others to see things in a different light; sometimes the purpose is to persuade readers to change their views or behavior. Of the Malik essay, it might be said that the author had the following intentions:

- To illustrate that, yes, many of the 6,000 languages spoken currently are on the verge of extinction.

- To argue that attempts to preserve dying languages in the name of linguistic diversity are futile and misguided.

- To impress upon the reader that the function of language most simply put is to communicate. Thus, the fewer languages spoken the more likely true communication can occur.

- To dispel the concept that the preservation of a particular language is an inalienable human right.

- To argue that if some languages are on the verge of extinction, "let them die in peace."

## How Well Does the Author Accomplish Those Purposes?

Determining how well an author accomplishes such purposes may seem subjective, but in reality it comes down to how well the case is presented. Is the thesis clear? Is it well laid out or argued? Are the examples sharp and convincing? Is the author's conclusion a logical result of what came before? Now let us return to Malik's essay:

- He paints a very clear picture of the reality that many languages are disappearing.

- He keeps to his point for most of his essay.

- He makes his major points in a style that is blunt, succinct, and often humorous.

- He cites quotations from books and articles of those he opposes to present their point of view.

- His opinions regarding language diversity are emphatically stated.

- He sometimes wanders into highly speculative territory. He points out similarities between the thinking of language campaigners and 19th-century Romantic notions about race. He then goes on to link the thinking of language campaigners to that of those responsible for the Holocaust. That is a sobering stretch.

## How Convincing Is the Evidence Presented? Is It Sufficient and Specific? Relevant? Reliable? Not Dated? Slanted?

Convincing writing depends on convincing evidence—that is, sufficient and relevant facts along with proper interpretations of facts. Facts are pieces of information that can be verified—such as statistics, examples, personal experience, expert testimony, and historical details. Proper interpretations of such facts must be logical and supported by relevant data. For instance, it is a fact that the SAT verbal scores in America slipped a few points in 2010. One interpretation might be that students are spending less time reading and more time on the Internet or watching TV than in the past. But without hard statistics documenting the viewing habits of a sample of students, that interpretation is shaky, the result of a writer jumping to conclusions.

*Is the Evidence Sufficient and Specific?* Writers use evidence on a routine basis, but sometimes it may not be sufficient. Sometimes the conclusions reached have too little evidence to be justified. Sometimes writers make hasty generalizations based solely on personal experience as evidence. How much evidence is enough? It is hard to say, but the more specific the details, the more convincing the argument. Instead of generalizations, good writers cite figures, dates, and facts; instead of paraphrases, they quote experts verbatim.

*Is the Evidence Relevant?* Good writers select evidence based on how well it supports the point being argued, not on how interesting, novel, or humorous it is. For instance, if you were arguing that Alex Rodriguez is the greatest living baseball player, you would not mention that he was born in New York City and was rumored in the press to have dated pop singer Madonna. Those are facts, but they have nothing to do with Rodriguez's athletic abilities. Irrelevant evidence distracts readers and weakens an argument.

***Is the Evidence Reliable? Not Dated?*** Evidence should not be so vague or dated that it fails to support one's claim. For instance, it would not be accurate to say that Candidate Jones fails to support the American worker because 15 years ago she purchased a foreign car. It is her current actions that are more important. Readers expect writers to be specific enough with data for them to verify. A writer supporting animal rights may cite cases of rabbits blinded in drug research, but such tests have been outlawed in the United States for many years. Another may point to medical research that appears to abuse human subjects, but not name the researchers, the place, or the year of such testing. Because readers may have no way of verifying evidence, suspicious claims will weaken an argument.

***Is the Evidence Slanted?*** Sometimes writers select evidence that supports their case while ignoring evidence that does not. Often referred to as "stacking the deck," this practice is unfair and potentially self-defeating for a writer. Although some evidence may have merit, an argument will be dismissed if readers discover that evidence was slanted or suppressed. For example, suppose you heard a classmate claim that he would never take a course with Professor Sanchez because she gives surprise quizzes, assigns 50 pages of reading a night, and does not grade on a curve. Even if these reasons are true, that may not be the whole truth. You might discover that Professor Sanchez is a dynamic and talented teacher whose classes are stimulating. Withholding that information may make an argument suspect. A better strategy is to acknowledge counterevidence and to confront it—that is, to strive for a balanced presentation by raising views and evidence that may not be supportive of your own.

## How Good Are the Sources of the Evidence Used? Were They Based on Personal Experience, Scientific Data, or Outside Authorities?

Writers enlist four basic kinds of evidence to support their views or arguments: personal experience (theirs and others'), outside authorities, factual references and examples, and statistics. In your own writing, you will be encouraged to use combinations of these.

*Personal testimony* should not be underestimated. Think of the books you have read or movies you have seen based on word-of-mouth recommendations. (Maybe even the school you are attending!) Personal testimony provides eyewitness accounts not available to you or readers—and sometimes eyewitness accounts are the most persuasive kind of evidence. Suppose you are writing about the rising alcohol abuse on college campuses. In addition to statistics and hard facts, quoting the experience of a first-year student who nearly died one night from alcohol poisoning would add dramatic impact. Although personal observations are useful and valuable, writers must not draw hasty conclusions from them. Because you and a couple of friends are in favor of replacing letter grades with a pass-fail system does not support the claim that the student body at your school is in favor of the conversion.

*Outside authorities* are people recognized as experts in a given field. The appeal to such authorities is a powerful tool in writing, especially for writers wanting to persuade readers of their views. We hear it all the time: "In a paper published in *Nature* magazine, scientists from MIT argued that . . . ," "Scholars inform us that . . . ," "According to his biographer, David Herbert Donald, Abraham Lincoln . . . ." Although experts try to be objective and fair-minded, sometimes their testimony is biased. You would not turn to scientists working for tobacco companies for unbiased opinions on lung cancer, for example.

*Factual references and examples* do as much to inform as to persuade. If somebody wants to sell you something, they will pour on the details. Think of the television commercials that show sport utility vehicles climbing rocky mountain roads while a narrator lists all the great standard features—permanent four-wheel drive, alloy wheels, second-generation airbags, power brakes, cruise control, and so on— or the cereal "infomercials" in which manufacturers explain how their new Yumm-Os now have 15 percent more fiber to help prevent cancer. Although readers may not have the expertise to determine which data are useful, they are often convinced by the sheer weight of the evidence—like courtroom juries judging a case.

*Statistics* impress people. Saying that 77 percent of your school's student body approves of women in military combat roles is much more persuasive than saying "a lot of people do." Why? Because statistics have a no-nonsense authority. Batting averages, polling results, economic indicators, medical and FBI statistics, demographic percentages—they are all reported in numbers. If accurate, they are hard to argue with, although they can be used to mislead. If somebody claims that 139 people on campus protested the appearance of a certain controversial speaker, it would be a distortion of the truth not to mention that another 1,500 attended the talk and gave the speaker a standing ovation. Likewise, the manufacturer that claims that its potato chips are 100 percent cholesterol free misleads the public, because no potato chips cooked in vegetable oil contain cholesterol—which is found only in animal fats. That is known as the "bandwagon" use of statistics—in other words, appealing to crowd-pleasing, healthy-eating awareness.

Now let's examine briefly Malik's sources of evidence:

- Malik uses statistics and personal experience very effectively in his opening paragraphs to establish the extent of language extinction.

- Malik uses common sense to persuasive effect when he defines the purpose of language—"The whole point of a language is to enable communication." To squelch the idea that the protection of fading languages is an inalienable human right, Malik uses the same blunt, commonsense approach, writing, "An individual certainly has the right to speak whatever language he or she wants. . . . But it is not incumbent on anyone to listen to them, nor to provide resources for the preservation of either their language or their culture."

- Malik cites and quotes directly from the works of those whose ideas he opposes.

- Malik risks losing his audience at times with a somewhat academic discussion of the similarities between the 19th-century Romantic idea of human differences and the campaign to preserve languages. He also links the idea that language identifies a people to some of the notions of racial differences responsible for the Holocaust.

- Malik evaluates the consequences of the recommendations of the "linguistic campaigners," as he calls them. He quotes their ideas that minority people and Third World people should follow "local ways of life" and "pursue traditional knowledge." He fires back, "This is tantamount to saying that such people should live a marginal life, excluded from the modern mainstream to which the rest of us belong."

## Did the Author Address Opposing Views on the Issue?

Many of the essays in this book will, in varying degrees, try to persuade you to agree with the author's position or argument. But, of course, any slant on a topic can have multiple points of view. In developing their ideas, good writers will anticipate different and opposing views. They will cite contrary opinions, maybe even evidence unsupportive of their own position. Not to do so leaves their own stand open to counterattack, as well as to claims of naïveté and ignorance. This is particularly damaging when arguing some controversial issue. Returning to the Malik essay:

- Malik establishes the opposing point of view by quoting extensively from books and articles written by linguists and anthropologists who are authorities in his field. He does not shy away from stating the points of view of those he disagrees with.

## Is the Author's Perspective Persuasive?

Style and content make for persuasive writing. Important points are how well a paper is composed—the organization, the logic, the quality of thought, the presentation of evidence, the use of language, the tone of discussion—and the details and evidence. Turning to Malik's essay, we might make the following observation:

- Malik is very persuasive in convincing his audience that language loss is a natural progression in the human experience. Rather than seeking to preserve dying languages, we should accept their loss as inevitable. Not only that, pressuring small minorities to hang on to their language actually hinders a people's progress by relegating them to a marginal lifestyle, outside the mainstream.

# Logical Fallacies—What They Are and How to Avoid Them

Sometimes writers make errors in logic. In fact, we have already pointed out a few of them. Such errors are called *logical fallacies,* a term derived from the Latin *fallere,* meaning "to deceive." Used unintentionally, these fallacies deceive writers into feeling that what they are saying is more persuasive than it really is. Even though an argument may be well developed and contain evidence, a fallacy creates a flaw in logic, thereby weakening the structure and persuasiveness.

Not all logical fallacies are unintentional. Sometimes a fallacy is deliberately employed—for example, when the writer's goal has more to do with persuading than arriving at the truth. Every day we are confronted with fallacies in commercials and advertisements. Likewise, every election year the airwaves are full of candidates' bloated claims and pronouncements rife with logical fallacies of all sorts.

Recognizing logical fallacies when they occur in a reading is an important step in critical thinking—assessing the effectiveness of the writer's argument. Following are some of the most common logical fallacies to look for.

## LOGICAL FALLACIES

**Ad Hominem Argument:** Attacks the opponent rather than the opponent's views.

*Of course she supports bilingual education. She's a bleeding-heart liberal.*

PROBLEM: Name-calling makes us question the writer's real motives or credibility.

**Ad Misericordium Argument (or so-called *pity appeal*):** Appeals to reader's emotions rather than reason.

*It makes no difference if he was guilty of Nazi war crimes. This man is 90 years old and in frail health, so he should not be made to stand trial.*

PROBLEM: Pity appeal feels like manipulation and distraction from the real issue.

**The Bandwagon Appeal:** Plays on our fears of being left out or different.

*Everybody knows he is the best candidate for the office.*

PROBLEM: We are asked to "get with it" without weighing the evidence.

**Begging the Question:** Assumes that something is a fact when it really has yet to be proven.

*That judge will probably go easy on that defendant because they are both women.*

PROBLEM: Assumes that because the judge is female she will be more compassionate to another female, which in itself assumes that women are more compassionate than men.

**Circular Reasoning:** Where the conclusion of an argument is hidden in the argument's premise.

*Steroids are dangerous because they ruin your health.*

PROBLEM: Steroids are dangerous because they are dangerous. Repetition of key terms or ideas is not evidence.

**False Analogy:** An analogy is a comparison. False analogies compare two things that seem alike but really are not.

*The 2001 attack on the World Trade Center was the Pearl Harbor of the 21st century.*

PROBLEM: Although the two have similarities, they are also very different events. For example, the attack on Pearl Harbor was a military attack on a naval base, while the attack on the World Trade Center was committed by terrorists on a civilian target.

**False Dilemma:** A claim or solution that presents only two extremes, when a possible or practical middle ground exists.

*I stumbled on my way up the aisle. My wedding was a disaster.*

PROBLEM: A single incident does not necessarily ruin the entire event. The rest of the wedding could have been quite satisfactory and enjoyable.

**Faulty Cause-and-Effect Reasoning:** (Also known as *post hoc, ergo propter hoc* reasoning, from the Latin "after this, therefore because of this.") Establishes a questionable cause-and-effect relationship between chronological events. It assumes that because one event happened before another, the first influenced the second.

*Every time Bill goes with me to Progressive Field, the Cleveland Indians lose.*

**PROBLEM:** Although the Indians lose whenever Bill joins you at Progressive Field, his presence does not cause the team to lose. It is just coincidence.

**Hasty Generalization:** A conclusion that is based on too little evidence, or reached when the evidence itself is too broad, not factual, or not substantiated.

*Television has caused a significant increase in violence and sexual promiscuity in America's youth.*

**PROBLEM:** This oversimplifies the relationship between television and violence and promiscuity in youth and discounts other factors that may be connected to the issue.

**Non Sequitur:** Draws a conclusion that does not follow logically from the premise or previous statement, leading to an error in deduction.

*Mrs. Marshall is a fabulous tennis player and knows how to dress with style. She comes from money.*

**PROBLEM:** The ability to play tennis or dress well has nothing to do with one's financial background.

**Red Herring:** A fact that is thrown into an argument in order to distract the reader from the real issue.

*Jennifer is not the sort of girl who shoplifts; she is on the girl's lacrosse team, the honor society, and she volunteers at the retirement home twice a month.*

**PROBLEM:** Simply because Jennifer is athletic, a good student, and a volunteer does not mean she is not capable of shoplifting.

**Slippery Slope:** Presumes one event will inevitably lead to a chain of other events that ends in a catastrophe—as one slip on a mountain will cause a climber to tumble down and bring with him or her all those in tow.

*Censorship of obscene material will spell the end of freedom of speech and freedom of the press.*

**PROBLEM:** This domino-effect reasoning is fallacious because it depends more on presumption than on hard evidence.

**Stacking the Deck:** Offers only the evidence that supports the premise while disregarding or withholding contrary evidence.

*Our Wonder Wieners all-beef hot dogs now contain 10 percent less fat.*

**PROBLEM:** Sounds like good news, but what the ad does not tell us is that Wonder Wieners still contain 30 percent fat.

# Exploring the Language of Visual Arguments

We have all heard the old saying, "A picture is worth a thousand words." In addition to many insightful and interesting articles on language, this edition of *Exploring Language* features even more visual arguments, editorial cartoons, and photographs to help illustrate the nonverbal ways we use and process language. We constantly react to nonverbal cues in our daily lives. Symbols, images, gestures, and graphics all communicate information instantly that we process as language.

Remember that most visual arguments, like written essays, are trying to convince you of something. Artists, photographers, advertisers, cartoonists, and designers approach their work with the same intentions that authors of written material do—they want to share a point of view, present an idea, inspire, or evoke a reaction. Think back to when you had your high school yearbook photo taken. The photographer didn't simply sit you down and start snapping pictures. More likely, the photographer told you how to sit, how to tilt your head, and where to gaze. You selected your clothing for the picture carefully and probably spent extra time on your hair that day. Lighting, shadow, and setting were also thoughtfully considered. You and your photographer crafted an image of how you wanted the world to see you— an image of importance because it would be forever recorded in your yearbook as well as distributed to family and friends as the remembrance of a milestone in your life. In effect, you were creating a visual argument. You may even apply this same type of energy when you post a new profile photo of yourself on Facebook—you are presenting a particular perspective to an audience—in this case, yourself.

While there are many different kinds of visual arguments, the most common ones take the form of artwork, advertisements, editorial cartoons, and news photos. These visual arguments often do not rely on an image alone to tell their story, although it is certainly possible for a thoughtfully designed visual argument to do so. More often, however, advertisements are accompanied by ad copy, editorial cartoons feature comments or statements, and news photos are placed near the stories they enhance.

# Analyzing Visual Arguments

Critical readers do not accept the author's point of view simply at face value. They consider the author's purpose and intent, audience, style, tone, and supporting evidence. You should apply these same analytical tools to "read" visual arguments effectively. As with written language, understanding the persuasive power of "visual language" requires a close examination and interpretation of the premise, claims, details, supporting evidence, and stylistic touches embedded in any visual piece. Ask yourself the following four questions when examining visual arguments:

- Who is the target audience?
- What are the claims made in the images?
- What shared history or cultural assumptions—or warrants—does the image make?
- What is the supporting evidence?

Considering these questions helps us to survey a visual piece critically and enables us to formulate reasoned assessments of its message and intent. For example, let's apply these questions to a famous painting by artist Norman Rockwell.

*Norman Rockwell,* Freedom of Speech, *1943*

## Norman Rockwell's *Freedom of Speech*

Norman Rockwell (1894–1978) was an artist whose work was featured on the covers of magazines, most notably *The Saturday Evening Post,* a publication he considered "the greatest show window in America." In 47 years, Rockwell contributed 321 paintings to the magazine and became an American icon.

On January 6, 1941, President Franklin Delano Roosevelt addressed Congress, delivering his famous "Four Freedoms" speech. Against the background of the Nazi domination of Europe and the Japanese oppression of China, Roosevelt described the four essential human freedoms—freedom of speech, freedom of worship, freedom from want, and freedom from fear. Viewing these freedoms as the fundamental basis on which our society was formed, Roosevelt called upon Americans to uphold these liberties at all costs. Two years later, Rockwell, inspired by Roosevelt's speech, created his famous series of paintings on these "Four Freedoms," reproduced in four consecutive issues of *The Saturday Evening Post*. So popular were the images that they were used by the U.S. government to sell war bonds, to inspire public support for the war effort, and to remind people of the ideals for which they were fighting. The paintings serve as an example of how art can sometimes extend into advertising.

Let's take a closer look at one of the four paintings, *Freedom of Speech,* on page 28. Before he took a brush to his canvas, Rockwell consciously or unconsciously asked himself some of the same questions writers do when they stare at a blank piece of paper while preparing to create a written argument. After determining that he would use the American small-town vehicle of democracy, the town meeting, as the means to express the theme of freedom of speech, he then painted his "argument."

**Who Is Rockwell's Audience?** *The Saturday Evening Post* was widely read in America in the 1930s and 1940s. Rockwell would have wanted his work to appeal to a wide audience—readers of the magazine. If we examine the people in the painting—presumably based on Rockwell's Arlington, Vermont, friends and neighbors—we can deduce the kind of audience the artist was hoping to touch: small-town citizens from a middle-income, working-class environment. Like the language of an argument written for a general audience, the figures represent what Rockwell considered all-American townsfolk.

The venue is a meetinghouse or town hall because people are sitting on benches. The figures represent a generational cross-section of men and women, from the elderly white-haired man to the left of the central standing figure to the young woman behind him. Style of dress reinforces the notion of class diversity, from the standing man in work clothes to the two men dressed in white shirts, ties, and suit jackets. The formality of the seated figures also opens audience identity to life beyond a small, rural community. That is, some of the men's formal attire and the woman in a stylish hat broaden the depiction to include white-collar urban America. While diversity in age and class is suggested, diversity of race is not. There are no Asians, African Americans, or other nonwhites in the scene. This exclusion might be a reflection of the times and, perhaps, the popular notion of what constituted small-town America 70 years ago. While such exclusion would be unacceptable today, it should be noted that in the years following this painting's completion, Rockwell used his considerable talent and fame to champion the civil rights struggle.

**What Is Rockwell's Claim?** It has been said that Norman Rockwell's paintings appeal to a dreamy-eyed American nostalgia and at the same time project a world where the simple acts of common folk express high American ideals. In this painting, we have one of the sacred liberties dramatized by a working-class man raised to the figure of a political spokesperson in the assembly of others. Clearly expressing his opinion as freely as anybody else, he becomes both the illustration and defender of the democratic principles of freedom and equality.

**What Are Rockwell's Assumptions?** As with written arguments, the success of a visual argument depends on whether the audience accepts the assumptions (the values, legal or moral principles, commonsense knowledge, or shared beliefs) projected in the image. One assumption underlying Rockwell's illustration is that freedom of speech is desirable for Americans regardless of gender, class, or position in society. We know this instantly from the facial expressions and body language of the figures in the canvas. For example, the face of the man standing seems more prominent because it is painted against a dark, blank background and is brighter than any others, immediately capturing our attention. His face tilts upward with a look of pride, lit as if by the inspiration of the ideals he represents—freedom of expression.

One might even see suggestions of divine inspiration on his face as it rises in the light and against the night-blackened window in the background. The lighting and man's posture are reminiscent of religious paintings of past centuries. Additionally, the man's body is angular and rough, while his facial characteristics strongly resemble those of a young Abraham Lincoln—which suggests a subtle fusion of the patriotic with the divine. The implied message is that freedom of speech is a divine right.

As for the surrounding audience, we take special note of the two men looking up at the speaker. The older man appears impressed and looks on with a warm smile of approval, while the other man on the right gazes up expectantly. In fact, the entire audience supports the standing man with reasonable, friendly, and respectful gazes. The speaker is "Everyman." And he has the support and respect of his community. Rockwell's audience, subscribers of *The Saturday Evening Post,* saw themselves in this image—an image that mirrored the values of honest, decent, middle America.

***What Is Rockwell's Supporting Evidence?*** The key supporting image in Rockwell's painting is the sharp contrast between the standing man and those sitting around him. Not only is he the only one on his feet, but he is the only working-class person clearly depicted. He stands out from the others in the room; and it is significant that they look up to him—a dramatic illustration of what it means to give the common person his or her say. Were the scene reversed—with the central figure formally dressed and those looking up approvingly attired in work clothes—we would have a completely different message: that is, a representative of the upper class perhaps "explaining" higher concepts to a less-educated people. The message would be all wrong. In the painting, class barriers are transcended as the "common man" has risen to speak his mind with a face full of conviction, while upper-class people look on in support. That's the American ideal in action.

Because this is a painting instead of a newspaper photograph, every detail is selected purposely and thus is open to interpretation. One such detail is the fold of papers sticking out of the man's jacket pocket. What might those papers represent? And what's the point of such a detail? What associations might we make with it? There are words printed on the paper, but we cannot read them, so we're left to speculate. The only other paper in the painting is in the hand of the man on the right. The words *report* and *town* are visible. We might conclude that the speaker's pocket contains the same pamphlet, perhaps a summary report of the evening's agenda or possibly a resolution to be voted on. Whatever the documentation, the man clearly doesn't need it; his remarks transcend whatever is on that paper. And here lies more evidence of Rockwell's claim and celebration of the unaided articulation of one man's views out of many—the essence of freedom of speech.

## Advertisements

Norman Rockwell sought to embody a concept through his art; as a result, his painting tries to prompt reflection and self-awareness. In other words, his artwork serves to open the mind to a new discovery or idea. Advertising also selects and crafts visual images. However, advertising has a different objective. Its goal is not to stimulate expansive and enlightened thought but to direct the viewer to a single basic response: Buy this product!

Images have clout, and none are so obvious or so craftily designed as those from the world of advertising. Advertising images are everywhere—television, newspapers, the Internet, magazines, the sides of buses, and highway billboards. Each year, companies collectively spend more than $150 billion on print ads and television commercials (more than the gross national product of many countries). Advertisements comprise at least a quarter of each television hour and form the bulk of most newspapers and magazines. Tapping into our most basic emotions, their appeal goes right to the quick of our fantasies: happiness, material wealth, eternal youth, social acceptance, sexual fulfillment, and power.

Like a written argument, every print ad or commercial has an audience and is developed using claims, assumptions, and evidence. Sometimes these elements are obvious; sometimes they are understated; sometimes they are implied. Ads may boast testimonials by average folk or celebrities or cite hard scientific evidence. And sometimes they simply manipulate our desire to be happy or socially accepted. But common to every ad and commercial, no matter what the medium, is the claim that you should buy this product.

Print ads are potentially complex mixtures of images, graphics, and text. So in analyzing an ad, you should be aware of the use of photography, the placement of the images, and the use of text, company logos, and other graphics such as illustrations, drawings, sidebar boxes, and so on. You should also keep in mind that every aspect of the image has been thought about and carefully designed. Let's take a look at how a recent magazine ad for Toyota uses some of these elements, including social appeal, the use of color and light, and setting, to convince us to buy the Toyota Prius hybrid car.

When analyzing a print ad, we should try to determine what first captures our attention. In the Toyota Prius ad on page 32, it is the bold, white outline of a car. The instant suggestion is a compact vehicle with a simple and streamlined design. The outline format barely intrudes upon our view of the beach scene; and, ironically, we're not even shown the actual vehicle the ad is selling. Second, we note a smiling, ethnically diverse couple. The man and woman are not in contact with one another but with the outline of the vehicle, suggesting that in their relationship they share positive interest in the car outline they are leaning on. Their attire is sporty and casual, and their smiles are relaxed and content. We wonder: Are they potential buyers? Did they design the car? Are they simply feeling good about what the car represents? But the small print at the bottom identifies them as "Toyota Associates," perhaps meaning that they had something to do with the design or production of the Prius.

The third component we notice is the beach itself. The soft lighting signals approaching dusk; the sand, dunes, sea, and sky are quiet, pristine, and undisturbed. We see a simple and unblemished image of nature. The fourth aspect we note is the text. The slogan, "WE SEE BEYOND CARS," is rendered in a large-font, bold print; the lower expository text is in a smaller font; and the last segment of the ad identifying the couple is smaller still. The last item our eye moves to is in the upper right-hand corner: Toyota and the URL: toyota.com/beyondcars.

TOYOTA
toyota.com/beyondcars

WE SEE BEYOND CARS.

WE SEE A GREENER TOMORROW. At Toyota, we believe that the best way to have an impact on the environment is to have as little impact as possible. It's why we have a zero emissions vision for our vehicles, not to mention a drive towards zero waste in all our plants. In fact, we spend $23 million every day researching future technologies. Can a car company help improve the environment? Why not? To us, it's all part of the big picture.

Pictured: Roxanna De Maria & Jesse Blanc, Toyota Associates
Toyota Prius, the world's first mass-produced hybrid

© 2009

One of the most striking aspects of this ad is how it doesn't look like other car ads. We are accustomed to images that show the actual vehicles—images that highlight particular features that manufacturers want consumers to associate with their cars: power, speed, ruggedness, luxury, handling, durability, and so forth. This ad defies those traditional approaches. Instead, we see a clean-cut twosome—who may or may not be romantically involved—leaning against the outline of a car we cannot see, though know it to be the Prius from the text. The message is that the Prius is an idea as much as it is a car. And driving this low-emissions vehicle isn't just about transportation; it's about being part of a movement that will preserve the environment. The pristine environment, which the Prius will protect, is what shines through in this ad. In short, the Prius is desirable because it is barely there.

***Who Is the Audience for the Toyota Prius Ad?*** The ad attracts viewers not unlike the young couple in the ad—young to middle-aged men and women who are technologically savvy, educated, and concerned about the environment. In fact, the ad assumes that protection of the environment takes precedence over a more polluting, powerful, gas-guzzling vehicle. The appeal is to individuals seeking an alternative to the typically over-engineered powerhouse machines. In its understated approach, the ad also assumes that viewers appreciate nuance and subtlety. In fact, the ad does not talk about the car. Instead, the ad talks about Toyota's mission to protect the environment. In so doing, it invites viewers to explore the relationship between the visuals and the text.

***What Is the Claim Toyota Is Making About the Prius?*** The claim of this ad is that if you want to save the environment from the fallout of fossil-fuel consumption, you should buy a Prius. Further, by purchasing one, you become part of a community of responsible, "with-it," and technologically savvy people. The ad claims in its slogan, "WE SEE BEYOND CARS." Combined with the minimalist outline of the Prius and the undisturbed beauty of the beach, that slogan suggests that there is something beyond cars that you the consumer are really interested in: preserving the beauty and purity of nature. Beyond advertising a car, the ad makes the claim that you can be part of a transcendent movement, the green movement, simply by purchasing a Prius and helping make the world a better place. The ad claims that Toyota is devoted to protecting the environment, in fact, announcing that it spends $23 million per day on research. Such a claim rebrands Toyota as not just a manufacturer of cars but as a key player in the preservation of the environment.

***What Is the Evidence to Support the Claim That the Prius Is a Good Car?*** The evidence for the desirability of the Toyota Prius is in the visual elements and the text. If one goes to the website toyota.com/beyondcars, one sees a minimalist visual argument in the same style as this ad which presents evidence about Toyota's presence in the U.S. car market, its research funding and Toyota car production, and sales.

***What Assumptions Does Toyota Make About the Audience?*** The creators of this ad made several assumptions about us, the audience: (1) that we are familiar with the traditional car ads that showcase their vehicles; (2) that a significant segment of the car-buying public is conscious of the environment and looking for ways to save it; (3) that a company associated with protecting the environment via hybrid cars is admirable; and (4) that the audience cares less about a vehicle's power, glamour, or speed and more about the environmental impact of the vehicle. In short, the ad assumes people are as interested in supporting a cause as they are in buying a car.

## Editorial Cartoons

Editorial cartoons have been a part of American life for over a century. They are a mainstay feature on the editorial pages in most newspapers—those pages reserved for columnists, contributing editors, and illustrators to present their views in words and pen and ink. An editorial cartoon—as opposed to a comic strip on the funny pages—is a powerful and compact form of communication that combines pen-and-ink drawings with dialogue balloons and captions. Editorial cartoons are not just visual jokes, but visual humor that comments on social or political issues while drawing on viewers' experience and knowledge.

The editorial cartoon is the story of a moment in the flow of familiar current events. The key words here are *moment* and *familiar*. Although a cartoon captures a split instant in time, it also implies what came before and, perhaps, what may happen next—either in the next moment or in some indefinite future. And usually the cartoon depicts a specific moment in time and reflects upon current events.

For a cartoon to be effective it must make the issue clear at a glance, and it must establish where it stands on the argument. To convey issues and figures at a glance, cartoonists resort to images that are instantly recognizable, that we don't have to work hard to grasp. Locales are determined by giveaway props: an airplane out the window suggests an airport; a cactus and cattle skull, a desert; an overstuffed armchair and TV, the standard living room. Likewise, human emotions are instantly conveyed: pleasure is a huge toothy grin; fury is steam blowing out of a figure's ears; love is two figures making goo-goo eyes with floating hearts overhead. People themselves may have exaggerated features to emphasize a point or emotion.

In his essay "What Is a Cartoon?," Mort Gerberg says that editorial cartoons rely on such visual clichés to convey their messages instantly. That is, they employ stock figures for their representation—images instantly recognizable from cultural stereotypes like the fat-cat tycoon, the mobster thug, and the sexy female movie star. These come to us in familiar outfits and props that give away their identities and professions. The cartoon judge has a black robe and gavel; the prisoner wears striped overalls and a ball and chain; the physician dons a smock and holds a stethoscope; the doomsayer is a scrawny, long-haired guy carrying a sign saying, "The end is near." These are visual clichés known by the culture at large, and we instantly recognize them.

The visual cliché may be what catches our eye in the editorial cartoon, but the message lies in what the cartoonist does with it. As Gerberg observes, "The message is in twisting it, in turning the cliché around." Throughout this book we have included editorial cartoons connected to the subject matter of each chapter. When reviewing these cartoons, analyze them with the four questions for analyzing visuals, and think carefully about what point of view each is trying to convey.

As you review the various visual presentations throughout the text, consider the ways symbolism, brand recognition, stereotyping, and cultural expectations contribute to how such illustrations communicate their ideas. Try to think abstractly, taking into account the many different levels of consciousness that visuals use to communicate. Consider also the way shading, lighting, and subject placement in the photos all converge to make a point. "Read" them as you would any text, as part of the overall purpose of this book to "explore language."

In the chapters that follow, you will discover more than one hundred different selections—both written and visual—that range widely across contemporary language matters and that we hope you will find exciting and thought-provoking.

Arranged thematically into ten chapters, the writings represent widely diverse language topics—from the evolution of English to tribal dialects and cybernetic slang; from the dangers of political gobbledygook to the pleasures of language that makes us laugh; from the way language shapes our brain to gender differences in language; from arguments for a global language to arguments for and against campus speech codes. Some of the topics will be familiar; others will be first-time exposure. Regardless of how these language issues touch your experience, critical thinking, critical reading, and critical writing will open you up to a deeper understanding of our language, our culture, and yourself as a vital member of that language community.

# 1  Breaking Silences

anguage is the basis of thought and the highest intellectual activity we practice. It is also the way we define ourselves—who we are as a species, as individuals, as a society, and as a culture. How we use language—our word choice, style of expression, tone—can convey much about our background, education, personality, even values. Likewise, the success of communication between individuals tells much about the health of a society and its culture. In many ways, we are our language. The readings in this section examine the origins and history of language and its importance to human culture and identity.

## Beginnings: The Evolution of Language

We begin this chapter with a look at some fundamental aspects of language—from a biblical exploration of how the world's many languages came to be, to how our brains are hardwired to construct grammar instinctively. The opening discussion of the famed ancient Tower of Babel gives the Bible's explanation for the diversity of language, and through three famous Renaissance paintings we see how artists interpreted this legendary story of the origins of the world's languages. Michael C. Corballis then presents his theory on the evolution of language from gesture to spoken words in "From Hand to Mouth." Linguist Susanne K. Langer discusses the uniquely human phenomenon of language symbolism. In "Language and Thought," she explores the relationship between word and thought and the difference between symbols and signs—differences that separate humans from the rest of the animal kingdom. Linguist Steven Pinker explores the connection between the way children learn language and the origins of language in "Horton Heared a Who!" Children's acquisition of language is further discussed by Ben Zimmer in "Chunking." Then Margalit Fox, in "Another Language for the Deaf," takes a close look at a new type of pictographic writing that crosses the boundaries of language itself. Her essay is followed by some examples of the remarkable form of communication called "SignWriting."

## Personal Recollections: Coming into Language

Language is such an intricate part of culture that we often lose sight of its power: how language leads and misleads us, how it educates and informs us, and how it shapes our perception of the world and even our personal identity. We may also take for granted how language empowers us and how it can forge understanding, break silences, and inspire action. In this section, we explore the ways we "come into language" and how it can be used to "break silences"—that is, how the power of language moves us as individuals, as social beings, and as leaders.

As individuals, we come to language in different ways, yet we share in the magic that opens the world to us and us to it. The next four essays explore how people from diverse backgrounds discovered the power of the word to shape the world and the self within it. In "Homemade Education," the influential black leader Malcolm X explains how as a young man he was possessed by words. He did not discover the power of words in a school library or the cozy confines of a bedroom, but in a prison cell, where he taught himself how to read and write, liberating his mind while his body was behind bars. "A Word for Everything" describes how the blind and deaf Helen Keller literally broke her silence when she discovered "the key to all language" and connected the concept of words to the things around her. Next, Christine Marín provides an equally dramatic account of her discovery of the power of language to shape one's identity in "Spanish Lessons." The final essay in this section, by Maxine Hong Kingston, the daughter of Chinese immigrants, describes her traumatizing introduction to the English language. The section ends with a visual exploration of the way preschool and early elementary school children learn the elements of language and writing through an exercise called "independent writing" in which they are encouraged to write unhindered by spelling and grammar rules.

# BEGINNINGS: THE EVOLUTION OF LANGUAGE

## Exploring the Language of **VISUALS**

### The Tower of Babel: Artistic Interpretations

The tale of the Tower of Babel provides an explanation of why there are so many different languages in the world. The historical Tower of Babel was probably a stepped pyramid known as a ziggurat with a temple to the Babylonian god Marduk at the top. Chapter 11 in the book of Genesis describes the building of the Tower of Babel to reach the heavens. At the time of its construction, the tale tells us, humans spoke only one language. Angered by humanity's arrogance, God confused their speech so that the builders each spoke a different language. As a result of this "confusion of tongues" (languages), work ceased, and the people were scattered about the face of the earth. The tower, various nonbiblical sources tell us, was destroyed by a great wind.

■ The Tower of Babel, 1587, by unknown artist, Kurpfalzisches Museum, Heidelberg

■ The Little Tower, mid-16th century, by Pieter Brueghel the Elder,
Museum Bojimans van Beuningen, Rotterdam

There are many other ancient stories about the origins of diverse languages
that are similar to the biblical tale. It does not mention the tower by name, but
the Qur'an has a story with similarities to the biblical story of the Tower of Babel,
although it is set during the time Moses was in Egypt. There is also a similar story
in Sumerian mythology, called "Enmerkar and the Lord of Aratta," in which two rival
gods, Enki and Enlil, as a result of their fighting, confuse the language of humans.

Historical linguistics has long wrestled with the idea of a single original language. Current scholarship points to a branching of languages from
a single Indo-European tongue. The main issue of dispute is *when* this
branching occurred and *why,* which in any case would have happened several thousand years before the biblical date of the fall of the Tower of Babel.

The following reading is from the book of Genesis, Chapter 11, verses
1–9, from the King James Version of the Bible.

Now the whole earth had one language and few words. And as men migrated from
the east, they found a plain in the land of Shinar and settled there. And they said
to one another, "Come, let us make bricks, and burn them thoroughly." And they
had brick for stone, and bitumen for mortar. Then they said, "Come, let us build
ourselves a city, and a tower with its top in the heavens, and let us make a name
for ourselves, lest we be scattered abroad upon the face of the whole earth." And
the Lord came down to see the city and the tower, which the sons of men had built.

■ Construction of the Tower of Babel, 16th century, by Hendrick III van Cleve, Kroller-Muller Museum, Otterio

And the Lord said, "Behold, they are one people, and they have all one language; and this is only the beginning of what they will do; and nothing that they propose to do will now be impossible for them. Come, let us go down, and there confuse their language, that they may not understand one another's speech." So the Lord scattered them abroad from there over the face of all the earth, and they left off building the city. Therefore its name was called Babel, because there the Lord confused the language of all the earth; and from there the Lord scattered them abroad over the face of all the earth. (Genesis 11:1-9)

### THINKING CRITICALLY

1. These three pictures were all painted during the 1500s by different Flemish artists. What similarities and differences do you see among the paintings?

2. What message, if any, do you think each artist was trying to convey with his interpretation of the Tower of Babel tale? Explain.

3. Do you think language began with a single tongue spoken by everyone, or did it evolve in different locations spoken by different groups of people? Explain your viewpoint.

# From Hand to Mouth
*Michael C. Corballis*

You have probably heard the phrase "actions speak louder than words." In this essay, linguist Michael C. Corballis explores the connection between gestures and spoken language. Human language, he conjectures, evolved from gestures—a form of sign language that predated spoken speech. Drawing on evidence from anthropology, animal behavior, neurology, anatomy, linguistics, and evolutionary psychology, Corballis describes a few of the reasons why he believes language probably developed from gestures to a signed language, punctuated with grunts and other vocalizations, which eventually developed into the spoken word. While his hypothesis is still the subject of debate, anyone who also "speaks with their hands" is likely to understand his logic.

Michael Corballis is a professor of psychology and a member of the Research Center for Cognitive Science at the University of Auckland, in Australia. He is the author of several books, including *The Lopsided Ape: The Evolution of the Generative Mind* (1993) and *From Hand to Mouth* (revised in 2003), from which this essay is excerpted. His work has appeared in *Science*, *Nature*, *Scientific American*, and *American Scientist*.

1 Imagine trying to teach a child to talk without using your hands or any other means of pointing or gesturing. The task would surely be impossible. There can be little doubt that bodily gestures are involved in the development of language, both in the individual and in the species. Yet, once the system is up and running, it can function entirely on vocalizations, as when two friends chat over the phone and create in each other's minds a world of events far removed from the actual sounds that emerge from their lips. My contention is that the vocal element emerged relatively late in hominid evolution. If the modern chimpanzee is to be our guide, the common ancestor of 5 or 6 million years ago would have been utterly incapable of a telephone conversation but would have been able to make voluntary movements of the hands and face that could at least serve as a platform upon which to build a language.

2 Evidence suggests that the vocal machinery necessary for autonomous speech developed quite recently in hominid evolution. Grammatical *language* may well have begun to emerge around 2 million years ago but would at first have been primarily gestural, though no doubt punctuated with grunts and other vocal cries that were at first largely involuntary and emotional. The complex adjustments necessary to produce speech as we know it today would have taken some time to evolve, and may not have been complete until some 170,000 years ago, or even later, when *Homo sapiens* emerged to grace, but more often disgrace, the planet. These adjustments may have been incomplete even in our close relatives the Neanderthals; arguably, it was this failure that contributed to their demise.

3 The question now is what were the selective pressures that led to the eventual dominance of speech? On the face of it, an acoustic medium seems a poor way to convey information about the world; not for nothing is it said that a picture is worth a thousand words. Moreover, we have seen that signed language has all the lexical and grammatical complexity of spoken language. Primate evolution is itself a

testimony to the primacy of the visual world. We share with monkeys a highly so-phisticated visual system, giving us three-dimensional information in color about the world around us, and an intricate system for exploring that world through movement and manipulation. Further, in a hunter-gatherer environment, where predators and prey are of major concern, there are surely advantages in silent communication since sound acts as a general alert. And yet we came to communicate about the world in a medium that in all primates except ourselves is primitive and stereotyped—and noisy.

4      Before we consider the pressures that may have favored vocalization over ges-tures, it bears repeating that the switch from hand to mouth was almost certainly not an abrupt one. In fact, manual gestures still feature prominently in language; even as fluent speakers gesture almost as much as they vocalize, and of course deaf commu-nities spontaneously develop signed languages. It has also been proposed that speech itself is in many respects better conceived as composed of gestures rather than se-quences of those elusive phantoms called phonemes. In this view, language evolved as a system of gestures based on movements of the hands, arms, and face, includ-ing movements of the mouth, lips, and tongue. It would not have been a big step to add voicing to the gestural repertoire, at first as mere grunts, but later articulated so that invisible gestures of the oral cavity could be rendered accessible, but to the ear rather than the eye. There may therefore have been a continuity from a language that was almost exclusively manual and facial, though perhaps punctuated by involuntary grunts, to one in which the vocal component has a much more extensive repertoire and is under voluntary control. The essential feature of modern expressive language is not that it is purely vocal, but rather that the vocal component can function autono-mously and provide the grammar as well as the meaning of linguistic communication.

5      What, then, are the advantages of a language that can operate autonomously through voice and ear, rather than hand and eye? Why speech?

## Advantages of Arbitrary Symbols

6  One possible advantage of vocal language is its arbitrariness. Except in rare cases of onomatopoeia, spoken words cannot be iconic, and they therefore offer scope for creat-ing symbols that distinguish between objects or actions that look alike or might other-wise be confusable. The names of similar animals, such as cats, lions, tigers, cheetahs, lynxes, and leopards, are all rather different. We may be confused as to which animal is which, but at least it is clear which one we are talking about. The shortening of words over time also makes communication more efficient, and some of us have been around long enough to see this happen: *television* has become *TV* or *telly*, *microphone* has been reduced to *mike* (or *mic*), and so on. The fact that more frequent words tend to be shorter than less frequent ones was noted by the American philologist George Kingsley Zipf, who related it to a principle of "least effort." So long as signs are based on iconic resemblance, the signer has little scope for these kinds of calibration.

7      It may well have been very important for hunter-gatherers to identify and name a great many similar fruits, plants, trees, animals, birds, and so on, and attempts at iconic representation would eventually only confuse. Jared Diamond observes that people living largely traditional lifestyles in New Guinea can name hundreds of

birds, animals, and plants, along with details about each of them. These people are illiterate, relying on word of mouth to pass on information, not only about potential foods, but also about how to survive dangers, such as crop failures, droughts, cyclones, and raids from other tribes. Diamond suggests that the main repository of accumulated information is the elderly. He points out that humans are unique among primates in that they can expect to live to a ripe old age, well beyond the age of child bearing (although perhaps it was not always so). A slowing down of senescence may well have been selected in evolution because the knowledge retained by the elderly enhanced the survival of their younger relatives. An elderly, knowledgeable granny may help us all live a little longer, and she can also look after the kids.

8      In the naming and transmission of such detailed information, iconic representation would almost certainly be inefficient; edible plants or berries could be confused with poisonous ones, and animals that attack confused with those that are benign. This is not to say that gestural signs could not do the trick. Manual signs readily become conventionalized and convey abstract information. Nevertheless, there may be some advantage to using spoken words, since they have virtually no iconic content to begin with, and so provide a ready-made system for abstraction.

9      I would be on dangerous ground, however, if I were to insist too strongly that speech is linguistically superior to signed language. After all, students at Gallaudet University seem pretty unrestricted in what they can learn; signed language apparently functions well right through to university level—and still requires students to learn lots of vocabulary from their suitably elderly professors. It is nevertheless true that many signs remain iconic, or at least partially so, and are therefore somewhat tethered with respect to modifications that might enhance clarity or efficiency of expression. But there may well be a trade-off here. Signed languages may be easier to learn than spoken ones, especially in the initial stages of acquisition, in which the child comes to understand the linking of objects and actions with their linguistic representations. But spoken languages, once acquired, may relay messages more accurately, since spoken words are better calibrated to minimize confusion. Even so, the iconic component is often important, and as I look over the quadrangle outside my office I see how freely the students there are embellishing their conversations with manual gestures.

## In the Dark

10  Another advantage of speech over gesture is obvious: we can use it in the dark! This enables us to communicate at night, which not only extends the time available for meaningful communications but may also have proven decisive in the competition for space and resources. We of the gentle species *Homo sapiens* have a legacy of invasion, having migrated out of Africa into territories inhabited by other hominins who migrated earlier. Perhaps it was the newfound ability to communicate vocally, without the need for a visual component, that enabled our forebearers to plan, and even carry out, invasions at night, and so vanquish the earlier migrants.

11      It is not only a question of being able to communicate at night. We can also speak to people when objects intervene and you can't see them, as when you yell to your friend in another room. All this has to do, of course, with the nature of sound itself, which travels equally well in the dark as in the light and wiggles its

way around obstacles. The wall between you and the base drummer next door may attenuate the sound but does not completely block it. Vision, on the other hand, depends on light reflected from an external source, such as the sun, and is therefore ineffective when no such source is available. And the light reflected from the surface of an object to your eye travels in rigidly straight lines, which means that it can provide detailed information about shape but is susceptible to occlusion and interference. In terms of the sheer ability to reach those with whom you are trying to communicate, words speak louder than actions.

## Listen to Me!

12  Speech does have one disadvantage, though: it is generally accessible to those around you and is therefore less convenient for sending confidential or secret messages or for planning an attack on enemies within earshot. To some extent, we can overcome this impediment by whispering. And sometimes, people resort to signing. But the general alerting function of sound also has its advantages. When Mark Antony cried, "Friends, Romans, countrymen, lend me your ears," he was trying to attract attention as well as deliver a message.

13  In the evolution of speech, the alerting component of language might have consisted at first simply of grunts that accompany gestures to give emphasis to specific actions or encourage reluctant offspring to attend while a parent lays down the law. It is also possible that nonvocal sounds accompanied gestural communication. Russell Gray has suggested to me that clicking one's fingers, as children often do when putting their hands up in class to answer a question, may be a sort of "missing link" between gestural and vocal language. I know of no evidence that chimpanzees or other nonhuman primates are able to click their fingers as humans can, although lip smacking, as observed in chimpanzees, may have played a similar role. Sounds may therefore have played a similar and largely alerting role in the early evolution of language, gradually assuming more prominence in conveying the message itself.

14  For humans, visual signals can only attract attention if they occur within a fairly restricted region of space, whereas the alerting power of sound is more or less independent of where its source is located relative to the listener. And sound is a better alerting medium in other respects as well. No amount of gesticulation will wake a sleeping person, whereas a loud yell will usually do the trick. The alerting power of sound no doubt explains why animals have evolved vocal signals for sending messages of alarm. Notwithstanding the peacock's tail or the parrot's gaudy plumage, even birds prefer to make noises to attract attention, whether in proclaiming territory or warning of danger. Visual signals are relatively inefficient because they may elude our gaze, and in any case we can shut them out by closing our eyes, as we do automatically when we sleep. Our ears, in contrast, remain open and vulnerable to auditory assault.

15  Speech has another, and subtler, attentional advantage. Manual gesture is much more demanding of attention, since you must keep your eyes fixed on the gesturer in order to extract her meaning, whereas speech can be understood regardless of where you are looking. There are a number of advantages in being able to communicate with people without having to look at them. You can effectively divide attention, using speech to communicate with a companion while visual attention is deployed elsewhere, perhaps to watch a football game or to engage in some joint

activity, like building a boat. Indeed, the separation of visual and auditory attention may have been critical in the development of pedagogy.

## Three Hands Better Than Two?

16 Another reason why vocal language may have arisen is that it provides an extra medium. We have already seen that most people gesture with their hands, and indeed their faces, while they talk. One might argue then, that the addition of a vocal channel provides additional texture and richness to the message.

17 But it is perhaps not simply a matter of being better. Susan Goldin-Meadow and David McNeill suggest that speech may have evolved because it allowed the vocal and manual components to serve different and complementary purposes. Speech is perfectly adequate to convey syntax, which has no iconic or mimetic aspect, and can relieve the hands and arms of this chore. The hands and arms are, of course, well adapted to providing the mimetic aspect of language, indicating in analogue fashion the shapes and sizes of things, or the direction of movement, as in the gesture that might accompany the statement "he went that-a-way." By allowing the voice to take over the grammatical component, the hands are given free rein, as it were, to provide the mimetic component.

18 But speech may have evolved, not because it gave the hands freer rein for mimetic expression, but rather because it freed the hands for other activities. Charles Darwin, who seems to have thought of almost everything, wrote, "We might have used our fingers as efficient instruments, for a person with practice can report to a deaf man every word of a speech rapidly delivered at a public meeting; but the loss of our hands, while thus employed, would have been a serious inconvenience." It would clearly be difficult to communicate manually while holding an infant, or driving a car, or carrying the shopping, yet we can and do talk while doing these things.

19 Speech also has the advantage over manual gesture in that it can be accomplished in parallel with manual demonstrations. Demonstrations might themselves be considered gestures, of course, but the more explanatory aspects of pedagogy, involving grammatical structure and symbolic content, would interfere with manual demonstration if they too were conveyed manually. Clearly, it is much easier and more informative to talk while demonstrating than to try to mix linguistic signs in with the demonstrations. This is illustrated by any good TV cooking show, where the chef is seldom at a loss for either words or ingredients. It may not be far-fetched to suppose that the selective advantages of vocal communication emerged when the hominins began to develop a more advanced tool technology, and they could eventually verbally explain what they were doing while they demonstrated tool-making techniques. Moreover, if vocal language did not become autonomous until the emergence of *Homo sapiens*, this might explain why tool manufacture did not really begin to develop true diversity and sophistication, and indeed to rival language itself in these respects, until within the last 100,000 years.

20 Thus, it was not the emergence of language itself that gave rise to the evolutionary explosion that has made our lives so different from our near relatives, the great apes. Rather, it was the invention of autonomous speech, freeing the hands for more sophisticated manufacture and allowing language to disengage from other manual activities, so that people could communicate while changing the baby's diaper, and even explain to a novice what they were doing. The idea that language

may have evolved relatively slowly . . . seems much more in accord with biological reality than the notion of a linguistic "big bang" within the past 200,000 years. Language and manufacture also allowed cultural transmission to become the dominant mode of inheritance in human life. That ungainly bird, the jumbo jet, could not have been created without hundreds, perhaps thousands, of years of cultural evolution, and the brains that created it were not biologically superior to the brains that existed 100,000 years ago in Africa. The invention of speech may have merely been the first of many developments that have put us not only on the map, but all over it.

## THINKING CRITICALLY

1. Corballis begins his essay by asking his readers to "imagine trying to teach a child to talk without using your hands, or any other means of pointing or gesturing." Why do you think he opens his piece with this scenario? How does it set up the argument that follows? Explain.

2. In paragraph 4, Corballis notes "manual gestures still feature prominently in language." What communication role do gestures play in language? Are gestures essential to communication? Are they the natural precursor to language? Why or why not?

3. Corballis's argument is that gestures preceded spoken language. Do you agree with his premise? Why or why not?

4. What advantages, according to Corballis, does spoken language have over gestured communication? List the examples he provides and evaluate the logic of each one.

5. What assumptions does Corballis make about his readers/audience in this essay in order for his argument to be effective? What objections, if any, could his readers raise against his theory of "from hand to mouth"?

## WRITING ASSIGNMENTS

1. Corballis notes that spoken language allows us to come up with many different words for similar things, especially things occurring in nature. Write a short essay applying this aspect of language in a more modern sense. What advantages does spoken language provide over gesture that is essential to our survival in the 21st century?

2. Corballis notes that he would be "on dangerous ground" if he were to insist that spoken language is linguistically superior to signed language (paragraph 9). What do you think? The signing skills of teachers at Gallaudet University (an undergraduate institution of higher learning for the deaf and hard-of-hearing) notwithstanding, could higher learning, or education in general, be possible without any spoken language as part of our human evolution? Why or why not? Write a short essay explaining your viewpoint, using examples from this essay and from outside research.

3. In paragraph 9, Corballis observes students outside his office "embellishing their conversations with manual gestures." Repeat this exercise on your own. Watch two or more friends engage in a conversation and note how often and in what ways they use their hands to enhance the discussion. Are they merely waving their hands, or unconsciously making more deliberate gestures? Would the conversation lose something—clarity, vibrancy, etc.—if the speakers did not gesture? Write an essay based on your observations on the connection between hand and mouth in communication.

# Language and Thought

*Susanne K. Langer*

> Language is the highest intellectual activity we practice. It is the way we define ourselves—who we are as a species, as a society, as a culture, and as individuals. It is the basis of thought because it contains the symbols of thought. How are thought and language connected? How do signs, which even some animals respond to, differ from the symbols that constitute language? The following essay by Susanne K. Langer answers these and many other questions about language and thought.
>
> Susanne Langer was one of the 20th century's most influential philosophers. A graduate of Radcliffe and Harvard, she is the author of *Philosophy in a New Key: A Study in the Symbolism of Reason, Rite and Art* (1942) and *Language and Myth* (1946). She died in 1985, a few years after completing the culmination of her life's work, the three-volume *Mind: An Essay on Human Feeling* (1982).

1   A symbol is not the same thing as a sign; that is a fact that psychologists and philosophers often overlook. All intelligent animals use signs; so do we. To them as well as to us sounds and smells and motions are signs of food, danger, the presence of other beings, or of rain or storm. Furthermore, some animals not only attend to signs but produce them for the benefit of others. Dogs bark at the door to be let in; rabbits thump to call each other; the cooing of doves and the growl of a wolf defending his kill are unequivocal signs of feelings and intentions to be reckoned with by other creatures.

2   We use signs just as animals do, though with considerably more elaboration. We stop at red lights and go on green; we answer calls and bells, watch the sky for coming storms, read trouble or promise or anger in each other's eyes. That is animal intelligence raised to the human level. Those of us who are dog lovers can probably all tell wonderful stories of how high our dogs have sometimes risen in the scale of clever sign interpretation and sign using.

3   A sign is anything that announces the existence or the imminence of some event, the presence of a thing or a person, or a change in the state of affairs. There are signs of the weather, signs of danger, signs of future good or evil, signs of what the past has been. In every case a sign is closely bound up with something to be noted or expected in experience. It is always a part of the situation to which it refers, though the reference may be remote in space and time. Insofar as we are led to note or expect the signified event we are making correct use of a sign. This is the essence of rational behavior, which animals show in varying degrees. It is entirely realistic, being closely bound up with the actual objective course of history—learned by experience, and cashed in or voided by further experience.

4   If man had kept to the straight and narrow path of sign using, he would be like the other animals, though perhaps a little brighter. He would not talk, but grunt and gesticulate the point. He would make his wishes known, give warnings, perhaps develop a social system like that of bees and ants, with such a wonderful efficiency of communal enterprise that all men would have plenty to eat, warm apartments—all exactly alike and perfectly convenient—to live in, and everybody could and would sit in the sun or by the fire, as the climate demanded, not talking but just basking, with every want

satisfied, most of his life. The young would romp and make love, the old would sleep, the middle-aged would do the routine work almost unconsciously and eat a great deal. But that would be the life of a social, superintelligent, purely sign-using animal.

5    To us who are human, it does not sound very glorious. We want to go places and do things, own all sorts of gadgets that we do not absolutely need, and when we sit down to take it easy we want to talk. Rights and property, social position, special talents and virtues, and above all our ideas, are what we live for. We have gone off on a tangent that takes us far away from the mere biological cycle that animal generations accomplish; and that is because we can use not only signs but also symbols.

6    A symbol differs from a sign in that it does not announce the presence of the object, the being, condition, or whatnot, which is its meaning, but merely *brings this thing to mind*. It is not a mere "substitute sign" to which we react as though it were the object itself. The fact is that our reaction to hearing a person's name is quite different from our reaction to the person himself. There are certain rare cases where a symbol stands directly for its meaning: in religious experience, for instance, the Host is not only a symbol but a Presence. But symbols in the ordinary sense are not mystic. They are the same sort of thing that ordinary signs are; only they do not call our attention to something necessarily present or to be physically dealt with—they call up merely a conception of the thing they "mean."

7    The difference between a sign and a symbol is, in brief, that a sign causes us to think or act *in the face* of the thing signified, whereas a symbol causes us to think *about* the thing symbolized. Therein lies the great importance of symbolism for human life, its power to make this life so different from any other animal biography that generations of men have found it incredible to suppose that they were of purely zoological origin. A sign is always embedded in reality, in a present that emerges from the actual past and stretches to the future; but a symbol may be divorced from reality altogether. It may refer to what is not the case, to a mere idea, a figment, a dream. It serves, therefore, to liberate thought from the immediate stimuli of a physically present world; and that liberation marks the essential difference between human and nonhuman mentality. Animals think, but they think *of* and *at* things; men think primarily *about* things. Words, pictures, and memory images are symbols that may be combined and varied in a thousand ways. The result is a symbolic structure whose meaning is a complex of all their respective meanings, and this kaleidoscope of *ideas* is the typical product of the human brain that we call the "stream of thought."

8    The process of transforming all direct experience into imagery or into that supreme mode of symbolic expression, language, has so completely taken possession of the human mind that it is not only a special talent but a dominant, organic need. All our sense impressions leave their traces in our memory not only as signs disposing our practical reactions in the future but also as symbols, images representing our *ideas* of things; and the tendency to manipulate ideas, to combine and abstract, mix, and extend them by playing with symbols, is man's outstanding characteristic. It seems to be what his brain most naturally and spontaneously does. Therefore his primitive mental function is not judging reality, but *dreaming his desires*.

9    Dreaming is apparently a basic function of human brains, for it is free and unexhausting like our metabolism, heartbeat, and breath. It is easier to dream than

not to dream, as it is easier to breathe than to refrain from breathing. The symbolic character of dreams is fairly well established.

10 Symbol mongering, on this ineffectual, uncritical level, seems to be instinctive, the fulfillment of an elementary need rather than the purposeful exercise of a high and difficult talent.

11 The special power of man's mind rests on the evolution of this special activity, not on any transcendently high development of animal intelligence. We are not immeasurably higher than other animals; we are different. We have a biological need and with it a biological gift that they do not share.

12 Because man has not only the ability but also the constant need of *conceiving* what has happened to him, what surrounds him, what is demanded of him—in short, of symbolizing nature, himself, and his hopes and fears—he has a constant and crying need of *expression*. What he cannot express, he cannot conceive; what he cannot conceive is chaos, and fills him with terror.

13 If we bear in mind this all-important craving for expression, we get a new picture of man's behavior; for from this trait spring his powers and his weaknesses. The process of symbolic transformation that all our experiences undergo is nothing more nor less than the process of *conception*, underlying the human faculties of abstraction and imagination.

14 When we are faced with a strange or difficult situation, we cannot react directly, as other creatures do, with flight, aggression, or any such simple instinctive pattern. Our whole reaction depends on how we manage to conceive the situation—whether we cast it in a definite dramatic form, whether we see it as a disaster, a challenge, a fulfillment of doom, or a fiat of the Divine Will. In words or dreamlike images, in artistic or religious or even in cynical form, we must *construe* the events of life. There is great virtue in the figure of speech, "I can *make* nothing of it," to express a failure to understand something. Thought and memory are processes of *making* the thought content and the memory image; the pattern of our ideas is given by the symbols through which we express them. And in the course of manipulating those symbols we inevitably distort the original experience, as we abstract certain features of it, embroider and reinforce those features with other ideas, until the conception we project on the screen of memory is quite different from anything in our real history.

15 Conception is a necessary and elementary process; what we do with our conceptions is another story. That is the entire history of human culture—of intelligence and morality, folly and superstition, ritual, language, and the arts—all the phenomena that set man apart from, and above, the rest of the animal kingdom. As the religious mind has to make all human history a drama of sin and salvation in order to define its own moral attitudes, so a scientist wrestles with the mere presentation of "the facts" before he can reason about them. The process of *envisaging* facts, values, hopes, and fears underlies our whole behavior pattern; and this process is reflected in the evolution of an extraordinary phenomenon found always, and only, in human societies—the phenomenon of language.

16 Language is the highest and most amazing achievement of the symbolistic human mind. The power it bestows is almost inestimable, for without it anything properly called "thought" is impossible. The birth of language is the dawn of humanity. The line between man and beast—between the highest ape and the

lowest savage—is the language line. Whether the primitive Neanderthal man was anthropoid or human depends less on his cranial capacity, his upright posture, or even his use of tools and fire, than on one issue we shall probably never be able to settle—whether or not he spoke.

17    In all physical traits and practical responses, such as skills and visual judgments, we can find a certain continuity between animal and human mentality. Sign using is an ever evolving, ever improving function throughout the whole animal kingdom, from the lowly worm that shrinks into his hole at the sound of an approaching foot, to the dog obeying his master's command, and even to the learned scientist who watches the movements of an index needle.

18    This continuity of the sign-using talent has led psychologists to the belief that language is evolved from the vocal expressions, grunts and coos and cries, whereby animals vent their feelings or signal their fellows; that man has elaborated this sort of communion to the point where it makes a perfect exchange of ideas possible.

19    I do not believe that this doctrine of the origin of language is correct. The essence of language is symbolic, not signific; we use it first and most vitally to formulate and hold ideas in our own minds. Conception, not social control, is its first and foremost benefit.

20    Watch a young child that is just learning to speak play with a toy; he says the name of the object, e.g.: "Horsey! Horsey! Horsey!" over and over again, looks at the object, moves it, always saying the name to himself or to the world at large. It's quite a time before he talks to anyone in particular; he talks first of all to himself. This is his way of forming and fixing the *conception* of the object in his mind, and around this conception all his knowledge of it grows. *Names* are the essence of language; for the *name* is what abstracts the conception of the horse from the horse itself, and lets the mere idea recur at the speaking of the name. This permits the conception gathered from one horse experience to be exemplified again by another instance of a horse, so that the notion embodied in the name is a general notion.

21    To this end, the baby uses a word long before he *asks* for the object; when he wants his horsey he is likely to cry and fret, because he is reacting to an actual environment, not forming ideas. He uses the animal language of *signs* for his wants; talking is still a purely symbolic process—its practical value has not really impressed him yet.

22    Language need not be vocal; it may be purely visual, like written language, or even tactual, like the deaf-mute system of speech; but it *must be denotative.* The sounds, intended or unintended, whereby animals communicate do not constitute a language because they are signs, not names. They never fall into an organic pattern, a meaningful syntax of even the most rudimentary sort, as all language seems to do with a sort of driving necessity. That is because signs refer to actual situations, in which things have obvious relations to each other that require only to be noted; but symbols refer to ideas, which are not physically there for inspection, so their connections and features have to be represented. This gives all true language a natural tendency toward growth and development, which seems almost like a life of its own. Languages are not invented; they grow with our need for expression.

23    In contrast, animal "speech" never has a structure. It is merely an emotional response. Apes may greet their ration of yams with a shout of "Nga!" But they do not say "Nga" between meals. If they could *talk about* their yams instead of just saluting

them, they would be the most primitive men instead of the most anthropoid of beasts. They would have ideas, and tell each other things true or false, rational or irrational; they would make plans and invent laws and sing their own praises, as men do.

### THINKING CRITICALLY

1. Langer's opening statement is "A symbol is not the same thing as a sign." In your own words, what is the difference between signs and symbols? Give some examples from your own experience.

2. What would human beings be like if they used only signs? What would be the state of human communications?

3. According to Langer, how did language develop?

4. Langer says that symbols cause us to think about the thing symbolized. What do the following symbols make us think about, or what messages are communicated by them: clothes with the Tommy Hilfiger trademark on them; a dorm windowsill stacked with beer cans; a Coach handbag; an American flag pin; a peace sign window decal; a Harley-Davidson motorcycle; a swastika; a rainbow sticker?

5. In the opening paragraphs, Langer uses comparison to clarify the differences between signs and symbols. What comparisons does she specifically use? How effective are they in helping the reader understand her points?

6. In paragraph 2, Langer gives some examples of signs, yet she waits until paragraph 3 to define *sign*. Why do you think she uses this strategy? Is it effective for her purpose?

### WRITING ASSIGNMENTS

1. Write a paper entitled "A Sign of the Times" in which you choose and discuss an appropriate sign of the state of today's world.

2. Write an essay describing all the different symbols and signs to which you responded on your way to class today.

3. What are some of the signs and symbols of the Internet? Write an essay in which you describe how Internet symbols have changed our world.

4. The very clothes we wear convey symbolic messages of some sort—socioeconomic status, awareness, worldliness, sometimes even political statements. Describe some of the messages you like to project through your choice of clothing, boots, shoes, jewelry, and so on.

---

# Horton Heared a Who!

*Steven Pinker*

What can the grammatical slips of children as they learn to speak tell us about language, history, and the human mind? In this essay, linguist Steven Pinker explains that language acquisition follows regular, predictable patterns. Children are able to develop grammatical rules instinctually—not merely by imitating the language of adults—but they also can produce new words that they never heard before. How they do this, says Pinker, can give us a glimpse into the early origins of language.

Steven Pinker is a psychology professor at Harvard University. He is internationally recognized for his research on language and cognition. In addition to being published in scholarly journals, his essays have appeared in popular media, including *The New York Times, Time,* and *Slate.* He is author of several books, including *The Language Instinct* (1994), *How the Mind Works* (1999), *Words and Rules* (2000), and *The Stuff of Thought* (2007). This essay first appeared in the November 1, 1999, issue of *Time* magazine.

1   Kids say the darnedest things. "We holded the baby rabbits." "The alligator goed kerplunk." "Horton heared a Who!" These lapses, you might dimly recall, have something to do with irregular verbs. But please don't stop reading just yet. Children's errors are not just anecdotes for grandparents or reminders of long forgotten grammar lessons. They are windows into the workings of language, history, and the human mind.

2       Verbs in English come in two flavors. Regular verbs like *walk* and *smell* form the past tense by adding *–ed*: Today I walk, yesterday I walked. English has thousands of them, and new ones arise every day, thanks to our ability to apply rules instinctively. When people first heard *to spam, to mosh,* and *to diss,* they did not run to the dictionary to look up their past tenses; they knew they were spammed, moshed, and dissed.

3       Even children do it. Told that a man likes to wug, they will say that yesterday he wugged. Children are not sponges; they are constantly creating new sentences and words, and never more clearly or charmingly than when they run into the second flavor of verb, the quirky irregulars. The past of *spring* is *sprang*, but the past of *cling* is not *clang* but *clung*, and the past of *bring* is neither *brang* nor *brung* but *brought*. English has only 180 irregulars, a ragtag list that children simply have to memorize.

4       But when an irregular word is still fresh in the mind, it is fragile. If a child's memory cannot cough up *held* quickly enough, he or she adds *–ed* by default and says heared or holded instead.

5       Irregular and regular verbs embody the two underlying tricks behind the gift of articulate speech: words and rules. A word is a memorized link between a sound and a meaning. The word *duck* does not look, walk, or quack like a duck. But we can use it to convey the idea of a duck because we all once learned to connect the sound with the idea.

6       We also combine words into bigger words and sentences, using the second trick of language, rules. Journalists say that when a dog bites a man, that isn't news, but when a man bites a dog, that is news. Rules let us convey news, by reshuffling words in systematic ways.

7       Today's regular and irregular verbs have their roots in old border disputes between the word module and the rule module. Many irregulars can be traced back over 5,500 years, to a mysterious tribe that came to dominate Europe, western Asia, and northern India. Their language, Indo-European, is the ancestor of Hindi, Persian, Russian, Greek, Latin, Gaelic, and English. It had rules that replaced vowels: the past of *senkw-* (sink) was *sonkw-*.

8       Language as it evolves over the centuries is like the game of Broken Telephone, where a whispered phrase gets increasingly distorted as it passes from lip to

ear to lip. Eventually speakers can no longer discern the rule behind a motley set of mangled verbs. They just memorize them as a list, as do subsequent generations. These are the irregulars, the fossils of dead rules.

9    The irregulars are vulnerable, too, because they depend on fallible human memory. If a verb declines in popularity, speakers may not hear its irregular form often enough to stamp it securely in memory. They fall back on *–ed*, changing the language for following generations. That is why forms from Chaucer's time such as *chide-chid* and *writhe-wrothe* disappeared, replaced by *chided* and *writhed*.

10   You can feel that force of history acting today. *Smote, slew, bade, rent,* and *forsook* sound odd, and few people would use them in casual speech. In a century, they will probably go the way of *chid* and *wrothe*.

11   Do irregular and regular verbs really come out of a dictionary in one part of the brain and a grammar in another? Perhaps. Some neurological patients seem to have damaged dictionaries: they strain to retrieve words, but speak in fluent sentences. As expected, they have trouble producing irregular verbs, and like children (whose memory for words is also fragile), they make errors like heared and holded. New techniques in cognitive neuroscience have found that irregular and regular forms trigger signals in different parts of the brain, perhaps from the systems for memory and for computation.

12   Why pay so much attention to the lowly irregular verb? I see these studies as part of a trend in intellectual life that biologist E. O. Wilson calls "consilience": the bridging of the two cultures of science and humanities through an understanding of how the mind works. The link connecting the migrations of great prehistoric tribes to the brain-imaging technologies of the next millennium may lie in the slip of the child's tongue.

### THINKING CRITICALLY

1. How, according to Pinker, can young children's grammar lapses serve as "windows into the workings of language, history, and the human mind"? Explain.

2. In paragraph 2, Pinker observes that we are able to conjugate new verbs "instinctively." Do you think grammar is instinctual? Why or why not?

3. Pinker notes that when words fall out of regular use (such as *smote, slew, bade,* and *forsook*) we forget their irregular conjugations and fall back on the *–ed* of regular verbs. Can you think of any additional verbs besides the ones Pinker names that are undergoing this change now?

4. Why does Pinker think irregular verbs are worthy of study? Explain.

### WRITING ASSIGNMENTS

1. Create a list of irregular verbs (a Google search should make compiling this list easy) and ask a child between the ages of 3 and 4 to use them in a present and past-tense sentence. How often do they use the *–ed* ending? Do they use any words correctly? If so, which ones? Write a short essay on children's language acquisition or irregular and regular verbs based on your observations.

2. Write a personal narrative of your own recollections of learning language as a child. Did you use words like *brang* or *brung*? Did irregular verbs confuse you? Speak to people who knew you as a young child for their memories of any language "slips" you may have made as you learned to speak. When, if ever, did you become *aware* of language?

# Exploring the Language of V I S U A L S

## Gimme a Cookie

### THINKING CRITICALLY

1. What is the "joke" in this cartoon? What point is the artist trying to make?
2. Identify any visual clichés in the cartoon.
3. Editorial cartoons usually exploit current events or circumstances in politics, culture, and society. Would this cartoon be funny twenty years ago? Forty years ago? Explain.

# Chunking

*Ben Zimmer*

Anyone who has spent time with a young child knows how amazing its acquisition of language can be. From coos and gurgles, a baby begins speaking with just a few words, but then within the short span of a few years, becomes fluent in his or her native language—processing not only vocabulary, but grammar, internal ordering, and nuances of tone. In this essay, Ben Zimmer explores the mysterious ways children learn language and why the way they learn in early childhood may not be the way we learn language as adults.

Ben Zimmer is a linguist, lexicographer, language columnist, and a self-proclaimed "word nut." His column "On Language" appears in *The New York Times* magazine. He has served as editor for American dictionaries at Oxford University Press and as a consultant to the Oxford English Dictionary. In addition to the "On Language" column, he is the author of "Word Routes," a column appearing online at Visual Thesaurus. His work has appeared in *The Boston Globe,* Forbes.com, and Slate and he has been interviewed widely about words and language, including interviews by CNN, NPR's *Morning Edition*, CBS News, *U.S. News & World Report,* and ABC World News.

1   My ebullient 4-year-old son, Blake, is a big fan of the CDs and DVDs that the band *They Might Be Giants* recently produced for the kiddie market. He'll gleefully sing along to "Seven," a catchy tune from their 2008 album "Here Come the 123s" that tells of a house overrun by anthropomorphic number sevens. The first one is greeted at the door: "Oh, there's the doorbell. Let's see who's out there. Oh, it's a seven. Hello, Seven. Won't you come in, Seven? Make yourself at home."

2   Despite the song's playful surrealism (more and more sevens arrive, filling up the living room), the opening lines are routine and formulaic. The polite ritual of answering the door and inviting a guest into your house relies on certain fixed phrases in English: "Won't you come in?" "Make yourself at home."

3   As Blake learned these pleasantries through the song and its video, I wondered how much—or how little—his grasp of basic linguistic etiquette is grounded in the syntactical rules that structure how words are combined in English. An idiom like "Make yourself at home" is rather tricky if you stop to think about it: the imperative verb "make" is followed by a second-person reflexive pronoun ("yourself") and an adverbial phrase ("at home"), but it's difficult to break the phrase into its components. Instead, we grasp the whole thing at once.

4   Ritualized moments of everyday communication—greeting someone, answering a telephone call, wishing someone a happy birthday—are full of these canned phrases that we learn to perform with rote precision at an early age. Words work as social lubricants in such situations, and a language learner like Blake is primarily getting a handle on the pragmatics of set phrases in English, or how they create concrete effects in real-life interactions. The abstract rules of sentence structure are secondary.

5   In recent decades, the study of language acquisition and instruction has increasingly focused on "chunking": how children learn language not so much on a word-by-word basis but in larger "lexical chunks" or meaningful strings of words that are committed to memory. Chunks may consist of fixed idioms or conventional

speech routines, but they can also simply be combinations of words that appear together frequently, in patterns that are known as "collocations." In the 1960s, the linguist Michael Halliday pointed out that we tend to talk of "strong tea" instead of "powerful tea," even though the phrases make equal sense. Rain, on the other hand, is much more likely to be described as "heavy" than "strong."

6    A native speaker picks up thousands of chunks like "heavy rain" or "make yourself at home" in childhood, and psycholinguistic research suggests that these phrases are stored and processed in the brain as individual units. As the University of Nottingham linguist Norbert Schmitt has explained, it is much less taxing cognitively to have a set of ready-made lexical chunks at our disposal than to have to work through all the possibilities of word selection and sequencing every time we open our mouths.

7    Cognitive studies of chunking have been bolstered by computer-driven analysis of usage patterns in large databases of texts called "corpora." As linguists and lexicographers build bigger and bigger corpora (a major-league corpus now contains billions of words, thanks to readily available online texts), it becomes clearer just how "chunky" the language is, with certain words showing undeniable attractions to certain others.

8    Many English-language teachers have been eager to apply corpus findings in the classroom to zero in on salient chunks rather than individual vocabulary words. This is especially so among teachers of English as a second language, since it's mainly the knowledge of chunks that allows non-native speakers to advance toward nativelike fluency. In his 1993 book, "The Lexical Approach," Michael Lewis set out a program of action, and the trend has continued in such recent works as "From Corpus to Classroom: Language Use and Language Teaching" and "Teaching Chunks of Language: From Noticing to Remembering."

9    Not everyone is on board, however. Michael Swan, a British writer on language pedagogy, has emerged as a prominent critic of the lexical-chunk approach. Though he acknowledges, as he told me in an e-mail, that "high-priority chunks need to be taught," he worries that "the 'new toy' effect can mean that formulaic expressions get more attention than they deserve, and other aspects of language— ordinary vocabulary, grammar, pronunciation and skills—get sidelined."

10    Swan also finds it unrealistic to expect that teaching chunks will produce nativelike proficiency in language learners. "Native English speakers have tens or hundreds of thousands—estimates vary—of these formulae at their command," he says. "A student could learn 10 a day for years and still not approach native-speaker competence."

11    Besides, Swan warns, "overemphasizing 'scripts' in our teaching can lead to a phrase-book approach, where formulaic learning is privileged and the more generative parts of language—in particular the grammatical system—are backgrounded." Formulaic language is all well and good when talking about the familiar and the recurrent, he argues, but it is inadequate for dealing with novel ideas and situations, where the more open-ended aspects of language are paramount.

12    The methodology of the chunking approach is still open to this type of criticism, but data-driven reliance on corpus research will most likely dominate English instruction in coming years. Lexical chunks have entered the house of language teaching, and they're making themselves at home.

## THINKING CRITICALLY

1. Why does Zimmer reference his 4-year-old son, Blake, at the beginning of the essay? How does his story about Blake connect to the point of Zimmer's essay?

2. What is "chunking?" How does it relate to how children learn language?

3. Would learning language in chunks, as it appears young children do, be a good way for adults to learn a foreign language? Why or why not?

4. What drawbacks, if any, can come from learning language in chunks? Explain.

## WRITING ASSIGNMENTS

1. Research the work of one of the linguists mentioned in this essay, such as Michael Halliday, and write a summary of his position on language acquisition.

2. If you have learned a foreign language (or are currently studying one), describe the process you undertook to understand its vocabulary, grammar and syntax, and construction. Connect your experiences to points Zimmer makes in this essay.

---

# Another Language for the Deaf
*Margalit Fox*

While sign language opened the doors of language to the deaf, the thousands of people who use it still must learn two languages to communicate in their world: the language of signing and the alphabet of the general population. For years, the primary language of the deaf—signing—could not be written down. Sign-Writing hopes to change this situation. In the next piece, Margalit Fox explains how SignWriting, a system of graphic symbols based on dance notation, aims to capture the world's signed languages in written form. But as Fox explains, the concept faces many challenges.

Margalit Fox is a reporter for *The New York Times* and an editor for that paper's *Book Review*. This article first appeared in the April 14, 2002, edition of *The New York Times*.

1 Imagine a language that can't be written. Hundreds of thousands of people speak it, but they have no way to read a newspaper or study a schoolbook in the language they use all day long.

2 That is the situation of the quarter-million or more deaf people in North America whose primary language is American Sign Language. Although they form a vast linguistic minority, their language, as complex as any spoken one, has by its very nature defied most attempts to write it down. In recent years, however, a system of graphic symbols based on dance notation has allowed the world's signed languages to be captured on paper. What's more, the system's advocates say, it may furnish deaf children with a long-sought bridge to literacy in English and other spoken languages, often a great struggle for signers.

3    But despite its utility, the system, called SignWriting, has yet to be widely adopted by deaf people: for many, the issue of whether signed languages need to be written at all remains an open question. "The written form is used by a small number of educated people," Valerie Sutton, the creator of SignWriting, said in a telephone interview from her office in La Jolla, Calif.

4    Little by little, though, SignWriting is gaining footholds in individual homes and classrooms in America and abroad. Disseminated by Ms. Sutton's nonprofit organization <www.signwriting.org>, it can now be found in 27 countries, including Italy, South Africa, Nicaragua, Japan, and Saudi Arabia.

5    American Sign Language is not English. Spoken in the United States and parts of Canada, it uses word orders and grammatical constructs not found in English (in certain respects it resembles Navajo).

6    For a deaf child whose first language is A.S.L., English—that is, written English—must be learned as a foreign language, just as a hearing person might study Sanskrit. But there is a catch: "The letters of the alphabet are based on sounds they can't hear," Ms. Sutton explained. For this reason, many deaf students never become fully literate in English, a perennial concern of educators. According to a long-term study by the Gallaudet Research Institute in Washington, deaf high school seniors score, on average, just below the fourth-grade level on standardized reading tests.

7    Dawn McReynolds of Clinton Township, MI, ran into the problem three years ago, when she discovered her 12-year-old did not know what "bread" meant. Born deaf, and fluent in A.S.L., Nicole McReynolds, then a sixth-grader in public school, was clearly bright. But standardized tests put her academic skills at a first- to second-grade level. As her stunned mother discovered after she pulled Nicole from the classroom and began home schooling, though Nicole had learned by rote to spell simple English words—"bread," "map," "yell"—she had little idea what they actually meant.

8    "Anything I could draw a picture for, she was O.K. with," Mrs. McReynolds said. "But things like 'what,' 'where,' 'when,' 'who'—she had no idea. It was horrible. It was as if she'd never been educated."

9    Advocates of SignWriting hope the system can help bridge the literacy gap. Though no formal studies have been published, anecdotal evidence from parents and teachers suggests its potential. "It's made English come alive for her," said Mrs. McReynolds, who introduced Nicole to SignWriting two and a half years ago, after seeing it on local television.

10    Where spoken languages operate acoustically, signed languages work spatially. Each sign is a compact bundle of data, conveying linguistic information by three primary means at once: the shape of the signer's hands, the location of the hands in space, and the direction in which the hands move. (Facial expression also matters.)

11    Devising a writing system that can capture this blizzard of data for each of A.S.L.'s thousands of signs is no simple task. "When you write English, we're using two-dimensional paper to represent a one-dimensional language, because English is just a series of sounds in a sequence, and we write down the sounds in the order we say them," said Karen van Hoek, a linguist who helped develop SignWriting. "But with sign language, it's the reverse: we're trying to get a three-dimensional language compressed down onto two-dimensional, flat paper."

12    Other writing systems have been created for A.S.L. during its century-and-a-half-long history. Some, used by linguists, are too abstract for everyday communication. Another, developed recently at the University of Arizona, is meant to help teach written English but not to handle literary traffic, like novel-writing, entirely in A.S.L.

13    SignWriting, which grew out of a system for transcribing movement that Ms. Sutton developed in the 1970s to notate choreography, can be handwritten, or typed using special software. Written vertically, it uses simple geometric forms to collapse a sign's three basic parameters—hand shape, location, and movement—into a streamlined icon, topped by a stylized face.

14    Few embraced the system at first. Many signers, mindful of a long paternalistic history of hearing people tampering with A.S.L., questioned Ms. Sutton's motives. Educators feared it would deter the deaf from learning English.

15    Though hostility has subsided, SignWriting is used today by only a small fraction of the deaf population, between 5,000 and 8,000 people worldwide, Ms. Sutton estimates. As Jane Fernandes, the provost of Gallaudet University, the prestigious school for the hearing impaired, said in an e-mail interview: "There are many deaf adults who were raised with Sign Language in their homes and schools and who have learned to read and write English quite fluently. They were able to navigate between Sign Language and English, without a system for writing their signs down."

16    While acknowledging SignWriting's potential usefulness in teaching English, Dr. Fernandes, who is deaf, expressed doubt about the larger need for written A.S.L. "English is the language of society," she wrote. "It works well for us and I believe English will remain the language in which we write in America."

17    Nicole McReynolds mastered SignWriting fairly easily, and the English words that eluded her began gradually to fall into place. Now 15 and a ninth-grader, she is back in public school, maintaining a B average in a program for hearing-impaired students conducted in English.

18    Before SignWriting, Mrs. McReynolds said, "I didn't think she would be able to live an independent life." These days, Nicole talks of college. "We believe that SignWriting is going to accompany her through her life," her mother said. "There is so much more hope for the future for her because she has this ability now."

### THINKING CRITICALLY

1. How is sign language different from spoken languages? What challenges does sign language face in order to transition into written form? Explain.
2. In what ways is learning written English for a deaf child much like learning a foreign language? What literacy obstacles must deaf children address when trying to learn written English?
3. Why does SignWriting hold promise over other forms of A.S.L. writing systems? Explain.
4. Sign languages are true languages, with vocabularies of thousands of words and complex and sophisticated grammars. Attend a speech or watch a program that has an A.S.L. interpreter present and focus your attention on the interpreter. If you could not hear, could you understand the context of the speech based on the signing? How does the interpreter augment his or her signing to complement the meaning of the speech? Explain.

5. Fox explains that when Sutton first developed SignWriting, it was met with suspicion by many members of the deaf world "mindful of a long paternalistic history of hearing people tampering with A.S.L." What does Fox mean? Why would deaf people question Sutton's motives?

6. In what ways did SignWriting represent a "coming into language" for Nicole McReynolds? Explain.

## WRITING ASSIGNMENTS

1. Visit the website for SignWriting maintained by Sutton at www.signwriting.org and review how the system works. Prepare an analysis of the written system explaining its basic premise, how to read it, and its ease of use.

2. Interview at least one deaf person on campus and discuss his or her knowledge and opinions of SignWriting. Ask them to explain, if possible, Fox's statement that when SignWriting was first introduced, the deaf community viewed it with suspicion. Based on your interview, develop an essay on some of the social implications of SignWriting.

3. Explore the challenges of conveying a gestured language such as A.S.L. into a written form. Try to tell a simple story, such as "The Three Little Pigs" or "Goldilocks and the Three Bears," without using a phonetic alphabet (heard sounds), but with pictograms (visual depictions) instead. Describe your experience and how it connects to your understanding of language and communication in general in an exploratory essay.

## Exploring the Language of **V I S U A L S**

# SignWriting

To hearing individuals, the disconnect between written English and American Sign Language (A.S.L.) is hard to understand. But imagine trying to learn a language that you cannot hear. How would you know what "sh," "oo," or "ch" or any phonetic sound actually meant? In the preceding piece, Margalit Fox describes how SignWriting, developed by Valerie Sutton, is attempting to bridge the literacy gap between A.S.L. and written English.

SignWriting is a visually designed set of symbols that records sign language. It aims to capture the visual subtleties of sign language by recording body movement. Because it records sign language rather than spoken languages such as English or Spanish, SignWriting can be used internationally to communicate.

Valerie Sutton is the inventor of Sutton Movement Writing, a visual alphabet for writing the movements of the human body. Her system includes DanceWriting, used to record dance choreography, and SignWriting—which she developed in 1974—used to communicate sign languages used by the deaf. She is the author of several books on dance choreography, including *DanceWriting Shorthand for Modern and Jazz Dance* (1982) and *The Bournonville School* (1975, 1976). The article that follows, "SignWriting: A Deaf Perspective," employs Sutton's SignWriting alphabet. The article is written by born-deaf, native American Sign Language instructor Lucinda O'Grady Batch, who wrote her thoughts directly in A.S.L. in SignWriting. The English translation of the A.S.L. was done after the A.S.L. article was written. SignWriting gives the deaf the opportunity to write directly in their own language.

### THINKING CRITICALLY

1. Visit Sutton's website and read the section "What is SignWriting?" at www.signwriting.org. Then review some of the lessons on SignWriting featured on the website. Does the system seem easy to follow and understand? In your opinion, could the system forge stronger language connections between hearing and nonhearing people? Explain.

2. After reviewing the SignWriting alphabet featured at the SignWriting website, www.signwriting.org, write a short message using the SignWriting system. Exchange your message with a classmate, and try to translate. How easy or difficult did you find the system to use? Explain.

3. In your opinion, is SignWriting a language or merely a system of symbols? What constitutes "language"? What is an alphabet? Explain.

4. Sutton states on her website that SignWriting can be used to read, write, and learn sign language. Explore how SignWriting and sign language are connected. Using two or three examples, compare the movements of A.S.L. for certain words to their SignWriting counterparts.

# SignWriting®

# A Deaf Perspective...

by Lucinda O'Grady Batch

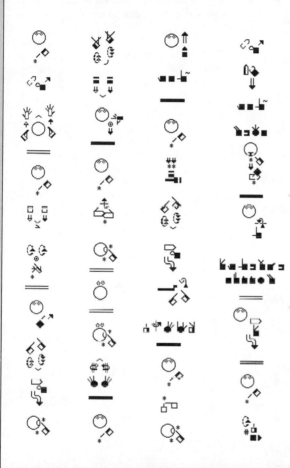

I am writing to tell you how strongly I feel about SignWriting and how much it can benefit Deaf people.

I was born Deaf to a Deaf family and I am a native American Sign Language (ASL) user. I have been working with Sign Writing since 1982. I was the first Deaf person to write articles in ASL, in SignWriting, for the SignWriter Newspaper. Later, Valerie Sutton and I established....

the Deaf Action Com-
mittee For SignWriting
(the DAC) in 1988.

I think it is very impor-
tant to spread the word
about SignWriting.
ASL is a language in its
own right, yet until
the development of
SignWriting, it was a
language without a
written form. When I
found out about Sign
Writing I was thrilled
to think that at last we
would have a way to
write our language.

Deaf Americans are one
of the very few linguis-
tic minorities that are
unable to get books
teaching English in

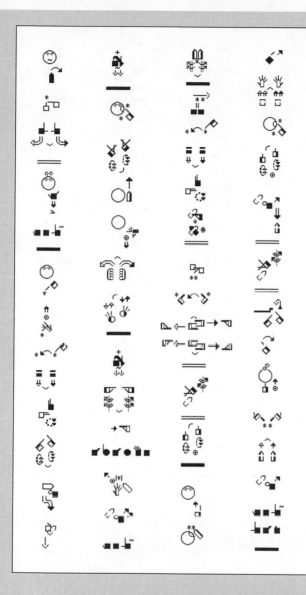

their native language. I feel that we can use SignWriting in order to learn English. Deaf people will benefit greatly from books explaining English grammar and idioms in written ASL.

We can also use it to write down and preserve our stories, poetry and plays. As you know, there are many Deaf playwrights and poets, and up until now, they have not had a way to write the ASL in their literature.

No matter what the project, SignWriting encourages us to read and write and I feel that is important.

All of us hope that you will enjoy learning SignWriting. Your interest and support is a great help to our Deaf community.

Lucinda
O'Grady
Batch

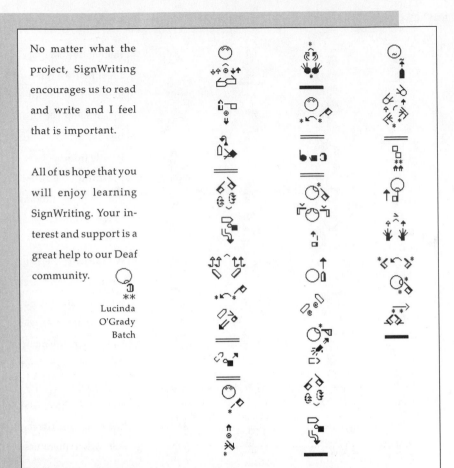

# PERSONAL RECOLLECTIONS: COMING INTO LANGUAGE

## Homemade Education
*Malcolm X*

It was said that he was the only man in America who could start a race riot—or stop one. A one-time street hustler, Malcolm X was born Malcolm Little in 1925. He rose to become one of the most articulate, fiery, and powerful leaders of black America during the 1960s. His writings and lectures taught African Americans that by taking action, they could take control over their own destiny. In 1946, Malcolm X was arrested for robbery. While in prison, Malcolm became a follower of Elijah Muhammad, the leader of the Nation of Islam (which was sometimes called the Black Muslim Movement). He rescinded his "slave name," Little, and was assigned the new name "X." It was during this time that he discovered the world of language and became obsessed with the written word and books, which he called "intellectual vitamins." After his release, he quickly rose through the ranks of the Nation of Islam and became one of its top administrators. In 1964, Malcolm X left the Nation of Islam to form his own organization, the Muslim Mosque, that articulated a more secular black nationalism. After a trip to Mecca, however, he began to change his views towards whites, considering the possibility that some whites could contribute to the struggle for racial equality. A year later, on February 21, 1965, Malcolm X was assassinated in the Audubon Ballroom in New York City while addressing a full house.

The following article is Malcolm X's account of coming to language—an inspiring glimpse of one man's struggle to find self-expression in the power of words. This excerpt comes from *The Autobiography of Malcolm X* (1965), an absorbing personal narrative written with the assistance of *Roots* author Alex Haley.

1   I've never been one for inaction. Everything I've ever felt strongly about, I've done something about. I guess that's why, unable to do anything else, I soon began writing to people I had known in the hustling world, such as Sammy the Pimp, John Hughes, the gambling house owner, the thief Jumpsteady, and several dope peddlers. I wrote them all about Allah and Islam and Mr. Elijah Muhammad. I had no idea where most of them lived. I addressed their letters in care of the Harlem or Roxbury bars and clubs where I'd known them.

2   I never got a single reply. The average hustler and criminal was too uneducated to write a letter. I have known many slick sharp-looking hustlers, who would have you think they had an interest in Wall Street; privately, they would get someone else to read a letter if they received one. Besides, neither would I have replied to anyone writing me something as wild as "the white man is the devil."

3   What certainly went on the Harlem and Roxbury wires was that Detroit Red was going crazy in stir, or else he was trying some hype to shake up the warden's office.

4    During the years that I stayed in the Norfolk Prison Colony, never did any official directly say anything to me about those letters, although, of course, they all passed through the prison censorship. I'm sure, however, they monitored what I wrote to add to the files which every state and federal prison keeps on the conversation of Negro inmates by the teachings of Mr. Elijah Muhammad.

5    But at that time, I felt that the real reason was that the white man knew that he was the devil.

6    Later on, I even wrote to the Mayor of Boston, to the Governor of Massachusetts, and to Harry S. Truman. They never answered; they probably never even saw my letters. I handscratched to them how the white man's society was responsible for the black man's condition in this wilderness of North America.

7    It was because of my letters that I happened to stumble upon starting to acquire some kind of a homemade education.

8    I became increasingly frustrated at not being able to express what I wanted to convey in letters that I wrote, especially those to Mr. Elijah Muhammad. In the street, I had been the most articulate hustler out there—I had commanded attention when I said something. But now, trying to write simple English, I not only wasn't articulate, I wasn't even functional. How would I sound writing in slang, the way I would *say* it, something such as, "Look, daddy, let me pull your coat about a cat. Elijah Muhammad—"

9    Many who today hear me somewhere in person, or on television, or those who read something I've said, will think I went to school far beyond the eighth grade. This impression is due entirely to my prison studies.

10    It had really begun back in the Charlestown Prison, when Bimbi first made me feel envy of his stock of knowledge. Bimbi had always taken charge of any conversation he was in, and I had tried to emulate him. But every book I picked up had few sentences which didn't contain anywhere from one to nearly all of the words that might as well have been in Chinese. When I just skipped those words, of course, I really ended up with little idea of what the book said. So I had come to the Norfolk Prison Colony still going through only book-reading motions. Pretty soon, I would have quit even these motions, unless I had received the motivation that I did.

11    I saw that the best thing I could do was get hold of a dictionary—to study, to learn some words. I was lucky enough to reason also that I should try to improve my penmanship. It was sad. I couldn't even write in a straight line. It was both ideas together that moved me to request a dictionary along with some tablets and pencils from the Norfolk Prison Colony school.

12    I spent two days just riffling uncertainly through the dictionary's pages. I'd never realized so many words existed! I didn't know *which* words I needed to learn. Finally, just to start some kind of action, I began copying.

13    In my slow, painstaking, ragged handwriting, I copied into my tablet everything printed on that first page, down to the punctuation marks.

14    I believe it took me a day. Then, aloud, I read back, to myself, everything I'd written on the tablet. Over and over, aloud, to myself, I read my own handwriting.

15    I woke up the next morning, thinking about those words—immensely proud to realize that not only had I written so much at one time, but I'd written words that I never knew were in the world. Moreover, with a little effort, I also could

remember what many of these words meant. I reviewed the words whose meanings I didn't remember. Funny thing, from the dictionary's first page right now, that "aardvark" springs to my mind. The dictionary had a picture of it, a long-tailed, long-eared, burrowing African mammal, which lives off termites caught by sticking out its tongue as an anteater does for ants.

16    I was so fascinated that I went on—I copied the dictionary's next page. And the same experience came when I studied that. With every succeeding page, I also learned of people and places and events from history. Actually the dictionary is like a miniature encyclopedia. Finally the dictionary's A section had filled a whole tablet—and I went on into the B's. That was the way I started copying what eventually became the entire dictionary. It went a lot faster after so much practice helped me pick up handwriting speed. Between what I wrote in my tablet, and writing letters, during the rest of my time in prison I would guess I wrote a million words.

17    I suppose it was inevitable that as my word-base broadened, I could for the first time pick up a book and read and now begin to understand what the book was saying. Anyone who has read a great deal can imagine the new world that opened. Let me tell you something: from then until I left that prison, in every free moment I had, if I was not reading in the library, I was reading on my bunk. You couldn't have gotten me out of books with a wedge. Between Mr. Muhammad's teachings, my correspondence, my visitors . . . and my reading of books, months passed without my even thinking about being imprisoned. In fact, up to then, I never had been so truly free in my life.

### THINKING CRITICALLY

1.  What exactly motivates Malcolm X to "get a hold of a dictionary—to study, to learn some words"?

2.  Explain how Malcolm X could be the "most articulate hustler" on the street, yet be unable to write simple English that was articulate and functional.

3.  In your own words, summarize what Malcolm X means when he says, "In fact, up to then, I never had been so truly free in my life." Can you in any way relate to his sense of freedom here? Have you ever had a similarly intense learning experience? If so, what was it like?

4.  Would this essay be likely to inspire an illiterate person to learn to read? Why or why not?

5.  Having read this essay, do you feel that studying a dictionary is or is not an effective way to improve language skills?

6.  Consider the introductory paragraph. What would you say is its function? Does it establish the thesis and controlling idea of the essay? Did it capture your attention and make you want to read on? Explain.

### WRITING ASSIGNMENTS

1.  Think of a situation in which you lacked the language skills you needed to communicate effectively. It may have been in a college interview, writing a letter to a friend, or expressing your ideas in class. Write an essay explaining the circumstances—how it made you feel and how you solved or coped with the problem. The tone of the piece may be serious, dramatic, or even humorous.

2. Do a little research to find out what kinds of services your community offers to adults who want to learn to read. You might start by contacting the town hall, the department of education, and reading clinics. After gathering information, write an essay outlining what is available and whether or not you feel these services are adequate.

3. Access the CMG website on Malcolm X at www.cmgww.com/historic/malcolm/index.html. Write an essay connecting his background to the excerpt from his autobiography. How did his determination to read lead to his success as a great orator? Would Malcolm X have been as successful if he had not had this experience in jail?

---

# A Word for Everything

*Helen Keller*

Most of us take for granted the ability to acquire language and communication skills. We develop these skills from infancy. As young children, we are constantly bombarded with visual and verbal stimuli, from which we begin to acquire language. But for Helen Keller (1880–1968), deaf and blind from the age of 19 months, a silent and dark world was her reality. She was unable to effectively communicate her needs and desires and to connect with the people around her.

When Helen was almost seven years old, her parents sought the help of Anne Mansfield Sullivan, a teacher familiar with communicating with the blind and deaf. Anne Sullivan changed Helen's world forever. The following excerpt is from Helen Keller's autobiography, *The Story of My Life*. In this essay, Keller remembers the arrival of her teacher and how Sullivan introduced her to the wonders of language. Specifically, Keller recalls the exact moment when she realized that everything had a name, and her joyous realization that she was connected to the world and the people around her.

1 The most important day I remember in all my life is the one on which my teacher, Anne Mansfield Sullivan, came to me. I am filled with wonder when I consider the immeasurable contrasts between the two lives which it connects. It was the third of March, 1887, three months before I was seven years old.

2 On the afternoon of that eventful day, I stood on the porch, dumb, expectant. I guessed vaguely from my mother's signs and from the hurrying to and fro in the house that something unusual was about to happen, so I went to the door and waited on the steps. The afternoon sun penetrated the mass of honeysuckle that covered the porch, and fell on my upturned face. My fingers lingered almost unconsciously on the familiar leaves and blossoms which had just come forth to greet the sweet southern spring. I did not know what the future held of marvel or surprise for me. Anger and bitterness had preyed upon me continually for weeks and a deep languor had succeeded this passionate struggle.

3 Have you ever been at sea in a dense fog, when it seemed as if a tangible white darkness shut you in, and the great ship, tense and anxious, groped her way toward the shore with plummet and sounding-line, and you waited with beating heart for something to happen? I was like that ship before my education began, only I was

without compass or sounding-line, and had no way of knowing how near the harbor was. "Light! Give me light!" was the wordless cry of my soul, and the light of love shone on me in that very hour.

4    I felt approaching footsteps. I stretched out my hand as I supposed to my mother. Some one took it, and I was caught up and held close in the arms of her who had come to reveal all things to me, and, more than all things else, to love me.

5    The morning after my teacher came she led me into her room and gave me a doll. The little blind children at the Perkins Institution had sent it and Laura Bridgman had dressed it; but I did not know this until afterward. When I had played with it a little while, Miss Sullivan slowly spelled into my hand the word "d-o-l-l." I was at once interested in this finger play and tried to imitate it. When I finally succeeded in making the letters correctly I was flushed with childish pleasure and pride. Running downstairs to my mother I held up my hand and made the letters for doll. I did not know that I was spelling a word or even that words existed; I was simply making my fingers go in monkey-like imitation. In the days that followed I learned to spell in this uncomprehending way a great many words, among them *pin, hat, cup* and a few verbs like *sit, stand* and *walk*. But my teacher had been with me several weeks before I understood that everything has a name.

6    One day, while I was playing with my new doll, Miss Sullivan put my big rag doll into my lap also, spelled "d-o-l-l" and tried to make me understand that "d-o-l-l" applied to both. Earlier in the day we had had a tussle over the words "m-u-g" and "w-a-t-e-r." Miss Sullivan had tried to impress it upon me that "m-u-g" is *mug* and that "w-a-t-e-r" is *water,* but I persisted in confounding the two. In despair she had dropped the subject for the time, only to renew it at the first opportunity. I became impatient at her repeated attempts and, seizing the new doll, I dashed it upon the floor. I was keenly delighted when I felt the fragments of the broken doll at my feet. Neither sorrow nor regret followed my passionate outburst. I had not loved the doll. In the still, dark world in which I lived there was no strong sentiment or tenderness. I felt my teacher sweep the fragments to one side of the hearth, and I had a sense of satisfaction that the cause of my discomfort was removed. She brought me my hat, and I knew I was going out into the warm sunshine. This thought, if a wordless sensation may be called a thought, made me hop and skip with pleasure.

7    We walked down the path to the well-house, attracted by the fragrance of the honeysuckle with which it was covered. Some one was drawing water and my teacher placed my hand under the spout. As the cool stream gushed over one hand she spelled into the other the word *water,* first slowly, then rapidly. I stood still, my whole attention fixed upon the motions of her fingers. Suddenly I felt a misty consciousness as of something forgotten—a thrill of returning thought; and somehow the mystery of language was revealed to me. I knew then that "w-a-t-e-r" meant the wonderful cool something that was flowing over my hand. That living word awakened my soul, gave it light, home, joy, set it free! There were barriers still, it is true, but barriers that could in time be swept away.

8    I left the well-house eager to learn. Everything had a name and each name gave birth to a new thought. As we returned to the house every object which I touched seemed to quiver with life. That was because I saw everything with the strange, new sight that had come to me. On entering the door I remembered the doll I had

broken. I felt my way to the hearth and picked up the pieces. I tried vainly to put them together. Then my eyes filled with tears; for I realized what I had done, and for the first time I felt repentance and sorrow.

9    I learned a great many new words that day. I do not remember what they all were; but I do know that *mother, father, sister, teacher* were among them—words that were to make the world blossom for me, "like Aaron's rod, with flowers." It would have been difficult to find a happier child than I was as I lay in my crib at the close of that eventful day and lived over the joys it had brought me, and for the first time longed for a new day to come.

10    I had now the key to all language, and I was eager to learn to use it. Children who hear acquire language without any particular effort; the words that fall from others' lips they catch on the wing, as it were, delightedly, while the little deaf child must trap them by a slow and often painful process. But whatever the process, the result is wonderful. Gradually, from naming an object we advance step by step until we have traversed the vast distance between our first stammered syllable and the sweep of thought in a line of Shakespeare.

11    At first, when my teacher told me about a new thing I asked very few questions. My ideas were vague, and my vocabulary was inadequate; but as my knowledge of things grew, and I learned more and more words, my field of inquiry broadened, and I would return again and again to the same subject, eager for further information. Sometimes a new word revived an image that some earlier experience had engraved on my brain. I remember the morning that I first asked the meaning of the word "love." This was before I knew many words. I had found a few early violets in the garden and brought them to my teacher. She tried to kiss me; but at that time I did not like to have any one kiss me except my mother. Miss Sullivan put her arm gently round me and spelled into my hand, "I love Helen."

12    "What is love?" I asked.

13    She drew me closer to her and said, "It is here," pointing to my heart, whose beats I was conscious of for the first time. Her words puzzled me very much because I did not then understand anything unless I touched it.

14    I smelt the violets in her hand and asked, half in words, half in signs, a question which meant, "Is love the sweetness of flowers?"

15    "No," said my teacher.

16    Again I thought. The warm sun was shining on us.

17    "Is this not love?" I asked, pointing in the direction from which the heat came, "Is this not love?"

18    It seemed to me that there could be nothing more beautiful than the sun, whose warmth makes all things grow. But Miss Sullivan shook her head, and I was greatly puzzled and disappointed. I thought it strange that my teacher could not show me love.

19    A day or two afterward I was stringing beads of different sizes in symmetrical groups—two large beads, three small ones, and so on. I had made many mistakes, and Miss Sullivan had pointed them out again and again with gentle patience. Finally I noticed a very obvious error in the sequence and for an instant I concentrated my attention on the lesson and tried to think how I should have arranged the beads. Miss Sullivan touched my forehead and spelled with decided emphasis, "Think."

20    In a flash I knew that the word was the name of the process that was going on in my head. This was my first conscious perception of an abstract idea.

21    For a long time I was still—I was not thinking of the beads in my lap, but trying to find a meaning for "love" in the light of this new idea. The sun had been under a cloud all day, and there had been brief showers; but suddenly the sun broke forth in all its southern splendor.

22    Again I asked my teacher, "Is this not love?"

23    "Love is something like the clouds that were in the sky before the sun came out," she replied. Then in simpler words than these, which at that time I could not have understood, she explained: "You cannot touch the clouds, you know; but you feel the rain and know how glad the flowers and the thirsty earth are to have it after a hot day. You cannot touch either; but you feel the sweetness that it pours into everything. Without love you would not be happy or want to play."

24    The beautiful truth burst upon my mind—I felt that there were invisible lines stretched between my spirit and the spirits of others.

25    From the beginning of my education Miss Sullivan made it a practice to speak to me as she would speak to any hearing child; the only difference was that she spelled the sentences into my hand instead of speaking them. If I did not know the words and idioms necessary to express my thoughts she supplied them, even suggesting conversation when I was unable to keep up my end of the dialogue.

26    This process was continued for several years; for the deaf child does not learn in a month, or even in two or three years, the numberless idioms and expressions used in the simplest daily intercourse. The little hearing child learns these from constant repetition and imitation. The conversation he hears in his home stimulates his mind and suggests topics and calls forth the spontaneous expression of his own thoughts. This natural exchange of ideas is denied to the deaf child. My teacher, realizing this, determined to supply the kinds of stimulus I lacked. This she did by repeating to me as far as possible, verbatim, what she heard, and by showing me how I could take part in the conversation. But it was a long time before I ventured to take the initiative, and still longer before I could find something appropriate to say at the right time.

27    The deaf and the blind find it very difficult to acquire the amenities of conversation. How much more this difficulty must be augmented in the case of those who are both deaf and blind! They cannot distinguish the tone of the voice or, without assistance, go up and down the gamut of tones that give significance to words; nor can they watch the expression of the speaker's face, and a look is often the very soul of what one says.

### THINKING CRITICALLY

1. Helen Keller was almost seven years old before her teacher Anne Sullivan began to teach her language. Would her experience have been different if she had been younger or older? Explain.

2. How do young children understand words such as *think, know,* or *feel* that have no physical or visual representation? How does Helen Keller begin to understand these terms?

3. Why doesn't the young Helen feel sorry for breaking her new doll? What accounts for her later remorse? What made the difference in Helen's emotional perspective? How are emotions connected to language?

4. What are the "amenities of conversation" that Keller alludes to in her final paragraph? Why are they important to communication? How can a look be "the very soul of what one says"?

5. How does Keller describe things that she has never seen or heard? How do her descriptions help her connect to her audience?

6. Evaluate Keller's tone in this essay. How does her tone help her audience relate to her essay? Who do you think her audience is, and what is she hoping to convey?

7. How does Keller use simile and metaphor in her writing? Why do you think she employs this literary convention?

## WRITING ASSIGNMENTS

1. How would you describe sound and sight to a person who could experience neither? Describe some everyday events such as a sunset or an ocean wave to a person who has never had sight or hearing. What descriptive alternatives would you use? After writing, explain the rationale behind your description.

2. Sit down with a friend and try to communicate using the Anne Sullivan and Helen Keller method of tracing letters into the palm of the hand. You may wish to use blindfolds for this exercise; do not speak throughout the exercise. Write an essay about your experience. Did it make you view your own method of communication differently?

3. Keller describes the moment when she first made the connection between Sullivan's palm tracings and the object described. She identifies this moment as the moment her soul was awakened and given "light, hope, [and] joy." Write about an experience of your own in which you had a moment of awakening that forever changed the way you understood your world. Following Keller's format, relate the events leading up to this moment. How did it change your life?

4. Read more about the life of Helen Keller. For a brief biographical sketch, try the Great Women Hall of Fame at www.greatwomen.org or read the autobiography from which this essay was taken. The American Foundation for the Blind's archives features more information about Keller, her teacher Anne Sullivan, and Keller's early experiences with language acquisition at www.afb.org/default. asp. Write a paper on how this remarkable woman became one of the most well-known and respected women in America. What role did language play in her fame?

# Exploring the Language of V I S U A L S

## American Sign Language Alphabet

Many of us take for granted the ability to communicate verbally—to shout a greeting across a courtyard, to hear a warning of imminent danger, to cluck baby talk to a giggling infant, or to whisper a secret in a friend's ear. However, many Americans who are hearing impaired must find alternative ways to communicate to others. Although sign language is one way of addressing this obstacle, it presents its own challenges. Few hearing people know sign language well enough to use it to communicate effectively. Moreover, it requires face-to-face contact between signers. The American Sign Language alphabet is a manual alphabet that augments the vocabulary of American Sign Language by allowing the speaker to sign the individual letters of a word such as with names, book titles, or when clarification is needed. Letters should be signed with the palm facing the viewer.

As you study this alphabet and answer the questions that follow, consider the ways you communicate verbally with others around you. What would happen if you could not verbally express yourself and, instead, had to rely on sign language to be understood? What advantages and disadvantages might you experience? For example, would sign language be more freeing—allowing you to communicate from distances or in loud areas where you may not be understood?

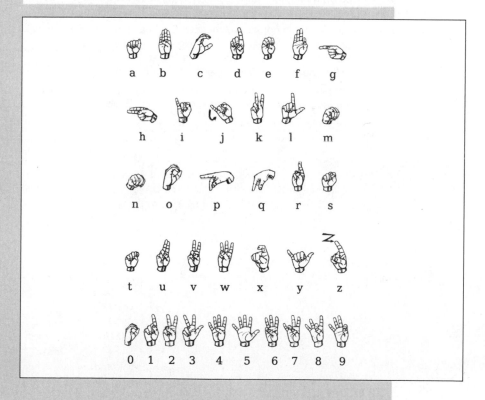

**THINKING CRITICALLY**

1. Study and learn the A.S.L. alphabet with a classmate or friend and spell out some names or titles. How easily are you understood? How quickly were you able to use the signed alphabet?

2. American Sign Language is taught in many colleges and universities to hearing students. Contrary to popular assumption, A.S.L. is not a signed form of English, but a language in its own right that developed gradually and still evolves, as many languages do. Find out if your school offers courses in A.S.L. If so, ask permission to attend a class and write about the experience. Try to apply some of the things you have learned about language in this class to your assessment of A.S.L.

3. If you have a hearing or speech impairment, discuss how this challenge affects your daily life and your communication with others. If you do not have any unique hearing or speech difficulties, discuss how you communicate with people who do. What issues do you confront, and how do you deal with them? Explain.

4. Sign languages are true languages, with vocabularies of thousands of words and complex and sophisticated grammars. Attend a speech or watch a program that has an A.S.L. interpreter present. Focus your attention on the interpreter. If you could not hear, could you understand the context of the speech based on the interpreter's signing? How does the interpreter augment his or her signing to complement the meaning of the speech? Explain.

5. Although many people do not know American Sign Language (A.S.L.), they do rely on some form of sign language to express themselves, such as by nodding or shaking their heads or through waving and other hand gestures. Discuss the ways you use sign language to convey meaning.

6. How could sign language improve the lives of hearing people? What advantages could signed languages offer over spoken ones? Explain.

# Spanish Lessons
*Christine Marín*

Christine Marín was born to bilingual Mexican-American parents in Globe, Arizona. Remembering the discrimination they encountered during their own childhoods, the elder Maríns determined that their children would speak English in their home. Her parents recognized the power of language—they told their children to "speak better English than the gringo, so that he could not ridicule [them] the way they had been ridiculed in school and work." In this environment, Christine Marín began to encounter some mixed messages. On the one hand, she was encouraged to be proud of her heritage and cultural background; on the other, she was discouraged from speaking Spanish. It was not until high school that she began to recognize the power of the Spanish tongue. The essay that follows describes Marín's gradual awakening to the power of her cultural language, her emerging respect for this language, and how it ultimately shaped her identity.

Christine Marín is the curator for the Chicano Research Collection at the University of Arizona, where she also teaches in the Women's Studies program. She is the author of *Latinos in Museums: Heritage Reclaimed* (1998).

1   The reality of being a Mexican-American whose mother tongue was English and who did not speak Spanish came in the form of a 1958 high school band trip and the song "La Bamba" by Ritchie Valens (I didn't even know he was Mexican-American!), which was quite popular. I wasn't any different from the other high school kids who learned the words of popular songs we heard on the radio. Anglo and Mexican-American kids would sit together in the back of the bus and sing loudly and attempt to drown out the singing of those kids who sat toward the front of the bus. The game was to see who could sing the best and the loudest, and consequently drown out the singing of those in front.

2   On one band trip we sang "La Bamba." I didn't realize we were singing so loudly and in Spanish! My "voice" came out in the form of Spanish lyrics, although I was unaware of it. My Mexican-American identity shone through. I remember how proud I was for singing in Spanish, even though I didn't understand all the words of the song. I didn't know what a *bamba* was or what a *marinero* was. I hadn't heard those words before, and I wondered if my Mexican-American girl-friends knew the meaning of the song. I stumbled over the words, mispronouncing many of them. Suddenly, one popular Anglo girl sitting toward the front of the bus stood up in the middle of the aisle and shouted out loud so that everyone could hear: "Hey, you Mexicans! This is America! Stop singing in Spanish!" She proceeded to loudly sing "God Bless America" and "My Country 'Tis of Thee." To my surprise, her Anglo friends joined her in singing those patriotic songs. Well, our group of Mexican-American girls was not to be outdone. We sang the words to "La Bamba" even louder, and this infuriated her even more! Eventually, our band director jumped up from his seat and demanded that we all shut up. That stopped the singing. I could see that our band director was agitated, but I wasn't sure if it was because of that stupid, racist remark from that little twerp or because of all the noise throughout the bus.

3    It didn't take me long to figure out what had happened. I realized that the girl and her friends did not resent being outsung but resented the fact that we were singing in Spanish, using words that weren't even a part of my everyday vocabulary! All I was doing was singing a song. I felt like getting up out of my seat and beating up that insensitive, stupid girl—and good! But I didn't. I learned the power of both the English and Spanish languages on that band trip. And what a lesson it was! The Spanish language posed a threat to that girl, and it made me feel proud of being a Mexican-American despite the fact that I didn't speak Spanish. I felt superior to her because I knew two languages and I could understand both English and Spanish, while she could only understand English.

4    In high school, I was an above-average student but certainly not one who made straight A's. I excelled in English and writing assignments, and my work was noticed by my English teachers, especially Mrs. Ethel Jaenicke. She hoped I would attend college after high school, something I hadn't thought was possible. She spent extra time with me and encouraged me to continue my writing. Unfortunately, my father's pay didn't stretch far enough to pay for a college education. My parents, however, knew the value and importance of a good education and wanted their children to continue on to college. They made great sacrifices to help all of us begin our college education and were encouraging, nurturing, and understanding about our struggles to stay in school. It was ultimately up to us to somehow find the money to stay in school and continue our education.

5    After graduation from Globe High School in 1961, I moved to Phoenix, where I lived with my older brother and his wife. A friend of his helped me get a job as a salesgirl at Jay's Credit Clothing, a Jewish-owned clothing store in downtown Phoenix. Customers bought their goods on credit. The clothing lines were fashionable, stylish, and overpriced. Most of the customers were African-Americans, Mexicans, Mexican-Americans, and some Anglos. Mexican-American saleswomen were paid a small weekly salary but earned most of their money through sales commissions. Making those sales was very competitive, and I didn't do so well. I couldn't speak Spanish well enough to assist Spanish-speaking customers who came into the store, which left me frustrated and embarrassed. One of the senior Mexican-American saleswomen felt sorry for me; she noticed how desperately I struggled with the language. She often gave me her own sales after she had assisted Spanish-speaking customers by putting my name on her sales tickets. She knew I would be attending Arizona State University in August and needed to save money for school. She took me under her wing and spoke to me of her childhood wishes of going to college, though her family couldn't afford to send her. This woman worked in that clothing store for many years. She taught me another lesson about the power of language: bilingualism paid well—monetarily well! I decided to recapture my lost native tongue and consciously worked on speaking more Spanish so that I could earn more money.

6    At ASU, I enrolled in liberal arts courses and had many interests. I took classes in psychology, sociology, history, and English, to name but a few. One college adviser even suggested that I major in Spanish because "Mexicans make good Spanish teachers and you could always find a job teaching it." If he only knew how badly I spoke the language! I didn't want to major in Spanish. Chalk up two

more lessons learned about the power of language. First, someone assumed I spoke Spanish simply because of my surname and brown-colored skin. Second, by knowing the Spanish language, I would always be guaranteed a teaching job. However, I didn't want to be a teacher. . . .

7    During my freshman year, an English professor insulted my character and intelligence when she accused me of taking credit for a writing assignment she believed was written by someone else. According to her, the essay was extremely well written, but I couldn't have written it because "Mexicans don't write that well." "You people don't even speak the language correctly." Another hard lesson to learn about the power of language! This time the lesson was that my skin color and Spanish surname—not my language proficiency and ability in English—served as criteria to discriminate against me. My English ability was questioned and discredited. The academy had silenced my English voice. No matter how hard I tried, I couldn't convince her I had written that essay and that I had not paid someone to write it for me, as she presumed. This incident angered me. I had done what my parents said—be better than the gringo through language. But since this gringa professor had power and status, she felt she could accuse me of cheating. Needless to say, I dropped the class and never spoke to her again. I didn't care whether she believed me or not. . . .

8    In 1970, I applied for and was hired for a bibliographer position, where I learned all aspects of verifying English-language bibliographic entries and citations for monographs, serials, periodicals, and government documents, among others. I learned the intricacies of checking and verifying library holdings and how to use bibliographic tools and sources. I grew intellectually in my work. Because of my knowledge of library-related information, I became the "expert" and "voice" for my classmates and their friends who either were unfamiliar with the library system or found learning how to use book or serial catalogs confusing. I taught them how to use the library's catalogs and reference tools and encouraged them to enjoy the library setting. My job empowered me. I had learned a new code—the library code.

9    The year 1970 was an important one for Mexican-American students at ASU in other ways. My friends were beginning to call themselves "Chicanos" as a term of self-identification and tossed aside the term "Mexican Americans." For them, the term "Chicano" meant empowerment, and they found a new identity as Chicanos. But it was not a new word to me. I had heard it used by my parents and their friends when I was growing up in Globe. My father called himself a Chicano, and so did his friends from his military service days in World War II. For them the word "Chicano" was used in friendship—as a term of endearment, as a term of identity.

10    Now my college friends were using the word "Chicano" differently and in a defiant manner, with the word "power" after it: "Chicano Power!" For them and for me, it became a term of self-identity. The word was an assertion of ethnic and cultural pride, a term heard in a new form of social protests and associated with student activism and civil rights militancy. Chicanos throughout the Southwest were caught up in the Chicano Movement, a civil rights movement. They made new demands—that they become visible rather than invisible on their college and university campuses—and wanted a voice. They demanded courses that described the history, culture, and experiences of Chicanos in the Southwest. They wanted

Chicano counselors and professors to teach bilingual-bicultural education courses and courses in social work on their campuses. Arizona State University was going to be at the forefront in making these changes. Two scholars, Dr. Manuel Patricio Servín and Dr. H. William Axford, played in integral role in this demand for change. Hayden Library was to be the setting that allowed students to legitimize history, culture, art, language, and literature by acknowledging the presence of Mexican-Americans, Chicanos, and Mexicans. . . .

11      Servín and Axford quickly became my friends; the scholar and the librarian took me under their wings. They anticipated what Chicano students were going to do: demand that their library have books *by* and *about* them. They were right, and they gave students their voice. This is where I came in. Not long after his arrival, Dr. Axford came to the bibliography department and asked if anyone was familiar with Chicano materials. Being the only Chicana in the department, I was the one who spoke up.

12      In 1969, my friends had organized the Mexican-American Students Organization (MASO) on the ASU campus, and I attended the meetings. MASO students came from various Arizona places, including mining towns, cities, and rural towns. The majority spoke English, so meetings were conducted in English; the MASO newsletter was written in English, with a few slogans in Spanish thrown in for effect, such as *¡Basta Ya!, ¡Viva La Raza!, Con Safos,* and *¡Viva La Huelga!* By 1970, I had attended Chicano Movement–related meetings, had participated in United Farmworker rallies in Phoenix, and had leafleted pro-union literature urging the boycott of lettuce sold at Safeway stores. I became well acquainted with Chicano Movement ideologies and with the events of the times.

13      I met with Drs. Axford and Servín and listened to a new idea that they proposed to me. Dr. Axford suggested that I become the bibliographer for the Chicano Studies Collection, with my first task being to conduct an inventory of the library's holdings of Chicano-related materials. Dr. Servín provided me with various bibliographies listing the Chicano Studies' holdings of university libraries in California. I kept a record of the library's strengths and weaknesses in Chicano Studies by searching publishers' catalogs, listing the titles we didn't have, and marking them as available for purchasing. In that meeting with Drs. Axford and Servín, I learned that it was their intent to build a Chicano Studies Collection that would support Servín's teaching and research needs in Chicano Studies and the needs of those students who would enroll in the American Studies program. Dr. Axford wanted to strengthen the library's holding in Chicano Studies so that he would be prepared to justify those holdings to Chicano students when they demanded that the library have them. I agreed to become the bibliographer for the Chicano Studies Collection. I was the staff of one. In essence, Axford and Servín empowered me to take over the Chicano Studies Collection. I became the expert, the liaison for scholars, students, and researchers. The Chicano Studies Collection became another means by which my voice was heard. I now had the opportunity to tell others of my culture, of which I was proud. . . .

14      Dr. Axford was open to the idea of meeting with MASO. I agreed to work with MASO representatives in selecting books for the Chicano Studies Collection. It was a positive relationship, reflective of Dr. Axford's philosophy of open

access to library materials and sources. Chicano students began to utilize the library, and brown faces were now appearing in greater numbers in the study areas in and around the collection. Soon I was collecting and saving MASO newsletters, leaflets, minutes from meetings, membership lists, and other Chicano movement materials for my own interest. Dr. Servín encouraged me to collect these materials for the library and planted the seed in my mind to someday build a Chicano Studies archives. What a great idea! He also encouraged me to return to school and enroll in his courses to familiarize myself with the historical literature of the Southwest. It was my fate and destiny to encounter Drs. Servín and Axford and to find a new direction that would satisfy my intellectual growth and development. I learned more about Chicano history from Dr. Servín's classes, where I was exposed to the writings, research, and thought of Chicano scholars and writers. He also gave me the opportunity to do research and helped me publish my first article about the Chicano Movement in a scholarly journal that he edited. In 1974, my scholarly voice came through.

15      Outside the classroom, I continued to be exposed to Chicano Movement ideas and activities, and I easily made friends and contacts who would lead me to those elusive materials that are archival prizes in academic libraries today. I was challenged to improve my Spanish language skills by those individuals who were community activists. They spoke in both English and Spanish, and I learned what the term "codeswitching" meant. As a reflection of the times, MASO students changed their name in 1971 to MECHA, which stands for Movimiento Estudiantil Chicano de Aztlán.

16      I've continued working at Hayden Library, where I am now the curator/archivist for the Chicano Research Collection. I have built the Chicano Studies Collection into an important archival repository. During the last ten years, I've been an adjunct faculty associate in the Women's Studies program, where I have taught the courses "La Chicana" and "Women in the Southwest." I have assigned my students to write about the history of Chicanas in their families, to become curious about their family histories, and to incorporate oral history into their research. Through this assignment, they give voice to their own family histories, and they acquire their own voices in the discovery of their identities. Their manuscripts, as well as those of others, are in the Chicano Research Collection. These materials provide information about the past. Students, researchers, and scholars from all over the world have access to records, documents, oral histories, photographs, diaries, correspondence, videos, pamphlets, leaflets, and posters about the history, culture, and heritage of Chicanos, Chicanas, and Mexican-Americans in the United States. I am proud and honored to preserve these records for future Chicana and Chicano scholars. It is these materials that transmit the voices of *nuestra raza* vis-à-vis the printed page.

17      As I conclude my journey and the sharing of my story of growing up in an Arizona mining town, I have come to discover the many voices and modes of communication I had available to me and how they have contributed to the formation of self and identity. These voices have empowered me, educated me, sensitized me. Empowerment came through my work as an archivist and MASO/MECHA student, my scholarship, and my work in academe. My English voices as a young

child, in school, and throughout ring clear: the discrimination in academe that I encountered in my English class and also my knowledge of the intricacies of library language. My Spanish voices are also evident: in the back of the band bus in high school; when, for economic survival, I was a salesclerk; and when, through activism, I worked for change in the Chicano community. My empowerment coming full circle is evident through the sharing of my voice in my scholarship and my roles as teacher, lecturer, and historian. From the back of the bus to the ivory tower, I have learned the power of language.

### THINKING CRITICALLY

1. What is the catalyst for Christine Marín's awareness of the power of Spanish in her life? How does she react to this event? How does it connect to her identity and her growing consciousness of the power of language?

2. How does Marín's physical appearance conflict with the expectations of the "Anglos" around her? Cite some examples in which her ethnic appearance causes cultural confusion, and explain how she deals with this.

3. How does Marín learn to appreciate her heritage? Having been raised in an English-only household as an American, how does her ancestry begin to blend with her identity? Review the changes described by Marín to the term *Chicano*. What did the word mean to her when she was a child in a Mexican-American household? How did the word change in the early 1970s while she was in college? What do you think accounts for this transition?

4. Until college, Marín says that she did not really feel that her Mexican heritage made her any different from her peers. What event does Marín experience as a freshman that changes her perspective? How does she react to it?

5. How does the Chicano Studies Collection at the University of Arizona become a means by which Marín's voice can be heard? What is this voice? How does it empower her?

6. What do you think is the meaning of the author's last sentence? Does it connect to her essay as a whole? Explain.

### WRITING ASSIGNMENTS

1. Marín details some of the experiences that contributed to her awareness of the power of her ancestral language and its connection to her identity. Can you recall any events in your life that made you realize the connections between your language and your sense of self? Write about your experience.

2. When Marín was a freshman, she encountered a teacher who refused to believe that she was capable of writing well because of her physical appearance. Have you ever experienced a similar situation in which someone judged you by your looks and not by your verbal or intellectual skills? Alternatively, have you ever made assumptions about another person's abilities based on what he or she looked like? Explain.

3. Is the way you personally use language something that you take for granted? Write an essay in which you explore the power of your own language. As you write, consider how language contributes to your identity and how you fit into your culture. How does your language empower you?

# The Language of Silence

*Maxine Hong Kingston*

Maxine Hong Kingston, born in 1940, was raised in a Chinese immigrant community in Stockton, California. As a first-generation American, she found herself having to adjust to two distinctly contrasting cultures. For a young girl, this was confusing and difficult, as she recalls in this selection from her highly praised and popular autobiography, *The Woman Warrior: Memoirs of a Girlhood Among Ghosts* (1976). To the Chinese immigrant, white Americans are "ghosts"—pale, threatening, and at times, comical specters who speak an incomprehensible tongue. For Kingston, becoming American meant adopting new values, defining a new self, and finding a new voice.

Before the publication of her award-winning autobiography, Kingston taught in several high schools and business schools. Since then, she has published *China Men* (1980); a novel, *The Tripmaster Monkey: His Fake Book* (1989); and reflections on writing, *To Be the Poet* (2002). She currently teaches English at the University of California, Berkeley.

1 Long ago in China, knot-makers tied string into buttons and frogs, and rope into bell pulls. There was one knot so complicated that it blinded the knot-maker. Finally an emperor outlawed this cruel knot, and the nobles could not order it anymore. If I had lived in China, I would have been an outlaw knot-maker.

2 Maybe that's why my mother cut my tongue. She pushed my tongue up and sliced the frenum. Or maybe she snipped it with a pair of nail scissors. I don't remember her doing it, only her telling me about it, but all during childhood I felt sorry for the baby whose mother waited with scissors or knife in hand for it to cry—and then, when its mouth was wide open like a baby bird's, cut. The Chinese say "a ready tongue is an evil."

3 I used to curl up my tongue in front of the mirror and tauten my frenum into a white line, itself as thin as a razor blade. I saw no scars in my mouth. I thought perhaps I had had two frena, and she had cut one. I made other children open their mouths so I could compare theirs to mine. I saw perfect pink membranes stretch ing into precise edges that looked easy enough to cut. Sometimes I felt very proud that my mother committed such a powerful act upon me. At other times I was terrified—the first thing my mother did when she saw me was to cut my tongue.

4 "Why did you do that to me, Mother?"

5 "I told you."

6 "Tell me again."

7 "I cut it so that you would not be tongue-tied. Your tongue would be able to move in any language. You'll be able to speak languages that are completely different from one another. You'll be able to pronounce anything. Your frenum looked too tight to do those things, so I cut it."

8 "But isn't 'a ready tongue an evil'?"

9 "Things are different in this ghost country."

10 "Did it hurt me? Did I cry and bleed?"

11 "I don't remember. Probably."

12    She didn't cut the other children's. When I asked cousins and other Chinese children whether their mothers had cut their tongues loose, they said "What?"

13    "Why didn't you cut my brothers' and sisters' tongues?"

14    "They didn't need it."

15    "Why not? Were theirs longer than mine?"

16    "Why don't you quit blabbering and get to work?"

17    If my mother was not lying she should have cut more, scraped away the rest of the frenum skin, because I have a terrible time talking. Or she should not have cut at all, tampering with my speech. When I went to kindergarten and had to speak English for the first time, I became silent. A dumbness—a shame—still cracks my voice in two, even when I want to say "hello" casually, or ask an easy question in front of the check-out counter, or ask directions of a bus driver. I stand frozen, or I hold up the line with the complete, grammatical sentence that comes squeaking out at impossible length. "What did you say?" says the cab driver, or "Speak up," so I have to perform again, only weaker the second time. A telephone call makes my throat bleed and takes up that day's courage. It spoils my day with self-disgust when I hear my broken voice come skittering out into the open. It makes people wince to hear it. I'm getting better, though. Recently I asked the postman for special-issue stamps; I've waited since childhood for postmen to give me some of their own accord. I am making progress, a little every day.

18    My silence was thickest—total—during the three years that I covered my school paintings with black paint. I painted layers of black over houses and flowers and suns, and when I drew on the background, I put a layer of chalk on top. I was making a stage curtain, and it was the moment before the curtain parted or rose. The teachers called my parents to school, and I saw they had been saving my pictures, curling and cracking, all alike and black. The teachers pointed to the pictures and looked serious, talked seriously too, but my parents did not understand English. ("The parents and teachers of criminals were executed," said my father.) My parents took the pictures home. I spread them out (so black and full of possibilities) and pretended the curtains were swinging open, flying up, one after another, sunlight underneath, mighty operas.

19    During the first silent year I spoke to no one at school, did not ask before going to the lavatory, and flunked kindergarten. My sister also said nothing for three years, silent in the playground and silent at lunch. There were other quiet Chinese girls not of our family, but most of them got over it sooner than we did. I enjoyed the silence. At first it did not occur to me I was supposed to talk or to pass kindergarten. I talked at home and to one or two of the Chinese kids in class. I made motions and even made some jokes. I drank out of a toy saucer when the water spilled out of the cup, and everybody laughed, pointing at me, so I did it some more. I didn't know that Americans don't drink out of saucers.

20    I liked the Negro students (Black Ghosts) best because they laughed the loudest and talked to me as if I were a daring talker too. One of the Negro girls had her mother coil braids over her ears Shanghai-style like mine; we were Shanghai twins except that she was covered with black like my paintings. Two Negro kids enrolled in Chinese school, and the teachers gave them Chinese names. Some Negro kids walked me to school and home, protecting me from the Japanese kids, who hit me and chased me and stuck gum in my ears. The Japanese kids were noisy and tough.

They appeared one day in kindergarten, released from concentration camp, which was a tic-tac-toe mark, like barbed wire, on the map.

21    It was when I found out I had to talk that school became a misery, that the silence became a misery. I did not speak and felt bad each time that I did not speak. I read aloud in first grade, though, and heard the barest whisper with little squeaks come out of my throat. "Louder," said the teacher, who scared the voice away again. The other Chinese girls did not talk either, so I knew the silence had to do with being a Chinese girl.

22    Reading out loud was easier than speaking because we did not have to make up what to say, but I stopped often, and the teacher would think I'd gone quiet again. I could not understand "I." The Chinese "I" has seven strokes, intricacies. How could the American "I," assuredly wearing a hat like the Chinese, have only three strokes, the middle so straight? Was it out of politeness that this writer left off strokes the way a Chinese has to write her own name small and crooked? No, it was not politeness; "I" is a capital and "you" is a lower-case. I stared at that middle line and waited so long for its black center to resolve into tight strokes and dots that I forgot to pronounce it. The other troublesome word was "here," no strong consonant to hang on to, and so flat, when "here" is two mountainous ideographs. The teacher, who had already told me every day how to read "I" and "here," put me in the low corner under the stairs again, where the noisy boys usually sat.

23    When my second grade class did a play, the whole class went to the auditorium except the Chinese girls. The teacher, lovely and Hawaiian, should have understood about us, but instead left us behind in the classroom. Our voices were too soft or nonexistent, and our parents never signed the permission slips anyway. They never signed anything unnecessary. We opened the door a crack and peeked out, but closed it again quickly. One of us (not me) won every spelling bee, though.

24    I remember telling the Hawaiian teacher, "We Chinese can't sing 'Land where our fathers died.'" She argued with me about politics, while I meant because of curses. But how can I have that memory when I couldn't talk? My mother says that we, like ghosts, have no memories.

25    After American school, we picked up our cigar boxes, in which we had arranged books, brushes, and an inkbox neatly, and went to Chinese school, from 5:00 to 7:30 P.M. There we chanted together, voices rising and falling, loud and soft, some boys shouting, everybody reading together, reciting together and not alone with one voice. When we had a memorization test, the teacher let each of us come to his desk and say the lesson to him privately, while the rest of the class practiced copying or tracing. Most of the teachers were men. The boys who were so well behaved in the American school played tricks on them and talked back to them. The girls were not mute. They screamed and yelled during recess, when there were no rules; they had fistfights. Nobody was afraid of children hurting themselves or of children hurting school property. The glass doors to the red and green balconies with the gold joy symbols were left wide open so that we could run out and climb the fire escapes. We played capture-the-flag in the auditorium, where Sun Yat-sen and Chiang Kai-shek's pictures hung at the back of the stage, the Chinese flag on their left and the American flag on their right. We climbed the teak ceremonial chairs and made flying leaps off the stage. One flag headquarters was behind the

glass door and the other on stage right. Our feet drummed on the hollow stage. During recess, the teachers locked themselves up in their office with the shelves of books, copybooks, inks from China. They drank tea and warmed their hands at a stove. There was no play supervision. At recess we had the school to ourselves, and also we could roam as far as we could go—downtown, Chinatown stores, home—as long as we returned before the bell rang.

26    At exactly 7:30 the teacher again picked up the brass bell that sat on his desk and swung it over our heads, while we charged down the stairs, our cheering magnified in the stairwell. Nobody had to line up.

27    Not all of the children who were silent at American school found voice at Chinese school. One new teacher said each of us had to get up and recite in front of the class, who was to listen. My sister and I had memorized the lesson perfectly. We said it to each other at home, one chanting, one listening. The teacher called on my sister to recite first. It was the first time a teacher had called on the second-born to go first. My sister was scared. She glanced at me and looked away; I looked down at my desk. I hoped that she could do it because if she could, then I would have to. She opened her mouth and a voice came out that wasn't a whisper, but it wasn't a proper voice either. I hoped that she would not cry, fear breaking up her voice like twigs underfoot. She sounded as if she were trying to sing through weeping and strangling. She did not pause or stop to end the embarrassment. She kept going until she said the last word, and then she sat down. When it was my turn, the same voice came out, a crippled animal running on broken legs. You could hear splinters in my voice, bones rubbing jagged against one another. I was loud, though. I was glad I didn't whisper. There was one little girl who whispered. . . .

28    How strange that the emigrant villagers are shouters, hollering face to face. My father asks, "Why is it I can hear Chinese from blocks away? Is it that I understand the language? Or is it they talk loud?" They turn the radio up full blast to hear the operas, which do not seem to hurt their ears. And they yell over the singers that wail over the drums, everybody talking at once, big arm gestures, spit flying. You can see the disgust on American faces looking at women like that. It isn't just the loudness. It is the way Chinese sounds, ching-chong ugly, to American ears, not beautiful like Japanese sayonara words with the consonants and vowels as regular as Italian. We make guttural peasant noise and have Ton Duc Thang names you can't remember. And the Chinese can't hear Americans at all; the language is too soft and western music unhearable. I've watched a Chinese audience laugh, visit, talk-story, and holler during a piano recital, as if the musician could not hear them. A Chinese-American, somebody's son, was playing Chopin, which has no punctuation, no cymbals, no gongs. Chinese piano music is five black keys. Normal Chinese women's voices are strong and bossy. We American-Chinese girls had to whisper to make ourselves American-feminine. Apparently, we whispered even more softly than the Americans. Once a year the teachers referred my sister and me to speech therapy, but our voices would straighten out, unpredictably normal, for the therapists. Some of us gave up, shook our heads, and said nothing, not one word. Some of us could not even

shake our heads. At times, shaking my head no is more self-assertion than I can manage. Most of us eventually found some voice, however faltering. We invented an American-feminine speaking personality.

## THINKING CRITICALLY

1. Kingston employed silence rather than language in the early grades. What accounts for the difference in attitude between kindergarten, where she "employed the silence," and first grade, where "silence became a misery"?

2. Kingston's teacher punished her for failing to read "I" and "here." How does this episode demonstrate the clash between Chinese and American cultures? Are there other episodes in the essay that also demonstrate this struggle?

3. How did Kingston's Chinese school differ from the American one? What impact did the former school have on her language development?

4. What do you make of Kingston's paintings? What was Kingston's personal view of her work? How do they relate to her "language of silence"?

5. Examine the conclusion of the essay. Would you say this is a moment of triumph or defeat for Kingston? Explain.

6. At what point in the essay do you know Kingston's focus? What are the clues to her purpose? Does this lead capture your attention? Explain.

7. Kingston writes this essay using the first person. How is this ironic in light of what she writes in the piece? Would this essay be as effective if it were told from a third-person point of view? Explain.

## WRITING ASSIGNMENTS

1. Assume that you are a teacher with Kingston as a pupil. How would you handle her? What different tactics would it take to get her to come out of herself? Write a paper in which you describe your role.

2. Did you have difficulties "coming to language" as a child? Do you remember resorting to protective silence because of your accent, a different primary language, or a different cultural identity? Did you feel fear and/or embarrassment because of your difference, and did you carry the results of your experience into your adult life? If so, in what way? In a personal narrative, describe your experience.

3. Kingston admits that even as an adult, she has "a terrible time talking." She says that she still freezes with shame, that she can hardly be heard, that her voice is broken and squeaky. What about her writing style? Do you see any reflection of her vocal difficulties—any signs of hesitation or uncertainty? In a paper, consider these questions as you try to describe her style as it relates to her experiences as a young girl.

4. Bilingual education is a controversial form of education designed to instill educational confidence in school children, allowing them to learn using the language spoken in their homes. See the National Clearinghouse for Bilingual Education's website, maintained by George Washington University, for more information on this form of education, at www.ncela.gwu.edu/. Kingston relates that she had to go to a separate Chinese school after her regular school day. Do you think Kingston's educational experience would have been different had she been taught in a bilingual classroom?

## MAKING CONNECTIONS

1. Which do we depend on more, signs or symbols? Which are we most apt to misconstrue? Can you think of any words that function as both signs and symbols?

2. Consider the ways we communicate without actually using words. Make a detailed report of a morning's activities in which information is relayed to and by you without speaking. Does a friend gesture for you to approach? Do you see a sign or even a color that warns you to stop? What other nonverbal cues communicate meaning to you? Connect your record to the points made by the authors in this section.

3. Most students take literacy for granted. Research the issue of illiteracy in this country. How does it impact the children of illiterate parents? Brainstorm and make a list of all the things you could not do. Prepare an essay exploring the issue of illiteracy in the United States, how prevalent the problem really is, and its impact on people today and over the next 20 years.

4. Recall any communication difficulties you had as a child. Perhaps you are bilingual or had difficulty pronouncing certain words, or maybe an older sibling prevented you from expressing yourself. Explain how your experience made you feel, recalling, if possible, any particularly telling experiences. Can you identify with any of the authors in this section? If so, which ones and why?

5. Did your parents or grandparents come to America from another country? If not, are you acquainted with anyone who did? Conduct an interview with this person about his or her language choices. What is his or her view about the importance of language? What happened to his or her language after moving to America? Provide a brief biographical sketch of the person you interviewed and present your research to the class.

6. Helen Keller writes that the acquisition of language "set her free." Malcolm X expresses similar views on the freeing power of language. In your journal, record your own feelings about the different ways that language provides freedom. In addition to drawing from some of the essays in this section, you may wish to add an experience of your own.

7. Each of the authors in this section recollects a moment in which they realized the power of language. For Malcolm X, it was when he realized how language could set him free. For Helen Keller, it was when she first connected words to abstract concepts. For Christine Marín, it was when she connected ethnic pride to the language of her ancestors. Write about a defining moment in your life when you felt the power of language.

8. Research the origins and development of American Sign Language. How does this system of communication qualify as a language? How has this language changed the lives of nonhearing people? Explain.

# Writers on Writing

Each of the essays in this textbook explores how language constructs reality for us: how it can be used to communicate, inform, lead, mislead, and even manipulate us. Although many pieces celebrate the joys of language, others lament its woes—that politicians and bureaucrats talk gobbledygook, that advertisers torture language to sell their goods, and that the ability of students to write clearly is deteriorating. In short, you hear a lot about bad writing.

This chapter offers insights and advice about good writing. From a practical point of view, the essays in this chapter are intended to help prepare you for the writing projects featured in this book and in your academic studies. The readings in this chapter also aim to provide the foundations of basic rhetorical principles and strategies so that you can participate with confidence in lively and informed debates about language.

Most college writing is an exercise in persuasion—an attempt to influence readers' attitudes about the subject matter. This is true whether you are discussing tragic irony in *Oedipus Rex,* analyzing the causes of World War I, writing a lab report on the solubility of salt, protesting next year's tuition increase, or explaining the joys of bungee jumping. How successful you are at persuading your readers will have a lot to do with the words you choose.

## The Writing Process

The first section considers the writing process—how we write, where we get our inspiration, and the techniques good writers use. The first essay, "Writing for an Audience" by Linda Flower, offers some key points of advice on establishing common ground with one's readers. The next two pieces, by critically acclaimed writers, describe how each author approaches the challenge of writing. Writer Anne Lamott explains how she helps her students find their muse in "Getting Started." In this age of many causes, good writing has the power to advance social change, a point that Mary Pipher explores in "Writing to Change the World." Then, fiction author Ayelet Waldman, in "Beware the Trap of 'Bore-geous' Writing," describes the balance between writing beautifully and writing *meaningfully.*

## Finding the Right Words

The second section features essays providing advice and suggestions on how to choose the right words to express your message effectively, and how to formulate that message so that your reader will be receptive and open to your ideas. Beginning writers often opt for cluttered expressions, empty jargon, and convoluted constructions to sound "smarter." However, all they achieve with this approach is poor writing. Richard Lederer explains in the section's first essay, "The Case for Short Words," that often the best way to say something is with short, clear, pure words that are rich with meaning. Patricia T. O'Conner builds on Lederer's tips by adding 13 more of her own in "Saying Is Believing," in which she explains that the best writers are the ones who are easily understood—ones you can read "without breaking a sweat." James Isaacs explains how not to communicate in his parody of what nearly every high school and college graduate must endure—the commencement speech—in "Clichés, Anyone?" The section closes with an essay addressing charged and strong language. "Selection, Slanting, and Charged Language" by Newman and Genevieve Birk describes how words can warp reality when writers bend them to achieve their own ends.

# THE WRITING PROCESS

## Writing for an Audience
*Linda Flower*

One of the most important tasks an educated person does is manage information. And writing is an important part of managing information. We write to keep track of things (lists, inventories, databases), to organize materials (outlines, tables of contents, indexes), and to develop ideas too complex to manage in our heads. We also write to tell people what we know, what conclusions we have drawn about a situation, and how we would like them to proceed. In the next essay, Linda Flower tells us that to be successful managers of information we need to know how our audience will see the information we present so that we can choose and shape information to help them understand our perspective.

Linda Flower is a professor of English at Carnegie-Mellon University and is, through her many books and articles, a prominent voice in the field of composition and rhetoric. She is the author of several textbooks, including *Problem Solving Strategies for Writing in College and the Community* (1985) and *The Construction of Negotiated Meaning: A Social Cognitive Theory of Writing* (1994). Her suggestions on creating common ground with your audience should be useful in writing situations you encounter in your college and professional career.

1 The goal of the writer is to create a momentary common ground between the reader and the writer. You want the reader to share your knowledge and your attitude toward that knowledge. Even if the reader eventually disagrees, you want him or her to be able for the moment to *see things as you see them*. A good piece of writing closes the gap between you and the reader.

### Analyze Your Audience

2 The first step in closing that gap is to gauge the distance between the two of you. Imagine, for example, that you are a student writing your parents, who have always lived in New York City, about a wilderness survival expedition you want to go on over spring break. Sometimes obvious differences such as age or background will be important, but the critical differences for writers usually fall into three areas: the reader's *knowledge* about the topic; his or her *attitude* toward it, and his or her

personal or professional *needs*. Because these differences often exist, good writers do more than simply express their meaning; they pinpoint the critical differences between themselves and their reader and design their writing to reduce those differences. Let us look at these three areas in more detail.

## Knowledge

3 This is usually the easiest difference to handle. What does your reader need to know? What are the main ideas you hope to teach? Does your reader have enough background knowledge to really understand you? If not, what would he or she have to learn?

## Attitudes

4 When we say a person has knowledge, we usually refer to his conscious awareness of explicit facts and clearly defined concepts. This kind of knowledge can be easily written down or told to someone else. However, much of what we "know" is not held in this formal, explicit way. Instead it is held as an attitude or image—as a loose cluster of associations. For instance, my image of lakes includes associations many people would have, including fishing, water skiing, stalled outboards, and lots of kids catching night crawlers with flashlights. However, the most salient or powerful parts of my image, which strongly color my whole attitude toward lakes, are thoughts of cloudy skies, long rainy days, and feeling generally cold and damp. By contrast, one of my best friends has a very different cluster of associations: to him a lake means sun, swimming, sailing, and happily sitting on the end of a dock. Needless to say, our differing images cause us to react quite differently to a proposal that we visit a lake. Likewise, one reason people often find it difficult to discuss religion and politics is that terms such as "capitalism" conjure up radically different images.

5 As you can see, a reader's image of a subject is often the source of attitudes and feelings that are unexpected and, at times, impervious to mere facts. A simple statement that seems quite persuasive to you, such as "Lake Wampago would be a great place to locate the new music camp," could have little impact on your reader if he or she simply doesn't visualize a lake as a "great place." In fact, many people accept uncritically any statement that fits in with their own attitudes—and reject, just as uncritically, anything that does not.

6 Whether your purpose is to persuade or simply to present your perspective, it helps to know the image and attitudes that your reader already holds. The more these differ from your own, the more you will have to do to make him or her *see* what you mean.

## Needs

7 When writers discover a large gap between their own knowledge and attitudes and those of the reader, they usually try to change the reader in some way. Needs, however, are different. When you analyze a reader's needs, it is so that you, the writer, can adapt to him. If you ask a friend majoring in biology how to keep your fish tank

from clouding, you don't want to hear a textbook recitation on the life processes of algae. You expect the friend to adapt his or her knowledge and tell you exactly how to solve your problem.

8      The ability to adapt your knowledge to the needs of the reader is often crucial to your success as a writer. This is especially true in writing done on a job. For example, as producer of a public affairs program for a television station, 80 percent of your time may be taken up planning the details of new shows, contacting guests, and scheduling the taping sessions. But when you write a program proposal to the station director, your job is to show how the program will fit into the cost guidelines, the FCC requirements for relevance, and the overall programming plan for the station. When you write that report your role in the organization changes from producer to proposal writer. Why? Because your reader needs that information in order to make a decision. He may be interested in your scheduling problems and the specific content of the shows, but he reads your report because of his own needs as station director of that organization. He has to act.

9      In college, where the reader is also a teacher, the reader's needs are a little less concrete but just as important. Most papers are assigned as a way to teach something. So the real purpose of a paper may be for you to make connections between two historical periods, to discover for yourself the principle behind a laboratory experiment, or to develop and support your own interpretation of a novel. A good college paper doesn't just rehash the facts; it demonstrates what your reader, as a teacher, needs to know—that you are learning the thinking skills his or her course is trying to teach.

10      Effective writers are not simply expressing what they know, like a student madly filling up an examination bluebook. Instead they are *using* their knowledge: reorganizing, maybe even rethinking their ideas to meet the demands of an assignment or the needs of their reader.

## THINKING CRITICALLY

1. Who does Flower assume to be her audience for this essay on audience? What evidence can you point to in the text that supports this answer?

2. Flower speaks of three areas of difference between a writer and his or her audience. List these three areas and, for each area, find two places in the text where Flower's writing seems designed to reduce those differences or to close the gap.

3. What is Flower's position on persuasiveness in writing? How is this attitude important to her point overall?

4. Do you find her discussion persuasive? Has she effectively closed the gaps between you, as audience, and herself, as writer? Discuss places in this text where she has been successful. Can you find places where she has not been successful, or where you think she might have done a better job? Write out any suggestions you have where you think she might have done a better job.

5. Make a list of different writing situations you have recently encountered or might expect to encounter in your work or profession. Identify a specific audience, then think very specifically about the knowledge, attitude, and needs of that audience and brainstorm a list of adjustments you will have to make in

order to bridge any gaps between you and your audience. Be ready to compare your answers with those of other students in the class.

6. Flower does not directly address what happens when an audience is comprised of different kinds of people. Can you think of instances where this has happened or might happen? What kinds of choices might an author make in order to meet the needs of many different kinds of people at one time? What happens when the writer fails to establish common ground with some part of his or her audience?

### WRITING ASSIGNMENTS

1. Flower is an expert on writing. Think of something you know really well and write an essay in which you explain writing (or some element of writing) to an audience that does not have your expertise.

2. Find samples of text (in the broadest sense of the word) on the same topic, but which are focused on different audiences. For your samples, you might look at an encyclopedia, news article, biography, textbook, expert opinion/testimonial, video clip, photograph or drawing, instruction manual, and so on. Consider differences in age, gender, culture, and educational backgrounds. Once you have gathered a range of materials, choose three that offer the most variety. Write an essay in which you describe the audience intended by the author(s) or creator(s) of each text; also discuss the strategies each author employed to bridge the presumed gaps in knowledge, attitude, and needs. Finally, draw conclusions about the relevance of these differences. Your focus should be on choices made with regard to language; organization; visual elements, including layouts; visual aids; and rhetorical elements such as narrative, exemplification, definition, comparison/contrast, exposition, and anything else that seems important.

3. Find a piece of text that is intended for an audience other than yourself. Perhaps find a journal from your major area that is targeted at professors/scholars, or find a discussion on a subject matter in which you have little or no background. Discuss the places where you have trouble and/or the different kinds of trouble you have. Explain what the author has done to meet the needs of his or her presumed audience. Then, talk about different strategies that might be employed in a revised version of the text aimed at you rather than at the intended audience. Append a one-page rewrite of this text (or some portion of it) to illustrate how the rewrite could be accomplished.

# Getting Started
*Anne Lamott*

For many students, the biggest writing challenge is simply getting started. In the next essay, writer and creative writing instructor Anne Lamott gives advice on how to get the ball rolling. The task of getting started, and feeling comfortable with what to write, is a challenge to students and published writers alike.

Anne Lamott is the author of several novels and memoirs, including *Hard Laughter* (1980), *All New People* (1989), *Operating Instructions* (1993), and *Crooked Little Heart* (1997). A past recipient of a Guggenheim fellowship, she has been a book review columnist for *Mademoiselle* magazine and a restaurant critic for *California* magazine. She teaches writing at the University of California–Davis and is a featured instructor at writing seminars throughout the state. The following piece is an excerpt from her 1995 book on writing, *Bird by Bird: Some Instructions on Writing and Life.*

1   The very first thing I tell my new students on the first day of a workshop is that good writing is about telling the truth. We are a species that needs and wants to understand who we are. Sheep lice do not seem to share this longing, which is one reason they write so very little. But we do. We have so much we want to say and figure out. Year after year my students are bursting with stories to tell, and they start writing projects with excitement and maybe even joy—finally their voices will be heard, and they are going to get to devote themselves to this one thing they've longed to do since childhood. But after a few days at the desk, telling the truth in an interesting way turns out to be about as easy and pleasurable as bathing a cat. Some lose faith. Their sense of self and story shatters and crumbles to the ground. Historically they show up for the first day of the workshop looking like bright goofy ducklings who will follow me anywhere, but by the time the second class rolls around, they look at me as if the engagement is definitely off.

2   "I don't even know where to start," one will wail.

3   Start with your childhood, I tell them. Plug your nose and jump in, and write down all your memories as truthfully as you can. Flannery O'Connor said that any one who survived childhood has enough material to write for the rest of his or her life. Maybe your childhood was grim and horrible, but grim and horrible is okay if it is well done. Don't worry about doing it well yet, though. Just start getting it down.

4   Now, the amount of material may be so overwhelming that it can make your brain freeze. When I had been writing food reviews for a number of years, there were so many restaurants and individual dishes in my brainpan that when people asked for a recommendation, I couldn't think of a single restaurant where I'd ever actually eaten. But if the person could narrow it down to, say, Indian, I might remember one lavish Indian palace, where my date had asked the waiter for the Rudyard Kipling sampler and later for the holy-cow tartare. Then a number of memories would come to mind, of other dates and other Indian restaurants.

5   So you might start by writing down every single thing you can remember from your first few years in school. Start with kindergarten. Try to get the words and memories down as they occur to you. Don't worry if what you write is no good, because no one is going to see it. Move on to first grade, to second, to third. Who were your teachers, your classmates? What did you wear? Who and what were you jealous of? Now branch out a little. Did your family take vacations during those years? Get these down on paper. Do you remember how much more presentable everybody else's family looked? Do you remember how when you'd be floating around in an inner tube on a river, your own family would have lost the little cap that screws over the airflow valve, so every time you got in and out of the inner tube, you'd scratch new welts in your thighs? And how other families never lost the caps?

6      If this doesn't pan out, or if it does but you finish mining this particular vein, see if focusing on holidays and big events helps you recollect your life as it was. Write down everything you can remember about every birthday or Christmas or Seder or Easter or whatever, every relative who was there. Write down all the stuff you swore you'd never tell another soul. What can you recall about your birthday parties—the disasters, the days of grace, your relatives' faces lit up by birthday candles? Scratch around for details: what people ate, listened to, wore—those terrible petaled swim caps, the men's awful trunks, the cocktail dress your voluptuous aunt wore that was so slinky she practically needed the Jaws of Life to get out of it. Write about the women's curlers with the bristles inside, the garters your father and uncles used to hold up their dress socks, your grandfathers' hats, your cousins' perfect Brownie uniforms, and how your own looked like it had just been hatched. Describe the trench coats and stoles and car coats, what they revealed and what they covered up. See if you can remember what you were given that Christmas when you were ten, and how it made you feel inside. Write down what the grown-ups said and did after they'd had a couple of dozen drinks, especially that one Fourth of July when your father made Fish House punch and the adults practically had to crawl from room to room.

7      Remember that you own what happened to you. If your childhood was less than ideal, you may have been raised thinking that if you told the truth about what really went on in your family, a long bony white finger would emerge from a cloud and point at you, while a chilling voice thundered, "We *told* you not to tell." But that was then. Just put down on paper everything you can remember now about your parents and siblings and relatives and neighbors, and we will deal with libel later on.

8      "But how?" my students ask. "How do you actually do it?"

9      You sit down, I say. You try to sit down at approximately the same time every day. This is how you train your unconscious to kick in for you creatively. So you sit down at, say, nine every morning, or ten every night. You put a piece of paper in the typewriter, or you turn on your computer and bring up the right file, and then you stare at it for an hour or so. You begin rocking, just a little at first, and then like a huge autistic child. You look at the ceiling, and over at the clock, yawn, and stare at the paper again. Then, with your fingers poised on the keyboard, you squint at an image that is forming in your mind—a scene, a locale, a character, whatever—and you try to quiet your mind so you can hear what that landscape or character has to say above the other voices in your mind. The other voices are banshees and drunken monkeys. They are the voices of anxiety, judgment, doom, guilt. Also, severe hypochondria. There may be a Nurse Ratched–like listing of things that must be done right this moment: foods that must come out of the freezer, appointments that must be canceled or made, hairs that must be tweezed. But you hold an imaginary gun to your head and make yourself stay at the desk. There is a vague pain at the base of your neck. It crosses your mind that you have meningitis. Then the phone rings and you look up at the ceiling with fury, summon every ounce of noblesse oblige, and answer the call politely, with maybe just the merest hint of irritation. The caller asks if you're working, and you say yeah, because you are.

10    Yet somehow in the face of all this, you clear a space for the writing voice, hacking away at the others with machetes, and you begin to compose sentences. You begin to string words together like beads to tell a story. You are desperate to communicate, to edify or entertain, to preserve moments of grace or joy or transcendence, to make real or imagined events come alive. But you cannot will this to happen. It is a matter of persistence and faith and hard work. So you might as well just go ahead and get started.

11    I wish I had a secret I could let you in on . . . some code word that has enabled me to sit at my desk and land flights of creative inspiration like an air-traffic controller. But I don't. All I know is that the process is pretty much the same for almost everyone I know. The good news is that some days it feels like you just have to keep getting out of your own way so that whatever it is that wants to be written can use you to write it. It is a little like when you have something difficult to discuss with someone, and as you go to do it, you hope and pray that the right words will come if only you show up and make a stab at it. And often the right words do come, and you—well—"write" for a while; you put a lot of thoughts down on paper. But the bad news is that if you're at all like me, you'll probably read over what you've written and spend the rest of the day obsessing, and praying that you do not die before you can completely rewrite or destroy what you have written, lest the eagerly waiting world learn how bad your first drafts are.

12    The obsessing may keep you awake, *or* the self-loathing may cause you to fall into a narcoleptic coma before dinner. But let's just say that you do fall asleep at a normal hour. Then the odds are that you will wake up at four in the morning, having dreamed that you have died. Death turns out to feel much more frantic than you had imagined. Typically you'll try to comfort yourself by thinking about the day's work—the day's excrementitious work. You may experience a jittery form of existential dread, considering the absolute meaninglessness of life and the fact that no one has ever really loved you; you may find yourself consumed with a free-floating shame, and a hopelessness about your work, and the realization that you will have to throw out everything you've done so far and start from scratch. But you will not be able to do so. Because you suddenly understand that you are completely riddled with cancer.

13    And then the miracle happens. The sun comes up again. So you get up and do your morning things, and one thing leads to another, and eventually, at nine, you find yourself back at the desk, staring blankly at the pages you filled yesterday. And there on page four is a paragraph with all sorts of life in it, smells and sounds and voices and colors and even a moment of dialogue that makes you say to yourself, very, very softly, "Hmmm." You look up and stare out the window again, but this time you are drumming your fingers on the desk, and you don't care about those first three pages; those you will throw out, those you needed to write to get to that fourth page, to get to that one long paragraph that was what you had in mind when you started, only you didn't know that, couldn't know that, until you got to it. And the story begins to materialize, and another thing is happening, which is that you are learning what you aren't writing, and this is helping you to find out what you *are* writing. Think of a fine painter attempting to capture an inner vision, beginning

with one corner of the canvas, painting what he thinks should be there, not quite pulling it off, covering it over with white paint, and trying again, each time finding out what his painting isn't, until finally he finds out what it is.

14     And when you do find out what one corner of your vision is, you're off and running. And it really is like running. It always reminds me of the last lines of *Rabbit, Run:* "his heels hitting heavily on the pavement at first but with an effortless gathering out of a kind of sweet panic growing lighter and quicker and quieter, he runs. Ah: runs. Runs."

15     I wish I felt that kind of inspiration more often. I almost never do. All I know is that if I sit there long enough, something will happen.

### THINKING CRITICALLY

1. What does Lamott mean when she says, "writing is about the truth"? Although she describes a creative writing workshop, how do you think this principle of truth could apply to other types of writing? Explain.

2. Who is "Nurse Ratched," and how can "she" interfere with your writing? What recommendations does Lamott give for stilling the voice of Nurse Ratched and other anxieties that may interfere with your writing?

3. Evaluate Lamott's style and tone in this essay. Does her writing reflect the lessons she teaches in this piece? How does her style connect with her audience? Do you think you would like to have her as a writing instructor? Why or why not?

4. Lamott observes that her class begins eager to begin writing, but soon grows frustrated with the actual mechanics of the process. Think about your own writing process. How do you write? Why do you write? Have you experienced frustrations similar to the students in Lamott's class? Explain.

5. What audience do you think Lamott is writing for? Support your answer by citing examples from her essay.

6. Lamott comments that one challenge many writers—including herself—face is dealing with a sense of "self-loathing" toward what they have written. Can you relate to this feeling? Why or why not?

### WRITING ASSIGNMENTS

1. Follow Lamott's advice to her class on getting started. Recall an incident from your childhood and write about it each day for a week. Focus on recalling memories, feelings, and impressions of the event. Return each day to add to and rework what you have written. At the end of the week, describe the experience of writing this way. Turn in both the creative writing piece you wrote and your analysis of the exercise to your instructor.

2. Have you ever had writer's block? How did you overcome it? What suggestions could you add to Lamott's advice for "getting started"?

3. The next time you have an essay assigned, keep a log or diary in which you can write about your own writing process. Include comments about how you approach and think about the assignment, how you prepare and actually write the piece, and how you revise and edit your essay. Be sure to include commentary on your feelings and impressions of the process as well as the actual mechanics of writing.

# Writing to Change the World
*Mary Pipher*

As a college student, you may not be thinking about how your writing may be viewed by posterity. In this next essay, Mary Pipher describes how one young girl's diary touched the world. Generations later, the words and thoughts of Anne Frank continue to move and inspire us. As you keep your own journals and record your own thoughts, think about how what you write can make an impact. How would you write to change the world?

Mary Pipher is a psychologist and family therapist. She is the author of many books, including *Reviving Ophelia* (1994), *The Shelter of Each Other* (1997), and *Another Country: Navigating the Emotional Terrain of Our Elders* (1999). This excerpt is from her 2006 book on writing, *Writing to Change the World*.

1   The first book to change my view of the universe was *The Diary of Anne Frank*. I read Anne's diary when I was a twelve-year-old, in Beaver City, Nebraska. Before I read it, I had been able to ignore the existence of evil. I knew a school had burned down in Chicago, and that children had died there. I had seen grown-ups lose their tempers, and I had encountered bullies and nasty school-mates. I had a vague sense that there were criminals—jewel thieves, bank robbers, and Al Capone-style gangsters—in Kansas City and Chicago. After reading the diary, I realized that there were adults who would systematically kill children. My comprehension of the human race expanded to include a hero like Anne, but also to include the villains who killed her. When I read Anne Frank's diary, I lost my spiritual innocence.

2   In September 2003, when I was fifty-five years old, I visited the Holocaust Museum, in Washington, D.C., to view the Anne Frank exhibit. I looked at the cover of her little plaid diary, and at the pages of her writing, at her family pictures. Miep Gies, Otto Frank's employee who brought food to the family, spoke on video about the people who hid in the attic. She said that Anne had always wanted to know the truth about what was going on. Others would believe the sugarcoated version of Miep's stories, but Anne would follow her to the door and ask, "What is really happening?"

3   The museum showed a short film clip of Anne dressed in white, her long hair dark and shiny. She is waving exuberantly from a balcony at a wedding party that is parading down the street. There are just a few seconds of film, captured by a filmmaker at the wedding who must have been entranced by her enthusiasm. The footage is haunting. Anne's wave seems directed at all of us, her small body casting a shadow across decades.

4   At the end of the exhibit, attendees hear the voice of a young girl reading Anne's essay, "Give," a piece inspired by her experience of passing beggars on the street. She wonders if people who live in cozy houses have any idea of the life of beggars. She offers hope: "How wonderful it is that no one has to wait, but can start right now to gradually change the world." She suggests action: "Give whatever you have to give, you can always give something, even it is a simple act of kindness." And she ends with "The world has plenty of room, riches, money

and beauty. God has created enough for each and every one of us. Let us begin by dividing it more fairly."

5   Even though Anne Frank was ultimately murdered, she managed, in her brief and circumscribed life, to tell the truth and bequeath the gift of hope. She searched for beauty and joy even in the harsh, frightened world of the attic in which her family hid from the Nazis. Her writing has lived on to give us all a sense of the potential largesse of the human soul, even in worst-case scenarios. It also reminds us that, behind the statistics about war and genocide, there are thousands of good people who have a responsibility to help.

6   All writing is designed to change the world, at least a small part of the world, or in some small way, perhaps a change in a reader's mood or in his or her appreciation of a certain kind of beauty. Writing to improve the world can be assessed by the goals of its writers and/or by its effects on the world. Most likely, Mary Oliver did not write her poem "Wild Geese" to inspire environmental activists and yet environmentalists have found it inspirational. Bob Dylan claims he had no intention of composing a protest song when he penned "Blowin' in the Wind," but it became the anthem for many of the causes of the last half of the twentieth century. On the other hand, musicians like Tori Amos, the Indigo Girls, and the band Ozomatli do hope to influence their listeners in specific ways, and they succeed. Looking back, Rachel Carson, in *Silent Spring*, satisfies both intent and effect: she wrote the book to stop the use of certain pesticides, and, following its publication, DDT was banned in the United States.

7   My dad told me about a rule that he and other soldiers followed in the Pacific during World War II. It was called the Law of 26, and it postulates that for every result you expect from an action there will be twenty-six results you do not expect. Certainly this law applies to writing. Sometimes a book intended to have one effect has quite another. For example, Upton Sinclair wrote *The Jungle* to call attention to the exploitation of the immigrant labor force and their working conditions in factories, yet it led to an outcry over unsanitary conditions in the meat industry and helped establish uniform standards for beef processing and inspection nationwide.

8   All writing to effect change need not be great literature. Some of it is art, of course, such as Walt Whitman's "I Hear America Singing" or Abraham Lincoln's Gettysburg Address. Some of it is relatively straightforward such as *Rampage: The Social Roots of School Shooting* by Katherine Newman, David Harding, and Cybelle Fox. And some of it is both artful and straightforward. For example, in *The Age of Missing Information*, Bill McKibben has a clever idea that he executes beautifully: he compares what he learns from a week in the mountains to what he learns from watching a week's worth of cable television. On the mountaintop, McKibben experiences himself as small yet connected to something large and awe-inspiring. He comes down from the mountain calm and clear-thinking. Watching cable for a week, he hears over and over that he has unmet needs, that he is grossly inadequate, yet he still is the center of the universe, deserving of everything he wants. McKibben ended the week feeling unfocused, agitated, and alone.

9   Many effective writers are not stylists, but they manage to convey a very clear message. Their writing is not directed toward sophisticates or literary critics. It is

designed to influence cousin Shirley, farmer Dale, coworker Jan, Dr. Lisa, neighbor Carol, businessman Carl, or voter Sylvia. Expository writing for ordinary people calls for a variety of talent—storytelling skills, clarity, and the ability to connect. Whether they are working on an op-ed piece, a speech, or a poem, skilled writers exercise creativity and conscious control. They labor to make the important interesting, and even compelling, to readers.

10      Change writers hope that readers will join them in what Charles Johnson calls "an invitation to struggle." Whereas writers of propaganda encourage readers to accept certain answers, writers who want to transform their readers encourage the asking of questions. Propaganda invites passive agreement; change writing invites original thought, openheartedness, and engagement. Change writers trust that readers can handle multiple points of view, contradictions, unresolved questions, and nuance. If, as André Gide wrote, "Tyranny is the absence of complexity," then change writers are founders of democracies.

11      Good writing astonishes its writer first. My favorite example of this phenomenon is Leo Tolstoy's *Anna Karenina*. Tolstoy planned to write a novel that condemned adultery, and his intention was to make the adulteress an unsympathetic character. But when he came to truly understand Anna as he wrote the book, he fell in love with her, and, a hundred years later, so do his readers. Empathy can turn contempt into love.

## THINKING CRITICALLY

1. How did Anne Frank's diary change the author and her view of the world? Can you think of a moment when you had a similar experience? How old were you? What was the piece that moved you, and how did it influence your view of the world?

2. What is the "Law of 26"? How might it apply to writing?

3. What distinctions does Pipher make among different types of writing? Explain.

4. Did this essay change how you feel about your own writing and its potential power? Why or why not?

5. Pipher describes how author Bill McKibben feels when he returns home from communing with nature on a mountaintop. Why does she use this example? How does it connect to the point she makes in her essay? Explain.

6. Many famous people have started to use online writing media, such as Facebook and Twitter, to advance awareness of various social and charitable causes. Describe what experience, if any, you have had with such campaigns. In your opinion, will blogs, tweets, and Facebook updates be the new journals of this century, as Anne Frank's diary functioned in the last?

## WRITING ASSIGNMENTS

1. Read the essay "How to Detect Propaganda" on page 427. How does propaganda compare to "change writing"? Based on what Pipher says here and your personal experience, how are the two different? How can you distinguish one from the other?

2. Select a poem or song that truly touched you and changed the way you thought about something. Identify the elements that influenced you and explain why you were moved by the words and the writing.

3. Anne Frank did not intend for her diary to "change the world," but her words have touched millions of people. Read or reread her diary and write an essay examining how and why her words and ideas have "changed the world."

---

# Beware the Trap of 'Bore-geous' Writing

*Ayelet Waldman*

Writers and professors of writing agree that good writing is essential to engaging readers and impressing your audience. But sometimes, as author Ayelet Waldman describes in the next piece, we can get so caught up in the weaving of our words that we forget our overarching point. Good writing isn't simply well-crafted sentences. Good writing makes a point. The key, notes Waldman, is finding the balance between crafting stylish prose and writing with intention.

Ayelet Waldman is the author of several novels, including *Red Hook Road, Bad Mother: A Chronicle of Maternal Crimes, Minor Calamities and Occasional Moments of Grace, Love and Other Impossible Pursuits, Daughter's Keeper,* and the *Mommy-Track* mysteries. Her essays have been published in a wide variety of newspapers and magazines, including *The New York Times,* the *Guardian, The San Francisco Chronicle,* and *Salon.com.* Her radio commentaries have appeared on "All Things Considered" and "The California Report." This essay appeared in the November 27, 2010 edition of *The Wall Street Journal.*

1 Recently, I found myself bored by the prospect of sitting down at the computer and getting to work on my unfinished novel, whose due date was fast approaching. I'd while away hours on Facebook, Twitter and email. I'd go for long walks. I'd been in love with this novel for so long, why had I suddenly lost interest?

2 One morning, instead of sending out tweets bemoaning my literary malaise, as had been my habit for the last few days, I scrolled up through the manuscript and began reading. The writing was good, I thought. Better than anything I'd done before. And that was the rub.

3 For the last month or so, I'd been spending my days crafting lush and richly imagined bits of narrative—long, lovely descriptions of characters and scenery, page after page of elegant prose in which nothing whatsoever was going on. No wonder I was bored. Though you won't find it in Webster's, there's a word to describe the kind of meticulously constructed writing that bores even its author. A "bore-geous" novel is one that is packed with gorgeous, finely wrought descriptions of places and people, with entire paragraphs extolling the slope of one character's nose, whole chapters describing another's perambulations through a city. These novels are often historical or set in foreign lands, their bore-geousness inspired by the author's anxiety about making an unfamiliar world feel convincing and true. It's not that the sentences aren't well-constructed, even lovely.

They are. That's part of the problem. Bore-geousness happens when you are writing beautifully but pointlessly.

4    This was not the first time I'd fallen prey to the disease, and I knew how to cure it. My solution was simple. This novel needed action. Not car chases and battles (though, just to be safe, I shoved in one of each). I needed to lift my characters' eyes from their navels, to stop indulging in long passages of description and contemplation. I needed to write scenes in which people did things, and said things and caused things to happen.

5    A scene, unlike a description, not only has a beginning, a middle and an end, but by the time it's over, something has changed, something has happened without which the story can't continue. Each scene must be necessary to the narrative. It's probably because I'm the mother of small children, but it often helps me to think of my novel as a building constructed of Legos of varying shapes, colors and sizes. Each scene is a single Lego piece that must snap into the larger edifice. Every Lego block of a scene both builds on and holds up the others.

6    When rewriting, I inevitably find passages that aren't necessary to the plot. They hang around like the random blocks left in the box when you're done building the Lego Atlantis Deep Sea Striker. Usually I'm convinced that these passages are among the most gorgeous things I've ever written. It's then that I remind myself of Faulkner's painful advice: "In writing, you must kill your darlings." I can no more include those bore-geous passages that do nothing to propel the story then I can snap a random red 3-by-2 Lego piece onto the head of my son's Deep Sea Salvage Crew Diver.

7    Good narrative writing must defend itself. Every sentence, even every word, must be there for a reason beyond its beauty. It must move the story along, pushing it toward what comes next. Good writing can and should be beautiful, but it must never be only beautiful. Bore-geous is always too much, and never enough.

## THINKING CRITICALLY

1. What does Waldman realize about her writing after leaving it for a few days? What writing trap does she find herself in? Explain.

2. Many books on writing instruction focus on form and style, with a focus on correct usage, grammar, and sentence construction. In what ways, if any, does too much focus on these elements expose us to the "bore-geous" trap? Have you ever found yourself in a similar situation? Explain.

3. Waldman describes the many other forms of writing she uses to distract her from her writer's block—Facebook, Twitter, and email. Do you easily get distracted and find yourself reading or doing something on the computer you did not intend to do? Explain.

4. Waldman notes, "Bore-geousness happens when you are writing beautifully but pointlessly." Can you think of examples of writing—novels, nonfiction, and essays—in which you were impressed by the writing but bored with the lack of a point? Explain.

5. Waldman is discussing the process of fiction writing. How might her points about writing fiction apply to other forms of writing, such as the personal narrative, the argument essay, and even electronic media like blogs? Explain.

### WRITING ASSIGNMENTS

1. In this essay, Waldman describes her personal approach to writing. Write your own narrative on how you write. Include any unique challenges you face or personal rituals you follow when you prepare to write. In your essay, describe how the way you approach writing influences the quality of your work.

2. If your school has a writing lab or writing resource center, interview its instructors and ask them about their own observations on effective writing. What recommendations do they have for avoiding "bore-geous" writing? What should you consider when aiming for the goals of both well-written *and* engaging prose?

# FINDING THE RIGHT WORDS

## The Case for Short Words
*Richard Lederer*

Sometimes students pull out the dictionary or thesaurus in an effort to find words that seem more "academic." We seem to think that the longer or more difficult the word is to pronounce, the more intelligent the writer must be. But this is not necessarily the case. In many situations, short words do the job better than long or complicated ones. In this essay, writer and former high school teacher Richard Lederer explains why small, short words can be the most powerful words of all.

Richard Lederer is the author of several best-selling books on words and language, including *Get Thee to a Punnery* (1988), *Crazy English* (1989), and *Fractured English* (1996). Lederer, who holds a PhD in linguistics, is a regular contributor to *Writer's Digest* and a language commentator on National Public Radio (NPR). The following essay was published in the August 1999 issue of the San Diego *Writers Monthly* and was featured in Lederer's 1991 book, *The Miracle of Language*.

1 When you speak and write, there is no law that says you have to use big words. Short words are as good as long ones, and short, old words—like sun and grass and home—are best of all. A lot of small words, more than you might think, can meet your needs with a strength, grace, and charm that large words do not have.

2 Big words can make the way dark for those who read what you write and hear what you say. Small words cast their clear light on big things—night and day, love and hate, war and peace, and life and death. Big words at times seem strange to the

eye and the ear and the mind and the heart. Small words are the ones we seem to have known from the time we were born, like the hearth fire that warms the home.

3      Short words are bright like sparks that glow in the night, prompt like the dawn that greets the day, sharp like the blade of a knife, hot like salt tears that scald the cheek, quick like moths that flit from flame to flame, and terse like the dart and sting of a bee.

4      Here is a sound rule: Use small, old words where you can. If a long word says just what you want to say, do not fear to use it. But know that our tongue is rich in crisp, brisk, swift, short words. Make them the spine and the heart of what you speak and write. Short words are like fast friends. They will not let you down.

5      The title of this essay and the four paragraphs that you have just read are wrought entirely of words of one syllable. In setting myself this task, I did not feel especially cabined, cribbed, or confined. In fact, the structure helped me to focus on the power of the message I was trying to put across.

6      One study shows that twenty words account for twenty-five percent of all spoken English words, and all twenty are monosyllabic. In order of frequency they are: *I, you, the, a, to, is, it, that, of, and, in, what, he, this, have, do, she, not, on,* and *they.* Other studies indicate that the fifty most common words in written English are each made of a single syllable.

7      For centuries our finest poets and orators have recognized and employed the power of small words to make a straight point between two minds. A great many of our proverbs punch home their points with pithy monosyllables: "Where there's a will, there's a way," "A stitch in time saves nine," "Spare the rod and spoil the child," "A bird in the hand is worth two in the bush."

8      Nobody used the short word more skillfully than William Shakespeare, whose dying King Lear laments:

> And my poor fool is hang'd! No, no, no life!
> Why should a dog, a horse, a rat have life,
> And thou no breath at all? . . .
> Do you see this? Look on her, look, her lips.
> Look there, look there!

9      Shakespeare's contemporaries made the King James Bible a centerpiece of short words—"And God said, Let there be light: and there was light. And God saw the light, that it was good." The descendants of such mighty lines live on in the twentieth century. When asked to explain his policy to parliament, Winston Churchill responded with these ringing monosyllables: "I will say: it is to wage war, by sea, land, and air, with all our might and with all the strength that God can give us." In his "Death of the Hired Man" Robert Frost observes that "Home is the place where, when you have to go there,/They have to take you in." And William H. Johnson uses ten two-letter words to explain his secret of success: "If it is to be,/ It is up to me."

10      You don't have to be a great author, statesman, or philosopher to tap the energy and eloquence of small words. Each winter I asked my ninth graders at St. Paul's School to write a composition composed entirely of one-syllable

words. My students greeted my request with obligatory moans and groans, but, when they returned to class with their essays, most felt that, with the pressure to produce high-sounding polysyllables relieved, they had created some of their most powerful and luminous prose. Here are submissions from two of my ninth graders:

> What can you say to a boy who has left home? You can say that he has done wrong, but he does not care. In spite of the breeze that made the vines sway, we all wished we could hide from the glare in a cool, white house. But, as there was no one to help dock the boat, we had to stand and wait.
>
> At last the head of the crew leaped from the side and strode to a large house on the right. He shoved the door wide, poked his head through the gloom, and roared with a fierce voice. Five or six men came out, and soon the port was loud with the clank of chains and creak of planks as the men caught ropes thrown by the crew; pulled them taut, and tied them to posts. Then they set up a rough plank so we could cross from the deck to the shore. We all made for the large house while the crew watched, glad to be rid of us.

### THINKING CRITICALLY

1. What, according to Lederer, are the "big things" that small words describe? Can you think of additional small words that describe "big things"?

2. In paragraph 7, Lederer points out several proverbs that use small words. Identify at least three or four more and test his observation. Do short words predominate? If so, what explains the high proportion of small words in proverbs?

3. Review the examples of student writing Lederer cites in his essay. What seems special about their writing? Does it seem constrained by the requirements of his assignment? Why or why not?

4. Why do so many students feel pressured to use long or complicated words instead of smaller ones? Do teachers reinforce the idea that big words are better? Do you think your grades would suffer if you opted for smaller words in your essays and homework assignments? Explain.

5. Evaluate Lederer's introductory paragraphs (1–4), which only use one-syllable words. Did you realize that he was using only short words when you first read these paragraphs? What impression did you have of his writing in these first four paragraphs? Explain.

### WRITING ASSIGNMENTS

1. Duplicate Lederer's assignment to his class. Write a full paragraph describing an everyday event, idea, or scene (getting up in the morning, viewing a sunrise, looking up at a night sky, a visit with your parents, how you feel about a significant other, etc.). After writing your paragraph and checking that it is indeed written using only one-syllable words, describe the challenges you faced and impressions you had of the composition processes.

2. Find a paragraph or two from an essay or freewriting assignment that you think is a good representation of your academic voice. Try rewriting the paragraph(s)

using only short words. In addition to comparing the two from your own perspective, give the two pieces to a friend or family member and ask them to
evaluate each. Ask your reviewer to explain what makes the piece they prefer
better in their opinion. Describe the results in a short essay, drawing your own
conclusions from your experiment.

# Saying Is Believing
## *Patricia T. O'Conner*

In the preceding piece, Richard Lederer made his case for short words. In this
essay, grammarian and writer Patricia T. O'Conner explains how to avoid some
of the pitfalls facing many college writers by embracing the principles of "plain
English." Too often, complexity, confusion, wordiness, and redundancy side-
track writers. Her solution is a list of 13 points that will improve your writing and
guide you through the writing blunders many students make.

A former editor of *The New York Times Book Review,* Patricia O'Conner is
the author of three books on writing and has published articles on grammar and
writing in many newspapers and journals, including *The New York Times* and
*Newsweek.* She is the author of *Words Fail Me: What Everyone Who Writes
Should Know About Writing* (2000) and of *You Send Me* (2002), written with
husband Stewart Kellerman. This essay was first published in her grammar
guidebook, *Woe Is I: The Grammarphobe's Guide to Better English in Plain
English* (1996).

1   A good writer is one you can read without breaking a sweat. If you want a workout,
you don't lift a book—you lift weights. Yet we're brainwashed to believe that the
more brilliant the writer, the tougher the going.

2       The truth is that the reader is always right. Chances are, if something you're
reading doesn't make sense, it's not your fault—it's the writer's. And if something
you write doesn't get your point across, it's probably not the reader's fault—it's
yours. Too many readers are intimidated and humbled by what they can't understand, and in some cases that's precisely the effect the writer is after. But confusion
is not complexity; it's just confusion. A venerable tradition, dating back to the ancient Greek orators, teaches that if you don't know what you're talking about, just
ratchet up the level of difficulty and no one will ever know.

3       Don't confuse simplicity, though, with simplemindedness. A good writer can
express an extremely complicated idea clearly and make the job look effortless. But
such simplicity is a difficult thing to achieve, because to be clear in your writing
you have to be clear in your thinking. This is why the simplest and clearest writing has the greatest power to delight, surprise, inform, and move the reader. You
can't have this kind of shared understanding if writer and reader are in an adversary
relationship.

4       Now, let's assume you know what you want to say, and the idea in your head is
as clear as a mountain stream. (I'm allowed a cliché once in a while.) How can you
avoid muddying it up when you put it into words?

5    There are no rules for graceful writing, at least not in the sense that there are rules for grammar and punctuation. Some writing manuals will tell you to write short sentences, or to cut out adjectives and adverbs. I disagree. The object isn't to simulate an android. When a sentence sounds nice, reads well, and is easy to follow, its length is just right. But when a sentence is lousy, you can take steps to make it more presentable. These are general principles, and you won't want to follow all of them all of the time (though it's not a bad idea).

## 1. Say what you have to say

6  Unless you're standing at a lectern addressing an audience, there's no need to clear your throat. Your listeners aren't finding their seats, putting down their forks, wrapping up a conversation, or whatever. Your audience—the reader—is ready. So get to it.

7    These are the kinds of throat-clearing phrases you can usually ditch:

> *At this juncture I thought you might be interested in knowing . . .*
> *Perhaps it would be valuable as we arrive at this point in time to recall . . .*
> *I can assure you that I'm sincere when I say . . .*
> *In light of recent developments the possibility exists that . . .*

8    (Of course, some messages could do with a bit of cushioning: *We at the bank feel that under the circumstances you would want us to bring to your attention as soon as possible the fact that . . . your account is overdrawn.*)

## 2. Stop when you've said it

9  Sometimes, especially when you're on a roll and coming up with your best stuff, it's hard to let go of a sentence (this one, for example), so when you get to the logical end you just keep going, and even though you know the reader's eyes are glazing over, you stretch one sentence thinner and thinner—with a semicolon here, a *however* or *nevertheless* there—and you end up stringing together a whole paragraph's worth of ideas before you finally realize it's all over and you're getting writer's cramp and you have to break down and use a period.

10    When it's time to start another sentence, start another sentence.

11    How do you know when it's time? Well, try breathing along with your sentences. Allow yourself one nice inhalation and exhalation per sentence as you silently read along. If you start to turn blue before getting to the end, either you're reading too slowly (don't move your lips) or the sentence is too long.

## 3. Don't belabor the obvious

12  Some writers can't make a point without poking you in the ribs with it. A voice isn't just pleasing; it's pleasing *to the ear.* You don't just give something away; you give it away *for free.* The reader will get the point without the unnecessary prepositional phrases (phrases that start with words like *by, for, in, of,* and *to*): pretty *in appearance,* tall *of stature,* blue *in color,* small *in size,* stocky *in build,* plan *in advance,* drive *by car,* assemble *in a group.* You get the picture.

## 4. Don't tie yourself in knots to avoid repeating a word

13 It's better to repeat a word that fits than to stick in a clumsy substitute that doesn't. Just because you've called something a spider once doesn't mean that the next time you have to call it an arachnid or a predaceous eight-legged creepy-crawly.

14 Editors sometimes call this attempt at elegant variation the Slender Yellow Fruit Syndrome. It is best explained by example: *Freddie was offered an apple and a banana, and he chose the slender yellow fruit.*

## 5. Be direct

15 Too many writers back into what they have to say. A straightforward statement like *He didn't intend to ruin your flower bed* comes out *His intention was not to ruin your flower bed.*

16 Don't mince words. If what you mean is, *Mom reorganized my closet brilliantly,* don't water it down by saying, *Mom's reorganization of my closet was brilliant.*

17 Here are a couple of other examples:

> *Their house was destroyed in 1993. Not: The destruction of their house occurred in 1993.*
> *We concluded that Roger's an idiot. Not: Our conclusion was that Roger's an idiot.*

18 If you have something to say, be direct about it. As in geometry, the shortest distance between two points is a straight line.

## 6. Don't make yourself the center of the universe

19 Of course we want to know what happened to you. Of course we care what you think and feel and do and say. But you can tell us without making every other word *I* or *me* or *my.* (Letter writers, who are fast becoming an endangered species, are often guilty of this. Next time you write a letter or memo, look it over and see how many sentences start with *I.*)

20 You can prune phrases like *I think that,* or *in my opinion,* or *let me emphasize that* out of your writing (and your talking, for that matter) without losing anything. Anecdotes can be told, advice given, opinions opined, all with a lot fewer first-person pronouns than you think.

21 This doesn't mean we don't love you.

## 7. Put descriptions close to what they describe

22 A television journalist in the Farm Belt once said this about a suspected outbreak of hoof-and-mouth disease: *The pasture contained several cows seen by news reporters that were dead, diseased, or dying.*

23 Do you see what's wrong? The words *dead, diseased, or dying* are supposed to describe the cows, but they're so far from home that they seem to describe the reporters. What the journalist should have said was: *Reporters saw a pasture containing several cows that were dead, diseased, or dying.*

24    When a description strays too far, the sentence becomes awkward and hard to read. Here's an adjective (*bare*) that has strayed too far from the noun (*cupboard*) it describes: *Ms. Hubbard found her* **cupboard,** *although she'd gone shopping only a few hours before,* **bare.** Here's one way to rewrite it: *Although she'd gone shopping only a few hours before, Ms. Hubbard found her* **cupboard bare.**

25    And here's an adverb (*definitely*) that's strayed too far from its verb (*is suing*): *She* **definitely,** *if you can believe what all the papers are reporting and what everyone is saying,* **is suing.** Put them closer together: *She* **definitely is suing,** *if you can believe what all the papers are reporting and what everyone is saying.*

26    The reader shouldn't need a map to follow a sentence.

## 8. Put the doer closer to what's being done

27 Nobody's saying that sentences can't be complex and interesting; they can, as long as they're easy to follow. But we shouldn't have to read a sentence twice to get it. Here's an example that takes us from Omaha to Sioux City by way of Pittsburgh:

> *The* **twins,** *after stubbornly going to the same high school despite the advice of their parents and teachers, chose different colleges.*

28    Find a way to say it that puts the doer (the subject, *twins*) closer to what's being done (the verb, *chose*): *The* **twins chose** *different colleges, after stubbornly going to the same high school despite the advice of their parents and teachers.*

29    If you need a compass to navigate a sentence, take another whack at the writing.

## 9. Watch out for pronounitis

30 A sentence with too many pronouns (*he, him, she, her, it, they, them,* and other words that substitute for nouns) can give your reader hives: *Fleur thinks that Judy told* **her** *boyfriend about* **their** *stupid little adventure and that* **she** *will come to regret it.*

31    Whose boyfriend? Whose stupid little adventure? Who'll regret what?

32    When you write things like this, of course, you know the cast of characters. It won't be so clear to somebody else. Don't make the reader guess.

## 10. Make sure there's a time and place for everything

> *While the merger specialist was vacationing in Aspen, she said she secretly put the squeeze on Mr. Buyout by threatening to go public with candid photos of him in one of those foil helmets, getting his hair streaked at Frederic Fekkai.*

33    Did the merger specialist tell this story when she was vacationing in Aspen, or is that where she put the squeeze on Mr. Buyout? Were the photos taken earlier? And where is Frederic Fekkai? This calls for two sentences:

> *While vacationing in Aspen, the merger specialist faxed us her secret. She had put the squeeze on Mr. Buyout in New York the week before by threatening to go public with candid photos of him in one of those foil helmets, getting his hair streaked at Frederic Fekkai.*

34    Where are we? What's going on? What time is it? These are questions the reader shouldn't have to ask.

## 11. Imagine what you're writing

35 Picture in your mind any images you've created.

Are they unintentionally funny, like this one? *The bereaved family covered the mirrors as a reflection of its grief.* If you don't see what's wrong, reflect on it for a moment.

36    Are there too many of them, as in this sentence? *The remaining bone of contention is a thorn in his side and an albatross around his neck:* Give the poor guy a break. One image at a time, please.

## 12. Put your ideas in order

37 Don't make the reader rearrange your messy sentences to figure out what's going on. The parts should follow logically. This doesn't mean they should be rattled off in chronological order, but the sequence of ideas should make sense. Here's how Gracie Allen might have talked about a soufflé recipe, for instance:

> *It is possible to make this soufflé with four eggs instead of eight. But it will collapse and possibly even catch fire in the oven, leaving you with a flat, burned soufflé. Now, you wouldn't want that, would you? So if you have only four eggs, reduce all the other ingredients in the recipe by half.*

38    Rearrange the ideas:

> *This soufflé recipe calls for eight eggs. If you want to use fewer, reduce the other ingredients accordingly. If the proportions aren't maintained, the soufflé could flatten or burn.*

## 13. Read with a felonious mind

39 Forget the details for a minute. Now step back and take a look at what you've written. Have you said what you wanted to say? After all, leaving the wrong impression is much worse than making a couple of grammatical boo-boos. Get some perspective.

40    Assuming you've made your point, ask yourself whether you could make it more smoothly. Somebody once said that in good writing, the sentences hold hands. See if you can give yours a helping hand. It may be that by adding or subtracting a word here or there, you could be even clearer. Or you could switch two sentences around, or begin one of them differently.

41    There's no easy way to raise your writing from competence to artistry. It helps, though, to read with a felonious mind. If you see a letter or memo or report that you admire, read it again. Why do you like it, and what makes it so effective? When you find a technique that works, steal it. Someday, others may be stealing from you.

## THINKING CRITICALLY

1. O'Conner comments in her first sentence, "A good writer is one you can read without breaking a sweat." Do you agree with this observation? Why or why not? What makes a writer "good"?

2. Evaluate O'Conner's tips as they compare to your own writing challenges. Which ones seem to be particularly helpful and why? If none of them seems relevant, explain why you hold this point of view.

3. O'Conner observes that many people are "brainwashed into believing that the more brilliant the writer, the tougher the going." What does she mean by this statement? Do you agree? Explain.

4. Which items in O'Conner's list endorse the use of "active voice"? What are the merits of active voice? How can using the active voice help writers and readers?

5. In paragraph 3, O'Conner warns, "don't confuse simplicity . . . with simplemindedness." Clear writing is the result of clear thinking. Think about your own writing process. How do you perceive the connection between your own thought process and your writing? Explain.

## WRITING ASSIGNMENTS

1. In her introduction, O'Conner comments that readers are "brainwashed" into thinking that brilliant writers are difficult to understand. Select two or three writers who you consider to be "brilliant," and evaluate how difficult their writing is to understand by analyzing a few pages of their writing. Based on your analysis, write an essay in which you agree or disagree with O'Conner's viewpoint.

2. Write with a "felonious mind." Pick two or three writers whose prose you admire and analyze their writing styles. Pick one writer to imitate, and, using that writer's particular style, write three or four paragraphs of your own. How does it "feel" to write like another writer? Did it make your writing stronger? Was it strange to write in another writer's voice? Explain.

3. Using an essay you have recently written, compare your writing to the 13 points O'Conner outlines in her article. Identify areas where you meet her recommendations and where you fall into some of the writing pitfalls she describes.

# Clichés, Anyone?

*James Isaacs*

Clichés are trite or overused expressions, and most writing books will tell you to avoid them. The problem with clichés is that they fail to have real substance— they are weakened by overuse. And because they are phrases on tap, users do not bother to come up with their own ideas or fresh wording. In this essay, James Isaacs presents a commencement speech; such speeches tend to serve as venues of packaged oratory. As you read this parody, try to identify the clichés and their intended meanings. You might even hear echoes of your own high school commencement!

James Isaacs is a writer, musician, and music critic for Microsoft's Side-walk Boston website. He was nominated for a Grammy in 1986 for coproducing the reissue of Frank Sinatra's work. For the past 15 years, Isaacs has hosted and produced jazz, soul, and pop-music programs for National Public Radio. This piece first appeared in *The Boston Globe* on May 8, 1998.

1  *Commencement fast approaches. On college campuses and in high school auditoriums and gymnasiums across the land, a parade of orators will loft the traditional airballs of homespun homilies, peppy locker room bromides, and windbaggery under many sails.*

2  *In recent years I have picked up extra income writing graduation ad-dresses for a few locally based notables, including a second-string television news anchor, several lieutenants of industry, and a minor pol or two.*

3  *The only instruction I received was that I should write in their voices, and this I think I did. However, as this spring finds me happily and inordinately busy at work on a made-for-community-access-TV musical "The Alchemy of Opie and Anthony," I hereby offer the following to any and all commencement speakers:*

4  Good morning (afternoon, evening), members of the Class of 1998 at (name of institution of learning) and your families and friends.

5  At this point in time, as we near the dawn of the new millennium and each of us seeks some sort of defining moment, it has never been more important to send a message, big time. Two words: "Work ethic." Or "speed bump." Or "role model." Whatever, as you young folks put it so succinctly.

6  That we're all on the same page and bring something to the table is the post-modern buzz that's on the cutting edge, you know what I'm saying? And in order to deconstruct the spin control, to be some kind of player—an icon, if you will—you will at some time in your life have to draw a line in the sand, even if your agenda is granularly challenged. So, do the math. Right there in the sand, go figure! It ain't rocket science.

7  It is then, and only then, once you step up to the plate, no matter how much you may have on your plate, that you'll get over it and start turning your life around by taking it to the next level. I know because I've been there, done that, while on my watch. And a fine Swiss watch it was until an 800-pound gorilla with in-your-face attitude hurled it almost over-the-top of Fenway Park's famous Green Monster.

8  So much for quality time.

9  And as you know, it ain't over till it's over. Or until the fat lady sings. But that's a story for another day.

10  To the young women among this year's graduates: Going out into the world can be a no-brainer, no problem, provided, of course, you have all your ducks in a row and they're in a full attack mode feeding frenzy, ready to push the envelope and deliver an awesome slam dunk that's in the zone.

11  It's also imperative that you keep this in mind: In order to distance yourself from every victim, enabler, and co-dependent on your radar screen, you might have to go right off the charts to reinvent yourself. And when it's time to move on, well,

you go, girl! Hey, even if it's on my dime, never forget that it's your call as to who will carry your water, no matter what he said or, for that matter, she said.

12    As for you young men, I recall that many years ago when I first expressed interest in a career in photojournalism, my father said, "Read my lips: Get a 'Life.'"

13    "Dad," I replied, "you just don't get it." Which certainly was true at the time, since we subscribed to *Collier's*. But when I also mentioned that I wanted to move to New York, his advice was equally blunt: "Don't go there." To which I answered: "Dad, even though you da man, you don't have a clue. But thanks for sharing."

14    So at the end of the day, life is face time. But it's also about show-me-the-money. And that's a good thing. First and foremost, however, I cannot stress strongly enough the notion that if you don't ask, don't tell, you will begin the healing process, get over it, and come to closure. It doesn't get any better than this.

15    End of story. To coin a phrase.

### THINKING CRITICALLY

1. Give your own definition of a cliché. How often do you use clichés in your own speech? How does Isaacs tap into our common knowledge of clichés in this commencement speech spoof?

2. Would this article be funny to a non-American audience? For example, would German- or Chinese-speaking people understand its humor? What about an English or Irish audience? Explain.

3. Although Isaacs pokes fun at the overuse of clichés during commencement speeches, clichés do enable speakers to connect to their audience. Identify some situations where clichés would be useful linguistic devices.

4. What is Isaacs's message in this article? What point is he trying to convey? Explain.

5. Recall your own commencement speech. Do you remember what was said? How does the memory of your commencement speech compare to your classmates' memories of it? As a group, how do the speeches compare in style and content?

6. What is Isaacs saying about the basic substance of the commencement speech? Do you agree with his perspective? Why or why not?

### WRITING ASSIGNMENTS

1. Write your own commencement speech. What would you say to connect to your audience? Would you use common linguistic conventions? Would you use clichés?

2. Write a letter to a friend using as many clichés as you can as long as they are appropriate to your message. Evaluate what you have written. Was this exercise easy or difficult? Explain.

3. Evaluate a political speech made by a politician. You may find it useful to record the speech or obtain a transcript of it. Did the official use any clichés? If so, identify and analyze them. Are some expressions more noticeable than others? Did any escape your notice the first time you heard the speech? Explain.

# Exploring the Language of **V I S U A L S**

## Writing Well

### THINKING CRITICALLY

1. What is the punch line of this cartoon? Explain.
2. What visual clichés does this cartoon use to convey a sense of place and character? Who is depicted in the cartoon, and what can we infer about the people based on what we understand about the scene?
3. What must the viewer know in order to understand the joke the cartoonist is trying to make? Explain.

# Selection, Slanting, and Charged Language

*Newman P. Birk and Genevieve B. Birk*

Language can shape our perception of reality. The way we use words—the exact language we select and the emphasis we give it—has the power of shaping another's judgment on a subject. What follows is a clear and revealing discussion of this fundamental principle that underlies all verbal communication. This piece is included for two simple reasons. First, as a writer, it is important to understand that the words you choose reflect your personal feelings, values, and attitudes toward a subject. Second, as a reader, you should be alert to the subtle powers of charged language to avoid being susceptible to those who control the words—whether they are propagandists, politicians, advertisers, or the editors of your local newspaper.

Newman P. Birk and Genevieve B. Birk are the authors of *Understanding and Using Language* (1972), from which this essay is taken.

## A. The principle of selection

1   *Before* it is expressed in words, our knowledge, both inside and outside, is influenced by the principle of selection. What we know or observe depends on what we notice; that is, what we select, consciously or unconsciously, as worthy of notice or attention. As we observe, the principle of selection determines which facts we take in.

2   Suppose, for example, that three people, a lumberjack, an artist, and a tree surgeon, are examining a large tree in a forest. Since the tree itself is a complicated object, the number of particulars or facts about it that one could observe would be very great indeed. Which of these facts a particular observer will notice will be a matter of selection, a selection that is determined by his interests and purposes. A lumberjack might be interested in the best way to cut the tree down, cut it up, and transport it to the lumber mill. His interest would then determine his principle of selection in observing and thinking about the tree. The artist might consider painting a picture of the tree, and his purpose would furnish his principle of selection. The tree surgeon's professional interest in the physical health of the tree might establish a principle of selection for him. If each man were now required to write an exhaustive, detailed report on everything he observed about the tree, the facts supplied by each would differ, for each would report those facts that his particular principle of selection led him to notice.[1]

3   The principle of selection holds not only for the specific facts that people observe but also for the facts they remember. A student suddenly embarrassed may remember nothing of the next ten minutes of class discussion but may have a vivid recollection of the sensation of the blood mounting, as he blushed, up his face and into his ears. In both noticing and remembering, the principle of selection applies,

---

[1] Of course, all three observers would probably report a good many facts in common—the height of the tree, for example, and the size of the trunk. The point we wish to make is that each observer would give us a different impression of the tree because of the different principle of selection that guided his observation.

and it is influenced not only by our special interest and point of view but by our whole mental state of the moment.

4     The principle of selection then serves as a kind of sieve or screen through which our knowledge passes before it becomes our knowledge. Since we can't notice everything about a complicated object or situation or action or state of our own consciousness, what we do notice is determined by whatever principle of selection is operating for us at the time we gain the knowledge.

5     It is important to remember that what is true of the way the principle of selection works for us is true also of the way it works for others. Even before we or other people put knowledge into words to express meaning, that knowledge has been screened or selected. Before an historian or an economist writes a book, or before a reporter writes a news article, the facts that each is to present have been sifted through the screen of a principle of selection. Before one person passes on knowledge to another, that knowledge has already been selected and shaped, intentionally or unintentionally, by the mind of the communicator.

## B. The principle of slanting

6 When we put our knowledge into words, a second process of selection, the process of slanting, takes place. Just as there is something, a rather mysterious principle of selection, which chooses for us what we will notice, and what will then become our knowledge, there is also a principle which operates, with or without our awareness, to select certain facts and feelings from our store of knowledge, and to choose the words and the emphasis that we shall use to communicate our meaning.[2] Slanting may be defined as the process of selecting (1) knowledge—factual and attitudinal; (2) words; and (3) emphasis, to achieve the intention of the communicator. Slanting is present in some degree in all communication: one may *slant for* (favorable slanting), *slant against* (unfavorable slanting), or *slant both ways* (balanced slanting). . . .

## C. Slanting by use of emphasis

7 Slanting by use of the devices of emphasis is unavoidable,[3] for emphasis is simply the giving of stress to subject matter, and so indicating what is important and what is less important. In speech, for example, if we say that Socrates was a *wise old man,* we can give several slightly different meanings, one by stressing *wise,* another by stressing *old,* another by giving equal stress to *wise* and *old,* and still another by giving chief stress to *man.* Each different stress gives a different slant (favorable or unfavorable or balanced) to the statement because it conveys a different attitude toward Socrates or a different judgment of him. Connectives and word order also slant by the emphasis they give: consider the difference in slanting or emphasis

---

[2]Notice that the "principle of selection" is at work as *we take in* knowledge, and that slanting occurs as *we express* our knowledge in words.
[3]When emphasis is present—and we can think of no instance in the use of language in which it is not— it necessarily influences the meaning by playing a part in the favorable, unfavorable, or balanced slant of the communicator. We are likely to emphasize by voice stress, even when we answer *yes* or *no* to simple questions.

produced by *old but wise, old and wise, wise but old.* In writing, we cannot indicate subtle stresses on words as clearly as in speech, but we can achieve our emphasis and so can slant by the use of more complex patterns of word order, by choice of connectives, by underlining heavily stressed words, and by marks of punctuation that indicate short or long pauses and so give light or heavy emphasis. Question marks, quotation marks, and exclamation points can also contribute to slanting.[4] It is impossible either in speech or in writing to put two facts together without giving some slight emphasis or slant. For example, if we have in mind only two facts about a man, his awkwardness and his strength, we subtly slant those facts favorably or unfavorably in whatever way we may choose to join them:

| MORE FAVORABLE SLANTING | LESS FAVORABLE SLANTING |
|---|---|
| He is awkward and strong. | He is strong and awkward. |
| He is awkward but strong. | He is strong but awkward. |
| Although he is somewhat awkward, he is very strong. | He may be strong, but he's very awkward. |

With more facts and in longer passages it is possible to maintain a delicate balance by alternating favorable emphasis and so producing a balanced effect.

8     All communication, then, is in some degree slanted by the *emphasis* of the communicator.

## D. Slanting by selection of facts

9 To illustrate the technique of slanting by selection of facts, we shall examine three passages of informative writing which achieve different effects simply by the selection and emphasis of material. Each passage is made up of true statements or facts about a dog, yet the reader is given three different impressions. The first passage is an example of objective writing or balanced slanting, the second is slanted unfavorably, and third is slanted favorably.

## 1. Balanced Presentation

Our dog, Toddy, sold to us a cocker, produces various reactions in various people. Those who come to the back door, she usually growls and barks at (a milkman has said that he is afraid of her); those who come to the front door, she whines at and paws; also she tries to lick people's faces unless we have forestalled her by putting a newspaper in her mouth. (Some of our friends encourage these actions; others discourage them. Mrs. Firmly, one friend, slaps the dog with a newspaper and says, "I know how hard dogs are to train.") Toddy knows and responds to a number of words and phrases, and guests sometimes remark that she is a "very intelligent dog." She has fleas in the summer, and she sheds, at times copiously, the year round. Her blond hairs are conspicuous

---

[4]Consider the slanting achieved by punctuation in the following sentences: He called the Senator an honest man? *He* called the Senator an honest man? He called the Senator an honest man! He said one more such "honest" senator would corrupt the state.

when they are on people's clothing or on rugs or furniture. Her color and her large brown eyes frequently produce favorable comment. An expert on cockers would say that her ears are too short and set too high and that she is at least six pounds too heavy.

10      The passage above is made up of facts, verifiable facts,[5] deliberately selected and emphasized to produce a *balanced* impression. Of course not all the facts about the dog have been given—to supply *all* the facts on any subject, even such a comparatively simple one, would be an almost impossible task. Both favorable and unfavorable facts are used, however, and an effort has been made to alternate favorable and unfavorable details so that neither will receive greater emphasis by position, proportion, or grammatical structure.

## 2. Facts Slanted Against

That dog put her paws on my white dress as soon as I came in the door, and she made so much noise that it was two minutes before she had quieted down enough for us to talk and hear each other. Then the gas man came and she did a great deal of barking. And her hairs are on the rug and on the furniture. If you wear a dark dress they stick to it like lint. When Mrs. Firmly came in, she actually hit the dog with a newspaper to make it stay down, and she made some remark about training dogs. I wish the Birks would take the hint or get rid of that noisy, short-eared, over-weight "cocker" of theirs.

11      This unfavorably slanted version is based on the same facts, but now these facts have been selected and given a new emphasis. The speaker, using her selected facts to give her impression of the dog, is quite possibly unaware of her negative slanting.

12      Now for a favorably slanted version:

## 3. Facts Slanted For

What a lively and responsive dog! When I walked in the door, there she was with a newspaper in her mouth, whining and standing on her hind legs and wagging her tail all at the same time. And what an intelligent dog. If you suggest going for a walk, she will get her collar from the kitchen and hand it to you, and she brings Mrs. Birk's slippers whenever Mrs. Birk says she is "tired" or mentions slippers. At a command she catches balls, rolls over, "speaks," or stands on her hind feet and twirls around. She sits up and balances a piece of bread on her nose until she is told to take it; then she tosses it up and catches it. If you are eating something, she sits up in front of you and "begs" with those

---

[5]*Verifiable facts* are facts that can be checked and agreed upon and proved to be true by people who wish to verify them. That a particular theme received a failing grade is a verifiable fact; one needs merely to see the theme with the grade on it. That the instructor should have failed the theme is not, strictly speaking, a verifiable fact, but a matter of opinion. That women on the average live longer than men is a verifiable fact; that they live better is a matter of opinion, a *value judgment*.

big dark brown eyes set in that light, buff-colored face of hers. When I got up to go and told her I was leaving, she rolled her eyes at me and sat up like a squirrel. She certainly is a lively and intelligent dog.

13    Speaker 3, like Speaker 2, is selecting from the "facts" summarized in balanced version 1, and is emphasizing his facts to communicate his impression.

14    All three passages are examples of *reporting* (i.e., consist only of verifiable facts), yet they give three very different impressions of the same dog because of the different ways the speakers slanted the facts. Some people say that figures don't lie, and many people believe that if they have the "facts," they have the "truth." Yet if we carefully examine the ways of thought and language, we see that any knowledge that comes to us through words has been subjected to the double screening of the principle of selection and the slanting of language. . . .

15    Wise listeners and readers realize that the double screening that is produced by the principle of selection and by slanting takes place even when people honestly try to report the facts as they know them. (Speakers 2 and 3, for instance, probably thought of themselves as simply giving information about a dog and were not deliberately trying to mislead.) Wise listeners and readers know too that deliberate manipulators of language, by mere selection and emphasis, can make their slanted facts appear to support almost any cause.

16    In arriving at opinions and values we cannot always be sure that the facts that sift into our minds through language are representative and relevant and true. We need to remember that much of our information about politics, governmental activities, business conditions, and foreign affairs comes to us selected and slanted. More than we realize, our opinions on these matters may depend on what newspaper we read or what news commentator we listen to. Worthwhile opinions call for knowledge of reliable facts and reasonable arguments for and against—and such opinions include beliefs about morality and truth and religion as well as about public affairs. Because complex subjects involve knowing and dealing with many facts on both sides, reliable judgments are at best difficult to arrive at. If we want to be fairminded, we must be willing to subject our opinions to continual testing by new knowledge, and must realize that after all they *are* opinions, more or less trustworthy. Their trustworthiness will depend on the representativeness of our facts, on the quality of our reasoning, and on the standard of values that we choose to apply.

17    We shall not give here a passage illustrating the unscrupulous slanting of facts. Such a passage would also include irrelevant facts and false statements presented as facts, along with various subtle distortions of fact. Yet to the uninformed reader the passage would be indistinguishable from a passage intended to give a fair account. If two passages (2 and 3) of casual and unintentional slanting of facts about a dog can give such contradictory impressions of a simple subject, the reader can imagine what a skilled and designing manipulation of facts and statistics could do to mislead an uninformed reader about a really complex subject. An example of such manipulation might be the account of the United States that Soviet propaganda has supplied to the average Russian. Such propaganda, however, would go beyond the mere slanting of the facts: it would clothe the selected facts in charged words and would make use of the many other devices of slanting that appear in charged language.

## E. Slanting by use of charged words

18 In the passages describing the dog Toddy, we were illustrating the technique of slanting by the selection and emphasis of facts. Though the facts selected had to be expressed in words, the words chosen were as factual as possible, and it was the selection and emphasis of facts and not of words that was mainly responsible for the two distinctly different impressions of the dog. In the passages below we are demonstrating another way of slanting—by the use of charged words. This time the accounts are very similar in the facts they contain; the different impressions of the subject, Corlyn, are produced not by different facts but by the subtle selection of charged words.

19 The passages were written by a clever student who was told to choose as his subject a person in action, and to write two descriptions, each using the "same facts." The instructions required that one description be slanted positively and the other negatively, so that the first would make the reader favorably inclined toward the person and the action, and the second would make him unfavorably inclined.

20 Here is the favorably charged description. Read it carefully and form your opinion of the person before you go on to read the second description.

### Corlyn

Corlyn paused at the entrance to the room and glanced about. A well-cut black dress draped subtly about her slender form. Her long blonde hair gave her chiseled features the simple frame they required. She smiled an engaging smile as she accepted a cigarette from her escort. As he lit it for her she looked over the flame and into his eyes. Corlyn had that rare talent of making every male feel that he was the one man in the world.

She took his arm and they descended the steps into the room. She walked with an effortless grace and spoke with equal ease. They each took a cup of coffee and joined a group of friends near the fire. The flickering light danced across her face and lent an ethereal quality to her beauty. The good conversation, the crackling logs, and the stimulating coffee gave her a feeling of internal warmth. Her eyes danced with each leap of the flames.

21 Taken by itself this passage might seem just a description of an attractive girl. The favorable slanting by use of charged words has been done so skillfully that it is inconspicuous. Now we turn to the unfavorably slanted description of the "same" girl in the "same" actions:

### Corlyn

Corlyn halted at the entrance to the room and looked around. A plain black dress hung on her thin frame. Her stringy bleached hair accentuated her harsh features. She smiled an inane smile as she took a cigarette from her escort. As he lit it for her she stared over the lighter and into his eyes. Corlyn had a habit of making every male feel that he was the last man on earth.

She grasped his arm and they walked down the steps and into the room. Her pace was fast and ungainly, as was her speech. They each reached for some coffee and broke into a group of acquaintances near the fire. The flickering light played across her face and revealed every flaw. The loud talk, the fire, and the coffee she had gulped down made her feel hot. Her eyes grew more red with each leap of the flames.

22    When the reader compares these two descriptions, he can see how charged words influence the reader's attitude. One needs to read the two descriptions several times to appreciate all the subtle differences between them. Words, some rather heavily charged, others innocent-looking but lightly charged, work together to carry to the reader a judgment of a person and a situation. If the reader had seen only the first description of Corlyn, he might well have thought that he had formed his "own judgment on the basis of the facts." And the examples just given only begin to suggest the techniques that may be used in heavily charged language. For one thing, the two descriptions of Corlyn contain no really good example of the use of charged abstractions; for another, the writer was obliged by the assignment to use the same set of facts and so could not slant by selecting his material.

## F. Slanting and charged language

23    . . . When slanting of facts, or words, or emphasis, or any combination of the three *significantly influences* feelings toward, or judgments about, a subject, the language used is charged language. . . .

24    Of course communications vary in the amount of charge they carry and in their effect on different people; what is very favorably charged for one person may have little or no charge, or may even be adversely charged, for others. It is sometimes hard to distinguish between charged and uncharged expression. But it is safe to say that whenever we wish to convey any kind of inner knowledge— feelings, attitudes, judgments, values—we are obliged to convey that attitudinal meaning through the medium of charged language; and when we wish to understand the inside knowledge of others, we have to interpret the charged language that they choose, or are obliged, to use. Charged language, then, is the natural and necessary medium for the communication of charged or attitudinal meaning. At times we have difficulty in living with it, but we should have even greater difficulty in living without it.

25    Some of the difficulties in living with charged language are caused by its use in dishonest propaganda, in some editorials, in many political speeches, in most advertising, in certain kinds of effusive salesmanship, and in blatantly insincere, or exaggerated, or sentimental expressions of emotion. Other difficulties are caused by the misunderstandings and misinterpretations that charged language produces. A charged phrase misinterpreted in a love letter; a charged word spoken in haste or in anger; an acrimonious argument about religion or politics or athletics or fraternities; the frustrating uncertainty produced by the effort to understand the complex attitudinal meaning in a poem or play or a short story— these troubles, all growing out of the use of charged language, may give us the

feeling that Robert Louis Stevenson expressed when he said, "The battle goes sore against us to the going down of the sun."

26    But however charged language is abused and whatever misunderstandings it may cause, we still have to live with it—and even by it. It shapes our attitudes and values even without our conscious knowledge; it gives purpose to, and guides, our actions; through it we establish and maintain relations with other people and by means of it we exert our greatest influence on them. Without charged language, life would be but half life. The relatively uncharged language of bare factual statement, though it serves its informative purpose well and is much less open to abuse and to misunderstanding, can describe only the bare land of factual knowledge; to communicate knowledge of the turbulencies and the calms and the deep currents of the sea of inner experience we must use charged language.

## THINKING CRITICALLY

1. The authors say that slanting is the process of selecting knowledge, words, and emphasis. Is it possible to communicate something without slanting it one way or another? Can you think of any kind of writing that is unslanted?

2. One of the best places to find charged and slanted language is on the editorial pages of a newspaper. Look through the various editorials, political columns, and letters to the editor. How many examples of slanted and charged language can you find? How deliberately were the verifiable facts selected? Were some facts given more emphasis than others?

3. How can we determine whether a report is charged?

4. Some of the most slanted writing we are exposed to comes in the form of advertising. Select some ads from magazines or newspapers (or television commercials) and consider the charged and slanted language used to sell the products.

5. What do the authors mean in paragraph 24 when they say that we have difficulty living with charged language and difficulty living without it?

## WRITING ASSIGNMENTS

1. The authors use the example of Toddy to illustrate how slanted reporting can bend judgment for or against something. Do the same. Select some innocuous item—an article of clothing, a toothbrush, your right shoe—and describe it, first slanting the language toward a favorable judgment, then toward an unfavorable judgment.

2. Write an essay using the authors' notion that "without charged language, life would be but half life" (paragraph 26).

3. Write three descriptions of the outfit you are wearing: as it might be seen by an artist, a tailor, and a nudist.

4. Reread this essay, noting the major charges made by the Birks regarding slanted writing. Conduct interviews with three or four instructors or students in the journalism or communications departments of your school, asking them whether they agree with the claims made by the Birks. How do slanting, selection, and charged language function in their own work? Write a paper analyzing your findings in terms of the Birks' article.

## MAKING CONNECTIONS

1. Select an essay you have already written and apply some of the principles of writing described by Lederer and O'Connor in their articles. Identify the parts of your essay that you changed and how the altered sections employ the techniques described in the two essays. How does your revised essay compare to its first version? Explain.

2. Find two magazine or newspaper articles covering the same event or person—maybe a movie star or political figure or athlete. How do they differ? How do they use the facts? How do they change and use language?

3. Which of the authors in this chapter provided you with the most useful information for improving your own writing, and why? Use examples from the article to support your response.

4. Several of the writers in this chapter provided lists of advice designed to improve your personal writing style. Create a list of your own in which you provide advice to less experienced writers, such as students just beginning junior high school. You may draw from the advice of the writers in this chapter, your own experience, and points made during class discussion. Remember to write to your audience when composing your list.

5. All writers put their personal stamp on their work. Write a short essay about how the words you choose—and how you express them—influence your audience's opinion of your message.

6. The authors in this chapter all describe different aspects of the writing process—from audience identification to finding your inspiration to editing the final product. During your next essay assignment, keep a journal of your impressions of each step of the writing process as you compose your essay. In your journal, consider your approach to the writing process during each step and the feedback you received from teachers and peers.

7. Many writing instructors encourage freewriting exercises that promote the unencumbered flow of ideas as a way to develop writing skills. Try to write about a topic—for example, teenage use of alcohol or a particular type of controversial music—for two different audiences. Keep your audience in mind as you write, but remain mindful of simply allowing your ideas to flow freely. After you complete this writing exercise, consider how freewriting compares to more structured methods of writing.

8. After reading the work of the authors featured in this chapter, do you have a better sense of the writing process? Explain why or why not.

9. In your own opinion, which stage of the writing process is the most important? Support your answer by drawing from material provided in this chapter as well as from your personal writing experiences.

10. What common advice or suggestions do the authors in this chapter make? Identify similarities and differences in their essays.

Approximately 400 million people speak English as their first language including the majority of citizens of the United States, the United Kingdom, Canada, Australia, South Africa, New Zealand, Ireland, and many islands in the Caribbean. Taught extensively throughout the world as a preferred second language, it is the dominant language for international communications, entertainment, science, diplomacy, medicine, and business. Interestingly, in some countries where English is not the preferred spoken language, it is the official language, including the Marshall Islands, Cameroon, the Philippines, and Zimbabwe.

This chapter takes a closer look at English usage locally in the United States and around the world. Is there such a thing as "American English"? And what about other "Englishes"? Is one form more correct than another? How is English influencing global communication, politics, and commerce? Is the dominance of the English language a good thing, moving us toward broader and clearer understanding, or invasive, pushing other languages and nations away?

## What Is "American" English?

The United States is comprised of people with many different racial origins, ethnic identities, religions, and languages. Our national motto, *e pluribus unum* ("out of many, one"), bespeaks the pride we feel in our multicultural heritage. Our unity is predicated on like-minded moral values, political and economic self-interest, and, perhaps, a common language. The first section of this chapter explores this common language and how it unifies and divides us. The section opens with a discussion of American English by Robert MacNeil in "Do You Speak American?" MacNeil sets out to understand why the English spoken in one part of the country can differ so much from that spoken in another. Even common words and expressions can be vastly different, begging the question, what exactly is "American English"? Linguist John Esling explores the way accents influence our perceptions of others and ourselves in "Everyone Has an Accent but Me." His essay is followed by an engaging discussion by Bill Bryson on just what is "good" and "bad" English in "Good English and Bad." Then John Simon, one of America's most famous and formidable language guardians, argues that good English is a serious social and personal issue in his essay, "Why Good English Is Good for You." The last reading in the section addresses English as a national language for the United States. Mauro E. Mujica, a Chilean immigrant, explains why he feels it is vitally important that the United States adopt English as its official language in "Why the U.S. Needs an Official Language."

## English as a Global Language

English is often referred to as the "lingua franca," or world language, of the modern world. English is the most often taught second language around the world. With so many different people from diverse backgrounds speaking English, the language itself is changing. It absorbs the influences of different cultures, with different dialects, inflections, usage, and meanings.

The second section in this chapter explores English as a global language—one that reflects the multicultural influences in a common tongue. The section begins with an essay by one of the leading linguistic authorities on the topic of the globalization of the English language, David Crystal. In "Why a Global Language?" Crystal explains the factors that drive a language to become global and why globalization—despite what some critics may claim—could be good for the planet. His piece is countered by another noted language authority, Barbara Wallraff, who argues in "What Global Language?" that English is not really the global language, at least not in the way many people think. There are different "Englishes" and they are not all the same, hindering our ability to understand each other. Then Keith Redfern blogs about how English has become a global language both insidiously through media and with intention as it is adopted by people around the world as the language of choice in "English as a Global Language: A Good Thing or a Bad Thing?" The final piece in this section questions what globalization of language might mean for American students in the future. Globalization, asserts Douglas McGray in "Lost in America," means that American students should be taking more foreign language classes rather than fewer. The reasons why may surprise you.

# WHAT IS "AMERICAN" ENGLISH?

## Do You Speak American?
*Robert MacNeil*

"Hoagie," "grinder," "bomb," "spukie," "po-boy," or "hero"—so many different names for pretty much the same thing, depending on where you place your order for a sub sandwich. While politicians may argue for or against the idea of a standard, national language, English-speaking Americans across the country are busy keeping the language vibrant and diverse. Robert MacNeil sets out to discover "why is the English spoken by Maine lobstermen so different from that spoken by cowboys in Texas?" How are regionalized words created? MacNeil traveled across the nation to try to find answers to these questions and to better understand the evolving and colorful language that is "American English."

Robert MacNeil is the former co-anchor of PBS's Emmy Award-winning *MacNeil/Lehrer NewsHour*. He is the author of several books, including *Do You Speak American?* (2004) and *The Story of English* (1986). This article first appeared in the January 2005 issue of *USA Today Magazine*. MacNeil wrote this essay as a companion piece to his PBS documentary, co-written by Bill Cran, "Do You Speak American?", which explores the country's linguistic diversity.

1 On Columbus Avenue in New York, a young waitress approaches our table and asks, "How are you guys doin'?" My wife and I are old enough to be her grandparents, but we are "you guys" to her. Today, in American English, guys can be guys, girls, or grandmothers. Girls call themselves guys, even dudes. For a while,

young women scorned the word girls, but that is cool again, probably because African-American women use it and it can be real cool—even empowering—to whites to borrow black talk, like the word cool. It is empowering to gay men to call themselves queer, once a hated homophobic term, but now used to satirize the whole shifting scene of gender attitudes in the TV reality show, "Queer Eye for the Straight Guy." As society changes, so does language, and American society has changed enormously in recent decades. Moreover, when new norms are resented or feared, language often is the target of that fear or resentment.

2　　How we use the English language became a hot topic during the 1960s, and it remains so today—a charged ingredient in the culture wars, as intensely studied and disputed as any other part of our society. That is appropriate because nothing is more central to our identity and sense of who we are and where we belong. "Aside from a person's physical appearance, the first thing someone will be judged by is how he or she talks," maintains linguist Dennis Baron.

3　　Many feel that the growing informality of American life, the retreat from fixed standards ("the march of casualization," *The New York Times* recently called it)— in clothing, manners, sexual mores—is reflected in our language and is corrupting it. They see schools lax about teaching grammar and hear nonstandard forms accepted in broadcasting, newspapers, politics, and advertising. They believe the slogan "Winston tastes good like a cigarette should" is so embedded in the national psyche that few Americans would now balk at the use of "like" (instead of "as") because that usage is fast becoming the new standard. They hate such changes in the language and they despair for our culture.

4　　Others, however, believe language is thriving—as inventive and vigorous as English was in the time of the Elizabethans—and they see American English as the engine driving what is now a global language.

5　　The controversies, issues, anxieties, and assumptions swirling around language today [can be] highly emotional and political. Why are black and white Americans speaking less and less like each other? Does Hispanic immigration threaten the English language? Is our exposure to national media wiping out regional differences and causing us all to speak the same? Is the language really in serious decline? Well, we have quite a debate about that.

6　　The people who believe so are known as prescriptivists: those who want us to obey prescribed rules of grammar. They do not mind being called curmudgeons and they alternate between pleasure and despair—pleasure in correcting their fellow citizens: despair that they cannot stop the language from going to hell in our generation.

## The Prince of Prescriptivists

7　One of the leading curmudgeons of our time—he has been called the Prince of Prescriptivists—is John Simon, theater critic for *New York Magazine*, and he comes to do battle in "Do You Speak American?" Simon sees the language today as "unhealthy, poor, sad, depressing, and probably fairly hopeless." In the foreword to a new book, *The Dictionary of Disagreeable English*, he writes: "No damsel was ever in such distress, no drayhorse more flogged, no defenseless child more drunkenly abused than the English language today."

8    The enemies for Simon are the descriptivists, those content to describe language as it actually is used. They include the editors of great dictionaries who, Simon charges, have grown dangerously permissive, abandoning advice on what is correct and what is not. He calls descriptivist linguists "a curse on their race."

9    One such individual is Jesse Sheidlower, American editor of the august *Oxford English Dictionary*. Does he believe the language is being mined by the great informality of American life? "No, it is not being ruined at all," he replies. Sheidlower believes that Simon and other language conservatives actually are complaining that linguists and dictionary writers no longer are focused on the language of the elite. They look at the old days and say, "Well, everything used to be very proper, and now we have all these bad words and people are being careless, and so forth." In fact, he insists people always have spoken that way. "It's just that you didn't hear them because the media would only report on the language of the educated upper middle class," Sheidlower points out. "Nowadays . . . we see the language of other groups, of other social groups, of other income levels, in a way that we never used to.

10    "Language change happens and there's nothing you can do about it." To which Simon replies, "Maybe change is inevitable—maybe. Maybe dying from cancer is also inevitable, but I don't think we should help it along."

11    Helping it along, to Simon, would mean surrendering to the word "hopefully," one of his pet peeves. "To say, 'Hopefully it won't rain tomorrow'—who, or what, is filled with hope? Nothing. So you have to say, 'I hope it won't rain tomorrow.' But you can say, 'I enter a room hopefully,' because you are the vessel for that hopefulness."

12    Sheidlower replies that modern computer databases make it possible to check texts back over the centuries: "We see that 'hopefully' is not in fact very new. . . . It goes back hundreds of years, and it has been very common even in highly educated speech for much of the time."

13    This battle—the stuff of angry skirmishes in books, magazines, and seminars—is only one part of what makes our language news today. Other findings may surprise many people because they challenge widely held popular conceptions, or misconceptions, about the language. . . .

14    While computers, information technology, globalization, digital communications, and satellites have revolutionized how we work, equally potent revolutions have occurred concerning the home, family structure and marriage, sexual mores, the role of women, race relations, and the rise of teenagers as a major consumer and marketing force. With this has come alterations in our public manners, eating habits, clothing, and tolerance of different lifestyles—all of which have been swept by a tide of informality.

## Linguists Spring into Action

15 Observing how these rapid social changes have altered our language have been the linguists, whose new branch of the social sciences really came into its own in the 1960s, followed more recently by sociolinguistics, the study of how language and society interact. They have produced a body of fascinating research that usually is

couched in technical language difficult for nonlinguists to understand. Dozens of linguists have lent their skills to help us translate their findings, and marry their scholarship to our sampling of the actual speech of ordinary Americans in all its variety, vitality, and humor, drawn from the widest social spectrum. They include waitresses, cowboys, hip-hop artists, Marine drill sergeants, Border Patrol agents, Mexican immigrants, Cajun musicians, African-American and Hispanic broadcasters, and Silicon Valley techies (who try to make computers talk like real people), as well as writers and editors, teachers and teenagers, surfers and snowboarders, actors and screenwriters, and presidents and politicians.

16      Did they all sound the same? One of the most common assumptions is that our total immersion in the same mass media is making us all speak in a similar manner. Not true, claim the linguists. We are not talking more alike, but less.

17      One of the enduring themes in American life is the pull of national against regional interests and regret for local distinctiveness erased in the relentless march of uniformity. It surfaced in the song "Little Boxes" by Pete Seeger, about people put into little boxes of identical houses made of "ticky tacky" and who all come out the same. Today, with more and more national franchising of basic elements— food, mobile homes, clothing, hotels, recreation—the U.S. can seem like one giant theme park endlessly reduplicated, the triumph of the cookie cutter culture and its distinctive art form, the national TV commercial.

18      Paradoxically, however, language is one fundamental aspect of our cultural identity in which growing homogenization is a myth. While some national trends are apparent, regional speech differences not only thrive, in some places they are becoming more distinctive. Local differences, pride, and identity with place are asserting themselves strongly, perhaps as instinctive resistance to the homogenizing forces of globalization. One remarkable example is the speech of urban African-Americans, which is diverging from standard mainstream English. After decades of progress in civil rights, and the growth of a large and successful black middle class, African-American speech in our big cities dramatically is going its own way.

19      Two linguists, Guy Bailey, provost of the University of Texas at San Antonio, and Patricia Cukor-Avila of the University of North Texas at Denton, have documented this. For 18 years, they have studied a small community in East Central Texas they named "Springville," which appears to live in a time warp from a century ago, when it was the center for local cotton sharecroppers, black and white. Little remains now but the original general store. During the late 1930s, the Works Progress Administration recorded the voices of elderly blacks, some former slaves, some the children of slaves.

20      One of them, Laura Smalley, was born to a slave mother. She was nine at the time of Emancipation in 1863. She told how the slave owner kept them ignorant of Lincoln's Proclamation for six months. "An' I thought ol' master was dead, but he wash'. . . . He'd been off to the war an' come back. All the niggers gathered aroun' to see ol' master again. You know, an' ol' master didn' tell, you know, they was free. . . . They worked there, I think now they say they worked them six months after that, six months. And turn them loose on the 19th of June. That's why, you know, they celebrate that day. Colored folks celebrates that day."

## Black and White Dialects

21 Reviewing the speech of Smalley and others, the linguists were taken by how similar it was to the speech of rural whites of that time and place, but now dissimilar to the speech of blacks today. Features characteristic of modern black speech, what linguists call African-American vernacular English—such as the invariant "be," as in "they 'be' working," or the deleted copular, leaving out the auxiliary verb in "they working"—were absent.

22      Here are samples of modern speech of African-Americans in large cities:

> "When the baby be sleep, and the othe' kids be at school, and my husband be at work, then . . . I might can finally sit down."
>      "She told David they Mama had went to Chicago to see her sister and her sister's new baby."

These examples show the invariant "be," and the construction "had went." Bailey and Cukor-Avila say that these features did not exist in black speech before World War II. They conclude that, after the great migration to the North from World War I to the 1970s, blacks were segregated in urban ghettoes, had less contact with whites than they had in places like Springville, and their speech began to develop new features, as all human speech does when people are separated culturally and have little communication.

23      This has serious consequences in efforts to reduce the school dropout rate among blacks. Not only white teachers, but many African-American instructors, despise the "street talk" or "slang" as they call it, and often treat the children as if they were stupid or uneducable. In 1979, a Federal judge in Detroit ruled that an Ann Arbor, Mich., school, ironically named after Martin Luther King, Jr., was discriminating against black kids because of their language and ordered the school to remedy it. Yet, the prejudice lives on elsewhere.

24      In 1997, Oakland schools tried to get black speech recognized not as a dialect of English but a separate language, Ebonics, to qualify for Federal money to teach English as a second language. That backfired amid furious protests nationally from black and white educators.

25      What is shocking to linguists is the manner in which many newspaper columnists excoriate black English, using terms such as "gibberish." In the linguistic community, black English is recognized as having its own internal consistency and grammatical forms. It certainly is not gibberish (which means something unintelligible) because it works effectively for communication within the urban community.

26      One of the first to give black English this measure of respect was William Labov of the University of Pennsylvania, who testified at a Senate hearing during the Ebonics furor in 1997: "This African-American vernacular English . . . is not a set of slang words, or a random set of grammatical mistakes, but a well-formed set of rules of grammar and pronunciation that is capable of conveying complex logic and reasoning."

27      To linguists, the fault lies not in a particular dialect, but in what attitudes others bring to it. Steve Harvey, an African-American who hosts the most popular morning radio show in Los Angeles, told us: "I speak good enough American. You know, I think there's variations of speaking American. I don't think there's any one

set way, because America's so diverse." He added, "You do have to be bilingual in this country, which means you can be very adept at slang, but you also have to be adept at getting through the job interview."

28    Now, without fanfare, some Los Angeles schools have been trying a more sympathetic approach to help minority students become bilingual—by teaching them the differences between African-American Language, as they call it, and Mainstream American English. We visited PS 100 in Watts to watch fifth-graders play a "Jeopardy"-like game in which they won points for "translating" such sentences as "Last night we bake cookies."

> Teacher: "What language is it in?"
>
> Student: "AAL."
>
> Teacher: "It is in African-American Language. What linguistic feature is in AAL?"
>
> Student: "Past-tense marker-ed."
>
> Teacher: "Past-tense marker-ed. That's cool! And how do you code-switch it to Mainstream American English?"
>
> Student: "Last night we baked cookies."
>
> Teacher: "You got five hundred more points." Big cheers from the kids.

29    So, four decades after the passage of landmark legislation outlawing racial discrimination, the news is that it blatantly survives in language. Columnists would not dream of describing other attributes of being African-American with epithets like "gibberish." They could, however, get away with it in writing about black language, which remains a significant barrier to success in school and ultimately in the job market and housing—pathways to the American dream.

30    Ironically, as much as it is despised, black English is embraced and borrowed by whites, especially young whites in thrall to the appeal of hip hop music. There are divergences just as dramatic within the English of white Americans. Around the Great Lakes, people are making what Labov believes are "revolutionary changes in the pronunciation of short vowels that have remained relatively stable in the language for a thousand years."

31    Labov is director of an effort to determine the boundaries of different dialects within American speech. Traditionally, that was achieved by comparing distinctive local or regional words people used for everyday things. One surviving example is the different terms for the long sandwich that contains cold cuts, cheese, and lettuce—a grinder in some parts of New England; a wedge in Rhode Island: a spuky in Boston; a hero in New York; a hoagie in Philadelphia; a submarine in Ohio and farther west. By drawing lines around places where each term is used, linguists can form maps of dialect areas. Many such regional terms are dying out because old craft skills are replaced by products marketed nationally. Labov leads a new method in which the different ways people pronounce words are recorded with colored dots on a map of the U.S. Connecting the dots produces the Atlas of North American English.

32    Labov and his colleagues found startling pronunciation changes in cities such as Chicago, Cleveland, and Detroit and New York State's Rochester and Syracuse. On a computer in his office in Philadelphia, we heard a woman say the word

"black," then the complete phrase: "Old senior citizens living on one 'black,'" and it was apparent that she was pronouncing "block" like "black." Similarly, another woman mentions what sounds like "bosses." The full sentence reveals she means "buses:" "I can vaguely remember when we had 'bosses' with the antennas on top."

33    When one vowel changes, so do the neighboring ones: "caught" shifts toward "cot," "cot" toward "cat," "cat" toward "kit" or "keeyat." Labov thinks these changes are quite important. "From our point of view as linguists, we want to understand why people should become more different from each other. We're all watching the same radio and television; we live side by side. And it's important to recognize that people don't always want to behave in the same way."

34    Labov has a theory that, behind changes like these, are women, the primary transmitters of language. Traditionally enjoying less economic power than men, women rely on the symbolic power offered by words. Labov believes women are more apt than men to adopt "prestige forms" of language and symbols of nonconformism—new or "stigmatized forms" that can acquire a kind of "covert prestige." Labov writes that women are quicker and more forceful in employing the new social symbolism, whatever it may be. Working on his landmark study, "The Principles of Linguistic Change," he identifies a particular type of woman— working class, well-established in her community—who takes pleasure in being nonconformist and is strong enough to influence others. He sees parallels between leadership in fashion and language change. Most young women are alert to novelty in fashion; some have the confidence to embrace it and the natural authority to induce others to follow.

35    These are mysterious forces working on our language from underneath, as it were, and producing startling changes that, far from homogenizing our speech, actually create more diversity. Despite all the forces of global and national uniformity in products and trends, Americans clearly still want to do their own thing linguistically. An example is Pittsburgh, where the local dialect, or Pittsburghese, is celebrated, constantly talked about, and made a commodity. They know themselves as "Yinzers," from "yinz," the plural of "you," or "you ones." They use "slippy" for "slippery"; "red up" means to "tidy up"; and "anymore" as in "Anymore, there's so many new buildings you can't tell which is which." In downtown Pittsburgh—pronounced "dahntahn"—the question, "Did you eat yet?" sounds like "Jeet jet?" If you haven't, the response is, "No, 'jew?'"

36    Barbara Johnstone, a linguist from Pittsburgh, thinks the pride in their local speech is a way for Pittsburghers to talk about who they are and what it means to live there. People treasure their local accents, because where they come from, or where they feel they belong, still does matter. In the words of California linguist, Carmen Fought, "People want to talk like the people they want to be like." This contradicts the common assumption that media exposure is making everyone sound the same.

## Local Accents Prevail

37 Yet, amusingly, people often are quite unaware of how their own speech sounds to others. Linguists we met were full of stories about people in Texas or coastal North Carolina with strong local accents who were convinced they sounded like Walter

Cronkite. It happened to me. I grew up in the Canadian province of Nova Scotia, so fascinated with words that I called a memoir of my childhood *Wordstruck.* Even in my own family, I often heard the same words said differently. My grandfather, from Nova Scotia's south shore, said "garridge" while his daughter, my mother, said "gar-aghe."

38    Until I first came to the U.S. in 1952, I was unaware how different my speech was even from that of neighboring New England. I was 21 and (briefly, thank God!) an aspiring actor, thrilled to be working in a summer theater in Massachusetts. The first time I stepped on to the stage and opened my mouth, the director said, "You can't talk like that." I was stunned, not knowing until that moment that I was pronouncing "out" to rhyme with "oat," and "about" with "aboat"—still the common Nova Scotian pronunciation. Anxious not to close any career doors, I immediately began trying to modify the "oat" sound, but 50 years later, when I am tired or back with my brothers in Canada, I still slip into the pronunciations I grew up with.

39    What appears to be the determining force in whether regional dialects survive or disappear is not media influence, but rather the movements of people. We talked to John Coffin, a lobsterman in South Freeport, Maine. Once a quiet fishing and ship-building harbor but now a bustling outlet shopping center, the town has attracted so many new visitors and residents that Coffin fears the Maine way of speaking—with its characteristic "ayeh" for "yes"—is disappearing: "I think in this area it's going to be a lost thing," and that makes him sad. "I'd like to think my children and grandchildren talk that way, whether people laugh at you, wherever we go—whatever." Do people laugh at his Maine accent? "Oh, yes, lots of times. When I was in the military, they made fun of me wicked." "Wicked" is a typical Maine word, meaning "very," as in " 'wicked' good."

40    This homogenizing trend is obvious on some of the islands, like Ocrakoke, off the coast of North Carolina, home of the Hoi Toiders, people who pronounce "high tide" as "hoi toid." These islands have become meccas for individuals from elsewhere building vacation homes, displacing locals and their dialect.

41    Still, the national media are having some effect: Labov notes two sound changes that have spread nationally, probably from California. One is the vowel in "do," which increasingly sounds like "dew." Labov calls it "oo-fronting"; the sound is produced more to the front of the mouth. You also hear it in the word "so," which sounds like "so-ew." Another trend, more noticeable among young women, but also some men, is a rising inflection at the ends of sentences, making statements such as "The bus station is around the corner" sound like a query. One of the regions where "oo-fronting" is common is the South, where there are changes just as dramatic as those in the North. Southern ghosts do not say "boo," but "bew."

42    The most prevalent shift is that Southerners increasingly are pronouncing the "r" at the ends of words such as father. In part, this is due to the large migration of Northerners to Southern cities. Partly it is the historic decline in influence of the coastal Southern areas that once boasted the great slave-holding plantation culture, and the kind of r-less pronunciation we associated with languid belles posing in hoop skirts on the porches of ante-bellum houses. This advancing "r" marks the growing prestige of what linguists call Inland Southern, the speech deriving

from Appalachia. That pattern goes back to the earliest days of British settlement, when people from parts of England who did not pronounce "r" settled the coastal areas, while the Scots-Irish, settlers from Northern Ireland who spoke with a strong "r," moved into the hills of Appalachia because the easily-cultivated coastal land already was taken.

43    Their speech has been given a huge boost by the rise of country music, no longer a regional craze, but a national phenomenon. Those who "sing country," wherever they come from, "talk country" and "talkin' country" has become a kind of default way of speaking informal American. It is considered easygoing and friendly. President George W. Bush has made it his trademark, with no disadvantage politically because, like him, a great many Americans say, "Howya doin'? Doin' fine!" and they are not more particular than he is about making subject agree with verb in sentences such as, "There's no negotiations with North Korea."

44    The economic rise of the South has had another startling result. So many Americans have moved into the South and Southwest and happily adopted Southernisms—such as "y'all" and "fixin' to" and pronouncing "I" as "all," not the Northern "eye-ee"—that more Americans now speak some variety of Southern than any other dialect. That is the conclusion of linguist John Fought, who believes that, as the population shift to the Sun Belt continues, "In time, we should expect 'r-full' southern to become accepted as standard American speech."

45    That news will come as a shock to Northerners conditioned over generations to despise Southern talk, considering it evidence of stupidity and backwardness. In the film "Sweet Home Alabama," the good ol' boy played by Josh Lucas says to his Northernized wife, Reese Witherspoon, "Just because I talk slow, doesn't mean I'm stupid." The context leads the audience to believe him.

46    The comedian Jeff Foxworthy still fills huge theaters North and South with his hilarious routine ridiculing Southern speech and Northern attitudes towards it. He kills them with his list of Southern "words:"

> "May-o-naise. Man, a's a lotta people here tonight,"
> "Urinal. I told my brother, 'You're in a lotta trouble when Daddy gets home.'"
> "Wichadidja. Hey, you didn't bring your track with you, did you?"

47    Northern attitudes to Southerners may be ameliorating slightly, possibly because it no longer is uncool in Northern cities to like country music and the culture that goes with it. Yet, an ingrained sense of the prestige of some dialects and scorn for others is very much alive. Linguist Dennis Preston of Michigan State University has spent years studying the prejudices Americans have concerning speech different from their own. He joined us on a train west from Philadelphia, demonstrating his regular technique. Establishing quick rapport with other passengers, he got them to mark on a map of the U.S. where they thought people spoke differently. Almost without exception, they circled the South and New York to locate the worst English. Referring to New York, a Pennsylvania woman told Preston contemptuously, "They say waader!" Preston asked, "What do you say?" "Water!" she declared proudly.

## A Distinct New York Voice

48 Preston, though, detects another emotion creeping in beneath the scorn, and that is pleasure. People may think Southern or New York speech is not good, but they find them charming, and that must be partly an effect of media exposure, for instance, to the sympathetic New York characters in the TV series "Law and Order." Linguists believe that broadcasting and the movies help all Americans understand different dialects, perhaps appreciating the diversity in our culture. Moreover, no matter how they themselves speak, Americans learn to understand the language of network broadcasters, which is the closest thing to an overall American standard. That standard coincides with the speech that Preston's subjects inevitably identify as the best American speech—that of the Midwest—because it has the fewest regional features.

49     That Midwest standard is relevant to the cutting edge of computer research in Silicon Valley. There is heavy investment in efforts to make computers speak like us and understand us. The researchers believe they will achieve that in 10 to 15 years but it is an incredible challenge.

50     What these efforts demonstrate is how infinitely complex our language and understanding of it is, how meaning turns on the subtlest changes in intonation, how vast any computer data base must be to catch all the nuances we take for granted. How do you program a computer to avoid those charming errors in context which foreigners make in perfectly grammatical sentences? For instance, a sign in an Egyptian hotel states: "Patrons need have no anxiety about the water. It has all been passed by the management." Or, this in a Swiss hotel: "Due to the impropriety of entertaining guests of the opposite sex in the bedrooms, it is suggested that the lobby be used for this purpose."

51     The effort to make computers understand speech raises other questions about the future of language. Will the technology, and the business imperatives behind it, create an irresistible drive toward more standard speech? If so, which accents or varieties of American speech will that leave out? Whom will it disenfranchise because of their dialect—African-Americans, Hispanics, Cajuns in Louisiana? A couple of years ago, the police chief of Shreveport, La., complained that the computer voice-recognition system used to route nonemergency calls did not understand the local accent. Researchers point out, however, that if you speak like someone from the Midwest, computers will understand you.

52     The emerging technology is irresistible for business. When United Airlines introduced a computerized voice-recognition system for flight information—replacing live bodies—it saved a reported $25,000,000. As these systems become more sophisticated, a lot of companies will want them to replace expensive warm bodies. Inevitably, more and more of our lives will involve talking to and being understood by computers. Being understood will be increasingly important. Will the technology work to reinforce existing linguistic stereotypes—about your sex, race, ethnicity, gender, or where you live—or help to break them down? Will we have to talk as computers would like us to in order for them to obey us?

53     During the California portion of filming "Do You Speak American?" I drove a car equipped with an elaborate voice-recognition system. I speak a version of standard broadcast American English, and I tried to enunciate clearly. Occasionally, it

worked, but often it did not and the car kept saying, "Pardon me? Pardon me?" and I gave it up.

54    Everything in the American experience, each new frontier encountered—geographical, spiritual, technological—has altered our language. What kind of a frontier are we crossing by teaching computers our most fundamental human skill, that of the spoken word?

## THINKING CRITICALLY

1. In paragraph 2, linguist Dennis Baron comments, "Aside from a person's physical appearance, the first thing someone will be judged by is how he or she talks." Do you judge people based on how they speak? What assumptions do you make about people who have certain accents? Based on how they use standard grammar? What judgments do you think people make about you based on how you talk? Explain.

2. What is the difference between prescriptive and descriptive linguistics? Where do the prescriptivists and the descriptivists stand on the current state of American English? With which viewpoint do you agree?

3. To prepare for his documentary, MacNeil interviewed many people, including "waitresses, cowboys, hip-hop artists, Marine drill sergeants, Border Patrol agents, Mexican immigrants, Cajun musicians, African-American and Hispanic broadcasters, and Silicon Valley techies . . . writers and editors, teachers and teenagers, surfers and snowboarders, actors and screenwriters, and presidents and politicians." Why do you think he chose these people to represent the linguistic trends of American English? Do you think he chose an accurate cross-section of people? What linguistic patterns would you expect from these groups? Explain.

4. MacNeil notes that "one of the most common assumptions is that our total immersion in the same mass media is making us all speak in a similar manner." How could the mass media influence the way we speak? Has the mass media been successful in creating a standard form of American English? Explain.

5. What is Ebonics? Why did it backfire in 1997 in Oakland, California? What replaced the Ebonics concept, and why?

6. Linguist William Labov theorizes that regional linguistic trends are primarily transmitted by women. Review his ideas and explain why you agree or disagree, in whole or in part, with his theory.

7. MacNeil wonders what will happen if computers are able to speak and understand speech. In your own words, respond to his concerns. What do you think will happen to American English, and why?

## WRITING ASSIGNMENTS

1. MacNeil notes that some dialects and speech patterns are considered more "correct" than others. Review the results of his research and take the quiz he describes in his essay on PBS's "Do You Speak American?" website: http://www.pbs.org/speak/speech/mapping/map.html. What do your results tell you about your own language biases?

2. In his essay, MacNeil observes that rather than sounding more alike, Americans are more linguistically different than ever before. Listen to some local

dialects on PBS's "Do You Speak American?" website and review its "Myths and Realities" section at http://www.pbs.org/speak/seatosea/americanvarieties. Before reading MacNeil's results, did you accept as true any of the myths he debunks?

3. Write an essay in which you explain why it is better to support a descriptive or prescriptive position regarding American English.

---

# Everyone Has an Accent but Me
## *John Esling*

Everybody has an accent. Accent is the way we speak, pronounce our words, intone sounds, and inflect voice. From listening to others speak, we make judgments about their background, education, culture, nationality, and social status. In fact, we are far more likely to judge people by their accent than by how they dress or carry themselves, or with whom they socialize. As John Esling explains in the next essay, we all have an accent, even if we think we do not.

John Esling is a professor of linguistics at the University of Victoria in British Columbia. He is also secretary of the International Phonetic Association and author of the *University of Victoria Phonetic Database*. This essay first appeared in the book *Language Myths* (1999), edited by Laurie Bauer and Peter Trudgill.

1   "I don't have an accent!" wails the friend indignantly. And we are all amused because the pronunciation of the utterance itself demonstrates to our ears that the claim is false. The speaker who voices this common refrain believes absolutely that his or her speech is devoid of any distinguishing characteristics that set it apart from the speech of those around them. We listeners who hear it are for our part equally convinced that the speaker's accent differs in some significant respect from our own. The key to understanding this difference of opinion is not so much in the differences in speech sounds that the speakers use but in the nature of "own-ness"—what does it mean to be "one of us" and to sound like it? It all comes down to a question of belonging. Accent defines and communicates who we are. Accent is the map which listeners perceive through their ears rather than through their eyes to "read" where the speaker was born and raised, what gender they are, how old they are, where they might have moved during their life, where they went to school, what occupation they have taken up, and even how short or tall they are, how much they might weigh, or whether they are feeling well or ill at the moment.

2   The fact is that everyone has an accent. It tells other people who we are because it reflects the places we have been and the things we have done. But the construct of accent, like so many other things, is relative. We may only realize that others think we have an accent when we leave the place we came from and find ourselves among people who share a different background from our own, or when a newcomer to our local area stands out as having a distinctly different pronunciation from most of those in our group—that is, relative to us. The closer we are to our native place and the more people that are there who grew up like us, the more

likely we are to sound like those people when we talk. In other words, we share their local accent.

3   Some countries have one accent which is accepted as "standard" and which enjoys higher social prestige than any other. This is true of RP (Received Pronunciation) in the UK, of standard French in France and of many countries that have evolved a broadcast standard for radio and television. We may feel that this national standard is accentless and that non-standard speakers, by contrast, have accents. Nevertheless, it has to be recognized that standards that have evolved in the broadcast industry have their roots in language varieties that already exist in distinct social groups and their institutions. To use one particular group's accent in broadcasting is to give that accent a wider reach than perhaps it had before, but the accent itself is no "less" of an accent than any other, although it may represent groups and institutions with more political and economic power than groups whose members use another accent.

4   Our perceptions and production of speech also change with time. If we were to leave our native place for an extended period, our perception that the new accents around us were strange would only be temporary. Gradually, depending on our age, what job we are doing and how many different sorts of folks with different types of accents surround us, we will lose the sense that others have an accent and we will begin to fit in—to accommodate our speech patterns to the new norm. Not all people do this to the same degree. Some remain intensely proud of their original accent and dialect words, phrases and gestures, while others accommodate rapidly to a new environment by changing, among other things, their speech habits, so that they no longer "stand out in the crowd." Whether they do this consciously or not is open to debate and may differ from individual to individual, but like most processes that have to do with language, the change probably happens before we are aware of it and probably couldn't happen if we were.

5   So when we say, "I don't have an accent," we really mean, "You wouldn't think I had an accent if you knew who I was and knew where I'd been." It has more to do with acceptance—agreeing to stop listening to the other as "other"—than with absolute differences in the vowels, consonants or intonation patterns that a speaker uses. At the most basic level, we acknowledge that every individual will always have some speech characteristics that distinguish him or her from everyone else, even in our local community. This is the essence of recognition—we can learn to pick a friend's voice out of the crowd even though we consider everyone in our local crowd to have the same "accent" compared to outsiders. So what we call accent is relative not only to experience but also to the number of speech features we wish to distinguish at a time.

6   Human perception is categorical. When it comes to placing an accent, we listen and categorize according to accents we have heard before. We have a hard time placing an accent that we have never heard before, at least until we find out what to associate that accent with. Our experience of perceiving the sounds of human speech is very much a question of "agreeing" with others to construct certain categories and then to place the sounds that we hear into them. In contemporary constructivist psychology, this process is called the "co-construction of reality," in which differences can be said not to exist until we construct them. One result of these principles

is that we can become quite attuned to stereotypical accents that we have heard only occasionally and don't know very well, while we become "insensitive" to the common accents we hear all around us every day. The speech of our colleagues seems "normal" to our ears, while the speech of a stranger stands out as different from that norm. So we feel that we don't have an accent because of the weight of experience that tells us that we are the best possible example of the "norm."

7      Details of pronunciation conjure up stereotypes. A few consonants and vowels or the briefest of intonation melodies cause us to search our memories for a pattern that matches what we have just heard. This is how we place speakers according to dialect or language group. It is also how we predict what the rest of their consonants and vowels and intonational phrasing will be like. Sometimes we are wrong, but usually we make good guesses based on limited evidence, especially if we've heard the accent before. Because we are used to the word order and common expressions of our language, a stranger's exotic pronunciation of a word which we recognize and understand can be catalogued as foreign, and we may ascribe it to one familiar stereotype or another and predict what the speaker's pronunciation of other words will be like. In this way, we see others as having an accent—because we take ourselves as the norm or reference to compare and measure others' speech.

8      It is interesting for the student of phonetics to observe the various ways in which one person's accent can differ from another's. There are three "strands" of accent which Professor David Abercrombie of the Department of Linguistics of the University of Edinburgh for many years taught his students to distinguish: the very short consonant and vowel sounds which alternate in rapid succession; the longer waves of rhythmic and melodic groupings, which we call rhythm and intonation; and the longest-term, persistent features that change very little in a given individual's voice, which we call voice quality.

9      Consonants and vowels are the building blocks of linguistic meaning, and slight changes in their quality inherently carry large differences in meaning, which we detect immediately. *Bought, bat, bet, bait* is a four-way distinction for an English speaker, but may only be a two-way distinction for a Spanish or Japanese speaker. Differences in vowels can make dialects of English incomprehensible even to each other at first. An American pronunciation of "John" can sound like "Jan" to a Scot; and a Scots pronunciation of "John" can sound like "Joan" to an American. Consonants are also critical in deciding the meaning of a word. The American who asked if she could clear away some "bottles" was understood by the pub owner in Scotland to have said "barrels," not only because of the vowel but also because the d-like pronunciation of the t-sound is almost exactly like the d-like pronunciation of the rolled r in Scots. Again, it is the speaker generating the utterance who thinks primarily in terms of meaning and not in terms of the sounds being used to transmit that meaning. It is the hearer who must translate the incoming speech sounds into new, meaningful units (which we usually call words) and who cannot help but notice that the signals coming in are patterned differently from the hearer's own system of speech sounds. Confusion over the meaning of a word can only highlight these differences, making the translation of meaning more difficult and making each participant in the conversation feel that the other has an accent. The impression is therefore mutual.

10      Another meaningful component of accent is intonation or the "melody" of speech. Differences in the rises and falls of intonation patterns, and the rhythmic beat that accompanies them, can be as significant as differences in the melodies of tunes that we recognize or in the beat of a waltz compared to a jig. One of the characteristics of the American comedian Richard Pryor's ability to switch from "white talk" to "black talk" is the control of the height and of the rising and falling of the pitch of the voice. Even more rapid timing of these rises and falls is an indication of languages such as Swedish and languages such as Chinese which have different tones, that is, pitches that distinguish word meanings from each other. Pitch can have the greatest effect on our impression of an accent or on our ability to recognize a voice. Our mood—whether we are excited or angry or sad—can change the sound of our voice, as the tempo of our speech also speeds up or slows down, so that we may sound like a different person.

11      Voice quality is the ensemble of more or less permanent elements that appear to remain constant in a person's speech. This is how we recognize a friend's voice on the telephone even if they only utter a syllable. Some voices are nasal; others low and resonant; others breathy; and still others higher pitched and squeaky. Presumably, the better we know a person, the less we feel they have a noticeable accent. Naturally, however, if they didn't have a distinguishable ensemble of accent features, we couldn't tell their voice apart from other people's. Travelers to a foreign country often experience an inability to tell individual speakers of a foreign language apart. As it once did in our native language, this ability comes with practice, that is, with exposure. The reason is that we need time to distinguish, first, to which strand of accent each particular speech gesture belongs and, second, which speech details are common to most speakers of that language and which belong only to the individual. Unless the individual's speech stands out in some remarkable way, we are likely to perceive the collection of common, group traits first.

12      Much of our perception of accent could actually be visual. Hand and facial gestures which accompany speech could cue a listener that the speaker comes from a different place, so that we expect the person to sound different from our norm. If we expect to hear an accent, we probably will. Sooner or later, wherever they live, most people encounter someone from another place. A stranger from out of town, a foreigner, even a person who had moved away and returned. But even in the same community, people from different social groups or of different ages can be distinguished on the basis of their speech. One of the intriguing linguistic aspects of police work is to locate and identify suspects on the basis of their accent. Often, this technique comes down to the skill of being able to notice details of speech that other observers overlook. Sometimes, an academic approach such as broadcasting a voice to a large number of "judges" over the radio or on television is necessitated. In this case, an anonymous suspect can often be narrowed down as coming from a particular area or even identified outright. Computer programs are also having moderate success at verifying individual speakers on the basis of their accent. These techniques are sometimes called "voiceprints," implying that each individual is unique, but as with human listeners, success may depend on how much speech from the individual can be heard and in how many contexts.

13    One of the most popular characterizations of the notion of accent modification has been George Bernard Shaw's *Pygmalion*, revived on stage and screen as *My Fair Lady*. The phonetician, Professor Higgins, is renowned for tracing the course of people's lives from their accents, and Eliza Doolittle, at the opposite extreme, while probably aware of different accents and able to identify them to some degree, appears at first quite unable to produce speech in anything other than her local-dialect accent. The transformation of Eliza, explained in sociolinguistic terms, is the apparent result of her accommodation to a new social milieu and her acceptance of a new role for herself. In terms of constructivist psychology, she co-constructed a new reality—a new story—for her life and left the old story behind. The transformation had its physical effect (she was no longer recognized in her former neighborhood) as well as its linguistic realization (her accent changed to suit her new surroundings). We all leave parts of the speaking style of our early years behind, while we adopt new patterns more suited to our later years. Whether we change a lot or a little depends on individual choices within a web of social circumstance.

### THINKING CRITICALLY

1. What do we mean when we say that someone does not have an accent? Is there a type of English that we seem to recognize as "accentless"? Why, according to the author, is such a determination false?

2. Consider the title of Esling's essay. How does it connect to his essay's thesis? Why do so many people feel that they do not have an accent? Explain.

3. Before reading this essay, how would you have described your accent? Would you have said you had one? After responding to this question, ask a friend or classmate from a different part of the country if they would agree with your assessment.

4. What stereotypes are associated with accents? Try to identify as many accents as you can think of and what stereotypes you associate with them.

5. Have you ever made presumptions about a person based on his or her accent? How did the phonetic elements Esling describes, such as intonation, pronunciation of consonants and vowels, and voice quality, influence your judgment? Why do we use these phonetic cues to form opinions about other people?

6. According to the author, what makes it possible for us to distinguish accents? Why can we not distinguish our own?

### WRITING ASSIGNMENTS

1. In his opening paragraph, Esling comments that accent serves as a "map" that tells others many things about us, including where we come from, our age, gender, education, and background. Write an essay in which you explore the relationship between accent and how we judge others. Do you judge people by how they speak? Is it automatic? Have you ever been wrong? Why do we tend to judge people by their accents?

2. At the end of his essay, Esling refers to George Bernard Shaw's play *Pygmalion*. Read the preface Shaw wrote regarding the subject matter and the social commentary behind his story, in which he notes, "it is impossible for an Englishman to open his mouth without making some other Englishman hate or despise him." What did Shaw mean by this statement? Does his observation hold any truth for Americans today? Why or why not? Explain.

# Good English and Bad
*Bill Bryson*

More than one billion people in the world speak English, and much of the rest of the world is attempting to. But the English language, with its various historical influences, is deceptively complex. Even language authorities will stumble over its idiosyncrasies. And the reason is simple: in an effort to establish criteria for *good* English for generations to come, 17th-century grammarians wrote rules of English modeled on those of Latin, which, though dead, was considered the most admirable and purest tongue. But as Bill Bryson explains, imposing Latin rules on English is like asking people to play baseball according to the rules of football. They do not go together; likewise, ancient standards of usage do not always describe how the language works today. In this lively and engaging discussion, Bryson explains how the distinction of *good* English from *bad* English is mostly a matter of conditioning and prejudice.

Bill Bryson is an American journalist living in England. He has worked for the *Times* of London and the *Independent,* also of London, and has written articles for *The New York Times, Esquire, GQ,* and other magazines. His books include *A Dictionary of Troublesome Words* (2004), *A Short History of Nearly Everything* (2003), and the highly acclaimed *The Mother Tongue* (1990), from which this essay comes. His most recent book is *Shakespeare: The World as Stage* (2007).

1 Consider the parts of speech. In Latin, the verb has up to 120 inflections. In English it never has more than five (e.g., *see, sees, saw, seeing, seen*) and often it gets by with just three (*hit, hits, hitting*). Instead of using loads of different verb forms, we use just a few forms but employ them in loads of ways. We need just five inflections to deal with the act of propelling a car—*drive, drives, drove, driving*, and *driven*—yet with these we can express quite complex and subtle variations of tense: "I drive to work every day," "I have been driving since I was sixteen," "I will have driven 20,000 miles by the end of this year." This system, for all its ease of use, makes labeling difficult. According to any textbook, the present tense of the verb *drive* is *drive*. Every junior high school pupil knows that. Yet if we say, "I used to drive to work but now I don't," we are clearly using the present tense *drive* in a past tense sense. Equally if we say, "I will drive you to work tomorrow," we are using it in a future sense. And if we say, "I would drive if I could afford to," we are using it in a conditional sense. In fact, almost the only form of sentence in which we cannot use the present tense form of *drive* is, yes, the present tense. When we need to indicate an action going on right now, we must use the participial form *driving*. We don't say, "I drive the car now," but rather "I'm driving the car now." Not to put too fine a point on it, the labels are largely meaningless.

2 We seldom stop to think about it, but some of the most basic concepts in English are naggingly difficult to define. What, for instance, is a sentence? Most dictionaries define it broadly as a group of words constituting a full thought and containing, at a minimum, a subject (basically a noun) and predicate (basically a verb). Yet if I inform you that I have just crashed your car and you reply, "What!" or "Where?" or "How!" you have clearly expressed a complete thought, uttered a sentence. But where are the subject and predicate? Where are the noun and verb,

not to mention the prepositions, conjunctions, articles, and other components that we normally expect to find in a sentence? To get around this problem, grammarians pretend that such sentences contain words that aren't there. "What!" they would say, really means "What are you telling me—you crashed my car?" while "Where?" is a shorthand rendering of "Where did you crash it?" and "How?" translates as "How on earth did you manage to do that, you old devil you?" or words to that effect. The process is called *ellipsis* and is certainly very nifty. Would that I could do the same with my bank account. Yet the inescapable fact is that it is possible to make such sentences conform to grammatical precepts only by bending the rules. When I was growing up we called that cheating.

3    In English, in short, we possess a language in which the parts of speech are almost entirely notional. A noun is a noun and a verb is a verb largely because the grammarians say they are. In the sentence "I am suffering terribly" *suffering* is a verb, but in "My suffering is terrible," it is a noun. Yet both sentences use precisely the same word to express precisely the same idea. *Quickly* and *sleepily* are adverbs but *sickly* and *deadly* are adjectives. *Breaking* is a present tense participle, but as often as not it is used in a past tense sense ("He was breaking the window when I saw him"). *Broken*, on the other hand, is a past tense participle but as often as not it is employed in a present tense sense ("I think I've just broken my toe") or even future tense sense ("If he wins the next race, he'll have broken the school record"). To deal with all the anomalies, the parts of speech must be so broadly defined as to be almost meaningless. A noun, for example, is generally said to be a word that denotes a person, place, thing, action, or quality. That would seem to cover almost everything, yet clearly most actions are verbs and many words that denote qualities—*brave, foolish, good*—are adjectives.

4    The complexities of English are such that the authorities themselves often stumble. Each of the following, penned by an expert, contains a usage that at least some of his colleagues would consider quite wrong.

> "Prestige is one of the few words that has had an experience opposite to that described in 'Worsened Words.'" (H. W. Fowler, *A Dictionary of Modern English Usage,* second edition) It should be "one of the few words that *have* had."
>
> "Each of the variants indicated in boldface type count as an entry." (*The Harper Dictionary of Contemporary Usage*) It should be "each . . . *counts.*"
>
> "It is of interest to speculate about the amount of dislocation to the spelling system that would occur if English dictionaries were either proscribed or (as when Malory or Sir Philip Sidney were writing) did not exist." (Robert Burchfield, *The English Language*) Make it "*was* writing."
>
> "A range of sentences forming statements, commands, questions and exclamations cause us to draw on a more sophisticated battery of orderings and arrangements." (Robert Burchfield, *The English Language*) It should be *causes*.
>
> "The prevalence of incorrect instances of the use of the apostrophe . . . together with the abandonment of it by many business firms . . . suggest that the time is close at hand when this moderately useful device should be abandoned." (Robert Burchfield, *The English Language*) The verb should be *suggests*.

"If a lot of the available dialect data is obsolete or almost so, a lot more of it is far too sparse to support any sort of reliable conclusion." (Robert Claiborne, *Our Marvelous Native Tongue*) *Data* is a plural.

"His system of citing examples of the best authorities, of indicating etymology, and pronunciation, are still followed by lexicographers." (Philip Howard, *The State of the Language*) His system *are*?

"When his fellowship expired he was offered a rectorship at Boxworth . . . on condition that he married the deceased rector's daughter." (Robert McCrum, et al., *The Story of English*) A misuse of the subjunctive: It should be "on condition that he marry."

5 English grammar is so complex and confusing for the one very simple reason that its rules and terminology are based on Latin—a language with which it has precious little in common. In Latin, to take one example, it is not possible to split an infinitive. So in English, the early authorities decided, it should not be possible to split an infinitive either. But there is no reason why we shouldn't, any more than we should forsake instant coffee and air travel because they weren't available to the Romans. Making English grammar conform to Latin rules is like asking people to play baseball using the rules of football. It is a patent absurdity. But once this insane notion became established grammarians found themselves having to draw up ever more complicated and circular arguments to accommodate the inconsistencies. As Burchfield notes in *The English Language,* one authority, F. Th. Visser, found it necessary to devote 200 pages to discussing just one aspect of the present participle. That is as crazy as it is amazing.

6 The early authorities not only used Latin grammar as their model, but actually went to the almost farcical length of writing English grammars in that language, as with Sir Thomas Smith's *De Recta et Emendata Linguae Anglicae Scriptione Dialogus* (1568), Alexander Gil's *Logonomia Anglica* (1619), and John Wallis's *Grammatica Linguae Anglicanae* of 1653 (though even he accepted that the grammar of Latin was ill-suited to English). For the longest time it was taken entirely for granted that the classical languages *must* serve as models. Dryden spoke for an age when he boasted that he often translated his sentences into Latin to help him decide how best to express them in English.

7 In 1660, Dryden complained that English had "not so much as a tolerable dictionary or a grammar; so our language is in a manner barbarous." He believed there should be an academy to regulate English usage, and for the next two centuries many others would echo his view. In 1664, The Royal Society for the Advancement of Experimental Philosophy formed a committee "to improve the English tongue," though nothing lasting seems to have come of it. Thirty-three years later in his *Essay Upon Projects*, Daniel Defoe was calling for an academy to oversee the language. In 1712, Jonathan Swift joined the chorus with a *Proposal for Correcting, Improving and Ascertaining the English Tongue.* Some indication of the strength of feeling attached to these matters is given by the fact that in 1780, in the midst of the American Revolution, John Adams wrote to the president of Congress appealing to him to set up an academy for the purpose of "refining, correcting, improving and ascertaining the English language" (a title that closely echoes, not to say

plagiarizes, Swift's pamphlet of sixty-eight years before). In 1806, the American Congress considered a bill to institute a national academy and in 1820 an American Academy of Language and Belles Lettres, presided over by John Quincy Adams, was formed, though again without any resounding perpetual benefits to users of the language. And there were many other such proposals and assemblies.

8     The model for all these was the Académie Française, founded by Cardinal Richelieu in 1635. In its youth, the academy was an ambitious motivator of change. In 1762, after many years of work, it published a dictionary that regularized the spellings of some 5,000 words—almost a quarter of the words then in common use. It took the *s* out of words like *estre* and *fenestre*, making them *être* and *fenêtre*, and it turned *roy* and *loy* into *roi* and *loi*. In recent decades, however, the academy has been associated with an almost ayatollah-like conservatism. When in December 1988 over 90 percent of French schoolteachers voted in favor of a proposal to introduce the sort of spelling reforms the academy itself had introduced 200 years earlier, the forty venerable members of the academy were, to quote the London Sunday *Times*, "up in apoplectic arms" at the thought of tampering with something as sacred as French spelling. Such is the way of the world. Among the changes the teachers wanted and the academicians did not were the removal of the circumflex on *être, fenêtre*, and other such words, and taking the -*x* off plurals such as *bureaux, chevaux*, and *chateaux* and replacing it with an -*s*.

9     Such actions underline the one almost inevitable shortcoming of national academies. However progressive and far-seeing they may be to begin with, they almost always exert over time a depressive effect on change. So it is probably fortunate that the English-speaking world never saddled itself with such a body, largely because as many influential users of English were opposed to academies as favored them. Samuel Johnson doubted the prospects of arresting change and Thomas Jefferson thought it in any case undesirable. In declining an offer to be the first honorary president of the Academy of Language and Belles Lettres, he noted that had such a body been formed in the days of the Anglo-Saxons English would now be unable to describe the modern world. Joseph Priestley, the English scientist, grammarian, and theologian, spoke perhaps most eloquently against the formation of an academy when he said in 1761 that it was "unsuitable to the genius of a free nation. . . . We need make no doubt but that the best forms of speech will, in time, establish themselves by their own superior excellence: and in all controversies, it is better to wait the decisions of time, which are slow and sure, than to take those of synods, which are often hasty and injudicious." [Quoted by Baugh and Cable, page 269]

10     English is often commended by outsiders for its lack of a stultifying authority. Otto Jespersen as long ago as 1905 was praising English for its lack of rigidity, its happy air of casualness. Likening French to the severe and formal gardens of Louis XIV, he contrasted it with English, which he said was "laid out seemingly without any definite plan, and in which you are allowed to walk everywhere according to your own fancy without having to fear a stern keeper enforcing rigorous regulations." [*Growth and Structure of the English Language*, page 16]

11     Without an official academy to guide us, the English-speaking world has long relied on self-appointed authorities such as the brothers H. W. and F. G. Fowler and Sir Ernest Gowers in Britain and Theodore Bernstein and William Safire in

America, and of course countless others. These figures write books, give lectures, and otherwise do what they can (i.e., next to nothing) to try to stanch (not staunch) the perceived decline of the language. They point out that there is a useful distinction to be observed between *uninterested* and *disinterested*, between *imply* and *infer*, *flaunt* and *flout*, *fortunate* and *fortuitous*, *forgo* and *forego*, and *discomfort* and *discomfit* (not forgetting *stanch* and *staunch*). They point out that *fulsome*, properly used, is a term of abuse, not praise, that *peruse* actually means to read thoroughly, not glance through, that *data* and *media* are plurals. And from the highest offices in the land they are ignored.

12    In the late 1970s, President Jimmy Carter betrayed a flaw in his linguistic armory when he said: "The government of Iran must realize that it cannot flaunt, with impunity, the expressed will and law of the world community." *Flaunt* means to show off; he meant *flout*. The day after he was elected president in 1988, George Bush told a television reporter he couldn't believe the enormity of what had happened. Had President-elect Bush known that the primary meaning of *enormity* is wickedness or evilness, he would doubtless have selected a more apt term.

13    When this process of change can be seen happening in our lifetimes, it is almost always greeted with cries of despair and alarm. Yet such change is both continuous and inevitable. Few acts are more salutary than looking at the writings of language authorities from recent decades and seeing the usages that heightened their hackles. In 1931, H. W. Fowler was tutting over *racial*, which he called "an ugly word, the strangeness of which is due to our instinctive feeling that the termination -al has no business at the end of a word that is not obviously Latin." (For similar reasons he disliked *television* and *speedometer*.) Other authorities have variously—and sometimes hotly—attacked *enthuse, commentate, emote, prestigious, contact* as a verb, *chair* as a verb, and scores of others. But of course these are nothing more than opinions, and, as is the way with other people's opinions, they are generally ignored.

14    So if there are no officially appointed guardians for the English language, who sets down all those rules that we all know about from childhood—the idea that we must never end a sentence with a preposition or begin one with a conjunction, that we must use *each other* for two things and *one another* for more than two, and that we must never use *hopefully* in an absolute sense, such as "Hopefully it will not rain tomorrow"? The answer, surprisingly often, is that no one does, that when you look into the background of these "rules" there is often little basis for them.

15    Consider the curiously persistent notion that sentences should not end with a preposition. The source of this stricture, and several other equally dubious ones, was one Robert Lowth, an eighteenth-century clergyman and amateur grammarian whose *A Short Introduction to English Grammar,* published in 1762, enjoyed a long and distressingly influential life both in his native England and abroad. It is to Lowth we can trace many a pedant's most treasured notions: the belief that you must say *different from* rather than *different to* or *different than*, the idea that two negatives make a positive, the rule that you must not say "the heaviest of the two objects," but rather "the heavier," the distinction between *shall* and *will*, and the clearly nonsensical belief that *between* can apply only to two things and *among* to more than two. (By this reasoning, it would not be possible to say that St. Louis is

between New York, Los Angeles, and Chicago, but rather that it is among them, which would impart a quite different sense.) Perhaps the most remarkable and curiously enduring of Lowth's many beliefs was the conviction that sentences ought not to end with a preposition. But even he was not didactic about it. He recognized that ending a sentence with a preposition was idiomatic and common in both speech and informal writing. He suggested only that he thought it generally better and more graceful, not crucial, to place the preposition before its relative "in solemn and elevated" writing. Within a hundred years this had been converted from a piece of questionable advice into an immutable rule. In a remarkable outburst of literal-mindedness, nineteenth-century academics took it as read that the very name *pre-position* meant it must come before something—anything.

16    But then this was a period of the most resplendent silliness, when grammarians and scholars seemed to be climbing over one another (or each other; it doesn't really matter) in a mad scramble to come up with fresh absurdities. This was the age when, it was gravely insisted, Shakespeare's *laughable* ought to be changed to *laugh-at-able* and *reliable* should be made into *relionable*. Dozens of seemingly unexceptional words—*lengthy, standpoint, international, colonial, brash*—were attacked with venom because of some supposed etymological deficiency or other. Thomas de Quincey, in between bouts of opium taking, found time to attack the expression *what on earth*. Some people wrote *mooned* for *lunatic* and *foresayer* for *prophet* on the grounds that the new words were Anglo-Saxon and thus somehow more pure. They roundly castigated those ignoramuses who impurely combined Greek and Latin roots into new words like *petroleum* (Latin *petro* + Greek *oleum*). In doing so, they failed to note that the very word with which they described themselves, *grammarians*, is itself a hybrid made of Greek and Latin roots, as are many other words that have lived unexceptionably in English for centuries. They even attacked *handbook* as an ugly Germanic compound when it dared to show its face in the nineteenth century, failing to notice that it was a good Old English word that had simply fallen out of use. It is one of the felicities of English that we can take pieces of words from all over and fuse them into new constructions—like *trusteeship*, which consists of a Nordic stem (*trust*), combined with a French affix (*ee*), married to an Old English root (*ship*). Other languages cannot do this. We should be proud of ourselves for our ingenuity and yet even now authorities commonly attack almost any new construction as ugly or barbaric.

17    Today in England you can still find authorities attacking the construction *different than* as a regrettable Americanism, insisting that a sentence such as "How different things appear in Washington than in London" is ungrammatical and should be changed to "How different things appear in Washington from how they appear in London." Yet *different than* has been common in England for centuries and used by such exalted writers as Defoe, Addison, Steele, Dickens, Coleridge, and Thackeray, among others. Other authorities, in both Britain and America, continue to deride the absolute use of *hopefully*. *The New York Times Manual of Style and Usage* flatly forbids it. Its writers must not say, "Hopefully the sun will come out soon," but rather are instructed to resort to a clumsily passive and periphrastic construction such as "It is to be

hoped that the sun will come out soon." The reason? The authorities maintain that *hopefully* in the first sentence is a misplaced modal auxiliary—that it doesn't belong to any other part of the sentence. Yet they raise no objection to dozens of other words being used in precisely the same unattached way—*admittedly, mercifully, happily, curiously*, and so on. The reason *hopefully* is not allowed is because, well, because somebody at the *New York Times* once had a boss who wouldn't allow it because his professor had forbidden it, because *his* father thought it was ugly and inelegant, because *he* had been told so by his uncle who was a man of great learning . . . and so on.

18    Considerations of what makes for good English or bad English are to an uncomfortably large extent matters of prejudice and conditioning. Until the eighteenth century it was correct to say "you was" if you were referring to one person. It sounds odd today, but the logic is impeccable. *Was* is a singular verb and *were* a plural one. Why should *you* take a plural verb when the sense is clearly singular? The answer—surprise, surprise—is that Robert Lowth didn't like it. "I'm hurrying, are I not?" is hopelessly ungrammatical, but "I'm hurrying, aren't I?"—merely a contraction of the same words—is perfect English. *Many* is almost always a plural (as in "Many people were there"), but not when it is followed by *a*, as in "Many a man was there." There's no inherent reason why these things should be so. They are not defensible in terms of grammar. They are because they are.

19    Nothing illustrates the scope of prejudice in English better than the issue of the split infinitive. Some people feel ridiculously strong about it. When the British Conservative politician Jock Bruce-Gardyne was economic secretary to the Treasury in the early 1980s, he returned unread any departmental correspondence containing a split infinitive. (It should perhaps be pointed out that a split infinitive is one in which an adverb comes between *to* and a verb, as in *to quickly look*.) I can think of two very good reasons for not splitting an infinitive.

1. Because you feel that the rulers of English ought to conform to the grammatical precepts of a language that died a thousand years ago.

2. Because you wish to cling to a pointless affectation of usage that is without the support of any recognized authority of the last 200 years, even at the cost of composing sentences that are ambiguous, inelegant, and patently contorted.

20    It is exceedingly difficult to find any authority who condemns the split infinitive—Theodore Bernstein, H. W. Fowler, Ernest Gowers, Eric Partridge, Rudolph Flesch, Wilson Follett, Roy H. Copperud, and others too tedious to enumerate here all agree that there is no logical reason not to split an infinitive. Otto Jespersen even suggests that, strictly speaking, it isn't actually possible to split an infinitive. As he puts it: " 'To' . . . is no more an essential part of an infinitive than the definite article is an essential part of a nominative, and no one would think of calling 'the good man' a split nominative." [*Growth and Structure of the English Language,* page 222]

21    Lacking an academy as we do, we might expect dictionaries to take up the banner of defenders of the language, but in recent years they have increasingly shied away from the role. A perennial argument with dictionary makers is whether

they should be *prescriptive* (that is, whether they should prescribe how language should be used) or *descriptive* (that is, merely describe how it is used without taking a position). The most notorious example of the descriptive school was the 1961 *Webster's Third New International Dictionary* (popularly called *Webster's Unabridged*), whose editor, Philip Gove, believed that distinctions of usage were elitist and artificial. As a result, usages such as *imply* as a synonym for *infer* and *flout* being used in the sense of *flaunt* were included without comment. The dictionary provoked further antagonism, particularly among members of the U.S. Trademark Association, by refusing to capitalize trademarked words. But what really excited outrage was its remarkable contention that *ain't* was "used orally in most parts of the U.S. by many cultivated speakers."

22    So disgusted was *The New York Times* with the new dictionary that it announced it would not use it but would continue with the 1934 edition, prompting the language authority Bergen Evans to write: "Anyone who solemnly announces in the year 1962 that he will be guided in matters of English usage by a dictionary published in 1934 is talking ignorant and pretentious nonsense," and he pointed out that the issue of the *Times* announcing the decision contained nineteen words condemned by the *Second International.*

23    Since then, other dictionaries have been divided on the matter. *The American Heritage Dictionary,* first published in 1969, instituted a usage panel of distinguished commentators to rule on contentious points of usage, which are discussed, often at some length, in the text. But others have been more equivocal (or prudent or spineless depending on how you view it). The revised *Random House Dictionary of the English Language*, published in 1987, accepts the looser meaning for most words, though often noting that the newer usage is frowned on "by many"—a curiously timid approach that at once acknowledges the existence of expert opinion and yet constantly places it at a distance. Among the looser meanings it accepts are *disinterested* to mean *uninterested* and *infer* to mean *imply*. It even accepts the existence of *kudo* as a singular—prompting a reviewer from *Time* magazine to ask if one instance of pathos should now be a patho.

24    It's a fine issue. One of the undoubted virtues of English is that it is a fluid and democratic language in which meanings shift and change in response to the pressures of common usage rather than the dictates of committees. It is a natural process that has been going on for centuries. To interfere with that process is arguably both arrogant and futile, since clearly the weight of usage will push new meanings into currency no matter how many authorities hurl themselves into the path of change.

25    But at the same time, it seems to me, there is a case for resisting change— at least slapdash change. Even the most liberal descriptivist would accept that there must be *some* conventions of usage. We must agree to spell *cat* c-a-t and not e-l-e-p-h-a-n-t, and we must agree that by that word we mean a small furry quadruped that goes *meow* and sits comfortably on one's lap and not a large lumbering beast that grows tusks and is exceedingly difficult to housebreak. In precisely the same way, clarity is generally better served if we agree to observe a distinction between *imply* and *infer, forego* and *forgo, fortuitous* and

*fortunate, uninterested* and *disinterested,* and many others. As John Ciardi observed, resistance may in the end prove futile, but at least it tests the changes and makes them prove their worth.

26    Perhaps for our last words on the subject of usage we should turn to the last words of the venerable French grammarian Dominique Bonhours, who proved on his deathbed that a grammarian's work is never done when he turned to those gathered loyally around him and whispered: "I am about to—or I am going to—die; either expression is used."

### THINKING CRITICALLY

1. How did early grammarians help shape the rules of current usage? According to Bryson, how did they contribute to some of the idiosyncrasies of English rules? Give some examples of rules formulated by early grammarians that do not work.

2. Given all the anomalies in the English language, what is the author suggesting about standards of usage? How does his discussion make you feel about your own lapses in grammar?

3. What, according to Bryson, is the difference between "good English" and "bad English"? What is his basis of distinction? Do you agree with his views?

4. Bryson reports that for centuries grammarians called for the official regulation of English usage. What fundamental attitudes about language did these proposals underscore? What about the attitudes of Thomas Jefferson and Joseph Priestley? Where does Bryson stand on the issue of regulation?

5. What kind of personality does Bryson project in this essay? In other words, based on his tone, his word choice, his style, the examples he chooses, his comments, and so on, how would you describe him?

6. What examples of Bryson's sense of humor can you point to? How does his humor contribute to the essay? Is this a strategy you might employ in your writing?

7. How would you evaluate Bryson's own use of English? How might Bryson respond to the criticism that while defending nonstandard usage, his own writing strictly obeys the rules of traditional usage?

### WRITING ASSIGNMENTS

1. Do you think that dictionaries should be prescriptive instead of descriptive—that is, should they take a position on the traditional rules of proper grammar, usage, and spelling? Write a letter to Bill Bryson explaining how you feel about this and give three specific reasons.

2. Have you ever been bothered by someone's poor grammar or usage? If so, describe in a brief essay your experience and your feelings. Has this essay affected your attitude at all? Explain.

3. If you heard the president or some other official make grammatical and usage errors in an interview, would that affect your view of that person? Would it make him or her seem less deserving of your respect or seem more down-to-earth? Write out your thoughts in an essay, perhaps citing some examples of faulty presidential usage you have found on your own.

# Why Good English Is Good for You

*John Simon*

Is rule-based grammar going the way of the dinosaur? Does it hinder the creative voice and individual style? The author of the next essay, a staunch "prescriptivist," argues that grammatical rules keep language vibrant. "Language remains alive," explains John Simon, "because each speaker (or writer) can and must, within the framework of accepted grammar, syntax, and pronunciation, produce a style that is his very own." The next essay is not just a wry and incisive look at the way American English is abused; it is an argument in favor of using "good" English—an effort that improves not only communication but also memory and thinking.

John Simon served as a theatre critic at *New York Magazine* for nearly 40 years. A renowned critic of the arts and of what he views as the shoddy language of Americans, for years he wrote a regular language column for *Esquire,* from which some essays, including the one below, were published in a collection about the decline of literacy, *Paradigms Lost* (1980).

1 What's good English to you that . . . you should grieve for it? What good is correct speech and writing, you may ask, in an age in which hardly anyone seems to know, and no one seems to care? Why shouldn't you just fling bloopers riotously with the throng, and not stick out from the rest like a sore thumb by using the language correctly? Isn't grammar really a thing of the past, and isn't the new idea to communicate in *any* way as long as you can make yourself understood?

2 The usual, basic defense of good English (and here, again, let us not worry about nomenclature—for all I care, you may call it "Standard English," "correct American," or anything else) is that it helps communication, that it is perhaps even a *sine qua non* of mutual understanding. Although this is a crude truth of sorts, it strikes me as, in some ways, both more and less than the truth. Suppose you say, "Everyone in their right mind would cross on the green light" or "Hopefully, it won't rain tomorrow," chances are very good that the person you say this to will understand you, even though you are committing obvious solecisms or creating needless ambiguities. Similarly, if you write in a letter, "The baby has finally ceased it's howling" (spelling *its* as *it's*), the recipient will be able to figure out what was meant. But "figuring out" is precisely what a listener or reader should not have to do. There is, of course, the fundamental matter of courtesy to the other person, but it goes beyond that: why waste time on unscrambling simple meaning when there are more complex questions that should receive our undivided attention? If the many cooks had to worry first about which out of a large number of pots had no leak in it, the broth, whether spoiled or not, would take forever to be ready.

3 It is, I repeat, only initially a matter of clarity. It is also a matter of concision. Space today is as limited as time. If you have only a thousand words in which to convey an important message it helps to know that "overcomplicated" is correct and "overly complicated" is incorrect. Never mind the grammatical explanations; the two extra characters and one space between words are reason enough. But what about the more advanced forms of wordmongering that hold sway nowadays? Take redundancy, like the "hopes and aspirations" of Jimmy Carter, quoted by Edwin Newman

as having "a deeply profound religious experience"; or elaborate jargon, as when Charles G. Walcutt, a graduate professor of English at CUNY, writes (again as quoted by Newman): "The colleges, trying to remediate increasing numbers of . . . illiterates up to college levels, are being highschoolized"; or just obfuscatory verbiage of the pretentious sort, such as this fragment from a letter I received: "It is my impression that effective *inter*personal verbal communication depends on prior effective *intra*-personal verbal communication." What this means is that if you think clearly, you can speak and write clearly—except if you are a "certified speech and language patholo-gist," like the writer of the letter I quote. (By the way, she adds the letters Ph.D. after her name, though she is not even from Germany, where *Herr* and *Frau Doktor* are in common, not to say vulgar, use.)

4    But except for her ghastly verbiage, our certified language pathologist (what-ever that means) is perfectly right: there is a close connection between the ability to think and the ability to use English correctly. After all, we think in words, we conceptualize in words, we work out our problems inwardly with words, and using them correctly is comparable to a craftsman's treating his tools with care, keeping his materials in good shape. Would you trust a weaver who hangs her wet laundry on her loom, or lets her cats bed down in her yarn? The person who does not respect words and their proper relationships cannot have much respect for ideas—very possibly cannot have ideas at all. My quarrel is not so much with minor errors that we all fall into from time to time even if we know better as it is with basic sloppi-ness or ignorance or defiance of good English.

5    Training yourself to speak and write correctly—and I say "training yourself" because nowadays, unfortunately, you cannot depend on other people or on insti-tutions to give you the proper training, for reasons I shall discuss later—training yourself, then, in language, means developing at the very least two extremely useful faculties: your sense of discipline and your memory. Discipline because language is with us always, as nothing else is: it follows us much as, in the old morality play, Good Deeds followed Everyman, all the way to the grave; and, if the language is written, even beyond. Let me explain: if you keep an orderly apartment, if you can see to it that your correspondence and bill-paying are attended to regularly, if your diet and wardrobe are maintained with the necessary care—good enough; you are a disciplined person.

6    But the preliminary discipline underlying all others is nevertheless your speech: the words that come out of you almost as frequently and—if you are tidy—as regularly as your breath. I would go so far as to say that, immediately after your bodily functions, language is first, unless you happen to be an ascetic, an anchorite, or a stylite; but unless you are a sty*lite*, you had better be a sty*list*.

7    Most of us—almost all—must take in and give out language as we do breath, and we had better consider the seriousness of language pollution as second only to air pollution. For the linguistically disciplined, to misuse or mispronounce a word is an unnecessary and unhealthy contribution to the surrounding smog. To have taught ourselves not to do this, or—being human and thus also imperfect—to do it as little as possible, means deriving from every speaking moment the satisfaction we get from a cap that snaps on to a container perfectly, an elevator that stops flush with the landing, a roulette ball that comes to rest exactly on the number on which

we have placed our bet. It gives us the pleasure of hearing or seeing our words—because they are abiding by the rules—snapping, sliding, falling precisely into place, expressing with perfect lucidity and symmetry just what we wanted them to express. This is comparable to the satisfaction of the athlete or ballet dancer or pianist finding his body or legs or fingers doing his bidding with unimpeachable accuracy.

8      And if someone now says that "in George Eliot's lesser novels, she is not completely in command" is perfectly comprehensible even if it is ungrammatical, the "she" having no antecedent in the nominative (*Eliot's* is a genitive), I say, "Comprehensible, perhaps, but lopsided," for the civilized and orderly mind does not feel comfortable with that "she"—does not hear that desired and satisfying click of correctness—unless the sentence is restructured as "George Eliot, in her lesser novels, is not . . ." or in some similar way. In fact, the fully literate ear can be thrown by this error in syntax; it may look for the antecedent of that "she" elsewhere than in the preceding possessive case. Be that as it may, playing without rules and winning—in this instance, managing to communicate without using good English—is no more satisfactory than winning in a sport or game by accident or by disregarding the rules: which is really cheating.

9      The second faculty good speech develops is, as I have mentioned before, our memory. Grammar and syntax are partly logical—and to that extent they are also good exercisers and developers of our logical faculty—but they are also partly arbitrary, conventional, irrational. For example, the correct "compared to" and "contrasted with" could, from the logical point of view, just as well be "contrasted to" and "compared with" ("compared with," of course, is correct, but in a different sense from the one that concerns us here, namely, the antithesis of "contrasted with"). And, apropos *different*, logic would have to strain desperately to explain the exclusive correctness of "different from," given the exclusive correctness of "other than," which would seem to justify "different than," jarring though that is to the cultivated ear.

10      But there it is: some things are so because tradition, usage, the best speakers and writers, the grammar books and dictionaries have made them so. There may even exist some hidden historical explanation: something, perhaps, in the Sanskrit, Greek, Latin, or other origins of a word or construction that you and I may very easily never know. We can, however, memorize; and memorization can be a wonderfully useful thing—surely the Greeks were right to consider Mnemosyne (memory) the mother of the Muses, for without her there would be no art and no science. And what better place to practice one's mnemonic skills than in the study of one's language?

11      There is something particularly useful about speaking correctly and precisely because language is always there as a foundation—or, if you prefer a more fluid image, an undercurrent—beneath what is going on. Now, it seems to me that the great difficulty of life lies in the fact that we must almost always do two things at a time. If, for example, we are walking and conversing, we must keep our mouths as well as feet from stumbling. If we are driving while listening to music, we must not allow the siren song of the cassette to prevent us from watching the road and the speedometer (otherwise the less endearing siren of the police car or the ambulance

will follow apace). Well, it is just this sort of bifurcation of attention that care for precise, clear expression fosters in us. By learning early in life to pay attention both to what we are saying and to how we are saying it, we develop the much-needed life skill of doing two things simultaneously.

12   Put another way, we foster our awareness of, and ability to deal with, form and content. If there is any verity that modern criticism has fought for, it is the recognition of the indissolubility of content and form. Criticism won the battle, won it so resoundingly that this oneness has become a contemporary commonplace. And shall the fact that form *is* content be a platitude in all the arts but go unrecognized in the art of self-expression, whether in conversation or correspondence, or whatever form of spoken or written utterance a human being resorts to? Accordingly, you are going to be judged, whether you like it or not, by the correctness of your English as much as by the correctness of your thinking; there are some people to whom bad English is as offensive as gibberish, or as your picking your nose in public would be to their eyes and stomachs. The fact that people of linguistic sensibilities may be a dying breed does not mean that they are wholly extinct, and it is best not to take any unnecessary chances.

13   To be sure, if you are a member of a currently favored minority, many of your linguistic failings may be forgiven you—whether rightly or wrongly is not my concern here. But if you cannot change your sex or color to the one that is getting preferential treatment—Bakke case or no Bakke case—you might as well learn good English and profit by it in your career, your social relations, perhaps even in your basic self-confidence. That, if you will, is the ultimate practical application of good English; but now let me tell you about the ultimate impractical one, which strikes me as being possibly even more important.

14   Somewhere in the prose writings of Charles Péguy, who was a very fine poet and prose writer—and, what is perhaps even more remarkable, as good a human being as he was an artist—somewhere in those writings is a passage about the decline of pride in workmanship among French artisans, which, as you can deduce, set in even before World War I, wherein Péguy was killed. In the passage I refer to, Péguy bemoans the fact that cabinet-makers no longer finish the backs of furniture—the sides that go against the wall—in the same way as they do the ex posed sides. What is not seen was just as important to the old artisans as what is seen—it was a moral issue with them. And so, I think, it ought to be with language. Even if no one else notices the niceties, the precision, the impeccable sense of grammar and syntax you deploy in your utterances, you yourself should be aware of them and take pride in them as in pieces of work well done.

15   Now, I realize that there are two possible reactions among you to what I have said up to this point. Some of you will say to yourselves: what utter nonsense! Language is a flexible, changing, living organism that belongs to the people who speak it. It has always been changed according to the ways in which people chose to speak it, and the dictionaries and books on grammar had to, and will have to, adjust themselves to the people and not the other way around. For isn't it the glory of language that it keeps throwing up new inventions as surf tosses our differently polished pebbles and bits of bottle glass onto the shore, and that in this inexhaustible variety, in this refusal to kowtow to dry-as-dust scholars, lies its vitality, its beauty?

16     Others among you, perhaps fewer in number, will say to yourselves: quite so, there is such a thing as Standard English, or purity of speech, or correctness of expression—something worth safeguarding and fostering; but how the devil is one to accomplish that under the prevailing conditions: in a democratic society full of minorities that have their own dialects or linguistic preferences, and in a world in which television, advertising, and other mass media manage daily to corrupt the language a little further? Let me try to answer the first group first, and then come back to the questions of the second.

17     Of course language is, and must be, a living organism to the extent that new inventions, discoveries, ideas enter the scene and clamor rightfully for designations. Political, social, and psychological changes may also affect our mode of expression, and new words or phrases may have to be found to reflect what we might call historical changes. It is also quite natural for slang terms to be invented, become popular, and in some cases, remain permanently in the language. It is perhaps equally inevitable (though here we are on more speculative ground) for certain words to become obsolescent and obsolete, and drop out of the language. But does that mean that grammar and syntax have to keep changing, that pronunciations and meanings of words must shift, that more complex or elegant forms are obliged to yield to simpler or cruder ones that often are not fully synonymous with them and not capable of expressing certain fine distinctions? Should, for instance, "terrestrial" disappear entirely in favor of "earthly," or are there shades of meaning involved that need to remain available to us? Must we sacrifice "notwithstanding" because we have "in spite of" or "despite"? Need we forfeit "jettison" just because we have "throw overboard"? And what about "disinterested," which is becoming a synonym for "uninterested," even though that means something else, and though we have no other word for "disinterested"?

18     "Language has *always* changed," say these people, and they might with equal justice say that there has always been war or sickness or insanity. But the truth is that some sicknesses that formerly killed millions have been eliminated, that some so-called insanity can today be treated, and that just because there have always been wars does not mean that someday a cure cannot be found even for that scourge. And if it cannot, it is only by striving to put an absolute end to war, by pretending that it can be licked, that we can at least partly control it. Without such assumptions and efforts, the evil would be so widespread that, given our current weaponry, we would no longer be here to worry about the future of language.

19     But we are here, and having evolved linguistically this far, and having the means—books of grammar, dictionaries, education for all—to arrest unnecessary change, why not endeavor with might and mind to arrest it? Certain cataclysms cannot be prevented: earthquakes and droughts, for example, can scarcely, if at all, be controlled; but we can prevent floods, for which purpose we have invented dams. And dams are precisely what we can construct to prevent floods of ignorance from eroding our language, and, beyond that, to provide irrigation for areas that would otherwise remain linguistically arid.

20     For consider that what some people are pleased to call linguistic evolution was almost always a matter of ignorance prevailing over knowledge. There is no valid reason, for example, for the word *nice* to have changed its meanings so many

times—except ignorance of its exact definition. Had the change never occurred, or had it been stopped at any intermediate stage, we would have had just as good a word as we have now and saved some people a heap of confusion along the way. But if *nice* means what it does today—and it has two principal meanings, one of them, as in "nice distinction," alas, obsolescent—let us, for heaven's sake, keep it where it is, now that we have the means with which to hold it there.

21    If, for instance, we lose the accusative case *whom*—and we are in great danger of losing it—our language will be the poorer for it. Obviously, "The man, whom I had never known, was a thief" means something other than "The man who I had never known was a thief." Now, you can object that it would be just as easy in the first instance to use some other construction; but what happens if *this* one is used incorrectly? Ambiguity and confusion. And why should we lose this useful distinction? Just because a million or ten million or a billion people less educated than we are cannot master the difference? Surely it behooves us to try to educate the ignorant up to our level rather than to stultify ourselves down to theirs. Yes, you say, but suppose they refuse to or are unable to learn? In that case, I say, there is a doubly good reason for not going along with them. Ah, you reply, but they are the majority, and we must accept their way or, if the revolution is merely linguistic, lose our "credibility" (as the current parlance, rather confusingly, has it) or, if the revolution is political, lose our heads. Well, I consider a sufficient number of people to be educable enough to be capable of using *who* and *whom* correctly, and to derive satisfaction from this capability—a sufficient number, I mean, to enable us to preserve *whom*, and not to have to ask "for who the bell tolls."

22    The main problem with education, actually, is not those who need it and cannot get it, but those who should impart it and, for various reasons, do not. In short, the enemies of education are the educators themselves: miseducated, underpaid, overburdened, and intimidated teachers (frightened because, though the pen is supposed to be mightier than the sword, the switchblade is surely more powerful than the ferrule), and professors who—because they are structural linguists, democratic respecters of alleged minority rights, or otherwise misguided folk—believe in the sacrosanct privilege of any culturally underprivileged minority or majority to dictate its ignorance to the rest of the world. For, I submit, an English improvised by slaves and other strangers to the culture—to whom my heart goes out in every human way—under dreadfully deprived conditions can nowise equal an English that the best literary and linguistic talents have, over the centuries, perceptively and painstakingly brought to a high level of excellence.

23    So my answer to the scoffers in this or any audience is, in simplest terms, the following: contrary to popular misconception, language does not belong to the people, or at least not in the sense in which *belong* is usually construed. For things can rightfully belong only to those who invent or earn them. But we do not know who invented language: is it the people who first made up the words for *father* and *mother*, for *I* and *thou*, for *hand* and *foot*; or is it the people who evolved the subtler shadings of language, its poetic variety and suggestiveness, but also its unambiguousness, its accurate and telling details? Those are two very different groups of people and two very different languages, and I, as you must have guessed by now, consider the latter group at least as important as the former. As for *earning*

language, it has surely been earned by those who have striven to learn it properly, and here even economic and social circumstances are but an imperfect excuse for bad usage; history is full of examples of people rising from humble origins to learn, against all kinds of odds, to speak and write correctly—even brilliantly.

24    *Belong*, then, should be construed in the sense that parks, national forests, monuments, and public utilities are said to belong to the people: available for properly respectful use but not for defacement and destruction. And all that we propose to teach is how to use and enjoy the gardens of language to their utmost aesthetic and salubrious potential. Still, I must now address myself to the group that, while agreeing with my aims, despairs of finding practical methods for their implementation.

25    True enough, after a certain age speakers not aware of Standard English or not exceptionally gifted will find it hard or impossible to change their ways. Nevertheless, if there were available funds for advanced methods in teaching; if teachers themselves were better trained and paid, and had smaller classes and more assistants; if, furthermore, college entrance requirements were heightened and the motivation of students accordingly strengthened; if there were no structural linguists and National Councils of Teachers of English filling instructors' heads with notions about "Students' Rights to Their Own Language" (they have every right to it as a *second* language, but none as a *first*); if teachers in all disciplines, including the sciences and social sciences, graded on English usage as well as on specific proficiencies; if aptitude tests for various jobs stressed good English more than they do; and, above all, if parents were better educated and more aware of the need to set a good example to their children, and to encourage them to learn correct usage, the situation could improve enormously.

26    Clearly, to expect all this to come to pass is utopian; some of it, however, is well within the realm of possibility. For example, even if parents do not speak very good English, many of them at least can manage an English that is good enough to correct a very young child's mistakes; in other words, most adults can speak a good enough four-year-old's idiom. They would thus start kids out on the right path; the rest could be done by the schools.

27    But the problem is what to do in the most underprivileged homes: those of blacks, Hispanics, immigrants from various Asian and European countries. This is where day-care centers could come in. If the fathers and mothers could be gainfully employed, their small children would be looked after by day-care centers where— is this asking too much?—good English could be inculcated in them. The difficulty, of course, is what to do about the discrepancy the little ones would note between the speech of the day-care people and that of their parents. Now, it seems to me that small children have a far greater ability to learn things, including languages, than some people give them credit for. Much of it is indeed rote learning, but, where languages are concerned, that is one of the basic learning methods even for adults. There is no reason for not teaching kids another language, to wit, Standard English, and turning this, if desirable, into a game: "At home you speak one way; here we have another language," at which point the instructor can make up names and explanations for Standard English that would appeal to pupils of that particular place, time, and background.

28    At this stage of the game, as well as later on in school, care should be exercised to avoid insulting the language spoken in the youngsters' homes. There must be ways to convey that both home and school languages have their validity and uses and that knowing both enables one to accomplish more in life. This would be hard to achieve if the children's parents were, say, militant blacks of the Geneva Smitherman sort, who execrate Standard English as a weapon of capitalist oppression against the poor of all races, colors, and religions. But, happily, there is evidence that most black, Hispanic, and other non-Standard English-speaking parents want their children to learn correct English so as to get ahead in the world.

29    Yet how do we defend ourselves against the charge that we are old fogeys who cannot emotionally adjust to the new directions an ever-living and changing language must inevitably take? Here I would want to redefine or, at any rate, clarify, what "living and changing" means, and also explain where we old fogeys stand. Misinformed attacks on Old Fogeydom, I have noticed, invariably represent us as people who shudder at a split infinitive and would sooner kill or be killed than tolerate a sentence that ends with a preposition. Actually, despite all my travels through Old Fogeydom, I have yet to meet one inhabitant who would not stick a preposition onto the tail of a sentence; as for splitting infinitives, most of us O.F.'s are perfectly willing to do that, too, but tactfully and sparingly, where it feels right. There is no earthly reason, for example, for saying "to dangerously live," when "to live dangerously" sounds so much better; but it does seem right to say (and write) "What a delight to sweetly breathe in your sleeping lover's breath"; that sounds smoother, indeed sweeter, than to "breathe in sweetly" or "sweetly to breathe in." But infinitives begging to be split are relatively rare; a sensitive ear, a good eye for shades of meaning will alert you whenever the need to split arises; without that ear and eye, you had better stick to the rules.

30    About the sense in which language is, and must be, alive, let me speak while donning another of my several hats—actually it is not a hat but a cap, for there exists in Greenwich Village an inscription on a factory that reads "CRITIC CAPS." So with my drama critic's cap on, let me present you with an analogy. The world theater today is full of directors who wreak havoc on classic plays to demonstrate their own ingenuity, their superiority, as it were, to the author. These directors aborted playwrights, for the most part—will stage productions of *Hamlet* in which the prince is a woman, a flaming homosexual, or a one-eyed hunchback.

31    Well, it seems to me that the same spirit prevails in our approach to linguistics, with every newfangled, ill-informed, know-nothing construction, definition, pronunciation enshrined by the joint efforts of structural linguists, permissive dictionaries, and allegedly democratic but actually demagogic educators. What really makes a production of, say, *Hamlet* different, and therefore alive, is that the director, while trying to get as faithfully as possible at Shakespeare's meanings, nevertheless ends up stressing things in the play that strike him most forcefully; and the same individuality in production design and performances (the Hamlet of Gielgud versus the Hamlet of Olivier, for instance—what a world of difference!) further differentiates one production from another, and bestows on each its particular vitality. So, too, language remains alive because each speaker (or writer) can and must, *within the framework of accepted grammar, syntax, and pronunciation,* produce a

style that is his very own, that is as personal as his posture, way of walking, mode of dress, and so on. It is such stylistic differences that make a person's—or a nation's—language flavorous, pungent, alive, and all this without having to play fast and loose with the existing rules.

32    But to have this, we need, among other things, good teachers and, beyond them, enlightened educators. I shudder when I read in the *Birmingham* (Alabama) *Post-Herald* of October 6, 1978, an account of a talk given to eight hundred English teachers by Dr. Alan C. Purves, vice-president of the National Council of Teachers of English. Dr. Purves is quoted as saying things like "We are in a situation with respect to reading where . . . ," and culminating in the following truly horrifying sentence: "I am going to suggest that when we go back to the basics, I think what we should be dealing with is our charge to help students to be more proficient in producing meaningful language—language that says what it means." Notice all the deadwood, the tautology, the anacoluthon in the first part of that sentence; but notice especially the absurdity of the latter part, in which the dubious word "meaningful"—a poor relation of "significant"—is thought to require explaining to an audience of English teachers.

33    Given such leadership from the N.C.T.E., the time must be at hand when we shall hear—not just "Don't ask for who the bell rings" (*ask not* and *tolls* being, of course, archaic, elitist language), but also "It rings for you and I."

### THINKING CRITICALLY

1. In your own words, why is good English good for you?

2. Consider the two examples Simon gives in paragraph 2: "Everyone in their right mind would cross on the green light" and "Hopefully, it won't rain tomorrow." If they communicate perfectly well, why haggle over the minor grammatical errors?

3. How does Simon justify so strong a statement as that in paragraph 7: "Language pollution . . . [is] second only to air pollution"? Do you agree? Can you think of circumstances in which bad language might be a threat to health—mental or otherwise?

4. Simon argues that good speech develops memory. How does he explain that? Can you substantiate that based on your own experience and practice?

5. One counter-response to Simon's call for upholding the standards of correct English is the assertion: "Language is a flexible, changing, living organism that belongs to the people who speak it." (This statement is nearly identical to Bill Bryson's claim in the previous essay.) How does Simon answer that charge? Can the language have rigid standards and still allow natural changes to occur? If so, give examples.

6. Simon singles out the word *nice* as one of the many victims of too much change. What are some of the current meanings of *nice*? Can you think of other words that have suffered too much change? What about the words *awful, terrific, wonderful,* and *fantastic*? What changes have they undergone since their original meanings?

7. Simon claims that "the enemies of education are the educators themselves" (paragraph 22). How does he justify such an assertion? Do you agree, given your own educational experience?

8. According to Simon, who are linguistically "the most underprivileged" children? What suggestions does Simon make for dealing with them?

9. From the tone and attitude of this essay, what kind of man would you say Simon is? Does he sound cranky and pedantic or snobbish and elitist? Or does he sound reasonable and friendly? Cite passages to substantiate your answer.

## WRITING ASSIGNMENTS

1. Simon asserts that "you are going to be judged, whether you like it or not, by the correctness of your English as much as by the correctness of your thinking." Write an essay about an occasion when you judged people on the basis of their English—or an occasion when you were judged on that basis. Describe how the language used by others prejudiced you for or against them—or how such prejudices might have operated for or against you.

2. Simon criticizes parents strongly for not setting good language examples for their children. Write a paper describing the quality of language training in your own home. Did your parents encourage you to learn correct usage? Were they strict with you about it? Do you feel adequately trained in English usage, or handicapped because of your upbringing?

3. This essay by Simon was originally an address to a college audience. Imagine yourself addressing an audience on the same subject: "Why Good English Is Good for You." This time you are addressing not Simon's college audience, but a group of people who speak nonstandard, "uneducated" English. Write a speech that they might benefit from in language that they would understand and not be repelled by.

---

# Why the U.S. Needs an Official Language
## Mauro E. Mujica

The question of whether America should have an official language is highly controversial. The English-only movement is particularly troubling for many Spanish-speaking areas of the country, such as California, the Southwest, and Florida. Opponents to the movement fear that laws forbidding the use of Spanish could violate their civil liberties. English-only proponents insist that linguistic divisions prevent national unity, isolate ethnic groups, and reinforce the economic disparity between the haves and the have-nots. It may surprise Americans that outside the United States, many people believe the United States should adopt an official language: English. In the next essay, Mauro E. Mujica explains that Americans seem to be the last people to recognize the need for an official language and why that language should be English.

Mauro E. Mujica is chairman and CEO of U.S. English Inc., the nation's oldest and largest citizens' action group dedicated to preserving the unifying role of the English language. Mujica, who was born in Chile and immigrated to the United States in 1965, has appeared on many television and radio programs, including *Today, Good Morning America,* and *60 Minutes.* This essay was printed online in 2003 by *The World & I,* a publication that seeks to present a broad range of thought-provoking readings in politics, science, culture, and humanity.

1   In June 2003, the Pew Research Center announced the results of an extensive survey on global trends such as the spread of democracy, globalization, and technology. Titled "Views of a Changing World," it was conducted from 2001 to 2003 and polled 66,000 people from 50 countries. The survey received some publicity in the United States, mainly because it showed that anti-American sentiments were on the upswing around the world. Less publicized was the fact that there is a now a global consensus on the need to learn English.

2   One question in the Pew survey asked respondents to agree or disagree with the statement "Children need to learn English to succeed in the world today." Many nations showed almost unanimous agreement on the importance of learning English. Examples include Vietnam, 98 percent; Indonesia, 96 percent; Germany and South Africa, 95 percent; India, 93 percent; China and the Philippines, 92 percent; Honduras, Japan, Nigeria, and Uganda, 91 percent; and France, Mexico, and Ukraine, 90 percent.

3   To an immigrant like myself (from Chile), these results come as no surprise. Parents around the world know that English is the global language and that their children need to learn it to succeed. English is the language of business, higher education, diplomacy, aviation, the Internet, science, popular music, entertainment, and international travel. All signs point to its continued acceptance across the planet.

4   Given the globalization of English, one might be tempted to ask why the United States would need to declare English its official language. Why codify something that is happening naturally and without government involvement?

## The Retreat of English

5   In fact, even as it spreads across the globe, English is on the retreat in vast sections of the United States. Our government makes it easy for immigrants to function in their native languages through bilingual education, multilingual ballots and driver's license exams, and government-funded translators in schools and hospitals. Providing most essential services to immigrants in their native languages is expensive for American taxpayers and also keeps immigrants linguistically isolated.

6   Historically, the need to speak and understand English has served as an important incentive for immigrants to learn the language and assimilate into the mainstream of American society. For the last 30 years, this idea has been turned on its head. Expecting immigrants to learn English has been called "racist." Marta Jimenez, an attorney for the Mexican American Legal Defense and Educational Fund, speaks of "the historical use of English in the United States as a tool of oppression."

7   Groups such as the National Association for Bilingual Education complain about the "restrictive goal" of having immigrant children learn in English. The former mayor of Miami, Maurice Ferre, dismissed the idea of even a bilingual future for his city. "We're talking about Spanish as a main form of communication, as an official language," he averred. "Not on the way to English."

8   Perhaps this change is best illustrated in the evolving views of the League of United Latin American Citizens (LULAC). Started in 1929, the group was originally pro-English and pro-assimilation. One of the founding aims and purposes of

LULAC was "to foster the acquisition and facile use of the Official Language of our country that we may hereby equip ourselves and our families for the fullest enjoyment of our rights and privileges and the efficient discharge of our duties and obligations to this, our country." By the 1980s the executive director of LULAC, Arnoldo Torres, could proudly proclaim, "We cannot assimilate and we won't!"

9    The result of this is that the United States has a rapidly growing population of people—often native born—who are not proficient in English. The 2000 Census found that 21.3 million Americans (8 percent of the population) are classified as "limited English proficient," a 52 percent increase from 1990 and more than double the 1980 total. More than 5 million of these people were born in the United States.

10    Citing census statistics gives an idea of how far English is slipping in America, but it does not show how this is played out in everyday life. Consider the following examples:

- *The New York Times* reports that Hispanics account for over 40 percent of the population of Hartford, Connecticut, and that the city is becoming "Latinized." Last year, Eddie Perez became Hartford's first Hispanic mayor. The city Web page is bilingual, and after-hours callers to the mayor's office are greeted by a message in Spanish. Half of Hartford's Hispanics do not speak English. According to Freddy Ortiz, who owns a bakery in the city, "In the bank, they speak Spanish; at the hospital, they speak Spanish; my bakery suppliers arc starting to speak Spanish. Even at the post office, they are Americans, but they speak Spanish." Even Mayor Perez notes that "we've become a Latin city, so to speak. It's a sign of things to come."
- In May, about 20 percent of the students at Miami Senior High School, where 88 percent of the students speak English as a second language, failed the annual Florida Comprehensive Assessment Test (FCAT) exam, which is required for graduation. The poor results prompted protests and demands for the test to be given in Spanish as well as English. Over 200 students and teachers gathered outside the school waving signs and chanting "No FCAT." A state senator from Miami introduced a bill that would allow the FCAT to be given in Spanish.
- Just a day before the Pew survey was released, Gwinnett County in Georgia announced it will provide its own staff translators for parents of students who speak Spanish, Korean, and Vietnamese. The school board approved $138,000 for the new translators despite a tight budget. Donna Robertson, a principal at an elementary school in the county, claimed the translators are only a short-term solution. The real solution, she claims, is a multilingual school staff. There are 46 languages spoken among students in Gwinnett County.
- In May, a poll taken by NBC News and *The Sun-Sentinel* newspaper of Fort Lauderdale, Florida, found 83 percent of Hispanics in south Florida agreeing that "it is easy to get along day in and day out without speaking English well/at all."

## The Costs of Multilingualism

11  Multilingual government is not cheap. Bilingual education alone is estimated to cost taxpayers billions of dollars per year. The federal government has spent over $100 million to study the effectiveness of bilingual education, only to discover that

it is less effective at teaching English than English immersion programs are. Much of the cost for court and school translators, multilingual voting ballots, and multiple document translations is picked up at the local level. Even during good economic times, this is a burden. In lean years it is a budget breaker, taking funds away from education, health care, transportation, and police and fire services.

12    For example, Los Angeles County spent $3.3 million, 15 percent of the entire election budget, to print election ballots in seven languages and hire multilingual poll workers for the March 2002 primary. The county also spends $265 per day for each of 420 full-time court interpreters. San Francisco spends $350,000 per each language that documents must be translated into under its bilingual government ordinance. Financial officials in Washington, D.C., estimate that a proposed language access would cost $7.74 million to implement. The bill would require all city agencies to hire translators and translate official documents for any language spoken by over 500 non-English-speaking people in the city.

13    The health-care industry, already reeling from a shortage of nurses and the costs of treating the uninsured, was dealt another blow by President Clinton. Executive Order 13166 was signed into law on August 11, 2000. The order requires private physicians, clinics, and hospitals that accept Medicare and Medicaid to provide, at their own expense, translators for any language spoken by any patient. The cost of an interpreter can exceed the reimbursement of a Medicare or Medicaid visit by 13 times—costing doctors as much as $500 per translator.

14    Of course, there are also nonmonetary costs associated with a multilingual America. These expenses often have a human cost.

15    A 22-year-old immigrant won a $71 million settlement because a group of paramedics and doctors misdiagnosed a blood clot in his brain. The man's relatives used the Spanish word intoxicado to describe his ailment. They meant he was nauseated, but the translator interpreted the word to mean intoxicated.

16    Six children were killed when a loose tailgate from a tractor trailer fell off on a Milwaukee highway. The driver of the family's SUV could not avoid the tailgate, which punctured the gas tank and caused the vehicle to explode. An investigation found that other truckers had tried to warn the driver of the tractor trailer about his loose tailgate, but the driver did not understand English.

17    An immigrant in Orange County, California, died from a fall into a 175-degree vat of chemicals at an Anaheim metal-plating shop. Though the company's instructions clearly forbade walking on the five-inch rail between tanks, they were printed in English, a language that the worker did not understand. An inquiry into the accident found that many of the recent hires were not proficient in English.

18    Hispanics accounted for nearly one-third of Georgia's workplace deaths in 2000, despite making up only 5.3 percent of the state's population. The National Institute for Occupational Safety and Health, a branch of the U.S. Centers for Disease Control and Prevention, blamed "misunderstandings arising from language barriers" for the deaths and said they "could be prevented and don't have to happen."

## The Dis-United States

19 We need only look to Canada to see the problems a multilingual society can bring. America's northern neighbor faces a severe constitutional crisis over the issue of

language. In 1995, the predominately French-speaking province of Quebec came within a few thousand votes of seceding from Canada. The secessionist Parti Québécois ruled the province until this year. The national government must cater to Quebec to preserve order and maintain a cohesive government. This has spurred secessionist movements in English-speaking western Canada on the grounds that the Canadian government favors French speakers.

20      Of course, battles over language rage across the globe, but since Canada is so similar, it offers the most instructive warning for the United States. While the policy of official multilingualism has led to disunity, resentment, and near-secession, it is also very costly. Canada's dual-language requirement costs approximately $260 million each year. Canada has one-tenth the population of the United States and spent that amount accommodating only two languages. A similar language policy would cost the United States much more than $4 billion annually, as we have a greater population and many more languages to accommodate.

21      Unless the United States changes course, it is clearly on the road to a Canadian-style system of linguistic enclaves, wasteful government expenses, language battles that fuel ethnic resentments, and, in the long run, serious ethnic and linguistic separatist movements.

22      What is at stake here is the unity of our nation. Creating an American-style Quebec in the Southwest as well as "linguistic islands" in other parts of the United States will be a disaster far exceeding the Canadian problem. Now, over 8 percent of the population cannot speak English proficiently. What happens when that number turns to 10 percent, 20 percent, or more?

23      The American assimilation process, often called the melting pot, is clearly not working. Declaring English to be our official language would bring back the incentive to learn it. Specifically, this step would require that all laws, public proceedings, regulations, publications, orders, actions, programs, and policies are conducted in the English language. There would be some commonsense exceptions in the areas of public health and safety, national security, tourism, and commerce.

24      Of course, declaring English the official language would only apply to government. People can still speak whatever language they choose at home and in private life. Official English legislation should also be combined with provisions for more English classes for non-English speakers. This can be paid for with a fraction of the money saved by ending multilingual government.

25      A bill in Congress would make this a reality. . . . If it passes, we can start to rebuild the American assimilation process and lessen the amount of linguistic separation in the United States. If it fails, we might have lost the last best chance for a sensible and cohesive language policy in this country. If that happens we can say "hasta la vista" to the "United" States and "adelante" to Canadian-style discord over the issues of language and ethnicity.

### THINKING CRITICALLY

1. The Pew study reported that many people outside of the United States strongly feel that knowledge of English is necessary for success. What is the basis for this sentiment? Does it surprise you? Why or why not?

2. In paragraph 4, Mujica postulates, "one might be tempted to ask why the United States would need to declare English its official language. Why codify something that is happening naturally and without government involvement?" Evaluate his argument as to why it is indeed important that the United States adopt English as its official language.

3. What is the irony of the "retreat" of English in the United States? Explain.

4. According to Mujica, what are the costs of multilingualism? Include in your answer the cultural, political, intellectual, social, and economic ramifications of a nation that does not adopt an official language.

5. Other countries such as France, England, and Brazil are not deemed "racist" (paragraph 6) for having national languages. Is the United States different from other countries that have official languages? Why or why not? In your opinion, do you think that adopting English as the official language of the United States would be racist?

6. According to Mujica, what are the social issues behind opposition to English as the official language?

### WRITING ASSIGNMENTS

1. Interview a number of people who had to learn English as a second language. How did they do it? What difficulties did they encounter? What assistance were they given as they learned English? How did learning English affect their lives? Encourage your interviewees to share stories of success as well as of failure.

2. An argument in favor of bilingual education is that mother-tongue instruction increases cultural and ethnic pride in the heritage of the mother country. Immigrant children are allowed to take pride in their home culture while learning in their native tongue. Do you think denying them this heritage and forcing English upon people is, as Marta Jimenez, an attorney for the Mexican American Legal Defense and Educational Fund, asserts, "a tool of oppression"? Write a paper in which you explore your feelings on this pro-bilingual perspective.

# ENGLISH AS A GLOBAL LANGUAGE

## Why a Global Language?
*David Crystal*

Is English the most successful language ever? Almost everywhere in the world, you can find English—printed on signs, menus, radio, television broadcasts, printed media, on t-shirts, and spoken by hotel clerks, bank tellers, and computer help-desk staffers. What factors have contributed to making English one of the most successful languages in the history of civilization? Author David Crystal explains what causes a language to become global and why our world today might actually need a global language.

David Crystal is a linguist and author and currently teaches at Bangor University in North Wales, United Kingdom. He is the author of many books on language as well as the editor of numerous reference works, including the *Cambridge Encyclopedia of Language* (1987) and the *Cambridge Encyclopedia of the English Language* (1995). His most recent book, *Txtng: The Gr8 Db8*, focuses on text language and its impact on society (2008). This essay is an excerpt from his book *English as a Global Language* (2003).

1 "English is the global language." A headline of this kind must have appeared in a thousand newspapers and magazines in recent years. [It is] the kind of statement that seems so obvious that most people would give [it] hardly a second thought. Of course English is a global language, they would say. You hear it on television spoken by politicians from all over the world. Wherever you travel, you see English signs and advertisements. Whenever you enter a hotel or restaurant in a foreign city, they will understand English, and there will be an English menu. Indeed, if there is anything to wonder about at all, they might add, it is why such headlines should still be newsworthy.

2 But English *is* news. The language continues to make news daily in many countries. And the headline *isn't* stating the obvious. For what does it mean, exactly? Is it saying that everyone in the world speaks English? This is certainly not true. Is it saying, then, that every country in the world recognizes English as an official language? This is not true either. So what does it mean to say that a language is a global language? Why is English the language which is usually cited in this connection? How did the situation arise? And could it change? Or is it the case that, once a language becomes a global language, it is there for ever?

3 These are fascinating questions to explore, whether your first language is English or not. If English is your mother tongue, you may have mixed feelings about the way English is spreading around the world. You may feel pride, that your language is the one which has been so successful; but your pride may be tinged with concern, when you realize that people in other countries may not want to use the language in the same way that you do, and are changing it to suit themselves. We are all sensitive to the way other people use (it is often said, abuse) "our" language. Deeply held feelings of ownership begin to be questioned. Indeed, if there is one predictable consequence of a language becoming a global language, it is that nobody owns it any more. Or rather, everyone who has learned it now owns it—"has a share in it" might be more accurate—and has the right to use it in the way they want. This fact alone makes many people feel uncomfortable, even vaguely resentful. "Look what the Americans have done to English" is a not uncommon comment found in the letter-columns of the British press. But similar comments can be heard in the USA when people encounter the sometimes striking variations in English which are emerging all over the world.

4 And if English is not your mother tongue, you may still have mixed feelings about it. You may be strongly motivated to learn it, because you know it will put you in touch with more people than any other language; but at the same time you know it will take a great deal of effort to master it, and you may begrudge that effort. Having made progress, you will feel pride in your achievement, and savor the communicative power you have at your disposal, but may none the less feel that mother-tongue speakers of English have an unfair advantage over you. And if you live in a country where the survival of your own language is threatened by the

success of English, you may feel envious, resentful, or angry. You may strongly object to the naivety of the populist account, with its simplistic and often suggestively triumphalist tone.

5     These feelings are natural, and would arise whichever language emerged as a global language. They are feelings which give rise to fears, whether real or imaginary, and fears lead to conflict. Language marches, language hunger-strikes, language rioting and language deaths are a fact, in several countries. Political differences over language economics, education, laws and rights are a daily encounter for millions. Language is always in the news, and the nearer a language moves to becoming a global language, the more newsworthy it is. So how does a language come to achieve global status?

## What Is a Global Language?

6     A language achieves a genuinely global status when it develops a special role that is recognized in every country. This might seem like stating the obvious, but it is not, for the notion of "special role" has many facets. Such a role will be most evident in countries where large numbers of the people speak the language as a mother tongue—in the case of English, this would mean the USA, Canada, Britain, Ireland, Australia, New Zealand, South Africa, several Caribbean countries and a sprinkling of other territories. However, no language has ever been spoken by a mother tongue majority in more than a few countries (Spanish leads, in this respect, in some twenty countries, chiefly in Latin America), so mother-tongue use by itself cannot give a language global status. To achieve such a status, a language has to be taken up by other countries around the world. They must decide to give it a special place within their communities, even though they may have few (or no) mother-tongue speakers.

7     There are two main ways in which this can be done. Firstly, a language can be made the official language of a country, to be used as a medium of communication in such domains as government, the law courts, the media, and the educational system. To get on in these societies, it is essential to master the official language as early in life as possible. Such a language is often described as a "second language," because it is seen as a complement to a person's mother tongue, or "first language."[1] The role of an official language is today best illustrated by English, which now has some kind of special status in over seventy countries, such as Ghana, Nigeria, India, Singapore and Vanuatu. This is far more than the status achieved by any other language—though French, German, Spanish, Russian, and Arabic are among those which have also developed a considerable official use. New political decisions on the matter continue to be made: for example, Rwanda gave English official status in 1996.

8     Secondly, a language can be made a priority in a country's foreign-language teaching, even though this language has no official status. It becomes the language

---

[1] The term "second language" needs to be used with caution—as indeed do all terms relating to language status. The most important point to note is that in many parts of the world the term is not related to official status, but simply reflects a notion of competence or usefulness.

which children are most likely to be taught when they arrive in school, and the one most available to adults who—for whatever reason—never learned it, or learned it badly, in their early educational years. Russian, for example, held privileged status for many years among the countries of the former Soviet Union. Mandarin Chinese continues to play an important role in South-east Asia. English is now the language most widely taught as a foreign language—in over 100 countries, such as China, Russia, Germany, Spain, Egypt and Brazil—and in most of these countries it is emerging as the chief foreign language to be encountered in schools, often displacing another language in the process. In 1996, for example, English replaced French as the chief foreign language in schools in Algeria (a former French colony).

9      In reflecting on these observations, it is important to note that there are several ways in which a language can be official. It may be the sole official language of a country, or it may share this status with other languages. And it may have a "semi-official" status, being used only in certain domains, or taking second place to other languages while still performing certain official roles. Many countries formally acknowledge a language's status in their constitution (e.g., India); some make no special mention of it (e.g., Britain). In certain countries, the question of whether the special status should be legally recognized is a source of considerable controversy—notably, in the USA.

10     Similarly, there is great variation in the reasons for choosing a particular language as a favored foreign language: they include historical tradition, political expediency, and the desire for commercial, cultural or technological contact. Also, even when chosen, the "presence" of the language can vary greatly, depending on the extent to which a government or foreign-aid agency is prepared to give adequate financial support to a language-teaching policy. In a well-supported environment, resources will be devoted to helping people have access to the language and learn it, through the media, libraries, schools, and institutes of higher education. There will be an increase in the number and quality of teachers able to teach the language. Books, tapes, computers, telecommunication systems and all kinds of teaching materials will be increasingly available. In many countries, however, lack of government support, or a shortage of foreign aid, has hindered the achievement of language-teaching goals.

11     Distinctions such as those between "first," "second" and "foreign" language status are useful, but we must be careful not to give them a simplistic interpretation. In particular, it is important to avoid interpreting the distinction between "second" and "foreign" language use as a difference in fluency or ability. Although we might expect people from a country where English has some sort of official status to be more competent in the language than those where it has none, simply on grounds of greater exposure, it turns out that this is not always so. We should note, for example, the very high levels of fluency demonstrated by a wide range of speakers from the Scandinavian countries and the Netherlands. But we must also beware introducing too sharp a distinction between first-language speakers and the others, especially in a world where children are being born to parents who communicate with each other through a lingua franca learned as a foreign language. In the Emirates a few years ago, for example, I met a couple—a German oil industrialist and a Malaysian—who had courted through their only common language, English, and

decided to bring up their child with English as the primary language of the home. So here is a baby learning English as a foreign language as its mother tongue. There are now many such cases around the world, and they raise a question over the contribution that these babies will one day make to the language, once they grow up to be important people, for their intuitions about English will inevitably be different from those of traditional native speakers.

12    These points add to the complexity of the present-day world English situation, but they do not alter the fundamental point. Because of the three-pronged development—of first-language, second-language, and foreign-language speakers—it is inevitable that a global language will eventually come to be used by more people than any other language. English has already reached this stage. Statistics suggest that about a quarter of the world's population is already fluent or competent in English, and this figure is steadily growing—in the early 2000s that means around 1.5 billion people. No other language can match this growth. Even Chinese, found in eight different spoken languages, but unified by a common writing system, is known to "only" some 1.1 billion.

## What Makes a Global Language?

13  Why a language becomes a global language has little to do with the number of people who speak it. It is much more to do with who those speakers are. Latin became an international language throughout the Roman Empire, but this was not because the Romans were more numerous than the peoples they subjugated. They were simply more powerful. And later, when Roman military power declined, Latin remained for a millennium as the international language of education, thanks to a different sort of power—the ecclesiastical power of Roman Catholicism.

14    There is the closest of links between language dominance and economic, technological, and cultural power, too, and this relationship will become increasingly clear as the history of English is told. Without a strong power-base, of whatever kind, no language can make progress as an international medium of communication. Language has no independent existence, living in some sort of mystical space apart from the people who speak it. Language exists only in the brains and mouths and ears and hands and eyes of its users. When they succeed, on the international stage, their language succeeds. When they fail, their language fails.

15    This point may seem obvious, but it needs to be made at the outset, because over the years many popular and misleading beliefs have grown up about why a language should become internationally successful. It is quite common to hear people claim that a language is a paragon, on account of its perceived aesthetic qualities, clarity of expression, literary power, or religious standing. Hebrew, Greek, Latin, Arabic and French are among those which at various times have been lauded in such terms, and English is no exception. It is often suggested, for example, that there must be something inherently beautiful or logical about the structure of English, in order to explain why it is now so widely used. "It has less grammar than other languages," some have suggested. "English doesn't have a lot of endings on its words, nor do we have to remember the difference between masculine, feminine and neuter gender, so it must be easier to learn." In 1848, a reviewer in the British periodical *The Athenaeum* wrote:

16    In its easiness of grammatical construction, in its paucity of inflection, in its almost total disregard of the distinctions of gender excepting those of nature, in the simplicity and precision of its terminations and auxiliary verbs, not less than in the majesty, vigour and copiousness of its expression our mother-tongue seems well adapted by organization to become the language of the world.

17    Such arguments are misconceived. Latin was once a major international language, despite its many inflectional endings and gender differences. French, too, has been such a language, despite its nouns being masculine or feminine; and so—at different times and places—have the heavily inflected Greek, Arabic, Spanish and Russian. Ease of learning has nothing to do with it. Children of all cultures learn to talk over more or less the same period of time, regardless of the differences in the grammar of their languages. And as for the notion that English has "no grammar"—a claim that is risible to anyone who has ever had to learn it as a foreign language—the point can be dismissed by a glance at any of the large twentieth-century reference grammars. The *Comprehensive grammar of the English language*, for example, contains 1,800 pages and some 3,500 points requiring grammatical exposition.[2]

18    This is not to deny that a language may have certain properties which make it internationally appealing. For example, learners sometimes comment on the "familiarity" of English vocabulary, deriving from the way English has over the centuries borrowed thousands of new words from the languages with which it has been in contact. The "welcome" given to foreign vocabulary places English in contrast to some languages (notably, French) which have tried to keep it out, and gives it a cosmopolitan character which many see as an advantage for a global language. From a lexical point of view, English is in fact far more a Romance than a Germanic language. And there have been comments made about other structural aspects, too, such as the absence in English grammar of a system of coding social class differences, which can make the language appear more "democratic" to those who speak a language (e.g., Javanese) that does express an intricate system of class relationships. But these supposed traits of appeal are incidental and need to be weighed against linguistic features which would seem to be internationally much less desirable—notably, in the case of English, the accumulated irregularities of its spelling system.

19    A language does not become a global language because of its intrinsic structural properties, or because of the size of its vocabulary, or because it has been a vehicle of a great literature in the past, or because it was once associated with a great culture or religion. These are all factors which can motivate someone to learn a language, of course, but none of them alone, or in combination, can ensure a language's world spread. Indeed, such factors cannot even guarantee survival as a living language—as is clear from the case of Latin, learned today as a classical language by only a

---

[2] Largely points to do with syntax, of course, rather than the morphological emphasis which is what many people, brought up in the Latinate tradition, think grammar to be about. The figure of 3,500 is derived from the index which I compiled for Quirk, Greenbaum, Leech and Svartvik (1985), excluding entries which related solely to lexical items.

scholarly and religious few. Correspondingly, inconvenient structural properties (such as awkward spelling) do not stop a language achieving international status either.

20    A language has traditionally become an international language for one chief reason: the power of its people—especially their political and military power. The explanation is the same throughout history. Why did Greek become a language of international communication in the Middle East over 2,000 years ago? Not because of the intellects of Plato and Aristotle: the answer lies in the swords and spears wielded by the armies of Alexander the Great. Why did Latin become known throughout Europe? Ask the legions of the Roman Empire. Why did Arabic come to be spoken so widely across northern Africa and the Middle East? Follow the spread of Islam, carried along by the force of the Moorish armies from the eighth century. Why did Spanish, Portuguese, and French find their way into the Americas, Africa and the Far East? Study the colonial policies of the Renaissance kings and queens, and the way these policies were ruthlessly implemented by armies and navies all over the known world. The history of a global language can be traced through the successful expeditions of its soldier/sailor speakers. And English . . . has been no exception.

21    But international language dominance is not solely the result of military might. It may take a militarily powerful nation to establish a language, but it takes an economically powerful one to maintain and expand it. This has always been the case, but it became a particularly critical factor in the nineteenth and twentieth centuries, with economic developments beginning to operate on a global scale, supported by the new communication technologies—telegraph, telephone, radio— and fostering the emergence of massive multinational organizations. The growth of competitive industry and business brought an explosion of international marketing and advertising. The power of the press reached unprecedented levels, soon to be surpassed by the broadcasting media, with their ability to cross national boundaries with electromagnetic ease. Technology, chiefly in the form of movies and records, fuelled new mass entertainment industries which had a worldwide impact. The drive to make progress in science and technology fostered an international intellectual and research environment which gave scholarship and further education a high profile.

22    Any language at the centre of such an explosion of international activity would suddenly have found itself with a global status. And English was apparently "in the right place at the right time." By the beginning of the nineteenth century, Britain had become the world's leading industrial and trading country. By the end of the century, the population of the USA (then approaching 100 million) was larger than that of any of the countries of western Europe, and its economy was the most productive and the fastest growing in the world. British political imperialism had sent English around the globe, during the nineteenth century, so that it was a language "on which the sun never sets."[3] During the twentieth century, this world presence was maintained and promoted almost single-handedly through the economic

---

[3] An expression adapted from the nineteenth-century aphorism about the extent of the British Empire. It continued to be used in the twentieth century, for example by Randolph Quirk (1985: 1).

supremacy of the new American superpower. Economics replaced politics as the chief driving force. And the language behind the US dollar was English.

## Why Do We Need a Global Language?

23 Translation has played a central (though often unrecognized) role in human interaction for thousands of years. When monarchs or ambassadors met on the international stage, there would invariably be interpreters present. But there are limits to what can be done in this way. The more a community is linguistically mixed, the less it can rely on individuals to ensure communication between different groups. In communities where only two or three languages are in contact, bilingualism (or trilingualism) is a possible solution, for most young children can acquire more than one language with unselfconscious ease. But in communities where there are many languages in contact, as in much of Africa and South-east Asia, such a natural solution does not readily apply.

24     The problem has traditionally been solved by finding a language to act as a lingua franca, or "common language." Sometimes, when communities begin to trade with each other, they communicate by adopting a simplified language, known as a pidgin, which combines elements of their different languages.[4] Many such pidgin languages survive today in territories which formerly belonged to the European colonial nations, and act as lingua francas; for example, West African Pidgin English is used extensively between several ethnic groups along the West African coast. Sometimes an indigenous language emerges as a lingua franca—usually the language of the most powerful ethnic group in the area, as in the case of Mandarin Chinese. The other groups then learn this language with varying success, and thus become to some degree bilingual. But most often, a language is accepted from outside the community, such as English or French, because of the political, economic, or religious influence of a foreign power.

25     The geographical extent to which a lingua franca can be used is entirely governed by political factors. Many lingua francas extend over quite small domains—between a few ethnic groups in one part of a single country, or linking the trading populations of just a few countries, as in the West African case. By contrast, Latin was a lingua franca throughout the whole of the Roman Empire—at least, at the level of government (very few "ordinary" people in the subjugated domains would have spoken much Latin). And in modern times Swahili, Arabic, Spanish, French, English, Hindi, Portuguese and several other languages have developed a major international role as a lingua franca, in limited areas of the world.

26     The prospect that a lingua franca might be needed for the *whole* world is something which has emerged strongly only in the twentieth century, and since the 1950s in particular. The chief international forum for political communication—the United Nations—dates only from 1945. Since then, many international bodies have come into being, such as the World Bank (also 1945), UNESCO and UNICEF (both 1946), the World Health Organization (1948) and the International Atomic Energy Agency (1957). Never before have so many countries (around 190, in the

---

[4] For the rise of pidgin Englishes, see Todd (1984).

case of some UN bodies) been represented in single meeting places. At a more restricted level, multinational regional or political groupings have come into being, such as the Commonwealth and the European Union. The pressure to adopt a single lingua franca, to facilitate communication in such contexts, is considerable, the alternative being expensive and impracticable multi-way translation facilities.

27    Usually a small number of languages have been designated official languages for an organization's activities: for example, the UN was established with five official languages—English, French, Spanish, Russian and Chinese. There is now a widespread view that it makes sense to try to reduce the numbers of languages involved in world bodies, if only to cut down on the vast amount of interpretation/ translation and clerical work required. Half the budget of an international organization can easily get swallowed up in translation costs. But trimming a translation budget is never easy, as obviously no country likes the thought of its language being given a reduced international standing. Language choice is always one of the most sensitive issues facing a planning committee. The common situation is one where a committee does not have to be involved—where all the participants at an international meeting automatically use a single language, as a utilitarian measure (a "working language"), because it is one which they have all come to learn for separate reasons. This situation seems to be slowly becoming a reality in meetings around the world, as general competence in English grows.

28    The need for a global language is particularly appreciated by the international academic and business communities, and it is here that the adoption of a single lingua franca is most in evidence, both in lecture-rooms and board-rooms, as well as in thousands of individual contacts being made daily all over the globe. A conversation over the Internet between academic physicists in Sweden, Italy, and India is at present practicable only if a common language is available. A situation where a Japanese company director arranges to meet German and Saudi Arabian contacts in a Singapore hotel to plan a multi-national deal would not be impossible if each plugged in to a 3-way translation support system, but it would be far more complicated than the alternative, which is for each to make use of the same language.

29    As these examples suggest, the growth in international contacts has been largely the result of two separate developments. The physicists would not be talking so conveniently to each other at all without the technology of modern communication. And the business contacts would be unable to meet so easily in Singapore without the technology of air transportation. The availability of both these facilities in the twentieth century, more than anything else, provided the circumstances needed for a global language to grow.

30    People have, in short, become more mobile, both physically and electronically. Annual airline statistics show that steadily increasing numbers are finding the motivation as well as the means to transport themselves physically around the globe, and sales of faxes, modems, and personal computers show an even greater increase in those prepared to send their ideas in words and images electronically. It is now possible, using electronic mail, to copy a message to hundreds of locations all over the world virtually simultaneously. It is just as easy for me to send a message from my house in the small town of Holyhead, North Wales, to a friend in Washington

as it is to get the same message to someone living just a few streets away from me. In fact, it is probably easier. That is why people so often talk, these days, of the "global village."

31     These trends would be taking place, presumably, if only a handful of countries were talking to each other. What has been so impressive about the developments which have taken place since the 1950s is that they have affected, to a greater or lesser extent, every country in the world, and that so many countries have come to be involved. There is no nation now which does not have some level of accessibility using telephone, radio, television, and air transport, though facilities such as fax, electronic mail and the Internet are much less widely available.

32     The scale and recentness of the development has to be appreciated. In 1945, the United Nations began life with 51 member states. By 1956 this had risen to 80 members. But the independence movements which began at that time led to a massive increase in the number of new nations during the next decade, and this process continued steadily into the 1990s, following the collapse of the USSR. There were 190 member states in 2002—nearly four times as many as there were fifty years ago. And the trend may not yet be over, given the growth of so many regional nationalistic movements worldwide.

33     There are no precedents in human history for what happens to languages, in such circumstances of rapid change. There has never been a time when so many nations need to talk to each other so much. There has never been a time when so many people wished to travel to so many places. There has never been such a strain placed on the conventional resources of translating and interpreting. Never has the need for more widespread bilingualism been greater, to ease the burden placed on the professional few. And never has there been a more urgent need for a global language.

## THINKING CRITICALLY

1. Discuss which languages were mandatory for you to study in school and which languages you have willingly chosen to study, if any. Give the reasons why your educational system may have mandated that you study a certain language and then, if applicable, explain your reasons for studying a language not forced on you.

2. In the introduction to this essay, David Crystal explains the "mixed feelings" people have about English becoming a global language. He presents these feelings from the point of view of both native English speakers and those whose mother tongue is not English. Reread these two paragraphs and then discuss if these "mixed feelings" apply to you.

3. The author uses many concrete examples (actually listing country names or specific languages) to explain his point. Find two places in his essay where he uses a concrete example and then find two places where he did not use any example, but if he had, his explanation would have been more clear.

4. What is Crystal's ultimate answer to the question, "What makes a global language?"

5. From both the author's perspective and your own, explain why there may be a need for a global language in modern times.

**WRITING ASSIGNMENTS**

1. Write an argumentative paper in favor of or against English becoming the official language of international organizations such as the United Nations, the World Bank, and the World Health Organization.

2. Write a brief essay explaining why English as a global language is controversial.

3. Crystal asserts, "From a lexical point of view, English is in fact far more a Romance than a Germanic language." Make a list of 50 words found in the English language that are of foreign origins. Explain where these words are originally from and how they could have found their way into the English language.

# Exploring the Language of **V I S U A L S**

## English and Globish

### THINKING CRITICALLY

1. What is this cartoon saying about language? Explain.

2. What visual clichés are used in the cartoon to convey who is featured and what is happening?

3. What is the "joke" the cartoonist is trying to convey?

4. In this cartoon, what do you need to know in order to understand the humor? Do you think this cartoon would be effective in another language, such as French or Japanese? Why or why not?

# What Global Language?

*Barbara Wallraff*

While the statistics seem compelling—English is the most taught second language in the world, and the primary language of business, science, and technology—don't throw out your foreign language textbooks just yet. In this next essay, language expert Barbara Wallraff explains why English is not managing to sweep all else before it—and if it ever does become the universal language, many of those who speak it will not understand one another.

Barbara Wallraff is a senior editor and the back-page "Word Court" and "Word Fugitives" columnist for *The Atlantic,* in which this article appeared in November 2000. She is the author of *Word Court* (2000) and *Your Own Words* (2004). Wallraff has been interviewed about language on the *Nightly News with Tom Brokaw* and dozens of radio programs, including *Fresh Air, The Diane Rehm Show,* and *All Things Considered.* Her articles have appeared in many publications, including *The Washington Post, The Boston Globe, The Wilson Quarterly*, and *The New York Times Magazine.*

1  Because I am interested in what happens to the English language, over the past year or so I've been asking people, at dinner parties and professional gatherings and so on, whether they think that English is well on its way to being the global language. Typically, they look puzzled about why I would even bother to ask such an obvious question. They say firmly, Of course. Then they start talking about the Internet. We're just having a conversation, so I refrain from launching into everything I'm about to tell you. It's not that I believe they're actually wrong. But the idea of English as a global language doesn't mean what they think it does—at least, not according to people I've interviewed whose professions are bound up especially closely in what happens to the English language.

2  English has inarguably achieved some sort of global status. Whenever we turn on the news to find out what's happening in East Asia, or the Balkans, or Africa, or South America, or practically anyplace, local people are being interviewed and telling us about it in English. This past April the journalist Ted Anthony, in one of two articles about global English that he wrote for the Associated Press, observed, "When Pope John Paul II arrived in the Middle East last month to retrace Christ's footsteps and addressed Christians, Muslims and Jews, the pontiff spoke not Latin, not Arabic, not Hebrew, not his native Polish. He spoke in English."

3  Indeed, by now lists of facts about the amazing reach of our language may have begun to sound awfully familiar. Have we heard these particular facts before, or only others like them? English is the working language of the Asian trade group ASEAN. It is the de facto working language of 98 percent of German research physicists and 83 percent of German research chemists. It is the official language of the European Central Bank, even though the bank is in Frankfurt and neither Britain nor any other predominantly English-speaking country is a member of the European Monetary Union. It is the language in which black parents in South Africa overwhelmingly wish their children to be educated.

4  This little list of facts comes from British sources: a report, The Future of English? and a follow-up newsletter that David Graddol, a language researcher at

The Open University, and his consulting firm, The English Company U.K., wrote in 1997 and 1998 for the British Council, whose mission is to promote British culture worldwide; and *English as a Global Language* (1997), a book by David Crystal, who is a professor at the University of Wales.

5    And yet, of course, English is not sweeping all before it, not even in the United States. According to the U.S. Bureau of the Census, ten years ago about one in seven people in this country spoke a language other than English at home—and since then the proportion of immigrants in the population has grown and grown. Ever-wider swaths of Florida, California, and the Southwest are heavily Spanish-speaking. Hispanic people make up 30 percent of the population of New York City, and a television station there that is affiliated with a Spanish-language network has been known to draw a larger daily audience than at least one of the city's English-language network affiliates. Even Sioux City, Iowa, now has a Spanish-language newspaper. According to the census, from 1980 to 1990 the number of Spanish-speakers in the United States grew by 50 percent.

6    Over the same decade the number of speakers of Chinese in the United States grew by 98 percent. Today approximately 2.4 million Chinese-speakers live in America, and more than four out of five of them prefer to speak Chinese at home. The rate of growth of certain other languages in the United States has been higher still. From 1980 to 1990 the number of speakers of Korean increased by 127 percent and of speakers of Vietnamese by 150 percent. Small American towns from Huntsville, Alabama, to Meriden, Connecticut, to Wausau, Wisconsin, to El Cenizo, Texas—all sites of linguistic controversy in recent years—have been alarmed to find that many new arrivals do not speak English well and some may not even see the point of going to the trouble of learning it.

7    How can all of this, simultaneously, be true? How can it be that English is conquering the globe if it can't even hold its own in parts of our traditionally English-speaking country?

8    A perhaps less familiar paradox is that the typical English-speaker's experience of the language is becoming increasingly simplified, even as English as a whole grows more complex. If these two trends are occurring, and they are, then the globalization of English will never deliver the tantalizing result we might hope for: that is, we monolingual English-speakers may never be able to communicate fluently with everyone everywhere. If we want to exchange anything beyond rudimentary messages with many of our future fellow English-speakers, we may well need help from something other than English.

9    The evidence strongly suggests that the range of realistic hopes and fears about the English language is narrower than some may suppose. Much discussion of what is likely to happen to English is colored, sometimes luridly, by what people dread or desire—for their children, their neighborhoods, their nations, their world. Human aspirations, of course, have a great deal to do with what comes to pass. And language is very much tied up with aspirations.

10    Last fall I visited David Graddol at The English Company's headquarters, in Milton Keynes, England. Graddol has a rumpled appearance somewhat at odds with the crisp publications, replete with graphs and pie charts and executive summaries, for which he is responsible. Similarly, the appearance of The English Company's

offices, located in the ground-floor flat of a Victorian house and sparsely furnished with good Arts and Crafts antiques together with some flea-market stuff, is amiably out of keeping with the sophisticated, high-tech nature of the consultancy's work. Stuck on the wall above the stove, in the kitchen, were four clocks, each captioned with a big letter hand-drawn on a piece of paper: M, K, M, A. This was to help the staff remember what time it was in Malaysia, Kazakhstan, Mozambique, and Argentina, the four sites where officials and advisers on how to teach English throughout those countries were taking part in an online seminar moderated by The English Company.

11     "The main message," Graddol told me, "is that the globalization of English isn't going to happen the way people expect it to." He ticked off a dizzying array of eventualities that could transform the world language picture: political alliances that have yet to be formed; the probable rise of regional trading blocs, in such places as Asia, the Arab world, and Latin America, in which the United States and other primarily English-speaking countries will be little involved; the possibility that world-changing technological innovations will arise out of nations where English is little spoken; a backlash against American values and culture in the Middle East or Asia; or the triumph of our values and culture in those places.

12     To understand the fundamental paradoxes of global English, though, we should focus on two realms of possibility: demographics and technology—yes, the Internet, but much else that's technological besides.

### First, Second, or Foreign Language

13 People who expect English to triumph over all other languages are sometimes surprised to learn that the world today holds three times as many native speakers of Chinese as native speakers of English. "Chinese," as language scholars use the word, refers to a family of languages and dialects the most widely spoken of which is Mandarin, and which share a written language although they are not all mutually intelligible when spoken. "English" refers to a family of languages and dialects the most widely spoken of which is standard American English, and which have a common origin in England—though not all varieties of English, either, are mutually intelligible. The versions of English used by educated speakers practically anywhere can be understood by most Americans, but pidgins, creoles, and diverse dialects belong to the same family, and these are not always so generally intelligible. To hear for yourself how far English now ranges from what we Americans are used to, you need only rent a video of the 1998 Scottish film *My Name Is Joe*, which, though in English, comes fully subtitled.

14     "Native speaker" is no easier to define with any precision than "Chinese" or "English," although it means roughly what you'd think: a person who grew up using the language as his or her first. In terms of how demographic patterns of language use are changing, native speakers are not where the action is. And the difference between native speakers and second- or foreign-language speakers is an important one subjectively as well as demographically. The subjective distinction I mean will be painfully familiar to anyone who, like me, spent years in school studying a foreign language and is now barely able to summon enough of it to order dinner in a restaurant.

15    In any case, the numerical gap is impressive: about 1,113 million people speak Chinese as their mother tongue, whereas about 372 million speak English. And yet English is still the world's second most common native language, though it is likely to cede second place within fifty years to the South Asian linguistic group whose leading members are Hindi and Urdu. In 2050, according to a model of language use that The English Company developed and named "engco" after itself, the world will hold 1,384 million native speakers of Chinese, 556 million of Hindi and Urdu, and 508 million of English. As native languages Spanish and Arabic will be almost as common as English, with 486 million and 482 million speakers respectively. And among young people aged fifteen to twenty-four English is expected to be in fourth place, behind not only Chinese and the Hindi-Urdu languages but also Arabic, and just ahead of Spanish.

16    Certainly, projections of all kinds perch atop teetering stacks of assumptions. But assuming that the tallies of native languages in use today are roughly accurate, the footing for projections of who will speak what as a first language fifty years from now is relatively sturdy. That's because many of the people who will be alive in fifty years are alive now; a majority of the parents of people who will be here then are already here; and most people's first language is, of course, the first language of their parents.

17    Prod at this last idea, to see how it takes into account such things as immigration and bilingual or multilingual places, and you'll find that it is not rock-solid. By David Crystal's estimate, for example, two thirds of the world's children grow up in bilingual environments and develop competence in two languages—so it is an open question what the native language of a good many of those children is. Then, too, a range of population projections exists, and demographers keep tinkering with them all.

18    But it's undeniable that English-speakers now have lower birth rates, on average, than speakers of Hindi and Urdu and Arabic and Spanish. And the countries where these other languages are spoken are, generally, less well developed than native-English-speaking countries. In 1996, according to United Nations statistics, 21 percent of males and 38 percent of females in "less developed regions" were illiterate in every language, as were 41 and 62 percent in the "least developed countries." Nonetheless, the gains that everyone expects English to make must come because it is adopted as a second language or a foreign language by most of the people who speak it. According to "The Decline of the Native Speaker," a paper David Graddol published last year in the *AILA Review* (AILA is the French acronym for the International Association of Applied Linguistics; the review belongs to the minority of international scholarly journals that still make use of another language in addition to English), the proportion of native English-speakers in the world population can be expected to shrink over the century 1950–2050 from more than eight to less than five percent.

19    A few more definitions will be helpful here. "Second-language" speakers live in places where English has some sort of official or special status. In India, for instance, the national government sanctions the use of English for its business, along with fifteen indigenous languages. What proportion of India's population of a billion speaks English is hotly debated, but most sources agree it is well under

five percent. All the same, India is thought to have the fourth largest population of English-speakers in the world, after the United States, the United Kingdom, and Nigeria—or the third largest if you discount speakers of Nigerian pidgin English. English is a second language for virtually everyone in India who speaks it. And obviously the United States, too, contains speakers of English as a second language—some 30 million of them in 1995, according to an estimate by David Crystal.

20    "Foreign-language" speakers of English live in places where English is not singled out in any formal way, and tend to learn it to communicate with people from elsewhere. Examples might be Japanese who travel abroad on business and Italians who work in tourism in their own country. The distinction between the two categories of non-native speakers is sometimes blurry. In Denmark and Sweden the overwhelming majority of children are taught English in school—does that constitute a special status?

21    The distinction between categories of speakers matters, in part because where English is a first or second language it develops local standards and norms. India, for instance, publishes dictionaries of Indian English, whereas Denmark and Sweden tend to defer to Britain or the United States in setting standards of English pronunciation and usage. The distinction also matters in relation to how entrenched English is in a given place, and how easy that place would find it to abandon the language.

22    One more surprise is how speculative any estimate of the use of English as a second or a foreign language must necessarily be. How large an English vocabulary and how great a command of English grammar does a person need in order to be considered an English-speaker? Generally, even the most rigorous attempts to determine how many people speak what, including the U.S. Census, depend on self-reporting. Do those years of French in high school and college entitle us to declare ourselves bilingual? They do if we want them to. Language researchers readily admit that their statistics on second- and foreign-language use are, as Graddol put it in "The Decline of the Native Speaker," "educated guesswork."

23    David Crystal, in his *Cambridge Encyclopedia of the English Language* (1995), observed that only 98 million second-language speakers of English in the world could be totted up with certainty. In *English as a Global Language*, though, he argued that the true number was more nearly 350 million. Graddol put forward a variety of estimates in "The Decline of the Native Speaker," including Crystal's, and explained why each had its proponents. According to the most expansive of them, the number of second-language speakers was 518 million in 1995. From 98 million to 518 million is quite a range.

24    Estimates of the number of foreign-language speakers of English range more widely still. Crystal reports that these "have been as low as 100 million and as high as 1,000 million." The estimates would vary, because by definition foreign-language speakers live in places where English has no official or special status. They may or may not have been asked in a national census or other poll about their competence in English or other languages; they may or may not have had any formal schooling in English; their assessment of their ability to speak English may or may not be accurate.

25    This last point is particularly worth bearing in mind. According to recent "Eurobarometer" surveys described by Graddol, "77% of Danish adults and 75% of Swedish adults for example, say they can take part in a conversation in English." And "nearly one third of the citizens of the 13 'non English-speaking' countries in the EU 'can speak English well enough to take part in a conversation.'" However, Richard Parker, in his book *Mixed Signals: The Prospects for Global Television News* (1995), reported this about a study commissioned by Lintas, a major media buyer, in the early 1990s:

> When ad researchers recently tested 4,500 Europeans for "perceived" versus "actual" English-language skills, the results were discouraging. First, the interviewees were asked to evaluate their English-language abilities, and then to translate a series of sample English phrases or sentences. The study produced, in its own words, "sobering" results: "the number of people really fit for English-language television turned out to be less than half the expected audience." In countries such as France, Spain, and Italy, the study found, fewer than 3 percent had excellent command of English; only in small markets, such as Scandinavia and the Low Countries, did the numbers even exceed 10 percent.

26    So the number of people in the world who speak English is unknown, and how well many of them speak and understand it is questionable. No one is arguing that English is not widely spoken and taught. But the vast numbers that are often repeated—a billion English-speakers, a billion and a half—have only tenuous grounding in reality.

27    I have never seen any tables or charts that rank languages according to the proportions of the world's population expected to be using them as second or foreign languages ten or fifty years from now. The subject is just too hypothetical, the range of variables too great. Consider, for instance, the side effects that the breakup of the Soviet Union has had on the use of the Russian language. Now that no central authority seeks to impose Russian on schoolchildren throughout the Soviet bloc, few countries besides Russia itself require students to learn it, and for the most part the language is less and less used. However, in places including the Caucasus, Russian continues to be valued as a lingua franca, and fluency in it remains a hallmark of an educated person.

28    Consider, too, the slender thread by which Canada's linguistic fate hung not long ago. In November of 1995 Quebec held a referendum to determine whether most of its citizens were in favor of independence. If 27,000 of the 4.65 million Quebeckers who voted had cast their ballots for secession rather than against, by now Canada's entire population of some 30 million people, all of them in theory bilingual, might conceivably be on the way to being largely monolingual—the nation of Quebec in French and what remained of Canada in English.

29    In the United States, discounting the claims that antagonists make about the other side's position, it's hard to find anyone who doesn't think it would be nice if everyone in the United States spoke English. Virtually all the impassioned debate is about whose resources should be devoted to making this happen and whether people should be encouraged to speak or discouraged from speaking other languages, too. All kinds of things have the potential to change the rate at which English as

a second language is learned in the United States. Suppose that nationwide, English lessons were available free (as they already are in some parts of the country) and that employers offered workers, and schools offered parents, incentives to take them. Who can say what effect this would have?

30     Patterns of learning foreign languages are more volatile still. When I visited David Graddol, last fall, The English Company was reviewing materials the Chinese government had created to be used by 400,000 Chinese instructors in teaching English to millions of their compatriots. Maybe this was a step in an inexorable process of globalization—or maybe it wasn't. Plans to teach English widely in China might change if relations between our two countries took a disastrous turn. Or the tipping point could be something completely undramatic, such as the emergence of an array of Chinese-language Web sites. The information-technology expert Michael Dertouzos told me not long ago that at a conference he had attended in Taipei, the Chinese were grumbling about having to use English to take advantage of the Internet's riches.

## Several Languages Called English

31 Much of what will happen to English we can only speculate about. But let's pursue an idea that language researchers regard as fairly well grounded: native speakers of English are already outnumbered by second-language and foreign-language speakers, and will be more heavily outnumbered as time goes on.

32     One obvious implication is that some proportion of the people using English for business or professional purposes around the world aren't and needn't be fluent in it. Recently I talked with Michael Henry Heim, a professor of Slavic literatures at the University of California at Los Angeles and a professional translator who has rendered into English major works by Milan Kundera and Günter Grass. By his count, he speaks "ten or so" languages. He told me flatly, "English is much easier to learn poorly and to communicate in poorly than any other language. I'm sure that if Hungary were the leader of the world, Hungarian would not be the world language. To communicate on a day-to-day basis—to order a meal, to book a room— there's no language as simple as English."

33     Research, though, suggests that people are likely to find a language easier or harder to learn according to how similar it is to their native tongue, in terms of things like word order, grammatical structure, and cognate words. As the researcher Terence Odlin noted in his book *Language Transfer* (1989), the duration of full-time intensive courses given to English-speaking U.S. foreign-service personnel amounts to a rough measurement of how different, in these ways, other languages are from English. Today the courses for foreign-service employees who need to learn German, Italian, French, Spanish, or Portuguese last twenty-four weeks. Those for employees learning Swahili, Indonesian, or Malay last thirty-six weeks, and for people learning languages including Hindi, Urdu, Russian, and Hungarian, forty-four weeks. Arabic, Chinese, Japanese, and Korean take eighty-eight weeks. Note that all the world's other commonest native languages except Spanish are in the groups most demanding of English-speakers. It might be reasonable to suppose that the reverse is also true—that Arabic- and Chinese-speakers find fluency in English to be more of a challenge than Spanish-speakers do.

34    A variety of restricted subsets of English have been developed to meet the needs of nonfluent speakers. Among these is Special English, which the Voice of America began using in its broadcasts experimentally some forty years ago and has employed part-time ever since. Special English has a basic vocabulary of just 1,500 words (*The American Heritage Dictionary* contains some 200,000 words, and the *Oxford English Dictionary* nearly 750,000), though sometimes these words are used to define non-Special English words that VOA writers deem essential to a given story. Currently VOA uses Special English for news and features that are broadcast a half hour at a time, six times a day, seven days a week, to millions of listeners worldwide.

35    But restricted forms of English are usually intended for professional communities. Among the best known of these is Seaspeak, which ships' pilots around the world have used for the past dozen years or so; this is now being supplanted by SMCP, or "Standard Marine Communication Phrases," which is also derived from English but was developed by native speakers of a variety of languages. Airplane pilots and air-traffic controllers use a restricted form of English called Airspeak.

36    Certainly, the world's ships and airplanes are safer if those who guide them have some language in common, and restricted forms of English have no modern-day rivals for this role. The greatest danger language now seems to pose to navigation and aviation is that some pilots learn only enough English to describe routine situations, and find themselves at a loss when anything out of the ordinary happens.

37    Something else obviously implied by the ascendance of English as a second and a foreign language is that more and more people who speak English speak another language at least as well, and probably better. India may have the third or fourth largest number of English-speakers in the world, but English is thought to be the mother tongue of much less than one percent of the population. This is bound to affect the way the language is used locally. Browsing some English-language Web sites from India recently, I seldom had trouble understanding what was meant. I did, however, time and again come across unfamiliar words borrowed from Hindi or another indigenous Indian language. On the site called India World the buttons that a user could click on to call up various types of information were labeled "samachar: Personalised News," "dhan: Investing in India," "khoj: Search India," "khel: Indian Cricket," and so forth. When I turned to the *Afternoon Despatch & Courier of Bombay* (some of whose residents call it Mumbai) and called up a gossipy piece about the romantic prospects of the son of Rajiv and Sonia Gandhi, I read, "Sources disclose that before Rahul Gandhi left for London, some kind of a 'swayamvar' was enacted at 10, Janpath with family friend Captain Satish Sharma drawing up a short list of suitable brides from affluent, well-known connected families of Uttar Pradesh."

38    Of course, English is renowned for its ability to absorb elements from other languages. As ever more local and national communities use English, though, they will pull language in ever more directions. Few in the world will care to look as far afield as the United States or Britain for their standards of proper English. After all, we long ago gave up looking to England—as did Indians and also Canadians, South Africans, Australians, and New Zealanders, among others. Today each of these national groups is proud to have its own idioms, and dictionaries to define them.

39    Most of the world's English-speaking communities can still understand one another well—though not, perhaps, perfectly. As Anne Soukhanov, a word columnist for this magazine and the American editor of the *Encarta World English Dictionary*, explained in an article titled "The King's English It Ain't," published on the Internet last year, "Some English words mean very different things, depending on your country. In South Asia, a hotel is a restaurant, but in Australia, a hotel is an establishment selling alcoholic beverages. In South Africa, a robot is a traffic light."

40    David Graddol told me about visiting China to consult on another English-curriculum project (one that had to do with teaching engineers in the steel industry) and finding a university that had chosen a Belgian company to develop lessons for it. When Graddol asked those in charge why they'd selected Belgians, of all people, to teach them English, they explained they saw it as an advantage that the Belgians, like the Chinese, are not native speakers. The Belgians, they reasoned, would be likely to have a feel both for the intricacies of learning the language in adulthood and for using it to communicate with other non-native speakers.

41    But by now we have strayed far beyond the relationship between demographics and the use of English. Technology has much to teach us too.

## The Web in My Own Language

42 When the conversations I have with friends and acquaintances about the future of English veer immediately toward technology—especially the Internet—it's understandable. Much has been made of the Internet as an instrument for circulating English around the globe. According to one estimate that has been widely repeated over the past few years, 80 percent of what's available on the Internet is in English. Some observers, however, have recently been warning that this may have been the high-water mark. It's not that English-speakers are logging off—au contraire—but that other people are increasingly logging on, to search out or create content in their own languages. As the newsletter that The English Company prepared for the British Council asserted in September of 1998, "Non English speakers are the fastest growing group of new Internet users." The consensus among those who study these things is that Internet traffic in languages other than English will outstrip English-language traffic within the next few years.

43    There's no reason this should surprise us—particularly if we recall that there are about 372 million people in the world whose native language is English and about 5,700 million people whose native language is something else. According to the same newsletter, a recent study by Euro Marketing Associates estimated that nearly 44% of the world's online population now speak a language other than English at home. Although many of these Internet users are bilingual and speak English in the workplace, Euro Marketing suggest that advertisers of non-business products will more easily reach this group by using their home language. Of the 56 million people who speak languages on the Internet other than English, Spanish speakers represent nearly a quarter.

44    The study also estimated that 13.1 percent of all Internet users speak an Asian language at home—Japanese, for the most part. A surge in Internet use like the one

that began in the United States half a dozen or so years ago is now under way in a number of other populous and relatively well-off places.

45  As has been widely noted, the Internet, besides being a convenient vehicle for reaching mass audiences such as, say, the citizenry of Japan or Argentina, is also well suited to bringing together the members of small groups—for example, middle-class French-speaking sub-Saharan Africans. Or a group might be those who speak a less common language: the numbers of Dutch-speakers and Finnish-speakers on the Internet are sharply up.

46  The Internet is capable of helping immigrants everywhere to remain proficient in their first language and also to stay current with what is going on back home. Residents in the Basque communities of Nevada and émigrés from the Côte d'Ivoire, for instance, can browse the periodicals, and even listen to the radio stations, of their homeland—much as American expatriates anywhere with an Internet connection can check the Web sites for CNN, ABC, MSNBC, and their hometown papers and radio stations.

47  No matter how much English-language material there is on the Web, then, or even how much more English material there is than material in other languages, it is naive to assume that home computers around the world will, in effect, become the work stations of a vast English language lab. People could use their computers that way—just as we English-speaking Americans could enlist our computers to help us learn Italian, Korean, or Yoruba. But, the glories of learning for its own sake aside, why would we want to do that? Aren't we delighted to be able to gather information, shop, do business, and be entertained in our own language? Why wouldn't others feel the same way? Consider, too, that many people regard high technology as something very much like a new language. Surely it's enough for a person to try to keep his or her hardware and software more or less up-to-date and running smoothly without simultaneously having to grapple with instructions or content in an actual foreign language.

48  Studies of global satellite television—a realm that is several years more mature than the Internet—also point to the idea that most people like new technology better when it speaks their own language. As Richard Parker wrote in *Mixed Signals*,

> Satellites can deliver programming and advertising instantaneously and simultaneously across the more than two dozen languages spoken in Western Europe, but the viewers—as repeated market research shows—want their television delivered in local tongues. Contrary to a history in which both motion pictures and early television broadcasts relied heavily on dubbing of foreign (often U.S.) programming, an affluent and culturally confident Europe now appears to be more linguistically divided than ever before.

49  Parker distinguishes between the "technologically feasible supply" of foreign programming and the "economically viable demand" for it, warning that we should be careful not to confuse the two. A few years ago, for example, Sweden aired a "reality-based" TV series, *Expedition: Robinson* (the word expedition has entered Swedish from English), and it quickly became a national obsession. But its success did not inspire American television networks to import the series; rather, they developed new shows, such as *Big Brother* and *Survivor*.

50    In sum, the globalization of English does not mean that if we who speak only English just sit back and wait, we'll soon be able to exchange ideas with anyone who has anything to say. We can't count on having much more around the world than a very basic ability to communicate. Outside certain professional fields, if English-speaking Americans hope to exchange ideas with people in a nuanced way, we may be well advised to do as people elsewhere are doing: become bilingual. This is easier said than done. If learning a second language were so simple, no doubt many more of us would have picked up Spanish or Chinese by now. It is clear, though, that the young learn languages much more readily than adults. Surely, American children who are exposed to nothing but English would benefit from being taught other languages as well.

51    At the same time, English is flourishing, and people here and everywhere are eager to learn it to the extent that it is practical for them to do so. It would behoove us to make learning English as easy as possible, for both children and adults, in this country and abroad.

52    However unwelcome this news may be to some, not even headlong technological advances mean that computers will soon be doing all the hard work of coping with other languages for us. For the foreseeable future computers will be able to do no more than some of the relatively easy work. When it comes to subtle comprehension of our world and the other people in it, we are, as ever, on our own.

## THINKING CRITICALLY

1. In her introduction, Wallraff states "the idea of English as a global language doesn't mean what [professionals/experts] think." Based on the information in this essay, what do people seem to think about the globalization of English? Why does Wallraff disagree with the position of the people she has interviewed on the issue?

2. Statistics on the far-reaching impact of English seem to imply that English is on its way to truly becoming the lingua franca of the world. What ways might one read the data? Based on statistical information, what might one surmise about the future of the English language?

3. How are language and the aspirations and hopes of one generation for the future of the next connected? What role will English play in a global context in the shaping of cultures in the future?

4. What factors might slow the globalization of English? Explain.

5. What does Wallraff mean when she says there are "several languages called English"? Explain.

6. What influence does technology play in the globalization of English?

## WRITING ASSIGNMENTS

1. Wallraff opens her essay with the example of when the Pope addressed a mixed group of Christians, Muslims, and Jews in English. Is English the new language of diplomacy? Write a short essay exploring how the use of English could improve or harm international communication.

2. Write an essay exploring what would happen if English did indeed become the global language of choice. Would it change your life in any way? How could it affect the lives of the next generation? Explain.

# English as a Global Language: A Good Thing or a Bad Thing?

*Keith Redfern*

While some people feel that the globalization of English is a good thing, others are not so certain. Both sides, however, generally concede that the English language has become an essential means of communication in the areas of the Internet, commerce, finance, education, and politics. Interestingly enough, the United States and other English-speaking countries have not directly sought the globalization of their language. In this next blog-style essay, author Keith Redfern explores the pros and cons of English as a global language.

Keith Redfern is a retired teacher and author who trained at Westminster College, Oxford, England. He now lives in southwestern France. He has published two works of nonfiction, many magazine articles, short stories, and a novel. He is a writer for Helium, an online "knowledge co-operative" that promotes the exchange of ideas supported by good writing. This essay appeared on Helium.com.

1 Whether we think it is a good thing or not, English has virtually become the global language already, and not because an official decision was made. That is simply the way it has developed. It is difficult to isolate where or when this began to happen, but it probably has a lot to do with the world wide coverage of English language movies, of English language television programs and English soccer.

2 However, history must play its part and, like it or not, it is a remnant in some areas of a British colonial past. There are perhaps two threads to the development, one geographical and the other related to areas of expertise. English became the first language of North America once the English had gained dominance over the French and Spanish in that continent's settlement. It naturally became the first language of Australasia as its countries are members of the British Commonwealth. Variants of English have grown up across the Pacific Ocean and in South East Asia due to colonization, and the type of English which is taking shape over time in this area is likely to be the one spoken by the most people in future decades. Further north, in Japan and the Philippines, American influence led to English becoming a common second language.

3 Britain's presence in the countries of southern Asia, an area which has hundreds of native languages of its own, led to English becoming the common second language throughout the subcontinent. English is probably the most commonly taught second language in European schools, and so, as the European Union has taken shape, although debates are translated into all members' languages, English has become the most commonly shared language.

4 While the above geographical spread was taking place, in certain areas of study, English has become accepted as the common language of *choice*. In all areas of medicine for example, our local doctors, dentists, surgeons and other specialists in France, all understand English and most medical journals are published in English. In the skies, air traffic controllers speak English to each other. In many major international sports, English is the common language of choice. And that is the important phrase to use in this context—language of choice.

5    No international body has made a decision that English should become the global language, but that is what seems to be developing. In France, where the native language is protected like an endangered species, teenagers are learning English as hard as they can, as they know it will be hard for them to find work, even in their home country, without an ability to communicate in English.

6    Some people may consider the global use of English is a bad thing for their own languages. However, there is a feeling in many areas now that local languages and native dialects should not be allowed to die out. A global use of English does not imply that other languages are going to be lost.

7    What people speak in their own homes will not necessarily be the national language of the country in which they live, and is certainly unlikely to be English, except in particular parts of the world. Many children are growing up to be bilingual, and their ability to learn languages, which is most easy at an early age, is an enviable thing to many adults. Perhaps the children will have parents of mixed languages—if so, being bilingual will become natural to them. They will learn at school the national language of the country in which they live, and they will probably learn English as well.

8    And so English is gradually becoming a global language, not because of decisions to that effect, but because of choice. This is probably a good thing overall, as it means that people of different races, religions and ethnic groups should be able to understand each other more easily. That has got to be good for the future of the world.

### THINKING CRITICALLY

1. After reading Redfern's essay, what bit of information regarding the spread of English surprised you the most, and why?

2. According to the author, why are so many people the world over choosing to learn English?

3. Redfern notes that the spread of English is likely due to exportation of English-language movies and television programs. What other media might also be contributing to the widespread adoption of English?

4. Redfern concludes that the global spread of English "has got to be good for the future of the world." Respond to his statement with your own viewpoint.

### WRITING ASSIGNMENTS

1. Redfern shares some of the factors that contributed to the spread of English and its influence around the world. Research how the English language has evolved over time, and write an essay describing this evolution, connecting it to the trends we are now seeing as a result of globalization. You may wish to refer to the essays in the first chapter as you prepare your essay.

2. Write a brief essay in which you discuss why some countries are not as open-minded about English or its advance.

3. Jitka Prikrylova, director of a Prague English-language school, said, "The world has opened up for us, and English is its language." Brainstorm a list of the different ways that learning a foreign language can open up the world.

4. Redfern is a writer for Helium—an online writing site that propels good writing to the top of lists and supports the exchange of ideas in a wide area of subjects. Look up the discussions on the English language and language globalization and write your own blog-style essay in which you answer the question posed by Redfern's title: "English as a Global Language: A Good Thing or a Bad Thing?"

# Lost in America
*Douglas McGray*

Speak two languages and you are bilingual. Speak only one? You must be American. So goes the old joke. But globalization means that students can no longer remain blissfully unaware of the world and cultures around them. Can Americans open the classroom door, or will today's youth be unprepared to lead tomorrow's world? And with the prominence of English, do we still need to learn foreign languages anyway?

Douglas McGray is a contributing writer at *Foreign Policy* magazine and a fellow at the New America Foundation, a think tank that examines political and cultural issues. This essay appeared in the May–June 2006 issue of *Foreign Policy*.

1 Christina is a modern, multitasking, American 15-year-old—fiddling with her new iPod, sassing the tall boy slouched beside her, and getting an impromptu lesson in Filipino culture at an after-school program in Oakland, California. "I speak Tagalog and Filipino," says the group's counselor, Michelle Ferrer, "two languages from the Island where my family comes from." Christina is puzzled. "The Philippines is an island?" she asks skeptically. Ferrer nods and Christina frowns. I thought it was in China, she says. Ferrer tries not to laugh. "Girl, you thought I was Chinese?" she teases gently. "No," Christina clarifies, "I thought the Philippines was a country in China."

2 In California, where Christina lives, more than 1 in 4 of the state's residents were born outside the United States. Schoolchildren speak more than 60 languages at home. Globalization is everywhere you look. Here in Oakland, an 11-year-old African-American boy has impressed international audiences with his uncanny Chinese arias. In nearby Fruitvale, nearly 100,000 locals turned out last fall for a Mexican Dia de los Muertos celebration. To the south, in Silicon Valley, a Bollywood cineplex effortlessly sells out its Hindi screenings. A few blocks from my San Francisco apartment, a shop that specializes in goods from Brazil (the area around Goiania specifically) shares its block with a Vietnamese restaurant and a yoga studio, where yuppies chant in Sanskrit as they bend and sweat; outside, Caribbean reggaeton blares from the windows of Japanese tuner coupes.

3 But for all the changes globalization has brought to the average American kid's cultural and commercial ecosystem, the average classroom has lagged far behind, even in cosmopolitan California. Take foreign languages. In the late 1940s, more than 90 percent of kids who studied a foreign language learned French, Spanish, or Latin. At the end of the century, a radically different era, that figure remained

the same. At least two decades after political scientists decided China would be the world's next major power, only a little more than 1,300 public high school students studied Chinese—just 8 percent of the number studying American Sign Language. More than 25 years since the oil crisis showed the Middle East to be the world's most vital and volatile region, only about 500 American public high schoolers were enrolled in Arabic classes, while some 175,000 studied Latin instead. Two thirds of American students never studied a second language at all in the year 2000.

4      That's just the most obvious anachronism. Many U.S. states have introduced world history classes, but few find time for modern Africa, Asia, Latin America, or the Middle East. Islam, for instance, makes a single scheduled appearance in California's history and social studies curriculum, in a survey of ancient societies for 11- and 12-year-olds. That provincial tendency lingers into college. Although half of all college-bound Americans say they hope to study abroad, only 1 percent actually follow through on those plans. And nearly half of those students travel to just four countries in Western Europe: Britain, France, Italy, and Spain. In 2004, Italy attracted more American students than all of Africa, Asia, and the Middle East combined.

5      As a result, young Americans like Christina represent something of a paradox: surrounded by foreign languages, cultures, and goods, they remain hopelessly uninformed, and misinformed, about the world beyond U.S. borders. In 2002, with their troops occupying Kabul, Afghanistan, and both Washington and the rest of the world debating a possible invasion of Iraq, 85 percent of 18- to 24-year-old Americans surveyed by the National Geographic Society could not find either country on a map. And it gets worse: Sixty-nine percent failed to find Britain, 29 percent could not find the Pacific Ocean, and nearly a third believed the U.S. population to be somewhere between 1 and 2 billion.

6      For most of U.S. history, a clique of exclusive universities and military academies trained an elite group of bright young men to handle the nation's minimal foreign concerns. But America has a different role in the world today, and the world has a different role in America. The U.S. military maintains more than half a million soldiers, intelligence officers, staff, and contractors abroad, and employs some 50,000 foreigners. Together, they operate more than 700 bases in roughly 130 countries—the shadow of America's interests in the world. At the same time, foreign influence in the United States grows every year. In West Virginia, a state mocked by smug urbanites as a backwater, local businesses did more than $3.1 billion in foreign trade in 2005, and investment from some 75 global firms created more than 30,000 new jobs.

7      Of course, fretting about public education is something of a national pastime. Every few years a new survey comes out, showing that American schoolchildren lag behind their global counterparts in science and math. That inevitably sends lawmakers and the public into a panic. Soon, we hear, the United States will become a nation of baristas and retail clerks, while Asians leave their kids with the Nannybot, commute to work on cold fusion-powered monorails, and fine-tune the software that will put Microsoft and Google out of business.

8      And yet, for all the anxiety that science and math education inspires, the state of global languages, politics, history, and culture in U.S. schools may actually be

scarier. Whether it is translating and analyzing intelligence intercepts in Arabic and Farsi, guiding American industry through new markets in Asia, collaborating with research partners across the globe, or shaping the foreign policy of the world's only superpower at the ballot box, young Americans will struggle to bear their responsibilities.

## The Hermit Classroom

9 The United States was barely a toddler, in nation years, when public schoolhouses began to spread across the country. It was a radical notion: teaching every poor farm boy or miner's son to read, write, add, and learn about the great men who founded their democracy, at a time when European governments still considered primary education a privilege. But the movement was rooted in anxiety. America was suddenly a republic, but a republic of foreigners—disparate, multilingual, barely connected to a distant government in Washington, and ill-equipped to weigh matters of state when they cast a vote.

10 Public education was designed to manufacture citizens. American textbooks appeared, scrubbed clean of continental influence. Georgia legislators actually banned study abroad before the age of 16. Even bitter political rivals of men such as George Washington and Thomas Jefferson saw the utility in building up a few common heroes. If Americans had nothing in common but America, then public education would unite them.

11 A homogenizing civic education prevailed without much dissent for more than a century, mostly because new waves of immigrants—Italians, Irish, Eastern Europeans—kept arriving. That ethos did face challenges. When, in the 1840s, German Americans in Cincinnati, Ohio, lobbied for their children to learn German, school administrators feared losing this wealthy, educated community to private schools, so they squeezed German into the curriculum. Later, Italian immigrants put pressure on New York City schools, and in the 1930s, an Italian-American principal offered his kids the country's first Italian class. Still, traditional ideals endured.

12 It took two world wars, the rise of an ambitious Soviet Union, and the birth of technologies that exploded any notion of safe distance for the United States to re-think its isolationist bent. Public education would change, too. But if the world out-side demanded American attention, American classrooms mostly resisted the call. After all, when the Germans rose in World War I, Americans did not rush to learn the enemy's language; they banned it from public schools. (By 1922, just 13,000 American public school students studied German, down from nearly 325,000 in 1915, when only Latin was more popular.) Why would the Cold War proceed any differently?

13 American education did react to the 20th century's growing internationalism, at least for a moment, after the Soviet Union launched the Sputnik program in the late 1950s. Shaken by Moscow's achievement, American legislators passed the National Defense Education Act, funding everything from advanced scientific research to foreign-language study. For more than a decade after Sputnik's flight, language education boomed in a way it never has since. But most of the money went to French and Spanish. And the largesse was short-lived. When budgets

tightened in the 1970s, international courses were the first to go, and the number of students in foreign-language classes dropped every year. By 1980, less than 1 in 10 universities required any foreign-language study for admission, down from one third in the 1960s. Nobody seemed concerned.

14 The globe-spanning perils and opportunities of the Cold War may have preoccupied Washington, D.C., but in education, the fight was at home, and over the past. Take California's world history curriculum (fairly thorough, by American standards). Children in the seventh and eighth grades study a culturally diverse history of the world, up through the Middle Ages. Due credit is paid to the contributions of great African, Asian, Middle Eastern, and Latin American civilizations. But by the time students hit the 10th grade, they reach the Industrial Revolution, and "world" history turns into the history of the United States and Western Europe. "The conservatives will say it's OK to include the traditions of ancient and medieval cultures," explains Ross Dunn, a history professor at San Diego State University and coauthor of an influential draft of national history standards in the 1990s, "but that once you get to 1500, the focus should be on the West, because that's where the action is."

15 University campuses, too, became battlegrounds in the 1990s, as students and professors staked out new American identities that put race, gender, or foreign heritage on equal footing with American citizenship. Conservatives lashed out at this "political correctness." Ironically, though, these fights over what it means to be American rarely considered American identity in a wider world. For all the heart-warming talk about respecting diverse cultures, 92 percent of American undergraduates never take a foreign-language class.

## An Incomplete Grade

16 Sputnik fell to Earth and faded from memory. But there would be other opportunities to shake schools out of their provincialism. None seems more striking, in hindsight, than a report commissioned by the White House in 1978. Pointing to unrest in the Middle East, and a line in the 1975 Helsinki Accords that compelled signatories to promote the study of foreign languages, Congressmen Paul Simon and Leon Panetta called on President Jimmy Carter to appoint a commission to assess the state of international studies. Their report, Strength through Wisdom, was blistering. "Americans' incompetence in foreign languages is nothing short of scandalous," the authors wrote. "The United States requires far more reliable capacities to communicate with its allies, analyze the behavior of potential adversaries, and earn the trust and sympathies of the uncommitted." And yet, the report argues, "our schools graduate a large majority of students whose knowledge and vision stops at the American shoreline, whose approach to international affairs is provincial, and whose heads have been filled with astonishing misinformation."

17 The report's authors, 25 luminaries of American academia, politics, and the media, proposed more than 100 pages of possible reforms, from requiring international education courses for all teachers in training, to launching regional language centers across the country that would support foreign-language instruction. Congress shrugged. "People who either were children of immigrants, or had language ability, or members [of Congress] who traveled abroad got it," Panetta

recalls. "But there wasn't broad support for what we were doing, either from the administration or from the congress." None of the reforms were adopted.

18    A generation of Americans grew up and left for college. The Cold War ended. The Internet came of age. Falling airfares turned foreign continents into weekend getaway spots. Average Americans developed strong opinions on everything from outsourcing, foreign pharmaceuticals, and global warming, to pandemic disease, terrorism, and the politics of oil. Globalization became a buzzword, and then a simple fact of life.

19    Unsurprisingly, American college students began to seek out new foreign languages and study abroad in greater numbers. But they did so with little encouragement. In 1996, congress actually chopped 20 percent from the budget of the Fulbright Program, which sends American graduates around the world for advanced study. Education reformers devoted most of their energy to math, English literacy, and standardized testing, and many primary schools dropped social studies and foreign languages altogether.

20    Earlier this year, President George W. Bush finally revived some of the ideas in Strength through Wisdom, with a new National Security Language Initiative. The modestly funded measure encourages foreign-language study as early as kindergarten, and requests new money to train and certify foreign-language teachers, particularly in so-called critical languages such as Arabic, Chinese, Farsi, Hindi, and Russian. It also promises to subsidize foreign study for high school and college students, and bring native speakers from abroad to teach in U.S. classrooms.

21    The business community, too, has started to champion the cause. According to a Committee for Economic Development study, 30 percent of large U.S. firms surveyed in 2002 believed a provincial, monolingual workforce had cost them business opportunities overseas. Even the College Board, a nonprofit organization that administers U.S. exams for college admissions and credit, has started to come around. Only six years ago, it offered two Advanced Placement (AP) exams on the writings of the Roman poet Virgil, and none on the politics, economics, history, and literature of five of the world's continents. It finally introduced a world history exam in 2002, and next year it will offer its first exams in non-European languages—Chinese and Japanese. The College Board's executive director for the AP program, Trevor Packer, also revealed that test planners are considering a shift that would put much more emphasis on the United States in a global context for a major update to their flagship U.S. History exam. "We have to reflect best practices at the university level," Packer says. "What we're finding are courses that do a better job than in the past of integrating U.S. history into global themes." Because the College Board defines educational rigor in American high schools, any shift in its outlook would have wide repercussions.

22    It could all begin to add up to another moment for international education in the United States. But the previous moments have been just that—moments. And there are reasons to worry this one will be no different. As *The New Republic* pointed out in January, the president's language initiative may promise $24 million to promote foreign-language instruction in K-12 schools, but that seems pretty paltry compared to the $206 million he requested to fund abstinence-only sex education. And ultimately, what happens in American classrooms today is driven by standardized tests,

administered by state governments. In California, teachers know that contemporary global themes such as disease, information technology, migration, and environmental policy make up about 10 percent of the "standards" they are supposed to teach in 10th grade world history, but they represent only one question on the 60-question state exam. With so much history to cover, and so much emphasis on test scores, teachers are under pressure to cut out extras. For now, foreign languages and global politics, economics, history, and culture are dispensable.

## World Class

23 That is not to say there are no bright spots. Ask around, and you will hear stories of individual teachers who slip global context into the curriculum, often with a lot of imagination. "It's mostly individuals who, because of their personal experiences, value international education, and try to find ways to fit it in," says Peter Hammer, social studies content specialist for the San Francisco Unified School District. "It takes a great deal of determination on the individual teacher's part, and support from outside the schools."

24     Some adventurous school districts have let their foreign-language programs evolve with the times. When the Washington, D.C., suburb of Fairfax, Virginia, began to attract new immigrants in the 1980s, schools reflected the change. Today, students can study Arabic, Chinese, French, German, Japanese, Latin, Russian, and Spanish. New York's Henry Street School takes Chinese-language students on field trips to Chinatown, where they speak Mandarin with curious shopkeepers and restaurant owners, and benefit from an easy and inexpensive study abroad-like experience. And then there is the spread of two-way bilingual immersion schools. At the public Alice Fong Yu elementary school in San Francisco, children learn everything from math to social studies in both Cantonese and English. By the time they reach high school, they are totally bilingual—cognitively wired to learn more languages, and culturally wired to understand America's place in the world.

25     A few schools are experimenting even further. At the Vaughn Next Century Learning Center, an influential public charter school in the sprawl north of Los Angeles, Eugene Astilla stands at the head of a classroom full of high school freshmen. His students, overwhelmingly Latino and overwhelmingly poor, are dressed in black and white (red and blue are gang colors, and banned in class). Astilla teaches world history at a new satellite school, the Vaughn International Studies Academy. It's one of eight pilot programs nationwide, funded by the nonprofit Asia Society and the Bill and Melinda Gates Foundation, to try to bring the contemporary world to every class in the school day, even science and math.

26     Today, Astilla asks his kids to compare Benito Mussolini, Adolf Hitler, and Saddam Hussein. All used violence to stay in power, several suggest. "They used propaganda," one student points out. "Good one!" Astilla says approvingly. He quizzes the class on facts. "Can someone tell me the name of Saddam's party?" he asks. "Sunni?" one kid says, hesitantly. "No, but good guess," Astilla says. "I'll give you a clue. It's something you kids don't take often enough." A boy in the back raises his hand. "The Shower Party?" he asks, and half the room jumps in at once: "Baath!"

27      The readings on Hitler and Mussolini are in the standard textbook. The readings on Saddam are downloaded from the Web. And that is how it goes in every class—teachers hit the stuff the state expects kids to know but lead detours out of the textbook to try and put things in a global context. Take a lesson going on next door, on plant biology, where the teacher, Noah DeLeon, mixes overhead slides on photosynthesis with world agriculture maps. He goes over the mechanics of plant reproduction, but also prompts kids to think about the wider meaning of plants, from the debate over corn-derived ethanol as a fuel source to food security around the world. "There's no curriculum out there," explains Principal Yvonne Chan. "There isn't any model."

28      All the students at Vaughn take Spanish and Chinese. Because many of them are fluent Spanish speakers, or native Spanish speakers who had to master English, they pick up Chinese quickly—a second foreign language always comes more easily. Next year, the school will begin to offer Arabic as an elective. Neighborhood parents, many of whom speak only Spanish, are among the school's biggest supporters. "Our children need languages other than Spanish and English to compete globally," says Imelda Sierra, whose daughter attends the school.

29      Large American cities have always been international and multicultural, but the nation's 2000 Census was something of a landmark. For the first time, new immigrants were more likely to settle in a suburb than in a big city such as Los Angeles, Miami, or New York. States that were home to very few recent immigrants a generation ago, including Maine, Minnesota, and North Carolina, are finding new languages and new cultures in their midst.

30      Of course, cultural diversity does not automatically give a community a global outlook. Many American children of immigrants reluctantly speak two or three languages, but otherwise stay willfully ignorant of their parents' native countries. White suburbanites may hear Hindi in the neighborhood for the first time, notice a new sari shop at the corner strip mall, develop a regular craving for takeout tandoori, and still think Kashmir is for sweaters. But new immigrants make foreignness immediate for Americans, in a way that citizens of small countries on crowded continents take for granted.

31      That may be the best hope for a broader commitment to international education in U.S. schools. Whether the United States looks to its growing and dispersing immigrant communities as a resource, though, may depend on how well the nation overcomes some longstanding ideas—namely, that Americans are easily drawn to foreign loyalties, and that public education should be a defense against cultural dissolution. Many critics, for instance, still rail against bilingual education as an un-American accommodation to foreigners. Just look at conservative pundit Tucker Carlson's reaction to the Bush administration's National Security Language Initiative. "People are really influenced by their study abroad," he argued. "Do we want, in other words, the federal government paying, possibly to create more converts to radical Islam? Because that is actually what's going to happen."

32      An inward-looking education system didn't stop the United States from becoming rich and powerful in the 20th century. It would be a mistake, though, to assume that what worked for previous generations will still work in the future. Scientific research teams have become multilingual, multinational, and multidisciplinary.

Businesses are staking out suppliers, partners, and storefronts overseas. Teachers and students must welcome and integrate a growing number of new immigrants into their communities. Soldiers, often teenagers with no education beyond high school, deploy alongside allies from dozens of different countries, and negotiate language and cultural barriers in situations where time and precision can make the difference between lives saved and lives lost. In the 21st century, everyone is a potential diplomat.

33    But it isn't just the world that's changing; it's the very nature of knowledge. Grammar, spelling, and multiplication tables may remain comfortingly constant, but theories in science, technology, politics, and economics can become dated by the time a textbook publisher goes to press. "What's different today," says Marcelo Suarez-Orozco, professor of globalization and education at New York University, "is the rapid rate in which knowledge becomes obsolete. That means that learning has to be focused on cognitive skills." Think about good computer education: It doesn't just teach kids to perform a task, it teaches them how to learn unfamiliar technology. The same holds true in global economics, politics, and society, which can shift—and shift the world's competitive landscape—as fast as a new operating system can turn a two-year-old laptop into an expensive typewriter.

34    We may live in a democratic age, but the international system is no democracy. The United States can solve crises that entire continents, working together, cannot. It can also sink most treaties, veto any global consensus, undermine the United Nations, and make far-reaching decisions that the rest of the world must live with. Savvy countries have realized that, and angled for influence with American youth. The Chinese government put up funding to encourage the College Board to develop its new AP Chinese exam, and Saudi Prince Alwaleed bin Talal recently donated $40 million to introduce ambitious Georgetown and Harvard students to the Arab world. Americans should be grateful for their concern. In a few years, Christina's disoriented peers will land jobs in Washington, get their first set of business cards from multinational firms, and sit in judgment of U.S. foreign policy every four years. The United States can no longer afford an isolationist education system, any more than the world can afford an isolationist American public.

### THINKING CRITICALLY

1. McGray beings his essay with an anecdote about a teenager and her lack of geographical knowledge. Do you think this is a fair example of most 15-year-olds? How would you rate your own knowledge of geography and foreign culture? Explain your rating.

2. This article points out, "Two thirds of American students never studied a second language at all in the year 2000." Are you part of this majority? Have you ever studied a foreign language? If so, which ones and why? If not, why did you chose not to learn a foreign language?

3. Do you hope to study or travel abroad during your college career? If so, where would you want to visit and if not, why not? How important is language in deciding where you would go?

4. Reread the first and last paragraphs of this essay. In what way does the author come full-circle, tying the introduction to the conclusion? Do you find this an effective writing technique?

5. Discuss the reasons why recent immigrants prefer to settle in the suburbs rather than settling in the big cities. What has changed over the past several years to make the suburbs a feasible option for immigrants?

## WRITING ASSIGNMENTS

1. Write an essay arguing that colleges and universities should—or should not—require foreign language study for admission or graduation.

2. The author of this article gives examples of how some teachers have taken the teaching of standard textbooks and incorporated outside sources in order to put this information into a global context. Reread paragraph 27, and create a lesson plan for your major in which you include a connection to global issues.

3. Write a brief essay agreeing or disagreeing with the following statement: "Americans are easily drawn to foreign loyalties, and . . . public education should be a defense against cultural dissolution."

## MAKING CONNECTIONS

1. As best as you can, try to describe your own English usage. Do you think that you speak "good English"? How would the various authors from this section respond to your form of usage? Explain.

2. Now that you have read the different perspectives concerning "standard English," write an essay about where you stand on the issue. Do you think we need language guardians such as John Simon? Is English a changing and malleable medium to which we must adapt according to popular opinion? Do you think we have a right to use whatever form of English we choose?

3. Consider the English language education you received in school. Was it prescriptive, or did it allow for more flexibility? Did you learn the rules of grammar and sentence structure? Has this instruction helped you in your daily life? Was your academic language useful to you as a writer and thinker, or has it proven largely unnecessary? Explain.

4. What is the difference between "good English" and "real English"? In your opinion, should one be used in certain cases and not in others? Explain.

5. Do you think you have an accent? Can you hear yourself speak it? Do you know anyone who claims not to have an accent? What do they mean? Are they accurate in their assessment of their speech? Write an essay in which you explore the concept of the accent in your local area and the way people react to speech. Is one way of speaking considered more educated or intelligent than another?

6. A global language is the language of public discourse, control, and power. Do you think that English instruction for non-English-speaking children should be left to chance or be approached by early, intensive instruction in school? Write a paper in which you explore your thoughts on this question. Consider in your discussion the effects of home language and culture on personal pride.

7. Have you ever been in a place where you did not speak the language? At a social gathering? Traveling in a non-English-speaking region or country? In an educational setting? With your classmates, discuss these situations. If you have been in one of these situations, discuss how your experience influences your opinion about bilingual education.

8. Many of the essays in this section refer to the concept of "mainstream" society, and how English is the language of mainstream society. Write an essay in which you identify and describe mainstream society. Who is part of it, and how do they belong in it? Who decides what is mainstream and what is not? Or if you wish, you may argue that such an entity does not exist in modern America.

9. What factors have driven the English language toward globalization? Based on the information provided by the authors in this section, review the reasons behind the prevalence of English and project the future of English as a global language in 20, 50, and 100 years.

10. What impact does the globalization of English have on the language itself? How is globalization influencing the evolution of English?

11. Research the issue of English as a lingua franca online. What do people think of English as the primary language of science and technology? Of commerce?

12. What challenges do nonnative speakers face as they try to compete in a global economy that seems to be dominated by a single language? Write an essay exploring the impact of English on the global economy and how different cultures are responding.

# Technology and Language 4

**H**uman languages are usually referred to as natural languages—they live, die, shift in location, and evolve with time. They are deeply influenced by our culture, and they reflect the times we live in. Actively used languages that change and grow are known as "living" languages. Conversely, those that are fixed or cease to develop further are known as "dead," as in the case of Latin.

Perhaps the strongest influence on our language today is technology. Technology has introduced new words, changed the meanings of others, and has even introduced new forms of language and communication. From office software such as Word and PowerPoint, to email, texting, tweeting, and blogs, technological innovations are changing the way we live our lives, the way we communicate, and language itself.

Before 1990, very few people had ever heard of the Internet. And fewer still could have guessed its impact on American culture, education, social networking, and business. More than 20 years later, the Internet has shaped a generation—and for many of us, life without it seems unimaginable. The Internet has made possible entirely new forms of social interaction. We can connect with friends and family nearby or across the globe. We can meet new people, build social networks, and even date. Social networking websites such as Facebook and Twitter have created new ways for us to connect and socialize. Users of these sites can build groups of current and new friends, arrange for on- and offline gatherings, share photos, create diaries, exchange messages, and build networks based on common interests. They can keep track of their friends' activities and plans on an hourly basis, and with messages sent to cell phones, be connected at all times anywhere. Yet, some social critics have observed, despite being so connected, technology seems to be pushing us further apart—into an isolated world where text shorthand replaces a human voice, and a webcam stands in for face-to-face human contact.

This chapter examines how technology influences language and communication—for better or worse. The first unit of essays examines the impact of different electronic media on the way we communicate with each other. First, we open with Christine Rosen, who wonders about the impact the virtual word is having on our language. The book, she observes, seems rigid and passé as we consume a daily diet of information bytes and digital images. What does this shift mean for our ability to absorb information and for the future of the book itself? Next we explore the influence of modern software systems on our communications skills in the boardroom and the classroom in "Is PowerPoint the Devil?" Julia Keller describes the history of PowerPoint and its hold on us. Her essay is supported by a demonstration of what a famous speech might have looked like if accompanied by PowerPoint slides in "Lincoln's Gettysburg Address in PowerPoint." The presentation is followed by an explanation by its creator, Peter Norvig. The section closes with an essay on blogs by word guru Geoffrey Nunberg, "Blogging in the Global Lunchroom," in which he observes that blogging has its own unique style that, according to the author, just adds to the fragmentation of thought that seems to be a trend in modern communication.

The next section reviews the ways technology is changing the way we talk to each other. The first three readings focus on the phenomenon of "texting"—what it is, how we use it, and how it may impede communication when inappropriately used. Linguist David Crystal describes how texting is shaping the communication style of a generation in his academic paper "Texting." His essay includes two poems by Norman Silver, who uses text language as the medium for his poetry. The next piece provides a review of some common IM (instant messaging) and text messaging terms and slang in "r u online?" by Kris Axtman. Then, in "The Keypad Solution," Ammon Shea describes how text messaging is reforming the spelling of English, which many English speakers admit doesn't always make much sense. Then Robert Kuttner discusses what he feels are the detrimental effects of the instant and often impersonal nature of email in "The Other Side of E-Mail." The section ends with two pieces on the popular social networking and microblogging service Twitter. First, economics professor Tyler Cowen explains that rather than viewing "tweeting" as detrimental to language, as critics fear, we should recognize it is reinvigorating communication, in "Three Tweets for the Web." Then Peggy Orenstein describes how tweeting makes her think about herself and her place in the world—maybe a bit too much—in "I Tweet, Therefore I Am."

# MAKING CONNECTIONS IN A MODERN WORLD

# In the Beginning Was the Word
*Christine Rosen*

The book, that fusty old technology, seems almost passé as we redirect our attention to text messages, sound bites, and summaries. E-readers are changing the way we interact with reading material. Entire school libraries have done away with books in favor of electronic downloads available on the Kindle or Nook. It is easy to blame technology for the seeming reduction of our literacy. But the fault, says sociologist Christine Rosen, is not in our books but In ourselves. And the price we pay for the ease of technology could be our imaginations and creativity.

Christine Rosen is a senior editor of *The New Atlantis* and resident fellow at the Ethics and Public Policy Center in Washington, D.C. She writes about the history of genetics, bioethics, the fertility industry, and the social impact of technology. She is the author of *Preaching Eugenics: Religious Leaders and the American Eugenics Movement* (2004). She has been widely published in many journals and newspapers, including *The New York Times Magazine, The Wall Street Journal, The Washington Post, The New Republic, National Review, The Weekly Standard, Commentary,* and *The New England Journal of Medicine.* This essay appeared in the Autumn 2009 issue of *Wilson Quarterly.*

1 In August, the company that owns *Reader's Digest* filed for bankruptcy protection. The magazine, first cobbled together with scissors and paste in a Greenwich Village basement in 1922 by De Witt Wallace and his wife, Lila, was a novel experiment in abridgement—in 62 pages, it offered Americans condensed versions of

current articles from other periodicals. The formula proved wildly successful, and by midcentury *Reader's Digest* was a publishing empire, with millions of subscribers and ventures including *Reader's Digest* Condensed Books, which sold abridged versions of best-selling works by authors such as Pearl Buck and James Michener. *Reader's Digest* both identified and shaped a peculiarly American approach to reading, one that emphasized convenience, entertainment, and the appearance of breadth. An early issue noted that it was "not a magazine in the usual sense, but rather a co-operative means of rendering a time-saving device."

2   The fate of *Reader's Digest* would have been of interest to the late historian and Librarian of Congress Daniel Boorstin. In his renowned 1962 book *The Image: A Guide to Pseudo-Events in America*, Boorstin used *Reader's Digest* as an example of what was wrong with a culture that had learned to prefer image to reality, the copy to the original, the part to the whole. Publications such as the *Digest*, produced on the principle that any essay can be boiled down to its essence, encourage readers to see articles as little more than "a whiff of literary ectoplasm exuding from print," he argued, and an author's style as littered with unnecessary "literary embellishments" that waste a reader's time.

3   Today, of course, abridgement and abbreviation are the norm, and our impatience for information has trained even those of us who never cracked an issue of *Reader's Digest* to prefer 60-second news cycles to 62 condensed pages per month. Free "aggregator" Web sites such as The Huffington Post link to hundreds of articles from other publications every day, and services such as DailyLit deliver snippets of novels directly to our e-mail in-boxes every morning.

4   Our willingness to follow a writer on a sustained journey that may at times be challenging and frustrating is less compelling than our expectation of being conveniently entertained. Over time, this attitude undermines our commitment to the kind of "deep reading" that researcher Maryanne Wolf, in *Proust and the Squid: The Story and Science of the Reading Brain* (2007), argues is important from an early age, when readers learn to identify with characters and to "expand the boundaries of their lives."

5   As Boorstin surveyed the terrain nearly half a century ago, his overarching concern was that an image-saturated culture would so distort people's sense of judgment that they would cease to distinguish between the real and the unreal. He criticized the creation of what he called "pseudo-events" such as politicians' staged photo-ops, and he traced the ways in which our pursuit of illusion transforms our experience of travel, clouds our ability to discern the motivations of advertisers, and encourages us to elevate celebrities to the status of heroes. "This is the appealing contradiction at the heart of our passion for pseudo-events: for made news, synthetic heroes, prefabricated tourist attractions, homogenized interchangeable forms of art and literature (where there are no 'originals,' but only the shadows we make of other shadows)," Boorstin wrote. "We believe we can fill our experience with new-fangled content."

6   Boorstin wrote *The Image* before the digital age, but his book still has a great deal to teach us about the likely future of the printed word. Some of the effects of the Internet appear to undermine Boorstin's occasionally gloomy predictions. For example, an increasing number of us, instead of being passive viewers of images,

are active participants in a new culture of online writing and opinion mongering. We comment on newspaper and magazine articles, post our reviews of books and other products online, write about our feelings on personal blogs, and bombard our friends and acquaintances with status updates on Facebook. As the word migrates from printed page to pixilated screen, so too do more of our daily activities. Online we find news, work, love, social interaction, and an array of entertainment. We have embraced new modes of storytelling, such as the interactive, synthetic world of video games, and found new ways to share our quotidian personal experiences, in hyperkinetic bursts, through micro-blogging services such as Twitter.

7      Many observers have loudly and frequently praised the new technologics as transformative and democratic, which they undoubtedly are. But their widespread use has sparked broader questions about the relevance and value of the printed word and the traditional book. The book, like the wheel, is merely a technology, these enthusiasts argue, and thus we should welcome improvements to it, even if those improvements eventually lead to the book's obsolescence. After all, the deeply felt human need for storytelling won't fade; it will merely take on new forms, forms we should welcome as signs of progress, not decay. As Boorstin observed in the foreword to the 25th-anniversary edition of *The Image*, "We Americans are sensitive to any suggestion that progress may have its price."

8      Our screen-intensive culture poses three challenges to traditional reading: distraction, consumerism, and attention-seeking behavior. Screen technologies such as the cell phone and laptop computer that are supposedly revolutionizing reading also potentially offer us greater control over our time. In practice, however, they have increased our anxiety about having too little of it by making us available anytime and anywhere. These technologies have also dramatically increased our opportunities for distraction. It is a rare Web site that presents its material without the clutter of advertisement, and a rare screen reader who isn't lured by the siren song of an incoming e-mail's "ping!" to set aside her work to see who has written. We live in a world of continuous partial attention, one that prizes speed and brandishes the false promise of multitasking as a solution to our time management challenges. The image-driven world of the screen dominates our attention at the same time that it contributes to a kind of experience pollution that is challenging our ability to engage with the printed word.

9      The digital revolution has also transformed the experience of reading by making it more consumer-oriented. With the advent of electronic readers (and cell phones that can double as e-readers), the book is no longer merely a thing you purchase, but a service to which you subscribe. With the purchase of a traditional book, your consumer relationship ends when you walk out of the bookstore. With a wirelessly connected Kindle or iPhone, or your Wi-Fi–enabled computer, you exist in a perpetual state of potential consumerism. To be sure, for most people reading has never been a pure, quasi-monastic activity; everyday life has always presented distractions to the person keen on losing herself in a book. But for the first time, thanks to new technologies, we are making those distractions an integral part of the experience of reading. Embedded in these new versions of the book are the means for constant and elaborate demands on our attention. And as our experience with other screen media, from television to video games to the Internet, suggests, such distractions are difficult to resist.

10    Finally, the transition from print reading to screen reading has increased our reliance on images and led to a form of "social narcissism" that Boorstin first identified in his book. "We have fallen in love with our own image, with images of our making, which turn out to be images of ourselves," he wrote. We become viewers rather than readers, observers rather than participants. The "common reader" Virginia Woolf prized, who is neither scholar nor critic but "reads for his own pleasure, rather than to impart knowledge or correct the opinions of others," is a vanishing species. Instead, an increasing number of us engage with the written word not to submit ourselves to another's vision or for mere edification, but to have an excuse to share our own opinions.

11    In August, Stanford University released preliminary results from its Stanford Study of Writing, which examined in-class and out-of-class writing samples from thousands of students over five years. One of the study's lead researchers, Andrea Lunsford, concluded, "We're in the midst of a literacy revolution the likes of which we haven't seen since Greek civilization." The source of this revolution, Lunsford proposed, is the "life writing" students do every day online: The study found that 38 percent of their writing occurred outside the classroom.

12    But as Emory University English professor Mark Bauerlein pointed out in a blog post on *The Chronicle of Higher Education's* Web site, this so-called revolution has not translated into concrete improvements in writing skills as measured by standardized tests such as the ACT; nor has it led to a reduction in the number of remedial writing courses necessary to prepare students for the workplace. Of greater concern was the attitude students expressed about the usefulness of writing: Most of them judged the quality of writing by the size of the audience that read it rather than its ability to convey ideas. One of the most prolific contributors to the study, a Stanford undergraduate who submitted more than 700 writing samples ranging from Facebook messages to short stories, told the *Chronicle* that for him a class writing assignment was a "soulless exercise" because it had an audience of one, the professor. He and other students in the study, raised on the Internet, consistently expressed a preference for writing that garnered the most attention from as many people as possible.

13    Our need for stories to translate our experience hasn't changed. Our ability to be deeply engaged readers of those stories is changing. For at least half a century, the image culture has trained us to expect the easily digestible, the quickly paced, and the uncomplicated. As our tolerance for the inconvenient or complex fades, images achieve even more prominence, displacing the word by appealing powerfully to a different kind of emotional sensibility, one whose vividness and urgency are undeniable but whose ability to explore nuance are not the same as that of the printed word.

14    What Boorstin feared—that a society beholden to the image would cease to distinguish the real from the unreal—has not come to pass. On the contrary, we acknowledge the unique characteristics of the virtual world and have eagerly embraced them, albeit uncritically. But Boorstin's other concern—that a culture that craves the image will eventually find itself mired in solipsism and satisfied by secondhand experiences—has been borne out. We follow the Twitter feeds of protesting Iranians and watch video of Michael Jackson's funeral and feel connected to

the rest of the world, even though we lack context for that feeling and don't make much effort to achieve it beyond logging on. The screen offers us the illusion of participation, and this illusion is becoming our preference. As Boorstin observed, "Every day seeing there and hearing there takes the place of being there."

15 This secondhand experience is qualitatively different from the empathy we develop as readers. "We read to know we are not alone," C.S. Lewis once observed, and by this he meant that books are a gateway to a better understanding of what it means to be human. Because the pace is slower and the rewards delayed, the exercise of reading on the printed page requires a commitment unlike that demanded by the screen, as anyone who has embarked on the journey of an ambitiously long novel can attest. What the screen gives us is pleasurable, but it is not the same kind of experience as deeply engaged reading; the "screen literacy" praised by techno-enthusiasts should be seen as a complement to, not a replacement of, traditional literacy.

16 Since the migration of the word from page to screen is still in its early stages, predictions about the future of print are hazardous at best. When *TIME* magazine named "YOU!" its person of the year in 2006, the choice was meant as a celebratory recognition of our new digital world and its many opportunities for self-expression. We are all writers now, crafters of our own images and creators of our own online worlds. But so far this power has made us less, not more, willing to submit ourselves to the singular visions of writers and artists and to learn from the difficult truths about the human condition. It has encouraged us to substitute images and simplistic snippets of text for the range, precision, and peculiar beauty of written language, with its unique power to express complex and abstract ideas. Recent surveys by the National Endowment for the Arts reveal that fewer Americans read literature for pleasure than in the past; writers of serious fiction face a daunting publishing market and a reading public that has come to prefer the celebrity memoir to the new literary novel.

17 There is a reason that the metaphor so often invoked to describe the experience of reading is one of escape: An avid reader can recall the book that first unlocked the door of his imagination or provided a sense of escape from the everyday world. The critic Harold Bloom has written that he was forever changed by his early encounters with books. "My older sisters, when I was very young, took me to the library, and thus transformed my life." As Maryanne Wolf notes, "Biologically and intellectually, reading allows the species to go 'beyond the information given to create endless thoughts most beautiful and wonderful.'"

18 The proliferation of image and text on the Internet has exacerbated the solipsism Boorstin feared, because it allows us to read in a broad but shallow manner. It endorses rather than challenges our sensibilities, and substitutes synthetic images for our own peculiar form of imagination. Over time, the ephemeral, immediate quality of this constant stream of images undermines the self-control required to engage with the written word. And so we find ourselves in the position of living in a highly literate society that chooses not to exercise in the privilege of literacy—indeed, it no longer views literacy as a privilege at all.

19 In *Essays on His Own Times* (1850), Samuel Taylor Coleridge observed, "The great majority of men live like bats, but in twilight, and know and feel the philosophy

of their age only by its reflections and refractions." Today we know our age by its tweets and text messages, its never-ending litany of online posts and ripostes. Judging by the evidence so far, the content we find the most compelling is what we produce about ourselves; our tastes, opinions, and habits. This has made us better interpreters of our own experience, but it has not made us better readers or more empathetic human beings.

### THINKING CRITICALLY

1. Do you own an e-reader such as a Kindle or a Nook? Does an e-reader offer the same experience as a paper volume? Why or why not? Why does Rosen object to e-readers on principle?

2. Rosen extensively references Daniel Boorstin. Specifically, Boorstin was critical of "pseudo-events" that make it difficult to distinguish the real from the unreal. How does modern communication technology challenge our ability to critically assess the world around us? Provide some examples from both the essay and your personal experience.

3. According to Rosen, what challenges to traditional reading does our screen-intensive culture pose? How is it changing the way we think?

4. One goal of persuasive writing is to encourage readers to think about something differently and to get them to take a new position or action. After reading this article, did Rosen change the way you view digital technology? Did her article encourage you to take any action or consider an issue in a different light? Why or why not?

5. According to Rosen, why is reading a text on a screen different from reading it on paper? Do you agree with her viewpoint?

6. Rosen states, "We find ourselves in the position of living in a highly literate society that chooses not to exercise in the privilege of literacy—indeed, it no longer views literacy as a privilege at all." Respond to her comment with your own view. Do you agree that society in general no longer chooses to "exercise the privilege of literacy"? Why or why not?

### WRITING ASSIGNMENTS

1. Deep reading is the process by which readers become immersed in the stories of the people and narratives they read, especially in works of fiction. The term is used by researcher Maryanne Wolf, in *Proust and the Squid: The Story and Science of the Reading Brain* (2007), who argues that deep reading is important from an early age, when readers learn to identify with characters and to "expand the boundaries of their lives." Write about a time when your engagement with the situation and characters in a book expanded the boundaries of your own experience.

2. "We read to know we are not alone," observed author C. S. Lewis. In what ways does the seemingly solitary act of reading, especially reading fiction, make us feel "not alone"? In your opinion, is there a difference between reading literature and reading text online? In your response, connect back to Lewis's point about the inclusive, communal nature of reading.

3. Rosen asserts, "we are all writers now, crafters of our own images and creators of our own online worlds." Write a short essay exploring how you are a writer.

What do you write? To whom and in what context? Do you write "outside of yourself"—that is, about other people, places, experiences, or ideas-or does your writing focus on yourself as an individual—your own ideas, thoughts, and views you wish others to consider? Explain.

4. Rosen fears that online writing has "encouraged us to substitute images and simplistic snippets of text for the range, precision, and peculiar beauty of written language, with its unique power to express complex and abstract ideas." Respond to her statement with your own viewpoint. Support your opinion with concrete examples and evidence.

# Is PowerPoint the Devil?
*Julia Keller*

PowerPoint, a presentation program by Microsoft, has changed the way businesses, educators, and students convey information and even share ideas. Some critics also believe it is changing the way we think—and not for the better. Designed as a time-saving tool that allows users to convey information quickly in an organized and attractive manner, PowerPoint, some argue, encourages us to reduce ideas and concepts into a series of bullet points. What accounts for the widespread and pervasive popularity of this program? How is it shaping business and academia? And what might we expect in the future?

Julia Keller is a Pulitzer Prize–winning journalist who currently works for the *Chicago Tribune* as its cultural critic. She has taught writing at Princeton University and is often a guest essayist on the PBS program "The NewsHour with Jim Lehrer." She is the author of *Mr. Gatling's Terrible Marvel: The Gun That Changed Everything and the Misunderstood Genius Who Invented It* (2008). This article appeared in the *Chicago Tribune* on January 22, 2003.

1 Halftime.

2 Your football team is behind—way, way behind—and there's a feeling in the locker room of heavy, clotted gloom. Everyone slouches on the floor against lockers and benches. Doom-induced lethargy pervades the place. Even the towels are too limp to swat at a teammate's derriere. And then the coach appears. Moving purposefully to the center of the room, he eyes the despairing players. He rubs his hands together as if they were kindling for inspiration.

3 At this point, the coach can:

• Deliver a rousing, emotion-laced speech exhorting the players to press on in the face of tremendous adversity and daunting odds, or
• Cue up a PowerPoint presentation on the six keys to victory, including bulleted items such as "Proper blocking and tackling," "Exhibiting a winning attitude," "Turning weaknesses into strengths" and "Don't focus on the scoreboard," along with a multimedia photo montage of memorable game-winning plays set to the soundtrack of "Rudy."

4 Which approach is more likely to send the team back onto the field poised for a comeback?

5      Your answer instantly drop-kicks you into one of two camps:

- Those who believe in the power of a freewheeling address, full of digressions and personal chemistry, to change hearts and minds most effectively.
- Those who believe in PowerPoint.

6      And while the cultural scoreboard may be invisible, this much is indisputable: The PowerPoint people are winning.

7      Actually, it's not even close. PowerPoint, the public-speaking application included in the Microsoft Office software package, is one of the most pervasive and ubiquitous technological tools ever concocted. In less than a decade, it has revolutionized the worlds of business, education, science and communications, swiftly becoming the standard for just about anybody who wants to explain just about anything to just about anybody else. From corporate middle managers reporting on production goals to fourth graders fashioning a show-and-tell on the French and Indian War to church pastors explicating the seven deadly sins—although seven is a trifle too many bullet points for an audience to absorb comfortably, as any veteran PowerPoint user will tell you—the software seems to be everywhere.

8      The phenomenon parallels the rise of the presentation as the basic unit of group communication. To be sure, there have always been presentations—although Martin Luther managed to get his 95 theses across just by nailing them to a church door—but they used to be low-key affairs accompanied by chalkboards or large pads of paper on easels. A great deal of interpersonal communication got done simply by means of that reviled but effective tool known as the memo.

9      Then came the 1970s, the era that brought us role-playing games, bonding and the sharing of feelings, soon to be followed by the 1980s, an epoch of networking, business retreats and mission statements. Communal settings began to be seen as the ideal venue for the transfer of information, not only because of various economies of scale but because the shoulder-to-shoulder atmosphere seemed to add validation to the material and a general bonhomie that helped cement the organization. Suddenly, like oaks toppling unheard in the forest, ideas seemed to lack existence if they weren't first trotted out in front of a large group of colleagues by a presenter armed with "visual aids"—overhead transparencies or photographic slides.

10     But slides and transparencies are often difficult to create. Moreover, the thought of presenting was enough to paralyze many people trying to make their way unobtrusively through the shoals of large organizations and research establishments. Nobody could possibly have enough slides to fill an entire presentation without verbal content. Sooner or later the speaker would have to . . . talk! . . . doing so from either a dry, prepared text or, God help them, from memory or even off the cuff.

11     It was into this breach that PowerPoint leaped. With PowerPoint, you could fit your entire presentation onto a computer disk and use a laptop to project it, in sequential order, onto a screen that the audience could watch. All your information and visuals could be arranged on discrete "pages" or "slides" full of headings and bulleted points that broke your talk down into coherent bits, similar to the outlines that your elementary school teacher tried vainly to teach you in the days when the only networking you wanted to do was watch "Scooby-Doo" and "The Munsters."

12    All at once, no more slides, no more overheads. Visuals could be scanned directly into the computer and inserted at appropriate places in your program. If you wished, PowerPoint had a variety of graphics you could also nab. Best of all, while you couldn't put all your spoken text onto the screen, you could get enough up there to quell your fears of public speaking.

13    At best, you could embellish upon the bullet points, confident that nerves wouldn't cause you to lose your place as your talk proceeded. At worst, you could stand up there and just recite the bullets as your entire speech, reading them aloud off the screen as if your audience were a tribe of illiterate backwoodsmen who had somehow wandered into a presentation on "A Stochastic Approach to Inelastic Demand for Durable Goods Using a Multifarious Economic Model."

14    But PowerPoint has a dark side. It squeezes ideas into a preconceived format, organizing and condensing not only your material but—inevitably, it seems—your way of thinking about and looking at that material. A complicated, nuanced issue invariably is reduced to headings and bullets. And if that doesn't stultify your thinking about the subject, it may have that effect on your audience—which is at the mercy of your presentation.

15    Eerily, PowerPoint was invented in 1984, that iconic year of Orwellian mind control. That was when Bob Gaskins and Dennis Austin of the Silicon Valley software company Forethought created a PowerPoint precursor called Presenter, which soon was renamed PowerPoint. Forethought and its promising software brainchild were acquired in 1987 by Microsoft, and a Macintosh version of PowerPoint went on sale that year. A Windows version was added in 1990.

16    PowerPoint has been the subject of a jauntily amusing New Yorker profile, a distinction generally reserved for heads of state, notorious criminals or controversial entertainers. The program is so widely used that it needs no introduction, no surrounding nest of associative explanation. Nobody tells the audio-visual guy at the university that has booked him or her to speak, "I'm going to use PowerPoint—you know, that software application that lets you use your computer to put cool stuff up on a screen with neat graphics and even a soundtrack if you want." And the software said something about you. Just to show up for a talk toting an old-fashioned carousel of slides is to label yourself the kind of individual who still has a bag telephone.

17    PowerPoint is way beyond branding. It left branding in the dust long ago. With more than 300 million users worldwide, according to a Microsoft spokesperson, with a share of the presentation software market that is said to top 95 percent and with an increasing number of grade school students indoctrinated every day into the PowerPoint way—chopping up complex ideas and information into bite-sized nuggets of a few words, and then further pureeing those nuggets into bullet items of even fewer words—PowerPoint seems poised for world domination.

18    Its astonishing popularity, the way it has spread exponentially through the culture, seems analogous, in a way, to drugs. Think of it as technological cocaine—so effortless to embrace initially, so difficult to relinquish after that. People who once use PowerPoint generally don't stop using it.

19    People who don't use it can't quite understand what all the fuss is about. And then they use it. And neither they nor their relationship to information is ever quite the same again.

20     Those who harbor reservations about PowerPoint, the iconoclasts who dare to question whether technology is always an unalloyed good, are difficult to coax into the open, so powerful is technology's grip on the human imagination in the 21st century. Anyone who asks, "Yes, we can—but should we?" about any technology risks being branded an antediluvian.

21     Author Lewis Mumford neatly captured this prejudice in a 1970 essay in which he lamented a widespread "technological compulsiveness." Western culture, he said, "has accepted as unquestionable a technological imperative that is quite as arbitrary as the most primitive taboo: not merely (is it) the duty to foster invention and constantly to create technological novelties, but equally the duty to surrender to these novelties unconditionally just because they are offered, without respect to their human consequences."

22     PowerPoint may be an easier, spiffier way to present information, but is it a better way? As the software spreads into more schools, as an increasing number of teachers employ it in their lectures and require students to use it in their class presentations, certain questions hover persistently just to one side of the glowing screen:

23     Is PowerPoint changing not only the way we do business and educate our young, but also the way we think?

24     "I hate PowerPoint," said Jay Phelan, an evolutionary biologist who teaches at the University of California at Los Angeles and is co-author of "Mean Genes" (2000), a study of how brain structure affects behavior. "I'm one of the few," he added ruefully.

25     Most of Phelan's colleagues use PowerPoint in their lectures and his students often request such presentations from him. But he resists distilling the contents of his lectures—the creative interplay of a teacher's knowledge and the students' hunger for ideas, as manifested in rhetorical display—into a series of bullet items.

26     "I spend a lot of time identifying what works in lectures," said Phelan. "It's not about a content transfer from the teacher to the other person. The students have the information. It's something else that gets conveyed in a good lecture. That gets lost when you use PowerPoint."

27     Is it changing our brains, though? Hard to say, Phelan replies, since evolutionary changes occur over millennia, not decades. Yet it is certainly affecting our creativity, he believes.

28     The point of PowerPoint—making presentations simple to prepare, so simple that a second grader can do it during commercial breaks of "SpongeBob SquarePants"—is what makes it dangerous to our imaginations, Phelan warns. "In their (Microsoft's) attempts to make PowerPoint easier to use, they have all these templates. They totally limit your ability to express yourself. Everybody's using the same color palette. It's one more way to choke the life out of creativity."

29     Indeed, the program helpfully provides something called AutoContent Wizard, which all but writes the presentation for you. From a hefty list of potential speech topics, you click on the one you want, say, "Project Overview," "Selling Your Ideas" or "Managing HR's Changing Role," and the software burps out some 10 to 12 slides with prompts and even some virtual text.

30     Such principled contrariness as Phelan's may be fine for a high-minded professor trailing an Ivy League Ph.D.—Phelan studied under renowned Harvard biologist

E. O. Wilson—but for businesswomen and men, resistance to PowerPoint is futile, said Clarke L. Caywood, associate professor of integrated marketing at Northwestern University. "No one in business today could pretend to be facile in business communications without PowerPoint," he declared. "It's like being able to read."

31    Caywood, an early fan of the software whose passion has remained strong, said his own lectures and speeches are all done on PowerPoint, and soon the whole world may be doling out information in bullet items with diverting graphics thrown in. "I don't see anything on the horizon that's going to bump it," he said. "This (PowerPoint) is really smoking."

32    More than 80 percent of the presentations given by business-school students rely on PowerPoint rather than the old-fashioned flowing narrative, Caywood said. And that's fortuitous, because once in the business world, those students will be employing PowerPoint on a regular basis, he added. Indeed, a Microsoft spokesman once estimated that some 30 million PowerPoint presentations are made daily by business professionals around the world.

33    "I'm not guilty of any crime in asking my students to develop this expertise," Caywood said. "Every business requires it now."

34    But what's fine for a business professional might not be so fine for a child just learning how to think, how to connect ideas, said Sherry Turkle, a professor at the Massachusetts Institute of Technology and director of MIT's Initiative on Technology and Self.

35    "These technologies are changing the way we think," said Turkle. "They change how our kids grow up and how they process information. They're not passive."

36    Software such as PowerPoint tends to prize "binary assumptions," Turkle noted, by jamming complex thoughts into brief snippets. "We have a technology that is encouraging us to see things in black and white—but is this a time when we need to see things in black and white? Good and bad? This kind of 'three bullets up and down' isn't helping us come up with the right kinds of arguments. It's not particularly what third graders need."

37    Turkle's reservations are not about PowerPoint per se—she uses it all the time, she admits—but about the increasing cultural mandate to have grade-school children become proficient in its use.

38    "It's one of the most popular softwares in elementary and secondary schools," she said. "But PowerPoint doesn't teach children to make an argument. It teaches them to make a point, which is quite a different thing. It encourages presentation, not conversation. Students grow accustomed to not being challenged. A strong presentation is designed to close down debate, rather than open it up."

39    Turkle, author of seminal books on the cultural consequences of technology such as "The Second Self: Computers and the Human Spirit" (1984) and "Life on the Screen: Identity in the Age of the Internet" (1995), added, "I don't want to make PowerPoint the motor for an apocalyptic future. But it's part of a general trend. It's one element among others that keep us from complexity. We face a very complex world. History is quite complex. Current events and literature are complex. Students are thinking and doing presentations on complicated things, and we need them to be able to think about them in complicated ways.

40      "PowerPoint is not a step in the right direction. It's an exemplar of a technology we should be quite skeptical about as a pedagogical tool."

41      How pervasive is PowerPoint among grade-school children? Exact numbers of PowerPoint users among the LePage's-and-Crayola set are hard to come by because, explains Eric Herzog, a product manager at Microsoft, individual school districts and sometimes even individual schools within those districts make their own decisions about technology use in the classroom.

42      "Overseas, we see more top-level decision-making. But in the United States, all states and all districts do it differently," said Herzog, who works in the company's Education Solutions division.

43      Microsoft supplies PowerPoint and other applications to schools at a substantial discount, Herzog said. Although the software originally was intended for the business market, by 1998 "teachers had discovered it," he said. They used it to present lessons and, more recently, to help students hone their proficiency with computers.

44      "Teachers like it because it's a content-empty tool," Herzog continued. "It's an open-ended tool. All the ideas, all the creativity, comes from the kids. PowerPoint is a tool they can use to express their creative ideas."

45      But what about the charges that PowerPoint slices and dices complexity and ambiguity? That it changes kids' thinking from a flowering tree of associative learning and rapturous discovery to the grim lockstep of an outline with one-size-fits-all clip art? That its fancy graphics can mask a lack of actual content?

46      "It's important to make sure it's used in the proper way," Herzog stated. "It's certainly not a replacement for other tools in the classroom."

47      Elizabeth Cochran, of the Chicago Public Schools, makes a similar point—a verbal point, that is, not a PowerPoint point: Technology is not inherently good or bad. Only its usage can be labeled that way.

48      "A PowerPoint presentation is not going to replace a long-term research paper," insisted Cochran, an instructional technology coordinator. Technology is now part of the curriculum as early as prekindergarten classes, she said. "It supports engaged learning. The research does show that when teaching is used in ways that make students participants in their own learning experience, it enhances the educational experience. It's a way of capitalizing on student interest."

49      No one doubts that kids love gadgets and gizmos, but, critics ask, since when do we let students decide what's good for them? Isn't that like replacing spinach on the school lunch menu with Oreos?

50      At any rate, Cochran noted, "We live in the digital age. It's important to incorporate it. Regardless of what career a student goes into, be it a restaurateur or the president of IBM, there will be a level of technology they'll need.

51      "As I said, PowerPoint will not replace a research paper," she added, "but if a student writes a paper, PowerPoint might be a way to deliver that paper in front of a group of people. It can always be used in a way that's not effective. But a chalkboard can be used in a way that's not effective, too."

52      The world of cultural observers, then, is large enough to contain both those enthralled by PowerPoint and those appalled by it, those who readily welcome new technologies and those who believe that all technologies need to be interrogated as relentlessly as murder suspects.

53 "I'm surprised at how resistant I've become to PowerPoint and such classroom technologies," mused Todd Parker, an English professor at DePaul University. "When they were first introduced, I thought I'd be happy to use such aids, but after trying several of them, especially PowerPoint, I've come to loathe them all with a passion—in particular because they easily become a crutch for the poor student and a stumbling block to students already too disengaged from the act of learning.

54 "My biggest complaint," Parker said, "is that they come between the teacher and his or her students. The danger is that class tends to devolve into a slide show from which students too often retreat to that room behind their eyeballs. My seven years at DePaul have taught me that the most valuable relationship between teacher and student is charismatic and immediate, one in which the teacher actively engages the students personally. This is hard to do when you turn the effort of instruction over to a machine.

55 "I even think that it's less important what I teach my students than how I challenge them morally and intellectually." Hard to imagine a PowerPoint presentation doing that.

56 Yet Roger Graves, Parker's colleague in the DePaul English department, is a PowerPoint enthusiast. "The educational evidence in support of the use of this technology is too strong," said Graves, who routinely posts his PowerPoint-fueled lectures on the Internet for students to peruse at their leisure. "Used properly, this technology changes what goes on in classrooms . . . The core teaching skill is not lecturing or even orchestrating class discussion, but instead creating a learning environment and motivating students. The focus becomes more on learning and less on teaching."

57 Howard Gardner, the well-known developmental psychologist who has written extensively about children's creativity and pioneered the concept of multiple intelligences, might seem like a perfect candidate to lead the anti-PowerPoint charge, especially in public schools, where rote use of the software might channel kids' minds into preordained pathways. But he's a PowerPoint man to the bone.

58 "I certainly don't see it as bad for students and learners," declared Gardner, who uses PowerPoint regularly in his public lectures. "I certainly don't think that it stifles creativity, and might even stimulate it if the technology is used imaginatively and synergistically with other paraphernalia."

59 "Like any other technology, it can be overused and distorted," cautioned Gardner, the John H. and Elizabeth A. Hobbs Professor of Cognition and Education at the Harvard University Graduate School of Education. "(But) PowerPoint is itself quite flexible and so there is no need for it to simplify or oversimplify students' presentations. If a student falls into a bad habit or uses it in a rigid fashion, teachers should give helpful feedback, just as if a student always wrote a paper in exactly the same way."

60 Others, however, bristle at the fact that PowerPoint presentations can be stamped out like machine parts. An essay by Thomas A. Stewart in an issue of *Fortune* last year was titled, "Ban It Now! Friends Don't Let Friends Use PowerPoint." Stewart argued that the software was turning business presentations into boring assembly-line products. "Why in the world would you want a uniform look?" Stewart asked, adding theatrically: "Never put more than three bullet points in a

PowerPoint show, experts say. It confuses people. Keep it simple." Then with rich sarcasm: "You know that life is."

61    The *Wall Street Journal* reported in December on PowerPoint's relentless march into grade-school classrooms, raising a few mild concerns among educators that the software's bells and whistles, its dazzling doodads, could transform mediocre student work into triumphs—at least on a superficial level.

62    And it's the superficiality, not the fact that PowerPoint may dumb down complex ideas, that bothers Larry Nighswander.

63    "People get overwhelmed with what they can do and forget that moderation is an important part," said Nighswander, director of the School of Visual Communications at Ohio University and a former *National Geographic* photographer.

64    PowerPoint is now the preferred software of photographers making presentations of their work to professors or prospective employers, Nighswander said. "But it can become visual noise. Nobody sees the content anymore. They're thinking, 'I wonder if this screen is going to blast out of the corner or break into little pieces?' When you're first shown what sophisticated software can do, you think, 'Oh, wow, I'll be able to do this or that.' It takes time to figure out if that can make a better presentation or if it's all just decoration.

65    "There's the old axiom in design that said, 'Less is more.' They should have that printed on the outside of the PowerPoint box. It needs a warning label."

66    So should all technologies, even the most benign-seeming ones, Neil Postman would say. Postman is the New York University professor who has turned out book after book asking us to stop and reflect before rushing headlong into technology's chilly embrace.

67    "Technology is ideology," he writes in his most famous polemic, "Amusing Ourselves to Death: Public Discourse in the Age of Show Business" (1985). "To be unaware that a technology comes equipped with a program for social change, to maintain that technology is neutral, to make the assumption that technology is always a friend to culture is, at this late hour, stupidly plain and simple."

68    What sort of world is reflected in PowerPoint? A world stripped down to briefly summarized essences, a world snipped clean of the annoying underbrush of ambiguity and complication. But is that the world in which we want to live? And are the values prized by businesses—succinctness, directness, manipulation of symbols—also the values we want running our schools and nurturing our children?

69    On the other hand, don't computers help everyone to work smarter and faster, and aren't students immeasurably enriched by an easy familiarity with technologies such as PowerPoint?

70    What do you think?—assuming that you still can, that is, after prolonged exposure to PowerPoint.

### THINKING CRITICALLY

1. What is the author's personal opinion of PowerPoint? Identify areas of her article that reveal her viewpoint.

2. Have you used PowerPoint? Taken classes in which it was used by an instructor? By other students? Describe your own views on the strengths and weaknesses of this program, connecting your thoughts to points made in Keller's article.

3. What social changes lead to PowerPoint's conquest of the American board-room? What accounts for its popularity?

4. What are some of the drawbacks to PowerPoint? Do you agree with any of the criticism leveled against it?

5. Do you think that PowerPoint is indeed influencing the way we think and process information? Explain.

6. Evaluate the author's conclusion and answer the questions she poses in her final two paragraphs.

## WRITING ASSIGNMENTS

1. Create your own PowerPoint deck for the "losing team" described in Keller's introduction. Use the titles Keller provides as well as any others you think need to be added.

2. Read "Is Google Making Us Stoopid?" by Nicholas Carr on page 509 and compare his points to ones raised by Keller and Norvig. Write an essay in which you address the ways technology may be influencing how we think. Drawing on information provided in both essays, explore whether these changes may be for the better—or for the worse.

## Exploring the Language of V I S U A L S

## Lincoln's Gettysburg Address—A PowerPoint Presentation

**And now please welcome President Abraham Lincoln**
Good morning. Just a second while I get this connection to work. Do I press this button here? Function-F7? No, that's not right. Hmmm. Maybe I'll have to reboot. Hold on a minute. Um, my name is Abe Lincoln and I'm your president. While we're waiting, I want to thank Judge David Wills, chairman of the committee supervising the dedication of the Gettysburg cemetery. It's great to be here, Dave, and you and the committee are doing a great job. Gee, sometimes this new **technology** does have glitches, but **we couldn't live without it, could we?** Oh—is it ready? OK, here we go:

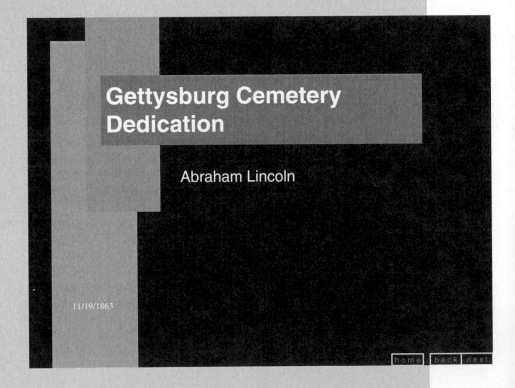

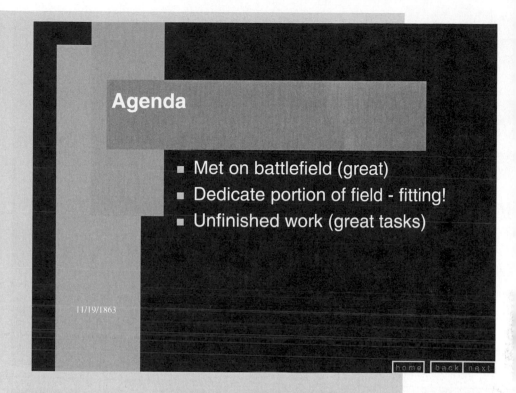

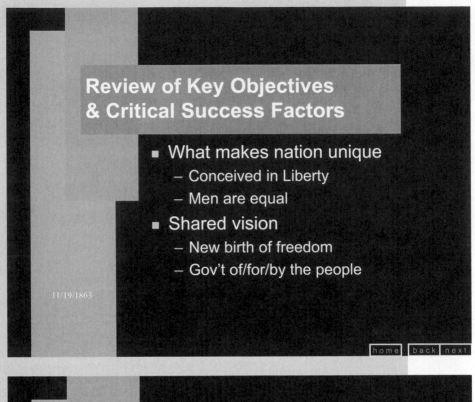

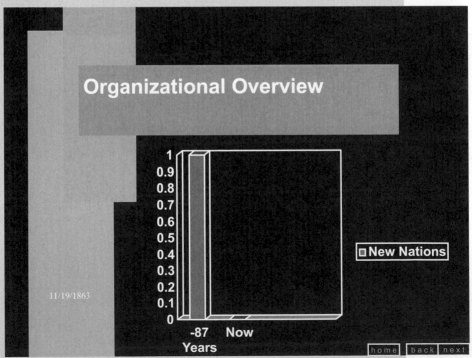

## Summary

- New nation
- Civil war
- Dedicate field
- Dedicated to unfinished work
- New birth of freedom
- Government not perish

11/19/1863

home   back   next

## PowerPoint Speaker Notes

*[Transcribed from voice recording by A. Lincoln, 11/18/63]*

*These are some notes on the Gettysburg meeting. I'll whip them into better shape when I can get on to my computer.*

"Four score and seven years ago our fathers brought forth on this continent a new nation, conceived in liberty and dedicated to the proposition that all men are created equal. Now we are engaged in a great civil war, testing whether that nation or any nation so conceived and so dedicated can long endure. We are met on a great battlefield of that war. We have come to dedicate a portion of that field as a final resting-place for those who here gave their lives that that nation might live. It is altogether fitting and proper that we should do this. But in a larger sense, we cannot dedicate, we cannot consecrate, we cannot hallow this ground. The brave men, living and dead, who struggled here have consecrated it far above our poor power to add or detract. The world will little note nor long remember what we say here, but it can never forget what they did here. It is for us the living rather to be dedicated here to the unfinished work which they who fought here have thus far so nobly advanced. It is rather for us to be here dedicated to the great task remaining before us—that from these honored dead we take increased devotion to that cause for which they gave the last full measure of devotion—that we here highly resolve that these dead shall not have died in vain, that this nation under God shall have a new birth of freedom, and that government of the people, by the people, for the people shall not perish from the earth."

# The Making of the *Gettysburg PowerPoint Presentation*
*Peter Norvig*

Peter Norvig is director of research at Google Inc. He is a fellow of the American Association for Artificial Intelligence and the Association for Computing Machinery and coauthor of *Artificial Intelligence: A Modern Approach*. Before joining Google, he served as head of computational sciences at NASA, an assistant professor at the University of Southern California, and a research faculty member at the University of California at Berkeley Computer Science Department, as well as a faculty member at USC and Berkeley. He created the Gettysburg PowerPoint Presentation, which has received critical acclaim in many academic and professional circles. In the next essay, Norvig explains why he created the PowerPoint presentation and discusses some of the perils of PowerPoint. You may view the presentation in color at http://www.norvig.com/Gettysburg/index.htm, where you can also read Norvig's entire description of the creation of the presentation and its success over the last 10 years.

## Why I Did It

*"Doesn't he realize this presentation is a waste of time? Why doesn't he just tell us what matters and get it over with?"*

1   How many times have you heard (or muttered) that? How many of us have been frustrated at seeing too many presentations where PowerPoint or other visual aids obscure rather than enhance the point? After one too many bad presentations at a meeting in January 2000, I decided to see if I could *do* something about it.

## How I Did It

2   Back in my hotel room I imagined what Abe Lincoln might have done if he had used PowerPoint rather than the power of oratory at Gettysburg. (I chose the Gettysburg speech because it was shorter than, say, the Martin Luther King "I have a dream" speech, and because I had an idea for turning "four score and seven years" into a gratuitous graph.) A Google search easily found the text of the Gettysburg address, and several articles echoing my frustration, including *USA Today* writer Kevin Maney's PowerPoint obsession takes off, which notes that PowerPoint was banned at Sun, and includes the Lincoln idea: *"Put another way, imagine if Abe Lincoln had PowerPoint for the Gettysburg Address. 'OK, this slide shows our nation four score and seven years ago.'"*

3       But as far as I could tell, nobody had actually *written* and published a Gettysburg PowerPoint presentation. (Note: a reader pointed out that John S. Rigden had an article in the March 1990 issue of *Physics Today* entitled "The Lost Art of Oratory: Damn the Overhead Projector" that also used the Gettysburg Address concept. David Wittenberg and Susan Hessler were nice enough to send me copies.) I started up PowerPoint and let the "Autocontent Wizard" help me create a new presentation. I selected the "Company Meeting (Online)" template, and figured from there I'd be creative in adding bad design wherever possible. I was surprised that the Autocontent Wizard had anticipated my desires so well that I had to make very few

changes. Four of the slide titles were taken directly from the template; I only had to delete a few I didn't need, and add "Not on the Agenda" after "Agenda."

4    I wasn't a professional designer, so I thought I'd be in for a late night doing some serious research: in color science to find a truly garish color scheme; in typography to find the worst fonts; and in overall design to find a really bad layout. But fortunately for me, the labor-saving Autocontent Wizard took care of all this for me! It suggested a red-on-dark-color choice for the navigation buttons that makes them very hard to see; it chose a serif font for the date that is illegible in low-resolution web mode, and of course Excel outdid itself on the graph, volunteering the 0.1 to 0.9 between the 0 and 1 new nations. All I had to do was take Lincoln's words and break them into pieces, making sure that I captured the main phrases of the original, while losing all the flow, eloquence, and impact.

5    I posted the presentation on my web site that night and promptly forgot about it. But some people noticed, and it began to spread by word of mouth (and link, and email).

## Press

6    Early citers include Daniel Dern's newsletter (he's Executive Editor at Byte.com), memepool, Phil Greenspun, Bill St. Clair, and the Gadwell group. Paul E. Schindler wrote *"OK, now all my website of the week recommendations are worth going to, but this one especially so, if for no other reason that the slide headed, "Things We Aren't Going To Do," (sic) with the bullet points "Dedicate. Consecrate. Hallow." Now that's funny. Is PowerPoint the medium Bob Newhart would be working in if he were just starting out today?"* I'm deeply honored by the comparison to Newhart (and I appreciate that Paul has resisted the temptation to call his recommendations "Schindler's list"). Later, Sherif Ghali wrote *"I haven't laughed this much since Roberto Benigni's Il Mostro."* Ed Tufte, the reigning guru of visual interface design, called it *"the trump card of subversive and ironic PP productions."*

7    On November 20, 2000, just six score and 17 years and 1 day after the original Gettysburg address, Tom Weber of the *Wall Street Journal* published an article on user interface design, focusing on the web and on the topic of the day, ballot design (remember butterfly ballots and pregnant chad?). Weber cited the usual suspects: Tufte, Don Norman and Jakob Nielsen, but also threw in the parenthetical remark: *(For a hilarious look at how Lincoln's Gettysburg Address would have fared in PowerPoint form, visit Peter Norvig's Web site at www.norvig.com (norvig.com) and see "all men are created equal" reduced to a bullet point.)* I quickly learned that *WSJ* readers are an early-rising bunch: by 7:00 AM east coast time web hits started rolling in, and my site was overwhelmed and shut down for the first and only time. Fortunately I was able to quickly set up a mirror site.

8    It is clear I struck a chord that reverberates with many people out there. (To me the really amazing thing is not that many people have seen it, but that 80% make it all the way through the six slides; experts will tell you it is unusual to get more than half to click through to the second page.) My immediate reaction was that maybe I had a hidden talent. Maybe I was a kind of *idiot savant* of bad design. I was also reminded of the time I saw the movie *The Big Picture* in LA with my friends in "the

industry," Gary and Rachel. *The Big Picture* starts with a scene about bad student movies, which was amusing to me as a naive viewer, but apparently hilarious to industry insiders, who recognize how all the rules had been broken. I had succeeded in breaking all the rules, but incredibly, the Autocontent Wizard did most of the work for me.

## Email

9  Hundreds of people have taken the time to write me a nice note, and dozens have asked permission to use my presentation in a course or presentation of their own. I particularly like Reading Great Speeches, Making Great Speeches by Shery Kearney. I got a piece of customized junk mail showing a version of the presentation that had been "improved" by some fancy graphics, another company that wanted to add a voice-over to it, a macromedia version by Raffaele Sena, and a clever version of the Declaration of Independence.

10  In all this, there have been only four negative comments. One echoed back the opening words of this page ("Doesn't he realize this presentation is a waste of time? Why doesn't he just tell us what matters and get it over with?"). Two came from civil war buffs who thought that the battle of Gettysburg was just too serious and solemn an event to be the subject of satire. I replied that it really wasn't about Gettysburg, it was about PowerPoint, but I can empathize with their point of view. Some things are just too sacred to mess with, no matter what. I mean, can you imagine if someone wanted to make a musical about Hitler? The final criticism came from someone who wrote:

> *Is this a high school attempt at something. Someone should take the time to review color combinations to make a presentation that is pleasant to the viewer. Red lettering on a black background works well in print, but not on computers as the color generation is lacking. It's not very readable.*

11  Oh well, as someone once said, you can't fool (or please) all of the people all of the time.

### THINKING CRITICALLY

1.  Why did Norvig create the Gettysburg Address PowerPoint presentation? What point was he trying to make?

2.  What makes the presentation funny? Why does it work? Explain.

3.  Why does Norvig include the criticism for his presentation as well as the praise? What is notable about it? Explain.

### WRITING ASSIGNMENT

1.  Create your own PowerPoint satire in which you distill a (short) famous speech into a PowerPoint presentation. You may use the "Autocontent Wizard," as Norvig did with his presentation, or embellish and enhance your presentation in any way you wish. Remember to include a copy of the speech in the Notes section of the presentation.

# Blogging in the Global Lunchroom
*Geoffrey Nunberg*

Millions of Americans have blogged at some point in their lives—either through creating their own blogs or responding to one. A blog ("Web log") is an online diary or commentary site that features regular entries that describe events, impressions, and viewpoints. Blogs may contain text, images, and video and often link to other websites, blogs, and online media. Most blogs allow readers to comment on the content of the post and to each other. As of 2007, the Blog Search Engine estimated there were over 112 million blogs. While many blogs are maintained by individuals, some are run by journals, newspapers, and other media outlets. Most blogs are not monitored for factual accuracy and often express the opinion and views of the blogger writing the content. Now that blogging has become its own genre, it is beginning to influence more creative types of writing. Author Geoffrey Nunberg explores how blogging may have begun and gives his readers insight into what we may expect next from the blogging culture.

Geoffrey Nunberg is an American linguist and a professor at the UC Berkeley School of Information. He has written extensively about the cultural and social implications of new technologies and language. Nunberg has been commenting on language, usage, and culture for National Public Radio's *Fresh Air* program since 1988. His commentaries on language also appear frequently in *The New York Times*. He serves as chair of the American Heritage Dictionary usage panel. Nunberg is the author of several books, including *The Way We Talk Now: Commentaries on Language and Culture* (2001) and *Talking Right* (2006). This essay is transcribed from a commentary broadcast on *Fresh Air* that aired on April 20, 2004.

1 Over the last couple of months, I've been posting on a group blog called languagelog.org, which was launched by a couple of linguists as a place where we could vent our comments on the passing linguistic scene.

2 Still, I don't quite have the hang of the form. The style that sounds perfectly normal in a public radio feature or an op-ed piece comes off as distant and pontifical when I use it in a blog entry. Reading over my own postings, I recall what Queen Victoria once said about Gladstone: "He speaks to me as if I were a public meeting."

3 I'm not the only one with this problem. A lot of newspapers have been encouraging or even requiring their writers to start blogs. But with some notable exceptions, most journalists have the same problems that I do. They do all the things you should do in a newspaper feature. They fashion engaging ledes, they develop their arguments methodically, they give context and background, and tack helpful IDs onto the names they introduce—"New York Senator Charles E. Schumer (D)."

4 That makes for solid journalism, but it's not really blogging. Granted, that word can cover a lot of territory. A recent Pew Foundation study found that around three million Americans have tried their hands at blogging, and sometimes there seem to be almost that many variants of the form. Blogs can be news summaries, opinion columns, or collections of press releases, like the official blogs of the presidential candidates. But the vast majority are journals posted by college students, office workers, or stay-at-home moms, whose average readership is smaller than

a family Christmas letter. (The blog hosting site livejournal.com reports that two thirds of bloggers are women—I'm not sure what to make of that proportion.)

5     But when people puzzle over the significance of blogs nowadays, they usually have in mind a small number of A-List sites that traffic in commentary about politics, culture, or technology—blogs like Altercation, Instapundit, Matthew Yglesias, Talking Points or Doc Searls. It's true that bloggers like these have occasionally come up with news scoops, but in the end they're less about breaking stories than bending them. And their language is a kind of anti-journalese. It's informal, impertinent, and digressive, casting links in all directions. In fact one archetypal blog entry consists entirely of a cryptic comment that's linked to another blog or a news item—"Oh, *please*," or "*He's* married to *her*?"

6     That interconnectedness is what leads enthusiasts to talk about the blogosphere, as if this were all a single vast conversation—at some point in these discussions, somebody's likely to trot out the phrase "collective mind." But if there's a new public sphere assembling itself out there, you couldn't tell from the way bloggers address their readers—not as anonymous citizens, the way print columnists do, but as co-conspirators who are in on the joke.

7     Taken as a whole, in fact, the blogging world sounds a lot less like a public meeting than the lunchtime chatter in a high-school cafeteria, complete with snarky comments about the kids at the tables across the room. (Bloggers didn't invent the word *snarky*, but they've had a lot to do with turning it into the metrosexual equivalent of *bitchy*. On the Web, blogs account for more than three times as large a share of the total occurrences of *snarky* as of the occurrences of *irony*.)[1]

8     Some people say this all started with Mickey Kaus's column in *Slate*, though Kaus himself cites the old *San Francisco Chronicle* columns of Herb Caen. And Camille Paglia not surprisingly claims that her column in Salon.com was the first true blog, and adds that the genre has been going downhill ever since.

9     But blogs were around on the Web well before Kaus or Paglia first logged in.[2] And if you're of a mind to, you can trace their print antecedents a lot further back than Caen or Hunter S. Thompson. That informal style recalls the colloquial voice that Addison and Steele devised when they invented the periodical essay in the early 18th century, even if few blogs come close to that in artfulness. Then too, those essays were written in the guise of fictive personae like Isaac Bickerstaff and Sir Roger de Coverly, who could be the predecessors of pseudonymous bloggers like Wonkette, Atrios, or Skippy the Bush Kangaroo, not to mention the mysterious conservative blogger who goes by the name of Edward Boyd.[3]

10     For that matter, my languagelog co-contributor Mark Liberman recalls that Plato always had Socrates open his philosophical disquisitions with a little diary entry, the way bloggers like to do: "I went down yesterday to see the festival at the Peiraeus with Glaucon, the son of Ariston, and I ran into my old buddy Cephalus and we got to talking about old age . . ."

11     Of course whenever a successful new genre emerges, it seems to have been implicit in everything that preceded it. But in the end, this is a mug's game, like asking whether the first SUV was a minivan, a station wagon, or an off-road vehicle.

12     The fact is that this is a genuinely new language of public discourse—and a paradoxical one. On the one hand, blogs are clearly a more democratic form

of expression than anything the world of print has produced. But in some ways they're also more exclusionary, and not just because they only reach about a tenth of the people who use the Web.[4] The high, formal style of the newspaper op-ed page may be nobody's native language, but at least it's a neutral voice that doesn't privilege the speech of any particular group or class. Whereas blogspeak is basically an adaptation of the table talk of the urban middle class—it isn't a language that everybody in the cafeteria is equally adept at speaking. Not that there's anything wrong with chewing over the events of the day with the other folks at the lunch table, but you hope that everybody in the room is at least reading the same newspapers at breakfast.[5]

## Notes

1. This is a rough estimate, arrived at by taking the proportion of total Google hits for a word that occur in a document that also contains the word blog:

   *snarky*: 87,700
   *snarky* + *blog*: 32,600 (37%)
   *irony*: 1,600,000
   *irony* + *blog*: 168,000 (10.5%)

   Of course the fact that the word *blog* appears in a page doesn't necessarily mean that it is a blog, but it turns out that more than 90 percent of the pages containing the word are blog pages, and in any case, the effect would be the same for both terms. And while some part of this variation no doubt reflects the status of *snarky* as a colloquial word that is less likely to show up in serious literary discussions and the like, the effect is nowhere near so marked when we look at the word *bitchy*:

   *bitchy*: 250,000
   *bitchy* + *blog*: 43,700 (17.5%)

   That is, the specialization to blogs is more than twice as high for *snarky* as for *bitchy*, even though both are colloquial items.

2. Many have given credit for inventing the genre to Dave Winer, whose Scripting News was one of the earliest weblogs, though Winer himself says that the first weblog was Tim Berners-Lee's page at CERN. But you could argue that *blog* has moved out from under the derivational shadow of its etymon—the word isn't just a truncation of *weblog* anymore. In which case, the identity of the first "real blog" is anybody's guess—and it almost certainly will be.

3. James Wolcott makes a similar comparison in the current *Vanity Fair,* and goes so far as to suggest that "If Addison and Steele, the editors of *The Spectator* and *The Tatler*, were alive and holding court at Starbucks, they'd be WiFi-ing into a joint blog."

   That's cute, but I think it gets Addison and Steele wrong—the studied effusions of Isaac Bickerstaff and Sir Roger de Coverly may have sounded like blogs, but they were fashioned with an eye towards a more enduring literary fame. Which is not to say that blogs couldn't become the basis for a genuine literary form. As I noted in a "Fresh Air" piece a few years ago that dealt more with blogs as personal journals:

> There's something very familiar about that accretion of diurnal detail. It's what the novel was trying to achieve when eighteenth-century writers cobbled it together out of subliterary genres like personal letters, journals, and newspapers, with the idea of reproducing the inner and outer experience that makes up daily life. You wonder whether anything as interesting could grow up in the intimate anonymity of cyberspace. (See "I Have Seen the Future, and It Blogs," in *Going Nucular*, PublicAffairs, May 2004.)

So it's not surprising that a number of fictional blogs ("flogs"? "blictions"?) have begun to emerge, adapting the tradition of the fictional diary that runs from *Robinson Crusoe* to *Bridget Jones's Diary*. As to whether that will ultimately amount to "anything as interesting" as the novel, the jury is likely to be out for a while.

4. The Pew study found that 11% of Internet users have read the blogs or diaries of other Internet users.

5. For a diverting picture of the blogosphere-as-lunchroom, see Whitney Pastorek's recent piece in the *Village Voice*, "Blogging Off."

## THINKING CRITICALLY

1. What experience have you had with blogging? If you have written or read blogs, give details about where you went to blog and why. If you have never blogged, explain why you have not.

2. Why do you suppose "that two thirds of bloggers are women"? The author is not sure what to make of this proportion. What do you make of this statistic?

3. What argument is Nunberg making in his last paragraph?

4. How does the title set up the tone for this piece? Do you find his tone and metaphor to be an effective way to get his point across?

5. Nunberg questions whether blogging will lead to "'anything as interesting' as the novel." What is your opinion? Do you think blogging can lead to a new genre? Why or why not?

## WRITING ASSIGNMENTS

1. The author equates blogging with Socrates' philosophical disquisitions and with Addison' and Steele's periodical essays. Do research on these other forms of discourse, and then write a brief essay stating whether you agree that these are the antecedents of blogging.

2. Study a few of your favorite blogging sites and then write an essay analyzing the language used on these sites. Does the language differ from other forms of writing? If so, how and why?

3. Find two recent (within the past year) commentaries written about blogging. Summarize each article and state whether the authors criticize or praise the blogging culture. End by explaining why you agree or disagree with the authors.

# VIRTUALLY SPEAKING

## Texting

*David Crystal*

It may come as a surprise to teens who run up huge cell phone bills texting their friends every month, but text messaging was never meant to be a means of communication between individuals. Conceived for commercial purposes, the first text message, "Merry Christmas," was sent in December 1992 over the Vodafone GSM network. During the late 1990s, text messaging became gradually available commercially, and it exploded in usage by 2002. Language teachers Jill and Charles Hadfield have observed that "textspeak is largely the language of the young—and a lively controversy has sprung up around its use mainly from the older generation who seek to variously analyze, interpret, or decry its use." In the next essay, linguist David Crystal comments on the phenomenon of texting, referring to two poems by author and poet Norman Silver.

David Crystal is a linguist and author and currently teaches at Bangor University in North Wales, United Kingdom. He is the author of many books on language as well as the editor of numerous reference works, including the *Cambridge Encyclopedia of Language* (1987) and the *Cambridge Encyclopedia of the English Language* (1995). His most recent book, *Txtng: The Gr8 Db8*, focuses on text language and its impact on society (2008). This essay is an excerpt from his book *English as a Global Language* (2003).

### txt commndmnts

1  u shall luv ur mobil fone with all ur hart
2  u & ur fone shall neva b apart
3  u shall nt lust aftr ur neibrs fone nor thiev
4  u shall b prepard @ all times 2 tXt & 2 recv
5  u shall use LOL & othr acronyms in conversatns
6  u shall be zappy with ur ast*r*sks & exc!matns!!
7  u shall abbrevi8 & rite words like theyr sed
8  u shall nt speak 2 sumI face2face if u cn msg em insted
9  u shall nt shout with capitls XEPT IN DIRE EMERGNCY +
10  u shall nt consult a ninglish dictnry

Norman Silver: *Laugh Out Loud :-D txt café.* 2006.

### langwij

langwij
is hi-ly infectious

children
the world ova
catch it
from parence
by word of mouth

the yung
r specially vulnerable
so care
shud b taken how langwij
is spread

symptoms include acute
goo-goo
& the equally serious ga-ga

if NE child
is infected with langwij
give em
3 Tspoons of txt
b4 bedtime
& ½ a tablet of verse
after every meal

Norman Silver: *Age, Sex, Location txt café.* 2006.

## LANGUAGE NOTES

| | |
|---|---|
| & | and |
| @ | at |
| 2 | to |
| a ninglish | an English |
| abbrevi8 | abbreviate |
| aftr | after |
| ast*r*sks | asterisks |
| b | be |
| b4 | before |
| capitls | capitals |
| cn | can |
| conversatns | conversations |
| dictnry | dictionary |
| em | them |
| emergncy | emergency |
| equllay | equally |
| exclmatns | exclamations |
| face2face | face-to-face |
| fone | phone |
| hart | heart |
| hi-ly | highly |
| insted | instead |
| langwij | language |
| LOL | laughing out loud |
| luv | love |
| mobil | mobile |

| msg | message |
| NE | any |
| neibrs | neighbour's |
| neva | never |
| nt | not |
| othr | other |
| ova | over |
| parence | parents |
| prepard | prepared |
| r | are |
| recv | receive |
| rite | write |
| sed | said |
| shud | should |
| sumI | someone |
| theyr | they're |
| thiev | thieve |
| Tspoons | teaspoons |
| tXt, txt | text |
| u | you |
| ur | your |
| xept | except |
| yung | young |

## Commentary

1 A new medium for language doesn't turn up very often, which is why the linguistic effects of electronic communications technology have attracted so much attention. And with mobile phones, where the small-screen technology is so constraining, the effects have generated one of the most idiosyncratic varieties in the history of language. I call it Textspeak.

2     Textspeak is characterized by its distinctive graphology. Its chief feature is rebus abbreviation. Words are formed in which letters represent syllables, as seen in "b," "b4," "NE," "r," "Tspoons," "u," "ur," "xcept." Use is made of logograms, such as numerals and symbols, as seen in "&," "@," "2," "abbrevi8," "b4," "face-2face," and "sumI." Punctuation marks and letters are adapted to express attitudes (the so-called smileys, or emoticons), as seen in the ':-D' after the title *Laugh Out Loud*—you have to read the symbols sideways to see the point.

3     Such forms are by no means restricted to Textspeak; they turn up in other electronic domains, such as emails, chatgroups, and blogs. Indeed, rebuses have a much longer linguistic history. The Victorians played games with them, and children's Christmas annuals have long contained puzzles using them. The only type of traditional rebus that does not appear in Textspeak is the use of picture—such as a bee representing the word "be." But in Textspeak something more radical has taken place.

4     The nature of telephony, plus the on-screen limitation to 160 characters, has motivated a much more wide-ranging and innovative set of conventions. Textspeak

has its own range of direct-address items, such as "F2T" ("free to talk?"), "PCM" ("please call me"), "MMYT" ("Mail me your thoughts"), and "RUOK" ("are you OK?"). Multi-word sentences and response sequences can be used, reduced to a sequence of initial letters. "LOL" is used in the poem, and is explained in the title of the book in which it appears; other examples are "SWDYT" ("So what do you think?"), "BTDT" ("Been there, done that"), and "YYSSWW" ("Yeah, yeah, sure, sure, whatever"). Even more ingenious coded abbreviations have been devised, especially among those for whom argot is a desirable safeguard against unwelcome surveillance.

5  Texters seem to be aware of the high information value of consonants as opposed to vowels. It is fairly unusual to lose consonants, unless the words are likely to be easily recognized, as in the case of "hi-ly" and "rite." But there are lots of instances where one vowel is dropped ("aftr," "capitls," "cn," "emergncy," "hart," "insted," "mobil," "nt," "othr," "prepard," "theyr," "thiev," "txt," "yung"), or two ("conversatns"), or three ("dictnry"), or four ("recv"). "Neibrs" is an interesting example, losing two consonants and two vowels (only one in American English, of course). "Msg" loses three vowels and one consonant. "Equllay" seems to be doing something different—making a word look strange for its own sake (the standard spelling contains the same letters, "equally"). "A ninglish" is also different: by moving the position of the word-break, the spelling suggests a non-standard pronunciation—though in fact running the "n" into the "e" of English is a perfectly standard practice.

6  Texters also seem to be well aware of the low information value of punctuation marks. There is no sentence punctuation at all in the poems, with the exception of the double exclamation-mark in the sixth commandment, and apostrophes are dropped in "neibrs" and "theyr." On the other hand, certain punctuation marks are given new functions, being used ludically in "ast*r*sks" and "exc!matns," and there is a contrastive use of space (in the second commandment), type-size (in the fifth and seventh), and colour ("hart" in the first and "XEPT IN DIRE EMERGNCY +" in the ninth are printed in red). Hyphens are sometimes respected (three uses in the "langwij" poem). Capital letters are conspicuous by their absence at the beginning of sentences, but are often used for effect—in the ninth commandment, for example, and also in some of the acronyms (such as "LOL").

7  Why abbreviate? There is ergonomic value in abbreviation, given that the number of key-strokes saved bears a direct relationship to time and energy—and formerly (depending on your service-provider) even the eventual size of your telephone bill. In a creation such as "ru2cnmel8r" ("Are you two seeing me later?"), the full form uses over twice as many key-strokes.

8  In 2004 I published *A Glossary of Textspeak and Netspeak,* and—ignoring the difference between upper-case and lower-case usage—collected about 500 Textspeak abbreviations. However, only a small number of these actually turn out to be in regular use. The vast majority are there just to be "clever," illustrating the possibilities of language play. "ROTFL" ("rolling on the floor laughing") may have had some use at the outset, but its later developments (such as "ROTFLMAO" and "ROTFLMAOWTIME"—"rolling on the floor laughing my ass off . . . with tears in my eyes") illustrate idiosyncratic communicative one-upmanship rather than

genuine community usage. And I doubt whether many texters actually use such creations as "LSHMBB" ("laughing so hard my belly is bouncing").

9      The method isn't without its difficulties. Leaving out letters always runs the risk of ambiguity. From the receiver's point of view, a single sequence can have more than one meaning: "BN"—"been" or "being," "CID"—"consider it done" or "crying in disgrace," "CYA"—"see you" or "cover your ass," "N"—"and" or "no," "Y"—"why" or "yes." If a message of transmitted love gets the reply "LOL," it is up to you to decide whether it means "laughing out loud" or "lots of love." It could make a big difference to an emerging relationship. And you have to know your recipient before you decode "GBH," which can be either a "great big hug" or "grievous bodily harm." There are similar ambiguities in the Textspeak of other languages.

10      From the sender's point of view there are also choices to be made. "Good to see you" can be "GTCY," "GTSY," "G2CY," or "G2SY"; "I love you" can be "ILU," "ILUVY," or "ILY"; "thanks" can be "THNX," "THX," "TX," or "TNX." I found a remarkable eight variants for "talk to you later": "TTUL," "TTUL8R," "TTYL," "TTYL8R," "T2UL," "T2UL8R," "T2YL," and "T2YL8R," and there are probably others. Even more exist for "what's up?"—depending on how many U's you bother to send: "WASSUP," "SUP?," "WU?," "WSU?," "WSUU?," "WSUUU?," etc. Doubtless text-messaging dialects are already evolving.

11      No texter is entirely consistent, and no two texters use identical conventions. While a few abbreviations are widely (possibly universally) used, such as "txt" and "msg," others are not. I have seen texters write "shl" or "shll" for "shall," but Silver doesn't. Some would write "consult" as "cnsult" or "cnslt." The seventh commandment is only partly respected, in these poems: "em," "fone," "langwij," "luv," "parence," "sed," and "shud" are indeed quasi-phonetic representations of the way these words are pronounced, presumably in Silver's accent. (That the spelling reflects a particular accent is clear from such words as "neva" and "ova," where there is no "r." A West-Country speaker would presumably not want to leave the "r" out—nor, for that matter, would most Americans.) But other words are not given a phonetic form. The full standard English spelling given to "infectious," "children," "vulnerable," "symptoms," "serious," and so on indicates that we are dealing here with a literary genre, not a real text situation at all.

12      To my mind, this is one of the most interesting things about the way texting has evolved. It is a new genre. It began to be used in poetry very early on, in *The Guardian*'s text-messaging poetry competitions. It was only a matter of time before a texting poet arrived on the scene, and a website (www.txtcafe.com) where doubtless the genre will be fully exploited and explored as time goes by. Text-message stories—even novels—are also already being circulated.

13      The Silver poems illustrate the strengths of texting, and also its limitations. The more unusual the word, the more it needs to be spelt out in full. There must be a serious limit to the amount of information which can be conveyed using abbreviation, and a real risk of ambiguity as soon as people try to go beyond a stock set of social phrases. The set of possible messages is really very small, and only a few abbreviations—such as "C" ("see"), "B" ("be"), "2" ("to, too, two"), "4" ("for, four, -fore"), and "U" ("you") can be used in lots of sentences.

14    Will Textspeak have an effect on the language as a whole? This is unlikely. The whole point of the style is to suit a particular technology where space is at a premium: and when that constraint is dropped, abbreviated language no longer has any purpose. Its "cool" associations amongst young (or at least, young-minded) people will allow some of its idiosyncrasy to achieve a use elsewhere, and there are occasional reports of Textspeak creeping into other forms of writing, such as school essays. But these are minor trends, part of the novelty of the medium. They can be controlled as part of the task of developing in children a sense of linguistic appropriateness—in the UK, one of the basic principles behind the National curriculum in English. The genre could gain strength from its literary applications, but it is too soon to say whether these have a long-term future.

15    Some people object to Textspeak. Some are bemused by it. I am fascinated by it, for it is the latest manifestation of the human ability—and young human ability, at that—to be linguistically creative and to adapt language to suit the demands of diverse settings. In Textspeak, we are seeing, in a small way, language in evolution.

## References

Baker, P. quoted in BBC News 15 April 2002: available online at http://news.bbc.co.uk/ I/hi/sci/tech/1926272.stm.

Crystal, D. 2004. *A Glossary of Textspeak and Netspeak*. Edinburgh University Press.

Crystal, D. 2008. *Txting: the Gr8 Db8*. Oxford: Oxford University Press, forthcoming.

Mobile Data Association statistics available online at www.text.it/home.cfm.

Silver, N. 2006. Laugh Out Loud :-D. *Age, Sex, Location*, both published by txt café, 57 Priory Street, Colchester, CO1 2QE.

Sutherland, J. 2002. 'Cn u txt?' *The Guardian* November 11 2002: available online at www.guardian.co.uk.

Thurlow, C. 2005. *Generation Txt: The Sociolinguistics of Young People's Text Messaging*, available online at www.txt2nite.com.

### THINKING CRITICALLY

1. What distinguishes textspeak from other forms of communication? Explain.

2. Why do some people object to textspeak? To what do they object, and why do they think it has the potential to "ruin" the English language? What does Crystal think of these objections? What do *you* think?

3. What communication challenges does textspeak pose for users? Recipients of messages? Explain.

4. Are there grammatical rules in textspeak? Is it merely shorthand, or is it something else?

5. Do you use textspeak or frequently send text messages? Describe your usage and feelings about the medium.

### WRITING ASSIGNMENTS

1. Write your own poem in text message language. Share your composition with the class. Describe what challenges you had in using this medium, if any.

2. David Crystal thinks that textspeak is unlikely to have an effect on the English language as a whole. Write an essay exploring the impact of textspeak on the

English language based on this essay and outside research. You may wish to interview some peers who use this communication medium for their views as you formulate your essay.

---

# "r u online?": The Evolving Lexicon of Wired Teens
*Kris Axtman*

As instant messaging (IM) and texting become a preferred method of communication, the English language is being used in new and creative ways. What does this phenomenon mean for how the younger generation communicates?

Kris Axtman is a staff writer at *The Christian Science Monitor*, in which this article appeared in the December 12, 2002 edition.

1 The conversation begins on the computer, nothing too atypical for a pair of teenage boys bored on a Friday night:

**Garret:** hey

**Josh:** sup

**Garret:** j/cu

**Josh:** same

**Garret:** wut r u doing 2nite

**Josh:** n2m

**Garret:** cool

Need a translation? Not if you're a 13-year-old who's been Internet-connected since birth. For the rest of us, welcome to the world of Net Lingo—the keyboard generation's gift to language and culture. "sup" is not a call to supper, but a query: "What's up?" And Josh's "n2m" reply? "Not too much."

2 As in every age, teenagers today are adapting the English language to meet their needs for self-expression. But this time, it's happening online—and at lightning speed. To some, it's a creative twist on dialogue, and a new, harmless version of teen slang. But to anxious grammarians and harried teachers, it's the linguistic ruin of Generation IM (instant messenger).

3 Whatever it is, the result fills Internet chat rooms, e-mail, and the increasingly popular instant messenger, on which correspondents fire off confessions, one-liners, and blather in real-time group chats or, more often, fleet-fingered tête-a-têtes.

4 "This is really an extension of what teenagers have always done: recreate the language in their own image. But this new lingo combines writing and speaking to a degree that we've never seen before," says Neil Randall, an English professor at the University of Waterloo and author of "Lingo Online: A Report on the Language of the Keyboard Generation."

5 The result, he says, is the use of writing to simulate speech—a skill not formally taught. In the process, typed communication has entered a new era of speed.

6 In a third-floor bedroom in Houston, Garret Thomas has three online conversations going at once. That's nothing, he says. Sometimes he chats with as many as

20 people at a time—chosen from his 200-plus "buddy list" that shows which of his friends are online and available. "I'm a really fast typer," says the redhead.

7    Though creating unique speech patterns is nothing new for the younger set, this generation is doing it in a novel way.

8    New acronyms, abbreviations, and emoticons—keyboard characters lined up to resemble human gestures or expressions, such as smiling :)—are coined daily. Indeed, almost 60 percent of online teenagers under age 17 use IM services, offered free by Internet providers such as Yahoo and America Online, according to Nielsen/NetRatings.

9    "All of my friends are on instant messenger," says Garret, not looking up from his cryptic chat with Josh. "It's just easier to talk to them this way."

10    Not like the fate of the universe depends on what they're saying. With one friend, he's talking about his rotten Spanish teacher who actually expects the class to participate. With another, he's debating the evening's options: the mall, a movie, chillin' at his house. With a third, he's deep in a discussion about how he never gives more than one-word answers. "who cares," Garret types.

11    "hey, that's two getting better," comes the reply.

12    In between all this, there's a whole bunch of "j/j" (just joking), "lol" (laughing out loud), and brb ("be right back"). In other words, typical teen chatter.

13    "Instant messaging has just replaced the phone . . . for their generation," says Mary Anne Thomas, a Houston mother on the other side of town, with two teen boys addicted to IM. She has noticed that her oldest son, who's normally quite shy around girls, feels more comfortable talking to them online—a positive, she thinks.

14    A negative, though, is that their grammar is becoming atrocious, and Net lingo is starting to show up on school assignments: "They talk with these abbreviated words and run-on sentences with no punctuation. I call it speed talking, and it's starting to carry over into their homework," she says. That's an issue that teachers around the country have been struggling with recently as instant messaging grows in popularity.

15    Another double-edged consequence comes in a culture of multitasking. Mrs. Thomas's oldest son spends about three hours on instant messenger each night. He'll talk to friends, download music, do homework, surf the Internet—all at the same time.

16    Because of the Internet, experts say, kids today are able to multitask like no other generation. But with that frenetic multitasking, others say, comes easy distraction—and the shrinking of already-short attention spans.

17    Garret says he gets onto IM when he's doing homework, and manages about eight different tasks at one time. Showing incredible focus—or frenzy—he flips from one screen to the next, rapidly firing off messages while surfing the Net and gabbing on the phone. (No, IM hasn't replaced the phone entirely.)

18    Now a high-school freshman, he says most of his friends were on IM by junior high, and he picked up the lingo as he went along. New terms get passed between friends, and different groups and regions of the country have their own IM lexicons, with particular acronyms, abbreviations, and emoticons that mirror their inside jokes and experience. Tonight, he tells a friend that he's "j/c." She asks, "what is j/c."

19    "just chillin'," he types, certain that she will use it in the future.

20    Experts say the intent of lingo—in any generation—is to signify "inness" with a particular group. And while teens have long pushed the boundaries of language, they are now doing it in written form.

21    "This is a new kind of slang, a written slang. We've never had anything like it before," says Robert Beard, professor emeritus of linguistics at Bucknell University in Lewisburg, Pa., and creator of yourDictionary.com.

22    Some parents worry that teens could get into trouble by talking to so many different—and sometimes unknown—buddies. Certainly, that's happened. But Dr. Randall says he found in his study that teens are quite aware of that issue and know how to protect themselves.

23    Even with his large buddy list, Garret gets it. He begins chatting with someone he hasn't talked to in a while, and when that person attacks him and uses profanity, he quickly ends the conversation.

24    "I'm not talking to him anymore," he says, slightly shaken, and then uses the software to block all incoming messages from that screen name. "I guess it's time to clean out my buddy list."

### SOME COMMON IM LINGO

AFK: Away From Keyboard
BBL: Be Back Later
BRB: Be Right Back
IMHO: In My Humble Opinion
JK: Just Kidding
LOL: Laughing Out Loud
LYLAS: Love You Like a Sister
NP: No Problem
OMG: Oh My God
OTP: On the Phone
ROFL: Rolling on Floor Laughing
TTFN: Ta-Ta for Now
TTYL: Talk to You Later
YW: You're Welcome

### THINKING CRITICALLY

1. Do you use IM and text messaging slang and shorthand to communicate with your friends? If so, do you ever use IM acronyms in spoken speech or in note-taking or class assignments? Explain.

2. Visit Netlingo.com or www.abbreviations.com. Review the different terms used in IM and text messaging. How many terms are you familiar with? Would you use these terms in any other situation besides electronic communication? Why or why not?

3. In your opinion, should educators be concerned that the younger generation's frequent usage of IM acronyms, slang, and emoticons will affect their language use and ability to communicate offline? Should teachers allow this new form of communication to be used offline, such as in school assignments? Explain.

## WRITING ASSIGNMENTS

1. Evaluate your own online communication style. Are you brief and to the point, or do you compose in more detail? What do you think your style says about you? What does it communicate to others? Do you have different styles for different situations? Explain.

2. Write about a relationship, romantic or merely friendly, in which online networking was an essential component of the connection you had with the other person. Cite examples of how social networking contributed to your relationship and how it enriched its quality.

3. How are Web-based relationships different from face-to-face ones? How would your life—and the relationships that enrich it—be different without the Internet and social networking sites?

# Exploring the Language of **V I S U A L S**

**THINKING CRITICALLY**

1. What is happening in this cartoon? What is the joke?

2. What do you need to understand about the issue this cartoon is addressing to understand the humor in the cartoon? Explain.

3. Would this cartoon be effective 10 years ago? Is it likely to be funny 10 years from now?

4. What visual cues does the cartoonist use to convey who the people in the picture are, and what is happening in the cartoon? Explain.

# The Keypad Solution

*Ammon Shea*

Is text messaging reforming the spelling of English? Most English-speaking (and writing) people agree that English spelling makes little sense. Every child who has struggled with silent "e" or the interchangeable nature of "i," "e," and "y" knows that spelling has less to do with common sense and more to do with tradition and convention. Many people have tried to reform English spelling, but to little avail. Will texting finally conquer the spelling bee?

Ammon Shea is the author of *Reading the O.E.D.: One Man, One Year, 21,730 Pages* (2008) and *Phone Book: The Curious History of the Book That Everyone Uses But No One Reads* (2010). He is a consulting editor of American dictionaries for Oxford University Press. This essay appeared in the January 22, 2010 edition of *The New York Times Magazine.*

1   There is a long and noble history of trying to change the English language's notoriously illogical system of spelling. The fact that through, rough, dough, plough, hiccough and trough all end with -ough, yet none of them sound the same as any of the others, is the sort of thing that has been vexing poets and learners of English for quite some time. Proponents of "fixing" this wayward orthography have included some of the most prominent names in American history. Benjamin Franklin suggested changing the alphabet, and Andrew Carnegie provided money for people to study the problem. President Theodore Roosevelt issued an edict in 1906 that gave the Government Printing Office a list of 300 words with new spellings: problem cases like artisan, kissed and woe were to be changed to artizan, kist and wo. Roosevelt was largely ignored by the G.P.O., and the matter was soon dropped. Although this issue has been extensively studied and argued over by these and other eminent thinkers, there has been an almost complete lack of success in effecting any substantial progress.

2   And so it is rather bizarre that the first widespread change in how people spell English words appears to have come from a group of (largely) young people sending text messages to one another with cellular phones and other electronic devices. You may not like seeing the phrase "LOL—U R gr8" on the page, but it is common enough that you are likely to understand it. Why have such inadvertent "reforms" succeeded where generations of dedicated intellectual attempts have not? And will they last?

3   For most of the history of the language, English speakers took a lackadaisical approach to spelling; the notion that a word should always be spelled the same way is a much more recent invention than the language itself. The standardization of English spelling began in the 16th century, and although it is unclear at exactly what point our spelling became set, what is certain is that ever since it happened, people have complained that the rules of spelling, such as they are, just don't make sense.

4   Perhaps the most successful attempt at spelling reform (at least in America) was wrought by Noah Webster, who managed to forever make Americans view the British honour and theatre as off-kilter. Some portion of Webster's determination to change -our to -or and -re to -er was due to nationalist fervor; he wanted his countrymen to break free of the orthographic bonds of their oppressors. He was noticeably

less successful in convincing Americans of the utility of many of his other ideas, like spelling oblique as obleek, machine as masheen and prove as proov.

5        I contacted several of the spelling-reform organizations in operation today to ask them about their feelings on adopting text-messaging shorthands as a kind of spelling reform. Alan Mole, the president of the American Literacy Council, when asked if his group had ever considered allying itself with the texters, said that it had not, although he added that text messaging "does serve the purpose of raising consciousness" about the fact "that there are different ways of making people spell." The council, which has picketed the Scripps National Spelling Bee, prefers its own phonetic method of spelling reform, called SoundSpel. The group offers a downloadable version of SoundSpel (ententetranslator.com/IDL.htm) that can instantly translate an entire novel's worth of standard English into a more spellable, if less recognizable, form.

6        The sister organization of the council, the British-based Spelling Society, does not advocate adopting texting conventions, either, but this is less surprising, because it does not advocate adopting any particular approach at all. Jack Bovill, the society's president, wrote in an e-mail message: "Our present aim is to raise awareness of the problems caused by the irregularity of English spelling. We DO NOT support solutions."

7        Whether texting conventions are supported by organized spelling reformists or not, can they possibly solve the difficulty of spelling our troublesome language? David Crystal, the author of "Txtng: The Gr8 Db8," told me in an e-mail message that "there's nothing in texting to suggest spelling reform," noting that texting relies heavily on abbreviations, which he sees as creative stylings, not systematic improvements. He added that there is very little that is new about most of the abbreviations and lexical shortenings that make texting so maddening to so many. In fact, he said, with the exception of a few recent coinages like LOL, "virtually all the commonly used ones can be found in English a century ago." For example, bn (been), btwn (between) and wd (would) can all be found in a 1942 dictionary of abbreviations.

8        Naomi Baron, a professor of linguistics at American University and author of "Always On: Language in an Online and Mobile World," shares Crystal's view. She predicts that the number of "textisms" will stop growing as people continue to develop more proficiency in using handheld devices and as the devices continue to grow more sophisticated than simple telephone touch pads. She adds that part of the appeal of texting shorthands is their novelty, and that that will fade.

9        Crystal did say that a certain amount of spelling reform might eventually come from the Internet: "People who try to impose reform 'top down' rarely succeed. But a 'bottom up' movement might well have some permanent effects." Given that the general attitude toward text messaging is that it comes from the linguistic bottom, it may well be that this masheen-sent lingua franca may proov to one day be less obleek than it is now.

## THINKING CRITICALLY

1. Shea observes that English spelling conventions make little sense. Share your own observations on English spelling and the challenges it presents.

2. David Crystal notes that "there's nothing in texting to suggest spelling reform," noting that texting relies heavily on abbreviations, which he sees as creative

stylings, not systematic improvements. In your experience, is texting a new way of spelling or a more efficient way of communicating through a hand-held device? Would you advocate for using texting conventions in an essay? In a book? Why or why not?

3. Linguistic professor Naomi Baron believes that the novelty of texting will eventually fade as people become more used to hand-held devices. Explore the validity of this statement with a survey. Ask at least 10 people who have used (or even grown up with) hand-held devices about their texting habits. How did they learn to text? What shortcuts do they use? Are they likely to change how they text friends and family in the future? Discuss your results in class as part of group discussion.

4. Visit the SoundSpel website (ententetranslator.com/IDL.htm) and read some of the "corrected" spelling it provides. How difficult is it to read English spelled phonetically? Does changing English spelling to be more phonetic make sense? Do you think it will ever happen? Why or why not?

### WRITING ASSIGNMENTS

1. Write a brief essay exploring your personal use of hand-held devices and their influence, if any, on your communication style. How old were you when you first started texting? How did you learn texting conventions? Has texting ever spilled over into other areas of communication in your daily life (like email, your job, or schoolwork?) Conclude with some observations about the future influence texting will likely have (or not have) on your life in the coming decade.

2. Write an essay in which you either agree or disagree, in whole or in part, with the idea of using texting conventions to reform spelling of English.

---

# The Other Side of E-Mail
*Robert Kuttner*

Few people would disagree that email is revolutionizing how we communicate. Individuals who never wrote an ordinary letter before now spend hours online composing and sending electronic messages. We can communicate to virtually every corner of the world with the push of a button. But what is the price of this easy and efficient new mode of communication? Robert Kuttner contends that instead of freeing our time, email is, in fact, a time "thief." He declares that although email has many uses, there is a darker side to it that we must consider when employing this medium.

Founder and co-editor of *The American Prospect,* a bimonthly journal of policy and politics, Robert Kuttner is also one of five contributing columnists to *Business Week*'s "Economic Viewpoint." His work has appeared in many publications, including *The New York Times*, the *Atlantic Monthly*, and *Harvard Business Review*. Kuttner is the author of five books, including *The End of Laissez Faire* (1991) and *Everything for Sale: The Virtues and Limits of Markets* (1997). The following editorial appeared in *The Boston Globe*.

1 A few years ago, when my daughter was a college freshman, I wrote a column singing the praises of e-mail. We were, suddenly, corresponding. It was, I decided,

the revenge of print on electronics—a whole generation raised on the tube and the phone, rediscovering the lost art of writing letters. How utterly charming.

2     Now I'm not so sure. E-mail has a dark side. To be sure, it saves a great deal of time and paperwork and has facilitated new, unimagined forms of affinity. However, e-mail is also a thief. It steals our time and our privacy. It deceives us into thinking we have endless additional hours in the day to engage in far-flung communications that we may or may not need or want.

3     On top of everything else we have to do, e-mail is one more garden demanding tending.

4     E-mail brings a kind of pseudo-urgency that demands an instant response. It creates false intimacies. Recently, I got an e-mail message from a perfect stranger, a student who had read one of my articles and wanted help on a term paper. I was touched, but alas, there aren't enough hours in the day. Yet something about the message made me feel I needed to apologize for not being able to do her homework. With e-mail, it's too easy to hit the reply key, with results you may regret. One acquaintance, thinking she was just responding to a note from a close friend, accidentally sent a highly personal message to the friend's entire mailing list.

5     I recently had a painful quarrel triggered by e-mail messages. A dear friend and I were both having a very busy week and imposing on each other's time. Without quite intending to, we ended up firing salvos of e-mail back and forth of escalating testiness until we had quite insulted each other. We apologized, in person.

6     This mishap could not have occurred either by phone or by ordinary mail. When talking to someone, you pay attention to tonality. And when you write a letter, you read it over a few times before sending it. But e-mail is tone-deaf and all too instant. It is ephemeral, yet irrevocable. Once you've banged out your message and sent it into the ether, you can't take it back.

7     E-mail is a great convenience—for the sender. The recipient is presumed to have infinite time and interest. It is the equivalent of endless Christmas letters from boring distant relatives all year long.

8     Bosses get in the habit of sending down incessant e-mail messages from on high, as if anyone cared. (Now hear this . . .) A large corporation with which I am vaguely affiliated sends me more messages than I could possibly want to have, let alone answer.

9     E-mail is also not secure. The magazine that I edit regularly gets highly personal missives, sent by mistake to the wrong e-mail address thanks to a typo. With the phone, you know as soon as you have a wrong number. And mis-addressed letters either get returned or end up in the dead letter office.

10     At one company, two people carrying on an affair were incautiously sending each other intimate e-mail, which a supervisor discovered. To make matters worse, they were making snide comments about the supervisor. Security escorted them from the premises.

11     E-mail is also easily forwarded and deliberately or mistakenly put into mass circulation. Don't e-mail anything private unless you are prepared to see it crop up all over the World Wide Web. E-mail, like talk radio, reduces inhibitions; it is democratic to the point of moronic. And I've not even gotten to mass junk e-mail, known in the trade as spam.

12    I know, I know, the Internet is a marvel. And it is. And, sure, e-mail is great for scheduling meetings, for sending and receiving research materials, for allowing people in remote locations to collaborate on projects. But novelty and low cost tend to breed excess.

13    Like every new tool, from the wheel to nuclear energy, electronic communication will take a while to find its proper etiquette and niche. In the meantime, it is an awkward adolescent that has borrowed the family car, hormones raging and radio blaring, with little regard for the rules of the road.

14    Of course, some fans of e-mail may find these words controversial or offensive. So if you have any comments on this column, my e-mail address is . . . no, actually, send me a letter.


### THINKING CRITICALLY

1. According to Kuttner, how does email transcend the generation gap? Can you think of other ways that email bridges gaps between groups of people?

2. How is email a "thief"? Do you agree with Kuttner's assessment? Describe the ways email can complicate life rather than simplify it. Would you have more or less time without email access? Explain.

3. How does email "reduce inhibitions" (paragraph 11)? What are the social perils of email? Describe the complications of email that are not found in other communication mediums, such as the telephone or ordinary face-to-face conversation.

4. What function does email have in today's society? How have our lives changed because of it? What influence has it had on our communication style and habits? Is it being replaced by text messaging? Explain.

5. What could be the long-term effects of email on social discourse? On how we converse with each other? Explain.

6. Kuttner compares the Internet to a garden that requires constant tending. How effective is this metaphor? Explain.


### WRITING ASSIGNMENTS

1. A popular television commercial for an Internet employment agency features a man writing an insulting letter to his boss only to have a toy fall off his monitor and hit the "enter" key, sending his message. Have you ever had a mishap with email such as the ones described by Kuttner in this article? Describe your experience. How did it influence your use of email in the future?

2. How does email differ from ordinary conversation? Drawing from your personal experience, write a paper in which you predict the influence of email on social discourse and how we converse with each other offline.

3. Track all of your online correspondence—received and sent—for a period of one week. This should include email, IM, text messaging, and posting on social networking sites. Develop categories for the communication (social, family, work, school, junk, etc.) and chart how many of each you receive and send in each category. Keep track of how much time you spend online. Write an essay evaluating the results of your online communication profile. Discuss how the

Internet both enhances and complicates life and whether it is indeed changing our personal relationships for better or for worse.

---

# Three Tweets for the Web
*Tyler Cowen*

It's an age-old grievance: the older generation grumbles that the younger one has so many problems—they have limited attention spans, they have no manners, they lack culture, they sit around all day, they don't read, and now, with texting and Twitter, they can't even write a coherent sentence. In the next essay, economics professor Tyler Cowen explains that the younger generation may be different not because they are lazy, but because they are doing things in new and exciting ways. They navigate information and communication in ways their grandparents could not have imagined. The future is now, and they are steering a new course through the information age. Cowen encourages everyone to welcome the new world with open arms—and browsers.

Tyler Cowen is an economics professor at George Mason University. He is the co-author of the popular economics blog *Marginal Revolution*. He currently writes the "Economic Scene" column for *The New York Times* and writes for such magazines as *The New Republic* and *The Wilson Quarterly,* in which this essay appeared in the Autumn 2009 issue.

1 The printed word is not dead. We are not about to see the demise of the novel or the shuttering of all the bookstores, and we won't all end up on Twitter. But we are clearly in the midst of a cultural transformation. For today's younger people, Google is more likely to provide a formative cultural experience than *The Catcher in the Rye* or *Catch-22* or even the Harry Potter novels. There is no question that books are becoming less central to our cultural life.

2 The relative decline of the book is part of a broader shift toward short and to the point. Small cultural bits—written words, music, and video—have never been easier to record, store, organize, and search, and thus they are a growing part of our enjoyment and education. The classic 1960s rock album has given way to the iTunes single. On YouTube, the most popular videos are usually just a few minutes long, and even then viewers may not watch them through to the end. At the extreme, there are Web sites offering five-word movie and song reviews, six-word memoirs ("Not Quite What I Was Planning"), seven-word wine reviews, and 50-word minisagas.*

3 The new brevity has many virtues. One appeal of following blogs is the expectation of receiving a new reward (and finishing off that reward) every day. Blogs

---

*Not everything is shorter and more to the point. The same modern wealth that encourages a proliferation of choices also enables very long performances and spectacles. In the German town of Halberstadt, a specially built organ is playing the world's longest concert ever, designed to clock in at 639 years. This is also the age of complete boxed sets, DVD collector's editions, extended "director's cut" versions of movies, and the eight- or sometimes even 10-year Ph.D. But while there is an increasing diversity of length, shorter is the trend. How many of us have an interest in hearing more than a brief excerpt from the world's longest concert?

feature everything from expert commentary on politics or graphic design to reviews of new Cuban music CDs to casual ruminations on feeding one's cat. Whatever the subject, the content is replenished on a periodic basis, much as 19th-century novels were often delivered in installments, but at a faster pace and with far more authors and topics to choose from. In the realm of culture, a lot of our enjoyment has always come from the opening and unwrapping of each gift. Thanks to today's hypercurrent online environment, this is a pleasure we can experience nearly constantly.

4    It may seem as if we have entered a nightmarish attention-deficit culture, but the situation is not nearly as gloomy as you have been told. Our culture of the short bit is making human minds more rather than less powerful.

5    The arrival of virtually every new cultural medium has been greeted with the charge that it truncates attention spans and represents the beginning of cultural collapse—the novel (in the 18th century), the comic book, rock 'n' roll, television, and now the Web. In fact, there has never been a golden age of all-wise, all-attentive readers. But that's not to say that nothing has changed. The mass migration of intellectual activity from print to the Web has brought one important development: We have begun paying more attention to information. Overall, that's a big plus for the new world order.

6    It is easy to dismiss this cornucopia as information overload. We've all seen people scrolling with one hand through a BlackBerry while pecking out instant messages (IMs) on a laptop with the other and eyeing a television (I won't say "watching"). But even though it is easy to see signs of overload in our busy lives, the reality is that most of us carefully regulate this massive inflow of information to create something uniquely suited to our particular interests and needs—a rich and highly personalized blend of cultural gleanings.

7    The word for this process is *multitasking*, but that makes it sound as if we're all over the place. There is a deep coherence to how each of us pulls out a steady stream of information from disparate sources to feed our long-term interests. No matter how varied your topics of interest may appear to an outside observer, you'll tailor an information stream related to the continuing "stories" you want in your life—say, Sichuan cooking, health care reform, Michael Jackson, and the stock market. With the help of the Web, you build broader intellectual narratives about the world. The apparent disorder of the information stream reflects not your incoherence but rather your depth and originality as an individual.

8    My own daily cultural harvest usually involves listening to music and reading—novels, nonfiction, and Web essays—with periodic glances at the *New York Times* Web site and an e-mail check every five minutes or so. Often I actively don't want to pull apart these distinct activities and focus on them one at a time for extended periods. I *like* the blend I assemble for myself, and I like what I learn from it. To me (and probably no one else, but that is the point), the blend offers the ultimate in interest and suspense. Call me an addict, but if I am torn away from these stories for even a day, I am very keen to get back for the next "episode."

9    Many critics charge that multitasking makes us less efficient. Researchers say that periodically checking your e-mail lowers your cognitive performance level to that of a drunk. If such claims were broadly correct, multitasking would pretty rapidly disappear simply because people would find that it didn't make sense to do it. Multitasking is flourishing, and so are we. There are plenty of lab experiments that

show that distracting people reduces the capacity of their working memory and thus impairs their decision making. It's much harder to show that multitasking, when it results from the choices and control of an individual, does anyone cognitive harm. Multitasking is not a distraction from our main activity, it is our main activity.

10    Consider the fact that IQ scores have been rising for decades, a phenomenon known as the Flynn effect. I won't argue that multitasking is driving this improvement, but the Flynn effect does belie the common impression that people are getting dumber or less attentive. A harried multitasking society seems perfectly compatible with lots of innovation, lots of high achievers, and lots of high IQ scores.

11    With the help of technology, we are honing our ability to do many more things at once and do them faster. We access and absorb information more quickly than before, and, as a result, we often seem more impatient. If you use Google to look something up in 10 seconds rather than spend five minutes searching through an encyclopedia, that doesn't mean you are less patient. It means you are creating more time to focus on other matters. In fact, we're devoting more effort than ever before to big-picture questions, from the nature of God to the best age for marrying and the future of the U.S. economy.

12    Our focus on cultural bits doesn't mean we are neglecting the larger picture. Rather, those bits are building-blocks for seeing and understanding larger trends and narratives. The typical Web user doesn't visit a gardening blog one day and a Manolo Blahnik shoes blog the next day, and never return to either. Most activity online, or at least the kind that persists, involves continuing investments in particular long-running narratives—about gardening, art, shoes, or whatever else engages us. There's an alluring suspense to it. *What's next?* That is why the Internet captures so much of our attention.

13    Indeed, far from shortening our attention spans, the Web *lengthens* them by allowing us to follow the same story over many years' time. If I want to know what's new with the NBA free-agent market, the debate surrounding global warming, or the publication plans of Thomas Pynchon, Google quickly gets me to the most current information. Formerly I needed personal contacts—people who were directly involved in the action—to follow a story for years, but now I can do it quite easily.

14    Sometimes it does appear I am impatient. I'll discard a half-read book that 20 years ago I might have finished. But once I put down the book, I will likely turn my attention to one of the long-running stories I follow online. I've been listening to the music of Paul McCartney for more than 30 years, for example, and if there is some new piece of music or development in his career, I see it first on the Internet. If our Web surfing is sometimes frantic or pulled in many directions, that is because we care so much about so many long-running stories. It could be said, a bit paradoxically, that we are impatient to return to our chosen programs of patience.

15    Another way the Web has affected the human attention span is by allowing greater specialization of knowledge. It has never been easier to wrap yourself up in a long-term intellectual project without at the same time losing touch with the world around you. Some critics don't see this possibility, charging that the Web is destroying a shared cultural experience by enabling us to follow only the specialized stories that pique our individual interests. But there are also those who argue

that the Web is doing just the opposite—that we dabble in an endless variety of topics but never commit to a deeper pursuit of a specific interest. These two criticisms contradict each other. The reality is that the Internet both aids in knowledge specialization and helps specialists keep in touch with general trends.

16    The key to developing your personal blend of all the "stuff" that's out there is to use the right tools. The quantity of information coming our way has exploded, but so has the quality of our filters, including Google, blogs, and Twitter. As Internet analyst Clay Shirky points out, there is no information overload, only filter failure. If you wish, you can keep all the information almost entirely at bay and use Google or text a friend only when you need to know something. That's not usually how it works. Many of us are cramming ourselves with Web experiences—videos, online chats, magazines—and also fielding a steady stream of incoming e-mails, text messages, and IMs. The resulting sense of time pressure is not a pathology; it is a reflection of the appeal and intensity of what we are doing. The Web allows you to enhance the meaning and importance of the cultural bits at your disposal; thus you want to grab more of them, and organize more of them, and you are willing to work hard at that task, even if it means you sometimes feel harried.

17    It's true that many people on the Web are not looking for a cerebral experience, and younger people especially may lack the intellectual framework needed to integrate all the incoming bits into a meaningful whole. A lot of people are on the Web just to have fun or to achieve some pretty straightforward personal goals—they may want to know what happened to their former high school classmates or the history of the dachshund. "It's still better than watching TV" is certainly a sufficient defense of these practices, but there is a deeper point: The Internet is supplementing and intensifying real life. The Web's heralded interactivity not only furthers that process but opens up new possibilities for more discussion and debate. Anyone can find space on the Internet to rate a product, criticize an idea, or review a new movie or book.

18    One way to understand the emotional and intellectual satisfactions of the new world is by way of contrast. Consider Mozart's opera *Don Giovanni*. The music and libretto express a gamut of human emotions, from terror to humor to love to the sublime. With its ability to combine so much in a single work of art, the opera represents a great achievement of the Western canon. But, for all *Don Giovanni*'s virtues, it takes well over three hours to hear it in its entirety, perhaps four with an intermission. Plus, the libretto is in Italian. And if you want to see the performance live, a good seat can cost hundreds of dollars.

19    Instead of experiencing the emotional range of *Don Giovanni* in one long, expensive sitting, on the Web we pick the moods we want from disparate sources and assemble them ourselves. We take a joke from YouTube, a terrifying scene from a Japanese slasher movie, a melody from iTunes, and some images—perhaps our own digital photos—capturing the sublime beauty of the Grand Canyon. Even if no single bit looks very impressive to an outsider, to the creator of this assemblage it is a rich and varied inner experience. The new wonders we create are simply harder for outsiders to see than, say, the fantastic cathedrals of Old Europe.

20    The measure of cultural literacy today is not whether you can "read" all the symbols in a Rubens painting but whether you can operate an iPhone and other Web-related technologies. One thing you can do with such devices is visit any

number of Web sites where you can see Rubens's pictures and learn plenty about them. It's not so much about having information as it is about knowing how to get it. Viewed in this light, today's young people are very culturally literate indeed—in fact, they are very often cultural leaders and creators.

21    To better understand contemporary culture, consider an analogy to romance. Although many long-distance relationships survive, they are difficult to sustain. When you have to travel far to meet your beloved, you want to make every trip a grand and glorious occasion. Usually you don't fly from one coast to another just to hang out and share downtime and small talk. You go out to eat and to the theater, you make passionate love, and you have intense conversations. You have a lot of thrills, but it's hard to make it work because in the long run it's casually spending time together and the routines of daily life that bind two people to each other. And of course, in a long-distance relationship, a lot of the time you're not together at all. If you really love the other person you're not consistently happy, even though your peak experiences may be amazing.

22    A long-distance relationship is, in emotional terms, a bit like culture in the time of Cervantes or Mozart. The costs of travel and access were high, at least compared to modern times. When you did arrive, the performance was often very exciting and indeed monumental. Sadly, the rest of the time you didn't have that much culture at all. Even books were expensive and hard to get. Compared to what is possible in modern life, you couldn't be as happy overall but your peak experiences could be extremely memorable, just as in the long-distance relationship.

23    Now let's consider how living together and marriage differ from a long-distance relationship. When you share a home, the costs of seeing each other are very low. Your partner is usually right there. Most days include no grand events, but you have lots of regular and predictable interactions, along with a kind of grittiness or even ugliness rarely seen in a long-distance relationship. There are dirty dishes in the sink, hedges to be trimmed, maybe diapers to be changed.

24    If you are happily married, or even somewhat happily married, your internal life will be very rich. You will take all those small events and, in your mind and in the mind of your spouse, weave them together in the form of a deeply satisfying narrative, dirty diapers and all. It won't always look glorious on the outside, but the internal experience of such a marriage is better than what's normally possible in a long-distance relationship.

25    The same logic applies to culture. The Internet and other technologies mean that our favorite creators, or at least their creations, are literally part of our daily lives. It is no longer a long-distance relationship. It is no longer hard to get books and other written material. Pictures, music, and video appear on command. Culture is there all the time, and you can receive more of it, pretty much whenever you want.

26    In short, our relationship to culture has become more like marriage in the sense that it now enters our lives in an established flow, creating a better and more regular daily state of mind. True, culture has in some ways become uglier, or at least it would appear so to the outside observer. But when it comes to how we actually live and feel, contemporary culture is more satisfying and contributes to the happiness of far more people. That is why the public devours new technologies that offer extreme and immediate access to information.

27    Many critics of contemporary life want our culture to remain like a long-distance relationship at a time when most of us are growing into something more mature. We assemble culture for ourselves, creating and committing ourselves to a fascinating brocade. Very often the paper-and-ink book is less central to this new endeavor; it's just another cultural bit we consume along with many others. But we are better off for this change, a change that is filling our daily lives with beauty, suspense, and learning.

28    Or if you'd like the shorter version to post to your Twitter account (140 characters or less): "Smart people are doing wonderful things."

### THINKING CRITICALLY

1. How many complete novels have you read in the past year? Do you agree or disagree with the author "that books are becoming less central to our cultural life"? Explain. Could books still be seen as a part of our social lives? Explain.

2. Cowen explains his daily multitasking as involving "listening to music and reading—novels, nonfiction, and Web essays—with periodic glances at *The New York Times* Web site and an e-mail check every five minutes or so." Describe your own "daily cultural harvest." Do you agree with the author that "Multitasking is not a distraction from our main activity, it is our main activity"? Explain.

3. According to the author, the Web actually lengthens our attention spans "by allowing us to follow the same story over many years' time." Which stories have you been following consistently for at least a year? Does the author's statement seem to be consistent with your own experience?

4. Define what it means to be cultured. Which analogy does Cowen use to support his point that today's young people are indeed cultured?

5. Evaluate your own online communication style. Are you brief and to the point, or do you compose in more detail? What do you think your style says about you? What does it communicate to others? Do you have different styles for different situations? Explain.

### WRITING ASSIGNMENTS

1. At the conclusion of his essay, Cowen jokingly sums up his main point for a posting to a Twitter account—in 140 characters or less. Do you agree with Cowen's own summation of his article? Write your own version of Cowen's essay in 140 characters or less.

2. This essay is in direct opposition to Nicholas Carr's article "Is Google Making Us Stoopid?" on page 509. For instance, Cowen argues that the Internet helps us think creatively and encourages debate, whereas Nicholas Carr feels that the Internet is taking away our ability to be deeply involved in lengthy prose, curtailing our creative thinking. After reading both articles, determine who makes the stronger overall argument and write a short comparison/contrast essay discussing your analysis.

3. In which ways does modern technology help enhance and deepen our life experiences? Can you imagine your life without a cell phone, hand-held communication devices, the Internet, or social networking tools like Facebook and Twitter? How would your life be different? Write a personal narrative describing how your life would be altered—or unchanged—by the loss of technology.

# I Tweet, Therefore I Am

*Peggy Orenstein*

Most people agree that social networking sites have allowed users to connect to people in ways they never could before. The social networking site Twitter allows people to share, almost instantly, moments in time (as long as we can summarize these moments into 140 characters or fewer). What do our online postings reveal about us and how we view ourselves? More than simply connecting us, social networking sites allow us to present a persona to the world—publicly sharing who we know, what we think, what we do, and even who we wish to be. Are social networking sites distracting us from living fully in the moment? Or are they enabling us to share our moments with our friends? In the next essay, Peggy Orenstein explains why she thinks the answer is a little of both.

Peggy Orenstein is the author of *Waiting for Daisy: A Tale of Two Continents, Three Religions, Five Infertility Doctors, an Oscar, an Atomic Bomb, a Romantic Night, and One Woman's Quest to Become a Mother* (2007). Her most recent book is *Cinderella Ate My Daughter* (2011). Her essays have appeared in such publications as *The Los Angeles Times, USA Today, Vogue, Discover, Mother Jones, Salon.com,* and *The New Yorker,* and she has contributed commentaries to National Public Radio's *All Things Considered.* She is a contributing writer for *The New York Times,* in which this essay appeared on July 30, 2010.

1   On a recent lazy Saturday morning, my daughter and I lolled on a blanket in our front yard, snacking on apricots, listening to a download of E. B. White reading "The Trumpet of the Swan." Her legs sprawled across mine; the grass tickled our ankles. It was the quintessential summer moment, and a year ago, I would have been fully present for it. But instead, a part of my consciousness had split off and was observing the scene from the outside: this was, I realized excitedly, the perfect opportunity for a tweet.

2   I came late to Twitter. I might have skipped the phenomenon altogether, but I have a book coming out this winter, and publishers, scrambling to promote 360,000-character tomes in a 140-character world, push authors to rally their "tweeps" to the cause. Leaving aside the question of whether that actually boosts sales, I felt pressure to produce. I quickly mastered the Twitterati's unnatural self-consciousness: processing my experience instantaneously, packaging life as I lived it. I learned to be "on" all the time, whether standing behind that woman at the supermarket who sneaked three extra items into the express check-out lane (you know who you are) or despairing over human rights abuses against women in Guatemala.

3   Each Twitter post seemed a tacit referendum on who I am, or at least who I believe myself to be. The grocery-store episode telegraphed that I was tuned in to the Seinfeldian absurdities of life; my concern about women's victimization, however sincere, signalled that I also have a soul. Together they suggest someone who is at once cynical and compassionate, petty yet deep. Which, in the end, I'd say, is pretty accurate.

4   Distilling my personality provided surprising focus, making me feel stripped to my essence. It forced me, for instance, to pinpoint the dominant feeling as I sat

outside with my daughter listening to E. B. White. Was it my joy at being a mother? Nostalgia for my own childhood summers? The pleasures of listening to the author's quirky, underinflected voice? Each put a different spin on the occasion, of who I was within it. Yet the final decision ("Listening to E. B. White's 'Trumpet of the Swan' with Daisy. Slow and sweet.") was not really about my own impressions: it was about how I imagined—and wanted—others to react to them. That gave me pause. How much, I began to wonder, was I shaping my Twitter feed, and how much was Twitter shaping me?

5    Back in the 1950s, the sociologist Erving Goffman famously argued that all of life is performance: we act out a role in every interaction, adapting it based on the nature of the relationship or context at hand. Twitter has extended that metaphor to include aspects of our experience that used to be considered off-set: eating pizza in bed, reading a book in the tub, thinking a thought anywhere, flossing. Effectively, it makes the greasepaint permanent, blurring the lines not only between public and private but also between the authentic and contrived self. If all the world was once a stage, it has now become a reality TV show: we mere players are not just aware of the camera; we mug for it.

6    The expansion of our digital universe—Second Life, Facebook, MySpace, Twitter—has shifted not only how we spend our time but also how we construct identity. For her coming book, "Alone Together," Sherry Turkle, a professor at M.I.T., interviewed more than 400 children and parents about their use of social media and cellphones. Among young people especially she found that the self was increasingly becoming externally manufactured rather than internally developed: a series of profiles to be sculptured and refined in response to public opinion. "On Twitter or Facebook you're trying to express something real about who you are," she explained. "But because you're also creating something for others' consumption, you find yourself imagining and playing to your audience more and more. So those moments in which you're supposed to be showing your true self become a performance. Your psychology becomes a performance." Referring to "The Lonely Crowd," the landmark description of the transformation of the American character from inner- to outer-directed, Turkle added, "Twitter is outer-directedness cubed."

7    The fun of Twitter and, I suspect, its draw for millions of people, is its infinite potential for connection, as well as its opportunity for self-expression. I enjoy those things myself. But when every thought is externalized, what becomes of insight? When we reflexively post each feeling, what becomes of reflection? When friends become fans, what happens to intimacy? The risk of the performance culture, of the packaged self, is that it erodes the very relationships it purports to create, and alienates us from our own humanity. Consider the fate of empathy: in an analysis of 72 studies performed on nearly 14,000 college students between 1979 and 2009, researchers at the Institute for Social Research at the University of Michigan found a drop in that trait, with the sharpest decline occurring since 2000. Social media may not have instigated that trend, but by encouraging self-promotion over self-awareness, they may well be accelerating it.

8    None of this makes me want to cancel my Twitter account. It's too late for that anyway: I'm already hooked. Besides, I appreciate good writing whatever the form:

some "tweeple" are as deft as haiku masters at their craft. I am experimenting with the art of the well-placed "hashtag" myself (the symbol that adds your post on a particular topic, like #ShirleySherrod, to a stream. You can also use them whimsically, as in, "I am pretending not to be afraid of the humongous spider on the bed. #lieswetellourchildren").

9     At the same time, I am trying to gain some perspective on the perpetual performer's self-consciousness. That involves trying to sort out the line between person and persona, the public and private self. It also means that the next time I find myself lying on the grass, stringing daisy chains and listening to E. B. White, I will resist the urge to trumpet about the swan.

## THINKING CRITICALLY

1. What does Orenstein mean when she refers to the "packaged self?" How do we "package" ourselves online? What does this mean for our communication with others?

2. Orenstein notes that when she tweets, she is projecting "who I am—or at least, who I believe myself to be." What does she mean? If we have to critically assess each communication for what it might say about us (and how we believe we are supposed to be), are we reflecting reality or a constructed image? Explain.

3. Do you use Twitter? If so, how often do you tweet and what do you tweet about? If not, explain why you choose not to participate in this social medium.

4. In your opinion, do Twitter and other social networking sites interfere with our ability to truly engage in the present? Do they distract us from our "live" moments, or do they allow us to live these moments more fully and with more engagement with others? Explain.

## WRITING ASSIGNMENTS

1. Is there a connection between how we communicate and relate to others online and how we develop our own sense of identity? How others perceive us? Print the profiles of at least 10 people you know (you may need to ask for permission if you are not part of a social network) and compare the profiles they present to the people you know in "real life." Alternatively, you could ask an acquaintance to share five profiles of people you do not know for analysis.

2. Write an essay exploring the consequences of social networking sites on the future of friendship and community.

3. Orenstein admits that when she tweets, she isn't necessarily conveying the truth of a moment as she lives it. She is, rather, creating tweets for how she imagines, and wants, people to react to what she says. What does this reveal about her tweeting? If you use Twitter to connect, do you think about what you are going to say and how it will reflect on the way people view you? How they will react to your words? Write a short essay exploring the connection between what we tweet and the "self-portraits" we create for our friends through our words.

## MAKING CONNECTIONS

1. Several of the writers in this unit are critical of social networking sites, noting that they promote self-centeredness, reduce our ability to cope with emotions, and cheapen what it means to be a "friend." Interview at least 10 people of different age groups about how they use online communication and their views of social networking sites. Create simple questions, but make them broad enough to allow for the expression of detailed viewpoints and opinions. Discuss the interviews as a group, and write a short essay evaluating the role of social networking on the lives of people today. Include any differences or similarities you noticed between age groups, professions, and/or social backgrounds. Based on your surveys, can you predict the role social networking will have in our lives in the next decade?

2. Are tweeting, texting, and other forms of abbreviated communication changing how we speak? Is there a difference between how you tweet or text and how you communicate in person, with live speech? Write an essay exploring the impact, if any, of texting and tweeting on the spoken word. Research the issue online, and identify at least three articles of merit that discuss the issue to support your view.

3. Research the pages of at least four different social networking sites (many are named in this unit). Describe how they are similar and how they are different. Do they attract different groups? Are some cooler than others? What groups do they attract, and how do they promote a sense of belonging and community? Explain.

4. What might the erosion of the real and virtual boundaries that social networking promotes eventually do to the way we communicate with each other? Will the way people define themselves now be different in 20 years as a result of this blending of online and offline relationships? Explain.

5. Anthropologist Margaret Mead once said that "civilization is the ever-widening circle of those whom we do not kill." Apply this statement to Internet relationships. Will the Internet revolutionize communication to the extent that it can prevent wars and human disagreement? Survey people for their opinions on this question and evaluate their responses in your essay. Draw from your own experience with the Internet as you formulate your evaluation.

6. What will the erosion of the real and virtual boundaries eventually do to our social consciousness? Will the way people define themselves now be different in 20 years as a result of this blending of realities?

7. Write an essay in which you explore the freedom Internet relationships grant. How are they different from face-to-face (F2F) relationships? Will the Internet replace many F2F relationships? If so, in what ways? What are the pros and cons of each?

# The Communication Gap: How We Speak to Each Other

Although language may be what separates us from other animals, it is conversation—the ability to communicate and interact with each other—that is at the heart of our humanity. As social animals, conversation forms the foundation of our daily interactions. But conversation is more than simply speaking; it is a collaborative exercise. How we interact with each other, in social groups, with our families, among friends and acquaintances, in work situations, and with our significant others, is a critical factor in our success as human beings. This chapter explores the social dynamics of conversation, differences between male and female communication styles, nonverbal communication, and the ways we relate and communicate with each other.

## He Says, She Says

Some sociologists and psychologists claim that men and women talk differently—either due to social conditioning or basic physiology—and that the "male" form of discourse is the preferred form of communication. With the great interest in communication, a growing number of scholars are attempting to prove that important differences distinguish the way men and women use language. Most researchers present theories that such differences are the results of either discriminatory socialization or genetic disposition.

The essays in this section address common assumptions about differences between how men and women communicate. First, in "Women Talk Too Much," Janet Holmes explains that the stereotype that women speak more than men is rooted in how our society values speech and claims this stereotype simply is not true. Then, in "Sex Differences," linguist Ronald Macaulay says that although some differences in expression reflect social and cultural conditioning, much of the controversy regarding gender-based linguistic differences are based on myths and age-old stereotypes. Linguist Deborah Cameron challenges the presumption that men and women speak so differently they seem as if they come from different planets, a theory publicized by John Gray over a decade ago. In "What Language Barrier?" Cameron explains why the myth of gender difference is really just a myth. But Tony Kornheiser seems to provide first-hand observational proof of gender difference as he compares conversations between himself and his daughter and son in "No Detail Is Too Small for Girls Answering a Simple Question." The section ends with an essay exploring parent/child communication dynamics. Linguist Deborah Tannen describes the communication challenges between people of the *same* gender—mothers and daughters—in "Oh, Mom. Oh, Honey."

## What We Say and How We Say It

Conversation forms the foundation of our social interactions. This section discusses the social elements of conversation and how men and women speak to each other. First, communications professors Teri Kwal Gamble and Michael W. Gamble project the discussion on gender styles to nonverbal behavior in "Nonverbal Behavior: Culture, Gender, and the Media," pointing out how this "gendered" sublanguage is influenced internally by culture and externally by the media. Jennifer Akin, in "Small-Scale Communication," then describes some of the barriers to communication and ways to address conflict in conversation. The next essay continues this exploration of obstacles to effective speech. David Grambs explains why he feels defeated by "uptalk" and misuse of the word "like," which seems to have permeated the speech of the younger generation. After years of trying to fight this insidious invader, Grambs reveals his fear that "like" is here to stay in "The Like Virus." The last essay explores the healing nature of talk. Margaret J. Wheatley discusses how conversation has the power to effect social change in "Some Friends and I Started Talking."

# HE SAYS, SHE SAYS

## Women Talk Too Much
*Janet Holmes*

Do women really talk more than men? Many people seem to think so, but is this assumption based on stereotypes or facts? And who determines how much talk is "too much"? In this essay, linguist Janet Holmes sets out to debunk the "language myth" that women talk too much. In fact, explains Holmes, women speak less than men do in situations where their talk is most "valued." She also asserts that the claim that "women talk too much" is inherently biased because it is men who tend to hold positions of power, who determine when there is too much talk (such as women speaking in informal settings) and when it is appropriate (men speaking in public forums).

Janet Holmes is a professor of sociolinguistics at the Victoria University of Wellington, New Zealand. Her publications include *An Introduction to Sociolinguistics* (2001) and *Women, Men and Politeness* (1995). She has published many articles on numerous sociolinguistic topics, including spoken New Zealand English, sexist language, humor, and workplace discourse.

1  Do women talk more than men? Proverbs and sayings in many languages express the view that women are always talking:

> *Women's tongues are like lambs' tails—they are never still. —English*
> *The North Sea will sooner be found wanting in water than a woman at a loss for words. —Jutlandic*
> *The woman with active hands and feet, marry her, but the woman with overactive mouth, leave well alone. —Maori*

Some suggest that while women talk, men are silent patient listeners.

> *When both husband and wife wear pants it is not difficult to tell them apart—he is the one who is listening. —American*

> *Nothing is so unnatural as a talkative man or a quiet woman. —Scottish*

Others indicate that women's talk is not valued but is rather considered noisy, irritating prattle:

*Where there are women and geese there's noise. —Japanese*

Indeed, there is a Japanese character which consists of three instances of the character for the concept "woman" and which translates as "noisy"! My favorite proverb, because it attributes not noise but rather power to the woman speaker is this Chinese one:

*The tongue is the sword of a woman and she never lets it become rusty.*

So what are the facts? Do women dominate the talking time? Do men struggle to get a word in edgewise, as the stereotype suggests?

## The Evidence

2   Despite the widespread belief that women talk more than men, most of the available evidence suggests just the opposite. When women and men are together, it is the men who talk most. Two Canadian researchers, Deborah James and Janice Drakich, reviewed sixty-three studies which examined the amount of talk used by American women and men in different contexts. Women talked more than men in only two studies.

3        In New Zealand, too, research suggests that men generally dominate the talking time. Margaret Franken compared the amount of talk used by female and male "experts" assisting a female TV host to interview well-known public figures. In a situation where each of three interviewers was entitled to a third of the interviewers' talking time, the men took more than half on every occasion.

4        I found the same pattern analyzing the number of questions asked by participants in one hundred public seminars. In all but seven, men dominated the discussion time. Where the numbers of women and men present were about the same, men asked almost two-thirds of the questions during the discussion. Clearly women were not talking more than men in these contexts.

5        Even when they hold influential positions, women sometimes find it hard to contribute as much as men to a discussion. A British company appointed four women and four men to the eight most highly paid management positions. The managing director commented that the men often patronized the women and tended to dominate meetings:

> *I had a meeting with a [female] sales manager and three of my [male] directors once . . . It took about two hours. She only spoke once and one of my fellow directors cut across her and said 'What Anne is trying to say Roger is . . .' and I think that about sums it up. He knew better than Anne what she was trying to say, and she never got anything said.*

6   There is abundant evidence that this pattern starts early. Many researchers have compared the relative amounts that girls and boys contribute to classroom talk. In a wide range of communities, from kindergarten through primary, secondary and tertiary education, the same pattern recurs—males dominate classroom talk. So on

this evidence we must conclude that the stereotype of the garrulous woman reflects sexist prejudice rather than objective reality.

## Looking for an Explanation

7  Why is the reality so different from the myth? To answer this question, we need to go beyond broad generalizations and look more carefully at the patterns identified. Although some teachers claim that boys are "by nature more spirited and less disciplined," there is no evidence to suggest that males are biologically programmed to talk more than females. It is much more likely that the explanation involves social factors.

## What Is the Purpose of the Talk?

8  One relevant clue is the fact that talk serves different functions in different contexts. Formal public talk is often aimed at informing people or persuading them to agree to a particular point of view (e.g., political speeches, television debates, radio interviews, public lectures, etc.). Public talk is often undertaken by people who wish to claim or confirm some degree of public status. Effective talk in public and in the media can enhance your social status—as politicians and other public performers know well. Getting and holding the floor is regarded as desirable, and competition for the floor in such contexts is common. (There is also some risk, of course, since a poor performance can be damaging.)

9      Classroom research suggests that more talk is associated with higher social status or power. Many studies have shown that teachers (regardless of their gender) tend to talk for about two-thirds of the available time. But the boys dominate the relatively small share of the talking time that remains for pupils. In this context, where talk is clearly valued, it appears that the person with most status has the right to talk most. The boys may therefore be asserting a claim to higher status than the girls by appropriating the majority of the time left for pupil talk.

10      The way women and men behave in formal meetings and seminars provides further support for this explanation. Evidence collected by American, British and New Zealand researchers shows that men dominate the talking time in committee meetings, staff meetings, seminars and task-oriented decision-making groups. If you are skeptical, use a stopwatch to time the amount of talk contributed by women and men at political and community meetings you attend. This explanation proposes that men talk more than women in public, formal contexts because they perceive participating and verbally contributing in such contexts as an activity which enhances their status, and men seem to be more concerned with asserting status and power than women are.

11      By contrast, in more private contexts, talk usually serves interpersonal functions. The purpose of informal or intimate talk is not so much status enhancement as establishing or maintaining social contact with others, making social connections, developing and reinforcing friendships and intimate relationships. Interestingly, the few studies which have investigated informal talk have found that there are fewer differences in the amount contributed by women and men in these contexts (though men still talked more in nearly a third of the informal studies reviewed by Deborah James and Janice Drakich). Women, it seems, are willing to talk more in relaxed

social contexts, especially where the talk functions to develop and maintain social relationships.

12  Another piece of evidence that supports this interpretation is the *kind* of talk women and men contribute in mixed-sex discussions. Researchers analyzing the functions of different utterances have found that men tend to contribute more information and opinions, while women contribute more agreeing, supportive talk, more of the kind of talk that encourages others to contribute. So men's talk tends to be more referential or informative, while women's talk is more supportive and facilitative.

13  Overall, then, women seem to use talk to develop personal relationships and maintain family connections and friendships more often than to make claims to status or to directly influence others in public contexts. Of course, there are exceptions, as Margaret Thatcher, Benazir Bhutto and Jenny Shipley demonstrate. But, until recently, many women seem not to have perceived themselves as appropriate contributors to public, formal talk.

14  In New Zealand we identified another context where women contributed more talk than men. Interviewing people to collect samples of talk for linguistic analysis, we found that women were much more likely than men (especially young men) to be willing to talk to us at length. For example, Miriam Meyerhoff asked a group of ten young people to describe a picture to a female and to a male interviewer. It was made quite clear to the interviewees that the more speech they produced the better. In this situation, the women contributed significantly more speech than the men, both to the male and to the female interviewer.

15  In the private but semi-formal context of an interview, then, women contributed more talk than men. Talk in this context could not be seen as enhancing the status of the people interviewed. The interviewers were young people with no influence over the interviewees. The explanation for the results seems to be that the women were being more cooperative than the men in a context where more talk was explicitly sought by the interviewer.

### Social Confidence

16  If you know a lot about a particular topic, you are generally more likely to be willing to contribute to a discussion about it. So familiarity or expertise can also affect the amount a person contributes to a particular discussion. In one interesting study the researcher supplied particular people with extra information, making them the "experts" on the topic to be discussed. Regardless of gender, these "experts" talked more in the subsequent discussions than their uninformed conversational partners (though male "experts" still used more talking time in conversation with uninformed women than female "experts" did with uninformed men).

17  Looking at people's contributions to the discussion section of seminars, I found a similar effect from expertise or topic familiarity. Women were more likely to ask questions and make comments when the topic was one they could claim expert knowledge about. In a small seminar on the current state of the economy, for instance, several women economists who had been invited to attend contributed to the discussion, making this one of the very few seminars where women's contributions exceeded men's.

18    Another study compared the relative amount of talk of spouses. Men dominated the conversations between couples with traditional gender roles and expectations, but when the women were associated with a feminist organization they
tended to talk more than their husbands. So feminist women were more likely to
challenge traditional gender roles in interaction.

19    It seems possible that both these factors—expert status and feminist philosophy—
have the effect of developing women's social confidence. This explanation also fits
with the fact that women tend to talk more with close friends and family, when
women are in the majority, and also when they are explicitly invited to talk (in an
interview, for example).

## Perceptions and Implications

20  If social confidence explains the greater contributions of women in some social
contexts, it is worth asking why girls in school tend to contribute less than boys.
Why should they feel unconfident in the classroom? Here is the answer which one
sixteen-year-old gave:

> *Sometimes I feel like saying that I disagree, that there are other ways of look-
> ing at it, but where would that get me? My teacher thinks I'm showing off,
> and the boys jeer. But if I pretend I don't understand, it's very different. The
> teacher is sympathetic and the boys are helpful. They really respond if they
> can show YOU how it is done, but there's nothing but "aggro" if you give any
> signs of showing THEM how it is done.*

Talking in class is often perceived as "showing off," especially if it is girl-talk.
Until recently, girls have preferred to keep a low profile rather than attract negative
attention.

21    Teachers are often unaware of the gender distribution of talk in their classrooms. They usually consider that they give equal amounts of attention to girls
and boys, and it is only when they make a tape recording that they realize that
boys are dominating the interactions. Dale Spender, an Australian feminist who
has been a strong advocate of female rights in this area, noted that teachers who
tried to restore the balance by deliberately "favoring" the girls were astounded to
find that despite their efforts they continued to devote more time to the boys in
their classrooms. Another study reported that a male science teacher who managed to create an atmosphere in which girls and boys contributed more equally to
discussion felt that he was devoting 90 per cent of his attention to the girls. And
so did his male pupils. They complained vociferously that the girls were getting
too much talking time.

22    In other public contexts, too, such as seminars and debates, when women and
men are deliberately given an equal amount of the highly valued talking time, there
is often a perception that they are getting more than their fair share. Dale Spender
explains this as follows:

> *The talkativeness of women has been gauged in comparison not with men but
> with silence. Women have not been judged on the grounds of whether they talk
> more than men, but of whether they talk more than silent women.*

23    In other words, if women talk at all, this may be perceived as "too much" by men who expect them to provide a silent, decorative background in many social contexts. This may sound outrageous, but think about how you react when precocious children dominate the talk at an adult party. As women begin to make inroads into formerly "male" domains such as business and professional contexts, we should not be surprised to find that their contributions are not always perceived positively or even accurately.

## Conclusion

24 We have now reached the conclusion that the question "Do women talk more than men?" can't be answered with a straight "yes" or "no." The answer is rather, "It all depends." It depends on many different factors, including the social context in which the talk is taking place, the kind of talk involved and the relative social confidence of the speakers, which is affected by such things as their social roles (e.g., teacher, host, interviewee, wife) and their familiarity with the topic.

25    It appears that men generally talk more in formal, public contexts where informative and persuasive talk is highly valued, and where talk is generally the prerogative of those with some societal status and has the potential for increasing that status. Women, on the other hand, are more likely to contribute in private, informal interactions, where talk more often functions to maintain relationships, and in other situations where for various reasons they feel socially confident.

26    Finally, and most radically, we might question the assumption that more talk is always a good thing. "Silence is golden," says the proverb, and there are certainly contexts in all cultures where silence is more appropriate than talk, where words are regarded as inadequate vehicles for feelings, or where keeping silent is an expression of appreciation or respect. Sometimes it is the silent participants who are the powerful players. In some contexts the strong silent male is an admired stereotype. However, while this is true, it must be recognized that talk is very highly valued in western culture. It seems likely, then, that as long as holding the floor is equated with influence, the complexities of whether women or men talk most will continue to be a matter for debate.

### THINKING CRITICALLY

1. How do the proverbs at the beginning of Holmes's essay set the tone? What is remarkable about these proverbs? Have you heard any of them? Which one do you like or dislike the most, and why?

2. In what ways does the context and setting of the conversation influence men's and women's talking patterns? Explain.

3. Holmes explains that in situations where talk is valued—in the classroom or boardroom, for instance—males are likely to speak more than females. If this is true, what accounts for the excess of proverbs and sayings regarding women's talk? Explain.

4. In paragraph 20, Holmes cites a 16-year-old girl who explains why she does not speak more in class. Evaluate this girl's response in the context of your own social and classroom experiences in high school.

**5.** What, according to Holmes, are the differences between men's and women's use of talk? Do you agree or disagree with her conclusions? Explain.

## WRITING ASSIGNMENTS

**1.** Ben Jonson, a 17th-century writer and playwright, wrote a popular play called *Epicene, or, The Silent Woman.* Locate a copy of this play and write an essay in which you make connections between attitudes toward women's talk three hundred years ago and today. How have things changed, and how are they similar?

**2.** Do you think that understanding gender patterns in conversation will change the way men and women speak to each other? Do you think that such changes are necessary and healthy? Alternatively, do you think that some men and women have a need for the established patterns? Explain.

# Sex Differences
*Ronald Macaulay*

Contrary to popular belief, men and women do not speak different forms of English. Nor are there innate or genetic differences in the way men and women acquire or use language. So argues Ronald Macaulay, a professor of linguistics and an expert on language acquisition. Although social background can generate some differences in the way the sexes speak, it is pure myth and stereotyping that sex differences show up in language patterns. Males do not, for instance, instinctively gravitate to coarse language, and females are not proternaturally drawn to the language of nurturing.

Ronald Macaulay is professor of linguistics at Pitzer College in Claremont, CA. He is the author of *Generally Speaking: How Children Learn Language* (1980), *Locating Dialect in Discourse: The Language of Honest Men and Bonnie Lasses in Ayr* (1991), and *The Social Art: Language and Its Uses* (1996), from which this essay is taken.

*I think the English women speak awfy nice. The little girls are very feminine just because they've a nice voice. But the same voice in an Englishman—nae really. I think the voice lets the men down but it flatters the girls.*

*—Aberdeen housewife*

1 More nonsense has been produced on the subject of sex differences than on any linguistic topic, with the possible exception of spelling. Perhaps this is appropriate. The relations between the sexes have generally been considered a fit topic for comedy. In his book *Language: Its Nature, Development and Origin*, Otto Jespersen has a chapter entitled "The Woman" in which he manages to include every stereotype about women that was current at the time. It is almost unfair to quote directly but even in the 1920s Jespersen should have known better, particularly since he

lived in Denmark where women have traditionally shown an independent spirit. Here are a few examples:

> There can be no doubt that women exercise a great and universal influence on linguistic development through their instinctive shrinking from coarse and gross expressions and their preference for refined and (in certain spheres) veiled and indirect expressions.
>
> Men will certainly with great justice object that there is a danger of the language becoming languid and insipid if we are always to content ourselves with women's expressions.
>
> Women move preferably in the central field of language, avoiding everything that is out of the way or bizarre, while men will often either coin new words or expressions or take up old-fashioned ones, if by that means they are enabled, or think they are enabled, to find a more adequate or precise expression for their thoughts. Woman as a rule follows the main road of language, where man is often inclined to turn aside into a narrow footpath or even to strike out a new path for himself. . . .
>
> Those who want to learn a foreign language will therefore always do well at the first stage to read many ladies' novels, because they will there continually meet with just those everyday words and combinations which the foreigner is above all in need of, what may be termed the indispensable small-change of a language.
>
> Woman is linguistically quicker than man: quicker to learn, quicker to hear, and quicker to answer. A man is slower: he hesitates, he chews the cud to make sure of the taste of words, and thereby comes to discover similarities with and differences from other words, both in sound and in sense, thus preparing himself for the appropriate use of the fittest noun or adjective.
>
> The superior readiness of speech of women is a concomitant of the fact that their vocabulary is smaller and more central than that of men.

2    Such stereotypes are often reinforced by works of fiction. Since little information about prosodic features or paralinguistic features is contained in the normal writing system, novelists frequently try to indicate the tone of voice by descriptive verbs and adjectives to introduce dialogue. An examination of several novels revealed an interesting difference between the expression used to introduce men's or women's speech:

| MEN | WOMEN |
|---|---|
| said firmly | said quietly |
| said bluntly | asked innocently |
| said coldly | echoed obediently |
| said smugly | said loyally |
| urged | offered humbly |
| burst forth | whispered |
| demanded aggressively | asked mildly |
| said challengingly | agreed placidly |

| | |
|---|---|
| cried furiously | smiled complacently |
| exclaimed contemptuously | fumbled on |
| cried portentously | implored |
| grumbled | pleaded |

The surprising part is that the two lists are totally distinct. No doubt the novelists intended to be realistic in describing two very different styles of speech but, in doing so, they also reinforce the stereotypes of men and women.

3    In the past twenty years the question of sex differences in language has been a growth industry as scholars have attempted to claim and to counter claims that there are or are not important differences in the ways in which males and females use language. It would, of course, be surprising if there were not. Both men and women will use the forms of language, registers, and styles appropriate to the activities in which they are engaged. To the extent that these activities differ between males and females, it is to be expected that their language will differ. This much is obvious. There is no need to look for a genetic basis for such differences. It is also obvious that those in a position of power often expect to be treated with deference by those over whom they have power. To the extent that in Western industrialized societies men have more often been in positions of power over women rather than the reverse, it is hardly surprising if women are sometimes found to have used deferential language. There have also been certain violent activities, such as fighting or contact sports, that until recently have been exclusively a male province, and there are forms of language appropriate to them that may have been less common among women.

4    Even in making such banal statements, one must qualify them by reference to "Western industrialized societies" or by limiting them to a single section of the community. For example, it is probably true that in Britain until World War I middle-class women were less likely to swear in public than middle-class men, but working-class women were less inhibited. (G. K. Chesterton reported that in an argument with a fishwife he could not compete in obscenities with her but triumphed in the end by calling her "An adverb! A preposition! A pronoun!")

5    In sociolinguistic studies of complex communities such as Glasgow, New York, and Norwich, it has been shown that women in the lower middle class are likely to be closer in their speech to the women in the class immediately above them than are the men, who are likely to be closer to the men in the class immediately below them. It has been suggested that this is because lower-class speech is associated with toughness and virility and the men in the lower middle class choose to identify with this image rather than with the less "masculine" speech of the upper-class men. It may not be unimportant that in these studies the interviewers were all men.

6    There seems, however, to be a deep-seated desire to find essential differences between the speech of men and women that can either be attributed to some discriminatory kind of socialization or, even better, to genetic disposition. This can be seen in many references to sex differences in language development. Popular belief and scholarly opinion has generally maintained that girls are more advanced in

language development than boys at the same age. Jespersen, for example, claimed that girls learned to talk earlier and more quickly than boys, and that the speech of girls is more correct than that of boys.

7    For about fifty years after Jespersen this view was maintained in the scholarly literature on children's development. In 1954 Professor Dorothea McCarthy published an article summarizing what was known about children's language development at that time. Her conclusion about sex differences is:

> One of the most consistent findings to emerge from the mass of data accumulated on language development in American white children seems to be a slight difference in favor of girls in nearly all aspects of language that have been studied.

8  What McCarthy actually found, however, was that the differences were not large enough to be statistically significant. Although psychologists are normally very careful not to make claims about differences that could be the result of chance (that is, are not statistically significant), McCarthy was so convinced that girls were more advanced in their speech that she chose to interpret the evidence the way she did. In a survey of the literature up till 1975, I found that none of the studies provided convincing evidence of consistent sex differences in language development. I concluded that the burden of proof remained with those who wished to claim otherwise. To the best of my knowledge, the situation has not changed since then.

9    What I did find were many examples of preconceived notions of sex differences from the assertion that girls have an innate tendency toward sedentary pursuits to claims that it is easier and more satisfying for the girl baby to imitate the mother's speech than it is for the boy baby to imitate the father's. One example will illustrate the kind of attitude:

> The little girl, showing in her domestic play the over-riding absorption in personal relationships through which she will later fulfill her role of wife, mother and "expressive" leader of the family . . . learns language early in order to communicate. The kind of communication in which she is chiefly interested at this stage concerns the nurturant routines which are the stuff of family life. Sharing and talking about them as she copies and "helps" her mother about the house must enhance the mutual identification of mother and child, which in turn . . . will reinforce imitation of the mother's speech and promote further acquisition of language, at first oriented toward domestic and interpersonal affairs but later adapted to other uses as well. Her intellectual performance is relatively predictable because it is rooted in this early communication, which enables her (environment permitting) to display her inherited potential at an early age.

This is contrasted with the interests of boys:

> Their preoccupation with the working of mechanical things is less interesting to most mothers and fathers are much less available.

As a result the boy's language development is slower:

> His language, less fluent and personal and later to appear than the girl's, develops along more analytic lines and may, in favourable circumstances, provide the groundwork for later intellectual achievement which could not have been foreseen in his first few years.

Girls, of course, are more predictable:

> The girl, meanwhile, is acquiring the intimate knowledge of human reactions which we call feminine intuition. Perhaps because human reactions are less regular than those of inanimate objects, however, she is less likely to develop the strictly logical habits of thought that intelligent boys acquire, and if gifted may well come to prefer the subtler disciplines of the humanities to the intellectual rigor of science.

I am not sure whether the writer considered himself a scientist, but if his writing is an example of intellectual rigor, then give me the subtlety of the humanities any day. What makes his statement all the more incredible is that it comes after describing a longitudinal study of children that showed no important sex differences in language development.

10    One of the problems with attempting to demonstrate differences in language development is that measures of linguistic proficiency, particularly for young children, are extremely crude instruments. Thus it is not surprising that samples of linguistic behavior will reveal occasional differences between subgroups of the sample. Such sex differences that have shown up on tests are much smaller than those that have been shown to relate to social background. The fact that most studies show no sex differences and that many of the findings of small differences have been contradicted in other studies should be sufficient warning against drawing conclusions about the linguistic superiority of either sex.

11    There are some differences between males and females that do not depend upon unreliable tests of language development. Boys are much more likely to suffer from speech disorders, such as stuttering, than girls. Adult males on average have deeper voices than adult females because the vibrating part of the vocal cords is about a third longer in men. However, there may be social influences on this physiological difference. It has been claimed that in the United States women may speak as if they were smaller than they are (that is, with higher-pitched voices) and men as if they were bigger than they are (that is, with lower-pitched voices). The "Oxford voice" common among Oxford fellows (all male) at one time was remarkably high pitched, and other social groups have adopted characteristic pitch levels that are not totally "natural."

12    It was reported that once during a debate in the French parliament when a delegate pointed out that there were differences between men and women, another delegate shouted out *Vive la difference!* It is not necessary to believe that men and women are the same to be skeptical about claims as to the differences in the way men and women speak. The desire to emphasize the differences seems to be

widespread. Jespersen's chapter remains as a warning signal to all who venture into this murky area that one's prejudices may show through. Jesperson obviously believed (and no doubt so did many of his readers) that what he was saying was self-evident. However, he ends the chapter by observing that "great social changes are going on in our times which may eventually modify even the linguistic relations of the two sexes." Eventually, even scholars following in Jespersen's footsteps may come to see that men and women are simply people and that what they have in common is more important than *la difference,* at least as far as their use of language is concerned.

13  It is, however, disturbing to find in a work published in 1991 the following passage by a distinguished and respected scholar:

> [I]t is clear why, as sociolinguists have often observed, women are more disposed to adopt the legitimate language (or the legitimate pronunciation): since they are both inclined towards docility with regard to the dominant usages both by the sexual division of labor, which makes them specialize in the sphere of consumption, and by the logic of marriage, which is their main if not their only avenue of social advancement and through which they circulate upwards, women are predisposed to accept, from school onwards, the new demands of the market in symbolic goods.

14  It is a salutary reminder that progress is often an illusion.

### THINKING CRITICALLY

1. Why does Macaulay refer to much of the work done on sex differences as "nonsense"?
2. Macaulay charges that fiction often reinforces sexual stereotypes as novelists attempt to introduce men's or women's speech. Are there any problems with the examples he cites? Support your answer.
3. What examples does Macaulay give to indicate how society influences male or female speech patterns?
4. Because Macaulay sees so many flaws in Jespersen's findings, why does he devote such a large portion of his article to discussing and even quoting Jespersen?
5. Does Macaulay feel that a lessening of sexist language indicates that society has made significant progress in the way it views the sexes?
6. Macaulay wrote his essay for a scholarly audience. In your opinion, is the language used in the essay more like that of a class lecture, a textbook, a radio talkshow, a professional journal, or a conference presentation? Why?

### WRITING ASSIGNMENTS

1. Keep a journal of the expressions writers you encounter use to introduce male and female characters' speech. What conclusions can you draw?
2. Watch a television program with a story line (e.g., a situation comedy, a drama, or a full-length movie). Write a brief critique of the program based on its presentation of linguistic sex differences.

# What Language Barrier?
*Deborah Cameron*

Do men and women really not communicate in the same way? It would seem that the consensus holds this view to be true. But is there scientific evidence to support this Mars-and-Venus theory? Oxford language professor Deborah Cameron investigates the controversy in this essay that challenges the idea that men and women don't understand each other.

Deborah Cameron is a feminist linguist and professor of language at Oxford University. Much of her academic research focuses on the relationship of language to gender and sexuality. She is the author of *The Myth of Mars and Venus* (2007), from which this essay is excerpted, appearing in *The Guardian* on October 1, 2007.

1 Do men and women speak the same language? Can they ever really communicate? These questions are not new, but since the early 1990s there has been a new surge of interest in them. Countless self-help and popular psychology books have been written portraying men and women as alien beings, and conversation between them as a catalogue of misunderstandings. The most successful exponents of this formula, such as Deborah Tannen, author of *You Just Don't Understand*, and John Gray, author of *Men Are From Mars, Women Are From Venus*, have topped the bestseller lists on both sides of the Atlantic. Advice on how to bridge the communication gulf between the sexes has grown into a flourishing multimedia industry. Gray's official website, for instance, promotes not only his various Mars and Venus books, but also seminars, residential retreats, a telephone helpline and a dating service.

2 Readers who prefer something a little harder-edged can turn to a genre of popular science books with titles such as *Brain Sex, Sex on the Brain, The Essential Difference*, and *Why Men Don't Iron*. These explain that the gulf between men and women is a product of nature, not nurture. The sexes communicate differently (and women do it better) because of the way their brains are wired. The female brain excels in verbal tasks whereas the male brain is better adapted to visual-spatial and mathematical tasks. Women like to talk; men prefer action to words.

3 Writers in this vein are fond of presenting themselves as latter-day Galileos, braving the wrath of the political correctness lobby by daring to challenge the feminist orthodoxy that denies that men and women are by nature profoundly different. Simon Baron-Cohen, the author of *The Essential Difference*, explains in his introduction that he put the book aside for several years because "the topic was just too politically sensitive". In the chapter on male-female differences in his book about human nature, *The Blank Slate*, Steven Pinker congratulates himself on having the courage to say what has long been "unsayable in polite company." Both writers stress that they have no political axe to grind: they are simply following the evidence where it leads, and trying to put scientific facts in place of politically correct dogma.

4 Yet before we applaud, we should perhaps pause to ask ourselves: since when has silence reigned about the differences between men and women? Certainly not since the early 1990s, when the previous steady trickle of books began to develop into a raging torrent. By now, a writer who announces that sex-differences are

natural is not "saying the unsayable:" he or she is stating the obvious. The proposition that men and women communicate differently is particularly uncontroversial, with clichés such as "men never listen" and "women find it easier to talk about their feelings" referenced constantly in everything from women's magazines to humorous greeting cards.

5    The idea that men and women "speak different languages" has itself become a dogma, treated not as a hypothesis to be investigated or as a claim to be adjudicated, but as an unquestioned article of faith. Our faith in it is misplaced. Like the scientists I have mentioned, I believe in following the evidence where it leads. But in this case, the evidence does not lead where most people think it does. If we examine the findings of more than 30 years of research on language, communication and the sexes, we will discover that they tell a different, and more complicated, story.

6    The idea that men and women differ fundamentally in the way they use language to communicate is a myth in the everyday sense: a widespread but false belief. But it is also a myth in the sense of being a story people tell in order to explain who they are, where they have come from, and why they live as they do. Whether or not they are "true" in any historical or scientific sense, such stories have consequences in the real world. They shape our beliefs, and so influence our actions. The myth of Mars and Venus is no exception to that rule.

7    For example, the workplace is a domain in which myths about language and the sexes can have detrimental effects. A few years ago, the manager of a call centre in north-east England was asked by an interviewer why women made up such a high proportion of the agents he employed. Did men not apply for jobs in his centre? The manager replied that any vacancies attracted numerous applicants of both sexes, but, he explained: "We are looking for people who can chat to people, interact, and build rapport. What we find is that women can do this more . . . women are naturally good at that sort of thing." Moments later, he admitted: "I suppose we do, if we're honest, select women sometimes because they are women rather than because of something they've particularly shown in the interview."

8    The growth of call centers is part of a larger trend in economically advanced societies. More jobs are now in the service than the manufacturing sector, and service jobs, particularly those that involve direct contact with customers, put a higher premium on language and communication skills. Many employers share the call-centre manager's belief that women are by nature better qualified than men for jobs of this kind, and one result is a form of discrimination. Male job applicants have to prove that they possess the necessary skills, whereas women are just assumed to possess them. In today's increasingly service-based economy, this may not be good news for men.

9    But it is not only men who stand to lose because of the widespread conviction that women have superior verbal skills. Someone else who thinks men and women are naturally suited to different kinds of work is Baron-Cohen. In *The Essential Difference* he offers the following "scientific" careers advice: "People with the female brain make the most wonderful counselors, primary school teachers, nurses, caregivers, therapists, social workers, mediators, group facilitators or personnel staff . . . People with the male brain make the most wonderful scientists, engineers, mechanics, technicians, musicians, architects, electricians, plumbers, taxonomists, bankers, toolmakers, programmers or even lawyers."

10     The difference between the two lists reflects what Baron-Cohen takes to be the "essential difference" between male and female brains. The female-brain jobs make use of a capacity for empathy and communication, whereas the male ones exploit the ability to analyze complex systems. Baron-Cohen is careful to talk about "people with the female/male brain" rather than "men and women". He stresses that there are men with female brains, women with male brains, and individuals of both sexes with "balanced" brains. He refers to the major brain types as "male" and "female", however, because the tendency is for males to have male brains and females to have female brains. And at many points it becomes clear that in spite of his caveats about not confusing gender with brain sex, he himself is doing exactly that.

11     The passage reproduced above is a good example. Baron-Cohen classifies nursing as a female-brain, empathy-based job (though if a caring and empathetic nurse cannot measure dosages accurately and make systematic clinical observations she or he risks doing serious harm) and law as a male-brain, system-analyzing job (though a lawyer, however well versed in the law, will not get far without communication and people-reading skills). These categorizations are not based on a dispassionate analysis of the demands made by the two jobs. They are based on the everyday common-sense knowledge that most nurses are women and most lawyers are men.

12     If you read the two lists in their entirety, it is hard not to be struck by another "essential difference": the male jobs are more varied, more creative, and better rewarded than their female counterparts. Baron-Cohen's job-lists take me back to my schooldays 35 years ago, when the aptitude tests we had to complete before being interviewed by a careers adviser were printed on pink or blue paper. In those days we called this sexism, not science.

13     At its most basic, what I am calling "the myth of Mars and Venus" is simply the proposition that men and women differ fundamentally in the way they use language to communicate. All versions of the myth share this basic premise; most versions, in addition, make some or all of the following claims:

1. Language and communication matter more to women than to men; women talk more than men.

2. Women are more verbally skilled than men.

3. Men's goals in using language tend to be about getting things done, whereas women's tend to be about making connections to other people. Men talk more about things and facts, whereas women talk more about people, relationships and feelings.

4. Men's way of using language is competitive, reflecting their general interest in acquiring and maintaining status; women's use of language is cooperative, reflecting their preference for equality and harmony.

5. These differences routinely lead to "miscommunication" between the sexes, with each sex misinterpreting the other's intentions. This causes problems in contexts where men and women regularly interact, and especially in heterosexual relationships.

14    The literature of Mars and Venus, in both the self-help and popular science genres, is remarkably patronizing towards men. They come off as bullies, petulant toddlers; or Neanderthals sulking in their caves. One (male) contributor to this catalogue of stereotypes goes so far as to call his book *If Men Could Talk*. A book called *If Women Could Think* would be instantly denounced; why do men put up with books that put them on a par with Lassie or Skippy the Bush Kangaroo ("Hey, wait a minute—I think he's trying to tell us something!")?

15    Perhaps men have realized that a reputation for incompetence can sometimes work to your advantage. Like the idea that they are no good at housework, the idea that men are no good at talking serves to exempt them from doing something that many would rather leave to women anyway. (Though it is only some kinds of talking that men would rather leave to women: in many contexts men have no difficulty expressing themselves—indeed, they tend to dominate the conversation.)

16    This should remind us that the relationship between the sexes is not only about difference, but also about power. The long-standing expectation that women will serve and care for others is not unrelated to their position as the "second sex". But in the universe of Mars and Venus, the fact that we (still) live in a male-dominated society is like an elephant in the room that everyone pretends not to notice.

17    My father, like many men of his generation, held the belief that women were incompetent drivers. During my teenage years, family car journeys were invariably accompanied by an endless running commentary on how badly the women around us were driving. Eventually I became so irritated by this, I took to scouring passing traffic for counter-examples: women who were driving perfectly well, and men who were driving like idiots.

18    My father usually conceded that the men were idiots, but not because they were men. Whereas female idiocy was axiomatically caused by femaleness, substandard male drivers were either "yobbos"—people with no consideration for others on the road or anywhere else—or "Sunday drivers": older men whose driving skills were poor because they used their cars only at weekends. As for the women who drove unremarkably, my father seemed surprised when I pointed them out. It was as if he had literally not noticed them until that moment. At the time I thought my father was exceptional in his ability to make reality fit his preconceptions, but now I know he was not. Psychologists have found in experimental studies that when interpreting situations people typically pay most attention to things that match their expectations, and often fail to register counter-examples.

19    It is not hard to see how these tendencies might lead readers of Mars and Venus books to "recognize" generalizations about the way men and women use language, provided those generalizations fit with already familiar stereotypes. An anecdote illustrating the point that, say, men are competitive and women cooperative conversationalists will prompt readers to recall the many occasions on which they have observed men competing and women cooperating—while not recalling the occasions, perhaps equally numerous, on which they have observed the opposite. If counter-examples do come to mind ("What about Janet? She's the most competitive person I know"), it is open to readers to apply the classic strategy of putting them in a separate category of exceptions ("of course, she grew up with three brothers / is the only woman in her department / works in a particularly competitive business").

In relation to men and women, our most basic stereotypical expectation is simply that they will be different rather than the same. We actively look for differences, and seek out sources that discuss them. Most research studies investigating the behavior of men and women are designed around the question: is there a difference? And the presumption is usually that there will be. If a study finds a significant difference between male and female subjects, that is considered to be a "positive" finding, and has a good chance of being published. A study that finds no significant differences is less likely to be published.

20     Most people, of course, do not read academic journals: they get their information about scientific research findings from the reports that appear in newspapers, or from TV science documentaries. These sources often feature research on male-female differences, since media producers know that there is interest in the subject. But the criteria producers use when deciding which studies to report and how to present them introduce another layer of distortion. And sometimes headlines trumpet so-called facts that turn out, on investigation, to have no basis in evidence at all.

21     In 2006, for instance, a popular science book called *The Female Brain* claimed that women on average utter 20,000 words a day, while men on average utter only 7,000. This was perfect material for sound bite science—it confirmed the popular belief that women are not only the more talkative sex but three times as much—and was reported in newspapers around the world.

22     One person who found it impossible to believe was Mark Liberman, a professor of phonetics who has worked extensively with recorded speech. His skepticism prompted him to delve into the footnotes of *The Female Brain* to find out where the author had got her figures. What he found was not an academic citation but a reference to a self-help book. Following the trail into the thickets of popular literature, Liberman came across several competing statistical claims. The figures varied wildly: different authors (and sometimes even the same author in different books) gave average female daily word-counts ranging from 4,000 to 25,000 words. As far as Liberman could tell, all these numbers were plucked from thin air: in no case did anyone cite any actual research to back them up. He concluded that no one had ever done a study counting the words produced by a sample of men and women in the course of a single day. The claims were so variable because they were pure guesswork.

23     After Liberman pointed this out in a newspaper article, the author of *The Female Brain* conceded that her claim was not supported by evidence and said it would be deleted from future editions. But the damage was already done: the much-publicized sound bite that women talk three times as much as men will linger in people's memories and get recycled in their conversations, whereas the little-publicized retraction will make no such impression. This is how myths acquire the status of facts.

## Do Women and Men Really Speak So Differently?

24   In 2005, an article appeared in the journal *American Psychologist* with the title The Gender Similarities Hypothesis. This title stood out as unusual, because, as we have seen, the aim of most research studies is to find differences rather than similarities

between men and women. Yet, as the article's author Janet S. Hyde pointed out, on closer inspection, the results of these studies very often show more similarity than difference.

25 Hyde is a psychologist who specializes in "meta-analysis," a statistical technique that allows the analyst to collate many different research findings and draw overall conclusions from them. Scientists believe that one study on its own does not show anything: results are only considered reliable if a number of different studies have replicated them. Suppose that the question is: who interrupts more, men or women? Some studies will have found that men interrupt more, others that women do, and others may have found no significant difference. In some studies the reported gender difference will be large, while in others it will be much smaller. The number of people whose behavior was investigated will also vary from study to study. Meta-analysis enables you to aggregate the various results, controlling for things that make them difficult to compare directly, and calculate the overall effect of gender on interruption.

26 Hyde used this technique to review a large number of studies concerned with all kinds of putative male-female differences. In Table 1, I have extracted the results for just those studies that dealt with gender differences in linguistic and communicative behavior. To read this table you need to know that "d" is the formula indicating the size of the overall gender difference: minus values for "d" indicate that females are ahead of males, whereas plus values indicate that males are ahead of females.

27 So, for instance, the table tells us that when the findings of different studies are aggregated, the overall conclusion is that men interrupt more than women and women self-disclose more than men. However, the really interesting information is in the last column, which tells us whether the actual figure given for d indicates an effect that is very large, large, moderate, small, or close to zero. In almost every case, the overall difference made by gender is either small or close to zero. Two items, spelling accuracy and frequency of smiling, show a larger effect—but it is still only moderate.

28 There were a few areas in which Hyde did find that the effect of gender was large or very large. For instance, studies of aggression and of how far people can throw things have shown a considerable gap between the sexes (men are more aggressive and can throw further). But in studies of verbal abilities and behavior, the differences were slight. This is not a new observation. In 1988 Hyde and her colleague Marcia Linn carried out a meta-analysis of research dealing specifically with gender differences in verbal ability. The conclusion they came to was that the difference between men and women amounted to "about one-tenth of one standard deviation"—statistician-speak for "negligible". Another scholar who has considered this question, the linguist Jack Chambers, suggests that the degree of non-overlap in the abilities of male and female speakers in any given population is "about 0.25%". That's an overlap of 99.75%. It follows that for any array of verbal abilities found in an individual woman, there will almost certainly be a man with exactly the same array.

29 Chambers' reference to individual men and women points to another problem with generalizations such as "men interrupt more than women" or "women are

## Gender Differences in Verbal/Communicative Behaviour

| Focus of research | No. of studies analysed | Value of d | Effect size |
| --- | --- | --- | --- |
| Reading comprehension | 23 | –0.06 | Close to zero |
| Vocabulary | 44 | –0.02–+0.06 | Close to zero |
| Spelling | 5* | –0.45 | Moderate |
| Verbal reasoning | 5* | –0.02 | Close to zero |
| Speech production | 12 | –0.33 | Small |
| Conversational interruption | 70 | +0.15–+0.33 | Small |
| Talkativeness | 73 | –0.11 | Small |
| Assertive speech | 75 | +0.11 | Small |
| Affiliative speech | 46 | –0.26 | Small |
| Self disclosure | 205 | –0.18 | Small |
| Smiling | 418 | –0,40 | Moderate |

*Note:* Asterisks indicate cases where the small number of studies analysed is compensated for by the fact that they were conducted with very large controlled samples.

*Source:* Adapted from Hyde, 'The Gender Similarities Hypothesis'.

more talkative than men". As well as underplaying their similarities, statements of the form "women do this and men do that" disguise the extent of the variation that exists within each gender group.

30      Explaining why he had reacted with instant skepticism to the claim that women talk three times as much as men, Liberman predicted: "Whatever the average female versus male difference turns out to be, it will be small compared with the variation among women and among men." Focusing on the differences between men and women while ignoring the differences within them is extremely misleading but, unfortunately, all too common.

## Do Women Really Talk More Than Men?

31  If we are going to try to generalize about which sex talks more, a reliable way to do it is to observe both sexes in a single interaction, and measure their respective contributions. This cuts out extraneous variables that are likely to affect the amount of talk (like whether someone is spending their day at a Buddhist retreat or a high school reunion), and allows for a comparison of male and female behavior under the same contextual conditions. Numerous studies have been done using this

approach, and while the results have been mixed, the commonest finding is that men talk more than women. One review of 56 research studies categorizes their findings as shown here:

## Pattern of Difference Found / Number of Studies

Men talk more than women / 34 (60.8%)
Women talk more than men / 2 (3.6%)
Men and women talk the same amount / 16 (28.6%)
No clear pattern / 4 (7.0%)[1]

32    The reviewers are inclined to believe that this is a case of gender and amount of talk being linked indirectly rather than directly: the more direct link is with status, in combination with the formality of the setting (status tends to be more relevant in formal situations). The basic trend, especially in formal and public contexts, is for higher-status speakers to talk more than lower-status ones. The gender pattern is explained by the observation that in most contexts where status is relevant, men are more likely than women to occupy high-status positions; if all other things are equal, gender itself is a hierarchical system in which men are regarded as having higher status.

33    "Regarded" is an important word here, because conversational dominance is not just about the way dominant speakers behave; it is also about the willingness of others to defer to them. Some experimental studies have found that you can reverse the "men talk more" pattern, or at least reduce the gap, by instructing subjects to discuss a topic that both sexes consider a distinctively female area of expertise. Status, then, is not a completely fixed attribute, but can vary relative to the setting, subject and purpose of conversation.

34    That may be why some studies find that women talk more in domestic interactions with partners and family members: in the domestic sphere, women are often seen as being in charge. In other spheres, however, the default assumption is that men outrank women, and men are usually found to talk more. In informal contexts where status is not an issue, the commonest finding is not that women talk more than men, it is that the two sexes contribute about equally.

35    If it does not reflect reality, why is the folk-belief that women talk more than men so persistent? The feminist Dale Spender once suggested an explanation: she said that people overestimate how much women talk because they think that, ideally, women would not talk at all. While that may be rather sweeping, it is true that belief in female loquacity is generally combined with disapproval of it. The statement "women talk more than men" tends to imply the judgment "women talk too much". (As one old proverb charmingly puts it: "Many women, many words; many geese, many turds.")

---

[1]Source: Based on Deborah James and Janice Drakich, 'Understanding Gender Differences in Amount of Talk', in Deborah Tannen (ed.), *Gender and Conversational Interaction*, Oxford University Press (New York, 1993).

36     The folk-belief that women talk more than men persists because it provides a justification for an ingrained social prejudice. Evolutionary psychology is open to a similar criticism: that it takes today's social prejudices and projects them back into prehistory, thus elevating them to the status of timeless truths about the human condition.

37     Champions of the evolutionary approach often say it is their opponents whose arguments are based on prejudice rather than facts or logic. They complain that feminists and other "PC" types are unwilling even to consider the idea that sex-differences might have biological rather than social causes. Instead of judging the arguments on their merits, these politically motivated critics just denounce them, and those who advance them, as reactionary and bigoted.

38     But their stories have a basic flaw: they are based not on facts, but on myths.

## THINKING CRITICALLY

1. Cameron states that it is now "politically correct" to presume that men and women communicate differently. Why was it once thought inappropriate to do so? Explain.

2. What does Cameron mean when she states that the idea that men and women "speak different languages" is a "dogma"? What is a dogma? What happens to scientific inquiry when a theory becomes a dogma?

3. On what grounds does Cameron challenge the idea that men and women differ fundamentally in the way they use language? Why does she feel it is simply not true? What harm does she believe could come from accepting this "false belief"?

4. How does the human brain construct reality to match expectations? What examples does Cameron use to demonstrate this phenomenon? How does this tendency apply to our ideas about communication styles of men and women?

5. In what ways has the theory of male-female communication differences been based on pseudoscience or not on science at all? Explain.

6. Did anything Cameron report in her essay surprise you? How do you think Janet Holmes would respond to this essay? Ronald Macaulay? Explain.

## WRITING ASSIGNMENTS

1. Cameron lists the five claims surrounding the theory that men and women use language differently. Review each one and explain why you believe they are likely, or unlikely, to be true. Refer to information from Cameron's essay, as well as other sources she cites in her piece, such as Deborah Tannen and Stephen Pinker. If you wish, you may also review John Gray's book *Men Are from Mars, Women Are from Venus.*

2. Try an experiment. In a student recreation area, or in the cafeteria where there is a mix of men and women, observe the conversational styles of each gender. Note whether one indeed speaks more than the other and differences, if any, in what they say or how they say it. Try this experiment over several days with several different groups of people. Write an analysis of your results, addressing the five theories regarding male-female communication cited by Cameron in her essay.

3. Many people interested in gender and communication claim that women tend to speak more and men tend to try to dominate conversation. Cameron notes that much of our beliefs about conversational dominance and women speaking more in general come from "folk belief." Explain what these beliefs are and write a paper in which you support or refute Cameron's position that these beliefs are simply unfounded.

---

# No Detail Is Too Small for Girls Answering a Simple Question

*Tony Kornheiser*

A common complaint between the sexes is that men and women just do not speak the same language. In the next essay, sports columnist and humorist Tony Kornheiser observes the differences in the communication style of his daughter and son, and by extension, women and men. His conclusion is that "women have more to say on everything."

Tony Kornheiser writes for *The Washington Post,* hosts *The Tony Kornheiser Show* on ESPN radio, and co-hosts *Pardon the Interruption* with fellow *Post* sports columnist Mike Wilbon on ESPN2. He is the author of several books, including *Pumping Irony* (1995) and *Bald as I Want to Be* (1997).

1 The last time I ventured into my favorite column area—differences between men and women—was when the infamous Teen Talk Barbie doll came out. Barbie was given 270 things to say, and one of them was "Math class is tough!" This, of course, is infuriating, because it plays into the damaging sexual stereotype that girls are stupid in math.

2 Well, I got cute and wrote how everyone knows girls are stupid in math. I gave an example of my own daughter, whom I love dearly, and who is a sensitive and caring soul, and how when I ask her, "If a bus leaves Cleveland at 7 p.m. heading for Pittsburgh, 200 miles away, and traveling 50 miles per hour, when will it arrive?" she answers, "Do all the children have seat belts, Daddy?" I thought it was a pretty good line. But I received all kinds of nasty mail, much of it—so help me—from female mathematicians, and female actuaries and female physicists specializing in subatomic particle acceleration. In that same column, I wrote that boys are stupid in English, yet I didn't get a single letter of protest from boys. Obviously, they couldn't read the column.

3 Anyway . . . here we go again.

4 My daughter recently came home from sleep-away camp, where she'd spent five weeks. She looked great. And I was so proud of her, going away by herself.

5 The first question I asked her was "How was camp?"

6 She began by saying, "Well, the day I left, I got on the bus, and I sat next to Ashley, and she brought Goldfish, which was good because I forgot my Now and Laters, and then Shannon came over, and she's from Baltimore, and she gets her clothes at the Gap, and she had a Game Boy, but all she had was Tetris, which I have, so we asked Jenny, who was the counselor, if anybody had Sonic the Hedgehog, but . . ."

7      She went on like this for a few minutes, still talking about the bus ride up to camp five weeks ago, and I came to the horrifying realization that she was actually going to tell me how camp was, minute by minute. Because this is what girls do (and when they grow up and become women, they do it, too, as any man can vouch for). They gather information and dispense it without discrimination. Everything counts the same! It is not that women lack the ability to prioritize information, it is that they don't think life is as simple as men do, and so they are fascinated by the multiplicity of choices that they see.

8      This is why you have to be very specific with what you ask women. If, for example, you missed a Rams game, and you know a woman who saw it, never, ever ask, "What happened?" Unless you have nowhere to go until Thursday.

9      Ask:

1. Who won?

2. What was the score?

3. Was anyone carried out on a stretcher?

10     You must get them to fast-forward.

11     Left to their own devices, girls go through life volubly answering essay questions. And boys? Multiple choice is way too complicated. Boys restrict themselves to true/false.

12     Boys do not gather and retain information, they focus on results.

13     My son went to camp for six weeks—one week longer than my daughter. As I had with my daughter, I asked him, "How was camp?"

14     He said, "Good. I busted Jason's nose." Short and to the point.

15     This was followed by, "Can we go to McDonald's?"

16     Did I mention the cheers? My daughter came back with cheers. About 187,640 musical cheers, all of which are accompanied by an intricate series of hand, feet and hip movements. She went to camp a 10-year-old, she came back a Vandella.

17     It's amazing, the affinity of girls and cheers. If you've ever been to camp, you know that girls have a special gene for cheers and that even girls who have never been to camp before—or, for that matter, been to America or spoken English before—automatically know all the cheers the moment they step off the bus. As a boy at camp, I used to look at girls in amazement, wondering why they would waste their time like that, when they could be doing useful things like me—memorizing Willie Mays' doubles and sacrifice flies during an entire decade.

18     Boys don't do musical cheers.

19     Even during "color war," that traditional camp competition when cheering is supposed to result in points, here's how boys cheer on the way to the dining hall: They look at the other team and say, "Yo, Green Team, drop dead."

## THINKING CRITICALLY

1. Kornheiser, in the context of his daughter's communication style, states that women "gather information and dispense it without discrimination." Respond to Kornheiser's assertion. Is there truth to his stereotypical description of the way men and women relay information? Explain.

2. In his introduction, Kornheiser relates how his joking about girls and math resulted in angry letters from many women, yet his comments about boys and English received no such response. What accounts for this difference? Is it more important to dispel one stereotype than it is the other? Why or why not?

3. Based on his essay, can you determine which communication style Kornheiser prefers? As a writer and columnist, is Kornheiser more "male" or "female" in his communication style? Explain.

4. How would you characterize Kornheiser's tone and style? What assumptions does he make about his audience? Does his article appeal to both sexes? Why or why not?

## WRITING ASSIGNMENTS

1. Many of the authors in this section seem to defend their own gender's communication style. Write an essay in which you support your gender's communication style, or defend or analyze the style of the opposite sex. Is one better than the other? Why or why not? Remember to support your perspective with examples.

2. In his essay, Tony Kornheiser describes the differences between the way his children, one boy and one girl, communicate. How do his observations connect to stereotypes about how men and women communicate? Are these communication styles simply a fact of gender? Explain, using examples from Kornheiser's essay and from other authors in this section, such as Deborah Tannen and Janet Holmes.

# Exploring the Language of **V I S U A L S**

## Men Are from Belgium, Women Are from New Brunswick

*Roz Chast*

Almost 20 years ago, marriage counselor John Gray published a controversial but best-selling book, *Men Are from Mars, Women Are from Venus: A Guide to Getting What You Want in Your Relationships*. Humorously explaining that men and women come from different planets (Mars and Venus), Gray postulated that the genders must respect their differences to achieve harmony. Although men and women speak a common tongue, their construction of meaning differs. For example, Gray proposed that when a woman suggests to a man that they stop and ask for directions, what he actually hears is her not trusting him to find his way without help. The cartoon by Roz Chast plays with some of Gray's concepts of male/female interpretations of language meaning. Chast's cartoons appear regularly in *The New Yorker* and the *Harvard Review*. She has illustrated several children's books and is the author of a number of cartoon collections, including *Childproof: Cartoons about Parents and Children* (1997).

## THINKING CRITICALLY

1. What is Chast trying to convey in this cartoon? Does it operate on several levels? Explain.

2. Do you find this cartoon funny? Do you think that it may be more humorous to one gender than another? If so, which gender would find it funnier, and why?

3. Why does Chast claim men are from Belgium and women are from New Brunswick? Why do you think she chose these locations?

4. If you did not know the gender of the author of this cartoon, could you guess? Why or why not? Does gender matter to the success of the cartoon and the points it is trying to make? Explain.

# Oh, Mom. Oh, Honey.

*Deborah Tannen*

Much of this section addresses the theory that men and women communicate—
or don't communicate—differently. Here, Deborah Tannen explores the conversational differences within gender—that is, the words of mothers and daughters.
It would seem that for generations and across cultures, mothers and daughters
have battled to reconcile a love/hate relationship that is largely constructed by
what mothers speak and what daughters hear. Can the two ever get along?

Deborah Tannen is professor of linguistics at Georgetown University. She is
the author of many best-selling books on linguistics and social discourse, including *I Only Say This Because I Love You* (2001), *The Argument Culture* (1999),
*You Just Don't Understand* (1997), and *You're Wearing That? Understanding
Mothers and Daughters in Conversation* (2007). She has been a featured guest
on many news programs, including *20/20, 48 Hours,* and *The NewsHour with
Jim Lehrer*. This essay appeared in the January 22, 2006 edition of *The Washington Post*.

1   The five years I recently spent researching and writing a book about mothers and
daughters also turned out to be the last years of my mother's life. In her late eighties
and early nineties, she gradually weakened, and I spent more time with her, caring
for her more intimately than I ever had before. This experience—together with her
death before I finished writing—transformed my thinking about mother-daughter
relationships and the book that ultimately emerged.

2   All along I had in mind the questions a journalist had asked during an interview about my research. "What is it about mothers and daughters?" she blurted
out. "Why are our conversations so complicated, our relationships so fraught?"
These questions became more urgent and more personal, as I asked myself: What
had made my relationship with my mother so volatile? Why had I often ricocheted
between extremes of love and anger? And what had made it possible for my love
to swell and my anger to dissipate in the last years of her life?

3   Though much of what I discovered about mothers and daughters is also true
of mothers and sons, fathers and daughters, and fathers and sons, there is a special
intensity to the mother-daughter relationship because talk—particularly talk about
personal topics—plays a larger and more complex role in girls' and women's social
lives than in boys' and men's. For girls and women, talk is the glue that holds a
relationship together—and the explosive that can blow it apart. That's why you can
think you're having a perfectly amiable chat, then suddenly find yourself wounded
by the shrapnel from an exploded conversation. Daughters often object to remarks
that would seem harmless to outsiders, like this one described by a student of mine,
Kathryn Ann Harrison:

"Are you going to quarter those tomatoes?" her mother asked as Kathryn was
preparing a salad. Stiffening, Kathryn replied, "Well, I was. Is that wrong?"
"No, no," her mother replied. "It's just that personally, I would slice them."
Kathryn said tersely, "Fine." But as she sliced the tomatoes, she thought, can't

I do *anything* without my mother letting me know she thinks I should do it some other way?

4    I'm willing to wager that Kathryn's mother thought she had merely asked a question about a tomato. But Kathryn bristled because she heard the implication, "You don't know what you're doing. I know better."

5    I'm a linguist. I study how people talk to each other, and how the ways we talk affect our relationships. My books are filled with examples of conversations that I record or recall or that others record for me or report to me. For each example, I begin by explaining the perspective that I understand immediately because I share it: in mother-daughter talk, the daughter's, because I'm a daughter but not a mother. Then I figure out the logic of the other's perspective. Writing this book forced me to look at conversations from my mother's point of view.

6    I interviewed dozens of women of varied geographic, racial and cultural backgrounds, and I had informal conversations or e-mail exchanges with countless others. The complaint I heard most often from daughters was, "My mother is always criticizing me." The corresponding complaint from mothers was, "I can't open my mouth. She takes everything as criticism." Both are right, but each sees only her perspective.

7    One daughter said, for example, "My mother's eyesight is failing, but she can still spot a pimple from across the room." Her mother doesn't realize that her comments—and her scrutiny—make the pimple bigger.

8    Mothers subject their daughters to a level of scrutiny people usually reserve for themselves. A mother's gaze is like a magnifying glass held between the sun's rays and kindling. It concentrates the rays of imperfection on her daughter's yearning for approval. The result can be a conflagration—*whoosh*.

9    This I knew: Because a mother's opinion matters so much, she has enormous power. Her smallest comment—or no comment at all, just a look—can fill a daughter with hurt and consequently anger. But this I learned: Mothers, who have spent decades watching out for their children, often persist in commenting because they can't get their adult children to do what is (they believe) obviously right. Where the daughter sees power, the mother feels powerless. Daughters and mothers, I found, both overestimate the other's power—and underestimate their own.

10   The power that mothers and daughters hold over each other derives, in part, from their closeness. Every relationship requires a search for the right balance of closeness and distance, but the struggle is especially intense between mothers and daughters. Just about every woman I spoke to used the word "close," as in "We're very close" or "We're not as close as I'd like (or she'd like) to be."

11   In addition to the closeness/distance yardstick—and inextricable from it—is a yardstick that measures sameness and difference. Mothers and daughters search for themselves in the other as if hunting for treasure, as if finding sameness affirms who they are. This can be pleasant: After her mother's death, one woman noticed that she wipes down the sink, cuts an onion and holds a knife just as her mother used to do. She found this comforting because it meant her mother was still with her.

12    Sameness, however, can also make us cringe. One mother thought she was being particularly supportive when she assured her daughter, "I know what you mean," and described a matching experience of her own. But one day her daughter cut her off: "Stop saying you know because you've had the same experience. You don't know. This is my experience. The world is different now." She felt her mother was denying the uniqueness of her experience—offering *too* much sameness.

13    "I sound just like my mother" is usually said with distaste—as is the wry observation, "Mirror mirror on the wall, I am my mother after all."

14    When visiting my parents a few years ago, I was sitting across from my mother when she asked, "Do you like your hair long?"

15    I laughed, and she asked what was funny. I explained that in my research, I had come across many examples of mothers who criticize their daughters' hair. "I wasn't criticizing," she said, looking hurt. I let the matter drop. A little later, I asked, "Mom, what do you think of my hair?" Without hesitation, she said, "I think it's a little too long."

16    Hair is one of what I call the Big Three that mothers and daughters critique (the other two are clothing and weight). Many women I talked to, on hearing the topic of my book, immediately retrieved offending remarks that they had archived, such as, "I'm so glad you're not wearing your hair in that frumpy way anymore"; another had asked, "You did that to your hair on purpose?" Yet another told her daughter, after seeing her on television at an important presidential event, "You needed a haircut."

17    I would never walk up to a stranger and say, "I think you'd look better if you got your hair out of your eyes," but her mother might feel entitled, if not obligated, to say it, knowing that women are judged by appearance—and that mothers are judged by their daughters' appearance, because daughters represent their mothers to the world. Women must choose hairstyles, like styles of dress, from such a wide range of options, it's inevitable that others—mothers included—will think their choices could be improved. Ironically, mothers are more likely to notice and mention flaws, and their comments are more likely to wound.

18    But it works both ways. As one mother put it, "My daughters can turn my day black in a millisecond." For one thing, daughters often treat their mothers more callously than they would anyone else. For example, a daughter invited her mother to join a dinner party because a guest had bowed out. But when the guest's plans changed again at the last minute, her daughter simply uninvited her mother. To the daughter, her mother was both readily available and expendable.

19    There's another way that a mother can be a lightning rod in the storm of family emotions. Many mothers told me that they can sense and absorb their daughters' emotions instantly ("If she feels down, I feel down") and that their daughters can sense theirs. Most told me this to illustrate the closeness they cherish. But daughters sometimes resent the expectation that they have this sixth sense—and act on it.

20    For example, a woman was driving her mother to the airport following a visit, when her mother said petulantly, "I had to carry my own suitcase to the car." The daughter asked, "Why didn't you tell me your luggage was ready?" Her mother replied, "You knew I was getting ready." If closeness requires you to hear—and

obey—something that wasn't even said, it's not surprising that a daughter might crave more distance.

21   Daughters want their mothers to see and value what they value in themselves; that's why a question that would be harmless in one context can be hurtful in another. For example, a woman said that she told her mother of a successful presentation she had made, and her mother asked, 'What did you wear?' The woman exclaimed, in exasperation, "Who cares what I wore?!" In fact, the woman cared. She had given a lot of thought to selecting the right outfit. But her mother's focus on clothing—rather than the content of her talk—seemed to undercut her professional achievement.

22   Some mothers are ambivalent about their daughters' success because it creates distance: A daughter may take a path her mother can't follow. And mothers can envy daughters who have taken paths their mothers would have liked to take, if given the chance. On the other hand, a mother may seem to devalue her daughter's choices simply because she doesn't understand the life her daughter chose. I think that was the case with my mother and me.

23   My mother visited me shortly after I had taken a teaching position at Georgetown University, and I was eager to show her my new home and new life. She had disapproved of me during my rebellious youth, and had been distraught when my first marriage ended six years before. Now I was a professor; clearly I had turned out all right. I was sure she'd be proud of me—and she was. When I showed her my office with my name on the door and my publications on the shelf, she seemed pleased and approving.

24   Then she asked, "Do you think you would have accomplished all this if you had stayed married?" "Absolutely not," I said. "If I'd stayed married, I wouldn't have gone to grad school to get my PhD."

25   "Well," she replied, "if you'd stayed married you wouldn't have had to." Ouch. With her casual remark, my mother had reduced all I had accomplished to the consolation prize. I have told this story many times, knowing I could count on listeners to gasp at this proof that my mother belittled my achievements. But now I think she was simply reflecting the world she had grown up in, where there was one and only one measure by which women were judged successful or pitiable: marriage. She probably didn't know what to make of my life, which was so different from any she could have imagined for herself. I don't think she intended to denigrate what I had done and become, but the lens through which she viewed the world could not encompass the one I had chosen. Reframing how I look at it takes the sting out of this memory.

26   Reframing is often key to dissipating anger. One woman found that this technique could transform holiday visits from painful to pleasurable. For example, while visiting, she showed her mother a new purchase: two pairs of socks, one black and one navy. The next day she wore one pair, and her mother asked, "Are you sure you're not wearing one of each color?" In the past, her mother's question would have set her off, as she wondered, "What kind of incompetent do you think I am?" This time she focused on the caring: Who else would worry about the color of her socks? Looked at this way, the question was touching. If a daughter can recognize that seeming criticism truly expresses concern, a mother can acknowledge

that concern truly implies criticism—and bite her tongue. A woman who told me that this worked for her gave me an example: One day her daughter announced, "I joined Weight Watchers and already lost two pounds." In the past, the mother would have said, "That's great" and added, "You have to keep it up." This time she replied, "That's great"—and stopped there.

27 Years ago, I was surprised when my mother told me, after I began a letter to her "Dearest Mom," that she had waited her whole life to hear me say that. I thought this peculiar to her until a young woman named Rachael sent me copies of e-mails she had received from her mother. In one, her mother responded to Rachael's effusive Mother's Day card: "Oh, Rachael!!!!! That was so WONDERFUL!!! It almost made me cry. I've waited 25 years, 3 months and 7 days to hear something like that. . . ."

28 Helping to care for my mother toward the end of her life, and writing this book at the same time, I came to understand the emotion behind these parallel reactions. Caring about someone as much as you care about yourself, and the critical eye that comes with it, are two strands that cannot be separated. Both engender a passion that makes the mother-daughter relationship perilous—and precious.

## THINKING CRITICALLY

1. Why, according to Tannen, is the mother-daughter communication dynamic particularly volatile? If you are female, did Tannen's observations resonate? If you are male, do you think Tannen's observations apply to mother-son relationships as well? Why or why not?

2. Tannen observes that because she is a daughter, she explains the perspective that she understands because she shares it (she is a daughter). Does this make her qualified—or unqualified—to judge the difference between other types of relationships? Does it limit her research to presenting only one perspective?

3. How can interpersonal relationships between mothers and daughters interfere with their ability to communicate effectively with one another? Explain.

4. What does Tannen's essay reveal about her relationship with her own mother? In your opinion, does her relationship with her mother make her more or less qualified to write a book about this topic?

## WRITING ASSIGNMENTS

1. Write a brief essay demonstrating how the narrator learns something from her experience and then changes her thinking or views. What epiphany does she experience as a result of the two staring incidents (paragraph 7 and 14)?

2. Write a personal narrative in which you explore your own relationship with a parent or trusted adult who had an influence on you growing up. Focus on the way you communicated with this person. For example, you can write about a mother-daughter, mother-son, father-daughter, or father-son relationship, or perhaps a relationship with a grandparent or step-parent. In your essay, address points raised by Tannen in this essay, as well as observations of your own regarding what communication dynamic was present during your childhood and how that communication dynamic remains or changed in young adulthood.

# WHAT WE SAY AND HOW WE SAY IT

## Nonverbal Behavior: Culture, Gender, and the Media
*Teri Kwal Gamble and Michael W. Gamble*

Much of this chapter addresses how men and women use written and spoken language. But what about our nonverbal communication skills—the way we "speak" without words? Do men and women use different nonverbal cues? Are smiles and nods female communication traits, whereas interruptions and touching are male traits? These are just a few of the body-language questions addressed by this essay.

Teri Kwal Gamble is a professor of communication at the College of New Rochelle, and Michael W. Gamble is a professor of communication at New York Institute of Technology. They have coauthored many books, including *Communication Works* (1990), *Literature Alive!* (1994), and *Public Speaking in the Age of Diversity* (1998). The following article is an excerpt from their latest collaboration, *Contacts: Communicating Interpersonally* (1998).

1   Throughout the world, people use nonverbal cues to facilitate self-expression. To a great extent, however, the culture of a people modifies their use of such cues. For example, individuals who belong to contact cultures, which promote interaction and encourage displays of warmth, closeness, and availability, tend to stand close to each other when conversing, seek maximum sensory experience, and touch each other frequently. In contrast, members of noncontact cultures discourage the use of such behaviors. Saudi Arabia, France, and Italy are countries with contact cultures; their members relish the intimacy of contact when conversing. In contrast, Scandinavia, Germany, England, Japan, and the United States are low- or lower-contact cultures whose members value privacy and maintain more distance from each other when interacting.[1]

2       Individuals who grow up in different cultures may display emotion or express intimacy in different ways. It is normal, for example, for members of Mediterranean cultures to display highly emotional reactions that are uninhibited and greatly exaggerated; it is common for them to express grief or happiness with open facial displays, magnified gestures, and vocal cues that support the feelings. On the other hand, neither the Chinese nor the Japanese readily reveal their feelings in public, preferring to display less emotion, maintain more self-control, and keep their feelings to themselves; for these reasons, they often remain expressionless.

3       Even when different cultures use the same nonverbal cues, their members may not give the cues the same meaning. In the United States, for example, a nod symbolizes agreement or consent, while in Japan it means only that a message was received.

4       If we hope to interact effectively with people from different cultures, it is important that we make the effort to identify and understand the many ways culture shapes nonverbal communication. We need to acknowledge that one communication style is not intrinsically better than any other; it is that awareness that can help contribute to more successful multicultural exchanges.

5    Men and women commonly use nonverbal communication in ways that reflect
societal expectations. For example, men are expected to exhibit assertive behaviors that demonstrate their power and authority; women, in contrast, are expected
to exhibit more reactive and responsive behaviors. Thus, it should not surprise us
that men talk more and interrupt women more frequently than vice versa.[2]

6    Men are also usually more dominant during interactions than women. Visual
dominance is measured by comparing the percentage of time spent looking while
speaking with the percentage of time spent looking while listening. When compared with women, men display higher levels of looking while speaking than
women do, and lower levels than women when they are listening. Thus, the visual
dominance ratio of men is usually higher than that of women, and again reflects
the use of nonverbal cues to reinforce perceptions of social power.[3]

7    Men and women also differ in their use of space and touch. Men use space
and touch to assert their dominance over women. As a result, men are much more
likely to touch women than women are to touch men. Women are thus more apt
to be the recipients of touching actions than they are to be the initiators of such
actions. Men also claim more personal space than women usually do, and they
more frequently walk in front of women rather than behind them. Thus, in general,
males are the touchers, not the touchees, and the leaders rather than the followers.

8    There are nonverbal behaviors that women display more than men do. Women
tend to smile more than men. They also commonly display their feelings more
overtly than men. In general, women are more expressive than men and exhibit
higher levels of involvement when engaged in person-to-person interaction than
men. Women also use nonverbal signals to draw others into conversation to a
greater extent than men. While women demonstrate an interest in affiliation, men
are generally more interested in establishing the strength of their own ideas and
agendas than they are in sharing the floor with others.[4] Women also are better interpreters of nonverbal messages than men.

9    All too often, the media and technology help legitimize stereotypical nonverbal
displays. The contents of various media contain a plethora of open sexual appeals,
portrayals of women obsessed with men, and male-female interactions that portray
the man as physically dominant and the female as subordinate. They also include
numerous repetitions of the message that "thin is in."[5]

10    After repeated exposure to such media messages, men and women come to
believe and ultimately emulate what they see and hear. Thus, females are primed to
devote considerable energy to improving their appearance, preserving their youth-
fulness, and nurturing others, while males learn to display tougher, more aggressive
take-charge cues, trying all the while to control their emotions.

11    Nonverbal power cues echo the male dominance/female subservience-mediated
message. In advertisements, for example, men are typically portrayed superior to
women, who are usually shown in various stages of undress. In the media, nonverbal behaviors portray women as vulnerable and men in control.[6]

12    The repetition of such myths can make us feel dissatisfied and inadequate. If
we rely on the media as a reference point for what is and is not desirable in our relationships and interactions, we may find it difficult to be ourselves.

13     Even mediated vocal cues suggest that it is the male and not the female who is the authority. In up to 90 percent of all advertisements male voices are used in voice-overs—even when the product being sold is aimed at women.

14     Further complicating the situation is the continued growth of the use of computer-generated virtual reality simulations. In addition to allowing us to feel as if we were really interacting in different, but make-believe environments and even giving us the opportunity to change our gender, such simulations are also being used to enforce violent gender scenarios resulting in women being threatened and killed. Even when erotic rather than violent, the media offerings all too often reinforce the notion that men have physical control over women.[7]

## Notes

1. Peter Andersen, "Exploring Intercultural Differences in Nonverbal Communication," in L. Samovar and R. Porter (eds.), *Intercultural Communication: A Reader,* 5th ed., Belmont, CA: Wadsworth Publishing, 1988, pp. 272–282.
2. B. Veland, "Tell Me More: On the Fine Art of Listening," *Utne Reader* (1992): 104–109; A. Mulac, "Men's and Women's Talk in Some Gender and Mixed Gender Dyads: Power or Polemic?" *Journals of Language and Social Psychology,* 8 (1989): 249–270.
3. J. F. Dovidio, S. L. Ellyson, C. F. Keating, K. Heltman, and C. E. Brown, "The Relationship of Social Power to Visual Displays of Dominance between Men and Women," *Journal of Personality and Social Psychology,* 54 (1988): 233–242.
4. Julia T. Wood, *Gendered Lives,* Belmont, CA: Wadsworth, 1994, p. 154.
5. See for example, J. Leland and E. Leonard, "Back to Twiggy," *Newsweek,* February 1, 1993, pp. 64–65.
6. Wood, *Gendered Lives,* p. 239.
7. Suzanne Stefanic, "Sex and the New Media," *NewMedia* (April 1993): 38–45.

### THINKING CRITICALLY

1. How does culture influence nonverbal communication? What are contact cultures? How can our understanding of contact cultures likewise improve our understanding of nonverbal communication between genders?

2. In paragraph 5, Gamble and Gamble say "it should not surprise us that men talk more and interrupt women more frequently than vice versa." Why do they feel this statement to be true? Based on your own experience, does it seem like a reasonable assessment? Explain.

3. How can looking and listening behaviors of men and women reinforce perceptions of social power?

4. In the final sentence of paragraph 7, the authors connect the act of touching to the act of leading. "Thus, in general, males are the touchers, not the touchees, and the leaders rather than the followers." Evaluate the accuracy of this connection. Do you agree with their conclusion? Explain.

### WRITING ASSIGNMENTS

1. Try to identify some of the differences between the way men and women use language through cues that are connected with language but not necessarily

actual words—such as pitch, tone, volume, facial expression, and touch. Write an essay from your own personal perspective analyzing the nonverbal communication of men and women. Are they indeed speaking the same language?

2. The authors theorize that women are better interpreters of nonverbal messages than men are (paragraph 8). Why do you think they make this judgment? Do you agree? How does the media perpetuate gender–power issues? In what nonverbal ways do they communicate gender stereotypes? Write an essay exploring the connection between the media and the nonverbal communication style of men and women.

# Small-Scale Communication

## Jennifer Akin

When she wrote this essay, Jennifer Akin was a graduate student of computational linguistics working at the Conflict Research Consortium at University of Colorado as a research assistant. She is now pursuing a degree in nonprofit administration. This essay was published online by *Beyond Intractability*, edited by Guy Burgess and Heidi Burgess, in September of 2003.

*"I never saw an instance of one or two disputants convincing the other by argument."*

*—Thomas Jefferson*

*"Discussion is an exchange of knowledge; argument an exchange of emotion."*

*—Robert Quillen*

1 Here is a scene with which we are all familiar: Alex says or does something that Bob interprets as an insult or an attack. Bob retaliates in words or action. Alex, having meant no harm in the first place, now sees Bob's actions or words as an unprovoked attack. The situation can quickly escalate even though there was no real reason for a fight to begin in the first place. What has happened here is not a failure to communicate, but a failure to understand communication. More often than not, that is what lies at the root of conflicts, although in intractable conflicts there may be many other factors as well.

2 Of course, misunderstanding of ideas or intent can also occur when there is an absence of communication between two groups. When two parties are not speaking, there is no way to clarify positions, intentions, or past actions; rumors can spread unchecked. Sometimes both parties make a concerted effort to communicate as clearly as possible, but cultural differences or language barriers obstruct clear understanding.

3 Even within a cultural group, misunderstandings can arise because of different personal communication styles. One person will ask a lot of questions to show interest, while another person will find that to be disrespectful. Men and women, in particu-

lar, are thought to have different styles. Linguist Deborah Tannen notes that, for women, "talk creates intimacy . . . [b]ut men live in a hierarchical world, where talk maintains independence and status."[1] Her research has also shown that, when speaking, women tend to face each other and look each other in the eye, while men prefer to sit at angles and look elsewhere in the room. Women also express more agreement and sympathy with one another's problems, while men will dismiss each other's problems. Both sets of responses are meant to reassure, but do not have that effect when used with the opposite gender. For example, women often become angry if a man dismisses their problem.

4      Fortunately, breakdowns in communication are usually repairable. Misunderstandings can be explained, languages can be translated, relationships can be restored (though sometimes this takes great effort over a long period of time), rumors can be controlled, and escalation limited—all through clear, verbal communication, i.e., talking. Despite common admonishments to "improve communication skills," the majority of people are already very sophisticated at sending and interpreting messages. The improvement most people need is more akin to a concert pianist fine-tuning a particular technique than to a 10-year-old student heading off for her weekly piano lesson.

5      A popular misconception about communication is what Michael Reddy calls "the conduit metaphor."[2] This is the belief that language is like the postal service, that it can transfer packages (ideas) from person to person without corruption of the original message: person A puts his thought or feelings into words and "gives" or "sends" these words to B, who "extracts" or unpacks the message. The danger of this metaphor is that it leads one to believe that language is effortless. Misunderstandings are therefore extremely frustrating in that they are not supposed to occur, and if they do occur, then someone must be at fault—either the speaker did not correctly package the message or the listener erred in unpacking it, or both. However, no such exchange takes place. A more accurate description is that the speaker attempts to code ideas, feelings, and images with words. Those words are transmitted to the listener who then matches them with his/her own experiences. There is no universal codebook, so what A thinks of as "success" will not necessarily match person B's definition. Words correspond to different ideas and feelings for different people, and it can take multiple attempts before an idea has been understood satisfactorily. The more cultural differences there are between speakers, the more frequently they will have to stop and work out differences of meaning.

6      The "conduit metaphor" highlights two important aspects of language: metaphor and semantics. Semantics refers to the specific meanings of words, as well as the value they carry beyond their definition. For example, one could call a woman, "lady," "girl," "ma'am," "miss" or any of dozens of synonymous terms. The difference between these

---

[1]Tannen, Deborah. "Sex, Lies and Conversation; Why Is It So Hard for Men and Women to Talk to Each Other?" *The Washington Post.* 24 June 1990.
[2]Reddy, Michael. "The Conduit Metaphor—A Case of Frame Conflict in our Language about Language." *Metaphor and Thought.* Ed. Andrew Ortony, Cambridge, 1979.

terms, and the reason the addressee will prefer some of them and be offended by others, is based on the value she places on each definition.

7   A clear understanding of semantics is crucial to preventing misunderstandings. Arguments frequently occur when two people think they are talking about the same thing, but really are just using the same word for two different ideas or things. An exaggerated example of this would be a misunderstanding over the question "What state was he in?" where one person is talking about a state of mind and the other about a political region. Hopefully that is a misunderstanding that can be cleared up quickly, but for a few moments both parties are likely to be confused and possibly think the other is crazy. A subtler example would be an argument over the definition of the word "respect." One person may understand "respect" to signify a feeling, while another sees it as an attitude demonstrated through actions. Though Andrew feels respect for Betty, Betty is angry that Andrew did not demonstrate this respect through actions. Andrew, on the other hand, is convinced he was not at fault because he does (or did) genuinely feel respect for Betty. This type of argument can drag on indefinitely with both sides vehemently defending themselves.

8   Metaphor is one of the most powerful linguistic devices. Metaphor expands understanding by relating the unknown to the familiar. Complex or unfamiliar ideas, systems or relationships are often explained by comparison to something already well known. The heart, for example, is a complex muscle performing very specialized tasks, but it is easier to understand its function by thinking of it as a familiar mechanical device such as a pump. Some cognitive scientists hypothesize that much human knowledge is structured with metaphor. The hidden danger of these linguistic devices is that, while creating associations of function or meaning ("the heart is like a pump"), they also transmit value judgments ("a pump is an ugly utilitarian tool"). Sometimes a metaphor is so subtle or commonly used that one is unaware it is there. For example, to "waste time" is a common English phrase, but how does one actually waste time? It is impossible, unless we assume that time, like apples (or money!), is a physical commodity. For most Americans, time is indeed thought of as a commodity that can be measured out, spent, wasted, and valued. This conception of time becomes problematic when an American interacts with someone from a culture for whom time is not a commodity.

9   A final misleading idea about language is the belief that words are harmless. "Sticks and stones may break my bones, but words will never hurt me," is a children's rhyme in the United States. Yet words can hurt people very badly. A biting criticism or personal attack can stay vivid in one's memory for years. Some words can provoke a physical response; a punch in the face perhaps. The words themselves may seem weightless, but they can bring about concrete reactions and should be used with care.

10   The conflict resolution field specializes in helping people communicate more effectively and avoid some of the pitfalls listed above. Two of the most common techniques taught are active listening, or empathic listening, and the use of "I-messages" instead of "you-messages." Both of these focus on trying to communicate without placing blame and really trying to hear and understand what the other person is saying. When people are in conflict, making the extra effort to improve communication between the disputants is often helpful in reducing the intensity of the conflict, even if the conflict cannot be that easily resolved.

**THINKING CRITICALLY**

1. What issues contribute to communication barriers? What factors lie at the root of conflicts and pose obstacles to clear communication?

2. What is the "conduit metaphor"? Why is it a popular misconception about communication? Explain.

3. Akin observes that another misconception regarding communication is that "words are harmless." Do you think many people believe this? Do you believe this? Explain.

4. Have you ever experienced a time when communication broke down due to one of the factors Akin describes in her essay? Describe the experience and how you handled it.

5. What is the author's thesis, and how does she support it? How effective are her examples in supporting her claims? Can you think of other areas in the essay where examples would be useful? Explain.


**WRITING ASSIGNMENTS**

1. Record a conversation between two people discussing a charged topic on a current event. Analyze their discussion, paying attention for some of the barriers to communication Akin describes. For example, what assumptions do the conversationalists hold in common? How do they exhibit trust? Do they risk hurting one another by making a conversational blunder? Explain.

2. Write an essay exploring the concept of common ground or understanding. Why is trust so important to the success of social conversation? Describe situations from your own experience in which trust played an important role in the success or failure of a conversation.


# The Like Virus
*David Grambs*

For at least 25 years, the conversational filler "like" has permeated American dialogue to become part of the mainstream lexicon. "Like" is usually accompanied by "uptalk," in which statements sound like questions through a rising inflection of pitch at the end of the sentence or comment. From the language of teens and twenty-somethings, "like" has infected our conversational patterns, overrun our malls, and even invaded the workplace. In the next piece, David Grambs offers some insights on the phenomenon of "like," now that it appears to be here to stay, at least, like, for a while?

David Grambs is a writer and editor and served as a staff member of the first edition of the *American Heritage Dictionary* (1969). He is the author of several books on words, including *The Random House Dictionary for Writers and Readers* (1990), *Death by Spelling* (1989), and *The Endangered English Dictionary* (1997). This essay appeared in the August 2001 issue of *The Vocabula Review*.

1   And like I'm, like, really grossed out, like . . .

2       The L-word. A kind of weightless backpack word that's more and more giving us humpbacked spoken English, the lite like has been airily clogging American

sentences for years now. The war against the usage—well, it wasn't much of a war, alas—has been lost for some time, and we language-conscious losers are all trying to learn to live with the new, disjunctive babble.

3      Still, I believe the phenomenon is worth standing back from and taking a look at, as opposed to shrugging or winking at its growth. What does the new, gratuitous use of like really represent in our language, functionally and lexically? What do the purportedly authoritative dictionaries tell us? And, as I ask myself every time I hear it, what price is literate, listenable English paying for its increasing currency?

4      Like-speech, or like-orrhea, is a curious, self-contained medium. With its attendant (usually) limited vocabulary and all-thumbs expressiveness, it's almost a kind of verbal hand-gesturing or mimicry, if not a middle-class pidgin. The kids—and more and more adults—seem locked in a kind of cawing hyperpresent tense. Many have strangely unresonant, throat-blocked, or glottal voices and use "up-talk," the tendency to end all sentences in a rising, questioning inflection.

5      Yes, they're mostly young people (though again, increasingly, exponentially, by no means just young people). But at times I think I'm hearing the voices of Loony Tunes and Merry Melodies creatures, each lost in rote subjectivity. At my neighborhood café a few years ago, where some local prep school kids hung out, I particularly remember one tall, chain-smoking girl, always dressed in black, who couldn't go five or six words without coughing up a viral like. None of her peers batted an eye at this. She was speaking their language—a language in which the role of the indispensable L-word isn't so much to mean as it is to stylize. Or is it destylize?

6      Semantically, the viral like (in the new, ever-insertable usage) is far less a legitimate word than a form of coping punctuation, a lame, reflexive stalling tactic for the syntactically challenged. It's plainly what rigorous old teachers or editors might have called "an excrescence," and it's quickly becoming the verbal security blanket and a virtual speech impediment for an entire generation—and generations to come—of Americans, from Generation X to Generation Z and beyond. It adds as much to our fair English language as barnacles do to a wharf or calculi to a healthy kidney. Apologists for this speechway—rest assured, it has multitudes of shrugging, unblinking defenders—explain that the constantly repeated word serves as a wonderfully stylish form of ironic punctuation. And here I thought it was just a terribly bad speech habit.

7      As you well know, this linguistic fifth column has been settling in since the 1980s. Its mindless use is sadly symptomatic of our slack-tongued American zeitgeist, of what might be called our flailing, contemporary more-or-lessness or something-like-thatness. We live, after all, in the *Age of Or Whatever*. It's not cool to be too clear, articulate, or specific about things.

8      Where did it come from? A California beach cave? Those old Valley Girls? (A Moon Unit Zappa song has been cited as seminal.) Saddam Hussein? MTV? A brain softener in our reservoirs, related to the cause of attention deficit disorder? The new like-speech has been related to the colorful old hipster use of the word, but I think it's a horse of another, colorless color. There is doubtless an interestingly complicated rationale for its origins linguistically and sociologically, but I'll settle for a bluntly simple answer. I think it comes from a peculiarly infectious strain of

laziness, or mental or communicative slackness. Of course, it's hip and ironic laziness. It's, like, postmodern laziness.

9    Probably nothing has spread the L-word so quickly as American television has.
Turn on your set nowadays and see how far into a talk show or celebrity interview
you can go without hearing that hiccup vocable. (Most standup comedians can no
more do without it than they can without their lame, stock "Thanks—you've been
great!" exit escape.) It's a whiny bug in the ear to any plain-speaking person, yet
the word has acquired an almost emblematic force. It has become a watchword of
glibly media-driven American pop culture. Keeping it ceaselessly in play seems to
be a form of bonding between those who don't want to appear to be too threaten-
ingly to the point, or is it too old?

10   One of its defenders in the *New York Times* a few years ago said the new use
of like is really just a rhetorical device. Sometimes it is used as a phonic punctuation mark to signal "important information ahead." (When used two, three times
in one sentence? The important information is usually, oh, a subsequent noun or
an elusive adjective. It's exhausting to the rest of us to have to be so constantly
alert to momentous divulgence, or completion of a sentence.) It also replaces, the
writer noted, the dramatic, silent pause, which, he quickly added, is now "passé."
(To which remark I can only ask for a moment of silence.) Or an interlaced like is
really to provide a kind of postmodern "tempering" of any possible harshness of
meaning. (It's very important today to placate repeatedly in one's conversation.)
And of course it's also a pioneering "verb form," as in And I was like, "Whatever,
you liar." More recently, a reputable linguistics professor said we shouldn't get all
huffy about the "ironizing" usage: it now serves as a useful device to "distance"
oneself from one's own words. I must confess that distancing myself more and
more from what I say has never been one of my goals in life.

11   And what, pray tell, would somebody such as Jane Austen or Ernest Heming-
way—or H. L. Mencken—have had to say about this delightfully ironic linguistic
phenomenon? Or imagine, if you will, for a little grotesque perspective, a classic
play such as Oscar Wilde's *The Importance of Being Earnest* performed in like-
speak. Maybe ten years from now, an avant-garde director—who knows?

12   As cultural archcritic John Simon says in his introduction to the sobering book
*Dumbing Down*:

> To a muddled mind, like may constitute a grace note, a bit of appoggiatura
> with which to decorate or even authenticate one's discourse. To the simple
> soul, those likes are so many hard, gemlike rhinestones. But, as with most
> nonsensical things, opposite interpretations may apply just as well. Thus like
> may be a disavowal of responsibility: if you say "I was like minding my own
> business," the like may cover you if someone discovers that you weren't
> minding it. . . . Eventually, though, the like becomes a mere unthinking habit,
> a verbal rut.

13   When a usage inexorably takes root, so do its apologists, including those who
work on dictionaries. Language, and especially English, constantly changes, and
so it should. (I have worked on the staffs of two U.S. dictionaries.) Yet it won't
do to say like-orrhea is just another passing, trendy neologism or speech habit. It

won't do because it's not a mere slang or buzz word and because it's not passing. Above all, it won't do because of what all those likes replace or avoid, what, infectingly, they betoken: an increasingly lazy recourse to choppy, bland, dysfunctional English.

14    If your own speech is showing more and more lite likes, you might ask yourself why your generation is the first in more than 200 years of U.S. history to have a desperate, ongoing need for a single flavorless four-letter communicational rest stop.

15    Then there are the two million-dollar questions:

- What in fact does the lite like actually mean?
- What part of speech is it? Take the sentence (please) And she's like, "Like, it wasn't like anything I've, like, ever seen." Do the various (four) likes here all have the same part of speech?

Which is another way of inquiring, what do our contemporary lexicographers have to say about it?

16    The equivocal—downright waffling—way our current American dictionaries (hands-off descriptive, never prescriptive) handle the ever-morphing interloper is less than instructive, and somewhat depressing. Admittedly, dealing with it in definitional terms is not an enviable task. Unfortunately, the dictionaries' respective definitions of the usage are not even accurately descriptive.

17    The leading American lexicon says that the latter-day like has two parts of speech, adverb and conjunction. You will find this in the tenth edition of *Merriam Webster's Collegiate Dictionary* (1993):

> like adv. . . . 3. used interjectionally in informal speech often to emphasize a word or phrase (as in "He was, like, gorgeous") or for an apologetic, vague, or unassertive effect (as in "I need to, like, borrow some money") 4. NEARLY: APPROXIMATELY (the actual interest is more like 18 percent)—used interjectionally in informal speech with expressions of measurement (it was, like, five feet long) (goes there every day, like).

A curious definition. It doesn't so much provide a meaning for like as it does hold it at arm's length and note that it is used "interjectionally." It tells us that it is used to emphasize a word or—or?—for an apologetic, vague, or unassertive effect. A questionable, contradictory pairing of meanings to be covered under one definition. And for the dictionary to say that the word is used for an apologetic, vague, or unassertive effect suggests that it is used artfully by articulate people as some kind of intentional rhetorical device. No, not quite the truth of the matter.

18    Are these meanings, denotations? The word is "used," and it is used for an "effect." How many other adverbs used in midsentence have to be set off in print by commas (though they aren't in all cases), almost as if to say that the interruptive word has no clear purpose (or meaning) in the sentence? It's interjectional indeed.

19    Merriam Webster also parcels out an "interjectional" sense of the word under its entry for like as a conjunction. It says the viral like is used to "introduce" a quotation, paraphrase, or thought. ("And I'm like, go away!") True enough in practice, though this is an interesting, not to say inventive, notion. And why a word deemed

to "introduce" an expression would be considered a conjunction, or connective, I have no idea. What the lite like primarily introduces is an implicit admission that the speaker doesn't want to bother completing an unbroken grammatical clause, or maybe can't—or just can't stop using the word. Like doesn't introduce. It supplants or forestalls, with graceless urgency.

20      The unabridged Random House dictionary (1987) also gives the more and more acceptable adverbial sense of "nearly, closely, approximately," as well as another sense:

> like interj. . . . 28. Informal. used esp. in speech, esp. nonvolitionally or habitually, to preface a sentence, to fill a pause, to express uncertainty, or to intensify or neutralize a following adjective: Like, why didn't you write to me? The music was, like, really great, you know?

21      Here we read that the all-purpose, no-purpose like is not an adverb. It's not a conjunction. It's an interjection. Now, does like express uncertainty—or expose it? Or attempt to dress it up? Or interlard pure lard? Random House doesn't claim an "emphasizer" function for the word. Instead, it says it is used to intensify or neutralize a following adjective. Intensify or neutralize? Hmm. Another curiously contradictory pairing. Worth noting is the prefatory "used esp. in speech, esp. nonvolitionally or habitually, to preface a sentence." The most interesting, even amusingly give-away, word here is "nonvolitionally."

22      From these lexical tightrope acts, it's hard not to get the sense that assigning parts of speech to the viral like leaves one, if not between a rock and a hard place, between a slippery slope and a will-o'-the-wisp.

23      More recently, the handsome *American Heritage Dictionary* (fourth edition) has shown more common sense in its handling of the viral like and backed off a bit. Instead of trying torturously to allot the shifty, slack usage a part or parts of speech, it covers the phenomenon as an idiom:

> be like Informal To say or utter. Used chiefly in oral narration: "And he's like, 'Leave me alone!' "

24      A final "Our Living Language" note commendably points out that what follows an "I'm like . . ." expression may be an actual quotation, or a brief imitation of another person's behavior, or a summarization of a past attitude or reaction—or it might instead signify either the speaker's attitude at the time or what he "might have said." Which? Exactly—make that inexactly—the point. But the AHD has nothing to say about all the other, more gratuitous placements of like pretty much anywhere within sentences in this American day and age. But if it walks like a duck and talks like a duck . . . ?

25      If we're not going to recognize it for the duck that it is, I'd venture to say that one can, deductively, come up with quite a few more, or competing, meanings (as opposed to "uses") for the viral like, according to the context of its various encroachments in sentences.

26      It can mean "possibly" (He couldn't, like, be there). It can mean "let's say" or "say" or "for example" (If we were to, like, meet at the movie theater, there'd be no problem). It can mean "you know" (Yeah, like, the Holocaust, it was, like, a bad

thing). It can mean "responding by" or "reacting by" (And then they're, like, running and hiding in the woods). It can mean "the situation is" or "at the beginning" (Like, all the people have been wiped out by this Death Planet). It can mean "dare I ask it" (Would you, like, marry me?). It can mean "or something like that" (It's a social organization, like). It can mean "get this" or "I'm not kidding" (It was, like, ten below outside). And so, like, on. Similarly, I suspect, one could make a procrustean case for the intrusive like's being just about any part of speech.

27    If these jokers-wild meanings can be said to have any legitimacy, what does that say about the dictionaries' handling of the problem? Maybe that the new L-word additive is not so much a word as it is an uttered wild card, and that we are in for a long, babbling game ahead.

28    It will certainly be interesting to see how dictionary editions ten or twenty years from now categorize and define the compulsive, drop-in like. Possibly, I fear, by noting that it is the single word—shibboleth—that most instantly identifies or characterizes an American anywhere in the world.

29    For now, what is more interesting, perhaps, is what today's dictionaries, with their carefully nonjudgmental hedging or tenuous best shot, don't tell you: that this "informal" usage is fundamentally an egregious, wildly contagious oral tic, and one quite infra dig in standard written English. Like-orrhea in current television or movie dialogue is usually somewhat satirical (but probably less and less so, sadly). A character whose speech is laced with lallygagging likes is invariably being pegged as immature, uneducated, thoroughly self-involved, or ditsy, if not a voluble airhead.

30    Except for its sense of "about" or "approximately," one could say that the new like probably, most often, has one essential meaning, and, ironically, it's a complete thought: "Uh, bear with me." Or is it: "Whoa and whew, it's kind of exhausting to get the right words together without taking a little break between them"? Or possibly: "Please, take no offense from anything that precedes or follows until my next like"?

31    By now, like-speech is indisputably becoming for millions a veritable pseudo-speech style. But what the usage really is, of course, is a hesitation form, along the lines of uh, well, I mean, or um. Hesitation forms are sentence litter, indeterminate words or word elements, basically meaningless and interruptive filler locutions. (Utterance that is filled with such paltering signposts is called embolalia.) Like-orrhea, no matter how numbly glib its ring, usually betokens the incessant need to pause and recalibrate or dumb down even the simplest thoughts. It's analogous to the midsentence constructional shift called anacoluthon, and a little like those iterated watchwords of expressional (and so expressive) insecurity: you know? right? okay? you understand what I'm saying? Actually, it's far worse because it's a microchip version: it can be tucked inside sentences wherever and whenever rather than being a mere trailing irritant. (It is indeed an "in word.")

32    The "meaningless like" is for John Simon a dreadful piece of detritus:

> The I means, you knows, kind ofs, and sort ofs are bad enough; but they at least form a hesitation waltz to give the speaker time to gather his next thought, or focus more tightly on the current one. That bit of verbal litter,

like, however, is something else—"something else" in the slang sense as well: something unconscionable, weird. It must not be mistaken for a more elegant synonym of er, with which speakers formerly tried to carpet the interstices of thought. It is too frequent to be that; nobody erred that consistently—not even a lighter-than-airhead on Hollywood Boulevard.

33    To a nonlike-orrheac, hearing the speech of a like-ridden conversationalist is like enduring reflexive, repetitive name-dropping by somebody who hasn't a clue that the name being dropped, and dropped, and dropped, is known to nobody else. But well beyond its general emptiness and annoyingness, the like virus is deplorable because of what goes along with it—what it avoids, covers up for, or necessitates. Where you find like-orrhea, you'll usually find concomitant sins:

- A knee-jerk or anxious (take your pick) "filling in" of any moment of hesitation in speech. Momentary silence—reflectiveness, that little pause for the right word, a subtle change in speech rhythm—has never been more golden.
- An inability to articulate fundamental indirect discourse, to report simple and coherently what somebody else said. Like injections generally—very generally—leave blitheringly unclear whether what follows are actual, stated words, a paraphrase of those words, or just the like user's rounded-off, subjective impression of the other person's feelings. ("And she's like, I'm not going there!")
- An eager dependency on the present tense. There is in writing the so-called historical present, of course. Because the new penchant for framing the most banal discourse in the present tense comes out of insecurity in using—or impatience with formulating?—ordinary past tenses, one could call this the hysterical present.
- A reluctance or inability to use basic elements of our rich English syntax—that is, to articulate compound or complex sentences, sentences with dependent clauses, sentences with verbs in more than one tense.
- A begging-off from the challenge to be at all interesting or persuasive to intelligent others—to think on one's feet without that four-letter stall-mate. The drone of verbiage clotted with little like blockages guarantees that, whatever the content, one will be irritating or stupefying. Or a less than thrilling job applicant.
- A limited vocabulary. Like-orrhea signals flailing approximation and avoidance of any effort at being articulate, much less eloquent. Interesting or apt words don't usually go along with it. Those happily unconscious of speaking a kind of communicable but uncommunicative mush can't spend much time around dictionaries or Updike novels.
- More words. One thing we definitely don't need in our talk-engulfed multimedia age is extra verbiage, or pandemic overuse of one word that just doesn't pay its own way.

34    The great English writer George Orwell, still admired for his passion about clarity and truth in language, did not favor the particularly British fondness for using the "not un-" locution, with a kind of snobbish coyness, as in "It's not uninteresting,"

instead of, plainly, "It's interesting." Orwell proposed a remedy for the mannerism. "One can cure oneself of the not un- formation by memorizing this sentence: 'A not unblack dog was chasing a not unsmall rabbit across a not ungreen field.'"

35    If you've already caught the like virus, I suggest one of three ways to cure yourself:

- One way is to memorize (as a kind of linguistic memento mori) this sentence: "Like, like as not, to tell it like it is, like Jane has no, like, liking for the like, likes of, like Dick, like it or not."
- Or every time you catch yourself using the L-word crutch, stop—and punish yourself by repeating word for word what you just said but this time substituting for each like the word kumquat.
- Or—simplest of all—just say no. Pure abstinence. Can you do it?

36    Me, I'm willing to live with the viral like in the sense of about or approximately. Otherwise, it should be recognized for what it is. It's not an adverb. It's not a conjunction. It's not an interjection. It's not an artful piece of introductory rhetoric. It's not a valid replacement for the verb to say. It's not a compellingly hip and ironic postmodern conversational style. It's not a trendy word that will pass. It's contemporary America's favorite wad of verbal bubble gum, and it's getting stickier every day.

## THINKING CRITICALLY

1. How does Grambs describe the phenomenon of *like*? Are you familiar with the usage of this word in modern speech? If so, do you or any of your friends suffer from "like-orrhea"? From your observations, would you agree with Grambs that the use of *like* is on the rise?

2. According to Grambs, what are the origins of *like*? What groups have used *like* in the past, and who uses it now? How has it expanded over the last decade?

3. Grambs notes that some defenders of *like* claim it can help speakers "distance" themselves from their words. Why would we want to "distance" ourselves from our speech? Do you agree, as Grambs asserts in paragraph 7, that "it's not cool to be too clear, articulate, or specific about things"? Explain.

4. What is Grambs's opinion of *like* and its entrenchment in American discourse? What explanations does he give for his feelings regarding the use of the word?

5. Given that the phenomenon of *like* is an oral one, how well does Grambs explore its role linguistically and socially? Are you able to "hear" what he is talking about? Do his examples serve as effective "translations"? Explain.

6. Grambs claims that "a character whose speech is laced with lallygagging likes is invariably being pegged as immature, uneducated, thoroughly self-involved, or ditsy." Do you agree with this observation? If *like* has become as mainstream as Grambs fears, why does this stereotype of its usage remain?

7. Grambs offers several suggestions at the end of his essay for eliminating "like-orrhea." If you use *like* frequently in your own speech, would you attempt to eliminate it? Why or why not? As an exercise, test one of his suggestions—such as replacing the word *like* with *kumquat*—and see how pervasive the word is in your conversation.

## WRITING ASSIGNMENTS

1. Grambs identifies teenagers and young "twenty-somethings" as the most frequent users of *like,* but he finds that other, older groups are using it as well. Conduct interviews with other students to determine their familiarity with and usage of *like,* in their conversational style. Write a paper exploring your findings. Try to determine if different demographic groups have different responses. Also, what different theories do your respondents have as to the origins and popularity of the word *like* in conversation? Will it indeed become a mainstream part of speech?

2. Grambs wonders what *The Importance of Being Earnest* by Oscar Wilde would be like performed in like-speak. Locate a copy of the play and rewrite a portion of it, making strategic use of like-speak. What happens to the dialogue? Does it modernize it? Make it sound uneducated or ditsy? Explain.

3. Write a paper in which you question the idea of standard or proper American English. What does the definition mean? What groups or dialects fall outside the standard, and what are the consequences of this? Should there be a language standard in the United States? Explain.

---

# Some Friends and I Started Talking: Conversation and Social Change

*Margaret J. Wheatley*

We spend our lives having conversations. The huge explosion of cell phone use in the last five years is testimony to how much time and money we are willing to expend in search of conversation. Communication is fundamental to our survival. It is used not only to articulate our needs and wants but also our dreams, fears, and goals. We use conversation to argue, console, share beliefs, develop thoughts, and discover more about each other. And it is from discussion and the exchange of ideas that great social movements are born. In the next essay, Margaret J. Wheatley explains why conversation can be a compelling tool for change. As Wheatley explains, "all social change begins with a conversation."

Margaret Wheatley is a well-known authority on organizational development. She is president of the Berkana Institute in Provo, Utah. She is the author of several books, including *Leadership and the New Science* (1992, coauthored with Myron Kellner-Rogers) and *A Simpler Way* (1996). The following essay first appeared in the *Utne Reader* and is excerpted from her book *Turning to One Another* (2002).

1 A Canadian woman told me this story. She was returning to Vietnam to pick up her second child, adopted from the same orphanage as her first child. On her visit two years earlier she had seen challenging conditions at the orphanage and had vowed this time to take medical supplies. "They needed Tylenol, not T-shirts or trinkets," she said to a friend one day. The friend suggested that the most useful thing to take would be an incubator. The woman was surprised (she'd been thinking bandages

and pills), but she started making calls, looking for an incubator. Weeks later, she had been offered enough pediatric medical supplies to fill four 40-foot shipping containers! And 12 incubators. From a casual conversation between two friends, a medical relief effort for Vietnamese children emerged. And it all began when "some friends and I started talking."

2     Stories like this are plentiful. Nothing has given me more hope recently than to observe how simple conversations give birth to actions that can change lives and restore our faith in the future. There is no more powerful way to initiate significant social change than to start a conversation. When a group of people discover that they share a common concern, that's when the process of change begins.

3     Yet it's not easy to begin talking to one another. We stay silent and apart from one another for many reasons. Some of us never have been invited to share our ideas and opinions. From early school days we've been instructed to be quiet so others can tell us what to think. Others have soured on conversation, having sat through too many meetings that degenerated into people shouting, or stomping out angrily, or taking control of the agenda.

4     But true conversation is very different from those sorts of experiences. It is a timeless and reliable way for humans to think together. Before there were classrooms, meetings, or group facilitators, there were people sitting around talking. When we think about beginning a conversation, we can take courage from the fact that this is a process we all know how to do. We are reawakening an ancient practice, a way of being together that all humans intimately understand.

5     We also can take courage in the fact that many people are longing to converse again. We are hungry for a chance to talk. People want to tell their stories, and are willing to listen to yours. I find that it takes just one person to start a conversation, because everyone else is eager to talk once it has begun. "Some friends and I started talking. . . ." Change doesn't happen from a leader announcing the plan. Change begins from deep inside a system, when a few people notice something they will no longer tolerate, or when they respond to someone's dream of what's possible.

6     It's easy to observe this in recent history. The Solidarity trade union movement in Poland began with conversation—less than a dozen workers in a Gdansk shipyard in 1980 speaking to each other about despair, their need for change, their need for freedom. Within months, Solidarity grew to 9.5 million workers. There was no e-mail then, just people talking to each other about their own needs, and finding that millions of fellow citizens shared their feelings. In a short time, they shut down the country, and changed the course of history.

7     To make important changes in our communities, our society, our lives, we just have to find a few others who care about the same thing we do. Together we can figure out the first step, then the second, then the next. Gradually, we grow powerful. But we don't have to start with power, only with passion.

8     Even among friends, starting a conversation can take courage. But conversation also *gives* us courage. Thinking together, deciding what actions to take, more of us become bold. As we learn from each other's experiences and interpretations,

we see issues in richer detail. This clarity can help us see both when to act and when not to. In some cases, the right timing means doing nothing right now. Talking can be enough for the time being.

9    If conversation is the natural way that humans think together, what gets lost when we stop talking? Paulo Freire, the influential Brazilian educator who used education to support poor people in transforming their lives, said that we "cannot be truly human apart from communication. . . . To impede communication is to reduce people to the status of things."

10   When we don't talk to one another in a meaningful way, Freire believes, we never act to change things. We become passive and allow others to tell us what to do. Freire had a deep faith in every person's ability to be a clear thinker and a courageous actor. Not all of us share this faith, but it is necessary if we are to invite colleagues into conversation. Sometimes it is hard to believe that others have as much to offer as we do in the way of concern and skill. But I have found that when the issue is important to others, they will not disappoint us. If you start a conversation, others will surprise you.

11   Near my home in Utah, I watched a small group of mothers cautiously begin meeting about a problem in the community: They wanted their children to be able to walk to school safely. They were shocked when the city council granted their request for a pedestrian traffic light. Encouraged by this victory, they started other projects, each more ambitious than the last. After a few years, they participated in securing a federal grant for neighborhood development worth tens of millions of dollars. Today, one of those mothers has become an expert on city housing, won a seat on the city council, and completed a term as council chair. When she tells her story, it begins like so many others: "Some friends and I started talking. . . ."

12   For conversation to become a powerful tool in society, we must take it seriously and examine our own role in making it successful. Here are some basic principles I've learned over years of hosting formal conversations around the country.

13   We acknowledge one another as equals. One thing that makes us equal is that we need each other. Whatever any one of us knows alone, it is not enough to change things. Someone else is bound to see things that we need to know.

14   We try to stay curious about each other. I maintain my curiosity by reminding myself that everyone has something to teach me. When others are saying things I disagree with, or have never thought about, or that I consider foolish or wrong, I remind myself that I really can learn from them—if I stay open and do not shut them out.

15   We recognize that we need each other's help to become better listeners. The greatest barrier to good conversation is that as a culture we're losing the capacity to listen. We're too busy. We're too certain of our own views. We just keep rushing past each other. At the beginning of any conversation I host, I make a point of asking everyone to help each other listen. This is hard work for almost everyone, but if we talk about listening at the start of a conversation, it makes things easier. If someone hasn't been listening to us, or misinterprets what we say, we're less likely to blame that person. We can be a little gentler with the

difficulties we experience in a group if we make a commitment at the start to help each other listen.

16     We slow down so we have time to think and reflect. Most of us work in places where we rarely have time to sit together and think. We dash in and out of meetings where we make hurried, not thoughtful, decisions. Working to create conditions for a true spirit of conversation helps rediscover the joy of thinking together.

17     We remember that conversation is the natural way humans think together. Conversation is not a new invention for the 21st century; we're restoring a tradition from earlier human experience. It does, however, take time to let go of our modern ways of being in meetings, to get past the habits that keep us apart—speaking too fast, interrupting others, monopolizing the time, giving speeches or making pronouncements. Many of us have been rewarded for these behaviors, becoming more powerful by using them. But the blunt truth is that they don't lead to wise thinking or healthy relationships.

18     We expect it to be messy at times. Life doesn't move in straight lines; and neither does a good conversation. When a conversation begins, people always say things that don't connect. What's important at the start is that everyone's voice gets heard, that everyone feels invited into the conversation. If you're hosting the conversation, you may feel responsible for pointing out connections between these diverse contributions, but it's important to let go of that impulse and just sit with the messiness. The messy stage doesn't last forever. If we suppress the messiness at the beginning, it will find us later on and be more disruptive. The first stage is to listen well to whatever is being said, forgetting about neat thoughts and categories, knowing that all contributions add crucial elements to the whole. Eventually, we will be surprised by how much we share.

19     The practice of true talking takes courage, faith, and time. We don't always get it right the first time, and we don't have to. We need to settle into conversation: we don't just do it automatically. As we risk talking to each other about things we care about, as we become curious about each other, as we slow things down, gradually we remember this timeless way of being together. Our rushed and thoughtless behaviors fade away, and we sit quietly in the gift of being together, just as humans have always done.

20     Another surprising but important element of conversation is a willingness to be disturbed, to allow our beliefs and ideas to be challenged by what others think. No one person or perspective can solve our problems. We have to be willing to let go of our certainty and be confused for a time.

21     Most of us weren't trained to admit what we don't know. We haven't been rewarded for being confused, or for asking questions rather than giving quick answers. We were taught to sound certain and confident. But the only way to understand the world in its complexity is to spend more time in the state of *not* knowing. It is very difficult to give up our certainties—the positions, beliefs, and explanations that lie at the heart of our personal identities. And I am not saying that we have to give up what we believe. We only need to be curious about what others believe, and to acknowledge that their way of interpreting the world might be essential to us.

22    I think it's important to begin a conversation by listening as best you can for what's different, for what surprises you. We have many opportunities every day to be the one who listens, curious rather than certain. If you try this with several people, you might find yourself laughing in delight as you realize how many unique ways there are to be human. But the greatest benefit of all is that listening moves us closer. When we listen with as little judgment as possible, we develop better relationships with each other.

23    Sometimes we hesitate to listen for what's different because we don't want to change. We're comfortable with our lives, and if we listened to anyone who raised questions, we might feel compelled to engage in new activities and ways of thinking. But most of us do see things in our lives or in the world that we would like to be different. If that's true, it means we listen more, not less. And we have to be willing to move into the very uncomfortable place of uncertainty.

24    We may simply fear the confusion that comes with new ideas in unsettled forms. But we can't be creative if we refuse to be confused. Change always starts with confusion; cherished interpretations must dissolve to make way for what's new. Great ideas and inventions miraculously appear in the space of not knowing. If we can move through the fear and enter the abyss we are rewarded greatly. We rediscover we're creative.

25    As the world grows more puzzling and difficult, most of us don't want to keep struggling through it alone. I can't know what to do from my own narrow perspective. I need a better understanding of what's going on. I want to sit down with you and talk about all the frightening and hopeful things I observe, and listen to what frightens you and gives you hope. I need new ideas and solutions for the problems I care about. And I know I need to talk to you to discover them. I need to learn to value your perspective, and I want you to value mine. I expect to be disturbed by what I hear from you. I know we don't have to agree with each other in order to think well together. There is no need for us to be joined at the head. We are joined by our human hearts.

### THINKING CRITICALLY

1. How does Wheatley's introductory story about the Canadian woman set the tone and theme for the rest of her essay? Explain.

2. Did this essay change the way you think about the power of conversation? About how you listen and how you converse? Explain.

3. Why do we "stay silent and apart from one another" in today's society? What reasons does Wheatley give? Can you think of additional reasons for people's reluctance to engage in conversation?

4. What, according to the author, is "true conversation"? Identify the elements of true conversation. How do your own everyday conversations compare to her definition? Explain.

5. Compare the points Wheatley makes about speaking and listening to the points Deborah Tannen makes about "lecturing and listening" in her essay in the preceding section of this chapter. On what points do they agree? Do you think Tannen would disagree with any of Wheatley's suggestions? Why or why not?

6. What happens when people stop talking? Explain.

**WRITING ASSIGNMENTS**

1. Wheatley provides several examples of conversations that changed society. Can you think of other examples that would support her thesis? Identify at least two other examples and discuss how conversation led to change.

2. In making suggestions for productive conversation, Wheatley states that we also enter conversation with a "willingness to be disturbed," and to have our beliefs challenged. Write about a conversation from your personal experience in which your beliefs were challenged. Did you try to see the other viewpoint? Did you focus on defending your beliefs? After reading this essay, would you try to conduct the conversation differently? Explain.

3. Among the aristocracy of the 18th century, salons became the rage. Salons were rooms in which people of social or intellectual distinction would gather to discuss topics and exchange ideas. (Salons later gave way to the parlors of the 19th century. The root word of *parlor* is *parler,* which is Old French for "talk.") Many Internet salons have emerged online, reviving this tradition. Visit an Internet salon and read some of the exchanges (e.g., cafeutne.org or theworldcafe.com). Write an essay comparing some of the points Wheatley makes in this essay regarding the power of conversation and the dialogues you read online. In what ways are people using Internet salons to promote social change? Explain.

## MAKING CONNECTIONS

1. Do you think language itself can be gendered? For example, are there certain words that seem male and others that seem female? Review the essays by Kornheiser and Holmes, and evaluate the words they use to convey their ideas. Write an essay that considers the idea of gendered language.

2. Have you ever found yourself at an impasse with a member of the opposite sex because your communication styles were different? For example, did you think the person you were arguing with "just didn't get it" solely because of his or her sex? What about because of a generational difference, such as between a mother and daughter or father and son? Explain what accounted for the miscommunication if you solved it.

3. Many of the authors in this section explain that men and women use language differently. Develop a list of the ways you think men and women use language differently, and then develop your own theory, or expound on an existing one, to explain the communication differences. Think about the adjectives men and women use, their body language, why they speak, and how they present their information. If you wish, you may write about why you feel there is no difference between the ways men and women use language.

4. Write a response to one of the authors in this section in which you explain why you agree, disagree, or partially agree with his or her observations on conversation. Support your response with examples from your own experience, outside research using resources from the supplemental website, and other arguments presented in this section.

5. What effect has "political correctness" had on our everyday conversation? What issues of trust do we presume with politically correct language? Explain.

6. What nonverbal cues do you project to others? In a few paragraphs, analyze yourself and the "vibes" you give to those around you through your body language, the way you walk, your facial expressions, dress style, and mental attitude.

7. Nonverbal behavior can be influenced by gender, culture, and media cues that may cause people to misunderstand each other. Explore the ways you rely on nonverbal cues when communicating with others. How much do you depend on the actual words used in a conversation versus the tone, facial expressions, gestures, and mannerisms of the conversationalists? Do you think your nonverbal behavior is influenced by your gender? Explain.

# Censorship and Free Speech 6

309

"**C**ongress shall make no law . . . abridging the freedom of speech, or of the press." With these simple words, the writers of the Constitution created one of the pillars of our democratic system of government—the First Amendment guarantee of every American's right to the free exchange of ideas, beliefs, and political debate. Most Americans passionately support their right to express themselves without fear of government reprisal. However, over the years questions have arisen about whether limits should be imposed on our right to free expression when the exercise of that right imposes hardship or pain on others. What happens when the right of one person to state his or her beliefs conflicts with the rights of others to be free from verbal abuse? In this chapter, we look at two particular areas that have generated debate and dialogue recently: biased language and hate speech, and censorship and free speech.

## Biased Language and Hate Speech

America is the most diverse society on earth, home to people of every race, nation, religion, and creed. Because of this diverse mix, our ability to comprehend all that "otherness" is sometimes overwhelmed, and we fall into the trap of reducing different people to handy but offensive labels. Perhaps even more damaging than stereotypes are racial epithets, in which words are used to deliberately wound. Forged by ignorance, fear, and intolerance, these words that hurt damningly reduce people to nothing more than a race, religion, gender, or body type. Such words aim to make the victim seem less than human and less worthy of respect. This section examines how biased language and hate speech are used to belittle, demean, or marginalize a person or a group of people.

The first reading takes a close look at "hate speech" and "political correctness." Linguist Robin Tolmach Lakoff examines the connection between hate speech and the First Amendment, from right and left political viewpoints. Then the author of a popular "politically correct" language handbook, Rosalie Maggio, describes how English subtly perpetuates prejudice and offers some simple guidelines for avoiding offensive stereotypes and exclusionary expressions, in "Bias-Free Language." Arguing with Maggio's position is literary critic and journalist Michiko Kakutani, whose "The Word Police" vehemently condemns such "language-laundering" efforts. Gloria Naylor describes how her experience with perhaps the most inflammatory racially charged word of all, *nigger,* forced her to confront ugly racial prejudice while still a child.

## Censorship and Free Speech

The First Amendment protects speech—even unpopular speech. But what happens when free expression runs counter to community values? At what point does the perceived degree of offensiveness warrant censorship? And at what point does censorship threaten to undermine our constitutional rights? For example, the free and open exchange of ideas seems critical to the goals of higher education. However, when the ideas expressed are racist, sexist, or otherwise offensive toward specific groups on campus, some universities and colleges have tried to censor and punish such forms of speech. Alan Charles Kors finds this form of censorship objectionable and dangerous, arguing that it chills freedom of expression and opinion. Taking the opposite side in "Regulating Racist Speech on Campus," Charles R. Lawrence III argues that verbal harassment violates student victims' rights to an education. Colleges and universities must act to prevent such harassment from happening by restricting this form of speech, he believes.

The First Amendment seems to protect speech that may seem socially and morally deplorable. In 2010, the Westboro Baptist Church gained particular notoriety for its picketing of military funerals and its protests held outside the Holocaust Memorial Museum in Washington, D.C. The faction, which has been classified as a hate group, is noted for using the children of its followers to carry signs proclaiming that "God hates Jews" and "God hates fags." Tina Dupuy explains in "Freedom of Deplorable Speech" that while the group's views may have no place in a polite society, we must protect even offensive speech if we are to ultimately protect our own. The section ends with an alternative viewpoint by Richard Delgado on why hate speech is not acceptable in "Hate Cannot Be Tolerated."

# BIASED LANGUAGE AND HATE SPEECH

## Hate Speech
*Robin Tolmach Lakoff*

Although the First Amendment protects free speech, not all speech is truly protected. You cannot, for example, yell "fire" in a crowded theater just for kicks, threaten someone with bodily harm, commit perjury, or knowingly slander another individual. Less clear are attitudes toward "fighting words"—words that are "so very bad that, upon hearing them, an ordinary person must strike out," and words that hurt, such as racial epithets. This is the language that gave birth to the "politically correct"—or p.c.—movement. In this article, linguist Robin Tolmach Lakoff takes a look at both sides of the p.c. "hate speech" debate. Should hate speech be protected under the First Amendment? As Lakoff explains, how we feel about this issue is closely connected to how we view the power of language itself.

Robin Tolmach Lakoff is a professor of linguistics at the University of California, Berkeley. She is the author of several books on language and politics, most recently *Talking Power: The Politics of Language in Our Lives* (1990) and *The Language War* (2000), from which this essay is excerpted.

1 The jewel in the anti-p.c. crown is the First Amendment, newly claimed by the right as its own. Historically the First Amendment was a thorn in the conservative side: it offered protection to nonmajoritarian views, lost causes, and the disenfranchised—not to

mention, of course, Communists and worse. From the Sedition Act of the Adams administration to continual attempts to pass a constitutional amendment banning flag-desecration, conservatives have always tried to impose sanctions on free expression, while liberals have tried to keep the "marketplace of ideas" open to all traders. For most of this century it has been the liberal wing of the Supreme Court that has struck down constraints on expression, from Nazi marches to antiwar protests, and the conservative wing that has tried to keep them in effect. But when the shoe is on the other foot and language control is passing from them, conservatives rethink that position. If p.c. can be framed as an attempt to wrest from *us* our historical right to use whatever language we want, whenever we want, to whomever we want, its proponents can be made out to be opponents of free speech and—voilà—we are metamorphosed into all-American defenders of the First Amendment against the infidel Hun, or the p.c. professoriate.

2      No one is expressly demanding the right to make use of hateful slurs. As Mari Matsuda notes, those with media access, the educated upper classes, need not stoop so low: "The various implements of racism find their way into the hands of different dominant-group members. Lower- and middle-class white men might use violence against people of color, whereas upper-class whites might resort to private clubs or righteous indignation against 'diversity' and 'reverse discrimination'" (in Matsuda et al. 1993, 23). So a member of a higher caste might never actually be exposed to virulent racist or sexist language among his associates, and therefore might be able to claim that it didn't exist any more or need not be taken seriously (because *we* don't have to encounter it in its more distasteful forms). And while there do exist epithets to be hurled at males and whites ("phallocrat," "honky"), they lack the sting of slurs against women, blacks, Latinos, and Asians. That is because, according to Matsuda, "racist speech proclaims racial inferiority and denies the personhood of target-group members. All members of the target group are at once considered alike and inferior" (36).

3      But a proclamation of inferiority is meaningful, or even possible, only if it can piggyback on an older stereotype of one race (or gender) as inferior: the "Snark Rule," which states that repetition makes a statement "true." Judith Butler defines hate speech as working through the repetition of similar prior speech acts: "hate speech is an act that recalls prior acts, requiring a future repetition to endure" (1997, 20). So if your group, or you as an individual member of that group, have never been subjected to epithets in the past, no words directed at you, however irritating, can have the full noxious effect of true hate speech. That is not to say that such language is benign. But if you are not a member of a historically submerged group, "you just don't get it," since you don't have a visceral understanding of the harm such speech can do. So it's relatively easy for you to see racist and sexist language and behavior as "just kidding" or "childish horseplay" and not demand a remedy for it.

4      Those who don't have personal reasons to feel that hateful epithets are damaging and who at the same time feel that any challenge to the right to use such speech is a serious threat to the First Amendment are apt to feel not only permitted but obligated, as a sacred duty, to oppose any attempts to legislate language control—at least those that come from the other side and attempt to constrain *our*

preferred linguistic possibilities. Laws that might constrain *theirs* are still unproblematic. Hence the right's continuing attempts to outlaw flag-burning, and the loud ruckus on the right that followed the 1989 five-to-four Supreme Court decision (*Texas v. Johnson*) that flag-burning constituted permissible expression under the First Amendment.[1]

5    To listen to some born-again First Amendment advocates, you would believe that its guarantee of free speech is and has always been absolute. But that is far from the case. Courts have always recognized the validity of competing claims: "clear and present danger," "falsely shouting 'fire' in a crowded theater," imminent threat, "fighting words," national interest, libel, threats, subornation of perjury, perjury itself, and others. Even some speech rights we consider uncontroversial today—including the right to provide birth control information or the right to protest the government's involvement in a war—were guaranteed only after arduous struggles. Even if hate speech regulations were to be enforced, that would not be the first curtailment of the absolute right to say anything, under any circumstances. In pondering the need for legislation against hate speech, the first question to address is the validity of competing interests. Does the right to enjoy speech that is as free as possible outweigh the right to "the equal protection of the laws" guaranteed to each of us under the Fourteenth Amendment, or vice versa?

6    This argument pits supporters of the Fourteenth Amendment (Critical Race Theorists and anti-pornography feminists like Catharine MacKinnon) against the odd couple composed of card-carrying ACLU liberals and conservative First Amendment supporters. Everyone agrees that hate speech is deplorable, and no reasonable person would ever indulge in any form of it. But the sides differ on what is to be done and on the consequences of what is done. Is racism so pervasive across this country and on college campuses, and other remedies so ineffectual, that speech codes must be enforced to guarantee to all the equal protection mandated by the Fourteenth Amendment? Or is the problem exaggerated—are there other ways to combat it, and does the need for preserving the First Amendment outweigh the responsibility to enforce the Fourteenth?

7    As a card-carrying ACLU member who is also a member of a couple of historically targeted groups, and as a member of a profession that abhors an unqualified statement, I naturally straddle the line. Others are more decisive. The CRTists tend to see hate speech as deeply pervasive, an increasing "epidemic" that can only be stopped by the immunization of speech codes. In the introduction to *Words That Wound*, its four authors argue that "Incidents of hate speech and racial harassment are reported with increasing frequency and regularity, particularly on American college campuses, where they have reached near epidemic proportions" (Matsuda et al. 1993, 1).

8    Since no figures are given, it is difficult to assess the accuracy of the claim. Even reports of an increasing number of acts of hate speech on college campuses would not necessarily show that hate speech had reached "epidemic" proportions—and might not even be an unequivocally bad thing. First, the larger numbers might merely be the result of more such acts being reported, a sign that minorities are being listened to more and taken more seriously than they used to be and that they now feel safe enough to complain. Even if there actually are more acts committed,

that might merely mean that the presence of more minorities and women in places where they previously had not had entree creates more readily available targets, and arouses more resentment. But even if the authors of *Words That Wound* have identified a real problem of endemic racism and sexism in America, the remedy is still not obvious: to some it is not even apparent that any remedy is needed, much less what remedy will work and occasion the least interference with freedom of speech.

## Language: Thought or Action?

9 Once again language is the problem. We don't know how to legislate hate speech, because we don't really know how to classify any kind of speech, which we would have to do before we could safely legislate against it. We are pretty clear on other kinds of human activity. Most of us would agree that thought cannot be an object of legislation and should not become one even if science could develop ways to peer into our minds. On the other hand, overt actions are always subject to control by law, and we would agree that they have to be, if we are to live together more or less peaceably in a state of civilization. We may argue about what kinds of actions should be punishable, and how, but punished bad actions must be. Language is intermediate between thought and action: it is thought made observable. It straddles the line between the abstract and the concrete, the ethereal and the corporeal. Which of its aspects—the ethereal or the physical—should be the basis of our legal understanding of the capacity of language to do harm? Is language inconsequential and therefore immune to legislation? Or is language equivalent to action—world-changing and so capable of harm—in which case legal notice must be taken of injurious linguistic behavior?

10 We teach our children the proverb "Sticks and stones may break my bones, but words will never harm me." Do we offer this saying as truth or as wishful magic: believe it and the pain will go away? Probably we would not be so quick to teach our children these words if we did not fear that the opposite was true. In our natural desire to save our children from pain, we encourage them to deny their feelings. But denial doesn't make it so.

11 We have only recently become a psychologically conscious society. Only in the last hundred years or so have we talked about psychic *wounds* and mental *diseases*. We are never sure whether we mean those expressions as literal descriptions or metaphors. We know that an autopsy on someone suffering from psychic trauma would reveal no physical evidence of that "wound." Yet there now exist physical interventions in the form of drugs that "cure" these traumas, and this possibility of physical "cure" argues for the physical reality of the symptoms.

12 When our legal system was established, it seemed clear that words were not deeds, so only physical misbehaviors were legally actionable. The legal systems of all societies specify punishments or remedies for physical harm. The wound is visible; witnesses may have observed exactly what occurred. There may be disagreement among the parties about the interpretation of the events: Did the victim do anything to provoke the act? Did the perpetrator perform it intentionally? Did he mean to do harm? To do as much harm as he did? Are there other extenuating circumstances?

But all participants can agree that something took place that changed the physical world.

13 But what about "words that wound"? Is that expression even meaningful? Are those who feel verbally wounded describing a real interaction with real and adjudicable consequences, or are they merely oversensitive souls who should grow up and take it like a man? If outsiders can't observe the damage, how can anyone prescribe a legal remedy for it?

14 If observers can agree on the amount and kind of force employed to make a physical wound, they can agree on the amount of damage probably sustained by the victim: their conclusions are based on scientifically demonstrable physical laws. But words mean different things to different people in different contexts: a word that would shock and intimidate a woman uttered by a strange man on a dark street at night might be a delightful expression of intimacy between her and someone she loves and trusts. African Americans can call one another "nigger" with relative impunity under specific conditions, but a white person cannot do the same. Language by nature is ambiguous and sensitive to context. The law by necessity strives to be precise and decontextualized. There is a discontinuity between the two words in the expression "language crime." Yet the law recognizes several: threats, defamation, offers of bribes, and perjury, for example. To make these concepts workable, we need to reach a formal understanding of language and its relation to action.

## Speech Acts: "Only Theory" or Reality?

15 Relevant here is the discussion of J. L. Austin's theory of performative speech acts. Austin concluded that language was equivalent to action, in that all utterances were performative and all performatives were world-changing—that is, actions. That theory has had important consequences for several academic fields: philosophy and linguistics (naturally), as well as literary theory, anthropology, and education. As long as it is confined safely within academia, it is mere theory that applies only to ideas, with few actual consequences. But in recent years, it has been incorporated into the discourse of the law, by both legal scholars (as in several papers of Peter Tiersma [1986, 1987]) and sociolinguists (see, for example, Shuy 1993). But nowhere does speech act theory have such concrete and far-reaching consequences as in the definitions of hate speech and its legal status.

16 Those who believe in Austin's formulation are likely to follow it to its logical conclusion: that linguistic misbehavior is a type of bad action and should be treated as such by the law, criminally and civilly. A strict Austinian is likely to support speech codes. If problems of enforceability arise based on the vagueness or ambiguity of language, it is the job of the codifiers to rewrite their statutes clearly enough to solve the problem. Those who disagree with Austin are apt to treat words very differently from actions, beyond the reach of legal remedy in most or even all cases.

17 There are many mixed positions and evasions, depending on the ability to draw and maintain a distinction between those kinds of language that constitute action-equivalents and others that are closer to thought-equivalents. Since the 1920s First Amendment law has divided utterances along those lines: language that constitutes

"expression" and receives a high degree of protection under the First Amendment, versus language that constitutes "conduct" and doesn't. A political opinion like "the Republicans deserve to win" will be counted in the first set and be protected, while a threat (even in indirect form) like, "I have a gun and I know how to use it" will under many circumstances be judged "conduct" and treated as a criminal action.

18    A crucial concept is that of "fighting words," as addressed in the 1942 Supreme Court decision *Chaplinsky v. New Hampshire*, which established the category of "fighting words" as unprotected action-equivalents. Chaplinsky, a Jehovah's Witness, got into a verbal altercation with the town marshal of Rochester, New Hampshire, in the course of which he used language considered very shocking in its time, calling the marshal a "Goddamned racketeer" and a "damned Fascist."[2] He was arrested and found guilty under the town's speech code, which prohibited "fighting words." The case was appealed up to the U.S. Supreme Court, which found for the state. In its unanimous opinion, the Court defined "fighting words": "There are certain well-defined and narrowly limited classes of speech, the prevention and punishment of which have never been thought to raise any Constitutional problem. These include the lewd and obscene, the profane, the libelous, and the insulting or 'fighting' words—those which by their very utterance inflict injury or tend to incite an immediate breach of the peace."

19    Significantly *Chaplinsky*, as well as later decisions citing it as precedent, locate the justification for the "fighting words" exception in the government's duties to prevent injury to citizens and keep the peace. The former has been essentially negated by later opinions, while the latter has provided appellate courts with an enduring can of worms. If the danger of "fighting words" is that the addressee is apt to lose control and breach the peace (the "breach" is accomplished, in this perspective, only via actions, not via the offensive utterance itself), why not hold the breacher, not the utterer, responsible? The Court's assumption is that some words are so very bad that on hearing them, an ordinary person *must* strike out (as reflexively as, when the doctor taps your knee with a hammer, you *have* to jerk your leg). No psychological or other evidence is cited in support of this proposition.

20    *Chaplinsky* would seem to suggest that verbal aggressors should pick their targets carefully. Persons with less testosterone are known to be less likely than those with more to react physically to provocation. So, presumably, insulting women is more likely to be constitutional under *Chaplinsky* than insulting men, and it's probably better to insult someone smaller than you (who will be less likely to "breach the peace") than someone larger. Scholars who try to justify speech codes these days, like the authors of *Words That Wound,* avoid the morass by thinking in terms of psychic rather than physical trauma. But the "fighting words" exception was not meant to cover psychic wounds, and even if it were determining whether psychic trauma has occurred is—if possible at all—not the business of a court of law and a lay jury.

21    As fond as linguists are of Austinian doctrine (if words are actions, then what we linguists do is important), we must recognize that in fact words are not the same as actions. Most people given the choice between a vile epithet and a punch in the nose would opt for the former. Arguably this is because the second

has immediate and obvious painful consequences, while the effects of the first take longer to emerge and are harder to link directly to their cause. If, as the judge said in admitting *Ulysses* into the country, no woman was ever seduced by a book, so no one was ever killed by a word. If language is world-changing, the way it works is different from that of direct action, and less accessible to legal investigation.

22      Franklyn Haiman, in *"Speech Acts" and the First Amendment* (1993), proposes that language is "mediated" action. Austin is not quite right, he suggests, in equating performativity with action. When I give an order, you have to perform the mental act of *deciding* or *willing* to obey me. Even in the clearer case of excommunication, the recipient must determine that the appropriate conditions are met and decide to behave as an excommunicated person in the future, for it to succeed. The words alone, Haiman points out, are meaningless: they derive force through the agreement by all participants on the nature of the real-world circumstances in which they find themselves.

23      But Haiman is not quite right to dismiss the word-as-action theory entirely. While words are not directly as world-changing as actions are, they are indirectly or psychologically world-changing. If I make a promise to you, that utterance forever alters our relationship and the way I think about it and behave toward you, and you toward me, in the future. To say that speech is not action is to fall into the logical error of drawing a sharp distinction between mind and body.

24      How we feel about hate speech and the First Amendment reflects our view of language itself. If we believe that words are not world-changing, we are apt to be comfortable with an interpretation of the First Amendment that permits much more freedom of speech than is permitted to action. But this leeway comes at the price, ironically, of devaluing language—seeing it as non-action, essentially harmless.

## Notes

1.  At this writing, an anti-flag desecration law has passed the House of Representatives and is considered likely to pass the Senate.
2.  Chaplinsky admitted making the basic statement, but said that as a Jehovah's Witness, he would never have uttered the d-word.

### THINKING CRITICALLY

1.  This article comments on "right" and "left" attitudes toward the First Amendment. To what does this refer? In what ways have the political left and right used the First Amendment to forward their own agendas? Explain.

2.  In several places in this essay, Lakoff strategically puts certain words in italics, including pronouns. Why does she do this? How does her use of italics contribute to what she is trying to relay to the reader? Explain.

3.  What is the author's personal position on politically correct language and hate speech codes? When does her position become clear? Does she fairly describe both sides of the issue? Explain.

4.  Why does Lakoff say some racial epithets are worse than others? For example, are *phallocrat* and *honky* parallel to other racial slurs? Why or why not?

5. What is the "Snark rule"? How does it relate to the impact of hate speech on a population?

6. In paragraph 5, Lakoff cites several examples of kinds of speech not protected by the First Amendment. How can her examples be used to support both sides of the hate speech argument? Explain.

7. In her discussion of *Chaplinsky v. New Hampshire* (paragraphs 18–20), Lakoff concludes that the ruling on the case "would seem to suggest that verbal aggressors should pick their targets carefully. . . . So, presumably, insulting women is more likely to be constitutional than insulting men." Describe the case and how Lakoff draws such a conclusion. Do you agree? Why or why not?

8. In paragraph 21, Lakoff explains why she feels that words are not actions. On what does she base her assessment? Why does she feel that Austin and Haiman are incorrect in their presumption that action and speech are corollaries? Explain.

9. In her closing comments, Lakoff comments that how we feel about hate speech has a great deal to do with how we feel about language. In your own words, explain what she means by this statement.

### WRITING ASSIGNMENTS

1. In your experience, has anyone called you, or a member of a group to which you belong, a name you found offensive? How did that incident make you feel? What was your response? Write a paper based on your answer.

2. In this essay, Lakoff notes that individuals or groups who do not have a history of hearing hate speech "just don't get it." It is the historical repetition and legacy of such language that give racial and sexist epithets their sting. Write an essay exploring this idea from your own viewpoint.

---

# Bias-Free Language: Some Guidelines
*Rosalie Maggio*

The growing reality of America's multiculturalism has produced a heightened sensitivity to language that is offensive to members of minority groups. In response, a number of bias-free language guides have been written—guides that caution against terms that might offend not only racial and ethnic groups but also women, gays, senior citizens, the handicapped, animal lovers, and the overweight. One of the most successful guides is Rosalie Maggio's *The Dictionary of Bias-Free Usage: A Guide to Nondiscriminatory Language* (1991). In the following excerpt from that guide's introduction, the author discusses how to evaluate and recognize language bias and why it should be avoided.

Rosalie Maggio is also the author of *The Nonsexist Word Finder* (1987), *How to Say It: Words, Phrases, Sentences, and Paragraphs for Every Situation* (1990), and, most recently, *The Art of Talking to Anyone* (2005). She has edited many college textbooks and published hundreds of stories and articles in educational publications and children's magazines. Her work has received several literary honors and awards for children's fiction and research on women's issues.

1 Language both reflects and shapes society. The textbook on American government that consistently uses male pronouns for the president, even when not referring to a specific individual (e.g., "a president may cast his veto"), reflects the fact that all our presidents have so far been men. But it also shapes a society in which the idea of a female president somehow "doesn't sound right."

2 Culture shapes language and then language shapes culture. "Contrary to the assumption that language merely reflects social patterns such as sex-role stereotypes, research in linguistics and social psychology has shown that these are in fact facilitated and reinforced by language" (Marlis Hellinger, in *Language and Power*, ed., Cheris Kramarae et al.).

3 Biased language can also, says Sanford Berman, "powerfully harm people, as amply demonstrated by bigots' and tyrants' deliberate attempts to linguistically dehumanize and demean groups they intend to exploit, oppress, or exterminate. Calling Asians 'gooks' made it easier to kill them. Calling blacks 'niggers' made it simpler to enslave and brutalize them. Calling Native Americans 'primitives' and 'savages' made it okay to conquer and despoil them. And to talk of 'fishermen,' 'councilmen,' and 'longshoremen' is to clearly exclude and discourage women from those pursuits, to diminish and degrade them."

4 The question is asked: Isn't it silly to get upset about language when there are so many more important issues that need our attention?

5 First, it's to be hoped that there are enough of us working on issues large and small that the work will all get done—someday. Second, the interconnections between the way we think, speak, and act are beyond dispute. Language goes hand-in-hand with social change—both shaping it and reflecting it. Sexual harassment was not a term anyone used twenty years ago; today we have laws against it. How could we have the law without the language; how could we have the language without the law? In fact, the judicial system is a good argument for the importance of "mere words"; the legal profession devotes great energy to the precise interpretation of words—often with far-reaching and significant consequences.

6 On August 21, 1990, in the midst of the Iraqi offensive, front-page headlines told the big story: President Bush had used the word *hostages* for the first time. Up to that time, *detainee* had been used. The difference between two very similar words was of possible life-and-death proportions. In another situation—also said to be life-and-death by some people—the difference between *fetal tissue* and *unborn baby* (in referring to the very same thing) is arguably the most debated issue in the country. So, yes, words have power and deserve our attention.

7 Some people are like George Crabbe's friend: "Habit with him was all the test of truth, /it must be right: I've done it from my youth." They have come of age using *handicapped, black-and-white, leper, mankind*, and pseudogeneric *he*; these terms must therefore be correct. And yet if there's one thing consistent about language it is that language is constantly changing; when the *Random House Dictionary of the English Language,* 2nd Edition was published in 1988, it contained 50,000 new entries, most of them words that had come into use since 1966. There were also 75,000 new definitions. (Incidentally, *RHD-II* asks its readers to "use gender-neutral terms wherever possible" and it never uses *mankind* in definitions where *people* is meant, nor does it ever refer to anyone of unknown gender as *he*.) However,

few supporters of bias-free language are asking for changes; it is rather a matter of choice—which of the many acceptable words available to us will we use?

8    A high school student who felt that nonsexist language did demand some changes said, "But you don't understand! You're trying to change the English language, which has been around a lot longer than women have!"

9    One reviewer of the first edition commented, "There's no fun in limiting how you say a thing." Perhaps not. Yet few people complain about looking up a point of grammar or usage or checking the dictionary for a correct spelling. Most writers are very fussy about finding the precise best word, the exact rhythmic vehicle for their ideas. Whether or not these limits "spoil their fun" is an individual judgment. However, most of us accept that saying or writing the first thing that comes to mind is not often the way we want to be remembered. So if we have to think a little, if we have to search for the unbiased word, the inclusive phrase, it is not any more effort than we expend on proper grammar, spelling, and style.

10    Other people fear "losing" words, as though there weren't more where those came from. We are limited only by our imaginations; vague, inaccurate, and disrespectful words can be thrown overboard with no loss to society and no impoverishment of the language.

11    Others are tired of having to "watch what they say." But what they perhaps mean is that they're tired of being sensitive to others' requests. From childhood onward, we all learn to "watch what we say": we don't swear around our parents; we don't bring up certain topics around certain people; we speak differently to friend, boss, cleric, English teacher, lover, radio interviewer, child. Most of us are actually quite skilled at picking and choosing appropriate words; it seems odd that we are too "tired" to call people what they want to be called.

12    The greatest objection to bias-free language is that it will lead us to absurdities. Critics have posited something utterly ridiculous, cleverly demonstrated how silly it is, and then accounted themselves victorious in the battle against linguistic massacre. For example: "So I suppose now we're going to say: He/she ain't heavy, Father/Sister; he/she's my brother/sister." "I suppose next it will be 'ottoperson'." Cases have been built up against the mythic "woperson," "personipulate," and "personhole cover" (none of which has ever been advocated by any reputable sociolinguist). No grist appears too ridiculous for these mills. And, yes, they grind exceedingly small. Using a particular to condemn a universal is a fault in logic. But then ridicule, it is said, is the first and last argument of fools.

13    One of the most rewarding—and, for many people, the most unexpected—side effects of breaking away from traditional, biased language is a dramatic improvement in writing style. By replacing fuzzy, overgeneralized, cliché-ridden words with explicit, active words and by giving concrete examples and anecdotes instead of one-word-fits-all descriptions you can express yourself more dynamically, convincingly, and memorably.

14    "If those who have studied the art of writing are in accord on any one point, it is on this: the surest way to arouse and hold the attention of the reader is by being specific, definite, and concrete" (Strunk and White, *The Elements of Style*). Writers who talk about *brotherhood* or *spinsters* or *right-hand men* miss a chance to spark their writing with fresh descriptions; they leave their readers as uninspired as they are.

Unthinking writing is also less informative. Why use the unrevealing *adman* when we could choose instead a precise, descriptive, inclusive word like *advertising executive, copywriter, account executive, ad writer,* or *media buyer?*

15    The word *manmade*, which seems so indispensable to us, doesn't actually say very much. Does it mean artificial? Handmade? Synthetic? Fabricated? Machine-made? Custom-made? Simulated? plastic? Imitation? Contrived?

16    Communication is—or ought to be—a two-way street. A speaker who uses *man* to mean *human being* while the audience hears it as *adult male* is an example of communication gone awry.

17    Bias-free language is logical, accurate, and realistic. Biased language is not. How logical is it to speak of the "discovery" of America, a land already inhabited by millions of people? Where is the accuracy in writing "Dear Sir" to a woman? Where is the realism in the full-page automobile advertisement that says in bold letters, "A good driver is a product of his environment," when more women than men influence car-buying decisions? Or how successful is the ad for a dot-matrix printer that says, "In 3,000 years, man's need to present his ideas hasn't changed. But his tools have," when many of these printers are bought and used by women, who also have ideas they need to present? And when we use stereotypes to talk about people ("isn't that just like a welfare mother/Indian/girl/old man"), our speech and writing will be inaccurate and unrealistic most of the time.

## Definition of Terms

### Bias/Bias-Free

18    Biased language communicates inaccurately about what it means to be male or female; black or white; young or old; straight, gay, or bi; rich or poor; from one ethnic group or another; disabled or temporarily able-bodied; or to hold a particular belief system. It reflects the same bias found in racism, sexism, ageism, handicappism, classism, ethnocentrism, anti-Semitism, homophobia, and other forms of discrimination.

19    Bias occurs in the language in several ways.

1. Leaving out individuals or groups. "Employees are welcome to bring their wives and children" leaves out those employees who might want to bring husbands, friends, or same-sex partners. "We are all immigrants in this country" leaves out Native Americans, who were here well before the first immigrants.

2. Making unwarranted assumptions. To address a sales letter about a new diaper to the mother assumes that the father won't be diapering the baby. To write "Anyone can use this fire safety ladder" assumes that all members of the household are able-bodied.

3. Calling individuals and groups by names or labels that they do not choose for themselves (e.g., *Gypsy, office girl, Eskimo, pygmy, Bushman, the elderly, colored man*) or terms that are derogatory (*fairy, libber, savage, bum, old goat*).

4. Stereotypical treatment that implies that all lesbians/Chinese/women/people with disabilities/teenagers are alike.

5. Unequal treatment of various groups in the same material.

6. Unnecessary mention of membership in a particular group. In a land of supposedly equal opportunity, of what importance is a person's race, sex, age, sexual orientation, disability, or creed? As soon as we mention one of these characteristics—without a good reason for doing so—we enter an area mined by potential linguistic disasters. Although there may be instances in which a person's sex, for example, is germane ("A recent study showed that female patients do not object to being cared for by male nurses"), most of the time it is not. Nor is mentioning a person's race, sexual orientation, disability, age, or belief system usually germane.

20    Bias can be overt or subtle. Jean Gaddy Wilson (in Brooks and Pinson, *Working with Words*) says, "Following one simple rule of writing or speaking will eliminate most biases. Ask yourself: Would you say the same thing about an affluent, white man?"

## Inclusive/Exclusive

21 Inclusive language includes everyone; exclusive language excludes some people. The following quotation is inclusive: "The greatest revolution of our generation is the discovery that human beings, by changing the inner attitudes of their minds, can change the outer aspects of their lives" (William James). It is clear that James is speaking of all of us.

22    Examples of sex-exclusive writing fill most quotation books: "Man is the measure of all things" (Protagoras). "The People, though we think of a great entity when we use the word, means nothing more than so many millions of individual men" (James Bryce). "Man is nature's sole mistake" (W. S. Gilbert).

## Sexist/Nonsexist

23 Sexist language promotes and maintains attitudes that stereotype people according to gender while assuming that the male is the norm—the significant gender. Nonsexist language treats all people equally and either does not refer to a person's sex at all when it is irrelevant or refers to men and women in symmetrical ways.

24    "A society in which women are taught anything but the management of a family, the care of men, and the creation of the future generation is a society which is on the way out" (L. Ron Hubbard). "Behind every successful man is a woman— with nothing to wear" (L. Grant Glickman). "Nothing makes a man and wife feel closer, these days, than a joint tax return" (Gil Stern). These quotations display various characteristics of sexist writing: (1) stereotyping an entire sex by what might be appropriate for some of it; (2) assuming male superiority; (3) using unparallel terms (*man and wife* should be either *wife and husband/husband and wife* or *woman and man/man and woman*).

25    The following quotations clearly refer to all people: "It's really hard to be roommates with people if your suitcases are much better than theirs" (J. D. Salinger). "If people don't want to come out to the ball park, nobody's going to stop them" (Yogi Berra). "If men and women of capacity refuse to take part in politics and

government, they condemn themselves, as well as the people, to the punishment of living under bad government" (Senator Sam J. Ervin). "I studied the lives of great men and famous women, and I found that the men and women who got to the top were those who did the jobs they had in hand, with everything they had of energy and enthusiasm and hard work" (Harry S Truman).

### Gender-Free/Gender-Fair/Gender-Specific

26 Gender-free terms do not indicate sex and can be used for either women/girls or men/boys (e.g., *teacher, bureaucrat, employee, hiker, operations manager, child, clerk, sales rep, hospital patient, student, grandparent, chief executive officer*).

27 Writing or speech that is gender-fair involves the symmetrical use of gender-specific words (e.g., *Ms. Leinwohl/Mr. Kelly, councilwoman/councilman, young man/young woman*) and promotes fairness to both sexes in the larger context. To ensure gender-fairness, ask yourself often: Would I write the same thing in the same way about a person of the opposite sex? Would I mind if this were said of me?

28 If you are describing the behavior of children on the playground, to be gender-fair you will refer to girls and boys an approximately equal number of times, and you will carefully observe what the children do, and not just assume that only the boys will climb to the top of the jungle gym and that only the girls will play quiet games.

29 Researchers studying the same baby described its cries as "anger" when they were told it was a boy and as "fear" when they were told it was a girl (cited in Cheris Kramarae, *The Voices and Words of Women and Men*). We are all victims of our unconscious and most deeply held biases.

30 Gender-specific words (for example, *alderwoman, businessman, altar girl*) are neither good nor bad in themselves. However, they need to be used gender-fairly; terms for women and terms for men should be used an approximately equal number of times in contexts that do not discriminate against either of them. One problem with gender-specific words is that they identify and even emphasize a person's sex when it is not necessary (and is sometimes even objectionable) to do so. Another problem is that they are so seldom used gender-fairly.

31 Although gender-free terms are generally preferable, sometimes gender-neutral language obscures the reality of women's or men's oppression. *Battered spouse* implies that men and women are equally battered; this is far from true. *Parent* is too often taken to mean *mother* and obscures the fact that more and more fathers are very much involved in parenting; it is better here to use the gender-specific *fathers and mothers* or *mothers and fathers* than the gender-neutral *parents*.

### Generic/Pseudogeneric

32 A generic is an all-purpose word that includes everybody (e.g., *workers, people, voters, civilians, elementary school students*). Generic pronouns include: *we, you, they*.

33 A pseudogeneric is a word that is used as though it included all people, but that in reality does not. *Mankind, forefathers, brotherhood*, and *alumni* are not generic because they leave out women. When used about Americans, *immigrants* leaves out all those who were here long before the first immigrants. "What a christian

thing to do!" uses *christian* as a pseudogeneric for *kind* or *good-hearted* and leaves out all kind, good-hearted people who are not Christians.

34    Although some speakers and writers say that when they use *man* or *mankind* they mean everybody, their listeners and readers do not perceive the word that way and these terms are thus pseudogenerics. The pronoun *he* when used to mean *he and she* is another pseudogeneric.

35    Certain generic nouns are often assumed to refer only to men, for example, *politicians, physicians, lawyers, voters, legislators, clergy, farmers, colonists, immigrants, slaves, pioneers, settlers, members of the armed forces, judges, taxpayers.* References to "settlers, their wives, and children," or "those clergy permitted to have wives" are pseudogeneric.

36    In historical context it is particularly damaging for young people to read about settlers and explorers and pioneers as though they were all white men. Our language should describe the accomplishments of the human race in terms of all those who contributed to them.

## Sex and Gender

37 An understanding of the difference between sex and gender is critical to the use of bias-free language.

38    Sex is biological: people with male genitals are male, and people with female genitals are female.

39    Gender is cultural: our notions of "masculine" tell us how we expect men to behave and our notions of "feminine" tell us how we expect women to behave. Words like *womanly/manly, tomboy/sissy, unfeminine/unmasculine* have nothing to do with the person's sex; they are culturally acquired, subjective concepts about character traits and expected behaviors that vary from one place to another, from one individual to another.

40    It is biologically impossible for a woman to be a sperm donor. It may be culturally unusual for a man to be a secretary, but it is not biologically impossible. To say "the secretary . . . she" assumes all secretaries are women and is sexist because the issue is gender, not sex. Gender describes an individual's personal, legal, and social status without reference to genetic sex; gender is a subjective cultural attitude. Sex is an objective biological fact. Gender varies according to the culture. Sex is a constant.

41    The difference between sex and gender is important because much sexist language arises from cultural determinations of what a woman or man "ought" to be. Once a society decides, for example, that to be a man means to hide one's emotions, bring home a paycheck, and be able to discuss football standings while to be a woman means to be soft-spoken, love shopping, babies, and recipes, and "never have anything to wear," much of the population becomes a contradiction in terms—unmanly men and unwomanly women. Crying, nagging, gossiping, and shrieking are assumed to be women's lot; rough-housing, drinking beer, telling dirty jokes, and being unable to find one's socks and keys are laid at men's collective door. Lists of stereotypes appear silly because very few people fit them. The best way to ensure unbiased writing and speaking is to describe people as individuals, not as members of a set.

## Gender Role Words

42  Certain sex-linked words depend for their meanings on cultural stereotypes: *feminine/ masculine, manly/womanly, boyish/girlish, husbandly/wifely, fatherly/ motherly, unfeminine/unmasculine, unmanly/unwomanly*, etc. What a person understands by these words will vary from culture to culture and even within a culture. Because the words depend for their meanings on interpretations of stereotypical behavior or characteristics, they may be grossly inaccurate when applied to individuals. Some-where, sometime, men and women have said, thought, or done everything the other sex has said, thought, or done except for a very few sex-linked biological activities (e.g., only women can give birth or nurse a baby, only a man can donate sperm or impregnate a woman). To describe a woman as unwomanly is a contradiction in terms; if a woman is doing it, saying it, wearing it, thinking it, it must be—by definition—womanly.

43      F. Scott Fitzgerald did not use "feminine" to describe the unforgettable Daisy in *The Great Gatsby*. He wrote instead, "She laughed again, as if she said something very witty, and held my hand for a moment, looking up into my face, promising that there was no one in the world she so much wanted to see. That was a way she had." Daisy's charm did not belong to Woman: it was uniquely hers. Replacing vague sex-linked descriptors with thoughtful words that describe an individual instead of a member of a set can lead to language that touches people's minds and hearts.

## Naming

44  Naming is power, which is why the issue of naming is one of the most important in bias-free language.

## Self-Definition

45  People decide what they want to be called. The correct names for individuals and groups are always those by which they refer to themselves. This "tradition" is not always unchallenged. Haig Bosmajian (*The Language of Oppression*) says, "It isn't strange that those persons who insist on defining themselves, who insist on this elemental privilege of self-naming, self-definition, and self-identity encounter vigorous resistance. Predictably, the resistance usually comes from the oppressor or would-be oppressor and is a result of the fact that he or she does not want to relinquish the power which comes from the ability to define others."

46      Dr. Ian Hancock uses the term *exonym* for a name applied to a group by outsiders. For example, Romani peoples object to being called by the exonym *Gypsies*. They do not call themselves Gypsies. Among the many other exonyms are: the elderly, colored people, homosexuals, pagans, adolescents, Eskimos, pygmies, savages. The test for an exonym is whether people describe themselves as "red-men," "illegal aliens," "holy rollers," etc., or whether only outsiders describe them that way.

47      There is a very small but visible element today demanding that gay men "give back" the word *gay*—a good example of denying people the right to name them-selves. A late-night radio caller said several times that gay men had "stolen" this word from "our" language. It was not clear what language gay men spoke.

48     A woman nicknamed "Betty" early in life had always preferred her full name, "Elizabeth." On her fortieth birthday, she reverted to Elizabeth. An acquaintance who heard about the change said sharply, "I'll call her Betty if I like!"

49     We can call them Betty if we like, but it's arrogant, insensitive, and uninformed: the only rule we have in this area says we call people what they want to be called.

### "Insider/Outsider" Rule

50   A related rule says that insiders may describe themselves in ways that outsiders may not. "Crip" appears in *The Disability Rag*; this does not mean that the word is available to anyone who wants to use it. "Big Fag" is printed on a gay man's T-shirt. He may use that expression; a non-gay may not so label him. One junior-high student yells to another, "Hey, nigger!" This would be highly offensive and inflammatory if the speaker were not African American. A group of women talk about "going out with the girls," but a co-worker should not refer to them as "girls." When questioned about just such a situation, Miss Manners replied that "people are allowed more leeway in what they call themselves than in what they call others."

### "People First" Rule

51   Haim Ginott taught us that labels are disabling; intuitively most of us recognize this and resist being labeled. The disability movement originated the "people first" rule, which says we don't call someone a "diabetic" but rather "a person with diabetes." Saying someone is "an AIDS victim" reduces the person to a disease, a label, a statistic; use instead "a person with/who has/living with AIDS." The 1990 Americans with Disabilities Act is a good example of correct wording. Name the person as a person first, and let qualifiers (age, sex, disability, race) follow, but (and this is crucial) only if they are relevant. Readers of a magazine aimed at an older audience were asked what they wanted to be called (elderly? senior citizens? seniors? golden agers?). They rejected all the terms; one said, "How about 'people'?" When high school students rejected labels like kids, teens, teenagers, youth, adolescents, and juveniles, and were asked in exasperation just what they would like to be called, they said, "Could we just be people?"

### Women as Separate People

52   One of the most sexist maneuvers in the language has been the identification of women by their connections to husband, son, or father—often even after he is dead. Women are commonly identified as someone's widow while men are never referred to as anyone's widower. Marie Marvingt, a Frenchwoman who lived around the turn of the century, was an inventor, adventurer, stunt woman, superathlete, aviator, and all-around scholar. She chose to be affianced to neither man (as a wife) nor God (as a religious), but it was not long before an uneasy male press found her a fit partner. She is still known today by the revealing label "the Fiancée of Danger." If a connection is relevant, make it mutual. Instead of "Frieda, his wife of seventeen years," write "Frieda and Eric, married for seventeen years."

53     It is difficult for some people to watch women doing unconventional things with their names. For years the etiquette books were able to tell us precisely how

to address a single woman, a married woman, a divorced woman, or a widowed woman (there was no similar etiquette on men because they have always been just men and we have never had a code to signal their marital status). But now some women are Ms. and some are Mrs., some are married but keeping their birth names, others are hyphenating their last name with their husband's, and still others have constructed new names for themselves. Some women—including African American women who were denied this right earlier in our history—take great pride in using their husband's name. All these forms are correct. The same rule of self-definition applies here: call the woman what she wants to be called.

### THINKING CRITICALLY

1. Maggio begins her article with a discussion of the ways language has real effects on people's attitudes and actions. What are some of the examples she supplies? How does language create desirable or undesirable consequences?

2. What are the four excuses people make to avoid using unbiased language? How does Maggio counter those excuses? What additional counterargument does she supply in defense of nonbiased language?

3. What main idea links all the different ways in which bias can occur (see paragraph 10)? Does biased language refer to individuals or to groups of people? Would the following statement be an example of biased (or stereotyped) language? "Mary is wearing her hair in a French braid today, so she'll no doubt wear it that way tomorrow."

4. What are the categories Maggio specifically names as subject to biased language? Can you supply additional categories?

5. Maggio uses the term *symmetrical* several times (e.g., paragraphs 23 and 27). What does this term mean? Does Maggio want to encourage or discourage the use of symmetrical language? Does *symmetry* refer only to gender bias, or can it refer to other kinds of bias too?

6. What is the difference between gender-free, gender-fair, and gender-specific language in paragraphs 26 through 31? What examples does Maggio supply for each one? When is each kind of nonbiased language appropriate?

7. What does Maggio mean by a "generic" word? A "pseudogeneric" word? How might pseudogeneric references harm people?

8. What is an "exonym"? Are exonyms ever appropriate, according to Maggio's discussion? Did you recognize all the words Maggio lists in paragraph 46 as exonyms? Can you supply substitutes for all the exonyms? If not, what problems did you encounter? Can you supply examples of other exonyms from your own experience?

9. Why do you think Maggio considers naming "one of the most important [issues] in bias-free language" (paragraph 44)? What is so important about the ability to choose a name? What do you think the woman in paragraph 48 is communicating by choosing to be called Elizabeth? Why do you think Maggio links this announcement to the woman's 40th birthday celebration?

10. What did the high school student in paragraph 8 really mean to say? Why do you think Maggio includes this statement? What point is she trying to make? Do you think that this student was male or female? Would it make a difference? Why does Maggio not specify?

## WRITING ASSIGNMENTS

1. Locate an article in a contemporary newspaper that you think displays one or more of the biases Maggio describes. In a letter to the editor (no more than 500 words), persuade the newspaper editors to avoid such biased language in future articles. Remember that your writing will be more effective if you write in a calm, reasonable tone, use specific examples, and explain clearly the benefits of unbiased language.

2. Look back at Susanne K. Langer's essay, "Language and Thought," in Chapter 1. How is Maggio's understanding of biased language and the harm it can create based on an understanding of language as symbol (as Langer uses that term)? What are the distinguishing features of language as symbol that biased language uses? Pay special attention to Maggio's treatment of naming, because Langer claims that "names are the essence of language" (in Langer's paragraph 20).

3. How would you go about designing an advertising campaign for the magazine that Maggio says is "aimed at an older audience"? What words would you use to avoid offensive labeling and to avoid the vagueness of the broadly generic noun *people* (which is the same term the high school students ask to be designated by)?

---

# The Word Police
## Michiko Kakutani

Not everybody applauds the efforts of those hoping to rid the language of offensive terms. To detractors, all such linguistic sensitivity is no more than a symptom of political correctness—a kind of be-sensitive-or-else campaign. They complain that unlike standard dictionaries, which are meant to help people use words, the so-called *cautionary* guides warn people against using them. Such is the complaint of Michiko Kakutani, who specifically targets Rosalie Maggio's *The Bias-Free Word Finder* as an example of the menace of hypersensitivity. She complains that in the name of the "politics of inclusion," proponents hunt down users of "inappropriate" language like the thought police from George Orwell's *1984*. And, claims Kakutani, they fill the English language with sloppy, pious euphemisms.

Michiko Kakutani is Pulitzer Prize–winning literary critic for *The New York Times*. This article was first published by *The New York Times* in January of 1993.

1   This month's inaugural festivities, with their celebration, in Maya Angelou's words, of "humankind"—"the Asian, the Hispanic, the Jew/ The African, the Native American, the Sioux,/ The Catholic, the Muslim, the French, the Greek/ The Irish, the Rabbi, the Priest, the Sheik,/ The Gay, the Straight, the Preacher,/ The privileged, the homeless, the Teacher"—constituted a kind of official embrace of multiculturalism and a new politics of inclusion.

2       The mood of political correctness, however, has already made firm inroads into popular culture. Washington boasts a store called Politically Correct that sells pro-whale, anti-meat, ban-the-bomb T-shirts, bumper stickers and buttons, as well as a local cable television show called "Politically Correct Cooking" that features

interviews in the kitchen with representatives from groups like People for the Ethical Treatment of Animals.

3      The Coppertone suntan lotion people are planning to give their longtime cover girl, Little Miss (Ms?) Coppertone, a male equivalent, Little Mr. Coppertone. And even Superman (Super-person?) is rumored to be returning this spring, reincarnated as four ethnically diverse clones: an African-American, an Asian, a Caucasian and a Latino.

4      Nowhere is this P.C. mood more striking than in the increasingly noisy debate over language that has moved from university campuses to the country at large—a development that both underscores Americans' puritanical zeal for reform and their unwavering faith in the talismanic power of words.

5      Certainly no decent person can quarrel with the underlying impulse behind political correctness: a vision of a more just, inclusive society in which racism, sexism and prejudice of all sorts have been erased. But the methods and fervor of the self-appointed language police can lead to a rigid orthodoxy—and unintentional self-parody—opening the movement to the scorn of conservative opponents and the mockery of cartoonists and late-night television hosts.

6      It's hard to imagine women earning points for political correctness by saying "ovarimony" instead of "testimony"—as one participant at the recent Modern Language Association convention was overheard to suggest. It's equally hard to imagine people wanting to flaunt their lack of prejudice by giving up such words and phrases as "bull market," "kaiser roll," "Lazy Susan," and "charley horse."

7      Several books on bias-free language have already appeared, and the 1991 edition of the Random House *Webster's College Dictionary* boasts an appendix titled "Avoiding Sexist Language." The dictionary also includes such linguistic mutations as "womyn" (women, "used as an alternative spelling to avoid the suggestion of sexism perceived in the sequence m-e-n") and "waitron" (a gender-blind term for waiter or waitress).

8      Many of these dictionaries and guides not only warn the reader against offensive racial and sexual slurs, but also try to establish and enforce a whole new set of usage rules. Take, for instance, *The Bias-Free Word Finder: A Dictionary of Nondiscriminatory Language* by Rosalie Maggio (Beacon Press)—a volume often indistinguishable, in its meticulous solemnity, from the tongue in-cheek *Official Politically Correct Dictionary and Handbook* put out last year by Henry Beard and Christopher Cerf (Villard Books). Ms. Maggio's book supplies the reader intent on using kinder, gentler language with writing guidelines as well as a detailed listing of more than 5,000 "biased words and phrases."

9      Whom are these guidelines for? Somehow one has a tough time picturing them replacing Fowler's *Modern English Usage* in the classroom, or being adopted by the average man (sorry, individual) in the street.

10      The "pseudogeneric 'he,'" we learn from Ms. Maggio, is to be avoided like the plague, as is the use of the word "man" to refer to humanity. "Fellow," "king," "lord" and "master" are bad because they're "male-oriented words," and "king," "lord" and "master" are especially bad because they're also "hierarchical, dominator society terms." The politically correct lion becomes the "monarch of the jungle," new-age children play "someone on the top of the heap," and the "Mona Lisa" goes down in history as Leonardo's "acme of perfection."

11      As for the word "black," Ms. Maggio says it should be excised from terms with a negative spin: she recommends substituting words like "mouse" for "black eye," "ostracize" for "blackball," "payola" for "blackmail" and "outcast" for "black sheep." Clearly, some of these substitutions work better than others: somehow the "sinister humor" of Kurt Vonnegut or "Saturday Night Live" doesn't quite make it; nor does the "denouncing" of the Hollywood 10.

12      For the dedicated user of politically correct language, all these rules can make for some messy moral dilemmas. Whereas "battered wife" is a gender-biased term, the gender-free term "battered spouse," Ms. Maggio notes, incorrectly implies "that men and women are equally battered."

13      On one hand, say Francine Wattman Frank and Paula A. Treichler in their book *Language, Gender, and Professional Writing* (Modern Language Association), "he or she" is an appropriate construction for talking about an individual (like a jockey, say) who belongs to a profession that's predominantly male—it's a way of emphasizing "that such occupations are not barred to women or that women's concerns need to be kept in mind." On the other hand, they add, using masculine pronouns rhetorically can underscore ongoing male dominance in those fields, implying the need for change.

14      And what about the speech codes adopted by some universities in recent years? Although they were designed to prohibit students from uttering sexist and racist slurs, they would extend, by logic, to blacks who want to use the word "nigger" to strip the term of its racist connotations, or homosexuals who want to use the word "queer" to reclaim it from bigots.

15      In her book, Ms. Maggio recommends applying bias-free usage retroactively: she suggests paraphrasing politically incorrect quotations, or replacing "the sexist words or phrases with ellipsis dots and/or bracketed substitutes," or using "sic" "to show that the sexist words come from the original quotation and to call attention to the fact that they are incorrect."

16      Which leads the skeptical reader of *The Bias-Free Word Finder* to wonder whether *All the King's Men* should be retitled *All The Ruler's People; Pet Cemetery, Animal Companion Graves; Birdman of Alcatraz, Birdperson of Alcatraz;* and *The Iceman Cometh, The Ice Route Driver Cometh?*

17      Will making such changes remove the prejudice in people's minds? Should we really spend time trying to come up with non-male–based alternatives to "Midas touch," "Achilles' heel," and "Montezuma's revenge"? Will tossing out Santa Claus—whom Ms. Maggio accuses of reinforcing "the cultural male-as-norm system"—in favor of Belfana, his Italian female alter ego, truly help banish sexism? Can the avoidance of "violent expressions and metaphors" like "kill two birds with one stone," "sock it to 'em" or "kick an idea around" actually promote a more harmonious world?

18      The point isn't that the excesses of the word police are comical. The point is that their intolerance (in the name of tolerance) has disturbing implications. In the first place, getting upset by phrases like "bullish on America" or "the City of Brotherly Love" tends to distract attention from the real problems of prejudice and injustice that exist in society at large, turning them into mere questions of semantics. Indeed, the emphasis currently put on politically correct usage has uncanny

parallels with the academic movement of deconstruction—a method of textual analysis that focuses on language and linguistic pyrotechnics—which has become firmly established on university campuses.

19    In both cases, attention is focused on surfaces, on words and metaphors; in both cases, signs and symbols are accorded more importance than content. Hence, the attempt by some radical advocates to remove the *Adventures of Huckleberry Finn* from curriculums on the grounds that Twain's use of the word "nigger" makes the book a racist text—never mind the fact that this American classic (written in 1884) depicts the spiritual kinship achieved between a white boy and a runaway slave, never mind the fact that the "nigger" Jim emerges as the novel's most honorable, decent character.

20    Ironically enough, the P.C. movement's obsession with language is accompanied by a strange Orwellian willingness to warp the meaning of words by placing them under a high-powered ideological lens. For instance, the "Dictionary of Cautionary Words and Phrases"—a pamphlet issued by the University of Missouri's Multicultural Management Program to help turn "today's journalists into tomorrow's multicultural newsroom managers"—warns that using the word "articulate" to describe members of a minority group can suggest the opposite, "that 'those people' are not considered well educated, articulate and the like."

21    The pamphlet patronizes minority groups, by cautioning the reader against using the words "lazy" and "burly" to describe any member of such groups; and it issues a similar warning against using words like "gorgeous" and "petite" to describe women.

22    As euphemism proliferates with the rise of political correctness, there is a spread of the sort of sloppy, abstract language that Orwell said is "designed to make lies sound truthful and murder respectable, and to give an appearance of solidity to pure wind." "Fat" becomes "big boned" or "differently sized"; "stupid" becomes "exceptional"; "stoned" becomes "chemically inconvenienced."

23    Wait a minute here! Aren't such phrases eerily reminiscent of the euphemisms coined by the Government during Vietnam and Watergate? Remember how the military used to speak of "pacification," or how President Richard M. Nixon's press secretary, Ronald L. Ziegler, tried to get away with calling a lie an "inoperative statement"?

24    Calling the homeless "the underhoused" doesn't give them a place to live; calling the poor "the economically marginalized" doesn't help them pay the bills. Rather, by playing down their plight, such language might even make it easier to shrug off the seriousness of their situation.

25    Instead of allowing free discussion and debate to occur, many gung-ho advocates of politically correct language seem to think that simple suppression of a word or concept will magically make the problem disappear. In the *Bias-Free Word Finder*, Ms. Maggio entreats the reader not to perpetuate the negative stereotype of Eve. "Be extremely cautious in referring to the biblical Eve," she writes; "this story has profoundly contributed to negative attitudes toward women throughout history, largely because of misogynistic and patriarchal interpretations that labeled her evil, inferior, and seductive."

26    The story of Bluebeard, the rake (whoops!—the libertine) who killed his seven wives, she says, is also to be avoided, as is the biblical story of Jezebel. Of Jesus

Christ, Ms. Maggio writes: "There have been few individuals in history as completely androgynous as Christ, and it does his message a disservice to overinsist on
his maleness." She doesn't give the reader any hints on how this might be accomplished; presumably, one is supposed to avoid describing him as the Son of God.

27      Of course the P.C. police aren't the only ones who want to proscribe what
people should say or give them guidelines for how they may use an idea; Jesse
Helms and his supporters are up to exactly the same thing when they propose to
patrol the boundaries of the permissible in art. In each case, the would-be censor
aspires to suppress what he or she finds distasteful—all, of course, in the name of
the public good.

28      In the case of the politically correct, the prohibition of certain words, phrases
and ideas is advanced in the cause of building a brave new world free of racism and
hate, but this vision of harmony clashes with the very ideals of diversity and inclusion that the multicultural movement holds dear, and it's purchased at the cost of
freedom of expression and freedom of speech.

29      In fact, the utopian world envisioned by the language police would be bought
at the expense of the ideals of individualism and democracy articulated in "The
Gettysburg Address." "Fourscore and seven years ago our forefathers brought forth
on this continent a new nation, conceived in liberty and dedicated to the proposition
that all men are created equal."

30      Of course, the P.C. police have already found Lincoln's words hopelessly
"phallocentric." No doubt they would rewrite the passage: "Fourscore and seven
years ago our foremothers and forefathers brought forth on this continent a new
nation, formulated with liberty, and dedicated to the proposition that all humankind
is created equal."

### THINKING CRITICALLY

1. What kinds of people are mentioned in the lines of Maya Angelou's inauguration poem? What do these people symbolize, according to Kakutani? How
   many of these groups are represented in your classroom right now?

2. What specific substitutions of words does Kakutani complain about in paragraph 10?
   Can you supply the "biased" term that the "politically correct" phrase has
   replaced in the second half of the paragraph?

3. What are the three "messy moral dilemmas" Kakutani points out in paragraphs
   12–14? Why does she tag the examples she cites as *dilemmas*? Why does she
   object to following politically correct guidelines in each case?

4. What is wrong, according to Kakutani in paragraphs 15 and 16, with Maggio's
   recommendation that unbiased language be applied retroactively? Rewrite
   one or two of the titles using Maggio's suggestions as quoted by Kakutani in
   paragraph 15—that is, use ellipses, brackets, and so on. How well do these
   suggestions work?

5. What examples of euphemism does Kakutani provide in paragraphs 22–24?
   What objections does she raise about these euphemisms? Why does she
   compare the new politically correct terms with terms from Watergate?

6. Describe the tone in the first three paragraphs of the article. Based on these
   paragraphs, did you think this piece was going to be serious, playful, or sarcastic?
   Upon what evidence did you base your response?

7. Look closely at the wording of Kakutani's first sentence in paragraph 22. Why does she not say outright that political correctness causes "sloppy, abstract language"? What do you think Maggio would say about the cause-and-effect relationship of political correctness and language?

8. Kakutani interrupts herself twice to insert a "correction"—to substitute a politically correct term for an incorrect term she has inadvertently let slip. These appear in paragraphs 9 and 26. What is going on here—did she have enough time to edit her article?

### WRITING ASSIGNMENTS

1. Compare the views about language of Rosalie Maggio in "Bias-Free Language" and Kakutani in this article. What powers does each author believe language has? What power does language not have? Cite specific evidence from each author for your comparison.

2. Despite Kakutani's attack on Maggio's book, she agrees with at least some of Maggio's underlying assumptions—for example, about language and power, about the need to end prejudice, and other points. Identify and discuss at least three assumptions or values that both authors would agree on; then, discuss why they believe that different actions are appropriate.

3. Examine some samples of your own writing from earlier in the term or from previous terms. Where have you struggled with politically correct language use? Have you always been successful in using it? What substitutions or changes did you try that, on rereading, seem less than satisfactory?

---

# "Nigger": The Meaning of a Word
*Gloria Naylor*

Context can be everything when it comes to the meaning of a word, even a word recognized as an ugly epithet. As Gloria Naylor explains, when she was a little girl, the word *nigger* was spoken comfortably in front of her by relatives and family friends. She had heard it dozens of times, viewing it as a term of endearment. But she really did not "hear" the term until it was "spit out" of the mouth of a white boy in her third-grade class.

Gloria Naylor, a native of New York City, is an accomplished writer whose first novel, *The Women of Brewster Place* (1982), won an American Book Award. She is also the author of *Linden Hills* (1985), *Mama Day* (1988), and *Bailey's Cafe* (1992). Her most recent book is *1996* (2005). This essay first appeared in *The New York Times* in February 1986.

1 Language is the subject. It is the written form with which I've managed to keep the wolf away from the door and, in diaries, to keep my sanity. In spite of this, I consider the written word inferior to the spoken, and much of the frustration experienced by novelists is the awareness that whatever we manage to capture in even the most transcendent passages falls far short of the richness of life. Dialogue achieves its power in the dynamics of a fleeting moment of sight, sound, smell and touch.

2    I'm not going to enter the debate here about whether it is language that shapes reality or vice versa. That battle is doomed to be waged whenever we seek intermittent reprieve from the chicken and egg dispute. I will simply take the position that the spoken word, like the written word, amounts to a nonsensical arrangement of sounds or letters without a consensus that assigns "meaning." And building from the meanings of what we hear, we order reality. Words themselves are innocuous; it is the consensus that gives them true power.

3    I remember the first time I heard the word nigger. In my third-grade class, our math tests were being passed down the rows, and as I handed the papers to a little boy in back of me, I remarked that once again he had received a much lower mark than I did. He snatched his test from me and spit out that word. Had he called me a nymphomaniac or a necrophiliac, I couldn't have been more puzzled. I didn't know what a nigger was, but I knew that whatever it meant, it was something he shouldn't have called me. This was verified when I raised my hand, and in a loud voice repeated what he had said and watched the teacher scold him for using a "bad" word. I was later to go home and ask the inevitable question that every black parent must face—"Mommy, what does 'nigger' mean?"

4    And what exactly did it mean? Thinking back, I realize that this could not have been the first time the word was used in my presence. I was part of a large extended family that had migrated from the rural South after World War II and formed a close-knit network that gravitated around my maternal grandparents. Their ground-floor apartment in one of the buildings they owned in Harlem was a weekend mecca for my immediate family, along with countless aunts, uncles and cousins who brought along assorted friends. It was a bustling and open house with assorted neighbors and tenants popping in and out to exchange bits of gossip, pick up an old quarrel or referee the ongoing checkers game in which my grandmother cheated shamelessly. They were all there to let down their hair and put up their feet after a week of labor in the factories, laundries and shipyards of New York.

5    Amid the clamor, which could reach deafening proportions—two or three conversations going on simultaneously, punctuated by the sound of a baby's crying somewhere in the back rooms or out on the street—there was still a rigid set of rules about what was said and how. Older children were sent out of the living room when it was time to get into the juicy details about "you-know-who" up on the third floor who had gone and gotten herself "p-r-e-g-n-a-n-t!" But my parents, knowing that I could spell well beyond my years, always demanded that I follow the others out to play. Beyond sexual misconduct and death, everything else was considered harmless for our young ears. And so among the anecdotes of the triumphs and disappointments in the various workings of their lives, the word nigger was used in my presence, but it was set within contexts and inflections that caused it to register in my mind as something else.

6    In the singular, the word was always applied to a man who had distinguished himself in some situation that brought their approval for his strength, intelligence or drive:

7    "Did Johnny *really* do that?"

8    "I'm telling you, that nigger pulled in $6,000 of overtime last year. Said he got enough for a down payment on a house."

9   When used with a possessive adjective by a woman—"my nigger"—it became a term of endearment for husband or boyfriend. But it could be more than just a term applied to a man. In their mouths it became the pure essence of manhood—a disembodied force that channeled their past history of struggle and present survival against the odds into a victorious statement of being: "Yeah, that old foreman found out quick enough—you don't mess with a nigger."

10  In the plural, it became a description of some group within the community that have overstepped the bounds of decency as my family defined it: Parents who neglected their children, a drunken couple who fought in public, people who simply refused to look for work, those with excessively dirty mouths or unkempt households were all "trifling niggers." This particular circle could forgive hard times, unemployment, the occasional bout of depression—they had gone through all of that themselves—but the unforgivable sin was a lack of self-respect.

11  A woman could never be a "nigger" in the singular, with its connotation of confirming worth. The noun girl was its closest equivalent in that sense, but only when used in direct address and regardless of the gender doing the addressing. "Girl" was a token of respect for a woman. The one-syllable word was drawn out to sound like three in recognition of the extra ounce of wit, nerve or daring that the woman had shown in the situation under discussion.

12  "G-i-r-l, stop. You mean you said that to his face?"

13  But if the word was used in a third-person reference or shortened so that it almost snapped out of the mouth, it always involved some element of communal disapproval. And age became an important factor in these exchanges. It was only between individuals of the same generation, or from an older person to a younger (but never the other way around), that "girl" would be considered a compliment.

14  I don't agree with the argument that use of the word nigger at this social stratum of the black community was an internalization of racism. The dynamics were the exact opposite: the people in my grandmother's living room took a word that whites used to signify worthlessness or degradation and rendered it impotent. Gathering there together, they transformed "nigger" to signify the varied and complex human beings they knew themselves to be. If the word was to disappear totally from the mouths of even the most liberal of white society, no one in that room was naïve enough to believe it would disappear from white minds. Meeting the word head-on, they proved it had absolutely nothing to do with the way they were determined to live their lives.

15  So there must have been dozens of times that the word "nigger" was spoken in front of me before I reached the third grade. But I didn't "hear" it until it was said by a small pair of lips that had already learned it could be a way to humiliate me. That was the word I went home and asked my mother about. And since she knew that I had to grow up in America, she took me in her lap and explained.

## THINKING CRITICALLY

1. Does Naylor think that written or spoken words are more powerful? Why? What does she mean when she says that it is "consensus that gives [words] true power"?

2. What did Naylor do as a response to hearing the word *nigger*? In your judgment, were her actions appropriate and effective ways of handling the situation?

3. List four different meanings that Naylor says she has heard adults apply to the word *nigger*. How are these four meanings different from what she believed the boy in her class meant? Are all four meanings positive?

4. Why can a woman not be referred to as a *nigger*? What other term is used for a woman that achieves meaning similar to the term *nigger* for a man?

5. Naylor relates in some detail the circumstances surrounding the first time she heard the word *nigger*. Why does she paint such an elaborate picture? Why does she not simply list her age and the fact that she heard it used as an insult? What do you think prompted the boy to use this word?

6. Why does Naylor compare the word *nigger* specifically to *nymphomaniac* and *necrophiliac*? Why these words? How are they similar? How are they different? (Look them up in your dictionary if you are not sure what they mean.)

### WRITING ASSIGNMENTS

1. In paragraphs 4 and 5, Naylor provides a detailed discussion of her extended family: where they lived, how they were related, what kind of atmosphere these people created, what kinds of discussion children were permitted to eavesdrop on, and so on. How is this information related to the subject of Naylor's essay, the meaning of the word *nigger*? Can you think of any words or expressions that are used by your own circle—family, friends, and the like—that would be inappropriate for outsiders to use but acceptable by intimates? Explain.

2. Does Naylor approve of her family and friends' use of the word *nigger*? Why or why not? Does she approve of other people using the word? Why or why not?

# | CENSORSHIP AND FREE SPEECH

# The Betrayal of Liberty on America's Campuses
*Alan Charles Kors*

In the following essay, Alan Charles Kors argues that instituting sanctions on speech is a direct violation of students' right to free expression. Exactly where should the line be drawn as to what constitutes hate speech? The ambiguity of many university codes, says Kors, leads to sanctioning students for ridiculous and outrageous reasons. When students must consider every word they say, and even how they say it, they are prevented from engaging in honest intellectual inquiry, debate, and dialogue.

Alan Charles Kors is a professor of history at the University of Pennsylvania. He is the co-author with Harvey Silverglate of *The Shadow University: The Betrayal of Liberty on America's Campuses* (1998). Together with Silverglate, he founded the Foundation for Individual Rights in Education (FIRE), a nonprofit organization that addresses individual liberty and rights issues on campuses.

In 2005, President George W. Bush awarded Kors the National Humanities Medal for his "scholarship, devotion to the Humanities, and . . . defense of academic freedom." In 2006, he was the T. B. Davie Memorial Lecturer on academic freedom at the University of Cape Town, South Africa. The following essay was a feature of the Bradley Lecture Series of the American Enterprise Institute for Public Policy Research in October 1998.

1   Those things that threaten free and open debate and those things that threaten academic freedom are the direct enemy of liberty. Such threats exist most dangerously at universities not in curriculum and scholarship, but in the new university *in loco parentis* (the university standing in the place of parents), where our nation's colleges and universities, across the board, are teaching contempt for liberty and its components: freedom of expression and inquiry; individual rights and responsibilities over group rights and entitlements; equal justice under law; and the rights of private conscience. *That* assault upon liberty is occurring not in the sunlight of open decisions and advertised agendas, but in the shadows of an unaccountable middle-administration that has been given coercive authority over the lives, speech, consciences, and voluntary individuation and association of students.

2   Almost all colleges and universities, for example, have "harassment" policies that prohibit selective "verbal behavior" or "verbal conduct," but almost none has the honesty to call these "speech codes." These policies, adopted from employment law and catastrophic for universities, are applied to faculty and students, the latter not even being employees of a university, but, in fact, its clients. The core of these codes is the prohibition of the creation of "a hostile or offensive environment," with the remarkable variations and embellishments that follow from Hobbes's observation that to the learned it is given to be learnedly foolish. Within very recent times, Bowdoin College chose to outlaw jokes and ways of telling stories "experienced by others as harassing." Brown University banned verbal behavior that produced "feelings of impotence . . . anger . . . or disenfranchisement . . . [whether] intentional or unintentional." Colby prohibited speech that caused loss of "self-esteem." The University of Connecticut prohibited "inconsiderate jokes," "stereotyping," and even "inappropriately directed laughter." Indeed, a student at Sarah Lawrence College recently was convicted of laughing at something that someone else said, and was ordered as a condition of remaining in the college, for his laughter, to read a book entitled *Homophobia on Campus*, see a movie about "homophobia," and write a paper about "homophobia." Rutgers University included within the forbidden any "heinous act" of harassment, "communication" that is "in any manner likely to cause annoyance or alarm," which causes *me* a great deal of annoyance *and* alarm. The University of Maryland–College Park outlaws not only "idle chatter of a sexual nature" and "comments or questions about the sensuality of a person," but pointedly explains that these verbal behaviors "do not necessarily have to be specifically directed at an individual to constitute sexual harassment." Expression goes well beyond the verbal, however, because the University of Maryland also prohibits "gestures . . . that are expressive of an idea, opinion, or emotion," including "sexual looks such as leering and ogling with suggestive overtones; licking lips or teeth; holding or eating food provocatively."

3    At Carnegie Mellon University, a student called his female opponent in an election for the Graduate Student Organization a "megalomaniac." He was charged with sexual harassment. The Dean of Students explained the deeper meaning of calling a woman a megalomaniac, citing a vast body of what he termed feminist "victim theory" on the plaintiff's behalf, and the associate provost submitted a brief that stated, "I have no doubt that this has created a hostile environment which impacts Lara's productivity as a student leader and as a graduate student."

4    Many universities, such as Berkeley itself, no less, adopted speech codes that outlawed "fighting words." That term is taken from the U.S. Supreme Court decision of the 1940s, *Chaplinsky v. New Hampshire* (a decision surely mooted by later Supreme Court decisions), in which, leftists take note, the unprotected fighting word was, of all things, "fascist." Many universities also leave the determination of whether something was a fighting word or created a hostile environment to the plaintiff. Thus, the University of Puget Sound states that harassment "depends on the point of view of the person to whom the conduct is unwelcome." The City University of New York warns that "sexual harassment is not defined by intentions, but by its impact on the subject." "No one," Bowdoin College warns, "is entitled to engage in behavior that is experienced by others as harassing." At the University of Connecticut, criticizing someone's limits of tolerance toward the speech of others is itself harassment: its code bans "attributing objections to any of the above [instances of harassment] to 'hypersensitivity' of the targeted individual or group."

5    West Virginia University prohibited, among many other things, "insults, humor, jokes, and anecdotes that belittle or demean an individual's or a group's sexuality or sex," and, try this one on for vagueness, "inappropriate displays of sexually suggestive objects or pictures which may include but are not limited to posters, pin-ups, and calendars." If applied equally, of course, such a policy would leave no sex or race safe in its conversations or humor, let alone in its artistic taste, but such policies never are applied equally. Thus, students at West Virginia received the official policies of the "Executive Officer for Social Justice," who stated the institutional orthodoxy about "homophobia" and "sexism." The Officer of Social Justice warned that "feelings" about gays and lesbians could not become "attitudes": "Regardless of how a person feels about others, negative actions or attitudes based on misconceptions and/or ignorance constitute prejudice, which contradicts everything for which an institution of higher learning stands." Among those prejudices it listed "heterosexism . . . the assumption that everyone is heterosexual, or, if they aren't, they should be." This, of course, outlawed specific religious inner convictions about sexuality. Because everyone had the right to be free from "harassment," the policy specified "behaviors to avoid." These prohibitions affected speech and voluntary associations based upon beliefs. Thus, "DO NOT [in capital letters] tolerate 'jokes' which are potentially injurious to gays, lesbians and bisexuals. . . . DO NOT determine whether you will interact with someone by virtue of his or her sexual orientation." The policy also commanded specific prescriptions: "value alternate lifestyles . . . challenge homophobic remarks . . . [and] use language that is not gender specific. . . . Instead of referring to anyone's romantic partner as 'girlfriend' or 'boyfriend,' use positive generic terms such as a 'friend,' 'lover,' or 'partner.' Speak of your own romantic partner similarly." The "homophobia" policy

ended with the warning that "harassment" or "discrimination" based on sexual preference was subject to penalties that ranged "from reprimand . . . to expulsion and termination, and including public service and educational remediation." "Educational remediation," note well, is an academic euphemism for thought reform. Made aware of what their own university was doing, a coalition of faculty members threatened to expose West Virginia University for its obvious violations of the state and federal constitutions, and to sue the administration if need be. As I talk, the University has removed the offending codes from its freshmen orientation packages and from its website. We shall see if it has removed them from its operational policies.

6    When federal courts struck down two codes restricting "verbal behavior" at public universities and colleges, namely, at the University of Michigan and the University of Wisconsin, other public colleges and universities—even in those jurisdictions where codes had been declared unconstitutional—did not seek to abolish their policies. Thus, Central Michigan University, after the University of Michigan code had been struck down, maintained a policy whose prohibitions included "any intentional, unintentional, physical, verbal, or nonverbal behavior that subjects an individual to an intimidating, hostile or offensive educational . . . environment by demeaning or slurring individuals through . . . written literature because of their racial or ethnic affiliation or using symbols, epitaphs [sic, we hope] or slogans that infer [sic] negative connotations about an individual's racial or ethnic affiliation."

7    In 1993, this policy was challenged, successfully, in Federal District Court. The Court noted that the code applied to "all possible human conduct," and, citing internal University documents, ruled that Central Michigan intended to apply it to speech "which a person 'feels' has affronted him or some group, predicated on race or ethnicity." The Court ruled that if the policy's words had meaning, it banned, precisely, protected speech. If someone's "treatise, term paper or even . . . cafeteria bull session" about the Middle East, the Court observed, blamed one group more than another on the basis of "some ancient ethnic traditions which give rise to barbarian combativeness or . . . inability to compromise," such speech, the Court found, "would seem to be a good fit with the policy language." In fact, the Court ruled, "Any behavior, even unintentional, that offends any individual is to be prohibited under the policy. . . . If the speech gives offense it is prohibited." When the President of Central Michigan University offered assurances that the policy was not intended to be enforced in such a way as to "interfere impermissibly with individuals' rights to free speech," the Court declared itself "emphatically unimpressed" by such a savings clause, and it observed: "The university . . . says in essence, 'trust us; we may interfere, but not impermissibly.' The Court is not willing to entrust . . . the First Amendment to the tender mercies of this institution's discriminatory harassment/affirmative action enforcer."

8    Many in the academy insist that the entire phenomenon labeled "political correctness" is the mythical fabrication of opponents of "progressive" change. The authors of an American Association of University Professors' special committee report, the "Statement on the 'Political Correctness' Controversy" (1991), insisted, without irony, that claims of "political correctness" were merely smokescreens to

hide the true agenda of such critics—a racist and sexist desire to thwart the aspirations of minorities and women in the academic enterprise.

9    It is, in fact, almost inconceivable that anyone of good faith could live on a college campus unaware of the repression, legal inequality, intrusions into private conscience, and malignant double standards that hold sway there. In the Left's history of McCarthyism, the firing or dismissal of one professor or student, the inquisition into the private beliefs of one individual, let alone the demands for a demonstration of fealty to community standards stand out as intolerable oppressions that coerced people into silence, hypocrisy, betrayal, and tyranny.

10    In fact, in today's assault on liberty on college campuses, there is not a small number of cases, speech codes, nor apparatuses of repression and thought reform. Number aside, however, a climate of repression succeeds not by statistical frequency, but by sapping the courage, autonomy, and conscience of individuals who otherwise might remember or revive what liberty could be.

11    Most students respect disagreement and difference, and they do not bring charges of harassment against those whose opinions or expressions "offend" them. The universities themselves, however, encourage such charges to be brought. At almost every college and university, students deemed members of "historically oppressed groups"—above all, women, blacks, gays, and Hispanics—are informed during orientations that their campuses are teeming with illegal or intolerable violations of their "right" not to be offended. To believe many new-student orientations would be to believe that there was a racial or sexual bigot, to borrow the mocking phrase of McCarthy's critics, "under every bed." At almost every college and university, students are presented with lists of a vast array of places to which they should submit charges of such verbal "harassment," and they are promised "victim support," "confidentiality," and sympathetic understanding when they file such complaints.

12    What an astonishing expectation to give to students: the belief that, if they belong to a protected category and have the correct beliefs, they have a right to four years of never being offended. What an extraordinary power to give to administrative tribunals: the prerogative to punish the free speech and expression of people to whom they assign the stains of historical oppression, while being free, themselves, to use whatever rhetoric they wish against the bearers of such stains. While the world looks at issues of curriculum and scholarship, above all, to analyze and evaluate American colleges and universities, it is, in fact, the silencing and punishment of belief, expression, and individuality that ought to concern yet more deeply those who care about what universities are and could be. Most cases never reach the public, because most individuals accused of "verbal" harassment sadly (but understandably) accept plea-bargains that diminish their freedom but spare them Draconian penalties, including expulsion. Those settlements almost invariably involve "sensitivity training," an appalling term, "training," to hear in matters of the human mind and spirit. Even so, the files on prosecutions under speech codes are, alas, overflowing.

13    "Settlements," by the way, are one of the best-kept and most frightening secrets of American academic life, almost always assigned with an insistence upon confidentiality. They are nothing less than an American version of thought reform from

benighted offender into a politically correct bearer, in fact or in appearance, of an ideology that is the regnant orthodoxy of our universities *in loco parentis.*

14    From this perspective, American history is a tale of the oppression of all "others" by white, heterosexual, Eurocentric males, punctuated by the struggles of the oppressed. "Beneficiaries" see their lives as good and as natural, and falsely view America as a boon to humankind. Worse, most "victims" of "oppression" accept the values of their oppressors. A central task of education, then, is to "demystify" such arbitrary power. Whites, males, and heterosexuals must recognize and renounce the injustice of their "privilege." Nonwhites, women, gays, and lesbians must recognize and struggle against their victimization, both in their beliefs and in their behaviors.

15    Such "demystification" has found a welcome home in a large number of courses in the humanities and social sciences, but for the true believers, this is insufficient, because most courses remain optional, many professors resist the temptation to proselytize, and students, for the most part, choose majors that take them far from oppression studies.

16    Indeed, students forever disappoint the ideologues. Men and women generally see themselves neither as oppressor nor oppressed, and, far from engaging in class warfare, often quite love each other. Most women refuse to identify themselves as "feminists." Group-identity centers—although they can rally support at moments of crisis—attract few students overall, because invitees busily go about the business of learning, making friends, pursuing interests, and seeking love—all the things that 18- to 22-year-olds have done from time immemorial. Attendance at group-identity organizations is often miniscule as a percentage of the intended population, and militant leaders complain endlessly about "apathy." Whites don't feel particularly guilty about being white, and almost no designated "victims" adopt truly radical politics. Most undergraduates unabashedly seek their portion of American freedom, legal equality, and bounty. What to do with such benighted students? Increasingly, the answer to that question is to use the *in loco parentis* apparatus of the university to reform their private consciences and minds. For the generation that once said, "Don't trust anyone *over* 30," the motto now is "Don't trust anyone *under* 30." Increasingly, Offices of Student Life, Residence Offices, and residence advisors have become agencies of progressive social engineering whose mission is to bring students to mandatory political enlightenment.

17    Such practices violate more than honest education. Recognition of the sanctity of conscience is the single most essential respect given to individual autonomy. There are purely practical arguments for the right to avoid self-incrimination or to choose religious (or other) creeds, but there is none deeper than restraining power from intruding upon the privacy of the self. Universities and colleges that commit the scandal of sentencing students (and faculty) to "sensitivity therapy" do not even permit individuals to choose their therapists. The Christian may not consult his or her chosen counselor, but must follow the regime of the social worker selected by the Women's Center or by the Office of Student Life. . . .

18    Imagine a campus on which being denounced for "irreligious bigotry" or "un-Americanism" carried the same stigma that being denounced for "racism," "sexism," and "homophobia" now carries in the academic world, so that in such

hearings or trials, the burden of proof invariably fell upon the "offender." The common sign at pro-choice rallies, "Keep your rosaries off our ovaries," would be prima facie evidence of language used as a weapon to degrade and marginalize, and the common term of abuse, "born-again bigot," would be compelling evidence of the choice to create a hostile environment for evangelicals. What panegyrics to liberty and free expression we would hear in opposition to any proposed code to protect the "religious" or the "patriotic" from "offense" and "incivility." Yet what deafening silence we have heard, in these times, in the campus acceptance of the speech provisions of so-called harassment codes.

19    The goal of a speech code, then, is to suppress speech one doesn't like. The goal of liberty and equal justice is to permit us to live in a complex but peaceful world of difference, disagreement, debate, moral witness, and efforts of persuasion—without coercion and violence. Liberty and legal equality are hard-won, precious, and, indeed—because the social world is often discomforting—profoundly complex and troublesome ways of being human. They require, for their sustenance, men and women who would abhor their own power of censorship and their own special legal privileges as much as they abhor those of others. In enacting and enforcing speech codes, universities, for their own partisan reasons, have chosen to betray the human vision of freedom and legal equality. It was malignant to impose or permit such speech codes; to deny their oppressive effects while living in the midst of those effects is beyond the moral pale.

20    On virtually any college campus, for all of its rules of "civility" and all of its prohibitions of "hostile environment," assimilationist black men and women live daily with the terms "Uncle Tom" and "Oreo" said with impunity, while their tormenters live with special protections from offense. White students daily hear themselves, their friends, and their parents denounced as "racists" and "oppressors," while their tormenters live with special protections from offense. Believing Christians hear their beliefs ridiculed and see their sacred symbols traduced—virtually nothing, in the name of freedom, may not be said against them in the classroom, at rallies, and in personal encounters—while their tormenters live with special protection from offense. Men hear their sex abused, find themselves blamed for all the evils of the world, and enter classrooms whose very goal is to make them feel discomfort, while their tormenters live with special protections from "a hostile environment."

21    It is our liberty, above all else, that defines us as human beings, capable of ethics and responsibility. The struggle for liberty on American campuses is one of the defining struggles of the age in which we find ourselves. A nation that does not educate in freedom will not survive in freedom, and will not even know when it has lost it. Individuals too often convince themselves that they are caught up in moments of history that they cannot affect. That history, however, is made by their will and moral choices. There is a moral crisis in higher education. It will not be resolved unless we choose and act to resolve it.

22    It is easy, however, to identify the vulnerabilities of the bearers of this worst and, at the time, most marginal legacy of the '60s: they loathe the society that they believe should support them generously in their authority over its offspring; they are detached from the values of individual liberty, legal equality, privacy, and the

sanctity of conscience toward which Americans essentially are drawn; and, for both those reasons, they cannot bear the light of public scrutiny. Let the sunlight in.

## THINKING CRITICALLY

1. Why does Kors believe racist and inflammatory speech should be protected by the First Amendment? What examples does he use to prove his point? Do you agree? Can you think of circumstances in which racist speech should not be protected? Explain.

2. How has this article affected your thinking on the subject of free speech and censorship? Has it changed your mind about the use of racially or sexually abusive language? Explain your perspective.

3. How are colleges and university administrators dealing with incidents of verbal abuse on American campuses? What is Kors's reaction to their handling of such problems? According to Kors, how are students being manipulated by university censorship rules?

4. Explain what Kors means when he says, "Many in the academy insist that the entire phenomenon labeled 'political correctness' is the mythical fabrication of opponents of 'progressive' change" (paragraph 8). Do you agree with this view?

5. Consider the author's voice in this essay. What sense do you get of Kors as an individual? Write a paragraph characterizing the author. Take into consideration his stand in the essay, his style and tone of writing, and the examples he uses to support his view and how he presents them.

## WRITING ASSIGNMENTS

1. Summarize Kors's argument in one paragraph. Include the key points of his discussion and his concluding observations. Then, explain why you agree or disagree, in whole or in part, with his argument and conclusions.

2. Research the First Amendment and Americans' right to free speech. After reviewing it carefully, write an essay explaining why you believe First Amendment rights extend to college campuses. Conversely, you may explain why you think they do not.

---

# Regulating Racist Speech on Campus
*Charles R. Lawrence III*

Recent years have witnessed a disturbing rise in racist and sexist language on college campuses. Some administrations have dealt with the problem by banning outright offensive language on the grounds that racial slurs are violent verbal assaults that interfere with students' rights to an education. Others fear that placing sanctions on racist speech violates the First Amendment guarantee of free expression. In the following essay, law professor Charles R. Lawrence III argues for the restriction of free speech by citing the U.S. Supreme Court's landmark decision in the case of *Brown v. Board of Education.*

Charles R. Lawrence teaches law at Georgetown University. He is the co-author of *We Won't Go Back: Making the Case for Affirmative Action*

(1997), written with his wife and fellow Georgetown professor Mari J. Matsuda. Lawrence is best known for his work in antidiscrimination law, equal protection, and critical race theory. He is also a former president of the Society of American Law Teachers.

1  I have spent the better part of my life as a dissenter. As a high-school student, I was threatened with suspension for my refusal to participate in a civil-defense drill, and I have been a conspicuous consumer of my First Amendment liberties ever since. There are very strong reasons for protecting even racist speech. Perhaps the most important of these is that such protection reinforces our society's commitment to tolerance as a value, and that by protecting bad speech from government regulation, we will be forced to combat it as a community.

2  But I also have a deeply felt apprehension about the resurgence of racial violence and the corresponding rise in the incidence of verbal and symbolic assault and harassment to which blacks and other traditionally subjugated and excluded groups are subjected. I am troubled by the way the debate has been framed in response to the recent surge of racist incidents on college and university campuses and in response to some universities' attempts to regulate harassing speech. The problem has been framed as one in which the liberty of free speech is in conflict with the elimination of racism. I believe this has placed the bigot on the moral high ground and fanned the rising flames of racism.

3  Above all, I am troubled that we have not listened to the real victims, that we have shown so little understanding of their injury, and that we have abandoned those whose race, gender, or sexual preference continues to make them second-class citizens. It seems to me a very sad irony that the first instinct of civil libertarians has been to challenge even the smallest, most narrowly framed efforts by universities to provide black and other minority students with the protection the Constitution guarantees them.

4  The landmark case of *Brown v. Board of Education* is not a case that we normally think of as a case about speech. But *Brown* can be broadly read as articulating the principle of equal citizenship. *Brown* held that segregated schools were inherently unequal because of the *message* that segregation conveyed—that black children were an untouchable caste, unfit to go to school with white children. If we understand the necessity of eliminating the system of signs and symbols that signal the inferiority of blacks, then we should hesitate before proclaiming that all racist speech that stops short of physical violence must be defended.

5  University officials who have formulated policies to respond to incidents of racial harassment have been characterized in the press as "thought police," but such policies generally do nothing more than impose sanctions against intentional face-to-face insults. When racist speech takes the form of face-to-face insults, catcalls, or other assaultive speech aimed at an individual or small group of persons, it falls directly within the "fighting words" exception to First Amendment protection. The Supreme Court has held that words which "by their very utterance inflict injury or tend to incite an immediate breach of the peace" are not protected by the First Amendment.

6  If the purpose of the First Amendment is to foster the greatest amount of speech, racial insults disserve that purpose. Assaultive racist speech functions as a

preemptive strike. The invective is experienced as a blow, not as a proffered idea, and once the blow is struck, it is unlikely that a dialogue will follow. Racial insults are particularly undeserving of First Amendment protection because the perpetrator's intention is not to discover truth or initiate dialogue but to injure the victim. In most situations, members of minority groups realize that they are likely to lose if they respond to epithets by fighting and are forced to remain silent and submissive.

7    Courts have held that offensive speech may not be regulated in public forums such as streets where the listener may avoid the speech by moving on, but the regulation of otherwise protected speech has been permitted when the speech invades the privacy of the unwilling listener's home or when the unwilling listener cannot avoid the speech. Racist posters, fliers, and graffiti in dormitories, bathrooms, and other common living spaces would seem to clearly fall within the reasoning of these cases. Minority students should not be required to remain in their rooms in order to avoid racial assault. Minimally, they should find a safe haven in their dorms and in all other common rooms that are a part of their daily routine.

8    I would also argue that the university's responsibility for insuring that these students receive an equal educational opportunity provides a compelling justification for regulations that insure them safe passage in all common areas. A minority student should not have to risk becoming the target of racially assaulting speech every time he or she chooses to walk across campus. Regulating vilifying speech that cannot be anticipated or avoided would not preclude announced speeches and rallies—situations that would give minority-group members and their allies the chance to organize counter-demonstrations or avoid the speech altogether.

9    The most commonly advanced argument against the regulation of racist speech proceeds something like this: we recognize that minority groups suffer pain and injury as the result of racist speech, but we must allow this hate mongering for the benefit of society as a whole. Freedom of speech is the lifeblood of our democratic system. It is especially important for minorities because often it is their only vehicle for rallying support for the redress of their grievances. It will be impossible to formulate a prohibition so precise that it will prevent the racist speech you want to suppress without catching in the same net all kinds of speech that it would be unconscionable for a democratic society to suppress.

10    Whenever we make such arguments, we are striking a balance on the one hand between our concern for the continued free flow of ideas and the democratic process dependent on that flow, and, on the other, our desire to further the cause of equality. There can be no meaningful discussion of how we should reconcile our commitment to equality and our commitment to free speech until it is acknowledged that there is real harm inflicted by racist speech and that this harm is far from trivial.

11    To engage in a debate about the First Amendment and racist speech without a full understanding of the nature and extent of that harm is to risk making the First Amendment an instrument of domination rather than a vehicle of liberation. We have not known the experience of victimization by racist, misogynist, and homophobic speech, nor do we equally share the burden of the societal harm it inflicts. We are often quick to say that we have heard the cry of the victims when we have not.

12    The *Brown* case is again instructive because it speaks directly to the psychic injury inflicted by racist speech by noting that the symbolic message of segregation affected "the hearts and minds" of Negro children "in a way unlikely ever to be undone." Racial epithets and harassment often cause deep emotional scarring and feelings of anxiety and fear that pervade every aspect of a victim's life.

13    *Brown* also recognized that black children did not have an equal opportunity to learn and participate in the school community if they bore the additional burden of being subjected to the humiliation and psychic assault contained in the message of segregation. University students bear an analogous burden when they are forced to live and work in an environment where at any moment they may be subjected to denigrating verbal harassment and assault. The same injury was addressed by the Supreme Court when it held that sexual harassment that creates a hostile or abusive work environment violates the ban on sex discrimination in employment of Title VII of the Civil Rights Act of 1964.

14    Carefully drafted university regulations would bar the use of words as assault weapons and leave unregulated even the most heinous of ideas when those ideas are presented at times and places and in manners that provide an opportunity for reasoned rebuttal or escape from immediate injury. The history of the development of the right to free speech has been one of carefully evaluating the importance of free expression and its effects on other important societal interests. We have drawn the line between protected and unprotected speech before without dire results. (Courts have, for example, exempted from the protection of the First Amendment obscene speech and speech that disseminates official secrets, that defames or libels another person, or that is used to form a conspiracy or monopoly.)

15    Blacks and other people of color are skeptical about the argument that even the most injurious speech must remain unregulated because, in an unregulated marketplace of ideas, the best ones will rise to the top and gain acceptance. Our experience tells us quite the opposite. We have seen too many good liberal politicians shy away from the issues that might brand them as being too closely allied with us.

16    Whenever we decide that racist speech must be tolerated because of the importance of maintaining societal tolerance for all unpopular speech, we are asking blacks and other subordinated groups to bear the burden for the good of all. We must be careful that the ease with which we strike the balance against the regulation of racist speech is in no way influenced by the fact that the cost will be borne by others. We must be certain that those who will pay that price are fairly represented in our deliberations and that they are heard.

17    At the core of the argument that we should resist all government regulation of speech is the ideal that the best cure for bad speech is good, that ideas that affirm equality and the worth of all individuals will ultimately prevail. This is an empty ideal unless those of us who would fight racism are vigilant and unequivocal in that fight. We must look for ways to offer assistance and support to students whose speech and political participation are chilled in a climate of racial harassment.

18    Civil rights lawyers might consider suing on behalf of blacks whose right to an equal education is denied by a university's failure to insure a nondiscriminatory

educational climate or conditions of employment. We must embark upon the development of a First Amendment jurisprudence grounded in the reality of our history and our contemporary experience. We must think hard about how best to launch legal attacks against the most indefensible forms of hate speech. Good lawyers can create exceptions and narrow interpretations that limit the harm of hate speech without opening the floodgates of censorship.

19    Everyone concerned with these issues must find ways to engage actively in actions that resist and counter the racist ideas that we would have the First Amendment protect. If we fail in this, the victims of hate speech must rightly assume that we are on the oppressors' side.

### THINKING CRITICALLY

1. What reasons does Lawrence offer for protecting racist speech from governmental restrictions? Do you agree? How are university restrictions different from those imposed by the government?

2. According to the author, how in the debate over racist language does the fight against racism conflict with the fight for free speech? What fundamental problem does Lawrence have with this conflict? Are his reasons convincing?

3. Why, according to Lawrence, is racist speech "undeserving of First Amendment protection" (paragraph 6)? Do you agree? If not, why not? If so, can you think of any circumstances when racist speech should be protected?

4. Have you ever been the victim of abusive speech—speech that victimized you because of your race, gender, religion, ethnicity, or sexual preference? Do you agree with Lawrence's argument regarding "psychic injury" (paragraph 12)? Explain.

5. How convincingly does Lawrence argue that racist speech should not be protected by the First Amendment? What is the logic of his argument? What evidence does he offer as support?

6. Select one of Lawrence's arguments that you think is especially strong or especially weak, and explain why you think so.

7. Lawrence opens his essay saying that he has a long history as a "dissenter." What is his strategy? What assumptions does he make about his audience? What does his refusal to participate in a civil-defense drill have to do with the essay's central issues?

### WRITING ASSIGNMENTS

1. Imagine that you have been chosen to lead a student committee that must draft a speech code for your university or college. After discussing the issue with some of your students and a few members of the faculty, draft the code. Consider both students' rights to free speech and faculty's right to expression. Include what constitutes hate speech and what limits can be placed on it, if any.

2. Research arguments for and against campus speech codes as expressed in online university publications for at least four colleges and universities. How are the codes similar and how are they different? Are they open for interpretation? In your opinion, do any seem fairer than others? Less fair? If your own campus has a speech code, include it in your discussion.

# Freedom of Deplorable Speech

*Tina Dupuy*

The actions of the Westboro Baptist Church—a small group led by Pastor Fred Phelps and known for its picketing at the funerals of fallen soldiers—faced legal scrutiny at the end of 2010. The fanatic fringe group pickets funerals with signs reading "Thank God for Dead Soldiers" and "God Hates the USA" and claims that fatalities in Iraq and Afghanistan are God's punishment for our failure to prosecute homosexuality. At issue is the right of the group to picket. On the one hand, what they do is hurtful and cruel, but on the other hand, their actions are protected by the First Amendment. Legal scholars are quick to point out that the First Amendment would be worthless if it only protected the expression of reasonable opinions and likeable ideas. In this next essay, Tina Dupuy explains why the First Amendment needs to protect everyone.

Tina Dupuy is an award-winning writer, nationally syndicated op-ed columnist, investigative journalist, on-air commentator, and fill-in host at *The Young Turks*. Her work has appeared in such publications as *The Los Angeles Times, Fast Company, LA Weekly, Newsday, Orange County Register, The Beast,* and the *LA Daily News* among others. This opinion editorial appeared December 19, 2010, through GateHouse News Service.

1 Pastor Fred Phelps and his Westboro Baptist Church congregation—also known as the "God Hates Fags" picketers—have no place in a polite society. But we don't live in a polite society. We live in this one. And in this one we are guaranteed the freedom of speech.

2 If you're for free speech, which I am, you're proclaiming you can be offended and be reasonably okay with it. Freedom of speech isn't just saying what you want to say, it's also letting other people say heinous and indefensible things and accepting the government's inaction on the issue.

3 The Bill of Rights deals with the relationship you have between you and your government. It doesn't mean that I can't tell you to shut up. It also doesn't mean that people like "n-word" aficionado Dr. Laura Schlessinger is "losing her First Amendment rights" by being boycotted. It means she is so distasteful that corporations don't want to endorse her speech by giving her advertising money. She still has the right to say it—it's the wide broadcast and corporate sponsorship she mistakenly thinks is her constitutional right. It's the reason she quit her job as a syndicated radio host to go to Sirius XM . . . to be a satellite radio host. Makes sense.

4 The Westboro Baptist Church came on the national scene by picketing Matthew Shepard's funeral. Shepard was a 21-year-old student in Wyoming, who in 1998 was tortured and beaten to death because he was gay. The church showed up to point out the victim was a "sinner." At the time it reminded me of the bloodthirsty demonstrators outside prisons during an execution, but this wasn't a convict—Shepard's only "crime" was being a gay kid in a small town.

5 After that, capitalizing on a tragedy to make a religious point became a theme for Pastor Phelps and his small church.

6 Soon they started picketing soldiers' funerals, claiming our men and women in uniform die because our country tolerates homosexuality. The church sees this as

their mission: tell us we're going to hell. And to thwart any labeling by the media—the description they provide their website reads, "Site of anti-homosexual propagandist Fred Phelps of Topeka, Kansas."

7    What they do is hideous. But lots of hideous things are done in the name of religion: sheltering child rapists; advocating violence against women; not helping the poor. And becoming wealthy by preaching the gospel of an insolvent prophet is . . . well, not exactly practicing what He preached.

8    Every time I hear blowhards claim this is a Christian nation—I just point out the poverty rate is 14.3%. *Christian* nation? No, we're not.

9    Anyway, in 2007 Louis Theroux of the BBC made the documentary, "The Most Hated Family in America." He followed the Phelps congregation, which is mostly his own large family. It's a fascinating look inside this icon of intolerance, daughter Shirley Phelps-Roper explained that what they scream on the street corner is done out of love. Informing people they're going to hell for their sins and for tolerating others' sins is . . . *loving*. That's how they see what they do. They think they're spreading the word and all of us are over-sensitive and in denial about our impending perpetuity in hell.

10   It's almost street theatre the way our sacred cows are made into creamed chipped beef casserole right in front of us. Anything we as a country deem sacrosanct and beyond controversy—there's Westboro Baptist protest signs reading "Thank God for AIDS."

11   Which is why last week the group showed up at Elizabeth Edwards' funeral. Why? I'll paraphrase: It was because she didn't repent enough.

12   There are plenty who *think* they are against political correctness until faced with a Fred Phelps God Hates Parade at the gravesite of a marine who died from an IED. Then there's a PC pause.

13   Yes, it angers us. What they do is disgusting. Which is why the Supreme Court is going to decide a case brought against the church by a family of a soldier who died in combat.

14   But popular speech doesn't need protection. Nor does popular religious belief. Seeing the Westboro Baptist Church protesting is (at the very, very least) a sign of *our* freedom.


### THINKING CRITICALLY

1. Dupuy observes that when you support free speech, you acknowledge that this includes speech that you might not agree with or that offends you. Do you agree with this assessment? Explain.

2. In what ways does Dupuy engage her audience? Identify areas of her editorial in which she particularly seeks to connect with her readers and whether her technique is effective.

3. Dupuy states in her conclusion, "popular speech doesn't need protection. Nor does popular religious belief. Seeing the Westboro Baptist Church protesting is (at the very, very least) a sign of *our* freedom." Explain what she means in this final statement of her editorial.

4. What does Dupuy say about Christianity? Why does she highlight this religious group in her editorial?

## WRITING ASSIGNMENTS

1. Dupuy points out that free speech permits us to speak, but does not protect us from the fallout when we express an unpopular point of view. She notes that talk show host Dr. Laura Schlessinger was free to say her unpopular comments on the air, but the result of this was that companies decided not to underwrite her anymore. Write an essay in which you explore this dichotomy. Research the issue of Dr. Schlessinger's on-air comments. See http://mediamatters.org/blog/201008120045 for an audio recording and transcript of the controversial conversation.

2. When did you first become aware of a powerfully charged racist or hateful word used to demean or diminish a person or a group of people? Were your recognitions gradual or can you trace your recognition to a specific time and place? What did you do to try to understand the word or the problem? Write a personal narrative describing your memory of how racist language or hate speech could be used to hurt.

# Exploring the Language of **VISUALS**

## First Amendment
*Robert Mankoff*

*"The way I see it, the Constitution cuts both ways. The First Amendment gives you the right to say what you want, but the Second Amendment gives me the right to shoot you for it."*

### THINKING CRITICALLY

1. What is the artist trying to say in this cartoon? Based on the cartoon, what is his position on the issue of the First Amendment? Explain.

2. Who are the characters in the cartoon, and who or what do they represent? How does the cartoonist convey his feelings about the issue through these caricatures?

3. What must you know first before you are able to understand this cartoon? Explain.

# Hate Cannot Be Tolerated
*Richard Delgado*

Speech codes and harassment polices have been adopted by many U.S. universities and businesses in an effort to stop racist and sexist language that can offend and contribute to a stressful environment. The rationale is that offensive slurs are violent verbal assaults that interfere with personal rights. Many civil liberties activists, students, college faculty, and citizens fear that such codes limit free speech. Who decides what is offensive language? Is hate speech indeed an assault? And do speech codes promote greater good and safety, even if they do curtail personal expression?

Richard Delgado is a law professor at the University of Pittsburgh. He is widely published and often appears on television programs including *Good Morning America, NPR,* and the *MacNeil-Lehrer Report.* He has authored 15 books and has published in *The Nation, The New Republic, The New York Times, The Washington Post,* and *The Wall Street Journal.* He is the author of many scholarly books, including *Race and Races: Cases and Resources for a Diverse America* (2007) and *The Law Unbound!* (2008). This article appeared in *Insight on the News,* a national biweekly newsmagazine published as the sister publication of *The Washington Times.*

1 Anonymous vandals scrawl hate-filled graffiti outside a Jewish student center. Black students at a law school find unsigned fliers stuffed inside their lockers screaming that they do not belong there. At a third campus, a group of toughs hurls epithets at a young Latino student walking home late at night.

2 In response to a rising tide of such incidents, some colleges have enacted hate-speech codes or applied existing rules against individuals whose conduct interferes with the educational opportunities of others. Federal courts have extended "hostile environment" case law to schools that tolerate a climate of hate for women and students of color.

3 Despite the alarm these measures sometimes elicit, nothing is wrong with them. In each case, the usual and preferred response—"more speech"—is unavailable to the victim. With anonymous hate speech such as the flier or graffiti, the victim cannot talk back, for the hate speaker delivers his message in a cowardly fashion. And talking back to aggressors is rarely an option. Indeed, many hate crimes began just this way: The victim talked back—and paid with his life.

4 Hate speech is rarely an invitation to a conversation. More like a slap in the face, it reviles and silences. College counselors report that campuses where highly publicized incidents of hate speech have taken place show a decline in minority enrollment as students of color instead choose to attend schools where the environment is healthier.

5 A few federal courts have declared overly broad hate-speech codes unconstitutional, as well they should. Nothing is gained by a rule so broad it could be construed as forbidding the discussion of controversial subjects such as evolution or affirmative action. But this is not what most people mean by hate speech, nor are colleges barred from drafting narrow rules that hone in on the conduct they wish to control. And when they do, courts are very likely to find in their favor.

Recent Supreme Court rulings striking down laws that ban sodomy, upholding affirmative action and approving punishment for cross-burning show that the court is not unaware of current trends. Society is becoming more diverse. Reasonable rules aimed at accommodating that diversity and regulating the conduct of bullies and bigots are to be applauded—not feared.

## THINKING CRITICALLY

1. In your opinion, do you think hate speech should be banned speech in any situation, or does banning speech create a slippery slope that invites the restriction of other forms of speech? Explain.

2. This piece is an opinion editorial that allows the writer to offer an opinion on an issue. Summarize Delgado's points and respond with your own editorial, referring to the specific points he makes in his article.

3. What reasons does Delgado offer for banning hate speech? Should hate speech be banned from college campuses but not from other public places? Or should it be restricted everywhere, under all circumstances?

4. Do you think hate speech deserves First Amendment protection? Can you think of any circumstances or situations where it should be allowed?

5. Delgado observes that "hate speech is rarely an invitation to a conversation." Why do you think he makes this comment? To what free speech argument is he referring? Explain.

## WRITING ASSIGNMENTS

1. Many legal scholars view restrictions on hate speech as a form of censorship and contrary to the democratic spirit of pluralism and tolerance. Write a paper in which you argue that hate speech should be protected. Alternatively, you may write a paper in which you explain that the First Amendment does not apply to this form of speech.

2. Would you support the right of a controversial figure to speak at your school if that individual had made racist or hateful comments (such as Don Imus, Dr. Laura Schlessinger, Reverend Jeremiah Wright, etc.)? Why or why not? Write an essay in which you explore the right to speak and the right to protest speakers if you disagree with them. Should we be able to ban speakers? Why or why not?

## MAKING CONNECTIONS

1. How can the principles of gender-free, gender-fair, and gender-specific language be applied to language that is biased about handicap, religion, race, age, or other group characteristics? Supply one example for each principle and include a phrase that contains biased language and a revision resolving the problem.

2. Rosalie Maggio and Michiko Kakutani take strong positions on the issue of "politically correct" language, while Robin Tolmach Lakoff takes a more neutral position. Create a conversation between two or more of these authors that discusses the issues of language use. (Your conversation will be more effective if you focus on a particular topic or issue—perhaps choose a controversy in the

news, a controversial TV program or movie, or anything to do with your school's speech or behavior codes.)

3. The issues of hate speech and stereotypical language seem to be deeply intertwined. Write an essay in which you explore the connection between the two and likely outcomes for the future. Are we moving toward a culture where more sensitive forms of speech become the norm? Will hate speech become a thing of the past if speech codes preventing it are instituted and enforced? Why or why not?

4. Several of the authors in this chapter examine the issue of epithets and how context affects their meaning. Choose an epithet and research its denotation and connotation. First explore various source books—standard dictionaries (the *Oxford English Dictionary* provides the etymology of words), slang dictionaries, encyclopedias, and so forth. Then interview class members about how they define these words. Do you find a difference between how the books define the words and how your classmates define them? Organize your findings and report them to the class.

5. In this chapter, some authors have strong opinions about the nature of prejudice and stereotypes—opinions that you may or may not agree with. For this assignment, play devil's advocate and write a critique of one of the essays in this section. Be sure to refer to the writer's text when drafting your essay so that you can be specific about where you disagree.

6. Suppose that a leader of a known hate group were invited to your campus— someone certain to speak in inflammatory racist language. Would you defend that person's right to address the student body? Why or why not? Should the person be protected under the First Amendment? Why or why not?

7. Write a letter to the editor of your school newspaper advocating restricted or unlimited speech on campus. In your letter, explain your viewpoint and provide supporting material. How do you think your letter would be received by the student body? Explain.

8. In a January 2003 article in *Boston Magazine,* "The Thought Police," Boston lawyer Harvey Silverglate stated that the First Amendment should protect your right to say what you wish, but that you are not immune to what happens after that. You may be subjected to angry retorts, public shunning, and social pressure, but you should not be officially punished for your language. Write a response to Silverglate expressing your own opinion on this assessment of the First Amendment.

# Advertising and Print Media

Much of what we know about the world comes from what the media tell us through television, radio, newspapers, magazines, and movies. Similarly, how we perceive that world is influenced by the media's presentation of it. Underwriting most of that media is advertising. Nearly $400 billion is spent every year on television commercials and print ads—more than the gross national product of many countries in the world—which account for a quarter of each television hour and the bulk of most newspapers and magazines. Tremendous power lies in the hands of those who control the media and write the ads. In this chapter, we will examine the tremendous power of advertising and news media, explore how each uses and abuses the power of words, and conjecture about the future of print media in an electronic age.

## The Language of Advertising

Advertising is everywhere—television, newspapers, magazines, the Internet, the exterior of buses, and highway billboards; it is printed on T-shirts, hot dogs, postage stamps, and even license plates. It is the driving force of our consumer economy. Advertising is everywhere people are, and its appeal goes right to the quick of our fantasies: happiness, material wealth, eternal youth, social acceptance, sexual fulfillment, and power. And it does so in carefully selected images and words. It is the most pervasive form of persuasion in America and, perhaps, the single manufacturer of meaning in our consumer society. Yet most of us are so accustomed to advertising that we hear it without listening and see it without looking. But if we stopped to examine how it works, we might be amazed at just how powerful and complex a psychological force advertising is. In this section, we examine how a simple page in a magazine or a 15-second TV spot feeds our fantasies and fears with the sole intention of separating us from our money.

By its very nature, the language of advertising is a very special language—one that combines words cleverly and methodically. On that point, the authors of the first two essays are in agreement. But beyond that, their views diverge widely. In "With These Words, I Can Sell You Anything," language-watcher William Lutz argues that advertisers tyrannically twist simple English words so that they appear to promise just what the consumer desires. Taking a defensive posture in "The Language of Advertising," Charles A. O'Neill, a professional advertiser, admits that the language of ads can be very appealing. He makes a persuasive argument that no ad can force consumers to lay their money down. Marketing guru Frank Luntz describes how the most successful companies combine advertising with corporate identity in "Be All That You Can Be: The Company Persona and Language Alignment." Then Douglas Rushkoff confirms what parents have long suspected—that Madison Avenue is after their children by surrounding them with logos, labels, and ads literally from the day they are born. The section ends with a series of ads for discussion and review.

## The Future of Print Media

At the beginning of the 20th century, the written word was the prime mover of information and mass entertainment. Books, newspapers, literary journals, and tabloids were how people got information, shared the latest fashions, and were entertained. Now, a century later, we are a culture that is moving from the printed page to the electronic screen. What does this mean for language and the future of print media? Some critics claim that language is becoming slovenly and unimaginative as media attempt to reach mass audiences via blogs and online blurbs. Even the editorial cartoon, a mainstay in the pages of many newspapers and journals, seems to be a dying breed. Is the influence of print journalism being lost in an effort to please advertisers and an impatient reading public? This section takes a look at print media and its role in our culture and our future.

The section begins with a comprehensive examination of the history and future of print media by Eric Alterman, "Out of Print." Alterman explains why newspapers seem to be losing readership while the online content they provide (often free) is growing. The problem is that they may be putting themselves out of business. His serious essay is followed by a spoof interview appearing on *The Huffington Post* by J. A. Konrath in which the print industry is "interviewed" about its approaching demise. Iconic television producer Danny Schechter then discusses the decline of newspaper journalism and its connection to the youth market. Schechter contends in "Are We Reaching Da Youth?" that the next generation of 20-somethings does not care about the news because big journalism clearly does not care about them. But what happens when we get our news from *The Daily Show* and *The Onion?* Then, Frank Watson provides some insights on the connection between newspapers and our own freedom in "Will the Death of Newspapers Also Kill Our Freedoms?"

Editorial cartoons have been a part of American life for more than a century. They are a mainstay feature on the editorial pages in most newspapers—those pages reserved for columnists, contributing editors, and illustrators to present their views in words and pen and ink. They are not just visual jokes but also visual humor that comments on social and political issues. They often depict a moment in the flow of familiar current events. In the last essay in this section, Pulitzer Prize–winning cartoonist Doug Marlette explains why editorial cartoons serve as a litmus test for freedom of speech. If cartoonists are silenced, he fears for the First Amendment rights of us all in "Freedom of Speech and the Editorial Cartoon." Marlette notes that cartoonists push the envelope to hold up a situation for examination and critical thought.

# THE LANGUAGE OF ADVERTISING

## With These Words, I Can Sell You Anything
*William Lutz*

It has been argued that people will inflate language to give importance to insignificant matters—a practice we hear in political campaigns where the intention is to exploit and manipulate. But the same practice can be seen in advertising. At least that's the opinion of William Lutz, who assails the linguistic habits of hucksters. In this essay, he alerts readers to the special power of "weasel words"—those familiar and sneaky critters that "appear to say one thing when in fact they say the opposite, or nothing at all."

William Lutz has been called the George Orwell of the 1990s. Chair of the Committee on Public Doublespeak of the National Council of Teachers of English, Lutz edits the *Quarterly Review of Doublespeak,* a magazine dedicated to the eradication of misleading official statements. He also teaches in the English department at Rutgers University. He is the author of *Beyond Nineteen Eighty-Four* (1989); *Doublespeak* (1989), from which this essay is taken; and most recently, *Doublespeak Defined* (1999).

1 One problem advertisers have when they try to convince you that the product they are pushing is really different from other, similar products is that their claims are subject to some laws. Not a lot of laws, but there are some designed to prevent fraudulent or untruthful claims in advertising. Even during the happy years of non-regulation under President Ronald Reagan, the FTC did crack down on the more blatant abuses in advertising claims. Generally speaking, advertisers have to be careful in what they say in their ads, in the claims they make for the products they advertise. Parity claims are safe because they are legal and supported by a number of court decisions. But beyond parity claims there are weasel words.

2 Advertisers use weasel words to appear to be making a claim for a product when in fact they are making no claim at all. Weasel words get their name from the way weasels eat the eggs they find in the nests of other animals. A weasel will make a small hole in the egg, suck out the insides, then place the egg back in the nest. Only when the egg is examined closely is it found to be hollow. That's the way it is with weasel words in advertising: Examine weasel words closely and you'll find that they're as hollow as any egg sucked by a weasel. Weasel words appear to say one thing when in fact they say the opposite, or nothing at all.

## "Help"—The Number One Weasel Word

3 The biggest weasel word used in advertising doublespeak is "help." Now "help" only means to aid or assist, nothing more. It does not mean to conquer, stop, eliminate, end, solve, heal, cure, or anything else. But once the ad says "help," it can say just about anything after that because "help" qualifies everything coming after it. The trick is that the claim that comes after the weasel word is usually so strong and so dramatic that you forget the word "help" and concentrate only on the dramatic claim. You read into the ad a message that the ad does not contain. More importantly, the advertiser is not responsible for the claim that you read into the ad, even though the advertiser wrote the ad so you would read that claim into it.

4 The next time you see an ad for a cold medicine that promises that it "helps relieve cold symptoms fast," don't rush out to buy it. Ask yourself what this claim is really saying. Remember, "helps" means only that the medicine will aid or assist. What will it aid or assist in doing? Why, "relieve" your cold "symptoms." "Relieve" only means to ease, alleviate, or mitigate, not to stop, end, or cure. Nor does the claim say how much relieving this medicine will do. Nowhere does this ad claim it will cure anything. In fact, the ad doesn't even claim it will do anything at all. The ad only claims that it will aid in relieving (not curing) your cold symptoms,

which are probably a runny nose, watery eyes, and a headache. In other words, this medicine probably contains a standard decongestant and some aspirin. By the way, what does "fast" mean? Ten minutes, one hour, one day? What is fast to one person can be very slow to another. Fast is another weasel word.

5    Ad claims using "help" are among the most popular ads. One says, "Helps keep you young looking," but then a lot of things will help keep you young looking, including exercise, rest, good nutrition, and a facelift. More importantly, this ad doesn't say the product will keep you young, only "young *looking*." Someone may look young to one person and old to another.

6    A toothpaste ad says, "Helps prevent cavities," but it doesn't say it will actually prevent cavities. Brushing your teeth regularly, avoiding sugars in foods, and flossing daily will also help prevent cavities. A liquid cleaner ad says, "Helps keep your home germ free," but it doesn't say it actually kills germs, nor does it even specify which germs it might kill.

7    "Help" is such a useful weasel word that it is often combined with other action-verb weasel words such as "fight" and "control." Consider the claim, "Helps control dandruff symptoms with regular use." What does it really say? It will assist in controlling (not eliminating, stopping, ending, or curing) the *symptoms* of dandruff, not the cause of dandruff nor the dandruff itself. What are the symptoms of dandruff? The ad deliberately leaves that undefined, but assume that the symptoms referred to in the ad are the flaking and itching commonly associated with dandruff. But just shampooing with *any* shampoo will temporarily eliminate these symptoms, so this shampoo isn't any different from any other. Finally, in order to benefit from this product, you must use it regularly. What is "regular use"—daily, weekly, hourly? Using another shampoo "regularly" will have the same effect. Nowhere does this advertising claim say this particular shampoo stops, eliminates, or cures dandruff. In fact, this claim says nothing at all, thanks to all the weasel words.

8    Look at ads in magazines and newspapers, listen to ads on radio and television, and you'll find the word "help" in ads for all kinds of products. How often do you read or hear such phrases as "helps stop . . . ," "helps overcome . . . ," "helps eliminate . . . ," "helps you feel . . . ," or "helps you look . . . "? If you start looking for this weasel word in advertising, you'll be amazed at how often it occurs. Analyze the claims in the ads using "help," and you will discover that these ads are really saying nothing.

9    There are plenty of other weasel words used in advertising. In fact, there are so many that to list them all would fill the rest of this book. But, in order to identify the doublespeak of advertising and understand the real meaning of an ad, you have to be aware of the most popular weasel words in advertising today.

## Virtually Spotless

10  One of the most powerful weasel words is "virtually," a word so innocent that most people don't pay any attention to it when it is used in an advertising claim. But watch out. "Virtually" is used in advertising claims that appear to make specific, definite promises when there is no promise. After all, what does "virtually" mean? It means "in essence of effect, although not in fact." Look at that definition again.

"Virtually" means *not in fact*. It does *not* mean "almost" or "just about the same as," or anything else. And before you dismiss all this concern over such a small word, remember that small words can have big consequences.

11    In 1971 a federal court rendered its decision on a case brought by a woman who became pregnant while taking birth control pills. She sued the manufacturer, Eli Lilly and Company, for breach of warranty. The woman lost her case. Basing its ruling on a statement in the pamphlet accompanying the pills, which stated that, "When taken as directed, the tablets offer virtually 100% protection," the court ruled that there was no warranty, expressed or implied, that the pills were absolutely effective. In its ruling, the court pointed out that, according to *Webster's Third New International Dictionary,* "virtually" means "almost entirely" and clearly does not mean "absolute" (*Whittington v. Eli Lilly and Company,* 333 F. Supp. 98). In other words, the Eli Lilly company was really saying that its birth control pill, even when taken as directed, *did not in fact* provide 100 percent protection against pregnancy. But Eli Lilly didn't want to put it that way because then many women might not have bought Lilly's birth control pills.

12    The next time you see the ad that says that this dishwasher detergent "leaves dishes virtually spotless," just remember how advertisers twist the meaning of the weasel word "virtually." You can have lots of spots on your dishes after using this detergent and the ad claim will still be true, because what this claim really means is that this detergent does not *in fact* leave your dishes spotless. Whenever you see or hear an ad claim that uses the word "virtually," just translate that claim into its real meaning. So the television set that is "virtually trouble free" becomes the television set that is not in fact trouble free, the "virtually foolproof operation" of any appliance becomes an operation that is in fact not foolproof, and the product that "virtually never needs service" becomes the product that is not in fact service free.

## New and Improved

13 If "new" is the most frequently used word on a product package, "improved" is the second most frequent. In fact, the two words are almost always used together. It seems just about everything sold these days is "new and improved." The next time you're in the supermarket, try counting the number of times you see these words on products. But you'd better do it while you're walking down just one aisle, otherwise you'll need a calculator to keep track of your counting.

14    Just what do these words mean? The use of the word "new" is restricted by regulations, so an advertiser can't just use the word on a product or in an ad without meeting certain requirements. For example, a product is considered new for about six months during a national advertising campaign. If the product is being advertised only in a limited test market area, the word can be used longer, and in some instances has been used for as long as two years.

15    What makes a product "new"? Some products have been around for a long time, yet every once in a while you discover that they are being advertised as "new." Well, an advertiser can call a product new if there has been "a material functional change" in the product. What is "a material functional change," you ask? Good question. In fact it's such a good question it's being asked all the time. It's

up to the manufacturer to prove that the product has undergone such a change. And if the manufacturer isn't challenged on the claim, then there's no one to stop it. Moreover, the change does not have to be an improvement in the product. One manufacturer added an artificial lemon scent to a cleaning product and called it "new and improved," even though the product did not clean any better than without the lemon scent. The manufacturer defended the use of the word "new" on the grounds that the artificial scent changed the chemical formula of the product and therefore constituted "a material functional change."

16      Which brings up the word "improved." When used in advertising, "improved" does not mean "made better." It only means "changed" or "different from before." So, if the detergent maker puts a plastic pour spout on the box of detergent, the product has been "improved," and away we go with a whole new advertising campaign. Or, if the cereal maker adds more fruit or a different kind of fruit to the cereal, there's an improved product. Now you know why manufacturers are constantly making little changes in their products. Whole new advertising campaigns, designed to convince you that the product has been changed for the better, are based on small changes in superficial aspects of a product. The next time you see an ad for an "improved" product, ask yourself what was wrong with the old one. Ask yourself just how "improved" the product is. Finally, you might check to see whether the "improved" version costs more than the unimproved one. After all, someone has to pay for the millions of dollars spent advertising the improved product.

17      Of course, advertisers really like to run ads that claim a product is "new and improved." While what constitutes a "new" product may be subject to some regulation, "improved" is a subjective judgment. A manufacturer changes the shape of its stick deodorant, but the shape doesn't improve the function of the deodorant. That is, changing the shape doesn't affect the deodorizing ability of the deodorant, so the manufacturer calls it "improved." Another manufacturer adds ammonia to its liquid cleaner and calls it "new and improved." Since adding ammonia does affect the cleaning ability of the product, there has been a "material functional change" in the product, and the manufacturer can now call its cleaner "new," and "improved" as well. Now the weasel words "new and improved" are plastered all over the package and are the basis for a multimillion-dollar ad campaign. But after six months the word "new" will have to go, until someone can dream up another change in the product. Perhaps it will be adding color to the liquid, or changing the shape of the package, or maybe adding a new dripless pour spout, or perhaps a ——————. The "improvements" are endless, and so are the new advertising claims and campaigns.

18      "New" is just too useful and powerful a word in advertising for advertisers to pass it up easily. So they use weasel words that say "new" without really saying it. One of their favorites is "introducing," as in, "Introducing improved Tide," or "Introducing the stain remover." The first is simply saying, here's our improved soap: the second, here's our new advertising campaign for our detergent. Another favorite is "now," as in, "Now there's Sinex," which simply means that Sinex is available. Then there are phrases like "Today's Chevrolet," "Presenting Dristan," and "A fresh way to start the day." The list is really endless because advertisers are always finding new ways to say "new" without really saying it. If there

is a second edition of this book, I'll just call it the "new and improved" edition. Wouldn't you really rather have a "new and improved" edition of this book rather than a "second" edition?

## Acts Fast

19 "Acts" and "works" are two popular weasel words in advertising because they bring action to the product and to the advertising claim. When you see the ad for the cough syrup that "Acts on the cough control center," ask yourself what this cough syrup is claiming to do. Well, it's just claiming to "act," to do something, to perform an action. What is it that the cough syrup does? The ad doesn't say. It only claims to perform an action or do something on your "cough control center." By the way, what and where is your "cough control center"? I don't remember learning about that part of the body in human biology class.

20 Ads that use such phrases as "acts fast," "acts against," "acts to prevent," and the like are saying essentially nothing, because "act" is a word empty of any specific meaning. The ads are always careful not to specify exactly what "act" the product performs. Just because a brand of aspirin claims to "act fast" for headache relief doesn't mean this aspirin is any better than any other aspirin. What is the "act" that this aspirin performs? You're never told. Maybe it just dissolves quickly. Since aspirin is a parity product, all aspirin is the same and therefore functions the same.

## Works Like Anything Else

21 If you don't find the word "acts" in an ad, you will probably find the weasel word "works." In fact, the two words are almost interchangeable in advertising. Watch out for ads that say a product "works against," "works like," "works for," or "works longer." As with "acts," "works" is the same meaningless verb used to make you think that this product really does something, and maybe even something special or unique. But "works," like "acts," is basically a word empty of any specific meaning.

## Like Magic

22 Whenever advertisers want you to stop thinking about the product and to start thinking about something bigger, better, or more attractive than the product, they use that very popular weasel word, "like." The word "like" is the advertiser's equivalent of a magician's use of misdirection. "Like" gets you to ignore the product and concentrate on the claim the advertiser is making about it. "For skin like peaches and cream" claims the ad for a skin cream. What is this ad really claiming? It doesn't say this cream will give you peaches-and-cream skin. There is no verb in this claim, so it doesn't even mention using the product. How is skin ever like "peaches and cream"? Remember, ads must be read literally and exactly, according to the dictionary definition of words. (Remember "virtually" in the Eli Lilly case.) The ad is making absolutely no promise or claim whatsoever for this skin cream. If you think this cream will give you soft, smooth, youthful-looking skin, you are the one who has read that meaning into the ad.

23 The wine that claims "It's like taking a trip to France" wants you to think about a romantic evening in Paris as you walk along the boulevard after a wonderful

meal in an intimate little bistro. Of course, you don't really believe that a wine can take you to France, but the goal of the ad is to get you to think pleasant, romantic thoughts about France and not about how the wine tastes or how expensive it may be. That little word "like" has taken you away from crushed grapes into a world of your own imaginative making. Who knows, maybe the next time you buy wine, you'll think those pleasant thoughts when you see this brand of wine, and you'll buy it. Or, maybe you weren't even thinking about buying wine at all, but now you just might pick up a bottle the next time you're shopping. Ah, the power of "like" in advertising.

24    How about the most famous "like" claim of all, "Winston tastes good like a cigarette should"? Ignoring the grammatical error here, you might want to know what this claim is saying. Whether a cigarette tastes good or bad is a subjective judgment because what tastes good to one person may well taste horrible to another. Not everyone likes fried snails, even if they are called escargot. (*De gustibus non est disputandum*, which was probably the Roman rule for advertising as well as for defending the games in the Colosseum.) There are many people who say all cigarettes taste terrible, other people who say only some cigarettes taste all right, and still others who say all cigarettes taste good. Who's right? Everyone, because taste is a matter of personal judgment.

25    Moreover, note the use of the conditional, "should." The complete claim is, "Winston tastes good like a cigarette should taste." But should cigarettes taste good? Again, this is a matter of personal judgment and probably depends most on one's experiences with smoking. So, the Winston ad is simply saying that Winston cigarettes are just like any other cigarette: Some people like them and some people don't. On that statement R. J. Reynolds conducted a very successful multimillion-dollar advertising campaign that helped keep Winston the number-two-selling cigarette in the United States, close behind number one, Marlboro.

## Can It Be Up to the Claim

26    Analyzing ads for doublespeak requires that you pay attention to every word in the ad and determine what each word really means. Advertisers try to wrap their claims in language that sounds concrete, specific, and objective, when in fact the language of advertising is anything but. Your job is to read carefully and listen critically so that when the announcer says that "Crest can be of significant value . . ." you know immediately that this claim says absolutely nothing. Where is the doublespeak in this ad? Start with the second word.

27    Once again, you have to look at what words really mean, not what you think they mean or what the advertiser wants you to think they mean. The ad for Crest only says that using Crest "can be" of "significant value." What really throws you off in this ad is the brilliant use of "significant." It draws your attention to the word "value" and makes you forget that the ad only claims that Crest "can be." The ad doesn't say that Crest *is* of value, only that it is "able" or "possible" to be of value, because that's all that "can" means.

28    It's so easy to miss the importance of those little words, "can be." Almost as easy as missing the importance of the words "up to" in an ad. These words are

very popular in sale ads. You know, the ones that say, "Up to 50% Off!" Now, what does that claim mean? Not much, because the store or manufacturer has to reduce the price of only a few items by 50 percent. Everything else can be reduced a lot less, or not even reduced. Moreover, don't you want to know 50 percent off of what? Is it 50 percent off the "manufacturer's suggested list price," which is the highest possible price? Was the price artificially inflated and then reduced? In other ads, "up to" expresses an ideal situation. The medicine that works "up to ten times faster," the battery that lasts "up to twice as long," and the soap that gets you "up to twice as clean" all are based on ideal situations for using those products, situations in which you can be sure you will never find yourself.

## Unfinished Words

29  Unfinished words are a kind of "up to" claim in advertising. The claim that a battery lasts "up to twice as long" usually doesn't finish the comparison—twice as long as what? A birthday candle? A tank of gas? A cheap battery made in a country not noted for its technological achievements? The implication is that the battery lasts twice as long as batteries made by other battery makers, or twice as long as earlier model batteries made by the advertiser, but the ad doesn't really make these claims. You read these claims into the ad, aided by the visual images the advertiser so carefully provides.

30      Unfinished words depend on you to finish them, to provide the words the advertisers so thoughtfully left out of the ad. Pall Mall cigarettes were once advertised as "A longer, finer and milder smoke." The question is, longer, finer, and milder than what? The aspirin that claims it contains "Twice as much of the pain reliever doctors recommend most" doesn't tell you what pain reliever it contains twice as much of. (By the way, it's aspirin. That's right; it just contains twice the amount of aspirin. And how much is twice the amount? Twice of what amount?) Panadol boasts that "nobody reduces fever faster," but, since Panadol is a parity product, this claim simply means that Panadol isn't any better than any other product in its parity class. "You can be sure if it's Westinghouse," you're told, but just exactly what it is you can be sure of is never mentioned. "Magnavox gives you more" doesn't tell you what you get more of. More value? More television? More than they gave you before? It sounds nice, but it means nothing, until you fill in the claim with your own words, the words the advertisers didn't use. Since each of us fills in the claim differently, the ad and the product can become all things to all people, and not promise a single thing.

31      Unfinished words abound in advertising because they appear to promise so much. More importantly, they can be joined with powerful visual images on television to appear to be making significant promises about a product's effectiveness without really making any promises. In a television ad, the aspirin product that claims fast relief can show a person with a headache taking the product and then, in what appears to be a matter of minutes, claiming complete relief. This visual image is far more powerful than any claim made in unfinished words. Indeed, the visual image completes the unfinished words for you, filling in with pictures what the words leave out. And you thought that ads didn't affect you. What brand of aspirin do you use?

32      Some years ago, Ford's advertisements proclaimed "Ford LTD—700% quieter." Now, what do you think Ford was claiming with these unfinished words? What was the Ford LTD quieter than? A Cadillac? A Mercedes Benz? A BMW? Well, when the FTC asked Ford to substantiate this unfinished claim, Ford replied that it meant that the inside of the LTD was 700% quieter than the outside. How did you finish those unfinished words when you first read them? Did you even come close to Ford's meaning?

## Combining Weasel Words

33      A lot of ads don't fall neatly into one category or another because they use a variety of different devices and words. Different weasel words are often combined to make an ad claim. The claim, "Coffee-Mate gives coffee more body, more flavor," uses Unfinished Words ("more" than what?) and also uses words that have no specific meaning ("body" and "flavor"). Along with "taste" (remember the Winston ad and its claim to taste good), "body" and "flavor" mean nothing because their meaning is entirely subjective. To you, "body" in coffee might mean thick, black, almost bitter coffee, while I might take it to mean a light brown, delicate coffee. Now, if you think you understood that last sentence, read it again, because it said nothing of objective value; it was filled with weasel words of no specific meaning: "thick," "black," "bitter," "light brown," and "delicate." Each of those words has no specific, objective meaning, because each of us can interpret them differently.

34      Try this slogan: "Looks, smells, tastes like ground-roast coffee." So, are you now going to buy Taster's Choice instant coffee because of this ad? "Looks," "smells," and "tastes" are all words with no specific meaning and depend on your interpretation of them for any meaning. Then there's that great weasel word "like," which simply suggests a comparison but does not make the actual connection between the product and the quality. Besides, do you know what "ground-roast" coffee is? I don't, but it sure sounds good. So, out of seven words in this ad, four are definite weasel words, two are quite meaningless, and only one has any clear meaning.

35      Remember the Anacin ad—"Twice as much of the pain reliever doctors recommend most"? There's a whole lot of weaseling going on in this ad. First, what's the pain reliever they're talking about in this ad? Aspirin, of course. In fact, any time you see or hear an ad using those words "pain reliever," you can automatically substitute the word "aspirin" for them. (Makers of acetaminophen and ibuprofen pain relievers are careful in their advertising to identify their products as nonaspirin products.) So, now we know that Anacin has aspirin in it. Moreover, we know that Anacin has twice as much aspirin in it, but we don't know twice as much as what. Does it have twice as much aspirin as an ordinary aspirin tablet? If so, what is an ordinary aspirin tablet, and how much aspirin does it contain? Twice as much as Excedrin or Bufferin? Twice as much as a chocolate chip cookie? Remember those Unfinished Words and how they lead you on without saying anything.

36      Finally, what about those doctors who are doing all that recommending? Who are they? How many of them are there? What kind of doctors are they? What are their qualifications? Who asked them about recommending pain relievers? What other pain relievers did they recommend? And there are a whole lot more questions about this "poll" of doctors to which I'd like to know the answers, but you get the

point. Sometimes, when I call my doctor, she tells me to take two aspirin and call her office in the morning. Is that where Anacin got this ad?

## Read the Label, or the Brochure

37 Weasel words aren't just found on television, on the radio, or in newspaper and magazine ads. Just about any language associated with a product will contain the doublespeak of advertising. Remember the Eli Lilly case and the doublespeak on the information sheet that came with the birth control pills. Here's another example.

38 In 1983, the Estée Lauder cosmetics company announced a new product called "Night Repair." A small brochure distributed with the product stated that "Night Repair was scientifically formulated in Estée Lauder's U.S. laboratories as part of the Swiss Age-Controlling Skincare Program. Although only nature controls the aging process, this program helps control the signs of aging and encourages skin to look and feel younger." You might want to read these two sentences again, because they sound great but say nothing.

39 First, note that the product was "scientifically formulated" in the company's laboratories. What does that mean? What constitutes a scientific formulation? You wouldn't expect the company to say that the product was casually, mechanically, or carelessly formulated, or just thrown together one day when the people in the white coats didn't have anything better to do. But the word "scientifically" lends an air of precision and promise that just isn't there.

40 It is the second sentence, however, that's really weasely, both syntactically and semantically. The only factual part of this sentence is the introductory dependent clause—"only nature controls the aging process." Thus, the only fact in the ad is relegated to a dependent clause, a clause dependent on the main clause, which contains no factual or definite information at all and indeed purports to contradict the independent clause. The new "skincare program" (notice it's not a skin cream but a "program") does not claim to stop or even retard the aging process. What, then, does Night Repair, at a price of over $35 (in 1983 dollars) for a .87-ounce bottle do? According to this brochure, nothing. It only "helps," and the brochure does not say how much it helps. Moreover, it only "helps control," and then it only helps control the "*signs* of aging," not the aging itself. Also, it "encourages" skin not to *be* younger but only to "look and feel" younger. The brochure does not say younger than what. Of the sixteen words in the main clause of this second sentence, nine are weasel words. So, before you spend all that money for Night Repair, or any other cosmetic product, read the words carefully, and then decide if you're getting what you think you're paying for.

## Other Tricks of the Trade

41 Advertisers' use of doublespeak is endless. The best way advertisers can make something out of nothing is through words. Although there are a lot of visual images used on television and in magazines and newspapers, every advertiser wants to create that memorable line that will stick in the public consciousness. I am sure pure joy reigned in one advertising agency when a study found that children who were asked to spell the word "relief" promptly and proudly responded "r-o-l-a-i-d-s."

42    The variations, combinations, and permutations of doublespeak used in advertising go on and on, running from the use of rhetorical questions ("Wouldn't you really rather have a Buick?" "If you can't trust Prestone, who can you trust?") to flattering you with compliments ("The lady has taste." "We think a cigar smoker is someone special." "You've come a long way baby."). You know, of course, how you're *supposed* to answer those questions, and you know that those compliments are just leading up to the sales pitches for the products. Before you dismiss such tricks of the trade as obvious, however, just remember that all of these statements and questions were part of very successful advertising campaigns.

43    A more subtle approach is the ad that proclaims a supposedly unique quality for a product, a quality that really isn't unique. "If it doesn't say Goodyear, it can't be polyglas." Sounds good, doesn't it? Polyglas is available only from Goodyear because Goodyear copyrighted that trade name. Any other tire manufacturer could make exactly the same tire but could not call it "polyglas," because that would be copyright infringement. "Polyglas" is simply Goodyear's name for its fiberglass-reinforced tire.

44    Since we like to think of ourselves as living in a technologically advanced country, science and technology have a great appeal in selling products. Advertisers are quick to use scientific doublespeak to push their products. There are all kinds of elixirs, additives, scientific potions, and mysterious mixtures added to all kinds of products. Gasoline contains "HTA," "F–130," "Platformate," and other chemical-sounding additives, but nowhere does an advertisement give any real information about the additive.

45    Shampoo, deodorant, mouthwash, cold medicine, sleeping pills, and any number of other products all seem to contain some special chemical ingredient that allows them to work wonders. "Certs contains a sparkling drop of Retsyn." So what? What's "Retsyn"? What's it do? What's so special about it? When they don't have a secret ingredient in their product, advertisers still find a way to claim scientific validity. There's "Sinarest. Created by a research scientist who actually gets sinus headaches." Sounds nice, but what kind of research does this scientist do? How do you know if she is any kind of expert on sinus medicine? Besides, this ad doesn't tell you a thing about the medicine itself and what it does.

## Advertising Doublespeak Quick Quiz

46  Now it's time to test your awareness of advertising doublespeak. (You didn't think I would just let you read this and forget it, did you?) The following is a list of statements from some recent ads. Your job is to figure out what each of these ads really says:

DOMINO'S PIZZA: "Because nobody delivers better."
TUMS: "The stronger acid neutralizer."
LISTERMINT: "Making your mouth a cleaner place."
CASCADE: "For virtually spotless dishes nothing beats Cascade."
NUPRIN: "Little. Yellow. Different. Better."
ANACIN: "Better relief."
SUDAFED: "Fast sinus relief that won't put you fast asleep."
ADVIL: "Advanced medicine for pain."
PONDS COLD CREAM: "Ponds cleans like no soap can."

MILLER LITE BEER: "Tastes great. Less filling."
PHILIPS MILK OF MAGNESIA: "Nobody treats you better than MOM (Philips Milk of Magnesia)."
BAYER: "The wonder drug that works wonders."
CRACKER BARREL: "Judged to be the best."
KNORR: "Where taste is everything."
ANUSOL: "Anusol is the word to remember for relief."
DIMETAPP: "It relieves kids as well as colds."
LIQUID DRANO: "The liquid strong enough to be called Drāno."
JOHNSON & JOHNSON BABY POWDER: "Like magic for your skin."
PURITAN: "Make it your oil for life."
PAM: "Pam, because how you cook is as important as what you cook."
IVORY SHAMPOO AND CONDITIONER: "Leave your hair feeling Ivory clean."
TYLENOL: "Stop. Think. Tylenol."
ALKA-SELTZER PLUS: "Fast, effective relief for winter colds."

## The World of Advertising

47 In the world of advertising, people wear "dentures," not false teeth; they suffer from "occasional irregularity," not constipation; they need deodorants for their "nervous wetness," not for sweat; they use "bathroom tissue," not toilet paper; and they don't dye their hair, they "tint" or "rinse" it. Advertisements offer "real counterfeit diamonds" without the slightest hint of embarrassment, or boast of goods made out of "genuine imitation leather" or "virgin vinyl."

48 In the world of advertising, the girdle becomes a "body shaper," "form persuader," "control garment," "controller," "outerwear enhancer," "body garment," or "anti-gravity panties," and is sold with such trade names as "The Instead," "The Free Spirit," and "The Body Briefer."

49 A study some years ago found the following words to be among the most popular used in U.S. television advertisements: "new," "improved," "better," "extra," "fresh," "clean," "beautiful," "free," "good," "great," and "light." At the same time, the following words were found to be among the most frequent on British television: "new," "good-better-best," "free," "fresh," "delicious," "full," "sure," "clean," "wonderful," and "special." While these words may occur most frequently in ads, and while ads may be filled with weasel words, you have to watch out for all the words used in advertising, not just the words mentioned here.

50 Every word in an ad is there for a reason; no word is wasted. Your job is to figure out exactly what each word is doing in an ad—what each word really means, not what the advertiser wants you to think it means. Remember, the ad is trying to get you to buy a product, so it will put the product in the best possible light, using any device, trick, or means legally allowed. Your only defense against advertising (besides taking up permanent residence on the moon) is to develop and use a strong critical reading, listening, and looking ability. Always ask yourself what the ad is really saying. When you see ads on television, don't be misled by the pictures, the visual images. What does the ad *say* about the product? What does the ad *not* say?

What information is missing from the ad? Only by becoming an active, critical consumer of the doublespeak of advertising will you ever be able to cut through the doublespeak and discover what the ad is really saying.

### THINKING CRITICALLY

1. How did *weasel words* get their name? Does it sound like an appropriate label? Why, according to Lutz, do advertisers use them?
2. What regulations restrict the use of the word *new*? How can these regulations be sidestepped, according to the author? In your opinion, do these regulations serve the interests of the advertiser or the consumer?
3. Do you think that most people fail to comprehend how advertising works on them? When you read or watch ads, do you see through the gimmicks and weasel words?
4. Take a look at Lutz's Doublespeak Quick Quiz on pages 367–368. Select five items and write a language analysis explaining what the ad really says.
5. According to the author, how can consumers protect themselves against weasel words?
6. The author uses "you" throughout the article. Do you find the use of the second person stylistically satisfying? Do you think it is appropriate for the article?
7. What do you think about Lutz's writing style? Is it humorous? Informal? Academic? What strategies does he use to involve the reader in the piece?

### WRITING ASSIGNMENTS

1. The essays in this section deal with advertising language and its effects on consumers and their value systems. Describe how understanding the linguistic strategies of advertisers—as exemplified here by Lutz—will or will not change your reaction to advertising.
2. As Lutz suggests, look at some ads in a magazine or newspaper (or television and radio commercials). Then make a list of all uses of *help* you find over a 24-hour period. Examine the ads to determine exactly what is said and what the unwary consumer thinks is being said. Write up your report.
3. Invent a product and have some fun writing an ad for it. Use as many weasel words as you can to make your product shine.
4. Undertake a research project on theories of advertising. Find books by professional advertisers or texts for courses in advertising and marketing. Then go through them trying to determine how they might view Lutz's interpretation of advertising techniques. How would the authors view Lutz's claim that advertising language is loaded with weasel words?

# The Language of Advertising
*Charles A. O'Neill*

In this essay, marketing executive Charles A. O'Neill disputes William Lutz's criticism of advertising doublespeak. While admitting to some of the craftiness of his profession, O'Neill defends the huckster's language—both verbal and visual—against claims that it distorts reality. Examining some familiar television commercials and magazine ads, he explains why the language may be charming and seductive but far from brainwashing.

O'Neill is an independent marketing and advertising consultant in Boston. This essay first appeared in the textbook *Exploring Language* in 1998 and was updated for this edition in 2011.

1 In 1957, a short dozen years after World War II ended, many people had good reason to be concerned about Science. Giant American corporations offered the promise of "Better Living Through Chemistry." Labs and factories turned out new "miracle" fabrics, vaccines, and building materials to support the fast-growing, surging crest of consumer-centric, late 1950s America.

2 But World War II American Science had also yielded The Bomb. Specialists working in secret laboratories had figured out how to translate the theoretical work of Dr. Einstein and others into weapons that did exactly what they were intended to do, incinerating hundreds of thousands of civilian Japanese men, women, and children in the process. Soon after, the USSR and the USA were locked in an arms race. Despite winning a world war, Americans now feared nuclear retaliation from a new enemy, the USSR. The Cold War unleashed a new wave of fear, paranoia, and suspicion, soon to be capitalized on by advertising.

3 So when Vance Packard wrote his seminal book, *The Hidden Persuaders*, (D. Mackay & Co.) about a dark alliance of social scientists with product marketers and advertisers, he struck a resonant chord based on fear of undetected but dangerous forces. The scientists who had designed the weapons that won the war had now, apparently, turned their sights on the emerging consumer society, using market research and psychology to gain a better understanding of "people's subsurface desires, needs, and drives," to "find their points of vulnerability." By applying the principles of laboratory experimentation and scientific reasoning to learn about the fears, habits, and aspirations of John and Mary Public, they would help businesses create products whose sales would be fueled by ever-more powerful advertising.

4 The advertising business is as old as Western Civilization, and perhaps even older. Signs in ancient Rome advertised circuses and events at the Coliseum; and in Pompeii, wall paintings and signs promoted the equivalent of "For a good time, turn the corner and tell them Gallus sent you." But the post-WWII era was unique as wartime manufacturing capacity was refocused on consumer goods to support the millions of servicemen and women who had returned from overseas, and along with them the "Baby Boomer" generation they spawned. For advertising agencies, this was a dynamic era, a quality captured in the frantic energy of the fictional agency, Sterling Cooper Draper Pryce, of AMC's *Mad Men* series.

5 Mr. Packard is certainly not alone as a critic of advertising. We recognize the value of advertising, but on some level we can't quite fully embrace it as a "normal" part of our experience. At best, we view it as distracting. At worst, we view it as a pernicious threat to our health, wealth, and social values.

6 How does advertising work? Why is it so powerful? Why does it raise such concern? What case can be made for and against the advertising business? In order

to understand advertising, you must accept that it is not about truth, virtue, love, or positive social values. It is about selling a product.

7      But this simple fact does not explain the unique power of advertising. Whatever the product or creative strategy, advertisements derive their power from a purposeful, directed combination of images. Images can take the form of words, sounds, or visuals, used individually or together. The combination of images is the language of advertising, a language unlike any other.

8      Everyone who grows up in the Western world soon learns that advertising language is different from other languages. We may have forgotten the sponsors, but we certainly know that these popular slogans "sound like ads."

"The Real Thing" (Coca Cola)
"The Ultimate Driving Machine" (BMW)
"Life's Good" (LG)
"Intel Inside" (Intel)
"Just Do It" (Nike)
"Have it your way" (Burger King)

## Edited and Purposeful

9      At heart, advertising is nothing more than the delivery system for salesmanship, something that is woven into the fabric of our society. There is nothing a consumer can do to hide from sales messages. This is not limited to what we think of as advertising media. We encounter it face-to-face, too.

10      For example: When you stop at a fast-food restaurant for a breakfast sandwich and a cup of coffee in the morning, the smiling young man or woman who takes your order is more than likely going to try to "sell you." Not just sell you what you ordered, but sell you into buying *more*. The manager of one such restaurant left a laminated card on the counter following an early morning motivational session for his fast-food crew. The card shows order clerks how to "upsell" their customers; that is, increase the amount of the sale by promoting items the customers did not initially know they wanted. The clerks are told to follow a simple, scripted sales track laced with words designed to make the customer feel, well, *hungrier*. Simply order coffee, for example, and they might offer you *"piping hot, fresh pancakes to go with your coffee"* or the opportunity to *"top off your breakfast with something sweet. Maybe some yummy blueberry biscuits with a dollop of sweet butter churned from the fresh milk of cows that roam the green pastures of Vermont? They're my favorite."*

11      This is an example of perfectly ordinary language (albeit somewhat altered here for dramatic effect and to avoid copyright concerns), with words carefully selected and enlisted in the service of sales. Even a small increase in business for a national fast-food chain generates hundreds of millions of dollars of new revenue, in this case created by a few clever words printed on laminated paper, then memorized by sales clerks and delivered sincerely with a sparkling smile, right to you.

12      Like sales scripts, advertising slogans may seem casual, but in fact they are carefully engineered. Slogans and all other types of advertising messages have a clear purpose; they are intended to trigger a specific response.

13    If you listen to the radio, you have undoubtedly heard an ad for "Kars4Kids."
14    The first verse is sung by a child; and the second verse is the same as the first, but a man sings it. Both are accompanied by a strumming guitar.

> *1-877-kars for kids*
> *k-a-r-s kars for kids*
> *1-877-kars for kids*
> *donate your car today*

This is followed by two or three sentences of reassurance that Kars4Kids is a registered charity, and donors may be able to claim the value of their car as a tax deduction.

15    Now if this radio spot were presented at an advertising industry creative awards banquet, you would hear the sound of crickets out in the Vermont pasture sooner than you'd hear applause. It does not sound particularly artful, nothing that Sterling Cooper Draper Pryce partner Don Draper would likely toss out at a boozy client luncheon.

16    But it does attract attention, and it works, principally through mind numbing repetition. Never mind that some listeners have found it profoundly disturbing.

> In a comment on a Topix forum titled, "The most irritating radio commercial of all time" a poster from Houston said, "{This commercial} gave me the worst headache I've ever had and I couldn't stop it from playing in my head. I've heard about . . . people hearing voices in their head and trying to fight them, and I imagine that this is what that must feel like. I just wanted to take a power drill to my temple to drill out the awful repetition!"

17    The poor fellow! Maybe some piping hot pancakes would help. Vexing though this example may well be, repetition is a reliable and well worn tool in advertising. According to Answers.Com, "the average person needs to hear something twenty times before they truly learn it." So once you have heard about Kars4Kids a 21st time, it has been filed away in your neocortex. What else could an advertiser possibly hope to achieve?

18    Perhaps one day you'll need to move your grandfather's 1957 Edsel out of your barn so you can expand the dairy herd, enabling you to supply even more butter to fast-food restaurants—in which case, in the immortal words of the *Ghost Busters*, theme, "Who you gonna call?"

19    Lots of people have called. On its website, "Joy for Our Youth," parent of Kars4Kids, reports 2008 contributions of $23 million. Not bad for a charity that picks up old cars, then auctions them or sells them off as scrap.

## Rich and Arresting

20 Advertisements cannot succeed unless they capture our attention. Of the hundreds of advertising messages in store for us each day, very few will actually command our conscious attention. The rest are screened out. The people who design and write ads know about this screening process; they anticipate and accept it as a premise of their business.

21    Repetition works, but the classic, all-time favorite device used to breach the awareness barrier is sex. Except for perhaps the insatiable need for caffeine before an early morning lecture, the desire to be sexually attractive is our most powerful instinct. Flip through any popular magazine, and you will find it packed with ads that are unabashedly, unapologetically sexual. Victoria's Secret, Calvin Klein, and every other clothing and fragrance marketer uses sex to sell. Popular media is a veritable playground of titillation, abounding with images of barely clothed men and women in poses suggesting that if only you would wear one of our little padded brassieres or spray our product behind your ears, a world of sexual adventure will reveal itself to you—even if, like many Americans these days, your Body Mass Index places you squarely in the rippling embrace of Obesity, a disease some attribute to mass market advertising for fat-laden fast food, like, perhaps, "yummy blueberry biscuits."

22    If advertising created Obesity, it also offers the cure: Americans spend billions of dollars every year on "fat burning" nutritional supplements, principally because they see them advertised on television, the web, and in the pages of magazines. You may be a zaftig Size 12, but the spokesman in the white lab coat points to the girl in the bikini and in your mind you can soon become Size 000P, too. The manufacturer didn't quite say this, mind you. You did!

23    Every successful advertisement uses a creative strategy based on an idea intended to attract and hold the attention of the targeted consumer audience. The strategy may include a photo of a pretty girl, strong creative execution or a straight-forward list of product features, or as we've seen, even something as simple as mind-numbing repetition.

24    Soft drink and fast-food companies often take a distinctive approach. "Slice of life" ads (so-called because they purport to show people in "real-life" situations) created to sell Coke or Pepsi often placed their characters in Fourth of July parades or other family events. The archetypical version of this ad is a photograph or TV spot filled-to-overflowing with babies frolicking with puppies in the sunlit foreground while their youthful parents play touch football. On the porch, Grandma and Pops are seen quietly smiling as they wait for all of this affection to transform itself in a climax of warmth, harmony, and joy.

25    These ads seduced us into feeling that if we drank the right combination of sugar, preservatives, caramel coloring, and secret ingredients, we'd join the crowd that—in the words of Coca-Cola's ad from 1971—would help "teach the world to sing . . . in perfect harmony."

26    If you watch *Mad Men*, you've seen many episodes where Don Draper spontaneously generates slogans and headlines, but in the real world, ads do not often emerge like Botticelli's *Venus* from the sea, flawless and fully grown. Most often, the creative strategy is developed only after extensive research. "Who will be interested in our product? How old are they? Where do they live? How much money do they earn? What problem will our product solve?" Answers to these questions provide the foundation on which the creative strategy is built.

## Involving

27  We have seen that the language of advertising is carefully engineered; we have discovered a few of the devices it uses to get our attention. Coke and Pepsi have caught

our eye with visions of peace and love. An actress offers a winsome smile. Now that they have our attention, advertisers present information intended to show us that their product fills a need and differs from the competition. It is the copywriter's responsibility to express, exploit, and intensify product differences where they exist.

28    When product differences do not exist, the writer must glamorize the superficial differences—for example, differences in packaging. As long as the ad is working to get our attention, the "action" is mostly in the ad itself, in the words and visual images. But as we read an ad or watch it on our smartphones, we become more deeply involved. The action starts to take place in us. Our imagination is set in motion, and our individual fears and aspirations, quirks, and insecurities come into play.

29    Consider, once again, the running battle among soft drinks. The cola wars have spawned many "look-alike" advertisements, because the product features and consumer benefits are generic, applying to all products in the category. Substitute one cola brand name for another, and the messages are often identical, right down to the way the cans are photographed in the closing sequence. This strategy relies on mass saturation and exposure for impact.

30    Some companies have set themselves apart from their competitors by making use of bold, even disturbing, themes and images. For example, it was not uncommon not long ago for advertisers in the fashion industry to make use of gaunt, languid models—models who, in the eyes of some observers, displayed a certain form of "heroin chic." Something was most certainly unusual about the models appearing in ads for Prada and Calvin Klein products. A young woman in a Prada ad projects no emotion whatsoever; she is hunched forward, her posture suggesting that she is in a trance or drug-induced stupor. In a Calvin Klein ad, a young man is gaunt beyond reason. He is shirtless. As if to draw more attention to his peculiar posture and "zero body fat" status, he is shown pinching the skin next to his navel.

31    Do these ads cynically exploit the insecurities of the young and clueless? In fact, on one level, all advertising is about exploitation: the systematic, deliberate identification of our needs and wants, followed by the delivery of a carefully constructed promise that Brand X will satisfy them.

32    Another common device used to engage our attention is old but no less effective: the use of famous or notorious personalities as product spokespeople or models. Advertising writers did not invent the human tendency to admire or seek to identify with famous people. Once we have seen a famous person in an ad, we associate the product with the person: "Britney Spears drinks milk. She's a hottie. I want to be a hottie, too! 'Hey Mom, Got Milk?'" Nichole Ritchie pitches clothes by Jimmy Choo; Celine Dion pitches her own perfume; Sharon Stone sells Christal watches. The logic is faulty, but we fall under the spell just the same. Advertising works, not because Britney is a nutritionist, Celine is an expert perfumer-diva, or because Sharon is a horologist, but because we participate in it. The ads bring the words, sounds, and pictures. We bring the chemistry.

## A Simple Language

33  Advertising language differs from other types of language in its simplicity. To determine how the text of a typical advertisement rates on a "simplicity index" in comparison with text in a magazine article, for example, try this exercise: Clip a

typical story from the publication you read most frequently. Calculate the number of words in an average sentence. Count the number of words of three or more syllables in a typical 100-word passage, omitting words that are capitalized, combinations of two simple words, or verb forms made into three-syllable words by the addition of *–ed* or *–es*. Add the two figures (the average number of words per sentence and the number of three-syllable words per 100 words), then multiply the result by 0.4. According to Robert Gunning the result is the approximate grade level required to understand the content. He developed this formula, the "Fog Index," to determine the comparative ease with which any given piece of written communication can be read.

34    Let's apply the Fog Index to the lyrics in the Kars4Kids ad.

> *1-877-kars for kids*
> *k-a-r-s kars for kids*
> *1-877-kars for kids*
> *donate your car today*

35 Counting each digit in the phone number as a word, the average sentence in this ad is 6.25 words. There *are no three-syllable words*.

> 6.25 words per sentence
> 0 three syllable words/100
> -----
>   6.25
> $\times$ 0.4 =
>   **2.5**

According to Gunning's scale, the language of the Kars4Kids commercial is so simple that even Geico's cavemen—and children halfway through the second grade—could understand it.

36    Why do advertisers favor simple language? The answer lies with the consumer: People of every age are subject to an overwhelming number of commercial messages each day. As a practical matter, we would not notice many of these messages if engaging content or eloquence were counted among their virtues. Today's consumer cannot take the time to focus on anything for long. Every aspect of modern life runs at an accelerated pace. Voice mail, smartphones, tweets, Facebook updates, text messages—the world is always awake, always switched on, feeding our hunger for more information, now. Time generally, and TV-commercial time in particular, is experienced in increasingly smaller segments. Fifteen-second commercials are no longer unusual.

37    Advertising language is simple; in the engineering process, difficult words or images—which in other forms of communication may be used to lend color or fine shades of meaning—are edited out and replaced by simple words or images less vulnerable to misinterpretation.

## Who Is Responsible?

38 Some critics view the advertising business as a cranky, unwelcome child of the free enterprise system—a noisy, whining, brash kid who must somehow be kept in line,

but isn't quite old enough to be sent off to college. In reality, advertising mirrors the fears, quirks, and aspirations of the society that creates it (and is, in turn, sold by it). This fact alone exposes advertising to parody and ridicule. The overall level of acceptance and respect for advertising is also influenced by the varied quality of the ads themselves. Some ads are deliberately designed to provoke controversy. But this is only one of the many charges frequently levied against advertising. Others include:

1. Advertising encourages unhealthy habits.

2. Advertising feeds on human weaknesses and exaggerates the importance of material things, encouraging "impure" emotions and vanities.

3. Advertising sells daydreams—distracting, purposeless visions of lifestyles beyond the reach of the majority of the people who are most exposed to advertising.

4. Advertising warps our vision of reality, implanting in us groundless fears and insecurities.

5. Advertising downgrades the intelligence of the public.

6. Advertising debases English.

7. Advertising perpetuates racial and sexual stereotypes.

39    What can be said in advertising's defense? First, it's only a reflection of society. What about the charge that advertising debases the intelligence of the public? Those who support this particular criticism would do well to ask themselves another question: Exactly how intelligent is the public? Sadly, evidence abounds that "the public" at large is not particularly intelligent, after all. Johnny can't read. Susie can't write. And the entire family spends the night in front of the television, watching one mindless reality show after another. Ads are effective because they sell products. They would not succeed if they did not reflect the values and motivations of the real world. Advertising both reflects and shapes our perception of reality. Consider prominent brand names and the impressions they create: Absolut is cool. Mercedes represents quality. BMW is the ultimate driving machine. Our sense of what these brand names stand for has as much to do with advertising as with the objective "truth."

40    That said, advertising shapes our perception of the world as surely as architecture shapes our impression of a city. It is part of our environment. Good, responsible advertising can serve as a positive influence for change, and encourage product innovation, while generating profits. Of course, the problem is that the obverse is also true: Advertising, like any form of mass communication, can be a force for both "good" and "bad." It can just as readily reinforce or encourage irresponsible behavior, ageism, sexism, ethnocentrism, racism, homophobia—you name it—as it can encourage support for diversity and social progress. People living in society create advertising. Society isn't perfect.

41    Perhaps, by learning how advertising works, we can become better equipped to sort out content from hype, product values from emotions, and salesmanship from

propaganda. No one is forcing you to buy yummy biscuits just because they're the fast-food server's favorite. No one is holding you hostage until you call 1-877-kars for kids and give away your grandfather's car in exchange for a tax deduction and a vacation voucher. You must listen. You must read. And finally you must think—all by yourself.

## THINKING CRITICALLY

1. O'Neill says that advertisers create in consumers a sense of need for products. Do you think it is ethical for advertisers to create such a sense when their products are generic and do not differ from those of the competition? Consider ads for gasoline, beer, and instant coffee.

2. Toward the end of the essay, O'Neill anticipates potential objections to his defense of advertising. What are some of these objections? What does he say in defense of advertising? Which set of arguments do you find stronger?

3. O'Neill describes several ways in which the language of advertising differs from other kinds of language. Briefly list the ways he mentions. Can you think of any other characteristics of advertising language that set it apart?

4. In paragraph 32, O'Neill claims that celebrity endorsement of a product is "faulty" logic. Explain what he means. Why do people buy products sold by famous people?

5. William Lutz teaches English and writes books about the misuse of language. Charles O'Neill is a professional advertiser. How do their views about advertising reflect their occupations? Which side of the argument do you agree with?

6. How effective do you think O'Neill's introductory paragraphs are? How well does he hook the reader? What particular audience might he be appealing to early on? What attitude toward advertising is established in the introduction?

## WRITING ASSIGNMENTS

1. Obtain a current issue of each of the following publications: *The New Yorker, Time, GQ, Vogue,* and *People.* Choose one article from each periodical and calculate its Fog Index according to the technique described in paragraphs 33 through 35. Choose one ad from each periodical and figure out its Fog Index. What different reading levels do you find among the publications? What do you know about the readers of these periodicals from your survey of the reading difficulty of the articles? Write up your findings in a paper.

2. O'Neill believes that advertising language mirrors the fears, quirks, and aspirations of the society that creates it. Do you agree or disagree with this statement? Explain in a brief essay.

3. Working with a group of classmates, develop a slogan and advertising campaign for one of the following products: sneakers, soda, a candy bar, or jeans.

How would you apply the principles of advertising, as outlined in O'Neill's article, to market your product? After completing your marketing strategy, "sell" your product to the class. If time permits, explain the reasoning behind your selling technique.

---

# Be All That You Can Be: The Company Persona and Language Alignment

*Frank Luntz*

Dr. Frank Luntz was named the "hottest pollster in America" by *The Boston Globe*. He has consulted with many Fortune 100 companies, political candidates, public advocacy groups, and world leaders—just about anyone who wants to know how to say things better and more effectively. This article appeared in *Advertising in the Digital Age* on December 13, 2010, and is excerpted from his book, *Words That Work* (2007).

1  It's not just CEOs and corporate spokespeople who need effective language to be the message. The most successful advertising taglines are not seen as slogans for a product. They are the product. From M&M's "melts in your mouth, not in your hand" to "Please don't squeeze the Charmin" bathroom tissue, from the "plop, plop, fizz, fizz" of Alka-Seltzer to "Fly the friendly skies of United," there is no light space between the product and its marketing. Words that work reflect "not only the soul of the brand, but the company itself and its reason for being in business," according to Publicis worldwide executive creative director David Droga.

2  In the same vein, advertising experts identify a common quality among the most popular and long-lasting corporate icons: Rather than selling for their companies, these characters personify them. Ronald McDonald, the Marlboro Man, Betty Crocker, the Energizer Bunny—they aren't shills trying to talk us into buying a Big Mac, a pack of smokes, a box of cake mix, a package of batteries; they don't even personalize the product. Just like the most celebrated slogans, they are the product.

3  Walk through any bookstore and you'll find dozens of books about the marketing and branding efforts of corporate America. The process of corporate communication has been thinly sliced and diced over and over, but what you won't find is a book about the one truly essential characteristic in our twenty-first-century world: the company persona and how words that work are used to create and sustain it.

4  The company persona is the sum of the corporate leadership, the corporate ethos, the products and services offered, interaction with the customer, and, most importantly, the language that ties it all together. A majority of large companies do not have a company persona, but those that do benefit significantly. Ben & Jerry's attracts customers in part because of the funky names they gave to the conventional (and unconventional) flavors they offer, but the positive relationship between corporate management and their employees also plays a role, even after Ben and Jerry sold the company. McDonald's in the 1970s and Starbucks over the past decade

became an integral part of the American culture as much for the lifestyle they reflected as the food and beverages they offered, but the in-store lexicon helped by setting them apart from their competition. (Did any customers ever call the person who served them a cup of coffee a "barista" before Starbucks made the term popular?) Language is never the sole determinant in creating a company persona, but you'll find words that work associated with all companies that have one.

5    And when the message, messenger, and recipient are all on the same page, I call this rare phenomenon "language alignment," and it happens far less frequently than you might expect. In fact, virtually all of the companies that have hired my firm for communication guidance have found themselves linguistically unaligned.

6    This manifests itself in two ways. First, in service-oriented businesses, the sales force is too often selling with a different language than the marketing people are using. There's nothing wrong with individualizing the sales approach to each customer, but when you have your sales force promoting a message that has no similarity with the advertising campaign, it undermines both efforts. The language in the ads and promotions must match the language on the street, in the shop, and on the floor. For example, Boost Mobile, which caters to an inner city youth demographic, uses the slogan "Where you at?" Not grammatically (or politically) correct—but it's the language of their consumer.

7    And second, corporations with multiple products in the same space too often allow the language of those products to blur and bleed into each other. Procter & Gamble may sell a hundred different items, but even though each one fills a different need, a different space, and/or a different category, it is perfectly fine for them to share similar language. You can use some of the same verbiage to sell soap as you would to sell towels, because no consumer will confuse the products and what they do.

8    Not so for a company that is in a single line of work, say selling cars or selling beer, where companies use the exact same adjectives to describe very different products. In this instance, achieving linguistic alignment requires a much more disciplined linguistic segmentation. It is almost always a more effective sales strategy to divvy up the appropriate adjectives and create a unique lexicon for each individual brand.

9    An example of a major corporation that has confronted both of these challenges and still managed to achieve linguistic alignment, even as they are laying off thousands of workers, is the Ford Motor Company—which manages a surprisingly diverse group of brands ranging from Mazda to Aston Martin. The Ford corporate leadership recognized that it was impossible to separate the Ford name, corporate history, heritage, and range of vehicles—so why bother. They came as a package. Sure, Ford maintains individual brand identity, through national and local ad campaigns and by creating and maintaining a separate image and language for each brand. For example, "uniquely sensual styling" certainly applies when one is talking about a Jaguar S Type, but would probably not be pertinent for a Ford F 250 pickup truck. But the fact that the CEO carries the Ford name communicates continuity to the company's customers, and Bill Ford sitting in front of an assembly line talking about leadership and innovation in all of Ford's vehicles effectively puts all the individual brands into alignment.

380 Chapter 7 / Advertising and Print Media

10      The words he uses—"innovation," "driven," "re-committed," "dramatically," "dedicated"—represent the simplicity and brevity of effective communications, and they are wrapped around the CEO who is the fourth-generation Ford to lead the company—hence credibility. The cars are the message, Bill Ford is the messenger, the language is dead-on, and Ford is weathering the American automotive crisis far better than its larger rival General Motors. Again, the language of Ford isn't the only driver of corporate image and sales—but it certainly is a factor.

11      In fact, the brand-building campaign was so successful that GM jumped on board. But Ford quickly took it a step further. In early 2006, they began to leverage their ownership of Volvo (I wonder how many readers did not know that Ford bought Volvo in 1999 and purchased Jaguar a decade earlier) to communicate a corporate-wide commitment to automotive safety, across all of its individual brands and vehicles. Volvo is one of the most respected cars on the road today, and aligning all of Ford behind an industry leader is a very smart strategy indeed.

12      So what about the competition?

13      General Motors, once the automotive powerhouse of the world, has an equally diverse product line and arguably a richer history of technology and innovation, but their public message of cutbacks, buy-backs, and layoffs was designed to appeal to Wall Street, not Main Street, and it crushed new car sales. At the time of this writing, GM is suffering through record losses, record job layoffs, and a record number of bad stories about its failing marketing efforts.

14      It didn't have to be this way.

15      The actual attributes of many of the GM product lines are more appealing than the competition, but the product image itself is not. To own a GM car is to tell the world that you're so 1970s, and since what you drive is considered an extension and expression of yourself to others, people end up buying cars they actually like less because they feel the cars will say something more about them.

16      Think about it. Here's a company that was the first to develop a catalytic converter, the first to develop an advanced anti-tipping stabilization technology, the first to develop engines that could use all sorts of blended gasolines, and most importantly in today's market, the creator of OnStar—an incredible new-age computerized safety and tracking device. Yet most American consumers have no idea that any of these valuable innovations came from General Motors, simply because GM decided not to tell them. So instead of using its latest and greatest emerging technology to align itself with its customers, GM finds itself in a deteriorating dialogue with shareholders. No alignment = no sales.

17      Another problem with GM: No one knew that the various brands under the GM moniker were in fact . . . GM. Even such well-known brands as Corvette and Cadillac had become disconnected from the parent company. Worse yet, all the various brands (with the exception of Hummer, which couldn't get lost in a crowd even if the brand manager wanted it to) were using similar language, similar visuals, and a similar message—blurring the distinction between brands and turning GM vehicles into nothing more than generic American cars. Repeated marketing failures were just part of GM's recurring problems, but as that issue was completely within their control, it should have been the easiest to address. When products, services, and language are aligned, they gain another essential attribute: authenticity. In my own

market research for dozens of Fortune 500 companies, I have found that the best way to communicate authenticity is to trigger personalization: Do audience members see themselves in the slogan . . . and therefore in the product? Unfortunately, achieving personalization is by no means easy.

18      To illustrate how companies and brands in a competitive space create compelling personas for themselves while addressing the needs of different consumer groups, let's take a look at cereals. Anyone can go out and buy a box of cereal. But different cereals offer different experiences. Watch and listen carefully to their marketing approach and the words they use.

19      Most cereals geared toward children sell energy, excitement, adventure, and the potential for fun—even more than the actual taste of the sugar-coated rice or wheat puffs in the cardboard box. On the other hand, cereal aimed at grown-ups is sold based on its utility to the maintenance and enhancement of health—with taste once again secondary.

20      Children's cereals are pitched by nonthreatening cartoon characters—tigers, parrots, chocolate-loving vampires, Cap'ns, and a tiny trio in stocking caps—never an adult or authority figure. Adult cereals come at you head-on with a not-so-subtle Food Police message, wrapped in saccharine-sweet smiles, exclaiming that this cereal is a favorite of healthy and cholesterol-conscious adults who don't want to get colon cancer! Ugghhh. Kids buy Frosted Flakes because "They're grrrreat!" Adults buy Special K because we want to be as attractive and vigorous as the actors who promote it. When it comes to cereal, about the only thing parents and kids have in common is that the taste matters only slightly more than the image, experience, and product association—and if the communication appears authentic, they'll buy.

21      And cereal certainly sells. From Cheerios to Cinnamon Toast Crunch, more than $6 billion worth of cold cereal was sold in the United States alone in 2005. If you were to look at the five top-selling brands, you would see a diverse list targeted to a diverse set of customers. The language used for each of these five brands is noticeably different, but in all cases totally essential.

22      In looking at the first and third best-selling brands of cereal, one might initially think that only a slight variation in ingredients mark their distinctions. Cheerios and Honey Nut Cheerios are both based around the same whole-grain O shaped cereal, but are in fact two very different products, beyond the addition of honey and a nut-like crunch.

23      The language behind Cheerios is remarkably simple and all-encompassing—"The one and only Cheerios." Could be for kids . . . could be for young adults . . . could be for parents. Actually, Cheerios wants to sell to all of them. As its Web site states, Cheerios is the right cereal for "toddlers to adults and everyone in between." The subtle heart-shaped bowl on each box suggests to the older consumer that the "whole-grain" cereal is a healthy start to a healthy day. But the Web site also has a section devoted entirely to younger adults, complete with testimonials and "tips from new parents" talking about how Cheerios has helped them to raise happy, healthy children. The language behind Cheerios works because it transcends the traditional societal boundaries of age and adds a sense of authenticity to the product.

24    While you could probably live a happy and healthy existence with Cheerios as your sole cereal choice, there is a substantial segment of the cereal market that demands more. For the cereal-consuming public roughly between the ages of four and fourteen, a different taste and linguistic approach is required. Buzz the Bee, the kid-friendly mascot of Honey Nut Cheerios, pitches the "irresistible taste of golden honey," selling the sweetness of the product to a demographic that craves sweet foods. While the parent knows that his or her child wants the cereal because of its sweet taste (as conveyed through the packaging), Honey Nut Cheerios must still pass the parent test. By putting such statements as "whole-grain" and "13 essential vitamins and minerals" on the box, the product gains authenticity, credibility, and the approval of the parent.

25    Two different messages on one common box effectively markets the same product to both children and parents alike, helping to make Honey Nut Cheerios the number three top-selling cereal in 2004. So with the addition of honey and nuts, General Mills, the producer of the Cheerios line, has filled the gap between toddlers and young adults, and completed the Cheerios cradle-to-grave lifetime hold on the consumer.

26    To take another example, if you want people to think you're hip and healthy, you make sure they see you drinking bottled water—and the fancier the better. No one walking around with a Diet Dr Pepper in hand is looking to impress anybody. These days, there's almost a feeling that soft drinks are exclusively for kids and the uneducated masses. There's a cache to the consumption of water, and expensive and exclusive brands are all the rage. Now, there may be a few people who have such extremely refined, educated taste buds that they can taste the difference between Dasani and Aquafina (I certainly can't), but the connoisseurs of modish waters are more likely than not posers (or, to continue the snobbery theme, poseurs). You won't see many people walking around Cincinnati or Syracuse clutching fancy bottled water. Hollywood, South Beach, and the Upper East Side of New York City are, as usual, another story.

27    There's one final aspect of being the message that impacts what we hear and how we hear it. How our language is delivered can be as important as the words themselves, and no one understands this principle better than Hollywood.

28    At a small table tucked away in the corner of a boutique Italian restaurant on the outskirts of Beverly Hills, I had the opportunity to dine with legendary actors Charles Durning, Jack Klugman, and Dom DeLuise. The entire dinner was a litany of stories of actors, writers, and the most memorable movie lines ever delivered. (Says Klugman, an Emmy Award winner, "A great line isn't spoken, it is delivered.") Best known for his roles in *The Odd Couple* and *Quincy*, Klugman told a story about how Spencer Tracy was practicing his lines for a movie late in his career in the presence of the film's screenwriter. Apparently not pleased with the reading, the writer said to Tracy, "Would you please pay more attention to how you are reading that line? It took me six months to write it," to which Tracy shot back, "It took me thirty years to learn how to say correctly the line that took you only six months to write."

29    Spencer Tracy knew how to be the message—and his shelf of Academy Awards proved it.

**THINKING CRITICALLY**

1. Luntz notes that it is important that words used to describe a brand reflect the "soul" of the brand and its reason for being in business. Why is this element in advertising so important? What happens when the words don't match up with the brand? Explain.

2. What is the personification of a brand? Can you think of other examples in addition to the ones Luntz cites?

3. What is the "company persona"? What role does language play in the creation of an effective company persona? Can you think of some popular companies that have effectively created personas that have influenced our language? Explain.

4. What is "language alignment"? Why is it important? Explain.

5. Luntz notes that it is important to use the "language of [the] consumer" to promote and successfully sell a product. What does he mean? Why is it important?

6. Luntz reviews the success of several brands, such as Ford, and the failures of others, such as GM. Why did Ford succeed and GM fail? What role did language play in Ford's effective marketing and in GM's inability to reach the public?

7. How do companies use language differently to market to children and adults? Explain.

**WRITING ASSIGNMENTS**

1. Luntz explains how companies use language to successfully attract consumers and engender their loyalty. Identify a few companies that successfully meet his criteria for "company persona" and "language alignment." Using the points outlined in his essay, explain why the companies you selected are successful.

2. Write an essay evaluating the advertising techniques of several popular brands today. Select several ads and evaluate how they succeed, or fail, in creating the language alignment necessary to connect with consumers and keep the brand alive. What techniques seem to be the most effective? Be sure to explain your position and support it with examples from real advertisements.

# A Brand by Any Other Name
*Douglas Rushkoff*

Brand-name products target groups of consumers—sometimes large, diverse populations, such as Pepsi or Coke, or very elite ones, such as Fendi or Gucci. The very name of the brand—or its logo—promotes an image the consumer believes he or she will project by having the product. In many ways, brands are a nonverbal language that communicates something about the values of the user. For teens, brands can announce membership in a particular group, value system, and personality type. Douglas Rushkoff explains in the next article that brands are important to teens, who like to think they are hip to the advertising game. But as he explains, it is a game they cannot win.

Douglas Rushkoff is a writer and columnist who analyzes, writes, and speaks about the way people, cultures, and institutions create, share, and influence each other's values. He is the author of many books on new media and popular culture, including *Media Virus* and *Coercion: Why We Listen to What "They" Say,* and the novels *Ecstasy Club* and *Exit Strategy.* His commentaries have aired on *CBS Sunday Morning* and NPR's *All Things Considered* and he has appeared on NBC *Nightly News, Frontline,* and *Larry King Live.* This essay appeared in the April 30, 2000 edition of the *London Times* under the title "Which One of These Sneakers Is Me?"

1  I was in one of those sports "superstores" the other day, hoping to find a pair of trainers for myself. As I faced the giant wall of shoes, each model categorized by either sports affiliation, basketball star, economic class, racial heritage or consumer niche, I noticed a young boy standing next to me, maybe 13 years old, in even greater awe of the towering selection of footwear.

2  His jaw was dropped and his eyes were glazed over—a psycho-physical response to the overwhelming sensory data in a self-contained consumer environment. It's a phenomenon known to retail architects as "Gruen Transfer," named for the gentleman who invented the shopping mall, where this mental paralysis is most commonly observed.

3  Having finished several years of research on this exact mind state, I knew to proceed with caution. I slowly made my way to the boy's side and gently asked him, "What is going through your mind right now?"

4  He responded without hesitation, "I don't know which of these trainers is 'me.'" The boy proceeded to explain his dilemma. He thought of Nike as the most utilitarian and scientifically advanced shoe, but had heard something about third world laborers and was afraid that wearing this brand might label him as too anti-Green. He then considered a skateboard shoe, Airwalk, by an "indie" manufacturer (the trainer equivalent of a micro-brewery) but had recently learned that this company was almost as big as Nike. The truly hip brands of skate shoe were too esoteric for his current profile at school—he'd look like he was "trying." This left the "retro" brands, like Puma, Converse and Adidas, none of which he felt any real affinity for, since he wasn't even alive in the 70s when they were truly and non-ironically popular.

5  With no clear choice and, more importantly, no other way to conceive of his own identity, the boy stood there, paralyzed in the modern youth equivalent of an existential crisis. Which brand am I, anyway?

6  Believe it or not, there are dozens, perhaps hundreds of youth culture marketers who have already begun clipping out this article. They work for hip, new advertising agencies and cultural research firms who trade in the psychology of our children and the anthropology of their culture. The object of their labors is to create precisely the state of confusion and vulnerability experienced by the young shopper at the shoe wall—and then turn this state to their advantage. It is a science, though not a pretty one.

7  Yes, our children are the prey and their consumer loyalty is the prize in an escalating arms race. Marketers spend millions developing strategies to identify children's predilections and then capitalize on their vulnerabilities. Young people are fooled for a while, but then develop defense mechanisms, such as media-savvy attitudes or ironic dispositions. Then marketers research these defenses, develop new countermeasures, and on it goes. The revolutionary impact of a new musical

385 Rushkoff / A Brand by Any Other Name ■ 385

genre is co-opted and packaged by a major label before it reaches the airwaves. The ability of young people to deconstruct and neutralize the effects of one advertising technique are thwarted when they are confounded by yet another. The liberation children experience when they discover the Internet is quickly counteracted by the lure of e-commerce web sites, which are customized to each individual user's psychological profile in order to maximize their effectiveness.

8    The battle in which our children are engaged seems to pass beneath our radar screens, in a language we don't understand. But we see the confusion and despair that results—not to mention the ever-increasing desperation with which even three-year-olds yearn for the next Pokemon trading card. How did we get in this predicament, and is there a way out? Is it your imagination, you wonder, or have things really gotten worse?

9    Alas, things seem to have gotten worse. Ironically, this is because things had gotten so much better.

10    In olden times—back when those of us who read the newspaper grew up— media was a one-way affair. Advertisers enjoyed a captive audience, and could quite authoritatively provoke our angst and stoke our aspirations. Interactivity changed all this. The remote control gave viewers the ability to break the captive spell of television programming whenever they wished, without having to get up and go all the way up to the set. Young people proved particularly adept at "channel surfing," both because they grew up using the new tool, and because they felt little compunction to endure the tension-provoking narratives of storytellers who did not have their best interests at heart. It was as if young people knew that the stuff on television was called "programming" for a reason, and developed shortened attention spans for the purpose of keeping themselves from falling into the spell of advertisers. The remote control allowed young people to deconstruct TV.

11    The next weapon in the child's arsenal was the video game joystick. For the first time, viewers had control over the very pixels on their monitors. The television image was demystified.

12    Lastly, the computer mouse and keyboard transformed the TV receiver into a portal. Today's young people grew up in a world where a screen could as easily be used for expressing oneself as consuming the media of others. Now the media was up for grabs, and the ethic, from hackers to camcorder owners, was "do it yourself."

13    Of course, this revolution had to be undone. Television and Internet programmers, responding to the unpredictable viewing habits of the newly liberated, began to call our mediaspace an "attention economy." No matter how many channels they had for their programming, the number of "eyeball hours" that human beings were willing to dedicate to that programming was fixed. Not coincidentally, the channel surfing habits of our children became known as "attention deficit disorder"—a real disease now used as an umbrella term for anyone who clicks away from programming before the marketer wants him to. We quite literally drug our children into compliance.

14    Likewise, as computer interfaces were made more complex and opaque— think Windows—the do-it-yourself ethic of the Internet was undone. The original Internet was a place to share ideas and converse with others. Children actually had

to use the keyboard! Now, the Internet encourages them to click numbly through packaged content. Web sites are designed to keep young people from using the keyboard, except to enter in their parents' credit card information.

15    But young people had been changed by their exposure to new media. They constituted a new "psychographic," as advertisers like to call it, so new kinds of messaging had to be developed that appealed to their new sensibility.

16    Anthropologists—the same breed of scientists that used to scope out enemy populations before military conquests—engaged in focus groups, conducted "trend-watching" on the streets, in order to study the emotional needs and subtle behaviors of young people. They came to understand, for example, how children had abandoned narrative structures for fear of the way stories were used to coerce them. Children tended to construct narratives for themselves by collecting things instead, like cards, bottlecaps called "pogs," or keychains and plush toys. They also came to understand how young people despised advertising—especially when it did not acknowledge their media-savvy intelligence.

17    Thus, Pokemon was born—a TV show, video game, and product line where the object is to collect as many trading cards as possible. The innovation here, among many, is the marketer's conflation of TV show and advertisement into one piece of media. The show is an advertisement. The story, such as it is, concerns a boy who must collect little monsters in order to develop his own character. Likewise, the Pokemon video game engages the player in a quest for those monsters. Finally, the card game itself (for the few children who actually play it) involves collecting better monsters—not by playing, but by buying more cards. The more cards you buy, the better you can play.

18    Kids feel the tug, but in a way they can't quite identify as advertising. Their compulsion to create a story for themselves—in a world where stories are dangerous—makes them vulnerable to this sort of attack. In marketers' terms, Pokemon is "leveraged" media, with "cross-promotion" on "complementary platforms." This is ad-speak for an assault on multiple fronts.

19    Moreover, the time a child spends in the Pokemon craze amounts to a remedial lesson in how to consume. Pokemon teaches them how to want things that they can't or won't actually play with. In fact, it teaches them how to buy things they don't even want. While a child might want one particular card, he needs to purchase them in packages whose contents are not revealed. He must buy blind and repeatedly until he gets the object of his desire.

20    Worse yet, the card itself has no value—certainly not as a play-thing. It is a functionless purchase, slipped into a display case, whose value lies purely in its possession. It is analogous to those children who buy action figures from their favorite TV shows and movies, with *no intention of ever removing them from their packaging*! They are purchased for their collectible value alone. Thus, the imagination game is reduced to some fictional moment in the future where they will, presumably, be resold to another collector. Children are no longer playing. They are investing.

21    Meanwhile, older kids have attempted to opt out of aspiration, altogether. The "15–24" demographic, considered by marketers the most difficult to wrangle into submission, have adopted a series of postures they hoped would make them

impervious to marketing techniques. They take pride in their ability to recognize when they are being pandered to, and watch TV for the sole purpose of calling out when they are being manipulated. They are armchair media theorists, who take pleasure in deconstructing and defusing the messages of their enemies.

22    But now advertisers are making commercials just for them. Soft drink advertisements satirize one another before rewarding the cynical viewer: "image is nothing," they say. The technique might best be called "wink" advertising, for its ability to engender a young person's loyalty by pretending to disarm itself. "Get it?" the ad means to ask. If you're cool, you do.

23    New magazine advertisements for jeans, such as those created by Diesel, take this even one step further. The ads juxtapose imagery that actually makes no sense—ice cream billboards in North Korea, for example. The strategy is brilliant. For a media-savvy young person to feel good about himself, he needs to feel he "gets" the joke. But what does he do with an ad where there's obviously something to get that he can't figure out? He has no choice but to admit that the brand is even cooler than he is. An ad's ability to confound its audience is the new credential for a brand's authenticity.

24    Like the boy at the wall of shoes, kids today analyze each purchase they make, painstakingly aware of how much effort has gone into seducing them. As a result, they see their choices of what to watch and what to buy as exerting some influence over the world around them. After all, their buying patterns have become the center of so much attention!

25    But however media-savvy kids get, they will always lose this particular game. For they have accepted the language of brands as their cultural currency, and the stakes in their purchasing decisions as something real. For no matter how much control kids get over the media they watch, they are still utterly powerless when it comes to the manufacturing of brands. Even a consumer revolt merely reinforces one's role as a consumer, not an autonomous or creative being.

26    The more they interact with brands, the more they brand themselves.

### THINKING CRITICALLY

1. What does a brand communicate about the person who wears or uses it? What message does the wearer/user seek to convey to others? Explain.

2. Look up the phrase *Gruen transfer* on the Internet. Were you aware of this angle of marketing practice? Does it change the way you think about how products are sold to you?

3. While the boy's dilemma in Rushkoff's introduction is humorous on the surface, it is a serious situation for the teen. Why is his choice of sneaker so important to him? What expectations does he seem to connect with his choice? What could happen if he picks the wrong shoe? How would the wrong choice impact the message he wishes to send to others about who he is and what he values?

4. In paragraph 9, Rushkoff notes that things have gotten worse because they have gotten better. What does he mean? What is the irony of the youth consumer market?

5. Rushkoff notes in paragraph 15 that the youth generation "constitutes a new psychographic." What makes this generation different from previous

generations of consumers? If you are a part of this generation, explain why you think you indeed represent a "new psychographic" or not.

6. In his conclusion, Rushkoff predicts that even media-savvy kids will still "lose" the game. Why will they fail? Explain.

## WRITING ASSIGNMENTS

1. Teens and young adults covet certain brand-name clothing because they believe it communicates a particular message. What defines a brand? Is it something created by the company or by the people who use the product? How does advertising influence the social view we have of ourselves and the brands we use? Write an essay on the connections between advertising and our cultural values of what is "in" or popular and what is not.

2. What makes you want to buy a product? Is it peer influence, cultural pressure, or social status? Do generational marketing techniques, like the ones described by Rushkoff, influence you? Write an essay exploring the way advertising targets specific age groups. Support your essay with information from this article as well as your own consumer experience.

3. Interview several young people between the ages of 12 and 17 about the products they like and why. Inquire what they like about a brand and the reasons why they would not buy a particular brand. Remember to ask them about whether they think brands communicate to their peers something special about them. Evaluate the results in a short essay on the purchasing habits of young consumers.

# Exploring the Language of **V I S U A L S**

## Current Advertisements

Take a look at the following magazine advertisements for different products and services. The sales pitches and marketing techniques take different slants—some relying on hard-sell copy, others hoping to arrest your attention with creative visuals; some taking the informative, even chatty approach, and others making an appeal to emotions. Following each ad is a list of questions to help you analyze the individual spreads and strategies. These questions should help stimulate class discussion and provide ideas for future papers.

## *Nike*

## THINKING CRITICALLY

1. How does this ad for Nike differ from the other sneaker ad in this section, for Skechers? Include an analysis of the model, the language, and the overall impression each ad gives the viewer in your response.

2. Why are the words in the young woman's monologue presented in capital letters? What effect does this give the ad and the message it is trying to convey?

3. Would this ad convey a different message it if did not include the monologue on the right? How might it be different if you could see the entire body of the woman speaking? Explain.

4. Why does the woman in the ad say her butt "herds skinny women away from the best deals at clothing sales?" How could she do this, and why does she think it is important enough to mention?

## Mercedes Benz

Girl Catching Flies. Brighton, May 2000.

**THINKING CRITICALLY**

1. What is the woman looking at? What impact does the ad have as we see what she sees? Explain.

2. The name the photographer gave this photo is "Girl Catching Flies." How does this title connect to the ad and what the product is trying to sell?

3. In what magazines would you expect to see an ad like this? How would it best reach its target audience?

4. Would this ad be as effective if it were a man looking at the car? What if you could see the woman's eyes?

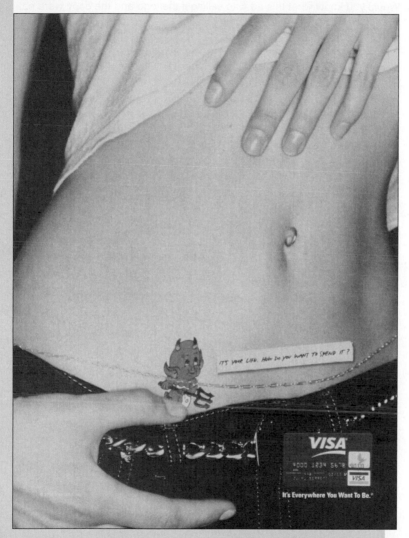

## THINKING CRITICALLY

1. Would you know what this ad was selling if the logo and the copy were not provided? Would there be any ambiguity about what was being sold? How much does this ad depend on name and image recognition? Explain.

2. Where would you expect to see an ad like this and why? If you were an advertising executive, where would you place this ad? How would you target your purchasing public? Explain.

3. This ad uses a fairly racy image to promote the product. What does this image say about Visa? About their feelings about the ad's target audience? Who are they hoping to attract to use their product?

4. In what sort of magazines and other print media would this ad be best placed? Would it work in *People* magazine or *Good Housekeeping*? Explain.

5. Would this ad be as effective if the tattoo were located on a different part of the body? On an arm or shoulder, for example? Why or why not?

## Skechers

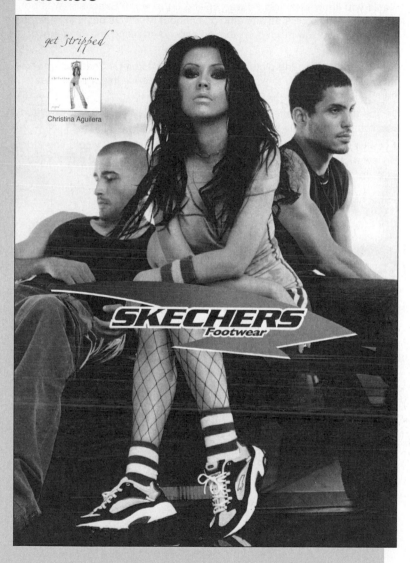

**THINKING CRITICALLY**

1. Would you know what this ad was selling if the word "Skechers" was not in the ad? Would there be any ambiguity about what was being sold in the advertisement? How much does this ad depend on name and image recognition? Explain.

2. Does the woman in the picture represent the product? What consumers are likely to be swayed to purchase Skechers because this woman "wears" them?

3. Do you think this ad effectively sells the product? What words would you use, if any, to make the ad more effective?

4. If you were leafing through a magazine and saw this ad, would you stop to view it? Why or why not? Would you remember the brand it promoted? Explain.

**THINKING CRITICALLY**

1. Review the caption featured in this ad. How does the caption connect to the person in the ad? What message does it convey? What do you need to already know to understand the caption, the message, and who the person in the ad is?

2. Who is the target audience for this ad? Where would you expect to see this ad?

3. How does this ad use Taylor Swift and her expression and pose to project an image about milk?

4. Who drinks milk? Do you think this ad would encourage kids to drink more milk? Adults? Why or why not?

| THE FUTURE OF PRINT MEDIA

## Out of Print
*Eric Alterman*

While newspapers in the United States have enjoyed a long and prosperous life of almost 300 years, it appears that their days may be numbered. Readership is down, with only 19 percent of Americans between the ages 18 and 34 admitting to even looking at a daily newspaper. In the last five years alone, industry giants such as the *Rocky Mountain News,* the *Baltimore Examiner,* and the *Cincinnati Post* have bit the dust. Others, such as the acclaimed *Christian Science Monitor* and the *Seattle Post-Intelligencer,* have been forced to adopt hybrid online/print or online-only models. Other forms of news have emerged, mostly online, as people increasingly turn to the Internet for their daily dose of information. Is print really dead?

Eric Alterman is a professor of English and a critically acclaimed journalist. He is a columnist for *The Nation,* a columnist for *Moment* magazine, and a regular contributor to *The Daily Beast.* He is the author of seven books, including the national bestsellers *What Liberal Media? The Truth About Bias and the News* (2004) and *The Book on Bush: How George W. (Mis)leads America* (2004). His articles have appeared in *Rolling Stone, Mother Jones,* and *The Sunday Express* among others. This article was first published by *The New Yorker* on March 31, 2008.

1   Few believe that newspapers in their current printed form will survive. Newspaper companies are losing advertisers, readers, market value, and, in some cases, their sense of mission at a pace that would have been barely imaginable just four years ago. Bill Keller, the executive editor of the *Times,* said recently in a speech in London, "At places where editors and publishers gather, the mood these days is funereal. Editors ask one another, 'How are you?,' in that sober tone one employs with friends who have just emerged from rehab or a messy divorce." Keller's speech appeared on the Web site of its sponsor, the *Guardian,* under the headline "NOT DEAD YET."

2   Perhaps not, but trends in circulation and advertising—the rise of the Internet, which has made the daily newspaper look slow and unresponsive; the advent of Craigslist, which is wiping out classified advertising—have created a palpable sense of doom. . . . America's most prized journalistic possessions are suddenly looking like corporate millstones. Rather than compete in an era of merciless transformation, the families that owned the Los Angeles *Times* and the *Wall Street Journal* sold off the majority of their holdings. The New York Times Company has seen its stock decline by fifty-four per cent since the end of 2004, with much of the loss coming in the past year; in late February, an analyst at Deutsche Bank recommended that clients sell off their Times stock. The Washington Post Company has avoided a similar fate only by rebranding itself an "education and media company"; its testing and prep company, Kaplan, now brings in at least half the company's revenue.

3    Until recently, newspapers were accustomed to operating as high-margin monopolies. To own the dominant, or only, newspaper in a mid-sized American city was, for many decades, a kind of license to print money. In the Internet age, however, no one has figured out how to rescue the newspaper in the United States or abroad. Newspapers have created Web sites that benefit from the growth of on-line advertising, but the sums are not nearly enough to replace the loss in revenue from circulation and print ads.

4    Most managers in the industry have reacted to the collapse of their business model with a spiral of budget cuts, bureau closings, buyouts, layoffs, and reductions in page size and column inches. Since 1990, a quarter of all American newspaper jobs have disappeared. The columnist Molly Ivins complained, shortly before her death, that the newspaper companies' solution to their problem was to make "our product smaller and less helpful and less interesting." That may help explain why the dwindling number of Americans who buy and read a daily paper are spending less time with it; the average is down to less than fifteen hours a month. Only nineteen per cent of Americans between the ages of eighteen and thirty-four claim even to look at a daily newspaper. The average age of the American newspaper reader is fifty-five and rising.

5    Philip Meyer, in his book "The Vanishing Newspaper" (2004), predicts that the final copy of the final newspaper will appear on somebody's doorstep one day in 2043. It may be unkind to point out that all these parlous trends coincide with the opening, this spring, of the $450-million Newseum, in Washington, D.C., but, more and more, what Bill Keller calls "that lovable old-fashioned bundle of ink and cellulose" is starting to feel like an artifact ready for display under glass.

6    Taking its place, of course, is the Internet, which is about to pass newspapers as a source of political news for American readers. For young people, and for the most politically engaged, it has already done so. As early as May, 2004, newspapers had become the least preferred source for news among younger people. According to "Abandoning the News," published by the Carnegie Corporation, thirty-nine per cent of respondents under the age of thirty-five told researchers that they expected to use the Internet in the future for news purposes; just eight per cent said that they would rely on a newspaper. It is a point of ironic injustice, perhaps, that when a reader surfs the Web in search of political news he frequently ends up at a site that is merely aggregating journalistic work that originated in a newspaper, but that fact is not likely to save any newspaper jobs or increase papers' stock valuation.

7    Among the most significant aspects of the transition from "dead tree" news-papers to a world of digital information lies in the nature of "news" itself. The American newspaper (and the nightly newscast) is designed to appeal to a broad audience, with conflicting values and opinions, by virtue of its commitment to the goal of objectivity. Many newspapers, in their eagerness to demonstrate a sense of balance and impartiality, do not allow reporters to voice their opinions publicly, march in demonstrations, volunteer in political campaigns, wear political buttons, or attach bumper stickers to their cars. . . .

8    Meanwhile, public trust in newspapers has been slipping at least as quickly as the bottom line. A recent study published by Sacred Heart University found that fewer than twenty per cent of Americans said they could believe "all or most"

media reporting, a figure that has fallen from more than twenty-seven per cent just five years ago. "Less than one in five believe what they read in print," the 2007 "State of the News Media" report, issued by the Project for Excellence in Journalism, concluded. "CNN is not really more trusted than Fox, or ABC than NBC. The local paper is not viewed much differently than the New York *Times*." Vastly more Americans believe in flying saucers and 9/11 conspiracy theories than believe in the notion of balanced—much less "objective"—mainstream news media. Nearly nine in ten Americans, according to the Sacred Heart study, say that the media consciously seek to influence public policies, though they disagree about whether the bias is liberal or conservative.

9    No less challenging is the rapid transformation that has taken place in the public's understanding of, and demand for, "news" itself. Rupert Murdoch, in a speech to the American Society of Newspaper Editors, in April, 2005—two years before his five-billion-dollar takeover of Dow Jones & Co. and the *Wall Street Journal*—warned the industry's top editors and publishers that the days when "news and information were tightly controlled by a few editors, who deigned to tell us what we could and should know," were over. No longer would people accept "a godlike figure from above" presenting the news as "gospel." Today's consumers "want news on demand, continuously updated. They want a point of view about not just what happened but why it happened. . . . And finally, they want to be able to use the information in a larger community—to talk about, to debate, to question, and even to meet people who think about the world in similar or different ways."

10    One month after Murdoch's speech, a thirty-one-year-old computer whiz, Jonah Peretti, and a former A.O.L. executive, Kenneth Lerer, joined the ubiquitous commentator-candidate-activist Arianna Huffington to launch a new Web site, which they called the Huffington Post. First envisaged as a liberal alternative to the Drudge Report, the Huffington Post started out by aggregating political news and gossip; it also organized a group blog, with writers drawn largely from Huffington's alarmingly vast array of friends and connections. Huffington had accumulated that network during years as a writer on topics from Greek philosophy to the life of Picasso, as the spouse of a wealthy Republican congressman in California, and now, after a divorce and an ideological conversion, as a Los Angeles-based liberal commentator and failed gubernatorial candidate.

11    Almost by accident, however, the owners of the Huffington Post had discovered a formula that capitalized on the problems confronting newspapers in the Internet era, and they are convinced that they are ready to reinvent the American newspaper. "Early on, we saw that the key to this enterprise was not aping Drudge," Lerer recalls. "It was taking advantage of our community. And the key was to think of what we were doing through the community's eyes."

12    On the Huffington Post, Peretti explains, news is not something handed down from above but "a shared enterprise between its producer and its consumer." Echoing Murdoch, he says that the Internet offers editors "immediate information" about which stories interest readers, provoke comments, are shared with friends, and generate the greatest number of Web searches. An Internet-based news site, Peretti contends, is therefore "alive in a way that is impossible for paper and ink."

13      Though Huffington has a news staff (it is tiny, but the hope is to expand in the future), the vast majority of the stories that it features originate elsewhere, whether in print, on television, or on someone's video camera or cell phone. The editors link to whatever they believe to be the best story on a given topic. Then they repurpose it with a catchy, often liberal-leaning headline and provide a comment section beneath it, where readers can chime in. Surrounding the news articles are the highly opinionated posts of an apparently endless army of both celebrity (Nora Ephron, Larry David) and non-celebrity bloggers—more than eighteen hundred so far. The bloggers are not paid. The over-all effect may appear chaotic and confusing, but, Lerer argues, "this new way of thinking about, and presenting, the news, is transforming news as much as CNN did thirty years ago." Arianna Huffington and her partners believe that their model points to where the news business is heading. "People love to talk about the death of newspapers, as if it's a foregone conclusion. I think that's ridiculous," she says. "Traditional media just need to realize that the online world isn't the enemy. In fact, it's the thing that will save them, if they fully embrace it."

14      It's an almost comically audacious ambition for an operation with only forty-six full-time employees—many of whom are barely old enough to rent a car. But, with about eleven million dollars at its disposal, the site is poised to break even on advertising revenue of somewhere between six and ten million dollars annually. What most impresses advertisers—and depresses newspaper-company executives—is the site's growth numbers. In the past thirty days, thanks in large measure to the excitement of the Democratic primaries, the site's "unique visitors"—that is, individual computers that clicked on one of its pages—jumped to more than eleven million, according to the company. And, according to estimates from Nielsen NetRatings and comScore, the Huffington Post is more popular than all but eight newspaper sites, rising from sixteenth place in December.

15      Arthur Miller once described a good newspaper as "a nation talking to itself." If only in this respect, the Huffington Post is a great newspaper. It is not unusual for a short blog post to inspire a thousand posts from readers—posts that go off in their own directions and lead to arguments and conversations unrelated to the topic that inspired them. Occasionally, these comments present original perspectives and arguments, but many resemble the graffiti on a bathroom wall.

16      The notion that the Huffington Post is somehow going to compete with, much less displace, the best traditional newspapers is arguable on other grounds as well. The site's original-reporting resources are minuscule. The site has no regular sports or book coverage, and its entertainment section is a trashy grab bag of unverified Internet gossip. And, while the Huffington Post has successfully positioned itself as the place where progressive politicians and Hollywood liberal luminaries post their anti-Bush Administration sentiments, many of the original blog posts that it publishes do not merit the effort of even a mouse click.

17      Additional oddities abound. Whereas a newspaper tends to stand by its story on the basis of an editorial process in which professional reporters and editors attempt to vet their sources and check their accuracy before publishing, the blogosphere relies on its readership—its community—for quality control. At the Huffington Post, Jonah Peretti explains, the editors "stand behind our front page" and do their

best to insure that only trusted bloggers and reliable news sources are posted there. Most posts inside the site, however, go up before an editor sees them. Only if a post is deemed by a reader to be false, defamatory, or offensive does an editor get involved.

18      The Huffington Post's editorial processes are based on what Peretti has named the "mullet strategy." ("Business up front, party in the back" is how his trend-spotting site BuzzFeed glosses it.) "User-generated content is all the rage, but most of it totally sucks," Peretti says. The mullet strategy invites users to "argue and vent on the secondary pages, but professional editors keep the front page looking sharp. The mullet strategy is here to stay, because the best way for Web companies to increase traffic is to let users have control, but the best way to sell advertising is a slick, pretty front page where corporate sponsors can admire their brands."

19      This policy is hardly without its pitfalls. During the Hurricane Katrina crisis, the activist Randall Robinson referred, in a post, to reports from New Orleans that some people there were "eating corpses to survive." When Arianna Huffington heard about the post, she got in touch with Robinson and found that he could not support his musings; she asked Robinson to post a retraction. The alacrity with which the correction took place was admirable, but it was not fast enough to prevent the false information from being repeated elsewhere. . . .

20      Traditional newspaper men and women tend to be unimpressed by the style of journalism practiced at the political Web sites. Operating on the basis of a Lippmann-like reverence for inside knowledge and contempt for those who lack it, many view these sites the way serious fiction authors might view the "novels" tapped out by Japanese commuters on their cell phones. Real reporting, especially the investigative kind, is expensive, they remind us. Aggregation and opinion are cheap.

21      And it is true: no Web site spends anything remotely like what the best newspapers do on reporting. Even after the latest round of new cutbacks and buyouts are carried out, the *Times* will retain a core of more than twelve hundred newsroom employees, or approximately fifty times as many as the Huffington Post. The Washington *Post* and the Los Angeles *Times* maintain between eight hundred and nine hundred editorial employees each. The *Times*' Baghdad bureau alone costs around three million dollars a year to maintain. And while the Huffington Post shares the benefit of these investments, it shoulders none of the costs.

22      Despite the many failures at newspapers, the vast majority of reporters and editors have devoted years, even decades, to understanding the subjects of their stories. It is hard to name any bloggers who can match the professional expertise, and the reporting, of, for example, the *Post*'s Barton Gellman and Dana Priest, or the *Times*' Dexter Filkins and Alissa Rubin.

23      In October, 2005, at an advertisers' conference in Phoenix, Bill Keller complained that bloggers merely "recycle and chew on the news," contrasting that with the *Times*' emphasis on what he called "a 'journalism of verification,' " rather than mere "assertion."

24      "Bloggers are not chewing on the news. They are spitting it out," Arianna Huffington protested in a Huffington Post blog. Like most liberal bloggers, she takes exception to the assumption by so many traditional journalists that their work

is superior to that of bloggers when it comes to ferreting out the truth. The ability of bloggers to find the flaws in the mainstream media's reporting of the Iraq war "highlighted the absurdity of the knee jerk comparison of the relative credibility of the so-called MSM and the blogosphere," she said, and went on, "In the run-up to the Iraq war, many in the mainstream media, including the New York *Times*, lost their veneer of unassailable trustworthiness for many readers and viewers, and it became clear that new media sources could be trusted—and indeed are often much quicker at correcting mistakes than old media sources."

25        But Huffington fails to address the parasitical relationship that virtually all Internet news sites and blog commentators enjoy with newspapers. The Huffington Post made a gesture in the direction of original reporting and professionalism last year when it hired Thomas Edsall, a forty-year veteran of the Washington *Post* and other papers, as its political editor. At the time he was approached by the Huffington Post, Edsall said, he felt that the *Post* had become "increasingly driven by fear—the fear of declining readership, the fear of losing advertisers, the fear of diminishing revenues, the fear of being swamped by the Internet, the fear of irrelevance. Fear drove the paper, from top to bottom, to corrupt the entire news operation." Joining the Huffington Post, Edsall said, was akin to "getting out of jail," and he has written, ever since, with a sense of liberation. But such examples are rare.

26        And so even if one agrees with all of Huffington's jabs at the *Times*, and Edsall's critique of the Washington *Post*, it is impossible not to wonder what will become of not just news but democracy itself, in a world in which we can no longer depend on newspapers to invest their unmatched resources and professional pride in helping the rest of us to learn, however imperfectly, what we need to know.

27        In a recent episode of "The Simpsons," a cartoon version of Dan Rather introduced a debate panel featuring "Ron Lehar, a print journalist from the Washington *Post*." This inspired Bart's nemesis Nelson to shout, "Haw haw! Your medium is dying!"

28        "Nelson!" Principal Skinner admonished the boy.

29        "But it is!" was the young man's reply.

30        Nelson is right. Newspapers are dying; the evidence of diminishment in economic vitality, editorial quality, depth, personnel, and the over-all number of papers is everywhere. What this portends for the future is complicated. Three years ago, Rupert Murdoch warned newspaper editors, "Many of us have been remarkably, unaccountably complacent . . . quietly hoping that this thing called the digital revolution would just limp along." Today, almost all serious newspapers are scrambling to adapt themselves to the technological and community-building opportunities offered by digital news delivery, including individual blogs, video reports, and "chat" opportunities for readers. Some, like the *Times* and the *Post*, will likely survive this moment of technological transformation in different form, cutting staff while increasing their depth and presence online. Others will seek to focus themselves locally. Newspaper editors now say that they "get it." Yet traditional journalists are blinkered by their emotional investment in their Lippmann-like status as insiders. They tend to dismiss not only most blogosphere-based criticisms but also the messy democratic ferment from which these criticisms emanate. The Chicago *Tribune* recently felt compelled to shut down comment boards on its Web site for

all political news stories. Its public editor, Timothy J. McNulty, complained, not without reason, that "the boards were beginning to read like a community of foul-mouthed bigots."

31    Arianna Huffington, for her part, believes that the online and the print newspaper model are beginning to converge: "As advertising dollars continue to move online—as they slowly but certainly are—HuffPost will be adding more and more reporting and the *Times* and *Post* model will continue with the kinds of reporting they do, but they'll do more of it originally online." She predicts "more vigorous reporting in the future that will include distributed journalism—wisdom-of-the-crowd reporting of the kind that was responsible for the exposing of the Attorneys General firing scandal." As for what may be lost in this transition, she is untroubled: "A lot of reporting now is just piling on the conventional wisdom—with important stories dying on the front page of the New York *Times*.". . .

32    And so we are about to enter a fractured, chaotic world of news, characterized by superior community conversation but a decidedly diminished level of first-rate journalism. The transformation of newspapers from enterprises devoted to objective reporting to a cluster of communities, each engaged in its own kind of "news"—and each with its own set of "truths" upon which to base debate and discussion—will mean the loss of a single national narrative and agreed-upon set of "facts" by which to conduct our politics. News will become increasingly "red" or "blue." This is not utterly new. Before Adolph Ochs took over the *Times*, in 1896, and issued his famous "without fear or favor" declaration, the American scene was dominated by brazenly partisan newspapers. And the news cultures of many European nations long ago embraced the notion of competing narratives for different political communities, with individual newspapers reflecting the views of each faction. It may not be entirely coincidental that these nations enjoy a level of political engagement that dwarfs that of the United States.

33    The transformation will also engender serious losses. By providing what Bill Keller, of the *Times*, calls the "serendipitous encounters that are hard to replicate in the quicker, reader-driven format of a Web site"—a difference that he compares to that "between a clock and a calendar"—newspapers have helped to define the meaning of America to its citizens. To choose one date at random, on the morning of Monday, February 11th, I picked up the paper-and-ink New York *Times* on my doorstep, and, in addition to the stories one could have found anywhere—Obama defeating Clinton again and the Bush Administration's decision to seek the death penalty for six Guantánamo detainees—the front page featured a unique combination of articles, stories that might disappear from our collective consciousness were there no longer any institution to generate and publish them. These included a report from Nairobi, by Jeffrey Gettleman, on the effect of Kenya's ethnic violence on the country's middle class; a dispatch from Doha, by Tamar Lewin, on the growth of American university campuses in Qatar; and, in a scoop that was featured on the Huffington Post's politics page and excited much of the blogosphere that day, a story, by Michael R. Gordon, about the existence of a study by the RAND Corporation which offered a harsh critique of the Bush Administration's performance in Iraq. The juxtaposition of these disparate topics forms both a baseline of knowledge for the paper's readers and a picture of the world they inhabit. In

"Imagined Communities" (1983), an influential book on the origins of nationalism, the political scientist Benedict Anderson recalls Hegel's comparison of the ritual of the morning paper to that of morning prayer: "Each communicant is well aware that the ceremony he performs is being replicated simultaneously by thousands (or millions) of others of whose existence he is confident, yet of whose identity he has not the slightest notion." It is at least partially through the "imagined community" of the daily newspaper, Anderson writes, that nations are forged.

34      Finally, we need to consider what will become of those people, both at home and abroad, who depend on such journalistic enterprises to keep them safe from various forms of torture, oppression, and injustice. "People do awful things to each other," the veteran war photographer George Guthrie says in "Night and Day," Tom Stoppard's 1978 play about foreign correspondents. "But it's worse in places where everybody is kept in the dark." Ever since James Franklin's *New England Courant* started coming off the presses, the daily newspaper, more than any other medium, has provided the information that the nation needed if it was to be kept out of "the dark." Just how an Internet-based news culture can spread the kind of "light" that is necessary to prevent terrible things, without the armies of reporters and photographers that newspapers have traditionally employed, is a question that even the most ardent democrat in John Dewey's tradition may not wish to see answered.

## THINKING CRITICALLY

1. What accounts for the rapid decline of America's newspapers? What support does Alterman provide to support this claim?

2. Alterman notes that many newspapers that still survive have "lost their sense of mission." What is a newspaper's mission? Can you think of missions ascribed to certain publications?

3. Do you read a newspaper? How do you locate news in general—on television? Online? Do you think about where news comes from and who writes it? Explain.

4. Alterman notes that many people who get their news from the Internet fail to realize that it is usually repackaged content from a printed newspaper report. If newspapers fail, what could happen to this content? To our ability to obtain information? Explain.

5. According to Alterman, why should we be concerned about the death of print?

6. What makes *The Huffington Post* different from other news sources? Do you read *The Huffington Post*?

7. Did anything about print media, both past and present, covered in this essay surprise you? Identify a point, fact, or connection highlighted by Alterman that you were unaware of. How did it influence your viewpoint on this subject? Why?

## WRITING ASSIGNMENTS

1. In your opinion, what is the future of printed media such as newspapers and magazines? In addition to facts presented in this article, draw upon your own experience. How might media be different in the next decade as a result of changes happening now? Include the positive as well as negative possibilities.

2. Select a breaking news story and research it via three media outlets—online, in print, and on the television news. Evaluate the details of the reporting, including the information and possible bias in the report. Which outlet provided the best reporting and why?

3. Research the "fourth estate" and freedom of the press. What implications, if any, does the loss of newspaper reporting have on our freedom of speech and access to information? Write an essay in which you explore what the future might be like, if, as Alterman suggests, by 2043 there were no newspapers.

---

# Is Print Dead?

*J. A. Konrath*

There is little doubt that technology changes things. Some inventions that seemed remarkable 20 years ago are now obsolete. Is print one such entity? On the one hand, print is where words are captured for posterity—from oral tradition to print, the words of Homer's *Iliad* and *Odyssey* still speak forth through millennia. On the other hand, in a digital world, fewer people seem to want to pay for words printed on paper. Will the words of Homer be captured forever on the screen of a Kindle? Or are e-books themselves just another step in the evolution of print? Here, J. A. Konrath "interviews" the print industry.

J. A. Konrath is the author of the Jack Daniels thriller series. The latest, *Stirred*, was published in 2011. Others in the series include *Bloody Mary* (2005), *Rusty Nail* (2006), *Dirty Martini* (2007), *Fuzzy Navel* (2008), *Cherry Bomb* (2009), and *Shaken* (2010). Under the name Jack Kilborn, Konrath wrote the horror novels *Afraid* (2009), *Trapped* (2010), *Endurance* (2010), and *Draculas* (2010). A true child of the digital revolution, Konrath has sold 46,000 self-published e-books on Kindle since April 2009. You can visit him at jakonrath.blogspot.com. This spoof interview with the print industry was published May 21, 2010 in *The Huffington Post*.

**MODERATOR:** Welcome to Obsolete Anonymous! I've gathered you all here to welcome our latest member, the Print Industry.

**PRINT INDUSTRY:** Hello, everyone. But there's been a mistake. I don't belong here.

(chuckles all around)

**PRINT INDUSTRY:** I'm serious. I'm not obsolete. I'm relevant. Print books have been around for hundreds of years. They're never going to be replaced.

**VHS TAPES:** Yeah, we all thought like that once.

**LP RECORDS:** It's called denial. It's tough to deal with at first.

**PRINT INDUSTRY:** Look, everyone, I assume you all think that ebooks are going to put me out of business. But that won't happen.

**PHONE COMPANY:** I remember when you couldn't walk twenty yards in a city without seeing a pay phone. Then those gosh darn cell phones came along. Do you know some people don't even have land lines anymore?

(Phone Company begins to cry. Print Phonebooks joins in. So does Dial Up Modems. Encyclopedia Set, wearing an I Hate Wikipedia T-Shirt, pops a few Prozac. A group hug ensues.)

**VIDEO RENTAL STORE:** What Phone Company is trying to say is that when a technology comes along that's faster, easier, and cheaper, the old technology—and all the companies that supported it—tends to fade away.

**PRINT INDUSTRY:** Why are you here, Video Rental Store? There are a lot of you around.

**CDS:** There were record stores everywhere once.

**CASSETTE TAPES:** Hell yeah! They sold cassettes, too! Someone give me a high five!

(no one gives Cassette Tapes a high five)

**VIDEO RENTAL STORE:** Things looked good for a while. I had a decent run. Then I got hit by all sides. Netflix. On Demand. Tivo. YouTube. But the nail in the coffin came in the past two years. Hulu. Roku—which allows subscribers to stream video instantly. iTunes and Amazon offering movie downloads. Red Box, which rents DVDs for 99 cents and takes up no more space than a candy machine . . .

**PRINT INDUSTRY:** But ebooks are just a tiny percentage of the market. People have been reading print since Gutenberg. They won't adapt to change that easily.

**SLR CAMERAS:** You're correct. It takes a few years for people to fully embrace new technology. Some never do. Instant Cameras never replaced me.

**INSTANT CAMERAS:** Shut up, SLR. We both got our butts kicked by digital. How much film did you sell last year?

**TV ANTENNAS:** I'm still big in some third world countries!

**TYPEWRITER:** The bottom line is, when technology improves, it becomes widely adopted. Me and Carbon Paper used to have a groovy thing going. I'd make the words, he would make the duplicates. Then Copy Machine got into the act, but he's not doing well now either.

**COPY MACHINE:** Effing computers.

**DOT MATRIX PRINTER:** Effing laser and inkjet. Doesn't anyone else miss tearing off the perforated hole punches on the side of paper? Don't they miss the feel and smell of that?

**FOLD-OUT PAPER MAPS:** I agree! Isn't it fun to open up a big map while you're driving, in hopes of figuring out where you are? Don't you miss the old days before cars came equipped with GPS and no one ever used that upstart, MapQuest?

**CDS:** Effing internet. That's the problem. Instant access to information and entertainment for the whole world. You guys want to talk about pirating and illegal downloads?

(everyone shouts out "no!")

**MODERATOR:** We all read on JA Konrath's blog that the way to fight piracy is with cost and convenience. Print Industry, are you lowering your prices and making it easier for customers to download your books?

**PRINT INDUSTRY:** Actually, we just raised prices on our ebooks.

(all-around sighs and head shaking)

**MODERATOR:** Well, far be it for you to learn from any of our mistakes. Are you making it easier at least?

**PRINT INDUSTRY:** Well, we've begun windowing titles, releasing them months after the hardcover comes out.

(collective head slapping)

**MUSIC INDUSTRY:** Have you at least tried selling from your own site? I wish I'd done that. But then Apple came along . . .

**PRINT INDUSTRY:** Uh . . . no. We haven't tried that. In fact, some ebooks—we'll use JA Konrath as an example since he was mentioned—aren't even available on all platforms and in all territories.

**MODERATOR:** What do you mean? Konrath's ebooks are available all over the place.

**PRINT INDUSTRY:** Those are the ones he uploads himself. The ones of his that we sell are missing from several key markets, and have been for years. But it's okay. We're paying him much smaller royalties and jacking the prices up high so we can still make a profit. Besides, ebooks are a niche market. Ereading devices are dedicated and expensive.

**ARCADES:** I used to be a thriving industry. Kids dropped millions of quarters in my thousands of locations. But then Nintendo, Sony, and Microsoft made home arcade machines, and now people play their videogames on dedicated devices. It's a multi-billion dollar business now, and I can only compete if I sell pizza and give out plastic trinkets to kids with the most foosball tickets. If people want the media, they buy the expensive device. Period.

**PRINT INDUSTRY:** None of you are listening to me. Print will always be around.

**NEWSPAPER INDUSTRY:** Yeah! What he said!

**PRINT INDUSTRY:** Let's not compare ourselves, okay Newspaper Industry? No offense.

**NEWSPAPER INDUSTRY:** None taken. Hey, maybe we can help each other. I'm selling advertising space for dirt cheap these days, and . . .

**PRINT INDUSTRY:** No thanks. No one reads you anymore. People get their news elsewhere.

**MODERATOR:** So why won't people get their novels elsewhere as well?

(Print Industry stands up, pointing a finger around the room.)

**PRINT INDUSTRY:** Look, this isn't about me. All of you guys have become irrelevant. Technology marched on, and you didn't march with it. But that WILL NOT happen to me. There will always be bookstores, and dead tree books. We'll continue to sell hardcovers at luxury prices, and pay artists 6% to 15% royalties on whatever list price WE deem appropriate. And the masses will buy our books BECAUSE WE SAID SO! WE SHALL NEVER BECOME OBSOLETE!!!

**BUGGY WHIP INDUSTRY:** Amen, brother! That's what I keep trying to tell these people!

**CDS:** (whispering to LPs) I give him six years, tops.

**THINKING CRITICALLY**

1. What issue is this spoof interview highlighting? How does the author use humor to make a point? What are the points he is trying to make?

2. What other obsolete products and industries are included in the spoof? What happened to them? What is likely to happen to the products and industries that replaced them?

3. What "arguments" does Print Industry give as to why "he" doesn't belong at Obsolete Anonymous? Why are his arguments invalid? What arguments, if any, would have been better for him to make in justifying his status as relevant? Explain.

4. The author of this piece distributes his work primarily through e-publishing. Does this influence his depiction of the print industry? Why or why not?

---

# Are We Reaching Da Youth?

*Danny Schechter*

Declining newspaper sales and fewer eyeballs on the evening news have media moguls worried. Where is everyone going for their news? For some, it is the Internet; for others, the radio; and in the case of the growing and vitally important youth market, it is nowhere at all. Why is the younger generation tuning out altogether? Danny Schechter believes that young adults "reject" the news because big journalism rejects *them*.

Danny Schechter is a television producer, independent filmmaker, blogger, and media critic who writes and lectures frequently about the media. His impressive background in media includes producing the ABC newsmagazine *20/20,* for which he won two Emmy Awards and was nominated for two others. Schechter joined the start-up staff at CNN. He is the executive editor of MediaChannel.org, for which he is the "blogger-in-chief" and writes a nearly 3,000-word daily blog entry on media and society. He is the author of several books, including *Media Wars: News at a Time of Terror* (2003) and *The More You Watch, The Less You Know* (1999). This essay was first published in the Winter 2003 issue of *The Neiman Report.*

1 First, a scene setter: Please don't call it a screed. Journalism tends to look up. Most news is about older people. It is about people in power. Presidents and potentates. Corporations. Celebrities. The Rich and Famous. It is about the people running things and the people who want to run things. And when it's not about their glories, it's about their darker sides, their scandals and deceits. And when it's not about them—the Innies—it's about estranged outsiders, losers and the lost-lone gunmen, suicide desperados, corporate criminals, everyday crooks, and ordinary victims. Body counts galore.

2 Victims are roadkill on the electronic highway to ratings heaven.

3 On TV, there's a daily parade of sound bites and press conferences brought to us by news guys who look like jocks with great haircuts and perky blondes standing in front of buildings yakking through thick makeup like political science majors. Presidential candidates compete with movie stars. Madonna is writing children's books. Cookbook connoisseur Martha Stewart is arranging flowers in courtrooms. A rap mogul is now a black political leader. Howard Stern is the King of All Media. Don Imus has become a caricature of himself. Jay Leno offers a launching pad for candidates.

4     And Fox News is anything but news.

5     Even the dream machine on the small screen has been reduced to inspiring us to survive "Temptation Island," not get thrown out of the "Big Brother" House, win a rose and a relationship from the hunk-like Bachelor or, if you are a "Bad Boy," delight in those 15 seconds of fame outrunning "Cops."

6     Reality television is anything but reality.

7     This is the media environment all in the know concede has been dumbed down for years. Even serious people can't take it seriously. As news biz merges into show biz, *Time* magazine calls war "militainent" and politics "electotainment." Facts are what they say they are like WMDs in Iraq or a fair vote in Florida. News-lite does not make Americans very bright. A recent study took note of pervasive misperceptions among TV news viewers.

8     When younger people are not downloading libraries of recorded music from the Internet, or piercing their noses and tattooing their behinds, they now get their "news" from late night TV, the Comedy Channel or "The Onion." Attitude is what excites them, not information. For most, it's not even cool to read newspapers or vote. The turnouts prove that.

9     There are so many distractions, so little time: DVDs, video games, comic books and video games. The channels are many. The choices are full. The voices are few. They don't watch news. How do I know? Watch the ads. The advertisers, whose business it is to watch who is watching, know. That's why there are so many commercials for Viagra, stomach remedies, and arthritis medications. In TV jargon, newscasts "skew old."

10     That's why Al Gore, who started out wanting to launch a liberal TV alternative, has been persuaded that a youth-oriented channel is the way to go. His new TV venture will use stealth "lifestyle" programming to politicize by appearing not to. If Fox News is the stern, finger-wagging, Archie Bunker-like, patriotically correct party-liner on the right, Gore, who has greened, pastel shirts and all, has become a permissive do-your-own-thinger. For him, depoliticizing politics is the only hope. He will learn that pandering won't work. Honesty and authenticity might.

## Meshing News and Music

11     I've written books, such as *The More You Watch, the Less You Know*, to explain what is going on with news these days. But I have also collaborated on some music projects hoping to zone into this apolitical zeitgeist to try to reach younger people who seem to have tuned out on so many fronts. (This does not include a whole generation of young activists crusading on the environment, human rights, peace and global justice issues.)

12     As the father of a hip media-savvy 20-something, I have had an up-close and personal education about why my orientation towards big ideas and political engagement doesn't always connect. ("If it's too loud, dad, you're too old.") When I was her age, I believed with Abbie Hoffman that "you can't trust anyone over 30." Now it sometimes feels like you can't trust anyone under 50.

13     Over the years, from my days in rock 'n' roll broadcasting, I have seen the way popular culture leads politics. As a result, I've been involved with multiartist

music benefits to promote awareness on important issues: from "No Nukes" in 1979 (about nuclear power) to "Sun City" in 1985 (against apartheid), from "Give Peace a Chance" in 1991 (trying to stop the first Gulf War) to "We Are Family" in the immediate aftermath of September 11th (an appeal for tolerance).

14    As the editor of Mediachannel.org, a global media Web site, I am now focusing on media issues by creating CDs with the musician/producer Polar Levine, who records as "polarity/1." Our first, in 1997, used hip-hop to take on what we call "News Goo." Here is a sample lyric:

> Communication Breakdown! Pause for this message. Wake up!
> Every station is identification
> Global syndication is shaping the nation. ABC-Disney, NBC-GE.
> Murdoch is Foxy and we're the hen, He owns the pen, the camera, the sword.
> Buy a Coke, buy a Ford. Gettin broke? Getting bored?
> Selling attitude like food for the masses. Junk consumption. We're lumpen
> A bumpkin to the corporate state.
> You cannot satiate what you can't negotiate
> Your will's been snatched, The bill's attached
> Flim-flam diagram, data-jam, handicam Caught it, Yo, ya bought it
> A mind is a profitable thing to waste. Ya want another taste, baby? We got
> CHORUS:
> News Goo—What we need to know
> News Goo—What we want to know
> News Goo—What we think we know
> Got remote control to choose the show.
> But the more we watch, the less we know
> Ignorance grows on the spirit like a tumor . . . till freedom is a rumor

15    The song is provocative and hard charging, but getting it on the air in this age of hyper media consolidation in radio is, shall we say, problematic. It has been played on alternative radio and Internet radio stations worldwide. Boston's WBCN, the radio station where I spent a decade dissecting news that is now owned by Viacom, which is one of the companies crusading for larger media monopolies, won't play it. No surprise there.

16    In 2003, at the height of the Iraq War, we went another way, making "Media Wars," named after another of my books. This track is an audio collage to a funky electronica groove track that uses comments of mine and some "rapping" that is intercut with bits of TV news broadcasts and presidential pronouncements. Levine explains on his popCULTmedia Web site: "The TV sound bites have—in no way—been manipulated to create a context different from that which was intended. The off-the-cuff remarks made by many of our leading, highly influential TV infotainers, who pass for presenters of news, reveal much about the current state of a once vigorous press. Fox News's 'fair, unbiased' commentary speaks for itself in the pride it takes in being 'unafraid' to serve as propagandists for Washington's right wing political establishment."

17    Songs like these won't transform the media or "elevate" a generation of news rejectors. How many will even hear them? They are an expression of a dissenting

point of view that tends to get marginalized anyway. But they do flow out of the theory that believes that if the news business is to reach this audience, it will have to speak its language and echo its concerns. Far too much of our news ignores young people or puts them down. All too often they are stereotyped as troublemakers to fear, not learn from. Their rejection of "the news" might be a reaction to big journalism's rejection of them.

18    Ya dig?

### THINKING CRITICALLY

1. According to Schechter, where do young people get the news? Why should it matter to big journalism? To society as a whole?

2. Do you consider yourself part of the "youth market" demographic? If so, where do you go for information? Do you read newspapers or watch television news? Why or why not? If you do not identify with this segment, explain where you get your information and why your generation differs from the current youth market.

3. Why does Schechter use the hip-hop song "News Goo" to illustrate his point? Is it effective? Why or why not?

4. Why is youth rejecting big journalism? What, if anything, can be done to entice youth back?

5. What is the meaning of Schechter's title? What is his use of language trying to do? Explain.

### WRITING ASSIGNMENTS

1. Most of us are aware of major events even if we fail to read a newspaper or watch the news regularly. Discuss the impact and role of TV news and newspaper reporting on informing you about events such as the war in Iraq, the civil rights movement, school shootings, the destruction of the Twin Towers of the World Trade Center, natural disasters in the United States and abroad, suicide bombings in Israel, or some other highly visible current event. How do you first learn of world events? Where do you turn for more information? How do you gauge what is reliable information and what is hype?

2. Conduct a poll on campus on where students get the news and their desire to remain informed about current events, local and national politics, and international happenings. Interview at least 25 people from a variety of majors and disciplines. Then write a response to Schechter's essay, answering his question "Are we reaching the youth?" and explain why his concerns are well-founded or in error.

# Will the Death of Newspapers Also Kill Our Freedoms?
*Frank Watson*

The term *the fourth estate* applies most commonly to news media and especially print journalism. The phrase is used to describe social or political forces "whose influence is not consistently or officially recognized." In the United States, it is often connected to the concept of freedom of the press, that is, the idea that the press is independent of government and able to speak the truth outside of political influences. In this next editorial, Frank Watson wonders what could happen to our freedoms when print media is no longer the primary way we obtain our information.

Frank Watson has been involved with the Web since it started. He has worked with most of the major web analytics companies and pioneered the ability to tie online marketing to offline conversion. He moderates many Internet industry forums. This editorial appeared in *Search Engine Watch* on September 24, 2010.

1 There has been much noise made about the shrinking circulation of printed newspapers and how the role of journalists will survive in this online age. Many people give it a moment's thought and continue with their daily lives, thinking it doesn't really apply to them. Yet if they would take a moment to think about it, they may see how the limited future of journalists could eventually result in the loss of a number of their freedoms.

## The Future of News

2 Would Bob Woodward and Carl Bernstein's stories about Watergate have found their way onto an online publication? Do stories of political corruption have any impact these days?

3 We re-elect dishonest politicians quite regularly. Many of the people who vote for them don't know what they have done in any great detail. And in this age of Enron and the like, such transgressions have become mere human frailties we're willing to overlook.

4 But people really should be concerned with the future of our news, online or otherwise. While I may not be a huge Rupert Murdoch fan and think some of his ideas are anachronistic, I share his concerns. The web has given people the belief that they shouldn't pay for information.

## Google Shock

5 Hey, Google is there for us to search and find what we really want to know, they even have a news tab up there on the right if we want to drill a little deeper in to an article we saw briefly as we surfed the endless cable TV stations we watch in the background as we Twitter or Facebook or play online games.

6 We live in the world Alvin Toffler wrote about in "Future Shock" more than 40 years ago. We're bombarded by information, with too many choices to make. So we segment, settle for shorter or more niched information, and forget about the basics we all as citizens of the world or a specific country need to keep up with to be truly involved with our "worlds."

7 How many people in the United States really understand what the Tea Party stands for? How many heard President Obama's speech the other day where it appeared he was calling on African Americans to take control of their destinies in an almost rise up and revolt tone reminiscent of the Black Panthers of old?

8 The reach of the ideologies of both of these opposed positions is lost in the noise of the banal items we must wade through to get to stories of worth. This isn't the fault just of our modern technological, distraction-filled lives. Economic factors also need to be considered.

## What Would Journalists Do?

9 The days of community newspapers is rapidly coming to an end. Well, at least the independent news gatherers of yore.

10   I'll be surprised if the journalism degree is even offered in 20 years. Where are reporters supposed to get their experience? Blogging? Writing press releases for various companies or politicians? Or maybe aggregating stories from the few remaining mainstream sources of news?

11   That last one I truly doubt. I recently interviewed for a position doing search engine optimization (SEO) for Reuters—one of the historical bastions of reporting. During the interview, I was told the company really didn't care about the numerous areas of news beyond those that appeal to their core demographic: men who pay for their financial information.

12   Reuters didn't have plans to concentrate on areas that didn't appeal to this demographic (e.g., social news, entertainment news, and even hard news) moving forward. The founders of this 200-year-old company must want to shoot lightening bolts from the heavens.

## Somebody Check My Brain

13 This dilution of what is actually covered is where we risk our freedom. People with influence can control what we get to see. The guilds and unions that have fought to keep the Fourth Estate alive have lost their power and we really don't seem to care.

14   And it is here that the voices of both the Tea Party and Obama's recent call to arms have true merit. Whatever your political alignment, there is a need to be aware of their meanings.

15   The World Wide Web isn't a savior. It needs us to interact with it thinkingly.

## Pay-Per-Freedom?

16 Would you pay for your online news? Current trends do not seem to support this idea. Interestingly, a local Hawaiian online paper that regularly charges its readers $20 a month allowed readers free access to the stories about politics to foster better informed citizenry. The broadcast television stations used to do the same thing until happy talk showed greater viewers and caught more advertising dollars.

17   True, there are alternative monetization models. Online advertising success can be tracked so well and so granularly. Unfortunately this isn't truly understood by the people who run major news sources.

## Newsosaurs

18 As newspapers watch the primary source of their income rapidly dwindling, their panic doesn't give them clear insight. The new media seem like upstarts—and they are.

19   Although newspapers were rocked by radio and television and survived, the new media is different. Many viewed it for far too long as just another medium they would slowly adapt to. Unfortunately, this is the one that will replace them, replace their form.

20   Kindles and iPads and all sorts of new distribution methods yet invented will take down the printed word. The printed word—if people in the right places, including the world's citizenry allow it—but not the word.

21    I hope there are always careers for writers who want to research and communicate to us the wrongs and ills and counter viewpoints we so need. I will never rely on 140 characters to tell me all about my world. But I will take tips and recommendations from the medium on what I should find out more about and see things from others' perspectives.

22    Hopefully, as printed newspapers disappear, reporters, publishing companies, and the general public continue to appreciate the need for independent writers.

### THINKING CRITICALLY

1. Watson states "people really should be concerned with the future of our news." Why does he think people should be paying attention to this issue? Do you agree? Why or why not?

2. How is the phenomenon of having too many choices leaving us with fewer choices? Explain.

3. Watson conjectures that journalism degrees will not even be offered in 20 years. Based on the information in his editorial, as well as others in this section, do you think he might be right? Why or why not?

4. In what ways does Watson tie the issue of print media to the security of our personal freedoms? Explain.

5. Watson asks, "Would you pay for your online news?" Answer his question with your own viewpoint, explaining why you would or would not.

### WRITING ASSIGNMENTS

1. One statistic notes that just under 20 percent of people under 35 read newspapers regularly. Over the course of a week, read several different newspapers (local, national, and even international) and explain why the reporting is (or is not) relevant to people under 35. If you wish, provide some solutions to help make newspapers more accessible to this segment of the population.

2. You have been hired as a newspaper editor who must turn around the dwindling readership of the local daily paper. Conduct a survey on what people want to read in the daily news. Consider your questions carefully. After gathering your information, design your revised paper (on paper or online) and explain in detail the rationale behind your new design. How much does your newspaper resemble others already in print? What distinguishes your paper? Or do you rely on popular conventions already in place? Explain.

# Freedom of Speech and the Editorial Cartoon
*Doug Marlette*

Editorial cartoons rely on visual clichés to convey their messages instantly. That is, they employ stock figures for their representation, images instantly recognizable from cultural stereotypes—the fat-cat tycoon, the mobster thug, the sexy female movie star. And these come to us in familiar outfits and with props that give away their identities and professions. The cartoon judge has a black robe and gavel; the prisoner wears striped overalls and a ball and chain; the physician dons a smock and forehead light; the doomsayer is a scrawny longhaired guy carrying a sign saying, "The end is near." These are visual clichés known by the culture at large, and we "get" them. Editorial cartoonists communicate their humor reliant upon the viewpoints and experiences of their audience.

Today, editorial cartoons are disappearing from the nation's newspapers. Some editors, fearful of angering their readers, are eliminating these features from newspapers or refusing to run editorial cartoons. As newspaper readership declines, cartoonists are often the positions first cut from the editorial pages. But in the next article, editorial cartoonist Doug Marlette, creator of "Kudzu" and of many single-frame cartoons, explains how editorial cartoonists provide the "acid test" of the First Amendment. What happens when the cartoonists, who convey unpopular sentiments, are finally silenced? The ramifications may be more far-reaching than we realize.

Doug Marlette is a Pulitzer Prize–winning artist who has worked for *The Charlotte Observer, The Atlanta Constitution*, and *New York Newsday*. He is the author of numerous books, including *Shred This Book: The Scandalous Cartoons of Doug Marlette* (1988), *Gone With the Kudzu* (1995), and *I Feel Your Pain* (1996). NBC's *Sunday Today Show* regularly animates his editorial cartoons to highlight current events. This article was first published in the Winter 2004 issue of the *Neiman Reports*.

1 Kurt Vonnegut once compared the artist to the canary in the coal mine, a hypersensitive creature who alerts hardier life forms to toxic gases by kindly dropping dead. Given the steady demise of editorial cartoonists during the past several years, newspapers might begin to wonder about the quality of the air.

2 Cartoonists have been keeling over in startling numbers—down from almost 200 just 20 years ago to fewer than 90 today. The poisonous fumes laying us low are the byproduct of the corporate culture that has engulfed newspapering during the past two decades. It is a bottom-line cult of efficiency that threatens not just my own profession but the integrity of journalism and hence the unruly spirit of democracy.

3 That is old news, and we've all heard reasons for the disappearance of the editorial cartoon. Circulation is down and budgets are tight. Newsprint costs soar. Editors forced to cut budgets look around and find the expendable employee, or the person least like them: the guy or gal who just draws pictures.

4 Newspapers have survived challenges for 200 years, from the rise of the telegraph to radio and television and now 24/7 cable news programming. That is because the newspaper's indispensable function has been to shape its community's very identity through the distinctive voices and personalities on its pages. Cartoons are the most accessible window into the character of the paper and its town. Yet more and more publishers are convincing themselves that they don't need a local pen or brush representing them on the editorial page. Instead of having an artist who will continue to shape and reflect the soul of their community, they get by cherry-picking canned (and cheap) cartoons from syndicates.

## Cartoons and the Bottom Line

5 When I started drawing editorial cartoons in the 1970s, the profit margins on which newspapers operated were 12 to 14 percent. Today, it's upwards of 25 percent. Most businesses—even Halliburton and Enron—have been content with five percent.

We are told that newspaper operating capital in the low-to-mid-20s—which, by the way, is on a par with that of pharmaceutical companies—is necessary because so much is required for production. By defining solvency up, the newspaper industry has switched its priorities from the public trust to the wealth of an increasingly centralized community of shareholders.

6    The fate of the editorial cartoonists demonstrates how this not only disserves society but also undermines the future the bottom-line watchers are trying to safeguard. Newspapers are playing not to lose when they should be playing to win.

7    Consider how the managers are pursuing the central mandate of their business model: to constantly expand readership. Their position is: "How can we expand readership if we make people mad? Anything that makes people think risks offending them and loses readership." That the editorial cartoonists' very reason for being is to provoke helps explain why they are the first to go. (From the same impulse, the old traditions of flirting, horseplay, razzing, smoking and drinking, have been filtered from the newsroom by means of human resources reeducation camps.)

8    Cartoonists represent the untidy, untamable forces that corporate suits have always waged war on. We represent instinct, and we work in the most powerful, primitive and unsettling of vocabularies: images. Cave painting is not the same as hunting and gathering. And cartoonists reach the reading public in a place where words just cannot go.

## Cartoons and the First Amendment

9    But what does the obsolescence of the editorial cartoonist have to do with the health of the democracy? Cartoons are the acid test of the First Amendment. They push the boundaries of free speech by the very qualities that have endangered them: Cartoons are hard to defend. They strain reason and logic. They can't say "on the other hand." And for as long as cartoons exist, Americans can be assured that we still have the right and privilege to express controversial opinions and offend powerful interests. The rise of a passive generation of parent-pleasing perfection monkeys makes preserving that prerogative seem more urgent than ever. "Minding" is an overrated virtue.

10    When we don't exercise our freedom of expression in troublesome ways, we may atrophy our best impulses. The First Amendment, the miracle of our system, is not just a passive shield of protection. In order to maintain our true, nationally defining diversity of ideas, it obligates journalists to be bold, writers to be full-throated and uninhibited, and those blunt instruments of the free press, cartoonists like me, not to self-censor. In order not to lose it, we must use it, swaggering and unapologetic.

11    The insidious unconsciousness of self-censorship can be discerned in the quality of editorial cartoons today. Increasingly in my profession, careerism seems to have replaced risk-taking. Proficiency stands in for talent. Too many cartoons look like art by committee. Emotional distancing has replaced the raw torque of yesterday's best. Nobody feels; nobody cares. Nothing is brought up. And the controversies that are generated seem to result as much from the cartoon's ineptness as its challenging content. Cartoonists have become victims of our cultural irony,

delivering postmodern sneers rather than true passion or outrage. Where do they stand? Nobody ever wondered that about Herblock or Conrad.

12    When I got into the business, American political cartooning was in the midst of a renaissance. The sixties, in all their cultural and political agitation, had reinvigorated the form. A generation of artists raised on television and *Mad* magazine was further egged on and taunted by Australian Pat Oliphant's juicy draftsmanship and incendiary content. Bob Dylan said recently that if he were starting out in today's sterile pop music world, he wouldn't go into music. I know just how he feels. I'm not sure that spirit can be revived, but I'd like to think so. My immodest proposal as I peek out of the slits in my bunker is that newspapers should save themselves by following not the business model but that model of survival, Mother Nature. A newspaper is an ecosystem, the health of which depends on the fitness of its symbiotic parts. When you eliminate one species, you threaten the vitality of the whole. If only cartoonists were valued as much as snail darters.

13    But we are only canaries.

### THINKING CRITICALLY

1. What connection does Kurt Vonnegut's comparison of artists to the "canary in the coal mine" have to editorial cartoonists? What is the canary to which he refers, and why is it an effective parallel to editorial cartoons?
2. According to Marlette, why are editorial cartoonists "the first to go" when cuts are made at newspapers? Why do editors feel they are expendable? Why does Marlette disagree?
3. How has our social consciousness of what we can and cannot say or communicate influenced editorial cartooning? Explain.
4. How is self-censorship affecting the quality of editorial cartoons?

### WRITING ASSIGNMENTS

1. Marlette notes that cartoonists' "very reason for being" is to provoke. Why is it important to do this? What role does provocation have in our society? How is it connected to freedom of speech? How would our culture be different if cartoonists were not allowed to provoke?
2. In his conclusion, Marlette observes that the "insidious unconsciousness of self-censorship can be discerned in the quality of editorial cartoons today." Research online the history of editorial cartoons and write an essay addressing Marlette's criticism. How do cartoons today compare to those 30, 50, and even 80 years ago?
3. Take a look at some political cartoons that deal with the same issue, such as immigration, the presidential race, gender, the economy, and so forth. How did different cartoonists present the situation? What perspectives do they offer?
4. After reading Marlette's article, collect five to ten cartoons from magazines and/or newspapers, such as from *The New Yorker's Cartoon Bank* or Daryl Cagle's *Cartoon Index*. Try to identify as many elements as you can for each cartoon and write a short essay on why cartoons are important—or not important—to our social consciousness.

# Exploring the Language of **V I S U A L S**

## Editorial Cartoons

For an editorial cartoon to be effective, it must make the issue clear at a glance and it must establish where it stands on the argument. Its success is often dependent on its audience sharing the cartoonist's political perspective, or at least the cartoonist's perspective of the issue, situation, or people it is trying to depict. As you view the cartoons, consider how they each make a claim and harbor certain assumptions about their audience. What "stand" is the cartoonist taking on the issue, event, or situation he or she depicts? And what evidence does the cartoonist offer to support this position?

### *Talk Now*

## THINKING CRITICALLY

1. What cultural assumptions does this cartoon make? What does its viewer need to know in order to understand it?

2. What is happening in this cartoon? What ironies does it present? What issue is it holding up for scrutiny?

## *Only a Theory*

MORIN
*THE MIAMI HERALD*
Miami
USA

DINOSAUR

HOWEVER, KEEP IN MIND THIS IS ONLY A THEORY...

MORIN
CWS/NYTS

### THINKING CRITICALLY

1. How does the cartoonist use visual clichés to tell a story in this cartoon? What background does the viewer need in order to understand the cartoon?

2. What issue is this cartoon addressing? What is the meaning of the woman's words? What is the twist?

## Best Student

### THINKING CRITICALLY

1. What is happening in this cartoon? What message is the cartoonist trying to convey? What "evidence" does the cartoonist provide to support his position?

2. Examine the characters in this cartoon. What is the meaning of all the awards in the background? What award is being conferred upon the graduate?

3. Would this cartoon be as funny 20 years ago? Twenty years in the future? Why or why not?

## MAKING CONNECTIONS

1. Choose a brand-name product you use regularly and one of its competitors—products whose differences are negligible, if they exist at all. Examine some advertisements for each brand. Write a short paper explaining what really makes you prefer your brand.

2. William Lutz characterizes the language used in ads as "weasel words"—that is, language that pretends to do one thing while really doing another. Explore your campus for examples of weasel words. Look not only at ads but also at material such as university brochures and pamphlets that are sent to prospective students and any political contests taking place (e.g., students running for the student government or candidates for office speaking at your campus). Write down all examples of weasel words and report back to your classmates.

3. Have you ever read a political cartoon that offended you? What was the nature of the cartoon, and why did it bother you? Explain.

4. One of life's little frustrations is reading a cartoon you just do not "get." You ask friends and family to explain the cartoon to you with little success. Locate a cartoon that you have difficulty understanding and bring it to class. In groups, discuss the cartoons and their possible meanings. If possible, suggest ways to clarify the joke either by refining the drawing or changing the wording.

5. What will happen to our freedom of information and objective truth if newspapers indeed go out of print? What about if newspapers were monopolized under one publisher? Describe what impact this situation could have on other media, such as the Internet.

6. Discuss the role editorial cartoons play in American culture. How are they used as a communication medium? How do they entertain? Refer to specific examples in your response. Are they indeed, as Marlette fears, endangered?

# Political Wordplay 8

425

Political language is a language of power. It influences government policy and action, identifies the dominant values of the moment, and wins votes. Likewise, it is language that is capable of making war, establishing peace, and electing presidents. However, political language also reflects the political needs of its users at a particular time. Thus, it has a reputation for being flexible and ambiguous or, worse, evasive and irresponsible as politicians shift the language to achieve their personal agendas. It is this "shifty" nature of political language that has contributed to the traditional American distrust of politicians and their promises. The essays in this chapter explore the various ways in which political language persuades the masses, manipulates words and meanings, promotes or supports certain value systems, and influences public opinion.

## Politically Speaking

The first section of this chapter examines how political language persuades the public by tapping into its common beliefs, fears, anxieties, hopes, and expectations. This political wordplay comes in many forms, some more damaging than others. If the fundamental objective of political wordplay is to bend minds, its misuse may have dangerous implications. That misuse of language is the subject of the first selection, "How to Detect Propaganda," composed in 1937 by members of the former Institute for Propaganda Analysis—a group that monitored the various kinds of political propaganda circulating before and during World War II. This timeless piece examines the particular rhetorical devices that constitute propaganda and serves as a tool for understanding the language of political manipulation. In the next selection, professional word-watcher William Lutz defines the different kinds of "doublespeak" used by government bureaucrats in "Doubts About Doublespeak." Propaganda and doublespeak are especially prevalent in times of conflict, as Jon Hooten discusses the language of war in "Fighting Words: The War Over Language."

The last two articles in this section work together with two speeches in the second section to focus on a special sort of political wordplay—the presidential speech. We know that such speeches are very important to how the public perceives the president. For example, the verbal mishaps of George W. Bush gave liberals a lot to squawk about, while making some conservatives feel more connected to a "real guy" who was just bumbling through like the rest of us. Barack Obama's campaign speeches were recognized by many as the making of the man—he reached the public through his visionary words and inspiring sentences. While most people know that speechwriters help the president's addresses to the public, this does not seem to detract from the power of the presidential speech. Anna Marie Trester explores the nuances of presidential speech in "Do You Speak Presidential?" in which she explains that it isn't just what you say but how you say it that distinguishes a successful speaker from a less memorable one. Then Richard O'Mara examines the speeches of the current man in the Oval Office, Barack Obama. It seems that everything this man says is scrutinized and dissected for meaning.

## Speaking Out: Language That Inspired Us

The second section of this chapter examines how language can be used to motivate and inspire us. Some of the people featured in these essays took great personal risk in using their voices to confront issues connected to racism, sexism, personal liberty, or inequality. Often speaking for a powerless or silenced segment of society, these speakers inspired their audiences and encouraged people to think about things differently through their speech. First, the matter of civil rights is addressed by Martin Luther King, Jr., in "Letter from Birmingham Jail," in which he argues compellingly that nonviolent protest can end racist hatred and bigotry. Sojourner Truth lends her voice as both a woman and a former slave to the issue of equality and fairness in "Ain't I a Woman?" The last readings in the section focus on two inaugural speeches: those of John F. Kennedy and Barack Obama, who, while separated by almost 50 years, are both recognized as young, charismatic speakers. John F. Kennedy's famous inaugural address, with its often quoted (and at times, misquoted) phrase, "Ask not what your country can do for you—ask what you can do for your country" comes first. From a former president to a more recent one, the next reading is Barack Obama's inaugural address, one of the most widely attended speeches in presidential history. As you read the articles and inspect the visuals in this section, consider how words and actions challenge us to think and how the power of language can change the world.

# | POLITICALLY SPEAKING

# How to Detect Propaganda
*Institute for Propaganda Analysis*

During the late 1930s, like today, political propaganda was rife, both in the United States and abroad. In 1937, Clyde R. Miller of Columbia University founded the Institute for Propaganda Analysis to expose propaganda circulating at the time. With the backing of several prominent businesspeople, the institute continued its mission for nearly five years, publishing various pamphlets and monthly bulletins to reveal its findings. The following essay is a chapter from one of its pamphlets. It presents a specific definition of propaganda, with an analysis of seven common devices necessary to bend truth—and minds—to political causes.

1 If American citizens are to have clear understanding of present-day conditions and what to do about them, they must be able to recognize propaganda, to analyze it, and to appraise it.

2    But what is propaganda?

3    As generally understood, *propaganda is expression of opinion or action by individuals or groups deliberately designed to influence opinions or actions of*

*other individuals or groups with reference to predetermined ends.* Thus propaganda differs from scientific analysis. The propagandist is trying to "put something across," good or bad, whereas the scientist is trying to discover truth and fact. Often the propagandist does not want careful scrutiny and criticism; he wants to bring about a specific action. Because the action may be socially beneficial or socially harmful to millions of people, it is necessary to focus upon the propagandist and his activities using the searchlight of scientific scrutiny. Socially desirable propaganda will not suffer from such examination, but the opposite type will be detected and revealed for what it is.

4    We are fooled by propaganda chiefly because we don't recognize it when we see it. It may be fun to be fooled but, as the cigarette ads used to say, it is more fun to know. We can more easily recognize propaganda when we see it if we are familiar with the seven common propaganda devices. These are:

1. The Name Calling Device

2. The Glittering Generalities Device

3. The Transfer Device

4. The Testimonial Device

5. The Plain Folks Device

6. The Card Stacking Device

7. The Band Wagon Device

5    Why are we fooled by these devices? Because they appeal to our emotions rather than to our reason. They make us believe and do something we would not believe or do if we thought about it calmly, dispassionately. In examining these devices, note that they work most effectively at those times when we are too lazy to think for ourselves; also, they tie into emotions which sway us to be "for" or "against" nations, races, religions, ideals, economic and political policies and practices, and so on through automobiles, cigarettes, radios, toothpastes, presidents, and wars. With our emotions stirred, it may be fun to be fooled by these propaganda devices, but it is more fun and infinitely more to our own interests to know how they work.

6    Lincoln must have had in mind citizens who could balance their emotions with intelligence when he made this remark ". . . but you can't fool all of the people all of the time."

## Name Calling

7    "Name Calling" is a device to make us form a judgment without examining the evidence on which it should be based. Here the propagandist appeals to our hate and fear. He does this by giving "bad names" to those individuals, groups, nations, races, policies, practices, beliefs, and ideals which he would have us condemn and reject. For centuries the name "heretic" was bad. Thousands were oppressed, tortured, or put to death as heretics. Anybody who dissented from popular or group

belief or practice was in danger of being called a heretic. In the light of today's knowledge, some heresies were bad and some were good. Many of the pioneers of modern science were called heretics; witness the cases of Copernicus, Galileo, Bruno. Today's bad names include: Fascist, demagogue, dictator, Red, financial oligarchy, Communist, muckraker, alien, outside agitator, economic royalist, Utopian, rabble-rouser, trouble-maker, Tory, Constitution-wrecker.

8    "Al" Smith called Roosevelt a Communist by implication when he said in his Liberty League speech, "There can be only one capital, Washington or Moscow." When "Al" Smith was running for the presidency many called him a tool of the Pope, saying in effect, "We must choose between Washington and Rome." That implied that Mr. Smith, if elected President, would take his orders from the Pope. Likewise Mr. Justice Hugo Black has been associated with a bad name, Ku Klux Klan. In these cases some propagandists have tried to make us form judgments without examining essential evidence and implications. "Al Smith is a Catholic. He must never be President." "Roosevelt is a Red. Defeat his program." "Hugo Black is or was a Klansman. Take him out of the Supreme Court."

9    Use of "bad names" without presentation of their essential meaning, without all their pertinent implications, comprises perhaps the most common of all propaganda devices. Those who want to *maintain the status quo* apply bad names to those who would change it. . . . Those who want to *change the status quo* apply bad names to those who would maintain it. For example, the *Daily Worker* and the *American Guardian* apply bad names to conservative Republicans and Democrats.

## Glittering Generalities

10    "Glittering Generalities" is a device by which the propagandist identifies his program with virtue by use of "virtue words." Here he appeals to our emotions of love, generosity, and brotherhood. He uses words like truth, freedom, honor, liberty, social justice, public service, the right to work, loyalty, progress, democracy, the American way, Constitution-defender. These words suggest shining ideals. All persons of good will believe in these ideals. Hence the propagandist, by identifying his individual group, nation, race, policy, practice, or belief with such ideals, seeks to win us to his cause. As Name Calling is a device to make us form a judgment to *reject and condemn* without examining the evidence, Glittering Generalities is a device to make us *accept and approve* without examining the evidence.

11    For example, use of the phrases, "the right to work" and "social justice," may be a device to make us accept programs for meeting labor-capital problems which, if we examined them critically, we would not accept at all.

12    In the Name Calling and Glittering Generalities devices, words are used to stir up our emotions and to befog our thinking. In one device "bad words" are used to make us mad; in the other "good words" are used to make us glad.

13    The propagandist is most effective in the use of these devices when his words make us create devils to fight or gods to adore. By his use of the "bad words," we personify as a "devil" some nation, race, group, individual, policy, practice, or ideal; we are made fighting mad to destroy it. By use of "good words," we personify as a godlike idol some nation, race, group, etc. Words which are "bad" to some are

"good" to others, or may be made so. Thus, to some the New Deal is "a prophecy of social salvation" while to others it is "an omen of social disaster."

14    From consideration of names, "bad" and "good," we pass to institutions and symbols, also "bad" and "good." We see these in the next device.

## Transfer

15    "Transfer" is a device by which the propagandist carries over the authority, sanction, and prestige of something we respect and revere to something he would have us accept. For example, most of us respect and revere our church and our nation. If the propagandist succeeds in getting church or nation to approve a campaign in behalf of some program, he thereby transfers its authority, sanction, and prestige to that program. Thus we may accept something which otherwise we might reject.

16    In the Transfer device, symbols are constantly used. The cross represents the Christian Church. The flag represents the nation. Cartoons like Uncle Sam represent a consensus of public opinion. Those symbols stir emotions. At their very sight, with the speed of light, is aroused the whole complex of feelings we have with respect to church or nation. A cartoonist by having Uncle Sam disapprove a budget for unemployment relief would have us feel that the whole United States disapproves relief costs. By drawing an Uncle Sam who approves the same budget, the cartoonist would have us feel that the American people approve it. Thus the Transfer device is used both for and against causes and ideas.

## Testimonial

17    The "Testimonial" is a device to make us accept anything from a patent medicine or a cigarette to a program of national policy. In this device the propagandist makes use of testimonials. "When I feel tired, I smoke a Camel and get the grandest 'lift.'" "We believe the John L. Lewis plan of labor organization is splendid; C.I.O. should be supported." This device works in reverse also; counter-testimonials may be employed. Seldom are these used against commercial products like patent medicines and cigarettes, but they are constantly employed in social, economic, and political issues. "We believe that the John L. Lewis plan of labor organization is bad; C.I.O. should not be supported."

## Plain Folks

18    "Plain Folks" is a device used by politicians, labor leaders, businessmen, and even by ministers and educators to win our confidence by appearing to be people like ourselves—"just plain folks among the neighbors." In election years especially do candidates show their devotion to little children and the common, homey things of life. They have front porch campaigns. For the newspaper men they raid the kitchen cupboard, finding there some of the good wife's apple pie. They go to country picnics; they attend service at the old frame church, they pitch hay and go fishing; they show their belief in home and mother. In short, they would win our votes by showing that they're just as common as the rest of us—"just plain folks"—and,

therefore, wise and good. Businessmen often are "plain folks" with the factory hands. Even distillers use the device. "It's our family's whiskey, neighbor; and neighbor, it's your price."

## Card Stacking

19 "Card Stacking" is a device in which the propagandist employs all the arts of deception to win our support for himself, his group, nation, race, policy, practice, belief, or ideal. He stacks the cards against the truth. He uses under-emphasis and over-emphasis to dodge issues and evade facts. He resorts to lies, censorship, and distortion. He omits facts. He offers false testimony. He creates a smoke screen of clamor by raising a new issue when he wants an embarrassing matter forgotten. He draws a red herring across the trail to confuse and divert those in quest of facts he does not want revealed. He makes the unreal appear real and the real appear unreal. He lets half-truth masquerade as truth. By the Card Stacking device, a mediocre candidate, through the "build-up," is made to appear an intellectual titan; an ordinary prize fighter, a probable world champion; a worthless patent medicine, a beneficent cure. By means of this device propagandists would convince us that a ruthless war of aggression is a crusade for righteousness. Some member nations of the Non-Intervention Committee send their troops to intervene in Spain. Card Stacking employs sham, hypocrisy, effrontery.

## The Band Wagon

20 The "Band Wagon" is a device to make us follow the crowd, to accept the propagandist's program en masse. Here his theme is: "Everybody's doing it." His techniques range from those of medicine show to dramatic spectacle. He hires a hall, fills a great stadium, marches a million men in parade. He employs symbols, colors, music, movement, all the dramatic arts. He appeals to the desire, common to most of us, to "follow the crowd." Because he wants us to "follow the crowd" in masses, he directs his appeal to groups held together by common ties of nationality, religion, race, environment, sex, vocation. Thus propagandists campaigning for or against a program will appeal to us as Catholics, Protestants, or Jews; as members of the Nordic race or as Negroes; as farmers or as school teachers; as housewives or as miners. All the artifices of flattery are used to harness the fears and hatreds, prejudices, and biases, convictions and ideals common to the group; thus emotion is made to push and pull the group on to the Band Wagon. In newspaper articles and in the spoken word this device is also found. "Don't throw your vote away. Vote for our candidate. He's sure to win." Nearly every candidate wins in every election—before the votes are in.

## Propaganda and Emotion

21 Observe that in all these devices our emotion is the stuff with which propagandists work. Without it they are helpless; with it, harnessing it to their purposes, they can make us glow with pride or burn with hatred, they can make us zealots in behalf of

the program they espouse. As we said at the beginning, propaganda as generally understood is expression of opinion or action by individuals or groups with reference to predetermined ends. Without the appeal to our emotion—to our fears and to our courage, to our selfishness and unselfishness, to our loves and to our hates—propagandists would influence few opinions and few actions.

22   To say this is not to condemn emotion, an essential part of life, or to assert that all predetermined ends of propagandists are "bad." What we mean is that the intelligent citizen does not want propagandists to utilize his emotions, even to the attainment of "good" ends, without knowing what is going on. He does not want to be "used" in the attainment of ends he may later consider "bad." He does not want to be gullible. He does not want to be fooled. He does not want to be duped, even in a "good" cause. He wants to know the facts and among these is included the fact of the utilization [of] his emotions.

23   Keeping in mind the seven common propaganda devices, turn to today's newspapers and almost immediately you can spot examples of them all. At election time or during any campaign, Plain Folks and Band Wagon are common. Card Stacking is hardest to detect because it is adroitly executed or because we lack the information necessary to nail the lie. A little practice with the daily newspapers in detecting these propaganda devices soon enables us to detect them elsewhere—in radio, newsreel, books, magazines, and in expression[s] of labor unions, business groups, churches, schools, and political parties.

### THINKING CRITICALLY

1.  Look at the definition of the word *propaganda* in paragraph 3. How many sets of people are involved—how many parties does it take to make propaganda? What are the roles or functions of each set of people?

2.  Supply an example of the way emotion overrides reason for each of the seven common propaganda devices the authors identify.

3.  Can you supply "bad names" from your own experience as a student? Some examples to get you started might include "geek," "nerd," and "teacher's pet" to refer to students; you can probably think of some generic terms for teachers as well. Compare these terms to the definition of propaganda. Do you think these terms qualify as propaganda?

4.  How are name calling and glittering generalities similar devices? How are they different? What do the authors of the document say? What additional features can you find?

5.  How do transfer, testimonial, and plain-folks devices all make use of power or prestige to influence our thinking? Can you think of something or someone you respect that could be used as a propaganda device—for example, a major sporting event, such as the Super Bowl, or a football hero?

6.  Give examples of times in your life when you have used the card stacking or band wagon devices to try to get something you wanted—such as permission from a parent or an excused absence from a teacher.

7.  What is the difference between "the propagandist" and "the scientist" in paragraph 3? What is their relationship to "truth and fact"? What is their relationship to each other? What is their relationship to the language they use?

8. What is "socially desirable propaganda"? Can you give examples from your own experience? Do you think that socially desirable propaganda uses the same devices that the authors of this article identify? Consider the safe-sex campaigns you have been exposed to.

**WRITING ASSIGNMENTS**

1. Based on your understanding of the whole article and on class discussion, develop your own definition of propaganda. Make sure you define each key term that you use.

2. Following the suggestions set down in the final paragraph of this essay, collect examples of propaganda from at least five different sources. Examine them, and then describe in a paper what devices they use. How do the creators of each kind of propaganda show that they are aware of their audience's emotions? What emotions do they appeal to? How much truth and fact do they seem to rely on?

3. Research and collect newspaper articles on an election—a race for student government on your campus, a recent town or state proposition, or even a national election. Be sure to collect a handful of articles from at least two major candidates or from two sides of the issue. What propaganda devices did each side use? Which side won? How much of a role do you think propaganda played in deciding the outcome?

4. Do you think the authors of this article would advocate getting rid of all propaganda? Why or why not? Be sure to include a discussion of what propaganda is and what function or role it serves.

# Doubts About Doublespeak
*William Lutz*

It has been said that the only sure things we cannot change are death and taxes. Well, that is not exactly right. We can call them "terminal living" and "revenue enhancement" to make people feel better about them. And that, in part, is the nature of what William Lutz rails against here: doublespeak. It is language intended not to reveal but to conceal, not to communicate but to obfuscate. In this essay, Lutz categorizes four kinds of doublespeak, distinguishing annoying though relatively harmless professional jargon from ruthlessly devious coinages such as "ethnic cleansing," which attempt to mask barbaric acts.

William Lutz is a professor of English at Rutgers University. He is the editor of the *Quarterly Review of Doublespeak* as well as author of *Beyond Nineteen Eighty-Four: Doublespeak in a Post-Orwellian Age* (1989) and *Doublespeak: From Revenue Enhancement to Terminal Living* (1990). "Doubts About Doublespeak" first appeared in *State Government News* in July 1993.

1 During the past year, we learned that we can shop at a "unique retail biosphere" instead of a farmers' market, where we can buy items made of "synthetic glass" instead of plastic, or purchase a "high velocity, multipurpose air circulator," or electric fan. A "waste-water conveyance facility" may "exceed the odor threshold"

from time to time due to the presence of "regulated human nutrients," but that is not to be confused with a sewage plant that stinks up the neighborhood with sewage sludge. Nor should we confuse a "resource development park" with a dump. Thus does doublespeak continue to spread.

2    Doublespeak is language which pretends to communicate but doesn't. It is language which makes the bad seem good, the negative seem positive, the unpleasant seem attractive, or at least tolerable. It is language which avoids, shifts or denies responsibility; language which is at variance with its real or purported meaning. It is language which conceals or prevents thought.

3    Doublespeak is all around us. We are asked to check our packages at the desk "for our convenience" when it's not for our convenience at all but for someone else's convenience. We see advertisements for "preowned," "experienced" or "previously distinguished" cars, not used cars and for "genuine imitation leather," "virgin vinyl" or "real counterfeit diamonds." Television offers not reruns but "encore telecasts." There are no slums or ghettos, just the "inner city" or "substandard housing" where the "disadvantaged" or "economically nonaffluent" live and where there might be a problem with "substance abuse." Nonprofit organizations don't make a profit, they have "negative deficits" or experience "revenue excesses." With doublespeak it's not dying but "terminal living" or "negative patient care outcome."

4    There are four kinds of doublespeak. The first kind is the euphemism, a word or phrase designed to avoid a harsh or distasteful reality. Used to mislead or deceive, the euphemism becomes doublespeak. In 1984 the U.S. State Department's annual reports on the status of human rights around the world ceased using the word "killing." Instead the State Department used the phrase "unlawful or arbitrary deprivation of life," thus avoiding the embarrassing situation of government-sanctioned killing in countries supported by the United States.

5    A second kind of doublespeak is jargon, the specialized language of a trade, profession or similar group, such as doctors, lawyers, plumbers or car mechanics. Legitimately used, jargon allows members of a group to communicate with each other clearly, efficiently and quickly. Lawyers and tax accountants speak to each other of an "involuntary conversion" of property, a legal term that means the loss or destruction of property through theft, accident or condemnation. But when lawyers or tax accountants use unfamiliar terms to speak to others, then the jargon becomes doublespeak.

6    In 1978 a commercial 727 crashed on takeoff, killing three passengers, injuring 21 others and destroying the airplane. The insured value of the airplane was greater than its book value, so the airline made a profit of $1.7 million, creating two problems: the airline didn't want to talk about one of its airplanes crashing, yet it had to account for that $1.7 million profit in its annual report to its stockholders. The airline solved both problems by inserting a footnote in its annual report which explained that the $1.7 million was due to "the involuntary conversion of a 727."

7    A third kind of doublespeak is gobbledygook or bureaucratese. Such doublespeak is simply a matter of overwhelming the audience with words—the more the better. Alan Greenspan, a polished practitioner of bureaucratese, once

testified before a Senate committee that "it is a tricky problem to find the particular calibration in timing that would be appropriate to stem the acceleration in risk premiums created by falling incomes without prematurely aborting the decline in the inflation-generated risk premiums."

8    The fourth kind of doublespeak is inflated language, which is designed to make the ordinary seem extraordinary, to make everyday things seem impressive, to give an air of importance to people or situations, to make the simple seem complex. Thus do car mechanics become "automotive internists," elevator operators become "members of the vertical transportation corps," grocery store checkout clerks become "career associate scanning professionals," and smelling something becomes "organoleptic analysis."

9    Doublespeak is not the product of careless language or sloppy thinking. Quite the opposite. Doublespeak is language carefully designed and constructed to appear to communicate when in fact it doesn't. It is language designed not to lead but mislead. Thus, it's not a tax increase but "revenue enhancement" or "tax-base broadening." So how can you complain about higher taxes? Those aren't useless, billion dollar pork barrel projects; they're really "congressional projects of national significance," so don't complain about wasteful government spending. That isn't the Mafia in Atlantic City; those are just "members of a career-offender cartel," so don't worry about the influence of organized crime in the city.

10    New doublespeak is created every day. The Environmental Protection Agency once called acid rain "poorly-buffered precipitation" then dropped that term in favor of "atmospheric deposition of anthropogenically-derived acidic substances," but recently decided that acid rain should be called "wet deposition." The Pentagon, which has in the past given us such classic doublespeak as "hexiform rotatable surface compression unit" for steel nut, just published a pamphlet warning soldiers that exposure to nerve gas will lead to "immediate permanent incapacitation." That's almost as good as the Pentagon's official term "servicing the target," meaning to kill the enemy. Meanwhile, the Department of Energy wants to establish a "monitored retrievable storage site," a place once known as a dump for spent nuclear fuel.

11    Bad economic times give rise to lots of new doublespeak designed to avoid some very unpleasant economic realities. As the "contained depression" continues so does the corporate policy of making up even more new terms to avoid the simple, and easily understandable, term "layoff." So it is that corporations "reposition," "restructure," "reshape," or "realign" the company and "reduce duplication" through "release of resources" that involves a "permanent downsizing" or a "payroll adjustment" that results in a number of employees being "involuntarily terminated."

12    Other countries regularly contribute to doublespeak. In Japan, where baldness is called "hair disadvantaged," the economy is undergoing a "severe adjustment process," while in Canada there is an "involuntary downward development" of the work force. For some government agencies in Canada, wastepaper baskets have become "user friendly, space effective, flexible, deskside sortation units." Politicians in Canada may engage in "reality augmentation," but they never lie. As part of their new freedom, the people of Moscow can visit "intimacy salons,"

or sex shops as they're known in other countries. When dealing with the bureaucracy in Russia, people know that they should show officials "normal gratitude," or give them a bribe.

13    The worst doublespeak is the doublespeak of death. It is the language, wrote George Orwell in 1946, that is "largely the defense of the indefensible . . . designed to make lies sound truthful and murder respectable, and to give an appearance of solidity to pure wind." In the doublespeak of death, Orwell continued, "defenseless villages are bombarded from the air, the inhabitants driven out into the countryside, the cattle machine-gunned, the huts set on fire with incendiary bullets. This is called pacification. Millions of peasants are robbed of their farms and sent trudging along the roads with no more than they can carry. This is called transfer of population or rectification of frontiers." Today, in a country once called Yugoslavia, this is called "ethnic cleansing."

14    It's easy to laugh off doublespeak. After all, we all know what's going on, so what's the harm? But we don't always know what's going on, and when that happens, doublespeak accomplishes its ends. It alters our perception of reality. It deprives us of the tools we need to develop, advance and preserve our society, our culture, our civilization. It breeds suspicion, cynicism, distrust and, ultimately, hostility. It delivers us into the hands of those who do not have our interests at heart. As Samuel Johnson noted in 18th century England, even the devils in hell do not lie to one another, since the society of hell could not subsist without the truth, any more than any other society.

### THINKING CRITICALLY

1. What is doublespeak, according to Lutz? What is its purpose?

2. Lutz divides doublespeak into four types. What are they? Give some of your own examples of each type. As best you can, rank these four types according to which are most offensive or harmful. Explain your choices.

3. In paragraph 4, Lutz classifies euphemisms as a form of doublespeak. In your opinion, are there instances when euphemisms are useful? Explain your answer.

4. Lutz says that "inflated language" is designed to make the ordinary seem extraordinary, as with elevated job titles. In your opinion, is there anything wrong with elevating job titles in this way? Why or why not?

5. In your opinion, is doublespeak as widespread as Lutz claims? Are its effects as serious as he perceives them to be?

6. Examine Lutz's introductory paragraph. How does this paragraph set the tone for the piece? Is it effective?

7. What is the opposing view in this piece? How does Lutz handle it in his argument? Are there counterarguments that Lutz has missed in his essay?

8. Are there any places in the essay where Lutz employs doublespeak in his own writing? If so, what effect does this have on your reading?

9. Consider Lutz's voice in this article. Is he a reliable narrator? Does he provide adequate documentation for his assertions? Cite specific examples from the text to support your answers.

**WRITING ASSIGNMENTS**

1. Write an essay in which you examine instances of doublespeak in the media, a particular profession, or among your acquaintances. Make a case either for or against its usage.

2. Was there ever a time when doublespeak had an impact on your life? Write a personal narrative reflecting on the effect, positive or negative, that doublespeak has had on your experience. You might consider having been swayed by advertising or political jargon.

3. Lutz defines doublespeak as "language which conceals or prevents thought" and "language which pretends to communicate but doesn't." Write an essay describing an experience wherein you used doublespeak. What was your goal in communicating as such? How was doublespeak useful to you in this situation?

4. Over the course of one day, record all the instances of doublespeak you encounter—from ads, TV shows, news articles, films, menus, and so on. (Whenever possible, photocopy these instances.) In a paper, try to classify the different kinds of doublespeak you found. Analyze the different functions of doublespeak and try to determine its effects on the intended audience.

5. Look through a newspaper or magazine for a short and clear discussion of an interesting topic. Then have some fun rewriting the piece entirely in doublespeak.

---

# Fighting Words: The War Over Language
*Jon Hooten*

Our everyday language is liberally sprinkled with the language of war—we "defend" our positions, "wage price wars" at discount stores, and "battle" termite "invasions." We get "bombed" or "blitzed" at parties. Perhaps we are so free with war language because over half the population has yet to experience a true war firsthand. But as we become more removed from the original meanings of the language of war, are we in danger of blurring metaphorical issues with ones of great consequence for humanity?

Jon Hooten is an educational administrator in the School of Communication at the University of Denver. He frequently writes on culture, religion, and environmental issues. This essay first appeared in the September 2002 issue of the online magazine *PopPolitics*.

1 Mine—perhaps, ours—is the first American generation that has yet to experience a full-blown, machine-gun shooting, prisoner-taking, horror-story war.

2     We youngsters sit wide-eyed while our shaky grandfathers and crusty uncles tell tales of enemy occupation, dead buddies, pretty gals and the joy of a fresh Lucky Strike on a rainy afternoon. To those born in the late 1960s and beyond, Nazis are nothing but cultural extremists (of the "femi-" or "soup" varieties), Vietnam makes a good setting for a summer blockbuster, and the Battle of the Bulge is a corny baby boomer punch line. Simply, the realities of the nation's major wars have been lost on one—going on two and three—generations of Americans.

3    That's not to say that my generation has not lived through skirmishes, conflicts and appalling battles. Those of us sitting in high school during the winter of 1991 watched the air strikes on Baghdad through the glassy eyes of CNN, with Peter Arnett and Wolf Blitzer calling the play-by-play. As Desert Storm eventually became known as the "Gulf War," many of us wondered if this was the future of the genre that we had read about in 11th grade history class.

4    From now on, it seemed, war would be a few nights of superpower smart-bombing and long-range tanks lobbing shells into ragtag militias commanded by egomaniacal dictators. It hardly seemed worthy of the designation "war."

5    Those of us who grew up after Vietnam simply cannot comprehend the dread that shaped older generations of Americans. Our experience of the Gulf War was an acutely sterile encounter. We watched replays of laser-guided missiles entering bunker windows, but seldom were we exposed to the sights of actual human collateral. Though tens—hundreds—of thousands of Iraqi casualties resulted, the televised images of precision war games grossly outnumbered the news clips of war's grisly human cost. Since many of us have not experienced the sights and sounds of war firsthand, we think about war rather thoughtlessly.

6    In our lack of true wartime experience, American culture has learned to deploy the images of war rather casually. The words of war were once the moral and emotional defense of the nation, corresponding with the real memories and motivations of an embattled citizenry. As war became less messy and more distant, the language of war invaded the common lexicon of America. Though you may have never noticed it, the extraordinary metaphor of war has infiltrated our quotidian use of language. (Can you count how many times "war words" are fired at you in this very paragraph?)

7    Our popular culture thinks nothing of invoking the language of conflict to describe most any topic. Pick up the morning's paper and browse through the headlines: "Mayor *Defends* New Budget." "Media *Blitz* Saves Kidnapped Girl." "Farmers *Battle* Summer Drought." "Browser *War* Heats Up." "Champ's Left Hook Right *on Target*."

8    Consider, for instance, the numerous ways in which the word 'bomb' is used: "Frat brothers get bombed on a Saturday night." "Your new car is 'the bomb.'" "Did you see that comedian bomb on Letterman last night?" "The quarterback threw a long bomb to win the game."

9    While we have haphazardly sprinkled our language with war's metaphors, is it possible that we have collectively forgotten how to think clearly about the literal phenomenon? Can the collective linguistic turn from the literal to the metaphorical be without consequence?

10    Throughout history, wars have usually followed a certain pattern: They have generally involved elaborate, enduring campaigns between at least two somewhat equal forces; they have resulted in mass casualties; and—this is the most important part—they have some sort of *conclusion*. Common sense would agree with this characterization, at least in the conventional sense of the phenomenon.

11    With this definition in mind, the latter half of the twentieth century has seen a proliferation of non-war–like wars. The war on poverty that Lyndon Johnson waged in the 1960s was an elaborate public policy initiative. The war on drugs

that swelled in the 1970s and 1980s became a tsunami of agencies, non-profit organizations, police action and international diplomacy. The Cold War, fought with national ideologies, economic posturing and infinite defense budgets, festered without any combat or mass casualties (at least among the superpowers) throughout the latter half of the twentieth century before finally coming to a head in the mid-1980s.

12    Now, after a decade's respite of new wars, we have another one on our hands: the war on terrorism.

13    After that inconceivable morning in September 2001, our media-sated political culture was quick to place the blame on those radicals who have become known as "the terrorists." Soon after, the "war on terror" was a go. President Bush promptly assembled his posse to round up the scoundrels who had done this—"Wanted," we were told by the president, "dead or alive." The weeks and months following that day were a slow and deliberate escalation of the war on terrorism, beginning internally with beefed up airports and FBI round-ups, then spreading—in a violent and explicit way—abroad in Afghanistan.

14    For several weeks, while the United States bombed that impoverished nation, the "war on terrorism" became known as the "war on Afghanistan." Quickly, this new war began to look like a war that the president's father fought ten years earlier. Though similar to the Gulf War in many ways, the mission in Afghanistan was very different. While Bush the Elder relied heavily on turkey-shoot combat fought from above, George W. sent in massive numbers of ground troops to hunt down "the evil ones."

15    A wobbly alliance with the locals in Afghanistan was also formed, so that fewer body bags would be sent back to the States full of our brothers and sisters. (Who knows how many Northern Alliance fighters were buried in their native soil.) And while his father had the modest goal of expelling Iraqi forces from Kuwait, Bush the Younger had grander plans of rounding up all the Al Qaeda and Taliban evil-doers he could find.

16    After the fighting in Afghanistan simmered down, and the immediate goal of capturing top terrorists was not met, the popular rhetoric of national affairs shifted away from geographic specifics to the more general "war on terrorism." No longer involving specific battles or well-defined goals, this war quickly began to look similar to other drawn-out wars with which my generation *is* familiar.

17    In 1981, first lady Nancy Reagan boldly advised us first-graders to "Just Say No to Drugs." (Abbie Hoffman is widely reported to have said, "To tell a drug addict to 'just say no' is like telling a manic depressive to 'just cheer up.'") Soon after, President Reagan instigated the all-out war on druggies. By 1988, the Anti-Drug Abuse Act had set its national sights on both the supply and demand of illegal substances in the United States. Though the DEA had been on the scene since 1973, the Reagans took seriously the evil scourge that they saw infecting America's children. The war on drugs was born, has thrived for more than 15 years, and continues in 2002 with an overall federal budget of $19.2 billion.

18    Last time I checked, however, people still buy and use drugs with relative ease. Though the statistics of drug use wax and wane like a Santa Cruz tide, it is safe to say that the war on drugs has not been won. What's more, the war is not a winnable affair. The war on drugs is a war on a perpetual opponent. Unlike a conventional

war, there will be no Normandy or Hiroshima, no crucial turning point or day of victory when all the pot heads and speed freaks will finally surrender.

19    Returning to our definition above, there is no doubt that the war on drugs largely fits the characterization of conventional war. The national strategy has certainly been a strategic battle of wits between two equally matched opponents (as the drug complex still manages to outfox the government with regularity and sophistication). This war has also lasted for more than two decades, and nobody doubts that real casualties have ensued, both domestically and abroad. The question remains, however, if this war will in fact ever come to completion. Can it be won?

20    If we put our heads to it, we will quickly recognize that a "war" of this type is nothing but a grand metaphor, a riding crop with which to whip patriotic Americans into action. In the case of the drug war, the United States has moved from metaphor to militarized efforts in the attempt to alter human habits. While these symbolic, rhetorical wars may seem to have few negative consequences, the conjuring of war's images, passions and emotions has real damaging effects. We are racing toward a finish line that doesn't exist.

21    The language of war, in all its urgency and obligation, will always motivate the patriotic and righteous. The metaphor necessarily creates an enemy, which, when characterized as such, becomes equally entrenched in the language of offense and defense. At its dark heart, a war demands division and opposition. Right vs. wrong. Good vs. evil.

22    Like the war on drugs, the war on terrorism is another overarching metaphor. Terrorism, like drug use, is an act unique to humanity, an action which will be with us for a long time. To war against terrorism is to war against an enemy that does not exist in only one place, that cannot be controlled by laws, that will perpetually be reborn in creative and cunning ways. Terrorism grows out of the fecund social and cultural and economic and religious and psychological slough that is civilization. Like the drug war, the war on terrorism can never be won.

23    By definition, terrorism is a concept or category that describes human actions. In most any dictionary, you will find no examples of what terrorism must be in order to be considered as such. In the dictionary, you will not find "hostage-taking," "suicide-bombing" and "the throwing of Molotov cocktails" under the definition of terrorism. Rather, you will find it described as systematic and violent acts to advance political ends. To war against terrorism, therefore, is to war against a classification, a description, in essence, a word.

24    How can bombs be dropped on a word?

25    At this point, you may be wondering, doesn't this guy know that the war on terrorism is actually a war on *terrorists?* That it is a war on their weapons supply, their finances, their training camps and the axis of evil that harbors them? Doesn't he realize that this exercise in logic has nothing to do with the reality of reality?

26    Well, yes. And no. I am well aware that acts of terrorism do not commit themselves. Of course, terrorism requires the personnel, training and weapons that make violence possible; limiting all of that should therefore logically decrease the instances of terrorist acts. However, the United States must realize that this war— while focused against terrorists, their weapons, etc.—is shaped and fought through the way we speak and write about it.

27     Fighting terrorism is different than fighting cavities. It is not a localized menace that can be brushed away, drilled or filled. On Sept. 9, 2001—two days before the events that sparked the Bush's new war—Alan Block wrote in *Pravda,* "When the metaphorical use of the term [war] is common and seldom challenged, resistance to actual war becomes more difficult and uncommon." Eventually, the verbal sparring becomes literal bombing.

28     When we generalize about the evils of terrorism, we shroud the faces, politics and religion behind the acts. That which motivates the militants has become opaqued by the wordiness of bumper sticker aphorisms and campaign stump speeches. While the war on terrorism has set its sights on the perpetrators and mechanisms therein, it has ignored that which initially provokes the violence. As a damning result, the evil, as it were, will always be with us. As long as the seeds of terrorism—ignorance, injustice, exploitation—are perpetually planted by the careless hand of the superpowers, the weeds of violence will continue to steal nutrients from the fruits of civilization.

29     Politicians, prosecutors and preachers alike invoke moving imagery of cosmic battles of good and evil. Yet, many public figures use this language in knowingly figurative ways. I get the sense, though, that President Bush takes seriously his war on evil, that with enough bombs, with plenty of firepower, and if the right people can be killed, then the axis of evil will fall. He does not seem to realize that evil is perennial, that the death of one season's crops will only fertilize the next season's seedlings. By creating martyrs of the evil-doers, he is signing the marching orders of their followers and inspiring a new impassioned generation of freedom fighters.

30     I would like nothing more than to eradicate the horror that is terrorism . . . along with poverty, hunger, ecocide and oppression. But invoking the language of war does more damage than it prevents. To war against anything will eventually allow the metaphors to become realities. If the twentieth century has taught us anything, it is that words have consequences. Words persuade, encourage and tyrannize. They convey power, passion and persecution. When we invoke the language of war, figurative battles against finances become literal battles against financiers. Symbolic warfare against weapons supplies becomes bloody warfare against weapons suppliers. While we arm ourselves for war, the roots of the violence go ignored, growing deeper into the fertile soils of culture and power.

31     In a famous article that was widely distributed on the Internet just before the first Gulf War, linguist George Lakoff wrote, "It is important to distinguish what is metaphorical from what is not. Pain, dismemberment, death, starvation, and the death and injury of loved ones are not metaphorical." Lakoff would agree that acts based on a metaphor will mirror the metaphor. Warring words will become warring deeds. Clearly, the metaphorical war on terrorism might just become a very real attack on Iraq, with real casualties and consequences.

32     When war is accepted in any form, it can be accepted in all forms. Oscar Wilde wrote in 1891, "As long as war is regarded as wicked, it will always have its fascination. When it is looked upon as vulgar, it will cease to be popular." Only when we choose to not invoke the words of war to address social ills will we begin to solve the problems that lead to violence. More often than not, we are our own worst enemy.

**THINKING CRITICALLY**

1. At the end of paragraph 6, Hooten asks his readers to count how many "war words" he has used. Identify these words, and discuss how these words have become mainstream in our regular speech.

2. In what ways, according to Hooten, has pop culture's use of war words influenced our thinking about the "war on terrorism"? Explain.

3. What is the author's tone in this piece? What is he trying to achieve by writing this essay? Explain.

4. According to Hooten, how have the wars of the last 20 years been "nothing but grand metaphors"? Do you agree with his assertions? Explain.

5. In paragraph 23, Hooten states, "By definition, terrorism is a concept or category that describes human actions. . . . To war against terrorism, therefore, is to war against a classification, a description, in essence, a word." What does Hooten mean by this statement? How does he qualify his claim in the paragraphs that follow?

6. In paragraph 9, Hooten asks, "is it possible that we have collectively forgotten how to think clearly about the literal phenomenon [of war]?" Write a response to his question, presenting your own perspective, while addressing some of the points Hooten raises in his essay.

**WRITING ASSIGNMENTS**

1. Identify as many war words as possible in today's lexicon. How are these words used in pop culture? Discuss whether the use of these words in common speech has diluted or influenced our view of war itself.

2. Write an essay in which you discuss your personal view of the "war on terrorism" as a label and a policy. Consider what the term means to you. What does it mean to the general population? To people from outside of the United States? Interview a spectrum of people for their view on what the phrase means and what their interpretations might mean.

3. Inflammatory political language carries tremendous power to influence national policy, laws, and social mores. What are our expectations of political language? How do we filter the fluff from the substance? Write an essay exploring the power of language to influence our feelings regarding the "war on terror" and the American military actions in the Middle East. You may also explore opposing viewpoints on how language is used—both nationally and internationally—to criticize the war and U.S. military activities abroad.

# Do You Speak Presidential?
*Anna Marie Trester*

Language is a powerful political tool, especially for presidents and presidential hopefuls. Presidents must convey a sense of empathy, strength, fortitude, and intelligence while also seeming to be approachable, trustworthy, and above all, truly "American." And in politics, it's not always what you say, but *how* you say it, that makes an impact. In this next article, Anna Marie Trester explains how, in America, presidential speech continues to reflect broader changes in our way of speaking.

She briefly reviews the language and style of presidents and explains how they "speak presidential." Students can hear the speeches mentioned in Trester's piece at www.pbs.org/speak/seatosea/standardamerican/presidential/voices.

Anna Marie Trester is a professor of communications at Georgetown University. Through presentations at such venues as the Smithsonian Associates, the Business Professional Women's Organization, and the annual meeting of the American Association of Applied Linguistics, she has explored topics including everyday language and how we talk to each other and why it matters. She also served as a linguistics researcher for Robert McNeill's documentary project *Do You Speak American?* from which this article is excerpted.

1 Ask most Americans what someone from Washington, D.C. sounds like, and they'll probably look at you blankly. American English as spoken in Washington, D.C. doesn't seem to be among the language's most recognizable or highly valued forms. This may have something to do with the city. It is not one of the nation's biggest and it is transitory; most inhabitants are not from D.C. and many do not stay long-term. When people move to D.C., they bring the speech of the communities in which they were raised, resulting in a mix of many norms.

2 Ironically, the American English that most Americans say is most acceptable may be entirely imaginary. Standard American is believed by Midwesterners and non-Midwesterners alike to have originated somewhere in the Midwest. Often these same people will point to broadcasting as playing an important role in the preference, but then what exactly is Broadcast English, and how does it relate to Standard American?

3 President Ronald Reagan is credited as speaking this variety, but he started as a professional actor. Reagan was a linguistic anomaly because his dramatic training made it difficult to tell where he was from based on how he spoke. Although he grew up in Illinois and moved to California, he was likely trained to have no appreciable regionalisms in his speech. Like many newscasters, Reagan used a form of speech that just sounds neutral. However, most Americans communicate information about where they come from every time they open their mouths. One of the most easily identifiable features is whether you pronounce the [r] sound. Let's consider three very different presidents.

## R-Lessness: JFK, Carter and FDR

### John F. Kennedy

4 *People "everywheah", in spite of occasional disappointments, look to us—not to "ouah" wealth or "powah", but to the splendor of our ideals. For "ouah" Nation is commissioned by history to be "eithah" an "observah" of freedom's "failuah" or the cause of its success.*

### Jimmy Carter

5 *But I'll always "remembah" that the best weapons "ah" the ones that "ah" "nevah" fired in combat, and the best soldier is one who "nevah" has to lay his life down on the field of battle. Strength is imperative "foah" peace, but the two must go hand in hand.*

6     Both Kennedy and Carter sometimes did not produce the [r] sound, particularly at the end of words. Both used a speech pattern known as Rless, in which speakers delete the [r] sound in certain contexts. This feature is typical in parts of New England (especially Boston), New York, New Jersey and in parts of the South. A feature may be interpreted differently depending upon a person's personal geography. Rless speech makes Kennedy sound more like an elite "Boston Brahman" but makes Carter sound like a Southerner.

7     The loss of the [r] sound by New Yorker Franklin Roosevelt on the other hand made him sound almost British. In the New York of his day, it sounded prestigious to drop [r]s at the ends of words such as water, sugar, ever. . . . The social significance of not pronouncing [r]s has changed several times in U.S. history.

## FDR's Fireside Chats

8 Franklin Delano Roosevelt used language as a powerful political tool, changing the way executive office holders speak to the nation. As president during the Great Depression and World War II, Roosevelt insisted on using plain direct speech, rather than the flourishing rhetoric of the presidents who had preceded him.

9     Roosevelt was the first president to use the mass media to regularly connect with the nation, in his famous "fireside chats." Roosevelt's evening radio addresses helped worried citizens stay informed on and involved with all matters of state. FDR intentionally used "direct, simple, calm language" to explain problems and his plans to solve them. He sensed that he would be most effective in communicating with the public if he "joined" citizens in their living rooms and kitchens for relaxed conversation. No president had ever made the effort to address his citizenry so directly and informally.

10     In changing how a president addressed the nation, and by educating and comforting the public with his speeches, FDR was able to bring about some of the most revolutionary changes in American and world history. These included the New Deal and the United Nations. Roosevelt's fireside chats also helped him convince Americans, in the years before Pearl Harbor, that they could not remain isolated.

11     Decades later, Ronald Reagan took Roosevelt's use of mass media to a new level, making the presidency seem even more accessible. Although not the first president to use television, Reagan is remembered as a master of the medium who delivered his vision dramatically, distilling it to its essential elements. Consider this powerful message delivered at the Brandenburg Gate in Berlin:

### Ronald Reagan

12     *"General Secretary Gorbachev, if you seek peace, if you seek prosperity for the Soviet Union and Eastern Europe, if you seek liberalization: Come here to this gate. Mr. Gorbachev, open this gate. Mr. Gorbachev—Mr. Gorbachev, tear down this wall!"*

## Bill Clinton's Style Shiftin'

13 Bill Clinton is known as a relaxed, disarming public speaker. It has been noted that from one speech to another he can sound almost like a different person. And in fact,

sociolinguists have found that speakers change their speaking style depending upon circumstances. Listen to the following speech excerpts, and see what differences in President Clinton's speaking style you notice:

### Bill Clinton

14      *Ma fellow citizens:*

15      *Today we celebrate the mystery of American renewal.*

16      *This ceremony is held in the depth of winter. But, by the words we speak and the faces we show the world, we force the spring.*

### Bill Clinton

17      *"You have to "disa:d" "wheder" we're "gonna" build a bridge to the future "ar" try to build a bridge to the "payst." You have to "disa:d" whether to tell the American people they have to get into that future on their own or whether that bridge is "gonna" be big enough and wide enough for all of us to walk across together. You have to "disa:d" "wheder" we're "gonna" say to "folks" 'you're on your own' or "wheder" we're "gonna" say 'yes it does "tayke" a village to raise our children and build our future'. Four years ago "a" came to Daytona Beach amid a "tam" of "ha" unemployment, rising frustration and increasing division."*

18      The first excerpt sounds a lot more formal than the second; Clinton also sounds less "Southern" in the inaugural address than in the campaign speech in the South. One of the contributing factors is the degree to which he produces the sound /ay/ as in "tired" as "tared"—or produces "my" as "ma." Changing the /ay/ sound to /a/ is commonly associated with traditional Southern American Speech, and partly why Clinton sounds more Southern at times. A Southerner may produce more of the "Southern" sounding variants when in a less formal situation, talking to other Southerners, or if the topic calls for less formality.

19      We all change the way that we speak depending on where we are, to whom we are talking and what we are talking about. This variation is style shifting. If we are hanging out with our friends we are much more likely to say *thinkin'*, *walkin'* or *talkin'* than if we are at a job interview, when we will carefully say *thinking*, *walking* or *talking*. Style shifts may be quite deliberate or unconscious.

## George W. Bush's Folksiness

20 Unlike Bill Clinton, George W. Bush sounds very much the same—folksy—to an audience at London's Whitehall Palace as to an audience in El Paso, Texas. Bush prides himself on speaking plainly and not sounding too highly educated, and as a result is called unstuffy, relaxed, down to earth. Sociolinguists know that his use of language plays a powerful role in this perception. Language is a powerful social tool that has the ability to draw people together or drive them apart.

### George W. Bush

21    *"Y y tambien voy a hablar un poquito en espanol"*

22    Speaking Spanish is meant to show that the president understands the concerns of Spanish speakers. It seems as if he is "one of them." Linguists talk about this use of language as *indexing an in-group membership*. Bush's Texan colloquialisms and informal speech, which may be deliberate, can achieve the same effect. He is not perceived as an imposing intellectual, projecting an image to which many people relate. They may feel that he is more like them because he says something that they might say in a way that they might say it themselves. Even speech errors seem to work in his favor, as they tend to promote the image of a down-to-earth man of the people.

## Language and Politics: Inside-Out

23 Another interesting recent development involves a rhetorical shift aimed at appealing to the voting power of the South and West. Presidents and presidential candidates have tried to distance themselves from the Washington, D.C. *establishment*— seen as a symbol of power, money, influence, big government, and waste and abuse. Much of the political discourse surrounding the 2000 presidential election touched on whether one was a "Washington Insider."

24    Although both men had somewhat similar linguistic backgrounds, the media often pegged Democratic candidate Al Gore as being too stuffy and not being "Southern enough," while George W. Bush never seemed to have that label stick to him. Because Bush sounded "more relaxed," he was perceived as having been— despite his obvious connections—less shaped by Washington. Language use reinforced that view. Gore frequently did not use contracted forms such as "I'm" or "It's," whereas candidate Bush almost always did. This tiny, almost imperceptible difference in their speaking styles as noted by linguist Geoffrey Nunberg may have been one reason listeners sensed that Gore was more "stuffy" or "arrogant" than Bush. Listeners could not have told you that Gore contracted less often, but rather that Gore somehow sounded more formal. A tiny linguistic choice had a perceptible social consequence.

25    The linguistic choices of 2004's Democratic nominee John Kerry, a non-Texan and non-Southerner, are also interesting to analyze. Midway through the Democratic primaries, Kerry—who had a privileged Boston upbringing—was observed to drop more of the [g] sound at the end of words such as talking, thinking and wanting. The result: Kerry began to sound less stuffy, more informal and possibly more approachable. Newspapers including the *Boston Globe* said this style change was one factor that helped turn around Kerry's campaign.

26    The issue of "Washington insiders" is negotiated in political campaigns and general political discourse. These rhetorical moves are positioning moves. George Bush noted of Al Gore's upbringing: "you can understand why, he was raised in a hotel in Washington."

27    In saying this, George W. Bush accomplishes a positioning of Gore as a Washington "insider" and simultaneously positions himself as an "outsider." Listeners

may infer that being an insider is undesirable; why else would Bush raise it in this manner? Gore could not respond until the next news cycle, by which time it may have been too late to alter voter perceptions. Bush's use of a Texan speech variety is another way to symbolically distance himself from the East Coast, making it easier to be perceived as an outsider and claim everything said to be positive about this identity.

28      We all use language daily to create an identity. The choices of people in the public eye are more visible and the stakes much higher. Language is and will continue to be an important tool for creating identity. This is no less true for presidents than for the rest of us.

## THINKING CRITICALLY

1. Think about the fact that politicians will often say a few words in the language of a group that they are trying to court. Why should they do this? What does this accomplish?

2. How can something as simple as the pronunciation of the letter "r" influence how we feel about the person speaking? How is the letter "r" pronounced in your area of the country? Do you feel more or less connected to people who pronounce "r" differently than you do? Would you respect the speaker less if he or she pronounced the letter "r" (or failed to pronounce it at all)? Explain.

3. Listen to the excerpts mentioned in this article online at www.pbs.org/speak/seatosea/standardamerican/presidential/voices. If you did not know the speakers were former presidents, how would you evaluate their speech? Does knowing where someone comes from and what someone does for a living influence your view of their speech style? Explain.

4. Trester notes that it is not just what presidents say that makes their speeches memorable, but also how they say it. Can you think of an instance in which you heard a political figure say something particularly memorable? What made it so?

5. Noted presidential political scientist George C. Edwards observed, "The greatest source of influence on the president is public approval." What role, if any, does presidential speech have on public approval? Explain.

6. In your opinion, what is more important for effective presidential communication: style or substance?

7. What is the importance of being an "outsider" instead of an "insider" when it comes to the presidency and the president's speech patterns? Explain.

## WRITING ASSIGNMENTS

1. Political scientist Doris Graber observed, "Politics is largely a word game." What makes language "political"? How can it be a "word game"? Expand on this idea based on information in this essay, your own experience, and points made by other authors in this section, such as William Lutz.

2. Do you think it is important for the President of the United States to be a good speaker? In an essay, define the language skills necessary to be an effective leader, and explain why you think these elements are important. Use examples to support your viewpoint.

3. Write an essay exploring how presidential communication has changed over the last 100 years. What influence has the media, beginning with newspapers, then radio, and then television and the Internet, had on presidential language? What about Twitter? What happens when presidential anecdotes are reduced to 140 characters?

---

# Deconstructing Obama's Oratorical Skills

*Richard O'Mara*

> Richard O'Mara observes that Obama can be a bit professorial, but he's part Reagan, part FDR, and maybe a lot of Teddy Roosevelt. The combination makes for an oratorical tour-de-force.
>
> Richard O'Mara worked for 40 years as an editorial writer, foreign correspondent, and foreign editor of the *Baltimore Sun.* While retired now from active journalism, he still writes for newspapers and journals such as *VQR, Antioch Review, Sewanee Review, Under the Sun, Cimarron Review,* and *High Plains Literary Review*. He also serves as a part-time correspondent for *The Christian Science Monitor,* in which this article appeared online on April 26, 2009.

1 There is much to be said about Barack Obama's oratorical skills. Much already has been, good and bad. Journalists launch their opinions and observations into the public airwaves and float them out into the cybernetic sea for whomever cares to fish them out. Mr. Obama's rhetoric is high octane fuel for debate among academics, political operatives, plain ordinary folk interested in knowing what's going on. In February, a columnist wrote in the *New York Sun* of how he had come away from a meeting with Obama "deeply impressed by his intelligence, forceful language," after which the writer changed his mind, and decided the new president was "largely a stage presence," another politician spewing promises unlikely to be kept.

2 Around the same time another pundit, this one on Slate, the online magazine, declared Obama's speeches "criminally short on specifics," and then cited a paper by an academic who "unpeeled" his speeches and claimed to have found a clue to his method: to tie his own life experience to various American icons, like Abraham Lincoln, Martin Luther King Jr., even Ronald Reagan.

3 David Frum, a conservative speechwriter for George Bush, inventor of the phrase "axis of evil," sees in Obama "an old fashioned speechmaker, one who is well prepared and who addresses his audience formally. His strength is in the set piece." His weakness? "He is lost in the modern, more free-wheeling sort of debate." To Mr. Frum, Obama won the presidency owing to the economic crisis that surfaced last year; his speeches helped him little.

4 Many who work and play in the varied fields of politics who dislike Obama are inclined, for some odd reason, to attack him at his strongest point: his manifest talent for speech-making. "People have been suspicious of rhetoric since Plato's time," says the writer and scholar, Garry Wills. "Some distrust Obama as a guy who just makes pretty speeches."

5　　But his speeches, Mr. Wills says, are hardly prettified, nor are they full of mesmerizing tricks and rhetorical flourishes; nor, as many think, "are they out of the black church culture of oratory, which produced Dr. King, Jesse Jackson and others like that."

6　　"Obama is professorial," says Wills. "His speeches manifest his time as a teacher."

7　　Richard Macksey, a humanities professor at Johns Hopkins University, expert on rhetoric, literary theory, and criticism, has identified his own clues to the Obama success: "He speaks in whole sentences. His body language gives the impression of relaxation. He listens." Mr. Macksey adds: "He's quick to admit when he's made a mistake. He is not quick to anger; his rhetoric is empty of fire and brimstone."

8　　Obama, when it comes to giving speeches, has been likened to John Kennedy, Ronald Reagan, F.D.R., even Abraham Lincoln. One Republican strategist, Frank Luntz, even said on network television, maybe in jest, "It's Bobby Kennedy he's channeling." Well, if Bobby Kennedy, why not Theodore Roosevelt, a personage whose name is not often found among those others with whom Obama is compared?

9　　It ought to be, says Jeffrey Tulis, author of "The Rhetorical Presidency." Mr. Tulis believes "Too much attention is often given to the style of oratory, the delivery of the speaker, the cadences of the speech. Obama is impressive in those dimensions, but what really carries him is the substance of his oratory."

10　　"If you have ever attended an Obama rally, you might have been surprised how little the powerful effect he had on his audience was due to so-called 'charisma,' and how much it was due to his treating his audience like adults capable of understanding an argument," he says. Tulis associates Obama with Teddy Roosevelt, not so much for the similarity of their rhetorical styles, but more for the similarity of the political situations they each encountered as president.

11　　Obama and Teddy Roosevelt, he says, "adopted moderation and pragmatic policies as their central mode or theme; each faced a serious threat to the functioning of the capitalist order, and each urged policies to fortify capitalism by modifying it with government regulation. Each claimed their policies were necessary for the long-term health of capitalism itself."

12　　"The form and content of the rhetoric of railroad regulation and trust busting to modify unfair shipping rates," initiated by Roosevelt in 1906, "is almost identical to that for banking regulation and financial sector reform for Obama," says Tulis.

13　　Strong forces gathered to block the efforts of both men: those of big business against Roosevelt, the Republican Party against Obama. Roosevelt resorted to strong, aggressive oratory, shocking, possibly dangerous for his time. (Twenty years earlier, President Andrew Johnson was impeached, in part, for his vituperative rhetoric, which shamed the presidency. But T.R. got his way.)

14　　Obama continues to deploy his verbal skills and to press, more gently, perhaps, for his own policies. He has advantages over the 26th president: He is unlikely to be impeached, no matter what he says. And he has a softer voice, unlike Roosevelt's, which was squeaky.

## THINKING CRITICALLY

1. O'Mara observes that Obama's speeches are "high octane fuel for debate among academics, political operatives, plain ordinary folk interested in knowing what's going on." What does he mean? What makes Obama's speeches particularly noteworthy and held up for scrutiny? Explain.

2. What is O'Mara's view of Obama's oratorical skills? Identify places where he expresses his view.

3. How has Obama's employment as a teacher helped his speech skills? Review a few of his speeches online and determine if you "hear" the teacher in him, as Wills suggests.

4. In what ways can Obama's oratorical style be compared to Teddy Roosevelt's? Locate a speech by Roosevelt and see if you can spot any similarities to Obama's substance and style.

5. O'Mara notes that much of the success of Obama's speeches is not so much the charisma for which he is known but "the substance of his oratory." What makes a speech substantial? Take a recent speech and deconstruct it in terms of substance and style. What strikes you about Obama's speech? Based on your observations, do you agree with O'Mara's assessment?

## WRITING ASSIGNMENTS

1. Write an essay exploring the connection between the president, his language, and the public perception of his leadership. Use examples from at least three different presidents, including Barack Obama, as you formulate your essay.

2. Select a political speech made by Barack Obama at www.whitehouse.gov/ briefing-room/speeches-and-remarks. After carefully reading the speech, try to summarize what Obama is promising the public or is saying about the issue. In what ways does he tap into common ideology to connect with his audience? Is any doublespeak used in the speech? Explain.

# Exploring the Language of **V I S U A L S**

## State of the Union

### THINKING CRITICALLY

1. What is the target audience for this cartoon? How does it convey a message to the viewer?

2. What is happening in this cartoon? Who is speaking? How can you tell who the speaker is? Explain.

3. Who is presumed to be on the "left" side of the cartoon, and who is on the "right"?

4. What is the message of this cartoon? What political position do you think the cartoonist holds?

# SPEAKING OUT:
# LANGUAGE THAT INSPIRED US

## Letter from Birmingham Jail
*Martin Luther King, Jr.*

> In 1963, Martin Luther King, Jr., was arrested at a sit-in demonstration in Birmingham, Alabama. Written from a jail cell, the famous letter reprinted here was addressed to King's fellow clergy, who were critical of his activities in the name of social justice. The letter, however, has a second audience in mind—the collective conscience of the American people. As such, the letter functions much like one of King's speeches, in which he applies both emotion and logic to strategically make his point.
>
> Martin Luther King, Jr., was one of the most prominent and charismatic leaders for black civil rights in America. An ordained minister with a doctorate in theology, King organized the Southern Christian Leadership Conference in 1957 to promote justice and equality for African Americans. Under King's leadership, the civil rights movement eventually eliminated racist laws that prohibited blacks from using restaurants, public swimming pools, and seats in the front sections of buses. For his efforts, King was awarded the Nobel Peace Prize in 1964. Four years later, while supporting striking sanitation workers in Memphis, Tennessee, King was assassinated.

My Dear Fellow Clergymen:

1 While confined here in the Birmingham city jail, I came across your recent statement calling my present activities "unwise and untimely." Seldom do I pause to answer criticism of my work and ideas. If I sought to answer all the criticisms that cross my desk, my secretaries would have little time for anything other than such correspondence in the course of the day, and I would have no time for constructive work. But since I feel that you are men of genuine good will and that your criticisms are sincerely set forth, I want to try to answer your statement in what I hope will be patient and reasonable terms.

2 I think I should indicate why I am here in Birmingham, since you have been influenced by the view which argues against "outsiders coming in." I have the honor of serving as president of the Southern Christian Leadership Conference, an organization operating in every southern state, with headquarters in Atlanta, Georgia. We have some eighty-five affiliated organizations across the South, and one of them is the Alabama Christian Movement for Human Rights. Frequently we share staff, educational and financial resources with our affiliates. Several months ago the affiliate here in Birmingham asked us to be on call to engage in a nonviolent direct-action program if such were deemed necessary. We readily consented, and when the hour came we lived up to our promise. So I, along with several members of my staff, am here because I was invited here, I am here because I have organizational ties here.

3 But more basically, I am in Birmingham because injustice is here. Just as the prophets of the eighth century B.C. left their villages and carried their "thus saith the Lord" far beyond the boundaries of their home towns, and just as the Apostle Paul left his village of Tarsus and carried the gospel of Jesus Christ to the far corners of the Greco-Roman world, so am I compelled to carry the gospel of freedom beyond my own home town. Like Paul, I must constantly respond to the Macedonian call for aid.

4 Moreover, I am cognizant of the interrelatedness of all communities and states. I cannot sit idly by in Atlanta and not be concerned about what happens in Birmingham. Injustice anywhere is a threat to justice everywhere. We are caught in an inescapable network of mutuality, tied in a single garment of destiny. Whatever affects one directly, affects all indirectly. Never again can we afford to live with the narrow, provincial "outside agitator" idea. Anyone who lives inside the United States can never be considered an outsider anywhere within its bounds.

5 You deplore the demonstrations taking place in Birmingham. But your statement, I am sorry to say, fails to express a similar concern for the conditions that brought about the demonstrations. I am sure that none of you would want to rest content with the superficial kind of social analysis that deals merely with effects and does not grapple with underlying causes. It is unfortunate that demonstrations are taking place in Birmingham, but it is even more unfortunate that the city's white power structure left the Negro community with no alternative.

6 In any nonviolent campaign there are four basic steps: collection of the facts to determine whether injustices exist; negotiation; self-purification; and direct action. We have gone through all these steps in Birmingham. There can be no gainsaying the fact that racial injustice engulfs this community. Birmingham is probably the most thoroughly segregated city in the United States. Its ugly record of brutality is widely known. Negroes have experienced grossly unjust treatment in the courts. There have been more unsolved bombings of Negro homes and churches in Birmingham than in any other city in the nation. These are the hard, brutal facts of the case. On the basis of these conditions, Negro leaders sought to negotiate with the city fathers. But the latter consistently refused to engage in good-faith negotiation.

7 Then, last September, came the opportunity to talk with leaders of Birmingham's economic community. In the course of the negotiations, certain promises were made by the merchants—for example, to remove the stores' humiliating racial signs. On the basis of these promises, the Reverend Fred Shuttlesworth and the leaders of the Alabama Christian Movement for Human Rights agreed to a moratorium on all demonstrations. As the weeks and months went by, we realized that we were the victims of a broken promise. A few signs, briefly removed, returned; the others remained.

8 As in so many past experiences, our hopes had been blasted, and the shadow of deep disappointment settled upon us. We had no alternative except to prepare for direct action, whereby we would present our very bodies as a means of laying our case before the conscience of the local and the national community. Mindful of the difficulties involved, we decided to undertake a process of self-purification.

We began a series of workshops on nonviolence, and we repeatedly asked ourselves: "Are you able to accept blows without retaliating?" "Are you able to endure the ordeal of jail?" We decided to schedule our direct-action program for the Easter season, realizing that except for Christmas, this is the main shopping period of the year. Knowing that a strong economic-withdrawal program would be the by-product of direct action, we felt that this would be the best time to bring pressure to bear on the merchants for the needed change.

9  Then it occurred to us that Birmingham's mayoralty election was coming up in March, and we speedily decided to postpone action until after election day. When we discovered that the Commissioner of Public Safety, Eugene "Bull" Connor, had piled up enough votes to be in the run-off, we decided again to postpone action until the day after the run-off so that the demonstrations could not be used to cloud the issues. Like many others, we waited to see Mr. Connor defeated, and to this end we endured postponement after postponement. Having aided in this community need, we felt that our direct-action program could be delayed no longer.

10  You may well ask: "Why direct action? Why sit-ins, marches and so forth? Isn't negotiation a better path?" You are quite right in calling for negotiation. Indeed, this is the very purpose of direct action. Nonviolent direct action seeks to create such a crisis and foster such a tension that a community which has constantly refused to negotiate is forced to confront the issue. It seeks so to dramatize the issue that it can no longer be ignored. My citing the creation of tension as part of the work of the nonviolent-resister may sound rather shocking. But I must confess that I am not afraid of the word "tension." I have earnestly opposed violent tension, but there is a type of constructive, nonviolent tension which is necessary for growth. Just as Socrates felt that it was necessary to create a tension in the mind so that individuals could rise from the bondage of myths and half-truths to the unfettered realm of creative analysis and objective appraisal, so must we see the need for nonviolent gadflies to create the kind of tension in society that will help men rise from the dark depths of prejudice and racism to the majestic heights of understanding and brotherhood.

11  The purpose of our direct-action program is to create a situation so crisis-packed that it will inevitably open the door to negotiation. I therefore concur with you in your call for negotiation. Too long has our beloved Southland been bogged down in a tragic effort to live in monologue rather than dialogue.

12  One of the basic points in your statement is that the action that I and my associates have taken in Birmingham is untimely. Some have asked: "Why didn't you give the new city administration time to act?" The only answer that I can give to this query is that the new Birmingham administration must be prodded about as much as the outgoing one, before it will act. We are sadly mistaken if we feel that the election of Albert Boutwell as mayor will bring the millennium to Birmingham. While Mr. Boutwell is a much more gentle person than Mr. Connor, they are both segregationists, dedicated to maintenance of the status quo. I have hope that Mr. Boutwell will be reasonable enough to see the futility of massive resistance to desegregation. But he will not see this without pressure from devotees of civil rights. My friends, I must say to you that we have not made a single gain in civil rights

without determined legal and nonviolent pressure. Lamentably, it is an historical fact that privileged groups seldom give up their privileges voluntarily. Individuals may see the moral light and voluntarily give up their unjust posture; but, as Reinhold Niebuhr has reminded us, groups tend to be more immoral than individuals.

13 We know through painful experience that freedom is never voluntarily given by the oppressor; it must be demanded by the oppressed. Frankly, I have yet to engage in a direct-action campaign that was "well timed" in the view of those who have not suffered unduly from the disease of segregation. For years now I have heard the word "Wait!" It rings in the ear of every Negro with piercing familiarity. This "Wait" has almost always meant "Never." We must come to see, with one of our distinguished jurists, that "justice too long delayed is justice denied."

14 We have waited for more than 340 years for our constitutional and God-given rights. The nations of Asia and Africa are moving with jet-like speed toward gaining political independence, but we still creep at horse-and-buggy pace toward gaining a cup of coffee at a lunch counter. Perhaps it is easy for those who have never felt the stinging darts of segregation to say, "Wait." But when you have seen vicious mobs lynch your mothers and fathers at will and drown your sisters and brothers at whim; when you have seen hate-filled policemen curse, kick and even kill your black brothers and sisters; when you see the vast majority of your twenty million Negro brothers smothering in an airtight cage of poverty in the midst of an affluent society; when you suddenly find your tongue twisted and your speech stammering as you seek to explain to your six-year-old daughter why she can't go to the public amusement that has just been advertised on television, and see tears welling up in her eyes when she is told that Funtown is closed to colored children, and see ominous clouds of inferiority beginning to form in her little mental sky, and see her beginning to distort her personality by developing an unconscious bitterness toward white people; when you have to concoct an answer for a five-year-old son who is asking: "Daddy, why do white people treat colored people so mean?"; when you take a cross-country drive and find it necessary to sleep night after night in the uncomfortable corners of your automobile because no motel will accept you; when you are humiliated day in and day out by nagging signs reading "white" and "colored"; when your first name becomes "nigger," your middle name becomes "boy" (however old you are) and your last name becomes "John," and your wife and mother are never given the respected title "Mrs."; when you are harried by day and haunted by night by the fact that you are Negro, living constantly at tiptoe stance, never quite knowing what to expect next, and are plagued with inner fears and outer resentments; when you are forever fighting a degenerating sense of "nobodiness"—then you will understand why we find it difficult to wait. There comes a time when the cup of endurance runs over, and men are no longer willing to be plunged into the abyss of despair. I hope, sirs, you can understand our legitimate and unavoidable impatience.

15 You express a great deal of anxiety over our willingness to break laws. This is certainly a legitimate concern. Since we so diligently urge people to obey the Supreme Court's decision of 1954 outlawing segregation in the public schools, at first

glance it may seem rather paradoxical for us consciously to break laws. One may well ask: "How can you advocate breaking some laws and obeying others?" The answer lies in the fact that there are two types of laws: just and unjust. I would be the first to advocate obeying just laws. One has not only a legal but a moral responsibility to obey just laws. Conversely, one has a moral responsibility to disobey unjust laws. I would agree with St. Augustine that "an unjust law is no law at all." Now, what is the difference between the two? How does one determine whether a law is just or unjust? A just law is a man-made code that squares with the moral law or the law of God. An unjust law is a code that is out of harmony with the moral law. To put it in the terms of St. Thomas Aquinas: An unjust law is a human law that is not rooted in eternal law and natural law. Any law that uplifts human personality is just. Any law that degrades human personality is unjust. All segregation statutes are unjust because segregation distorts the soul and damages the personality. It gives the segregator a false sense of superiority and the segregated a false sense of inferiority. Segregation, to use the terminology of the Jewish philosopher Martin Buber, substitutes an "I-it" relationship for an "I-thou" relationship and ends up relegating persons to the status of things. Hence segregation is not only politically, economically and sociologically unsound, it is morally wrong and sinful. Paul Tillich has said that sin is separation. Is not segregation an existential expression of man's tragic separation, his awful estrangement, his terrible sinfulness? Thus it is that I can urge men to obey the 1954 decision of the Supreme Court, for it is morally right; and I can urge them to disobey segregation ordinances, for they are morally wrong.

16 Let us consider a more concrete example of just and unjust laws. An unjust law is a code that a numerical or power majority group compels a minority group to obey but does not make binding on itself. This is *difference* made legal. By the same token, a just law is a code that a majority compels a minority to follow and that it is willing to follow itself. This is *sameness* made legal.

17 Let me give another explanation. A law is unjust if it is inflicted on a minority that, as a result of being denied the right to vote, had no part in enacting or devising the law. Who can say that the legislature of Alabama which set up that state's segregation laws was democratically elected? Throughout Alabama all sorts of devious methods are used to prevent Negroes from becoming registered voters, and there are some counties in which, even though Negroes constitute a majority of the population, not a single Negro is registered. Can any law enacted under such circumstances be considered democratically structured?

18 Sometimes a law is just on its face and unjust in its application. For instance, I have been arrested on a charge of parading without a permit. Now, there is nothing wrong in having an ordinance which requires a permit for a parade. But such an ordinance becomes unjust when it is used to maintain segregation and to deny citizens the First Amendment privilege of peaceful assembly and protest.

19 I hope you are able to see the distinction I am trying to point out. In no sense do I advocate evading or defying the law, as would the rabid segregationist. That would lead to anarchy. One who breaks an unjust law must do so openly, lovingly, and with a willingness to accept the penalty. I submit that an individual who breaks a

law that conscience tells him is unjust, and who willingly accepts the penalty of imprisonment in order to arouse the conscience of the community over its injustice, is in reality expressing the highest respect for law.

20 Of course, there is nothing new about this kind of civil disobedience. It was evidenced sublimely in the refusal of Shadrach, Meshach and Abednego to obey the laws of Nebuchadnezzar, on the grounds that a higher moral law was at stake. It was practiced superbly by the early Christians, who were willing to face hungry lions and the excruciating pain of chopping blocks rather than submit to certain unjust laws of the Roman Empire. To a degree, academic freedom is a reality today because Socrates practiced civil disobedience. In our own nation, the Boston Tea Party represented a massive act of civil disobedience. We should never forget that everything Adolf Hitler did in Germany was "legal" and everything the Hungarian freedom fighters did in Hungary was "illegal." It was "illegal" to aid and comfort a Jew in Hitler's Germany. Even so, I am sure that, had I lived in Germany at the time, I would have aided and comforted my Jewish brothers. If today I lived in a Communist country where certain principles dear to the Christian faith are suppressed, I would openly advocate disobeying that country's antireligious laws.

21 I must make two honest confessions to you, my Christian and Jewish brothers. First, I must confess that over the past few years I have been gravely disappointed with the white moderate. I have almost reached the regrettable conclusion that the Negro's great stumbling block in his stride toward freedom is not the White Citizen's Councilor or the Ku Klux Klanner, but the white moderate, who is more devoted to "order" than to justice; who prefers a negative peace which is the absence of tension to a positive peace which is the presence of justice; who constantly says: "I agree with you in the goal you seek, but I cannot agree with your methods of direct action"; who paternalistically believes he can set the timetable for another man's freedom; who lives by a mythical concept of time and who constantly advises the Negro to wait for a "more convenient season." Shallow misunderstanding from people of good will is more frustrating than absolute misunderstanding from people of ill will. Lukewarm acceptance is much more bewildering than outright rejection.

22 I had hoped that the white moderate would understand that law and order exist for the purpose of establishing justice and that when they fail in this purpose they become the dangerously structured dams that block the flow of social progress. I had hoped that the white moderate would understand that the present tension in the South is a necessary phase of the transition from an obnoxious negative peace, in which the Negro passively accepted his unjust plight, to a substantive and positive peace, in which all men will respect the dignity and worth of human personality. Actually, we who engage in nonviolent direct action are not the creators of tension. We merely bring to the surface the hidden tension that is already alive. We bring it out in the open, where it can be seen and dealt with. Like a boil that can never be cured so long as it is covered up but must be opened with all its ugliness to the natural medicines of air and light, injustice must be exposed, with all the tension its exposure creates, to the light of human conscience and the air of national opinion before it can be cured.

23 In your statement you assert that our actions, even though peaceful, must be condemned because they precipitate violence. But is this a logical assertion? Isn't this like condemning a robbed man because his possession of money precipitated the evil act of robbery? Isn't this like condemning Socrates because his unswerving commitment to truth and his philosophical inquiries precipitated the act by the misguided populace in which they made him drink hemlock? Isn't this like condemning Jesus because his unique God-consciousness and never-ceasing devotion to God's will precipitated the evil act of crucifixion? We must come to see that, as the federal courts have consistently affirmed, it is wrong to urge an individual to cease his efforts to gain his basic constitutional rights because the quest may precipitate violence. Society must protect the robbed and punish the robber.

24 I had also hoped that the white moderate would reject the myth concerning time in relation to the struggle for freedom. I have just received a letter from a white brother in Texas. He writes: "All Christians know that the colored people will receive equal rights eventually, but it is possible that you are in too great a religious hurry. It has taken Christianity almost two thousand years to accomplish what it has. The teachings of Christ take time to come to earth." Such an attitude stems from a tragic misconception of time, from the strangely irrational notion that there is something in the very flow of time that will inevitably cure all ills. Actually, time itself is neutral; it can be used either destructively or constructively. More and more I feel that the people of ill will have used time much more effectively than have the people of good will. We will have to repent in this generation not merely for the hateful words and actions of the bad people but for the appalling silence of the good people. Human progress never rolls in on wheels of inevitability; it comes through the tireless efforts of men willing to be co-workers with God, and without this hard work, time itself becomes an ally of the forces of social stagnation. We must use time creatively, in the knowledge that the time is always ripe to do right. Now is the time to make real the promise of democracy and transform our pending national elegy into a creative psalm of brotherhood. Now is the time to lift our national policy from the quicksand of racial injustice to the solid rock of human dignity. You speak of our activity in Birmingham as extreme. At first, I was rather disappointed that fellow clergymen would see my nonviolent efforts as those of an extremist. I began thinking about the fact that I stand in the middle of two opposing forces in the Negro Community. One is a force of complacency, made up in part of Negroes who, as a result of long years of oppression, are so drained of self-respect and a sense of "somebodiness" that they have adjusted to segregation; and in part of a few middle-class Negroes who, because of a degree of academic and economic security and because in some ways they profit by segregation, have become insensitive to the problems of the masses. The other force is one of bitterness and hatred, and it comes perilously close to advocating violence. It is expressed in the various black nationalist groups that are springing up across the nation, the largest and best known being Elijah Muhammad's Muslim movement. Nourished by the Negro's frustration over the continued existence of racial discrimination, this movement is made up of people who have lost faith in America, who have absolutely repudiated Christianity, and who have concluded that the white man is an incorrigible "devil."

25 I have tried to stand between these two forces, saying that we need emulate neither the "do-nothingism" of the complacent nor the hatred and despair of the black nationalist. For there is the more excellent way of love and nonviolent protest. I am grateful to God that, through the influence of the Negro church, the way of nonviolence became an integral part of our struggle.

26 If this philosophy had not emerged, by now many streets of the South would, I am convinced, be flowing with blood. And I am further convinced that if our white brothers dismiss as "rabble-rousers" and "outside agitators" those of us who employ nonviolent direct action, and if they refuse to support our nonviolent efforts, millions of Negroes will, out of frustration and despair, seek solace and security in black-nationalist ideologies—a development that would inevitably lead to a frightening racial nightmare.

27 Oppressed people cannot remain oppressed forever. The yearning for freedom eventually manifests itself, and that is what has happened to the American Negro. Something within has reminded him of his birthright of freedom, and something without has reminded him that it can be gained. Consciously or unconsciously, he has been caught up by the *Zeitgeist*, and with his black brothers of Africa and his brown and yellow brothers of Asia, South America and the Caribbean, the United States Negro is moving with a sense of great urgency toward the promised land of racial justice. If one recognizes this vital urge that has engulfed the Negro community, one should readily understand why public demonstrations are taking place. The Negro has many pent-up resentments and latent frustrations, and he must release them. So let him march; let him make prayer pilgrimages to the city hall; let him go on freedom rides—and try to understand why he must do so. If his repressed emotions are not released in nonviolent ways, they will seek expression through violence; this is not a threat but a fact of history. So I have not said to my people: "Get rid of your discontent." Rather, I have tried to say that this normal and healthy discontent can be channeled into the creative outlet of nonviolent direct action. And now this approach is being termed extremist.

28 But though I was initially disappointed at being categorized as an extremist, as I continued to think about the matter I gradually gained a measure of satisfaction from the label. Was not Jesus an extremist for love: "Love your enemies, bless them that curse you, do good to them that hate you, and pray for them which despitefully use you, and persecute you." Was not Amos an extremist for justice: "Let justice roll down like waters and righteousness like an everflowing stream." Was not Paul an extremist for the Christian gospel: "I bear in my body the marks of the Lord Jesus." Was not Martin Luther an extremist: "Here I stand; I cannot do otherwise, so help me God." And John Bunyan: "I will stay in jail to the end of my days before I make a butchery of my conscience." And Abraham Lincoln: "This nation cannot survive half slave and half free." And Thomas Jefferson: "We hold these truths to be self-evident, that all men are created equal. . . ." So the question is not whether we will be extremists, but what kind of extremists we will be. Will we be extremists for hate or for love? Will we be extremists for the preservation of injustice or for the existence of justice? In that dramatic scene on Calvary's hill, three men were crucified. We must never forget that all three were crucified for the same

crime—the crime of extremism. Two were extremists for immorality, and thus fell below their environment. The other, Jesus Christ, was an extremist for love, truth and goodness, and thereby rose above his environment. Perhaps the South, the nation and the world are in dire need of creative extremists. . . .

29  If I have said anything in this letter that overstates the truth and indicates an unreasonable impatience, I beg you to forgive me. If I have said anything that understates the truth and indicates my having a patience that allows me to settle for anything less than brotherhood, I beg God to forgive me.

30  I hope this letter finds you strong in the faith. I also hope that circumstances will soon make it possible for me to meet each of you, not as an integrationist or a civil-rights leader but as a fellow clergyman and a Christian brother. Let us all hope that the dark clouds of racial prejudice will soon pass away and the deep fog of misunderstanding will be lifted from our fear-drenched communities, and in some not too distant tomorrow the radiant stars of love and brotherhood will shine over our great nation with all their scintillating beauty.

Yours for the cause of Peace and Brotherhood,
Martin Luther King, Jr.

## THINKING CRITICALLY

1. King states in paragraph 24, "We will have to repent in this generation not merely for the hateful words and actions of the bad people but for the appalling silence of the good people." What does this statement mean to you? Do you agree? In what situations might silence be appalling?

2. Describe the voice and tone King uses in this letter. What does his voice reveal about his personality, and how does it affect his argument? How does he establish credibility, authority, and personality in his letter? Explain.

3. In paragraph 12, King states that the Birmingham officials at the time were "dedicated to maintenance of the status quo." What was the status quo in the Birmingham of 1963? What is the status quo today?

4. In paragraph 14, King provides a catalogue of reasons why the civil rights movement could not wait any longer. Analyze this technique in terms of King's argument. What effect does this cataloguing have on the reader?

5. Martin Luther King, Jr., was first and foremost a preacher. How does the language in his letter reveal his profession? Would this letter be as effective as a speech? Would it be better? How does the medium (letter or speech) affect the choice of language used?

6. In paragraphs 15 through 20, King provides proof regarding the differences between just and unjust laws. Examine the language in this section and decide whether his logic is effective. Explain your conclusions.

## WRITING ASSIGNMENTS

1. Some critics have commented that King was considered a great leader by the white status quo because he preached a program of nonviolence and used a rhetoric that reflected "acceptable American values." Explore this idea further by researching some additional speeches made by King. Then, drawing from your research, write an essay addressing this issue expressing your opinion.

2. Using the language techniques employed by King in his letter, write your own letter directed toward people you respect protesting an injustice that you feel they may not entirely understand. Consider the concerns of your audience as you explain the nature of the injustice, the history and sociology behind it, and why you feel your argument is valid and should be accepted by your readers.

3. In his letter, King justifies civil disobedience by arguing that the established laws are unjust. Are there any current laws that seem unjust to you? Would you demonstrate to protest a current unjust law or practice? Why or why not?

---

# Ain't I a Woman?

*Sojourner Truth*

Sojourner Truth was born into slavery with the name Isabella Baumfree around 1797. In 1826, she escaped to freedom with her infant daughter Sophia. In 1843, she changed her name to Sojourner Truth, which some biographers attribute to her intention to travel the country "telling the truth." Other historians report that her name change was connected to a religious experience. During her lifetime, she spoke for women's rights and prison reform and even addressed the Michigan Legislature speaking against capital punishment. She was highly respected among abolitionists and met Abraham Lincoln in 1864 at the White House. She also met Elizabeth Cady Stanton in 1867, while traveling through the South. After a long life fighting for human rights, Sojourner Truth died at her home in Battle Creek, Michigan, in 1883.

In May of 1851, Sojourner Truth attended a women's rights convention held in Akron, Ohio. The only black woman in attendance, on the second day of the convention, Truth rose from her seat and approached the podium. Nearly six feet tall, with a deep, clear voice, Truth systematically refuted the claims of some of the male speakers that day. What follows is a transcription of that speech as recorded by Frances D. Gage, who presided at the convention.

1   Well, children, where there is so much racket there must be something out o' kilter. I think that 'twixt the negroes of the South and the women of the North all a-talking about rights, the white man will be in a fix pretty soon. But what's all this here talking about?

2   That man over there says that women need to be helped into carriages, and lifted over ditches, and to have the best place everywhere. Nobody ever helps me into carriages, or over mud puddles, or gives me any best place *(and raising herself to her full height and her voice to a pitch like rolling thunder, she asked),* and ain't I a woman? Look at me! Look at my arm! *(And she bared her right arm to the shoulder, showing her tremendous muscular power.)* I have ploughed, and planted, and gathered into barns, and no man could head me—and ain't I a woman? I could work as much and eat as much as a man (when I could get it), and bear the lash as well—and ain't I a woman? I have borne thirteen children and seen them almost all sold off to slavery, and when I cried out with my mother's grief, none but Jesus heard—and ain't I a woman?

3   Then they talk about this thing in the head—what's this they call it? *("Intellect," whispered someone near.)* That's it, honey. What's that got to do with woman's rights or Negroes' rights? If my cup won't hold but a pint and yours holds a quart, wouldn't you be mean not to let me have my little half-measure full? *(And she pointed her*

*significant finger and sent a keen glance at the minister who had made the argument. The cheering was long and loud.)*

4    Then that little man in black there, he says women can't have as much rights as man, 'cause Christ wasn't a woman. Where did your Christ come from? *(Rolling thunder could not have stilled that crowd as did those deep, wonderful tones, as she stood there with outstretched arms and eye of fire. Raising her voice still louder, she repeated,)* Where did your Christ come from? From God and a woman. Man had nothing to do with Him. *(Oh! what a rebuke she gave the little man.)*

5    *(Turning again to another objector, she took up the defense of mother Eve. I cannot follower [sic] her through it all. It was pointed, and witty, and solemn, eliciting at almost every sentence deafening applause; and she ended [sic] by asserting that)* If the first woman God ever made was strong enough to turn the world upside down, all alone, these together *(and she glanced her eye over us),* ought to be able to turn it back and get it right side up again; and now they are asking to do it, the men better let them. *(Long-continued cheering.)*

6    'Bliged to you for hearing on me, and now old Sojourner hasn't got anything more to say.

## THINKING CRITICALLY

1. How does Truth prefix each of her answers to the male dissenters? Can you figure out what the men said from Truth's words? Explain.

2. What is the biblical argument against the equality of women? How does Truth address this argument?

3. According to historians, the women at the Akron convention asked Frances Gage to prevent Truth from speaking, fearing that it would "mix and confuse" causes. What do you think was the basis of their fear? How do you think they felt about Truth after she spoke?

4. What kind of courage did it take for Truth to speak at this convention, both as a woman and as an ex-slave? How does she use her background to assert her convictions? Is she effective in making her point? Explain.

## WRITING ASSIGNMENTS

1. Visit the Sojourner Truth Institute at http://www.sojournertruth.org and read more about this remarkable woman. Write an essay on how her achievements as a woman and as a former slave left their mark on our history. How do you think Truth would react to our society today?

2. Both Stanton and Truth addressed the "biblical argument" made against women's rights. Stanton called this argument "perverted," and Truth likewise challenged it. To what argument are they referring? Evaluate this "biblical argument" against women's rights. Then write an essay in which you address this issue. How does the biblical argument factor into our modern ideology?

3. Compare the general status of American women with that of women in other countries in order to demonstrate the wide range of women's rights and roles. Using library research and, if possible, personal testimony from people from other countries, develop your findings in a paper.

# John F. Kennedy's Inaugural Address

There are several presidential speeches that remain in American memory as truly great. Abraham Lincoln's Gettysburg Address is one, and John F. Kennedy's inaugural address is another. Heavy snow fell the night before the inauguration, but Kennedy insisted that the ceremony not be cancelled or postponed. So that his image would not be muffled with fussy overcoats, Kennedy wore long underwear so that he could remove his topcoat during his speech to the American people. The oath of office was administered by Chief Justice Earl Warren, and the poet Robert Frost read one of his poems at the ceremony. Kennedy made this speech, his inaugural address, on Friday, January 20, 1961.

1 "Vice President Johnson, Mr. Speaker, Mr. Chief Justice, President Eisenhower, Vice President Nixon, President Truman, reverend clergy, fellow citizens, we observe today not a victory of party, but a celebration of freedom—symbolizing an end, as well as a beginning—signifying renewal, as well as change. For I have sworn before you and Almighty God the same solemn oath our forebears prescribed nearly a century and three quarters ago.

2    The world is very different now. For man holds in his mortal hands the power to abolish all forms of human poverty and all forms of human life. And yet the same revolutionary beliefs for which our forebears fought are still at issue around the globe—the belief that the rights of man come not from the generosity of the state, but from the hand of God.

3    We dare not forget today that we are the heirs of that first revolution. Let the word go forth from this time and place, to friend and foe alike, that the torch has been passed to a new generation of Americans—born in this century, tempered by war, disciplined by a hard and bitter peace, proud of our ancient heritage—and unwilling to witness or permit the slow undoing of those human rights to which this Nation has always been committed, and to which we are committed today at home and around the world.

4    Let every nation know, whether it wishes us well or ill, that we shall pay any price, bear any burden, meet any hardship, support any friend, oppose any foe, in order to assure the survival and the success of liberty.

5    This much we pledge—and more.

6    To those old allies whose cultural and spiritual origins we share, we pledge the loyalty of faithful friends. United, there is little we cannot do in a host of cooperative ventures. Divided, there is little we can do—for we dare not meet a powerful challenge at odds and split asunder.

7    To those new States whom we welcome to the ranks of the free, we pledge our word that one form of colonial control shall not have passed away merely to be replaced by a far more iron tyranny. We shall not always expect to find them supporting our view. But we shall always hope to find them strongly supporting their own freedom—and to remember that, in the past, those who foolishly sought power by riding the back of the tiger ended up inside.

8    To those peoples in the huts and villages across the globe struggling to break the bonds of mass misery, we pledge our best efforts to help them help themselves, for whatever period is required—not because the Communists may be doing it, not

because we seek their votes, but because it is right. If a free society cannot help the many who are poor, it cannot save the few who are rich.

9   To our sister republics south of our border, we offer a special pledge—to convert our good words into good deeds—in a new alliance for progress—to assist free men and free governments in casting off the chains of poverty. But this peaceful revolution of hope cannot become the prey of hostile powers. Let all our neighbors know that we shall join with them to oppose aggression or subversion anywhere in the Americas. And let every other power know that this Hemisphere intends to remain the master of its own house.

10   To that world assembly of sovereign states, the United Nations, our last best hope in an age where the instruments of war have far outpaced the instruments of peace, we renew our pledge of support—to prevent it from becoming merely a forum for invective—to strengthen its shield of the new and the weak—and to enlarge the area in which its writ may run.

11   Finally, to those nations who would make themselves our adversary, we offer not a pledge but a request: that both sides begin anew the quest for peace, before the dark powers of destruction unleashed by science engulf all humanity in planned or accidental self-destruction.

12   We dare not tempt them with weakness. For only when our arms are sufficient beyond doubt can we be certain beyond doubt that they will never be employed.

13   But neither can two great and powerful groups of nations take comfort from our present course—both sides overburdened by the cost of modern weapons, both rightly alarmed by the steady spread of the deadly atom, yet both racing to alter that uncertain balance of terror that stays the hand of mankind's final war.

14   So let us begin anew—remembering on both sides that civility is not a sign of weakness, and sincerity is always subject to proof. Let us never negotiate out of fear. But let us never fear to negotiate.

15   Let both sides explore what problems unite us instead of belaboring those problems which divide us.

16   Let both sides, for the first time, formulate serious and precise proposals for the inspection and control of arms—and bring the absolute power to destroy other nations under the absolute control of all nations.

17   Let both sides seek to invoke the wonders of science instead of its terrors. Together let us explore the stars, conquer the deserts, eradicate disease, tap the ocean depths, and encourage the arts and commerce.

18   Let both sides unite to heed in all corners of the earth the command of Isaiah— to "undo the heavy burdens . . . and to let the oppressed go free."

19   And if a beachhead of cooperation may push back the jungle of suspicion, let both sides join in creating a new endeavor, not a new balance of power, but a new world of law, where the strong are just and the weak secure and the peace preserved.

20   All this will not be finished in the first 100 days. Nor will it be finished in the first 1,000 days, nor in the life of this Administration, nor even perhaps in our lifetime on this planet. But let us begin.

21   In your hands, my fellow citizens, more than in mine, will rest the final success or failure of our course. Since this country was founded, each generation of Americans has been summoned to give testimony to its national loyalty. The graves of young Americans who answered the call to service surround the globe.

22    Now the trumpet summons us again—not as a call to bear arms, though arms we need; not as a call to battle, though embattled we are—but a call to bear the burden of a long twilight struggle, year in and year out, "rejoicing in hope, patient in tribulation"—a struggle against the common enemies of man: tyranny, poverty, disease, and war itself.

23    Can we forge against these enemies a grand and global alliance, North and South, East and West, that can assure a more fruitful life for all mankind? Will you join in that historic effort?

24    In the long history of the world, only a few generations have been granted the role of defending freedom in its hour of maximum danger. I do not shrink from this responsibility—I welcome it. I do not believe that any of us would exchange places with any other people or any other generation. The energy, the faith, the devotion which we bring to this endeavor will light our country and all who serve it—and the glow from that fire can truly light the world.

25    And so, my fellow Americans: ask not what your country can do for you—ask what you can do for your country.

26    My fellow citizens of the world: ask not what America will do for you, but what together we can do for the freedom of man.

27    Finally, whether you are citizens of America or citizens of the world, ask of us the same high standards of strength and sacrifice which we ask of you. With a good conscience our only sure reward, with history the final judge of our deeds, let us go forth to lead the land we love, asking His blessing and His help, but knowing that here on earth God's work must truly be our own.

### THINKING CRITICALLY

1. Analyze the language of this speech, mindful of Kennedy's use of adjectives, grammar, repetition, and symbolism. Whom does he reference? What pronouns does he use? Explain.

2. This speech is recognized by many historians as particularly memorable and impactful. What elements make this speech great? What factors, besides the words themselves, could have contributed to the success of the speech?

3. At the time Kennedy was elected, the country was very politically divided. How does Kennedy try to encourage collaboration through his language? Explain.

4. Kennedy's approval rating jumped almost 25 percent after he gave this speech, despite a controversial election and politically divided parties. What elements do you think account for this jump? Explain.

5. Would Kennedy's speech be as effective today as it was 50 years ago? Would it be as effective if another charismatic leader spoke the words, such as Barack Obama?

6. What personal elements does Kennedy interject into his speech? Do you think adding such personal information makes his address more compelling? Why or why not?

### WRITING ASSIGNMENTS

1. Imagine you are a young American in 1961 hearing Kennedy's address for the first time on inauguration day. View Kennedy's speech at http://www.americanrhetoric.com/speeches/jfkinaugural.htm. Write an essay recording your impressions of the

speech, how it made you feel, and your emotional reactions, if any. Include notes on how he dressed, addressed the crowd, the people he had near him, and any emotion he projected as he spoke his famous words.

2. President Harry S. Truman once said, "the principle power that the president has is to bring people in and try to persuade them to do what they ought to do without persuasion." What did Truman mean? Write an essay exploring this statement as it applies to any speech that advocates for change. Analyze Kennedy's speech or another one in this section.

---

# Barack Obama's Inaugural Address

On January 20, 2009, Barack Obama was sworn in as the 44th president of the United States. Like Kennedy's inauguration, the day was very cold. But that didn't keep people from attending the historic event, which set a record attendance for any event held in Washington, D.C. The theme of the speech was "A New Birth of Freedom," a phrase from Abraham Lincoln's Gettysburg Address, which also reflected the 200th anniversary of the birth year of Abraham Lincoln.

1 My fellow citizens: I stand here today humbled by the task before us, grateful for the trust you have bestowed, mindful of the sacrifices borne by our ancestors.

2 I thank President Bush for his service to our nation, as well as the generosity and cooperation he has shown throughout this transition.

3 Forty-four Americans have now taken the presidential oath.

4 The words have been spoken during rising tides of prosperity and the still waters of peace. Yet, every so often the oath is taken amidst gathering clouds and raging storms. At these moments, America has carried on not simply because of the skill or vision of those in high office, but because We the People have remained faithful to the ideals of our forebears, and true to our founding documents.

5 So it has been. So it must be with this generation of Americans.

6 That we are in the midst of crisis is now well understood. Our nation is at war against a far-reaching network of violence and hatred. Our economy is badly weakened, a consequence of greed and irresponsibility on the part of some but also our collective failure to make hard choices and prepare the nation for a new age.

7 Homes have been lost, jobs shed, businesses shuttered. Our health care is too costly, our schools fail too many, and each day brings further evidence that the ways we use energy strengthen our adversaries and threaten our planet.

8 These are the indicators of crisis, subject to data and statistics. Less measurable, but no less profound, is a sapping of confidence across our land; a nagging fear that America's decline is inevitable, that the next generation must lower its sights.

9 Today I say to you that the challenges we face are real, they are serious and they are many. They will not be met easily or in a short span of time. But know this America: They will be met.

10 On this day, we gather because we have chosen hope over fear, unity of purpose over conflict and discord.

11 On this day, we come to proclaim an end to the petty grievances and false promises, the recriminations and worn-out dogmas that for far too long have strangled our politics.

12    We remain a young nation, but in the words of Scripture, the time has come to set aside childish things. The time has come to reaffirm our enduring spirit; to choose our better history; to carry forward that precious gift, that noble idea, passed on from generation to generation: the God-given promise that all are equal, all are free, and all deserve a chance to pursue their full measure of happiness.

13    In reaffirming the greatness of our nation, we understand that greatness is never a given. It must be earned. Our journey has never been one of shortcuts or settling for less.

14    It has not been the path for the faint-hearted, for those who prefer leisure over work, or seek only the pleasures of riches and fame.

15    Rather, it has been the risk-takers, the doers, the makers of things—some celebrated, but more often men and women obscure in their labor—who have carried us up the long, rugged path towards prosperity and freedom.

16    For us, they packed up their few worldly possessions and traveled across oceans in search of a new life. For us, they toiled in sweatshops and settled the West, endured the lash of the whip and plowed the hard earth.

17    For us, they fought and died in places like Concord and Gettysburg, Normandy and Khe Sanh.

18    Time and again these men and women struggled and sacrificed and worked till their hands were raw so that we might live a better life. They saw America as bigger than the sum of our individual ambitions; greater than all the differences of birth or wealth or faction.

19    This is the journey we continue today. We remain the most prosperous, powerful nation on Earth. Our workers are no less productive than when this crisis began. Our minds are no less inventive, our goods and services no less needed than they were last week or last month or last year. Our capacity remains undiminished. But our time of standing pat, of protecting narrow interests and putting off unpleasant decisions—that time has surely passed.

20    Starting today, we must pick ourselves up, dust ourselves off, and begin again the work of remaking America.

21    For everywhere we look, there is work to be done.

22    The state of our economy calls for action: bold and swift. And we will act not only to create new jobs but to lay a new foundation for growth.

23    We will build the roads and bridges, the electric grids and digital lines that feed our commerce and bind us together.

24    We will restore science to its rightful place and wield technology's wonders to raise health care's quality and lower its costs.

25    We will harness the sun and the winds and the soil to fuel our cars and run our factories. And we will transform our schools and colleges and universities to meet the demands of a new age.

26    All this we can do. All this we will do.

27    Now, there are some who question the scale of our ambitions, who suggest that our system cannot tolerate too many big plans. Their memories are short, for they have forgotten what this country has already done, what free men and women can achieve when imagination is joined to common purpose and necessity to courage.

28    What the cynics fail to understand is that the ground has shifted beneath them, that the stale political arguments that have consumed us for so long, no longer apply.

29    The question we ask today is not whether our government is too big or too small, but whether it works, whether it helps families find jobs at a decent wage, care they can afford, a retirement that is dignified.

30    Where the answer is yes, we intend to move forward. Where the answer is no, programs will end.

31    And those of us who manage the public's dollars will be held to account, to spend wisely, reform bad habits, and do our business in the light of day, because only then can we restore the vital trust between a people and their government.

32    Nor is the question before us whether the market is a force for good or ill. Its power to generate wealth and expand freedom is unmatched.

33    But this crisis has reminded us that without a watchful eye, the market can spin out of control. The nation cannot prosper long when it favors only the prosperous.

34    The success of our economy has always depended not just on the size of our gross domestic product, but on the reach of our prosperity; on the ability to extend opportunity to every willing heart—not out of charity, but because it is the surest route to our common good.

35    As for our common defense, we reject as false the choice between our safety and our ideals.

36    Our founding fathers, faced with perils that we can scarcely imagine, drafted a charter to assure the rule of law and the rights of man, a charter expanded by the blood of generations.

37    Those ideals still light the world, and we will not give them up for expedience's sake.

38    And so, to all other peoples and governments who are watching today, from the grandest capitals to the small village where my father was born: know that America is a friend of each nation and every man, woman, and child who seeks a future of peace and dignity, and we are ready to lead once more.

39    Recall that earlier generations faced down fascism and communism not just with missiles and tanks, but with the sturdy alliances and enduring convictions.

40    They understood that our power alone cannot protect us, nor does it entitle us to do as we please. Instead, they knew that our power grows through its prudent use. Our security emanates from the justness of our cause; the force of our example; the tempering qualities of humility and restraint.

41    We are the keepers of this legacy. Guided by these principles once more, we can meet those new threats that demand even greater effort, even greater cooperation and understanding between nations. We'll begin to responsibly leave Iraq to its people and forge a hard-earned peace in Afghanistan.

42    With old friends and former foes, we'll work tirelessly to lessen the nuclear threat and roll back the specter of a warming planet.

43    We will not apologize for our way of life nor will we waver in its defense.

44    And for those who seek to advance their aims by inducing terror and slaughtering innocents, we say to you now that, "Our spirit is stronger and cannot be broken. You cannot outlast us, and we will defeat you."

45    For we know that our patchwork heritage is a strength, not a weakness.

46    We are a nation of Christians and Muslims, Jews and Hindus, and nonbelievers. We are shaped by every language and culture, drawn from every end of this Earth.

47    And because we have tasted the bitter swill of civil war and segregation and emerged from that dark chapter stronger and more united, we cannot help but believe that the old hatreds shall someday pass; that the lines of tribe shall soon dissolve; that as the world grows smaller, our common humanity shall reveal itself; and that America must play its role in ushering in a new era of peace.

48    To the Muslim world, we seek a new way forward, based on mutual interest and mutual respect.

49    To those leaders around the globe who seek to sow conflict or blame their society's ills on the West, know that your people will judge you on what you can build, not what you destroy.

50    To those who cling to power through corruption and deceit and the silencing of dissent, know that you are on the wrong side of history, but that we will extend a hand if you are willing to unclench your fist.

51    To the people of poor nations, we pledge to work alongside you to make your farms flourish and let clean waters flow; to nourish starved bodies and feed hungry minds.

52    And to those nations like ours that enjoy relative plenty, we say we can no longer afford indifference to the suffering outside our borders, nor can we consume the world's resources without regard to effect. For the world has changed, and we must change with it.

53    As we consider the road that unfolds before us, we remember with humble gratitude those brave Americans who, at this very hour, patrol far-off deserts and distant mountains. They have something to tell us, just as the fallen heroes who lie in Arlington whisper through the ages.

54    We honor them not only because they are guardians of our liberty, but because they embody the spirit of service: a willingness to find meaning in something greater than themselves.

55    And yet, at this moment, a moment that will define a generation, it is precisely this spirit that must inhabit us all.

56    For as much as government can do and must do, it is ultimately the faith and determination of the American people upon which this nation relies.

57    It is the kindness to take in a stranger when the levees break; the selflessness of workers who would rather cut their hours than see a friend lose their job which sees us through our darkest hours.

58    It is the firefighter's courage to storm a stairway filled with smoke, but also a parent's willingness to nurture a child, that finally decides our fate.

59    Our challenges may be new, the instruments with which we meet them may be new, but those values upon which our success depends, honesty and hard work, courage and fair play, tolerance and curiosity, loyalty and patriotism—these things are old.

60    These things are true. They have been the quiet force of progress throughout our history.

61    What is demanded then is a return to these truths. What is required of us now is a new era of responsibility—a recognition, on the part of every American, that we

have duties to ourselves, our nation, and the world, duties that we do not grudgingly accept but rather seize gladly, firm in the knowledge that there is nothing so satisfying to the spirit, so defining of our character than giving our all to a difficult task.

62    This is the price and the promise of citizenship.

63    This is the source of our confidence: the knowledge that God calls on us to shape an uncertain destiny.

64    This is the meaning of our liberty and our creed, why men and women and children of every race and every faith can join in celebration across this magnificent mall. And why a man whose father less than 60 years ago might not have been served at a local restaurant can now stand before you to take a most sacred oath.

65    So let us mark this day in remembrance of who we are and how far we have traveled.

66    In the year of America's birth, in the coldest of months, a small band of patriots huddled by dying campfires on the shores of an icy river.

67    The capital was abandoned. The enemy was advancing. The snow was stained with blood.

68    At a moment when the outcome of our revolution was most in doubt, the father of our nation ordered these words be read to the people:

69    "Let it be told to the future world that in the depth of winter, when nothing but hope and virtue could survive, that the city and the country, alarmed at one common danger, came forth to meet it."

70    America, in the face of our common dangers, in this winter of our hardship, let us remember these timeless words; with hope and virtue, let us brave once more the icy currents, and endure what storms may come; let it be said by our children's children that when we were tested we refused to let this journey end, that we did not turn back nor did we falter; and with eyes fixed on the horizon and God's grace upon us, we carried forth that great gift of freedom and delivered it safely to future generations.

71    Thank you. God bless you. And God bless the United States of America.

### THINKING CRITICALLY

1. Consider how Obama describes the fight against terrorism, the need for a unified country, and issues connected to health care and the economy. How does he phrase his view of these issues?

2. Are there any phrases in this speech that fit William Lutz's definition of "doublespeak" (see page 433)? If so, identify them and explain why you think they serve as examples of this type of speech.

3. The White House website, where this speech is posted, chose to include areas where this speech met with applause (these annotations were edited out for this publication). In your opinion, does inclusion of applause influence your reception and interpretation of the speech?

4. Compare Obama's address to another speech given after he assumed the presidency (see the archives at www.whitehouse.gov). After this address, did the president's use of language change?

5. How does Obama recount historical events in this speech? Is it effective support for the points he makes in his address? Why or why not?

## WRITING ASSIGNMENTS

1. Compare and contrast Obama's speech to Kennedy's speech of almost 50 years before. In what ways, if any, are they similar? Different? Which, in your opinion, is more effective and why?

2. Presidential language serves to motivate us, persuade us, and rally us under a common cause. Have you ever found yourself influenced by a particular speech made by a U.S. president? If so, what was particularly compelling and why? Reflect on the speech and how it appealed to both your intellect and to your emotions.

## Exploring the Language of VISUALS

### Wordle of Barack Obama's Inaugural Address

A "wordle" is a tool for generating "word clouds" from text. The clouds give greater prominence to words that appear more frequently in the text. The word cloud that follows was made from Obama's inaugural address. Note what words were used most often. This word cloud was generated by wordle.net, focusing on the 100 most frequently used words in his speech.

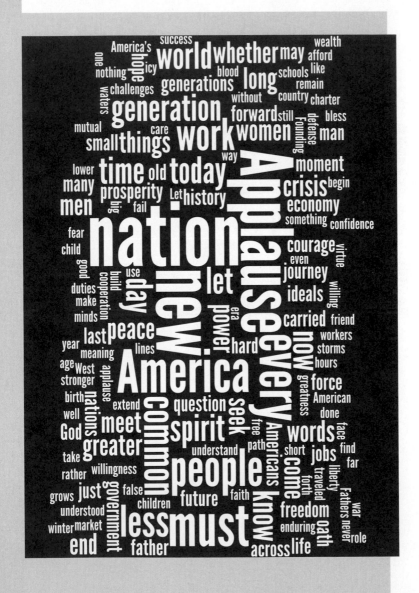

## THINKING CRITICALLY

1. This wordle focuses on the 100 most frequently used words in Obama's inaugural address. What words stand out? What, if anything, does this tell us about what points were particularly important for him to convey?

2. This word cloud was created on www.wordle.net/create. Cut and paste the words of Kennedy's inaugural address into the wordle generator. Remember to select "100 words" so that the word cloud uses the same parameters. How do the clouds compare to each other? Try this exercise with another famous speech, such as Lincoln's first or second inaugural address.

3. Is there a connection between the words a president uses and the way we view his presidency? Locate the speeches of three or four presidents, made at similar points in their careers (inaugural addresses, state of the union addresses, speeches made after a particular crisis, etc.). Generate word clouds for each and compare the results to how history has described their presidential leadership.

## MAKING CONNECTIONS

1. Have you ever been the victim of political propaganda? Have you ever voted for something or someone (or would have were you not underage) because of a campaigner's persuasive political language, or given to a cause for the same reason? Write an account of your experience and try to explain how the language influenced you.

2. Some of the most interesting examples of political language come from campaign debates. Find a campaign speech from either a local or national figure and evaluate it for the political doubletalk and avoidance tactics described by some of the authors in this section. You can find transcripts of presidential debates on the Internet. Discuss your research in an essay.

3. Compare some of the points made in "How to Detect Propaganda" with William Lutz's article, "With These Words, I Can Sell You Anything," and Charles O'Neill's article, "The Language of Advertising," both in Chapter 7. How are Lutz's "weasel words" similar to the propagandist's attempts to appeal to emotion that the Institute for Propaganda Analysis's authors identify? Do you think the Institute's authors would agree with O'Neill that the propaganda of advertising uses language in a way that is special or different from everyday use?

4. Try creating some political language of your own. Imagine you are running for office—president, senator, mayor, or school committee. Using some of the features and tricks of political language discussed in this section, write a campaign speech outlining why you, and not your opponent, should be elected. Have the class critique your speech.

5. Find political speeches from a recent campaign, either local or national. Try CNN's political pages at www.allpolitics.com or do a Google search for recent political speeches. Select one and try to identify the ways it manipulates language to sway the public. If you wish, create wordles to see which words dominate the speech.

6. Write a letter to the editor expressing your opinion about one of the speeches included in this section as if it had been recently delivered. Write your letter as if you were living in the historical period of the selection.

7. In paragraph 24 in his "Letter from Birmingham Jail," Martin Luther King, Jr., states, "We will have to repent in this generation not merely for the hateful words and actions of the bad people but for the appalling silence of the good people." Compare the implications of his statement to a speech given on April 22, 1999, by Nobel Peace Prize winner Elie Weisel, "The Perils of Indifference," at www.historyplace.com/speeches/wiesel.htm, given as part of the White House Millennium lecture series. Write an essay exploring the ideas expressed by each man, as well as your own perspective on "indifference" and "silence."

8. Select a current (within the last two years) photo, essay, or article that you think represents an example of someone challenging the status quo. Explain why you think your selection fits within the overall theme of this section. How does your photo or article compare and contrast with the selections featured in this

section? What do you think will be the long-term implications of your example of broken silence?

9. Compare the use of repetition in Martin Luther King, Jr.'s "Letter from Birmingham Jail" to that of Sojourner Truth's "Ain't I a Woman?" In what ways do they employ similar linguistic devices? How do you think each would respond to the other's oratory style? Subject matter? Explain.

# 9 Language and the Brain

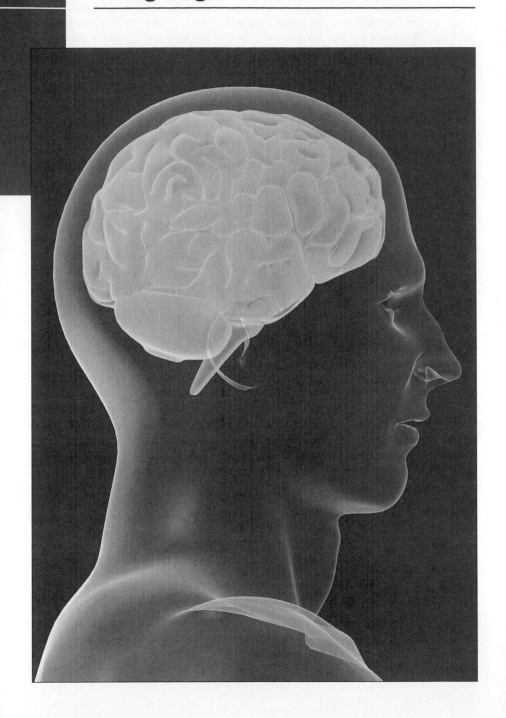

**H**umans communicate with one another with an amazing range of languages, many with different grammatical systems, nuances of tone and inflections of voice, and a wide array of sounds. While the acquisition of language is an amazing process, can the languages we speak shape the way we see the world, the way we think, and the way we live our lives? Can it influence how we interact with people of other cultures and how we view ourselves in the world? And more interestingly, does learning a new language change the way we think? And what happens when we introduce modern forms of communication into the equation, such as the Internet, texting, and e-books?

The question of whether language influences thought is not new. Linguists and neuroscientists tend to agree that the acquisition of language is a complex process that is influenced by natural forces as well as social and cultural ones— but they diverge regarding to what degree and to what extent. Over half a century ago, linguist Benjamin Lee Whorf put forth the theory that our native language significantly affects our experience of the world. Whorf even went so far as to assert that our language shapes our very thoughts. His view was challenged by many linguists, especially Noam Chomsky, who instead proposed that the human brain comes equipped at birth with a set of rules—a "universal grammar"—that organizes language no matter what country you are born in. While languages may seem very different, Chomsky argues that they are bound by the same set of neurological rules, just expressed differently.

And what effect, if any, is technology having on our language and our brain? If language influences the way we think, as some linguists believe, and technology is influencing our language, does that mean that technology is changing the way we think? The second part of this chapter explores the possible impact technology is having on the way we process thought and language.

## Language and Thought

The first section opens with a piece by Guy Deutscher, "Does Your Language Shape How You Think?" that describes the contributions of Benjamin Lee Whorf and his theories on the connections between language and thought. Whorf believed that language and thought are intertwined in profound ways, a theory that held popular until critics such as Noam Chomsky challenged the view with the theory of "universal grammar," explained in the next article by Bruno Dubuc. The argument is given a more personal viewpoint in Tom Munnecke's narrative "Nothing Is Missing," which describes the challenges and frustrations he faced as he tried to find the right words in different languages. The last two pieces in this section describe the work and findings of scientist Lera Boroditsky. First, Joan O'C. Hamilton provides an overview of Boroditsky's impact on cognitive linguistics in "You Say Up, I Say Yesterday." Then, a piece by Boroditsky herself describes her findings in "Lost in Translation."

## Digital Thought

Is technology changing our brains and how we communicate with each other? How we think? The second section in this chapter explores the influence of technology on our brains, for better or worse. First, Nicholas Carr explains why he feels our brains are suffering from digital overload in "Is Google Making Us Stoopid?" His essay is followed by a compilation of responses to his essay in "The Internet: Is It Changing the Way We Think?" pulled together by John Naughton. Finally, Steven Pinker explains why all the fuss over changing brains is really over nothing in "Mind Over Mass Media." Of course, our brains change with new experiences; that is its beauty. Pinker encourages us to consider all of the things the digital revolution has helped us achieve in a very short time as we evolve with technology.

# LANGUAGE AND THOUGHT

## Does Your Language Shape How You Think?
*Guy Deutscher*

Is language, with its varied forms, lexicons, and grammatical styles, a result of biological and neurological processes that occur naturally in the human mind? Or is language part biology and part sociology? Can our mother tongue affect how we think and perceive the world? In this next essay, linguist Guy Deutscher explains why he thinks that language plays an important role in how we think and how we view the world. Language, explains Deutscher, is more than an inherent set of rules fixed in our brain at birth. Language is the result of a matrix of cultural and social influences that help shape how we think about the world and perceive ourselves within it.

Guy Deutscher is an honorary research fellow at the School of Languages, Linguistics and Cultures at the University of Manchester. He is the author of *The Unfolding of Language*. His latest book, from which this article is adapted, is *Through the Language Glass: Why the World Looks Different in Other Languages* (2010). This article appeared in *The New York Times* on August 26, 2010.

1    Seventy years ago, in 1940, a popular science magazine published a short article that set in motion one of the trendiest intellectual fads of the 20th century. At first glance, there seemed little about the article to augur its subsequent celebrity. Neither the title, "Science and Linguistics," nor the magazine, M.I.T.'s Technology Review, was most people's idea of glamour. And the author, a chemical engineer who worked for an insurance company and moonlighted as an anthropology lecturer at Yale University, was an unlikely candidate for international superstardom. And yet Benjamin Lee Whorf let loose an alluring idea about language's power over the mind, and his stirring prose seduced a whole generation into believing that our mother tongue restricts what we are able to think.

2    In particular, Whorf announced, Native American languages impose on their speakers a picture of reality that is totally different from ours, so their speakers would simply not be able to understand some of our most basic concepts, like the

flow of time or the distinction between objects (like "stone") and actions (like "fall"). For decades, Whorf's theory dazzled both academics and the general public alike. In his shadow, others made a whole range of imaginative claims about the supposed power of language, from the assertion that Native American languages instill in their speakers an intuitive understanding of Einstein's concept of time as a fourth dimension to the theory that the nature of the Jewish religion was determined by the tense system of ancient Hebrew.

3    Eventually, Whorf's theory crash-landed on hard facts and solid common sense, when it transpired that there had never actually been any evidence to support his fantastic claims. The reaction was so severe that for decades, any attempts to explore the influence of the mother tongue on our thoughts were relegated to the loony fringes of disrepute. But 70 years on, it is surely time to put the trauma of Whorf behind us. And in the last few years, new research has revealed that when we learn our mother tongue, we do after all acquire certain habits of thought that shape our experience in significant and often surprising ways.

4    Whorf, we now know, made many mistakes. The most serious one was to assume that our mother tongue constrains our minds and prevents us from being able to think certain thoughts. The general structure of his arguments was to claim that if a language has no word for a certain concept, then its speakers would not be able to understand this concept. If a language has no future tense, for instance, its speakers would simply not be able to grasp our notion of future time. It seems barely comprehensible that this line of argument could ever have achieved such success, given that so much contrary evidence confronts you wherever you look. When you ask, in perfectly normal English, and in the present tense, "Are you coming tomorrow?" do you feel your grip on the notion of futurity slipping away? Do English speakers who have never heard the German word *Schadenfreude* find it difficult to understand the concept of relishing someone else's misfortune? Or think about it this way: If the inventory of ready-made words in your language determined which concepts you were able to understand, how would you ever learn anything new?

5    Since there is no evidence that any language forbids its speakers to think anything, we must look in an entirely different direction to discover how our mother tongue really does shape our experience of the world. Some 50 years ago, the renowned linguist Roman Jakobson pointed out a crucial fact about differences between languages in a pithy maxim: "Languages differ essentially in what they *must* convey and not in what they *may* convey." This maxim offers us the key to unlocking the real force of the mother tongue: if different languages influence our minds in different ways, this is not because of what our language *allows* us to think but rather because of what it habitually *obliges* us to think *about*.

6    Consider this example. Suppose I say to you in English that "I spent yesterday evening with a neighbor." You may well wonder whether my companion was male or female, but I have the right to tell you politely that it's none of your business. But if we were speaking French or German, I wouldn't have the privilege to equivocate in this way, because I would be obliged by the grammar of language to choose between *voisin* or *voisine*; *Nachbar* or *Nachbarin*. These languages compel me to inform you about the sex of my companion whether or not I feel it is remotely your

concern. This does not mean, of course, that English speakers are unable to understand the differences between evenings spent with male or female neighbors, but it does mean that they do not have to consider the sexes of neighbors, friends, teachers and a host of other persons each time they come up in a conversation, whereas speakers of some languages are obliged to do so.

7     On the other hand, English does oblige you to specify certain types of information that can be left to the context in other languages. If I want to tell you in English about a dinner with my neighbor, I may not have to mention the neighbor's sex, but I do have to tell you something about the timing of the event: I have to decide whether we *dined, have been dining, are dining, will be dining* and so on. Chinese, on the other hand, does not oblige its speakers to specify the exact time of the action in this way, because the same verb form can be used for past, present or future actions. Again, this does not mean that the Chinese are unable to understand the concept of time. But it does mean they are not obliged to think about timing whenever they describe an action.

8     When your language routinely obliges you to specify certain types of information, it forces you to be attentive to certain details in the world and to certain aspects of experience that speakers of other languages may not be required to think about all the time. And since such habits of speech are cultivated from the earliest age, it is only natural that they can settle into habits of *mind* that go beyond language itself, affecting your experiences, perceptions, associations, feelings, memories and orientation in the world.

9     But is there any evidence for this happening in practice?

10    Let's take genders again. Languages like Spanish, French, German and Russian not only oblige you to think about the sex of friends and neighbors, but they also assign a male or female gender to a whole range of inanimate objects quite at whim. What, for instance, is particularly feminine about a Frenchman's beard (*la barbe*)? Why is Russian water a she, and why does she become a he once you have dipped a tea bag into her? Mark Twain famously lamented such erratic genders as female turnips and neuter maidens in his rant "The Awful German Language." But whereas he claimed that there was something particularly perverse about the German gender system, it is in fact English that is unusual, at least among European languages, in not treating turnips and tea cups as masculine or feminine. Languages that treat an inanimate object as a he or a she force their speakers to talk about such an object as if it were a man or a woman. And as anyone whose mother tongue has a gender system will tell you, once the habit has taken hold, it is all but impossible to shake off. When I speak English, I may say about a bed that "it" is too soft, but as a native Hebrew speaker, I actually feel "she" is too soft. "She" stays feminine all the way from the lungs up to the glottis and is neutered only when she reaches the tip of the tongue.

11    In recent years, various experiments have shown that grammatical genders can shape the feelings and associations of speakers toward objects around them. In the 1990s, for example, psychologists compared associations between speakers of German and Spanish. There are many inanimate nouns whose genders in the two languages are reversed. A German bridge is feminine (*die Brücke*), for instance, but *el puente* is masculine in Spanish; and the same goes for clocks, apartments,

forks, newspapers, pockets, shoulders, stamps, tickets, violins, the sun, the world and love. On the other hand, an apple is masculine for Germans but feminine in Spanish, and so are chairs, brooms, butterflies, keys, mountains, stars, tables, wars, rain and garbage. When speakers were asked to grade various objects on a range of characteristics, Spanish speakers deemed bridges, clocks and violins to have more "manly properties" like strength, but Germans tended to think of them as more slender or elegant. With objects like mountains or chairs, which are "he" in German but "she" in Spanish, the effect was reversed.

12      In a different experiment, French and Spanish speakers were asked to assign human voices to various objects in a cartoon. When French speakers saw a picture of a fork (*la fourchette*), most of them wanted it to speak in a woman's voice, but Spanish speakers, for whom *el tenedor* is masculine, preferred a gravelly male voice for it. More recently, psychologists have even shown that "gendered languages" imprint gender traits for objects so strongly in the mind that these associations obstruct speakers' ability to commit information to memory.

13      Of course, all this does not mean that speakers of Spanish or French or German fail to understand that inanimate objects do not really have biological sex—a German woman rarely mistakes her husband for a hat, and Spanish men are not known to confuse a bed with what might be lying in it. Nonetheless, once gender connotations have been imposed on impressionable young minds, they lead those with a gendered mother tongue to see the inanimate world through lenses tinted with associations and emotional responses that English speakers—stuck in their monochrome desert of "its"—are entirely oblivious to. Did the opposite genders of "bridge" in German and Spanish, for example, have an effect on the design of bridges in Spain and Germany? Do the emotional maps imposed by a gender system have higher-level behavioral consequences for our everyday life? Do they shape tastes, fashions, habits and preferences in the societies concerned? At the current state of our knowledge about the brain, this is not something that can be easily measured in a psychology lab. But it would be surprising if they didn't.

14      The area where the most striking evidence for the influence of language on thought has come to light is the language of space—how we describe the orientation of the world around us. Suppose you want to give someone directions for getting to your house. You might say: "After the traffic lights, take the first left, then the second right, and then you'll see a white house in front of you. Our door is on the right." But in theory, you could also say: "After the traffic lights, drive north, and then on the second crossing drive east, and you'll see a white house directly to the east. Ours is the southern door." These two sets of directions may describe the same route, but they rely on different systems of coordinates. The first uses *egocentric* coordinates, which depend on our own bodies: a left-right axis and a front-back axis orthogonal to it. The second system uses fixed *geographic* directions, which do not rotate with us wherever we turn.

15      We find it useful to use geographic directions when hiking in the open countryside, for example, but the egocentric coordinates completely dominate our speech when we describe small-scale spaces. We don't say: "When you get out of the elevator, walk south, and then take the second door to the east." The reason the egocentric system is so dominant in our language is that it feels so much easier and

more natural. After all, we always know where "behind" or "in front of" us is. We don't need a map or a compass to work it out, we just feel it, because the egocentric coordinates are based directly on our own bodies and our immediate visual fields.

16   But then a remote Australian aboriginal tongue, Guugu Yimithirr, from north Queensland, turned up, and with it came the astounding realization that not all languages conform to what we have always taken as simply "natural." In fact, Guugu Yimithirr doesn't make any use of egocentric coordinates at all. The anthropologist John Haviland and later the linguist Stephen Levinson have shown that Guugu Yimithirr does not use words like "left" or "right," "in front of" or "behind," to describe the position of objects. Whenever we would use the egocentric system, the Guugu Yimithirr rely on cardinal directions. If they want you to move over on the car seat to make room, they'll say "move a bit to the east." To tell you where exactly they left something in your house, they'll say, "I left it on the southern edge of the western table." Or they would warn you to "look out for that big ant just north of your foot." Even when shown a film on television, they gave descriptions of it based on the orientation of the screen. If the television was facing north, and a man on the screen was approaching, they said that he was "coming northward."

17   When these peculiarities of Guugu Yimithirr were uncovered, they inspired a large-scale research project into the language of space. And as it happens, Guugu Yimithirr is not a freak occurrence; languages that rely primarily on geographical coordinates are scattered around the world, from Polynesia to Mexico, from Namibia to Bali. For us, it might seem the height of absurdity for a dance teacher to say, "Now raise your north hand and move your south leg eastward." But the joke would be lost on some: the Canadian-American musicologist Colin McPhee, who spent several years on Bali in the 1930s, recalls a young boy who showed great talent for dancing. As there was no instructor in the child's village, McPhee arranged for him to stay with a teacher in a different village. But when he came to check on the boy's progress after a few days, he found the boy dejected and the teacher exasperated. It was impossible to teach the boy anything, because he simply did not understand any of the instructions. When told to take "three steps east" or "bend southwest," he didn't know what to do. The boy would not have had the least trouble with these directions in his own village, but because the landscape in the new village was entirely unfamiliar, he became disoriented and confused. Why didn't the teacher use different instructions? He would probably have replied that saying "take three steps forward" or "bend backward" would be the height of absurdity.

18   So different languages certainly make us *speak* about space in very different ways. But does this necessarily mean that we have to *think* about space differently? By now red lights should be flashing, because even if a language doesn't have a word for "behind," this doesn't necessarily mean that its speakers wouldn't be able to understand this concept. Instead, we should look for the possible consequences of what geographic languages *oblige* their speakers to convey. In particular, we should be on the lookout for what habits of mind might develop because of the necessity of specifying geographic directions all the time.

19   In order to speak a language like Guugu Yimithirr, you need to know where the cardinal directions are at each and every moment of your waking life. You need to have a compass in your mind that operates all the time, day and night, without

lunch breaks or weekends off, since otherwise you would not be able to impart the most basic information or understand what people around you are saying. Indeed, speakers of geographic languages seem to have an almost-superhuman sense of orientation. Regardless of visibility conditions, regardless of whether they are in thick forest or on an open plain, whether outside or indoors or even in caves, whether stationary or moving, they have a spot-on sense of direction. They don't look at the sun and pause for a moment of calculation before they say, "There's an ant just north of your foot." They simply feel where north, south, west and east are, just as people with perfect pitch feel what each note is without having to calculate intervals. There is a wealth of stories about what to us may seem like incredible feats of orientation but for speakers of geographic languages are just a matter of course. One report relates how a speaker of Tzeltal from southern Mexico was blindfolded and spun around more than 20 times in a darkened house. Still blindfolded and dizzy, he pointed without hesitation at the geographic directions.

20      How does this work? The convention of communicating with geographic coordinates compels speakers from the youngest age to pay attention to the clues from the physical environment (the position of the sun, wind and so on) every second of their lives, and to develop an accurate memory of their own changing orientations at any given moment. So everyday communication in a geographic language provides the most intense imaginable drilling in geographic orientation (it has been estimated that as much as 1 word in 10 in a normal Guugu Yimithirr conversation is "north," "south," "west" or "east," often accompanied by precise hand gestures). This habit of constant awareness to the geographic direction is inculcated almost from infancy: studies have shown that children in such societies start using geographic directions as early as age 2 and fully master the system by 7 or 8. With such an early and intense drilling, the habit soon becomes second nature, effortless and unconscious. When Guugu Yimithirr speakers were asked how they knew where north is, they couldn't explain it any more than you can explain how you know where "behind" is.

21      But there is more to the effects of a geographic language, for the sense of orientation has to extend further in time than the immediate present. If you speak a Guugu Yimithirr-style language, your memories of anything that you might ever want to report will have to be stored with cardinal directions as part of the picture. One Guugu Yimithirr speaker was filmed telling his friends the story of how in his youth, he capsized in shark-infested waters. He and an older person were caught in a storm, and their boat tipped over. They both jumped into the water and managed to swim nearly three miles to the shore, only to discover that the missionary for whom they worked was far more concerned at the loss of the boat than relieved at their miraculous escape. Apart from the dramatic content, the remarkable thing about the story was that it was remembered throughout in cardinal directions: the speaker jumped into the water on the western side of the boat, his companion to the east of the boat, they saw a giant shark swimming north and so on. Perhaps the cardinal directions were just made up for the occasion? Well, quite by chance, the same person was filmed some years later telling the same story. The cardinal directions matched exactly in the two tellings. Even more remarkable were the spontaneous hand gestures that accompanied the story. For instance, the direction in which the

boat rolled over was gestured in the correct geographic orientation, regardless of the direction the speaker was facing in the two films.

22    Psychological experiments have also shown that under certain circumstances, speakers of Guugu Yimithirr-style languages even remember "the same reality" differently from us. There has been heated debate about the interpretation of some of these experiments, but one conclusion that seems compelling is that while we are trained to ignore directional rotations when we commit information to memory, speakers of geographic languages are trained not to do so. One way of understanding this is to imagine that you are traveling with a speaker of such a language and staying in a large chain-style hotel, with corridor upon corridor of identical-looking doors. Your friend is staying in the room opposite yours, and when you go into his room, you'll see an exact replica of yours: the same bathroom door on the left, the same mirrored wardrobe on the right, the same main room with the same bed on the left, the same curtains drawn behind it, the same desk next to the wall on the right, the same television set on the left corner of the desk and the same telephone on the right. In short, you have seen the same room twice. But when your friend comes into your room, he will see something quite different from this, because everything is reversed north-side-south. In his room the bed was in the north, while in yours it is in the south; the telephone that in his room was in the west is now in the east, and so on. So while you will see and remember the same room twice, a speaker of a geographic language will see and remember two different rooms.

23    It is not easy for us to conceive how Guugu Yimithirr speakers experience the world, with a crisscrossing of cardinal directions imposed on any mental picture and any piece of graphic memory. Nor is it easy to speculate about how geographic languages affect areas of experience other than spatial orientation—whether they influence the speaker's sense of identity, for instance, or bring about a less-egocentric outlook on life. But one piece of evidence is telling: if you saw a Guugu Yimithirr speaker pointing at himself, you would naturally assume he meant to draw attention to himself. In fact, he is pointing at a cardinal direction that happens to be behind his back. While we are always at the center of the world, and it would never occur to us that pointing in the direction of our chest could mean anything other than to draw attention to ourselves, a Guugu Yimithirr speaker points through himself, as if he were thin air and his own existence were irrelevant.

24    In what other ways might the language we speak influence our experience of the world? Recently, it has been demonstrated in a series of ingenious experiments that we even perceive colors through the lens of our mother tongue. There are radical variations in the way languages carve up the spectrum of visible light; for example, green and blue are distinct colors in English but are considered shades of the same color in many languages. And it turns out that the colors that our language routinely obliges us to treat as distinct can refine our purely visual sensitivity to certain color differences in reality, so that our brains are trained to exaggerate the distance between shades of color if these have different names in our language. As strange as it may sound, our experience of a Chagall painting actually depends to some extent on whether our language has a word for blue.

25    In coming years, researchers may also be able to shed light on the impact of language on more subtle areas of perception. For instance, some languages, like Matses in Peru, oblige their speakers, like the finickiest of lawyers, to specify exactly how they came to know about the facts they are reporting. You cannot simply say, as in English, "An animal passed here." You have to specify, using a different verbal form, whether this was directly experienced (you saw the animal passing), inferred (you saw footprints), conjectured (animals generally pass there that time of day), hearsay or such. If a statement is reported with the incorrect "evidentiality," it is considered a lie. So if, for instance, you ask a Matses man how many wives he has, unless he can actually see his wives at that very moment, he would have to answer in the past tense and would say something like "There were two last time I checked." After all, given that the wives are not present, he cannot be absolutely certain that one of them hasn't died or run off with another man since he last saw them, even if this was only five minutes ago. So he cannot report it as a certain fact in the present tense. Does the need to think constantly about epistemology in such a careful and sophisticated manner inform the speakers' outlook on life or their sense of truth and causation? When our experimental tools are less blunt, such questions will be amenable to empirical study.

26    For many years, our mother tongue was claimed to be a "prison house" that constrained our capacity to reason. Once it turned out that there was no evidence for such claims, this was taken as proof that people of all cultures think in fundamentally the same way. But surely it is a mistake to overestimate the importance of abstract reasoning in our lives. After all, how many daily decisions do we make on the basis of deductive logic compared with those guided by gut feeling, intuition, emotions, impulse or practical skills? The habits of mind that our culture has instilled in us from infancy shape our orientation to the world and our emotional responses to the objects we encounter, and their consequences probably go far beyond what has been experimentally demonstrated so far; they may also have a marked impact on our beliefs, values and ideologies. We may not know as yet how to measure these consequences directly or how to assess their contribution to cultural or political misunderstandings. But as a first step toward understanding one another, we can do better than pretending we all think the same.

### THINKING CRITICALLY

1. What language theory did Whorf propose? What did his theory challenge? Why did his theory fall so sharply out of favor? Explain.

2. In what ways do certain languages allow their speakers access to certain concepts and ways of thinking about things, and others do not? Provide some examples.

3. What does Deutscher mean when he observes, "if different languages influence our minds in different ways, this is not because of what our language *allows* us to think, but rather because of what it habitually *obliges* us to think *about*"?

4. In what ways does a gender system of language influence how we perceive technically neuter nouns? Provide some examples of how a gendered language system can impact how we think.

5. What is the difference between an egocentric-focused way of communicating location and a geographic one? How does it affect the brain and how we convey information about our place in space?

6. What are Guugu Yimithirr speakers? How do Guugu Yimithirr speakers experience the world?

### WRITING ASSIGNMENTS

1. Linguist Steven Pinker maintains that three things have to hold for the Whorfian hypothesis to be true: speakers of one language should find it nearly impossible to think like speakers of another language; the differences in language should affect actual reasoning; and the differences should be caused by language, not just correlated with it. Based on the information provided in this essay, respond to Pinker's challenge in which you either agree or disagree with him.

2. Deutscher describes the differences in egocentric versus geographic modes of communicating location in space and time. Create an invitation to a party, providing directions to the location as well as information on the date and time. What confusion, if any, would your invitation pose for a Chinese speaker? A Guugu Yimithirr speaker? Explain.

3. Consider the phrase, "you don't know what you don't know," in the context of language. Write a short essay exploring the way language confines us to the vocabulary of our native tongue. In what ways does it prevent us from "knowing" things?

# Chomsky's Universal Grammar
*Bruno Dubuc*

Universal grammar is a linguistic theory that argues that certain properties are inherent in all possible human languages possess. Often attributed to the linguist Noam Chomsky, the theory suggests that many of the rules of grammar are hardwired in the brain and will develop if a child is raised under normal conditions.

The following is from the online manual *The Brain from Top to Bottom,* explaining the fundamentals of universal grammar. The site was developed, researched, and written by Bruno Dubuc and funded by the Canadian Institutes of Health Research: Institute of Neurosciences, Mental Health and Addiction (INMHA).

1 During the first half of the 20th century, linguists who theorized about the human ability to speak did so from the behaviorist perspective that prevailed at that time. They therefore held that language learning, like any other kind of learning, could be explained by a succession of trials, errors, and rewards for success. In other words, children learned their mother tongue by simple imitation, listening to and repeating what adults said.

2 This view became radically questioned, however, by the American linguist Noam Chomsky. For Chomsky, acquiring language cannot be reduced to simply developing an inventory of responses to stimuli, because every sentence that anyone produces can be a totally new combination of words. When we speak, we combine a finite number of elements—the words of our language—to create an infinite number of larger structures—sentences.

3   Moreover, language is governed by a large number of rules and principles, particularly those of syntax, which determine the order of words in sentences. The term "generative grammar" refers to the set of rules that enables us to understand sentences but of which we are usually totally unaware. It is because of generative grammar that everyone says "that's how you say it" rather than "how that's you it say," or that the words "Bob" and "him" cannot mean the same person in the sentence "Bob loves him." but can do so in "Bob knows that his father loves him." (Note in passing that generative grammar has nothing to do with grammar textbooks, whose purpose is simply to explain what is grammatically correct and incorrect in a given language.)

4   Even before the age of 5, children can, without having had any formal instruction, consistently produce and interpret sentences that they have never encountered before. It is this extraordinary ability to use language despite having had only very partial exposure to the allowable syntactic variants that led Chomsky to formulate his "poverty of the stimulus" argument, which was the foundation for the new approach that he proposed in the early 1960s.

5   In Chomsky's view, the reason that children so easily master the complex operations of language is that they have innate knowledge of certain principles that guide them in developing the grammar of their language. In other words, Chomsky's theory is that language learning is facilitated by a predisposition that our brains have for certain structures of language.

6   But what language? For Chomsky's theory to hold true, all of the languages in the world must share certain structural properties. And indeed, Chomsky and other generative linguists like him have shown that the 5000 to 6000 languages in the world, despite their very different grammars, do share a set of syntactic rules and principles. These linguists believe that this "universal grammar" is innate and is embedded somewhere in the neuronal circuitry of the human brain. And that would be why children can select, from all the sentences that come to their minds, only those that conform to a "deep structure" encoded in the brain's circuits.

## Universal Grammar

7 Universal grammar, then, consists of a set of unconscious constraints that let us decide whether a sentence is correctly formed. This mental grammar is not necessarily the same for all languages. But according to Chomskyian theorists, the process by which, in any given language, certain sentences are perceived as correct while others are not, is universal and independent of meaning.

8   Thus, we immediately perceive that the sentence "Robert book reads the" is not correct English, even though we have a pretty good idea of what it means. Conversely, we recognize that a sentence such as "Colorless green ideas sleep furiously." is grammatically correct English, even though it is nonsense.

9   A pair of dice offers a useful metaphor to explain what Chomsky means when he refers to universal grammar as a "set of constraints." Before we throw the pair of dice, we know that the result will be a number from 2 to 12, but nobody would take a bet on its being 3.143. Similarly, a newborn baby has the potential to speak any of a number of languages, depending on what country it is born in, but it will not

just speak them any way it likes: it will adopt certain preferred, innate structures. One way to describe these structures would be that they are not things that babies and children learn, but rather things that happen to them. Just as babies naturally develop arms and not wings while they are still in the womb, once they are born they naturally learn to speak, and not to chirp or neigh.

## Observations That Support the Chomskyian View of Language

10 Until Chomsky propounded his theory of universal grammar in the 1960s, the empiricist school that had dominated thinking about language since the Enlightenment held that when children came into the world, their minds were like a blank slate. Chomsky's theory had the impact of a large rock thrown into this previously tranquil, undisturbed pond of empiricism.

11     Subsequent research in the cognitive sciences, which combined the tools of psychology, linguistics, computer science, and philosophy, soon lent further support to the theory of universal grammar. For example, researchers found that babies only a few days old could distinguish the phonemes of any language and seemed to have an innate mechanism for processing the sounds of the human voice.

12     Thus, from birth, children would appear to have certain linguistic abilities that predispose them not only to acquire a complex language, but even to create one from whole cloth if the situation requires. One example of such a situation dates back to the time of plantations and slavery. On many plantations, the slaves came from many different places and so had different mother tongues. They therefore developed what are known as pidgin languages to communicate with one another. Pidgin languages are not languages in the true sense, because they employ words so chaotically—there is tremendous variation in word order, and very little grammar. But these slaves' children, though exposed to these pidgins at the age when children normally acquire their first language, were not content to merely imitate them. Instead, the children spontaneously introduced grammatical complexity into their speech, thus in the space of one generation creating new languages, known as creoles.

## Chomsky and the Evolution of Language

13 Many authors, adopting the approach of evolutionary psychology, believe that language has been shaped by natural selection. In their view, certain random genetic mutations were thus selected over many thousands of years to provide certain individuals with a decisive adaptive advantage. Whether the advantage that language provided was in coordinating hunting parties, warning of danger, or communicating with sexual partners remains uncertain, however.

14     Chomsky, for his part, does not see our linguistic faculties as having originated from any particular selective pressure, but rather as a sort of fortuitous accident. He bases this view, among other things, on studies which found that recursivity—the ability to embed one clause inside another, as in "the person who was singing yesterday had a lovely voice"—might be the only specifically human component of language. According to the authors of these studies, recursivity originally developed not to help us communicate, but rather to help us solve other problems connected, for example, with numerical quantification or social relations, and humans

did not become capable of complex language until recursivity was linked with the other motor and perceptual abilities needed for this purpose. (Thus recursivity would meet the definition of a spandrel offered by Stephen Jay Gould.) According to Chomsky and his colleagues, there is nothing to indicate that this linkage was achieved through natural selection. They believe that it might simply be the result of some other kind of neuronal reorganization.

## The Minimalist Program

15 In the 1990s, Chomsky's research focused on what he called the "minimalist program," which attempted to demonstrate that the brain's language faculties are the minimum faculties that could be expected, given certain external conditions that are imposed on us independently. In other words, Chomsky began to place less emphasis on something such as a universal grammar embedded in the human brain, and more emphasis on a large number of plastic cerebral circuits. And along with this plasticity would come an infinite number of concepts. The brain would then proceed to associate sounds and concepts, and the rules of grammar that we observe would in fact be only the consequences, or side effects, of the way that language works. Analogously, we can, for example, use rules to describe the way a muscle operates, but these rules do nothing but explain what happens in the muscle; they do not explain the mechanisms that the brain uses to generate these rules.

## Criticisms of Chomsky's Theories

16 Chomsky thus continues to believe that language is "pre-organized" in some way or other within the neuronal structure of the human brain, and that the environment only shapes the contours of this network into a particular language. His approach thus remains radically opposed to that of Skinner or Piaget, for whom language is constructed solely through simple interaction with the environment. This latter, behaviorist model, in which the acquisition of language is nothing but a by-product of general cognitive development based on sensorimotor interaction with the world, would appear to have been abandoned as the result of Chomsky's theories.

17 Since Chomsky first advanced these theories, however, evolutionary biologists have undermined them with the proposition that it may be only the brain's general abilities that are "pre-organized." These biologists believe that to try to understand language, we must approach it not from the standpoint of syntax, but rather from that of evolution and the biological structures that have resulted from it. According to Philip Lieberman, for example, language is not an instinct encoded in the cortical networks of a "language organ," but rather a learned skill based on a "functional language system" distributed across numerous cortical and subcortical structures.

18 Though Lieberman does recognize that human language is by far the most sophisticated form of animal communication, he does not believe that it is a qualitatively different form, as Chomsky claims. Lieberman sees no need to posit a quantum leap in evolution or a specific area of the brain that would have been the seat of this innovation. On the contrary, he says that language can be described as a neurological system composed of several separate functional abilities.

19    For Lieberman and other authors, such as Terrence Deacon, it is the neural circuits of this system, and not some "language organ," that constitute a genetically predetermined set that limits the possible characteristics of a language. In other words, these authors believe that our ancestors invented modes of communication that were compatible with the brain's natural abilities. And the constraints inherent in these natural abilities would then have manifested themselves in the universal structures of language.

20    Another approach that offers an alternative to Chomsky's universal grammar is generative semantics, developed by linguist George Lakoff of the University of California at Berkeley. In contrast to Chomsky, for whom syntax is independent of such things as meaning, context, knowledge, and memory, Lakoff shows that semantics, context, and other factors can come into play in the rules that govern syntax. In addition, metaphor, which earlier authors saw as a simple linguistic device, becomes for Lakoff a conceptual construct that is essential and central to the development of thought.

21    Lastly, even among those authors who embrace Chomsky's universal grammar, there are various conflicting positions, in particular about how this universal grammar may have emerged. Steven Pinker, for instance, takes an adaptationist position that departs considerably from the exaptation thesis proposed by Chomsky.

### THINKING CRITICALLY

1. How did Chomsky challenge the prevalent linguistic viewpoint that children learn language through trial and error? Explain.

2. What does "generative grammar" mean? What role in language development does generative grammar play as children learn language? Explain.

3. Chomsky's theory seemed so compelling that it became the linguistic norm for many years. What evidence is provided to support Chomsky's theory? What made it so compelling?

4. What challenges have been made to Chomsky's theory? How might Deutscher respond to the theory?

5. In your opinion, which viewpoint seems more compelling, Whorf's linguistic theory or Chomsky's? A combination of both? Explain.

### WRITING ASSIGNMENTS

1. Steven Pinker has adopted an "adaptationist" position on language acquisition that diverges from Chomsky's exaptation thesis. Research Pinker's viewpoint and explain why it is stronger or less convincing than Chomsky's explanation.

2. Compare some of the linguistic theories presented in this section with points raised in the first chapter of this book on "coming into language." How does understanding of language development in the brain aid our understanding of "coming into language" as humans communicating with each other? Write an essay exploring the connection between our scientific understanding of what happens in our brains and our social understanding of how we might communicate with each other.

# Nothing Is Missing
*Tom Munnecke*

In the first essay in this section, Guy Deutscher described how our native language may influence how we think about the world and our place in it. In the personal narrative that follows, Tom Munnecke explains how speaking and thinking in different languages presented unique frustrations for him. While learning a new language such as German opened new doors of understanding and ways of viewing things, it also left him at a loss when trying to describe his new viewpoints in his native language, English, which lacked words for ideas and concepts that had words in German. The result was Tom's living within different linguistic "shells," each with its own opportunities and limitations.

Tom Munnecke is one of the world's leading experts in health information technology. He is particularly interested in innovation at the intersection of health care, personalization, and social network technologies. Although he has lived in Southern California most of his life, he has traveled to over 70 countries. He maintains a journal/blog, on which the following memoir was published.

1   I first noticed it when I was seven years old, attending school for a year in Canada. I had been living in the San Fernando valley, in Southern California, which a few decades later would be the epicenter of the "valley girl" dialect. It was the first trickle of intuition which would later become a flood over the years.

2   I attended school in rural route 9 in Crumblin, just outside of London, Ontario. The issue was the pronunciation of the letter Z. I had grown up from my earliest nursery school days pronouncing it zee. But in Canada, they pronounced it zed. The same letter had two different pronunciations. I could understand color becoming colour; this was two different symbols meaning the same thing. But Z was the same symbol working two different ways, depending on where I was living. This made an indelible impression on me as a seven-year-old. Language was not quite the rock solid foundation I had assumed.

3   I next experienced it in Göttingen, Germany. I was 15, and found myself sitting in a German *Gymnasium* classroom, listening to teachers speak in an entirely different language. Instead of one sound being different, I discovered a whole new world. As I gradually became fluent in German over the next 3 months, I realized that the German world was different from the English world. They had names for things and concepts which simply did not exist in English. Things which they took for granted, I struggled to understand.

4   When I came back to California after 9 months of immersion in the German world, I found myself stuttering when I tried to speak English. Thoughts would come to me in German, and I would have to translate them back into English. German was not just a sound or a language, but an entire culture—a language shell within which they lived. My German friends all expanded their German/English language shells together—so it became a shared cultural experience to them. I, on the other hand, had to build my own shell, making my own connections and associations.

5   I had a very hard time explaining this situation to my English-speaking friends. I could relate endless examples of the differences I noted, but I could not explain

the whole situation. It was as if I had words to describe the atoms, but not the molecules. Something was missing in my ability to express things about this situation. I could see things which I could not talk about. No one else had my particular amalgamation of language shells. Neither language could express things which were outside of it. It was as if I were living in a cognitive no-man's land.

6    Reality was not a perfectly precise, enclosed shell in which everything was rational: a word for every thought and a thought for every word. There were always holes in the fabric of reality, which normal people simply ignored in order to maintain their rationality.

7    For example, consider the sentence, "This sentence is false." Is the sentence true? If so, it must be false. Is the sentence false? If so, then it must be true. Paradoxes like this abound in any language which is capable of referring to itself. Somehow, we manage to construct a meaningful reality with language which uses both logic and self-referential logic. We ignore the paradoxes inherent in our language, and carry on as if the world is completely rational. There was something missing in our language shells which kept us from falling into irrational self referential gibberish. Like the blind spot we all have in our field of vision, we simply overlook what is missing and carry on.

8    I came to see my linguistic shell with great ambivalence. On the one hand, it provided a comfortable environment, safe from the paradoxical or the unknown. On the other hand, however, it trapped me and my thinking within a restricted, confined realm which did not allow the discussion of things outside of it.

9    Very few people realized this—that their entire linguistic reality was ensconced within a language shell in which they could think everything they could say, and say everything they could think. The problem is, there are very powerful things outside that speech/thought shell which are simply "nothing" to their normal reality.

10    Those who venture too far outside their shell do so at great peril. Rip the fabric too far, and we can not communicate with anyone, not even yourself. Language simply fails to operate when attempting to wrap words around these phantoms outside of language.

11    Travelling to Japan jolted me into understanding the "nothings" outside my Western linguistic shell. I spent the night in a ryokan, a traditional Japanese inn. Everything was perfect. The room was tiled perfectly with fragrant tatami mats, spotlessly clean. It seemed to float above the koi ponds outside, and had a delightful private garden outside the window.

12    However, the flower arrangement in the nook disturbed me greatly. The vase, to my Western sense of composition, was off-center. Why would they go through such a great effort to do the flower arrangement, then make the mistake of putting it off to one side of the nook? I almost moved it, but thought better of it—there must have been some reason for it. I went to sleep on the futon under the nook, pondering the problem. There must have been some reason for this off-center placement.

13    I woke up the next morning with fresh eyes. I knew, without even looking, why the vase was where it was. The flowers arched over the emptiness of the nook, creating a negative space that accentuated the flow of the arrangement. I saw the whole thing as *flowing* instead of just *sitting*. And somehow, the emptiness of the space the flower framed was connected to the emptiness of my linguistic shell.

Words created negative space, but we were blind to it. Words were *sitting*; reality was *flowing*.

14     The vase was in the perfect position. It had not moved, but rather my perception of it was kind of a cognitive earthquake.

15     I had changed.

16     This was a whole new way of seeing for me. I had never seen things flow like this before. It was as if I had been looking only at static views, snapshots of the world, and was now able to see a motion picture. I could play the frames in single image mode and analyze the difference between each frame, but now it was easier to let the movie play and see the whole picture. Things that previously could only be glimpsed with the greatest of analytical effort from the snapshots were now perfectly clear to me. I just needed to sit back and look at the flow. It was as if all of my culture, education and language had taught me to look only at the snapshots. Understanding flow required great specialization and understanding of the differences between two frames, and had to be repeated again for the third frame. People spend whole careers locked in this process, finding ever greater detail and differences between frames. They measured their progress by counting the degree of detail they discovered.

17     I began to see flow in all of the Japanese art. In Hokusai's "The Wave," I suddenly saw the canoeists in the water. Gardens suddenly had a path in them, which completely changed my vision of what they were about. Gardens flowed in time, in my position in them, in season, and in my perception of them.

18     I had no word for this experience. It was simply outside of my language shell, and the generally accepted Western languages. Flow was an extremely weak word for it, one of those specialized analyses of a single frame. Silence, "seeing the world from the outside in," "blacks and whites as shades of gray," "dichotomous things becoming one," are just some of the other definitions I might have chosen. It was related to the hypnotic effects of watching waves on the beach or a campfire. We are in a fixed place, watching a single thing, but it is constantly changing. And like trying to explain what I was thinking after 20 minutes of watching the surf or campfire, it is very difficult to express the experience in words.

19     The flower arrangement was but a weak prelude to what I would experience at the Nanzenji temple in Kyoto. There is a dry landscape garden there, called the "leaping tiger." At first glance, it is just a set of rocks and bushes set in a bed of gravel. It was set in such a beautiful setting, I knew that there was something more to it. I sat on the steps of the veranda, feeling much of the sense of tranquility I felt in the ryokan. But I could not see the flow. I could see the snapshot, and the stark simplicity had its hypnotic effect on me. It was not unlike watching the surf or a campfire, only it was fixed and the observer had to provide the motion.

20     I knew the garden was creating a negative space for something, like the nook in the ryokan. But where was the space, and what was the negative it was framing?

21     I stared at the garden, becoming increasingly aggravated at the scene. Something was flowing, I knew, but I could not see it. As much as I tried to put words and concepts together, even with my new-found "flower arrangement" eyes, I could not understand it. I began to see glimpses of the emptiness framed by the garden, but every time I focused on the glimpse, it disappeared.

22    I became ever more anxious about it. It seemed the harder I looked, the further away it got. It was as if it were an invisible chasm, pulling me towards it, but disappearing every time I looked at it.

23    Finally, in a snit of frustration, I turned away. I turned my back to the garden, and walked away.

24    And then I saw it.

25    All of the fabric piecing together my language shell simply dissolved away. Not looking at the garden, I saw it. Not understanding it, I understood its meaning. Being confused, I discovered the truth. Being hot, I was cold. Being public, I was private. Being outside, I was inside. Seeing the flow, I could see the snapshot. Having no language, I had a new language. Seeing time, I could lose it. Being weak, I was strong. Not struggling, I accomplished what I sought. Big was little, black was white, hard was soft, language was no language, up was down, left was right, light was dark. I understood everything by understanding nothing.

26    The negative space created by the garden was me and my own perceptions. I was at the center of a self-referential universe, one huge paradox. All of the distinctions and categories I used to describe it folded back on themselves, as if the universe were just a huge hall of mirrors, endlessly reflecting what we look at.

27    From the universe-as-hall-of-mirrors perspective, shining a light on a subject only increases the number of reflections you can see. Rather than making the original thing more visible, it makes it harder to see, lost in the reflections. Turning away from the mirrors manipulated by words, I could see the original object.

28    I could see my own linguistic shell—somehow, I had moved outside of it, and in the overwhelming confusion of the moment, it became clear to me that words were just a form of organizing and categorizing. The shell is a kind of prison within which we capture thought and language, in which we struggle to force them to behave in logical, consistent ways. We ostracize thoughts or language which escape the shell, calling them illogical, inconsistent, foolish, or childlike. Within our shell, it is legal to endlessly recite examples of things which are reflections of some thing just outside our shell. To reach out and grab the original thing, however, requires a huge amount of cognitive civil disobedience. The linguistic community permits only the most infrequent excursions, it exerts control over our thoughts which make even the most authoritative dictator pale in comparison.

29    I found that nearly every word I had was dozens of reflections away from its source in the hall of cognitive mirrors. Things were far more connected, and in far simpler ways, than my linguistic shell would allow. It was our way of creating words and thoughts which was creating the gulf between them. I could feel public and private at the same time, they were not dichotomous after all. Somehow, my linguistic shell conspired to force them apart, into an "If one, then not the other" relationship.

30    I became particularly skeptical of hierarchies. It seemed that the authority of the shell was driven by top-down delineation and categorization. In a hierarchical outline, the top left hand category was the most general. It controlled everything else below it, not unlike a general controlling an army. Everything below this most

general category is subservient to it. It got there in a process of elimination—it was not some other category. The hierarchy provides a tidy way to pigeonhole our thoughts. A place for every thought, and a thought for every place.

31    Our linguistic shells control us by these huge arrays of overlapping categories. We fix our thoughts and words according to these hierarchies, allowing us to ignore the scaffolding creating by the pigeonhole process.

32    This scheme works well in many cases. When I am asked for the location of the nearest rest room, I would be disappointed if I were shown a place where I could only rest. The commonly accepted English shell has bound "rest room" and "toilet" together in a commonly understood manner. It is necessary to categorize and bind specific concepts to specific words. These words and concepts support the snapshot world.

33    However, there are problems and domains in which this kind of cognitive pigeonholing breaks down. Frequently, it is related to the difference between snapshot and movie modes of viewing.

34    For example, we can look at a spider web and the moth as two snapshots in nature. The spider has a sticky web to collect moths, and the moth has powdery wings to defend against the stickiness of the web. The cleverness of these two survival schemes can be seen as a miracle of nature. We could analyze nature and find endless examples of this type of interaction between species, and create a huge hierarchically organized library of such effects—a photo album of all the snapshot interactions of nature, so to speak. Marveling at number and complexity of the collection, we would be tempted to assume that there had to be some centrally planned and controlled universe which could manage such a complex set of snapshots.

35    Or, we could see these things as merely examples of the flow of a movie, two species coevolving over time. Evolution is the flow view, creating the endless number of snapshots in nature.

36    What controls the waves on the ocean? They both existed before Newton's $F=ma$. Our laws of nature are descriptors, not controllers. One could create a law of jaywalking, which states stoplights create jaywalkers.

37    I am not denigrating Newton's $F=ma$. One cannot help to marvel at the bridges, skyscrapers, and trips to the moon which it has allowed. It is the kingpin of a linguistic shell used by scientists and engineers with huge success.

38    But Newton's shell, like all shells, is limited in its scope. It presumed a world in which things were moving at much less than the speed of light, for example. Considering motion of bodies at near the speed of light was nothing Newton was concerned about.

39    Newton's shell also assumed a certain sense of objectivity. Scientists could watch balls on a billiard table (or, in their mind's eye, construct a frictionless one) from the outside. They could watch a ball with a certain mass and velocity strike one another, and predict with uncanny precision the results of the collision. The scientists hovered over their virtual billiard table, assumed perfectly calibrated clocks, and watched the process as objective observers. It was repeatable and predictable.

40    If I were sitting on the top of a rocket to be launched to the moon, I would be very happy to know that all of the components of the rocket were operating in a repeatable and predictable manner. The whole rocket is the sum of each of the components; I would rather not have the rocket display some unexpected property during liftoff.

41    Much in the same manner as our linguistic shells exclude paradoxical sentences, Newton's shell excluded situations where the observer *is* the object. If, instead of inanimate billiard balls, we put Newton and LaPlace on the frictionless table, there would be no way to predict the outcome of a collision. The observers and the objects have become one.

42    Herein lies the most challenging unknown to our linguistic shells of today. How do we deal with systems which are so vast and comprehensive that they can change our entire physical world and our future generations? These systems have no central point of control. There is no king of the Internet, master of the weather, emperor of the rainforests, corporation owning the ocean, global health system, or a worldwide family planner.

43    In the past, we allowed these issues to be relegated to science or religion. Science dealt with matters which could be treated objectively, religion and superstition handled much the rest. A vast reservoir of emptiness, however, lies just beyond the linguistic shell which binds these two, waiting to be discovered.

44    The world is not shrinking, it is just that our notion of distance is collapsing. Satellite television and electronic mail are connecting people globally with little or no respect for geographical, political, or time-zone boundaries.

45    Distance is being replaced by the notion of connectivity. Two things are far away if they are not connected, close together if they are connected. Connection is not based on physical proximity, but rather the flow of bits.

46    Our notion of linguistic shells—the very foundation of how we use language and thought—is based on the notion of distance. We separate things, categorize them, and create our languages based on notions of proximity which have been true over the millennia. Today, however, the boundaries of these shells are both collapsing and exploding.

47    This implosion/explosion of our world as we know it will perhaps be the most significant process in our species' evolutionary lifespan. And it will all occur as a result of something which is invisible to us now, a missing nothing.

### THINKING CRITICALLY

1. How did Munnecke's experience as a young child in Canada with the letter "zee/zed" open his eyes to some of the challenges of language? Explain.

2. What does Munnecke mean by the term *linguistic shell*?

3. Munnecke observes, "Very few people realize . . . that their entire linguistic reality was ensconced within a language shell in which they could think everything they could say, and say everything they could think." What challenges does confinement in one "shell" present the speaker? The thinker?

4. What does Munnecke's experience in the Japanese inn reveal to him about language? About his view of the world?

5. Munnecke admits that "the flow" doesn't adequately explain his experience in Japan. Does this prevent the reader from understanding his experience? Why or why not?

6. What conclusions does Munnecke draw from his multiple experiences? Did any in particular strike you as particularly interesting or on point? If so, which ones and why?

## WRITING ASSIGNMENTS

1. If you speak another language in addition to your native tongue, can you relate to Munnecke's experience of having words or terminology to describe certain things in one language but not in another? If so, write a personal narrative describing your own experience with this quirk of language, and how, if at all, it impacted your ability to communicate.

2. Munnecke's experiences in Japan create a sort of epiphany for him in which he emerges seeing the world in a completely different way. Describe a time when you experienced something that completely changed your view of the world and yourself in it.

3. In what ways do words limit us? Write an essay in which you explore the idea that instead of helping us communicate, words can actually prevent us from experiencing the world fully.

# Exploring the Language of **V I S U A L S**

## Calvin and Hobbes

### THINKING CRITICALLY

1. What does Calvin mean when he says he likes to "verb" words? Have you ever "verbed"? Explain.

2. Calvin gives an example of a word that was a noun but now is a verb. Can you think of other examples?

3. Verbing often occurs when something in our lives requires a new word to describe an experience or action, usually because of the introduction of new technology or ways of doing something. Think of some examples of how technology has changed the way we live our lives and thus necessitated our creating new words to describe our activities.

# You Say Up, I Say Yesterday
*Joan O'C. Hamilton*

Can language really shape how we think? Stanford researcher Lera Boroditsky says yes, and her work speaks volumes about what makes people tick. Some languages provide nuances that others do not, such as intention, gender, and spatial relationships. The result is that the speaker of one language may think about things a little differently than the speaker of another language. These subtle differences could have larger implications for communication and the limitations as well as the full range of possibilities granted by human language.

Joan O'C. Hamilton is a writer with extensive experience in magazine journalism and is a former bureau chief, columnist, and correspondent for *Business Week* magazine. She helps high-profile people share their stories, including coauthoring e-Bay founder Meg Whitman's *The Power of Many*. Her articles have appeared in *The New York Times*, *Town & Country*, *Wired*, *Technology Review*, *Stanford Lawyer*, *Stanford Medicine*, *The Boston Globe*, and many other publications. This article first appeared in the May/June 2010 issue of *Stanford University Magazine*.

1 Lera Boroditsky's journey to answer one of psychology's most intriguing and fractious questions has been a curious one. She's spent hours showing Spanish-speakers videos of balloons popping, eggs cracking and paper ripping. She's scoured Stanford and MIT's math and computer science departments for Russian speakers willing to spend an hour sorting shades of blue. She's even traipsed to a remote aboriginal village in Australia where small children shook their heads at what they considered her pitiable sense of direction and took her hand to show her how to avoid being gobbled by a crocodile. Yet she needs little more than a teacup on her office coffee table to explain the essence of her research.

2 "In English," she says, moving her hand toward the cup, "if I knock this cup off the table, even accidentally, you would likely say, 'She broke the cup.'" However, in Japanese or Spanish, she explains, intent matters.

3 If one deliberately knocks the cup, there is a verb form to indicate as much. But if the act were an accident, Boroditsky explains, a smile dancing across her lips as she translates from Spanish, the speaker would essentially say, "The cup broke itself."

4 The question is: Does the fact that one language tends to play the blame game while the other does not mean speakers of those languages think differently about what happened? If so, what might linguistic differences tell us about cognition, perception and memory—and with what implications for such perennial debates as the influence of nature versus nurture? Welcome to the intensely spirited academic debate on which Boroditsky has spent the last decade shining a bright new light.

5 As anyone who's studied a new language understands well, languages differ in myriad ways beyond simply having, as comedian Steve Martin once observed, "a different word for everything." They may assign nouns different genders—in German, moon is masculine; in French and Spanish, feminine—or none. Others require specific verb choices depending on whether an action was completed or not, or whether the speaker witnessed it or is reporting secondhand.

6      But Boroditsky, PhD '01, is not a linguist. She is a cognitive scientist—specifically, an assistant professor of psychology, neuroscience and symbolic systems—who pays attention to what a speaker of a given language thinks, perceives and remembers about an event. In that realm, the answer to the blame-game question turns out not to be obvious at all.

7      Boroditsky's research suggests, for example, that the mechanics of using a language such as English, which tends to assign an agent to an action regardless of the agent's intent, also tends to more vividly imprint that agent in the speaker's memory. Other linguistic differences help young children in aboriginal cultures achieve powers of navigation that would confound a Harvard professor. She is amassing a body of intriguing and creative evidence that language influences how its speakers focus their attention, remember events and people, and think about the world around them. And these influences may provide insight to a given culture's conception of time, space, color or even justice.

8      Boroditsky's colleagues and mentors say her research is generating breakthrough insights. She is "one of the first to show truly convincing effects of language on cognitive processes," including mental imagery, reasoning, perception and problem solving, says Daniel Slobin, a professor emeritus of psychology and linguistics at UC-Berkeley. Slobin coined the term "thinking for speaking" to describe how the language-specific ways different cultures talk about space and time shape how they think about space and time. He adds that Boroditsky "has taken on some of the major dimensions of abstract thought."

9      Slobin, like Boroditsky, is often called a "neo-Whorfian" cognitive scientist. The connection between language and thought has long captivated poets, philosophers, linguists and thinkers of many sorts, but the modern debate has its roots in the work of the early 20th-century American linguist Benjamin Whorf and his Yale mentor, Edward Sapir. They thought that the structure of language was integral to both thought and cultural evolution, a notion sometimes called linguistic relativity.

10      However, others—most notably MIT linguist Noam Chomsky—later argued that all languages share the same deep structure of thought and that thought has a universal quality separate from language. (Babies think before they learn to speak, so thought is not dependent on language.) Those scientists believe that languages express thinking and perception in different ways but do not shape the thinking and perception. In the case of the teacup, that school would argue that surely a speaker of any language absorbs the same information at the scene regardless of the conventions of verb form used and, if pressed, can convey exactly what happened by adding more specific descriptions.

11      Boroditsky's research suggests that may not be so. She has shown that speakers of languages that use "non-agentive" verb forms—those that don't indicate an animate actor—are less likely to remember who was involved in an incident. In one experiment, native Spanish speakers are shown videos of several kinds of acts that can be classified as either accidental or intentional, such as an egg breaking or paper tearing. In one, for example, a man sitting at a table clearly and deliberately sticks a pin into the balloon. In another variation, the same man moves his hand toward the balloon and appears surprised when it pops. The Spanish speakers tend to remember the person who deliberately punctured the balloon, but they do not

as easily recall the person who witnesses the pop but did not deliberately cause it. English speakers tend to remember the individual in both the videos equally; they don't pay more or less attention based on the intention of the person in the video.

12    Almost a decade ago, Boroditsky, then a young assistant professor at MIT, conducted a study of Mandarin speakers that thrust her into the spotlight. English speakers, she explains, tend to see time on a horizontal plane: The best years are ahead; he put his past behind him. Speakers of Mandarin, however, tend to see time both horizontally and vertically, with new events emerging from the ground like a spring of water, the past above and the future below. Boroditsky's first paper on this work attracted what her colleagues say were unusually spirited rebuffs claiming the work was flawed and could not be duplicated. But later studies have shown the same results.

13    One vocal critic of neo-Whorfian ideas is Lila Gleitman, professor emerita of psychology and linguistics at the University of Pennsylvania. Gleitman argues that Boroditsky and other neo-Whorfians' results are highly dependent on the context in which these experiments take place. They neglect the reality that "linguistic representations under-determine the conceptual contents they are used to convey: Language is sketchy compared with the richness of our thoughts," Gleitman says. In other words, however precise and specific the conventions of one language may be, the lack of those conventions in another language does not mean a speaker's thinking or perception is similarly sparse.

14    Boroditsky's own journey began in Belarus, where she was the only child of parents who were both engineers. At 12, she says, she spoke Russian and struggled with Belarusian and Ukrainian. She was learning English in school when her parents got the opportunity to emigrate. A close friend had preceded them by three months and settled in Skokie, Ill., where they went as well. Boroditsky's background and passion for argument earned her the nickname "Red Fury" in high school, she says with a laugh. She recalls thinking even as a teenager about the degree to which language could shape an argument and exaggerate the differences between people.

15    She enrolled at Northwestern, where she intended to work on a larger-scale theory of cognitive science. Dedre Gentner, a professor of psychology, became a mentor. Gentner says Boroditsky immediately distinguished herself among undergraduates. "She asked just fabulous questions and I grabbed her and said, 'Are you doing research?'" Gentner brought her into her research group and says that from day one Boroditsky displayed courage and cleverness. "She is just fearless about pursuing information."

16    For her PhD, Boroditsky came to Stanford and worked with psychology professor Gordon Bower. She became an assistant professor in the department of brain and cognitive sciences at MIT before she returned to Stanford in 2004. "It's exceedingly rare for us to hire back our own graduate students," notes Bower, who was Boroditsky's thesis adviser. "She brought a very high IQ and a tremendous ability for penetrating analysis."

17    Boroditsky, 33, blends intellectual gravitas with an unmistakable love of whimsy. The day we meet, her sparkly silver shoes contrast nicely with her huge, bright aubergine couch, and photographs show her driving a banana-like vehicle around the Burning Man festival. She has dubbed her lab "Cognation," and her

tongue-in-cheek website includes funny profiles of her graduate students and an invitation to sing along to the "Cognation national anthem," a music clip of Groucho Marx singing, "Whatever it is, I'm against it."

18 The former Red Fury had to be fearless to pursue her research fascination. "Language influencing thought was extremely controversial for decades," explains Gentner. "If you talked about language's impact on cognition, you were considered an idiot or a lunatic. We talked about it in my lab, but I used to warn the students not to talk about it outside the lab. Lera," she adds with a chuckle, "was bold enough to ignore that warning. It's now a fully researched and discussed issue."

19 Boroditsky focuses on linguistic features that may inform more fundamental differences in how cultures convey their relationship to concepts such as space, time or gender. "What I'm really interested in are the ingredients of meaning. I don't believe we can explain how we construct meaning without understanding patterns in metaphor and language."

20 Consider space. About a third of the world's languages do not rely on words for right and left. Instead, their speakers use what are called absolute directions—north, south, east and west. For everything. In Australia, for example, if Tara VanDerveer were giving a basketball clinic to the aboriginal Thaayorre in their native language, she'd have to order her players to dribble up the south side of the court, fake east, go west, then make a layup on the west side of the basket.

21 This orientation to the compass points affects all sorts of tasks. When speakers of these languages are asked to arrange photographs showing a time sequence, they line them up east to west. English speakers tend to view time-sequence photographs as going from left to right, while Hebrew speakers line them up right to left. The upshot of the need to constantly stay oriented in order to communicate the simplest concept, says Boroditsky, is that in communities of these speakers, even small children can perform phenomenal feats of navigation, and everyone is constantly mentally synchronizing their spatial relationships.

22 Or consider: Is color perception linked to what we call colors? In another experiment, Boroditsky compared the ability of English speakers and Russian speakers to distinguish between shades of blue. She picked those languages because Russian does not have a single word for blue that covers all shades of what English speakers would call blue; rather, it has classifications for lighter blues and darker blues as different as the English words yellow and orange. Her hypothesis was that Russians thus pay closer attention to shades of blue than English speakers, who lump many more shades under one name and use more vague distinctions. The experiment confirmed her hypothesis. Russian speakers could distinguish between hues of blue faster if they were called by different names in Russian. English speakers showed no increased sensitivity for the same colors. This suggests, says Boroditsky, that Russian speakers have a "psychologically active perceptual boundary where English speakers do not."

23 Boroditsky also is fascinated with how cultures perceive and communicate ideas about time. Some languages require their speakers to include temporal information in every utterance. In the Yagua language of Peru, there are five distinct grammatical forms of the past tense, for example, to describe when an event occurred: a few hours prior; the day before; roughly one week to a month ago;

roughly two months to two years ago; and the distant or legendary past. English is not that precise, but it is true that every time you use a verb in English, you are conveying information about time. Depending on whether something has happened already (I made dinner), is happening now (I am making dinner), or will happen in the future (I will make dinner), the speaker must pick different verb forms. Without the temporal information, the utterance would feel incomplete, ungrammatical. You couldn't just say I make dinner in all three cases.

24    Not so in Indonesian. Unlike English, Indonesian verbs never change to express time: Make is always just make. Although Indonesian speakers can add words like already or soon, this is optional. It doesn't feel incomplete or ungrammatical to just say, I make dinner. This led to another fascinating experimental result—and to Boroditsky's opening up a laboratory in Indonesia. A student from Indonesia assured Boroditsky, who was still skeptical, that most Indonesians simply do not bother to mark time when they speak. So she challenged the student to set up an experiment where Indonesian speakers would be shown photographs of the same act in a time progression: a man about to kick a soccer ball, a man kicking a soccer ball, a man who has kicked the ball, which is flying away. Boroditsky and the student made a bet. Is it possible that Indonesian speakers wouldn't mark time progression? If they did not care about time, what would they pay attention to?

25    The student's hypothesis was proven right. Indonesian speakers, after looking at the three photographs, tended to not only use the same descriptions for each photograph with no time markers—the man kick the ball—but many also said later there was no difference between the photos. Realize that to English speakers, these were not subtle differences—each photograph of the man and the ball was distinctly different.

26    Moreover, when the researchers mixed in photographs of different individuals kicking the ball, the Indonesian participants were more likely to describe two photographs as similar when the person doing the kicking was the same, regardless of which of the three different actions was being performed. English speakers were more likely to say photographs were similar when the actors in the photos were doing the same action in time.

27    Similar to the balloon-popping experiment, Boroditsky's argument is that Indonesians' language structure cues their attention. If you need to figure something out to put it into words, then you pay attention to those details; but if you don't, you don't.

28    Boroditsky's results are attracting more and more researchers to the field and producing additional evidence for measured acceptance of Whorfian arguments. "I'm not sure I would have gone into this if I'd known it was so controversial," she says. But an emotional and intense response from psychologists who previously rejected the idea that language affects thinking is not surprising, she says.

29    "This work is at the center of some of the biggest debates in the study of the mind—nature versus nurture; is the mind divided into modular regions; is there a special encapsulated language 'organ' in the brain. It's pretty bothersome for someone to come along and say that perhaps many of the phenomena that we in psychology have been studying could differ from language to language. It would be much easier if we could just study American college sophomores and assume our observations would be the same everywhere."

30    One implication of Boroditsky's research is its relationship to what psychologists call "framing." In a paper due to be published this year, she and her team used the infamous 2004 Super Bowl halftime show in which singer Justin Timberlake seemed to pull off the front of Janet Jackson's costume, revealing her breast. Timberlake later described the incident as a "wardrobe malfunction" (conceptually not unlike that teacup breaking itself). Even when test subjects saw the same video of the event, and even when they had read and heard about the incident prior to the study, Boroditsky reports that when the researchers described the event then asked the subjects to assess a financial liability to Justin Timberlake, their responses were divided. The group that heard an "agentive" description, in which "Timberlake ripped the costume," recommended a much higher fine than the group that was told "the costume ripped." According to Boroditsky, "Linguistic framing affected people's judgments of blame and financial liability in all conditions; language mattered whether it was presented before, after or without video evidence."

31    She says other work has raised intriguing questions about the accuracy of translations—in courtrooms, for example—of languages such as Spanish that tend to be non-agentive. Might a Spanish-speaking juror interpret a phrase like "the gun went off" differently from an English-speaking juror? Might seemingly age-old conflicts around the world have any connection to language-based influences that render geographical neighbors somewhat inscrutable to one another?

32    Gleitman says there is no debate that specific word choice and use of language can influence other people's thinking—after all, that partly is what language is for, she notes. Boroditsky counters that there is nothing in human endeavor to which language is not connected. Thus, she argues, why not the very mechanisms of how we perceive, remember and process?

33    Just as genetic analysis of intelligence or aptitude can be controversial, research in this field can raise questions about underlying differences between cultures and spark debate about when "different" is implicitly a suggestion of "better." Gleitman, despite her own skepticism of the Whorfian arguments, nonetheless grants that increased work in this area is important. "The questions have been raised provocatively and usefully by Lera Boroditsky, among other scientists." The journey to find answers continues.

### THINKING CRITICALLY

1.  How could intention influence the way we think? Consider Boroditsky's example of Japanese speakers' ability to recount the intention of the person who broke a tea cup. How could the lack of such distinctions in English influence our thinking?

2.  In what ways is Boroditsky's research revealing "convincing effects of language on cognitive process?" How is she proving that language does indeed influence how we think?

3.  What challenges have Boroditsky's theories on language faced? Why?

4.  How can the language we speak influence our perception of time and events? What examples does Hamilton provide to demonstrate the difference in thinking?

5.  What is "framing"? How can it influence our thinking?

**WRITING ASSIGNMENTS**

1. Lawyers are often accused of playing with language. For example, consider a man—Mr. Jones—on trial for the vehicular homicide of Mary Smith. The defense attorney says, "The victim was hit by the car," and the prosecuting attorney says, "Mr. Jones hit Mary Smith with his car." Does one statement influence our thinking more than the other? Write an essay exploring this concept.

2. Hamilton describes how Boroditsky noticed from early on "the degree to which language could shape an argument and exaggerate the differences between people." Expand on this idea. Can you think of examples when language helped you or hurt you when another person used it?

# Lost in Translation
## Lera Boroditsky

For a long time, the idea that language might shape thought was considered at best untestable and more often simply wrong. Research in Lera Boroditsky's labs at Stanford University and at MIT has helped reopen this question. Using data collected from around the world, including Greece, China, Chile, Indonesia, Russia, and Aboriginal Australia, researchers in Boroditsky's lab determined that people who speak different languages do indeed think differently and that even flukes of grammar can profoundly affect how we see the world. Explains Boroditsky, "appreciating its role in constructing our mental lives brings us one step closer to understanding the very nature of humanity."

Lera Boroditsky, a native of Minsk, is a professor of psychology, neuroscience, and symbolic systems at Stanford University. She currently serves as editor in chief of *Frontiers in Cultural Psychology*. She also runs a satellite language lab in Jakarta, Indonesia. This article appeared in *The Wall Street Journal* on July 23, 2010.

1 Do the languages we speak shape the way we think? Do they merely express thoughts, or do the structures in languages (without our knowledge or consent) shape the very thoughts we wish to express?

2 Take "Humpty Dumpty sat on a . . ." Even this snippet of a nursery rhyme reveals how much languages can differ from one another. In English, we have to mark the verb for tense; in this case, we say "sat" rather than "sit." In Indonesian you need not (in fact, you can't) change the verb to mark tense.

3 In Russian, you would have to mark tense and also gender, changing the verb if Mrs. Dumpty did the sitting. You would also have to decide if the sitting event was completed or not. If our ovoid hero sat on the wall for the entire time he was meant to, it would be a different form of the verb than if, say, he had a great fall.

4 In Turkish, you would have to include in the verb how you acquired this information. For example, if you saw the chubby fellow on the wall with your own eyes, you'd use one form of the verb, but if you had simply read or heard about it, you'd use a different form.

**USE YOUR WORDS**

Some findings on how language can affect thinking.

Russian speakers, who have more words for light and dark blues, are better able to visually discriminate shades of blue.

Some indigenous tribes say north, south, east and west, rather than left and right, and as a consequence have great spatial orientation.

The Piraha, whose language eschews number words in favor of terms like few and many, are not able to keep track of exact quantities.

In one study, Spanish and Japanese speakers couldn't remember the agents of accidental events as adeptly as English speakers could. Why? In Spanish and Japanese, the agent of causality is dropped: "The vase broke," or "the vase was broken" rather than "John broke the vase."

5    Do English, Indonesian, Russian and Turkish speakers end up attending to, understanding, and remembering their experiences differently simply because they speak different languages?

6    These questions touch on all the major controversies in the study of mind, with important implications for politics, law and religion. Yet very little empirical work had been done on these questions until recently. The idea that language might shape thought was for a long time considered untestable at best and more often simply crazy and wrong. Now, a flurry of new cognitive science research is showing that in fact, language does profoundly influence how we see the world.

7    The question of whether languages shape the way we think goes back centuries; Charlemagne proclaimed that "to have a second language is to have a second soul." But the idea went out of favor with scientists when Noam Chomsky's theories of language gained popularity in the 1960s and '70s. Dr. Chomsky proposed that there is a universal grammar for all human languages—essentially, that languages don't really differ from one another in significant ways. And because languages didn't differ from one another, the theory went, it made no sense to ask whether linguistic differences led to differences in thinking.

8    The search for linguistic universals yielded interesting data on languages, but after decades of work, not a single proposed universal has withstood scrutiny. Instead, as linguists probed deeper into the world's languages (7,000 or so, only a fraction of them analyzed), innumerable unpredictable differences emerged.

9    Of course, just because people talk differently doesn't necessarily mean they think differently. In the past decade, cognitive scientists have begun to measure not just how people talk, but also how they think, asking whether our understanding of even such fundamental domains of experience as space, time and causality could be constructed by language.

10    For example, in Pormpuraaw, a remote Aboriginal community in Australia, the indigenous languages don't use terms like "left" and "right." Instead, everything is talked about in terms of absolute cardinal directions (north, south, east, west), which means you say things like, "There's an ant on your southwest leg." To say hello in Pormpuraaw, one asks, "Where are you going?", and an appropriate response might be, "A long way to the south-southwest. How about you?" If you don't know which way is which, you literally can't get past hello.

11    About a third of the world's languages (spoken in all kinds of physical environments) rely on absolute directions for space. As a result of this constant linguistic training, speakers of such languages are remarkably good at staying oriented and keeping track of where they are, even in unfamiliar landscapes. They perform navigational feats scientists once thought were beyond human capabilities. This is a big difference, a fundamentally different way of conceptualizing space, trained by language.

12    Differences in how people think about space don't end there. People rely on their spatial knowledge to build many other more complex or abstract representations including time, number, musical pitch, kinship relations, morality and emotions. So if Pormpuraawans think differently about space, do they also think differently about other things, like time?

13    To find out, my colleague Alice Gaby and I traveled to Australia and gave Pormpuraawans sets of pictures that showed temporal progressions (for example, pictures of a man at different ages, or a crocodile growing, or a banana being eaten). Their job was to arrange the shuffled photos on the ground to show the correct temporal order. We tested each person in two separate sittings, each time facing in a different cardinal direction. When asked to do this, English speakers arrange time from left to right. Hebrew speakers do it from right to left (because Hebrew is written from right to left).

14    Pormpuraawans, we found, arranged time from east to west. That is, seated facing south, time went left to right. When facing north, right to left. When facing east, toward the body, and so on. Of course, we never told any of our participants which direction they faced. The Pormpuraawans not only knew that already, but they also spontaneously used this spatial orientation to construct their representations of time. And many other ways to organize time exist in the world's languages. In Mandarin, the future can be below and the past above. In Aymara, spoken in South America, the future is behind and the past in front.

15    In addition to space and time, languages also shape how we understand causality. For example, English likes to describe events in terms of agents doing things. English speakers tend to say things like "John broke the vase" even for accidents. Speakers of Spanish or Japanese would be more likely to say "the vase broke itself." Such differences between languages have profound consequences for how their speakers understand events, construct notions of causality and agency, what they remember as eyewitnesses and how much they blame and punish others.

16    In studies conducted by Caitlin Fausey at Stanford, speakers of English, Spanish and Japanese watched videos of two people popping balloons, breaking eggs and spilling drinks either intentionally or accidentally. Later everyone got a surprise memory test: For each event, can you remember who did it? She discovered a striking cross-linguistic difference in eyewitness memory. Spanish and Japanese speakers did not remember the agents of accidental events as well as did English speakers. Mind you, they remembered the agents of intentional events (for which their language would mention the agent) just fine. But for accidental events, when one wouldn't normally mention the agent in Spanish or Japanese, they didn't encode or remember the agent as well.

17    In another study, English speakers watched the video of Janet Jackson's infamous "wardrobe malfunction" (a wonderful nonagentive coinage introduced into the English language by Justin Timberlake), accompanied by one of two written

reports. The reports were identical except in the last sentence where one used the agentive phrase "ripped the costume" while the other said "the costume ripped." Even though everyone watched the same video and witnessed the ripping with their own eyes, language mattered. Not only did people who read "ripped the costume" blame Justin Timberlake more, they also levied a whopping 53% more in fines.

18    Beyond space, time and causality, patterns in language have been shown to shape many other domains of thought. Russian speakers, who make an extra distinction between light and dark blues in their language, are better able to visually discriminate shades of blue. The Piraha, a tribe in the Amazon in Brazil, whose language eschews number words in favor of terms like few and many, are not able to keep track of exact quantities. And Shakespeare, it turns out, was wrong about roses: Roses by many other names (as told to blindfolded subjects) do not smell as sweet.

19    Patterns in language offer a window on a culture's dispositions and priorities. For example, English sentence structures focus on agents, and in our criminal-justice system, justice has been done when we've found the transgressor and punished him or her accordingly (rather than finding the victims and restituting appropriately, an alternative approach to justice). So does the language shape cultural values, or does the influence go the other way, or both?

20    Languages, of course, are human creations, tools we invent and hone to suit our needs. Simply showing that speakers of different languages think differently doesn't tell us whether it's language that shapes thought or the other way around. To demonstrate the causal role of language, what's needed are studies that directly manipulate language and look for effects in cognition.

21    One of the key advances in recent years has been the demonstration of precisely this causal link. It turns out that if you change how people talk, that changes how they think. If people learn another language, they inadvertently also learn a new way of looking at the world. When bilingual people switch from one language to another, they start thinking differently, too. And if you take away people's ability to use language in what should be a simple nonlinguistic task, their performance can change dramatically, sometimes making them look no smarter than rats or infants. (For example, in recent studies, MIT students were shown dots on a screen and asked to say how many there were. If they were allowed to count normally, they did great. If they simultaneously did a nonlinguistic task—like banging out rhythms—they still did great. But if they did a verbal task when shown the dots— like repeating the words spoken in a news report—their counting fell apart. In other words, they needed their language skills to count.)

22    All this new research shows us that the languages we speak not only reflect or express our thoughts, but also shape the very thoughts we wish to express. The structures that exist in our languages profoundly shape how we construct reality, and help make us as smart and sophisticated as we are.

23    Language is a uniquely human gift. When we study language, we are uncovering in part what makes us human, getting a peek at the very nature of human nature. As we uncover how languages and their speakers differ from one another, we discover that human natures too can differ dramatically, depending on the languages we speak. The next steps are to understand the mechanisms through which languages help us construct the incredibly complex knowledge systems we have. Understanding how

knowledge is built will allow us to create ideas that go beyond the currently think-able. This research cuts right to the fundamental questions we all ask about ourselves. How do we come to be the way we are? Why do we think the way we do? An impor-tant part of the answer, it turns out, is in the languages we speak.

### THINKING CRITICALLY

1. Boroditsky opens her essay with two questions. Answer her questions with information from her article and other articles in this section.

2. Consider Boroditsky's example of Humpty Dumpty and the many different nu-ances of information (or lack of information) that would be conveyed about this nursery rhyme in different languages. How could this information influence the speaker's way of thinking about the experience of Humpty Dumpty? Explain.

3. How do languages help us figure out time and space? Did it surprise you that not everyone organizes a sequence of events in a linearly left to right fashion? Could you think up and down, or having the future behind you? Why or why not?

4. In what ways do patterns in language provide a "window" to a particular cul-ture's dispositions and priorities? Explain.

### WRITING ASSIGNMENTS

1. Boroditsky quotes Charlemagne: "to have a second language is to have a sec-ond soul." Write an essay describing your own experiences learning another language (sign language included). What challenges did you face? Did you ever really master the other language? If not, what held you back? If so, did you have a breakthrough moment when you started thinking in that language as well as speaking it? Explain.

2. Interview several students for whom English is a second language. Ask them to describe what challenges, if any, they have encountered with language differ-ences. If you know someone who is a native speaker of one of the languages Boroditsky studied, ask them to expand on her points, if possible.

# DIGITAL THOUGHT

# Is Google Making Us Stoopid?

*Nicholas Carr*

Only a generation ago, researching information could take weeks or months and consisted of countless hours of reading through mounds of printed magazines, newspapers, and academic journals. To find original sources for research pa-pers students waded through microfiche, card catalogues, and volumes of refer-ence books, reading every detail, looking for just the right phrase or statistic that could prove their point or help make their case. Now researching takes only a few hours working with databases and search engines to find that perfect phrase or statistic to cut and paste into a research paper. The Internet has changed the way we work and study, and it may even be changing the way we think. Are we getting more efficient, or are our brains getting lazy? In this next essay, author Nicholas Carr discusses what the Internet is doing to our brains and how new ways of thinking will change us forever—for better or for worse.

Nicholas Carr writes on the social, economic, and business implications of technology. He is the author of the 2008 *Wall Street Journal* bestseller *The Big Switch: Rewiring the World, from Edison to Google,* and most recently, *The Shallows: What the Internet Is Doing to Our Brains* (2010). Carr has written for many periodicals, including *The Atlantic Monthly, The New York Times Magazine, Wired, The Financial Times, Die Zeit, The Futurist,* and *Advertising Age,* and has been a columnist for *The Guardian* and *The Industry Standard.* This essay appeared as the cover story of *The Atlantic*'s "Ideas" issue in the summer of 2008.

1   "Dave, stop. Stop, will you? Stop, Dave. Will you stop, Dave?" So the supercomputer HAL pleads with the implacable astronaut Dave Bowman in a famous and weirdly poignant scene toward the end of Stanley Kubrick's *2001: A Space Odyssey.* Bowman, having nearly been sent to a deep-space death by the malfunctioning machine, is calmly, coldly disconnecting the memory circuits that control its artificial "brain." "Dave, my mind is going," HAL says, forlornly. "I can feel it. I can feel it."

2   I can feel it, too. Over the past few years I've had an uncomfortable sense that someone, or something, has been tinkering with my brain, remapping the neural circuitry, reprogramming the memory. My mind isn't going—so far as I can tell—but it's changing. I'm not thinking the way I used to think. I can feel it most strongly when I'm reading. Immersing myself in a book or a lengthy article used to be easy. My mind would get caught up in the narrative or the turns of the argument, and I'd spend hours strolling through long stretches of prose. That's rarely the case anymore. Now my concentration often starts to drift after two or three pages. I get fidgety, lose the thread, begin looking for something else to do. I feel as if I'm always dragging my wayward brain back to the text. The deep reading that used to come naturally has become a struggle.

3   I think I know what's going on. For more than a decade now, I've been spending a lot of time online, searching and surfing and sometimes adding to the great databases of the Internet. The Web has been a godsend to me as a writer. Research that once required days in the stacks or periodical rooms of libraries can now be done in minutes. A few Google searches, some quick clicks on hyperlinks, and I've got the telltale fact or pithy quote I was after. Even when I'm not working, I'm as likely as not to be foraging in the Web's info-thickets reading and writing e-mails, scanning headlines and blog posts, watching videos and listening to podcasts, or just tripping from link to link to link. (Unlike footnotes, to which they're sometimes likened, hyperlinks don't merely point to related works; they propel you toward them.)

4   For me, as for others, the Net is becoming a universal medium, the conduit for most of the information that flows through my eyes and ears and into my mind. The advantages of having immediate access to such an incredibly rich store of information are many, and they've been widely described and duly applauded. "The

perfect recall of silicon memory," *Wired*'s Clive Thompson has written, "can be an enormous boon to thinking." But that boon comes at a price. As the media theorist Marshall McLuhan pointed out in the 1960s, media are not just passive channels of information. They supply the stuff of thought, but they also shape the process of thought. And what the Net seems to be doing is chipping away my capacity for concentration and contemplation. My mind now expects to take in information the way the Net distributes it: in a swiftly moving stream of particles. Once I was a scuba diver in the sea of words. Now I zip along the surface like a guy on a Jet Ski.

5    I'm not the only one. When I mention my troubles with reading to friends and acquaintances—literary types, most of them—many say they're having similar experiences. The more they use the Web, the more they have to fight to stay focused on long pieces of writing. Some of the bloggers I follow have also begun mentioning the phenomenon. Scott Karp, who writes a blog about online media, recently confessed that he has stopped reading books altogether. "I was a lit major in college, and used to be [a] voracious book reader," he wrote. "What happened?" He speculates on the answer: "What if I do all my reading on the web not so much because the way I read has changed, i.e., I'm just seeking convenience, but because the way I THINK has changed?"

6    Bruce Friedman, who blogs regularly about the use of computers in medicine, also has described how the Internet has altered his mental habits. "I now have almost totally lost the ability to read and absorb a longish article on the web or in print," he wrote earlier this year. A pathologist who has long been on the faculty of the University of Michigan Medical School, Friedman elaborated on his comment in a telephone conversation with me. His thinking, he said, has taken on a "staccato" quality, reflecting the way he quickly scans short passages of text from many sources online. "I can't read *War and Peace* anymore," he admitted. "I've lost the ability to do that. Even a blog post of more than three or four paragraphs is too much to absorb. I skim it."

7    Anecdotes alone don't prove much. And we still await the long-term neurological and psychological experiments that will provide a definitive picture of how Internet use affects cognition. But a recently published study of online research habits, conducted by scholars from University College London, suggests that we may well be in the midst of a sea change in the way we read and think. As part of the five-year research program, the scholars examined computer logs documenting the behavior of visitors to two popular research sites, one operated by the British Library and one by a U.K. educational consortium, that provide access to journal articles, e-books, and other sources of written information. They found that people using the sites exhibited "a form of skimming activity," hopping from one source to another and rarely returning to any source they'd already visited. They typically read no more than one or two pages of an article or book before they would "bounce" out to another site. Sometimes they'd save a long article, but there's no evidence that they ever went back and actually read it. The authors of the study report:

> It is clear that users are not reading online in the traditional sense; indeed there are signs that new forms of "reading" are emerging as users "power browse" horizontally through titles, contents pages and abstracts going for quick wins. It almost seems that they go online to avoid reading in the traditional sense.

8    Thanks to the ubiquity of text on the Internet, not to mention the popularity of text-messaging on cell phones, we may well be reading more today than we did in the 1970s or 1980s, when television was our medium of choice. But it's a different kind of reading, and behind it lies a different kind of thinking—perhaps even a new sense of the self. "We are not only what we read," says Maryanne Wolf, a developmental psychologist at Tufts University and the author of *Proust and the Squid: The Story and Science of the Reading Brain*. "We are how we read." Wolf worries that the style of reading promoted by the Net, a style that puts "efficiency" and "immediacy" above all else, may be weakening our capacity for the kind of deep reading that emerged when an earlier technology, the printing press, made long and complex works of prose commonplace. When we read online, she says, we tend to become "mere decoders of information." Our ability to interpret text, to make the rich mental connections that form when we read deeply and without distraction, remains largely disengaged.

9    Reading, explains Wolf, is not an instinctive skill for human beings. It's not etched into our genes the way speech is. We have to teach our minds how to translate the symbolic characters we see into the language we understand. And the media or other technologies we use in learning and practicing the craft of reading play an important part in shaping the neural circuits inside our brains. Experiments demonstrate that readers of ideograms, such as the Chinese, develop a mental circuitry for reading that is very different from the circuitry found in those of us whose written language employs an alphabet. The variations extend across many regions of the brain, including those that govern such essential cognitive functions as memory and the interpretation of visual and auditory stimuli. We can expect as well that the circuits woven by our use of the Net will be different from those woven by our reading of books and other printed works.

10    Sometime in 1882, Friedrich Nietzsche bought a typewriter—a Malling-Hansen Writing Ball, to be precise. His vision was failing, and keeping his eyes focused on a page had become exhausting and painful, often bringing on crushing headaches. He had been forced to curtail his writing, and he feared that he would soon have to give it up. The typewriter rescued him, at least for a time. Once he had mastered touch-typing, he was able to write with his eyes closed, using only the tips of his fingers. Words could once again flow from his mind to the page.

11    But the machine had a subtler effect on his work. One of Nietzsche's friends, a composer, noticed a change in the style of his writing. His already terse prose had become even tighter, more telegraphic. "Perhaps you will through this instrument even take to a new idiom," the friend wrote in a letter, noting that, in his own work, his " 'thoughts' in music and language often depend on the quality of pen and paper."

12    "You are right," Nietzsche replied, "our writing equipment takes part in the forming of our thoughts." Under the sway of the machine, writes the German media scholar Friedrich A. Kittler, Nietzsche's prose "changed from arguments to aphorisms, from thoughts to puns, from rhetoric to telegram style."

13    The human brain is almost infinitely malleable. People used to think that our mental meshwork, the dense connections formed among the 100 billion or so neurons inside our skulls, was largely fixed by the time we reached adulthood. But

brain researchers have discovered that that's not the case. James Olds, a professor of neuroscience who directs the Krasnow Institute for Advanced Study at George Mason University, says that even the adult mind "is very plastic." Nerve cells routinely break old connections and form new ones. "The brain," according to Olds, "has the ability to reprogram itself on the fly, altering the way it functions."

14      As we use what the sociologist Daniel Bell has called our "intellectual technologies"—the tools that extend our mental rather than our physical capacities—we inevitably begin to take on the qualities of those technologies. The mechanical clock, which came into common use in the 14th century, provides a compelling example. In *Technics and Civilization,* the historian and cultural critic Lewis Mumford described how the clock "disassociated time from human events and helped create the belief in an independent world of mathematically measurable sequences." The "abstract framework of divided time" became "the point of reference for both action and thought."

15      The clock's methodical ticking helped bring into being the scientific mind and the scientific man. But it also took something away. As the late MIT computer scientist Joseph Weizenbaum observed in his 1976 book, *Computer Power and Human Reason: From Judgment to Calculation,* the conception of the world that emerged from the widespread use of timekeeping instruments "remains an impoverished version of the older one, for it rests on a rejection of those direct experiences that formed the basis for, and indeed constituted, the old reality." In deciding when to eat, to work, to sleep, to rise, we stopped listening to our senses and started obeying the clock.

16      The process of adapting to new intellectual technologies is reflected in the changing metaphors we use to explain ourselves to ourselves. When the mechanical clock arrived, people began thinking of their brains as operating "like clockwork." Today, in the age of software, we have come to think of them as operating "like computers." But the changes, neuroscience tells us, go much deeper than metaphor. Thanks to our brain's plasticity, the adaptation occurs also at a biological level.

17      The Internet promises to have particularly far-reaching effects on cognition. In a paper published in 1936, the British mathematician Alan Turing proved that a digital computer, which at the time existed only as a theoretical machine, could be programmed to perform the function of any other information-processing device. And that's what we're seeing today. The Internet, an immeasurably powerful computing system, is subsuming most of our other intellectual technologies. It's becoming our map and our clock, our printing press and our typewriter, our calculator and our telephone, and our radio and TV.

18      When the Net absorbs a medium, that medium is re-created in the Net's image. It injects the medium's content with hyperlinks, blinking ads, and other digital gewgaws, and it surrounds the content with the content of all the other media it has absorbed. A new e-mail message, for instance, may announce its arrival as we're glancing over the latest headlines at a newspaper's site. The result is to scatter our attention and diffuse our concentration.

19      The Net's influence doesn't end at the edges of a computer screen, either. As people's minds become attuned to the crazy quilt of Internet media, traditional media have to adapt to the audience's new expectations. Television programs add text

crawls and pop-up ads, and magazines and newspapers shorten their articles, intro-duce capsule summaries, and crowd their pages with easy-to-browse info-snippets. When, in March of this year, *The New York Times* decided to devote the second and third pages of every edition to article abstracts, its design director, Tom Bodkin, ex-plained that the "shortcuts" would give harried readers a quick "taste" of the day's news, sparing them the "less efficient" method of actually turning the pages and reading the articles. Old media have little choice but to play by the new-media rules.

20    Never has a communications system played so many roles in our lives—or exerted such broad influence over our thoughts—as the Internet does today. Yet, for all that's been written about the Net, there's been little consideration of how, exactly, it's reprogramming us. The Net's intellectual ethic remains obscure.

21    About the same time that Nietzsche started using his typewriter, an earnest young man named Frederick Winslow Taylor carried a stopwatch into the Mid-vale Steel plant in Philadelphia and began a historic series of experiments aimed at improving the efficiency of the plant's machinists. With the approval of Mid-vale's owners, he recruited a group of factory hands, set them to work on various metalworking machines, and recorded and timed their every movement as well as the operations of the machines. By breaking down every job into a sequence of small, discrete steps and then testing different ways of performing each one, Tay-lor created a set of precise instructions—an "algorithm," we might say today—for how each worker should work. Midvale's employees grumbled about the strict new regime, claiming that it turned them into little more than automatons, but the fac-tory's productivity soared.

22    More than a hundred years after the invention of the steam engine, the Indus-trial Revolution had at last found its philosophy and its philosopher. Taylor's tight industrial choreography—his "system," as he liked to call it—was embraced by manufacturers throughout the country and, in time, around the world. Seeking max-imum speed, maximum efficiency, and maximum output, factory owners used time-and-motion studies to organize their work and configure the jobs of their workers. The goal, as Taylor defined it in his celebrated 1911 treatise, *The Principles of Sci-entific Management,* was to identify and adopt, for every job, the "one best method" of work and thereby to effect "the gradual substitution of science for rule of thumb throughout the mechanic arts." Once his system was applied to all acts of manual labor, Taylor assured his followers, it would bring about a restructuring not only of industry but of society, creating a utopia of perfect efficiency. "In the past the man has been first," he declared; "in the future the system must be first."

23    Taylor's system is still very much with us; it remains the ethic of industrial manufacturing. And now, thanks to the growing power that computer engineers and software coders wield over our intellectual lives, Taylor's ethic is beginning to govern the realm of the mind as well. The Internet is a machine designed for the efficient and automated collection, transmission, and manipulation of information, and its legions of programmers are intent on finding the "one best method"—the perfect algorithm—to carry out every mental movement of what we've come to describe as "knowledge work."

24    Google's headquarters, in Mountain View, California—the Googleplex—is the Internet's high church, and the religion practiced inside its walls is Taylorism.

Google, says its chief executive, Eric Schmidt, is "a company that's founded around the science of measurement," and it is striving to "systematize everything" it does. Drawing on the terabytes of behavioral data it collects through its search engine and other sites, it carries out thousands of experiments a day, according to the *Harvard Business Review*, and it uses the results to refine the algorithms that increasingly control how people find information and extract meaning from it. What Taylor did for the work of the hand, Google is doing for the work of the mind.

25    The company has declared that its mission is "to organize the world's information and make it universally accessible and useful." It seeks to develop "the perfect search engine," which it defines as something that "understands exactly what you mean and gives you back exactly what you want." In Google's view, information is a kind of commodity, a utilitarian resource that can be mined and processed with industrial efficiency. The more pieces of information we can "access" and the faster we can extract their gist, the more productive we become as thinkers.

26    Where does it end? Sergey Brin and Larry Page, the gifted young men who founded Google while pursuing doctoral degrees in computer science at Stanford, speak frequently of their desire to turn their search engine into an artificial intelligence, a HAL-like machine that might be connected directly to our brains. "The ultimate search engine is something as smart as people—or smarter," Page said in a speech a few years back. "For us, working on search is a way to work on artificial intelligence." In a 2004 interview with *Newsweek*, Brin said, "Certainly if you had all the world's information directly attached to your brain, or an artificial brain that was smarter than your brain, you'd be better off." Last year, Page told a convention of scientists that Google is "really trying to build artificial intelligence and to do it on a large scale."

27    Such an ambition is a natural one, even an admirable one, for a pair of math whizzes with vast quantities of cash at their disposal and a small army of computer scientists in their employ. A fundamentally scientific enterprise, Google is motivated by a desire to use technology, in Eric Schmidt's words, "to solve problems that have never been solved before," and artificial intelligence is the hardest problem out there. Why wouldn't Brin and Page want to be the ones to crack it?

28    Still, their easy assumption that we'd all "be better off" if our brains were supplemented, or even replaced, by an artificial intelligence is unsettling. It suggests a belief that intelligence is the output of a mechanical process, a series of discrete steps that can be isolated, measured, and optimized. In Google's world, the world we enter when we go online, there's little place for the fuzziness of contemplation. Ambiguity is not an opening for insight but a bug to be fixed. The human brain is just an outdated computer that needs a faster processor and a bigger hard drive.

29    The idea that our minds should operate as high-speed data-processing machines is not only built into the workings of the Internet, it is the network's reigning business model as well. The faster we surf across the Web—the more links we click and pages we view—the more opportunities Google and other companies gain to collect information about us and to feed us advertisements. Most of the proprietors of the commercial Internet have a financial stake in collecting the crumbs of data we leave behind as we flit from link to link—the more crumbs, the better.

The last thing these companies want is to encourage leisurely reading or slow, concentrated thought. It's in their economic interest to drive us to distraction.

30    Maybe I'm just a worrywart. Just as there's a tendency to glorify technological progress, there's a countertendency to expect the worst of every new tool or machine. In Plato's *Phaedrus,* Socrates bemoaned the development of writing. He feared that, as people came to rely on the written word as a substitute for the knowledge they used to carry inside their heads, they would, in the words of one of the dialogue's characters, "cease to exercise their memory and become forgetful." And because they would be able to "receive a quantity of information without proper instruction," they would "be thought very knowledgeable when they are for the most part quite ignorant." They would be "filled with the conceit of wisdom instead of real wisdom." Socrates wasn't wrong—the new technology did often have the effects he feared—but he was shortsighted. He couldn't foresee the many ways that writing and reading would serve to spread information, spur fresh ideas, and expand human knowledge (if not wisdom).

31    The arrival of Gutenberg's printing press, in the 15th century, set off another round of teeth gnashing. The Italian humanist Hieronimo Squarciafico worried that the easy availability of books would lead to intellectual laziness, making men "less studious" and weakening their minds. Others argued that cheaply printed books and broadsheets would undermine religious authority, demean the work of scholars and scribes, and spread sedition and debauchery. As New York University professor Clay Shirky notes, "Most of the arguments made against the printing press were correct, even prescient." But, again, the doomsayers were unable to imagine the myriad blessings that the printed word would deliver.

32    So, yes, you should be skeptical of my skepticism. Perhaps those who dismiss critics of the Internet as Luddites or nostalgists will be proved correct, and from our hyperactive, data-stoked minds will spring a golden age of intellectual discovery and universal wisdom. Then again, the Net isn't the alphabet, and although it may replace the printing press, it produces something altogether different. The kind of deep reading that a sequence of printed pages promotes is valuable not just for the knowledge we acquire from the author's words but for the intellectual vibrations those words set off within our own minds. In the quiet spaces opened up by the sustained, undistracted reading of a book, or by any other act of contemplation, for that matter, we make our own associations, draw our own inferences and analogies, foster our own ideas. Deep reading, as Maryanne Wolf argues, is indistinguishable from deep thinking.

33    If we lose those quiet spaces, or fill them up with "content," we will sacrifice something important not only in our selves but in our culture. In a recent essay, the playwright Richard Foreman eloquently described what's at stake:

> I come from a tradition of Western culture, in which the ideal (my ideal) was the complex, dense and "cathedral-like" structure of the highly educated and articulate personality—a man or woman who carried inside themselves a personally constructed and unique version of the entire heritage of the West. [But now] I see within us all (myself included) the replacement of complex inner density with a new kind of self—evolving under the pressure of information overload and the technology of the "instantly available."

34    As we are drained of our "inner repertory of dense cultural inheritance," Foreman concluded, we risk turning into " 'pancake people'—spread wide and thin as we connect with that vast network of information accessed by the mere touch of a button."

35    I'm haunted by that scene in *2001*. What makes it so poignant, and so weird, is the computer's emotional response to the disassembly of its mind: its despair as one circuit after another goes dark, its childlike pleading with the astronaut—"I can feel it. I can feel it. I'm afraid"—and its final reversion to what can only be called a state of innocence. HAL's outpouring of feeling contrasts with the emotionlessness that characterizes the human figures in the film, who go about their business with an almost robotic efficiency. Their thoughts and actions feel scripted, as if they're following the steps of an algorithm. In the world of *2001,* people have become so machinelike that the most human character turns out to be a machine. That's the essence of Kubrick's dark prophecy: as we come to rely on computers to mediate our understanding of the world, it is our own intelligence that flattens into artificial intelligence.

## THINKING CRITICALLY

1. In this essay, Nicholas Carr uses a full-circle approach in which he links his introduction to his conclusion. What hook does Carr use in the introduction and how does he revisit it in his conclusion? Do you find the full-circle approach to be an effective writing strategy? Explain.

2. The psychologist Maryanne Wolf is quoted as saying, "We are not only what we read . . . We are how we read." What does she mean by this statement? How might this effect the reading of literature for future generations?

3. The article illustrates several examples of how technology has given us great advancements, but in the process has taken something away from our ability to think. Find three textual examples of this phenomenon. In the author's opinion, is the price we are paying worth the gain? What do you think?

4. Sergey Brin, one of the founders of Google, says, "Certainly if you had all the world's information directly attached to your brain, or an artificial brain that was smarter than your brain, you'd be better off." What is Nicholas Carr's opinion of this statement? What is your opinion of this statement?

5. According to Carr, Google seeks to develop the perfect search engine that "understands exactly what you mean and gives you back exactly what you want." Which search engine do you commonly use? Try experimenting with at least three different search engines to see which one is most effective. What makes one search engine better than another?

## WRITING ASSIGNMENTS

1. How does Carr show that money may be the underlying cause of the recent change in the way we are reading and thinking? Summarize this section of the article, and then state if you find this business model to be ethical. What, if anything, can individuals do to influence the trend?

2. How is society affected by the media? How do new technologies change our way of thinking? Write an essay exploring the concept that technology can change the way our brains actually think. Will the Internet, e-books, or another technological device influence our physical evolution? Explain.

# The Internet: Is It Changing the Way We Think?

*John Naughton*

In the previous article, Nicholas Carr explains why he believes Google is changing our brains, and not necessarily for the better. His assertion that the Internet is not only shaping our lives but physically altering our brains has sparked a lively debate about the role of technology and its influence on our very biology. Are our minds being altered due to our increasing reliance on search engines, social networking sites, and other digital technologies? In this piece, John Naughton invites some popular writers to weigh in on the issue.

John Naughton is an Irish academic, journalist, and writer based in the United Kingdom. He is a professor of the Open University, where he holds the title Professor of the Public Understanding of Technology. He is director of the Wolfson College, Cambridge Press Fellowship Program, and also academic advisor to the Arcadia Fellowship Project at Cambridge University Library. This article was first published in the British newspaper *The Observer* on August 15, 2010.

1 Every 50 years or so, American magazine the *Atlantic* lobs an intellectual grenade into our culture. In the summer of 1945, for example, it published an essay by the Massachusetts Institute of Technology (MIT) engineer Vannevar Bush entitled "As We May Think". It turned out to be the blueprint for what eventually emerged as the world wide web. Recently, the *Atlantic* published an essay by Nicholas Carr, one of the blogosphere's most prominent (and thoughtful) contrarians, under the headline "Is Google Making Us Stupid?".

2 "Over the past few years," Carr wrote, "I've had an uncomfortable sense that someone, or something, has been tinkering with my brain, remapping the neural circuitry, reprogramming the memory. My mind isn't going—so far as I can tell—but it's changing. I'm not thinking the way I used to think. I can feel it most strongly when I'm reading. Immersing myself in a book or a lengthy article used to be easy. My mind would get caught up in the narrative or the turns of the argument and I'd spend hours strolling through long stretches of prose. That's rarely the case anymore. Now my concentration often starts to drift after two or three pages. I get fidgety, lose the thread, begin looking for something else to do. I feel as if I'm always dragging my wayward brain back to the text. The deep reading that used to come naturally has become a struggle." The title of the essay is misleading, because Carr's target was not really the world's leading search engine, but the impact that ubiquitous, always-on networking is having on our cognitive processes. His argument was that our deepening dependence on networking technology is indeed changing not only the way we think, but also the structure of our brains.

3 Carr's article touched a nerve and has provoked a lively, ongoing debate on the net and in print (he has now expanded it into a book, *The Shallows: What the Internet Is Doing to Our Brains*). This is partly because he's an engaging writer who has vividly articulated the unease that many adults feel about the way their modi operandi have changed in response to ubiquitous networking. Who bothers to write down or memorize detailed information any more, for example, when they

know that Google will always retrieve it if it's needed again? The web has become, in a way, a global prosthesis for our collective memory.

4    It's easy to dismiss Carr's concern as just the latest episode of the moral panic that always accompanies the arrival of a new communications technology. People fretted about printing, photography, the telephone and television in analogous ways. It even bothered Plato, who argued that the technology of writing would destroy the art of remembering.

5    But just because fears recur doesn't mean that they aren't valid. There's no doubt that communications technologies shape and reshape society—just look at the impact that printing and the broadcast media have had on our world. The question that we couldn't answer before now was whether these technologies could also reshape us. Carr argues that modern neuroscience, which has revealed the "plasticity" of the human brain, shows that our habitual practices can actually change our neuronal structures. The brains of illiterate people, for example, are structurally different from those of people who can read. So if the technology of printing—and its concomitant requirement to learn to read—could shape human brains, then surely it's logical to assume that our addiction to networking technology will do something similar?

6    Not all neuroscientists agree with Carr and some psychologists are skeptical. Harvard's Steven Pinker, for example, is openly dismissive. But many commentators who accept the thrust of his argument seem not only untroubled by its far-reaching implications but are positively enthusiastic about them. When the Pew Research Centre's Internet & American Life project asked its panel of more than 370 internet experts for their reaction, 81% of them agreed with the proposition that "people's use of the internet has enhanced human intelligence".

7    Others argue that the increasing complexity of our environment means that we need the net as "power steering for the mind". We may be losing some of the capacity for contemplative concentration that was fostered by a print culture, they say, but we're gaining new and essential ways of working. "The trouble isn't that we have too much information at our fingertips," says the futurologist Jamais Cascio, "but that our tools for managing it are still in their infancy. Worries about 'information overload' predate the rise of the web . . . and many of the technologies that Carr worries about were developed precisely to help us get some control over a flood of data and ideas. Google isn't the problem—it's the beginning of a solution."

## Sarah Churchwell, Academic and Critic

8  Is the internet changing our brains? It seems unlikely to me, but I'll leave that question to evolutionary biologists. As a writer, thinker, researcher and teacher, what I can attest to is that the internet is changing our habits of thinking, which isn't the same thing as changing our brains. The brain is like any other muscle—if you don't stretch it, it gets both stiff and flabby. But if you exercise it regularly, and cross-train, your brain will be flexible, quick, strong and versatile. In one sense, the internet is analogous to a weight-training machine for the brain, as compared with the free weights provided by libraries and books. Each method has its advantage, but used properly one works you harder. Weight machines are directive and enabling:

they encourage you to think you've worked hard without necessarily challenging yourself. The internet can be the same: it often tells us what we think we know, spreading misinformation and nonsense while it's at it. It can substitute surface for depth, imitation for originality, and its passion for recycling would surpass the most committed environmentalist.

9    In 10 years, I've seen students' thinking habits change dramatically: if information is not immediately available via a Google search, students are often stymied. But of course what a Google search provides is not the best, wisest or most accurate answer, but the most popular one.

10   But knowledge is not the same thing as information, and there is no question to my mind that the access to raw information provided by the internet is unparalleled and democratizing. Admittance to elite private university libraries and archives is no longer required, as they increasingly digitize their archives. We've all read the jeremiads that the internet sounds the death knell of reading, but people read online constantly—we just call it surfing now. What they are reading is changing, often for the worse; but it is also true that the internet increasingly provides a treasure trove of rare books, documents and images, and as long as we have free access to it, then the internet can certainly be a force for education and wisdom, and not just for lies, damned lies, and false statistics.

11   In the end, the medium is not the message, and the internet is just a medium, a repository and an archive. Its greatest virtue is also its greatest weakness: it is unselective. This means that it is undiscriminating, in both senses of the word. It is indiscriminate in its principles of inclusion: anything at all can get into it. But it also—at least so far—doesn't discriminate against anyone with access to it. This is changing rapidly, of course, as corporations and governments seek to exert control over it. Knowledge may not be the same thing as power, but it is unquestionably a means to power. The question is, will we use the internet's power for good, or for evil? The jury is very much out. The internet itself is disinterested: but what we use it for is not.

## Naomi Alderman, Novelist

12   If I were a cow, nothing much would change my brain. I might learn new locations for feeding, but I wouldn't be able to read an essay and decide to change the way I lived my life. But I'm not a cow, I'm a person, and therefore pretty much everything I come into contact with can change my brain.

13   It's both a strength and a weakness. We can choose to seek out brilliant thinking and be challenged and inspired by it. Or we can find our energy sapped by an evening with a "poor me" friend, or become faintly disgusted by our own thinking if we've read too many romance novels in one go. As our bodies are shaped by the food we eat, our brains are shaped by what we put into them.

14   So of course the internet is changing our brains. How could it not? It's not surprising that we're now more accustomed to reading short-form pieces, to accepting a Wikipedia summary, rather than reading a whole book. The claim that we're now thinking less well is much more suspect. If we've lost something by not reading 10 books on one subject, we've probably gained as much by being able to link together ideas easily from 10 different disciplines.

15   But since we're not going to dismantle the world wide web any time soon, the more important question is: how should we respond? I suspect the answer is as simple as making time for reading. No single medium will ever give our brains all possible forms of nourishment. We may be dazzled by the flashing lights of the web, but we can still just step away. Read a book. Sink into the world of a single person's concentrated thoughts.

16   Time was when we didn't need to be reminded to read. Well, time was when we didn't need to be encouraged to cook. That time's gone. None the less, cook. And read. We can decide to change our own brains—that's the most astonishing thing of all.

## Ed Bullmore, Psychiatrist

17 Whether or not the internet has made a difference to how we use our brains, it has certainly begun to make a difference to how we think about our brains. The internet is a vast and complex network of interconnected computers, hosting an equally complex network—the web—of images, documents and data. The rapid growth of this huge, manmade, information-processing system has been a major factor stimulating scientists to take a fresh look at the organization of biological information-processing systems like the brain.

18   It turns out that the human brain and the internet have quite a lot in common. They are both highly non-random networks with a "small world" architecture, meaning that there is both dense clustering of connections between neighboring nodes and enough long-range short cuts to facilitate communication between distant nodes. Both the internet and the brain have a wiring diagram dominated by a relatively few, very highly connected nodes or hubs; and both can be subdivided into a number of functionally specialized families or modules of nodes. It may seem remarkable, given the obvious differences between the internet and the brain in many ways, that they should share so many high-level design features. Why should this be?

19   One possibility is that the brain and the internet have evolved to satisfy the same general fitness criteria. They may both have been selected for high efficiency of information transfer, economical wiring cost, rapid adaptivity or evolvability of function and robustness to physical damage. Networks that grow or evolve to satisfy some or all of these conditions tend to end up looking the same.

20   Although there is much still to understand about the brain, the impact of the internet has helped us to learn new ways of measuring its organization as a network. It has also begun to show us that the human brain probably does not represent some unique pinnacle of complexity but may have more in common than we might have guessed with many other information-processing networks.

## Geoff Dyer, Writer

21 Sometimes I think my ability to concentrate is being nibbled away by the internet; other times I think it's being gulped down in huge, Jaws-shaped chunks. In those quaint days before the internet, once you made it to your desk there wasn't much to distract you. You could sit there working or you could just sit there. Now you sit

down and there's a universe of possibilities—many of them obscurely relevant to the work you should be getting on with—to tempt you. To think that I can be sitting here, trying to write something about Ingmar Bergman and, a moment later, on the merest whim, can be watching a clip from a Swedish documentary about Don Cherry—that is a miracle (albeit one with a very potent side-effect, namely that it's unlikely I'll ever have the patience to sit through an entire Bergman film again).

22    Then there's the outsourcing of memory. From the age of 16, I got into the habit of memorizing passages of poetry and compiling detailed indexes in the backs of books of prose. So if there was a passage I couldn't remember, I would spend hours going through my books, seeking it out. Now, in what TS Eliot, with great prescience, called "this twittering world", I just google the key phrase of the half-remembered quote. Which is great, but it's drained some of the purpose from my life.

23    Exactly the same thing has happened now that it's possible to get hold of out-of-print books instantly on the web. That's great too. But one of the side incentives to travel was the hope that, in a bookstore in Oregon, I might finally track down a book I'd been wanting for years. All of this searching and tracking down was immensely time-consuming—but only in the way that being alive is time-consuming.

## Colin Blakemore, Neurobiologist

24  It's curious that some of the most vociferous critics of the internet—those who predict that it will produce generations of couch potatoes, with minds of mush—are the very sorts of people who are benefiting most from this wonderful, liberating, organic extension of the human mind. They are academics, scientists, scholars and writers, who fear that the extraordinary technology that they use every day is a danger to the unsophisticated.

25    They underestimate the capacity of the human mind—or rather the brain that makes the mind—to capture and capitalize on new ways of storing and transmitting information. When I was at school I learned by heart great swathes of poetry and chunks of the Bible, not to mention page after page of science textbooks. And I spent years at a desk learning how to do long division in pounds, shillings and pence. What a waste of my neurons, all clogged up with knowledge and rules that I can now obtain with the click of a mouse.

26    I have little doubt that the printing press changed the way that humans used their memories. It must have put out of business thousands of masters of oral history and storytelling. But our brains are so remarkably adept at putting unused neurons and virgin synaptic connections to other uses. The basic genetic make-up of Homo sapiens has been essentially unchanged for a quarter of a million years. Yet 5,000 years ago humans discovered how to write and read; 3,000 years ago they discovered logic; 500 years ago, science. These revolutionary advances in the capacity of the human mind occurred without genetic change. They were products of the "plastic" potential of human brains to learn from their experience and reinvent themselves.

27    At its best, the internet is no threat to our minds. It is another liberating extension of them, as significant as books, the abacus, the pocket calculator or the Sinclair Z80.

Just as each of those leaps of technology could be (and were) put to bad use, we should be concerned about the potentially addictive, corrupting and radicalizing influence of the internet. But let's not burn our PCs or stomp on our iPads. Let's not throw away the liberating baby with the bathwater of censorship.

## Maryanne Wolf, Cognitive Neuroscientist

28 I am an apologist for the reading brain. It represents a miracle that springs from the brain's unique capacity to rearrange itself to learn something new. No one, however, knows what this reading brain will look like in one more generation.

29      No one today fully knows what is happening in the brains of children as they learn to read while immersed in digitally dominated mediums a minimum of six to seven hours a day (Kaiser report, 2010). The present reading brain's circuitry is a masterpiece of connections linking the most basic perceptual areas to the most complex linguistic and cognitive functions, like critical analysis, inference and novel thought (ie, "deep reading processes"). But this brain is only one variation of the many that are possible. Therein lies the cerebral beauty and the cerebral rub of plasticity.

30      Understanding the design principles of the plastic reading brain highlights the dilemma we face with our children. It begins with the simple fact that we human beings were never born to read. Depending on several factors, the brain rearranges critical areas in vision, language and cognition in order to read. Which circuit parts are used depends on factors like the writing system (eg English v Chinese); the formation (eg how well the child is taught); and the medium (eg a sign, a book, the internet). For example, the Chinese reading brain requires more cortical areas involved in visual memory than the English reader because of the thousands of characters. In its formation, the circuit utilizes fairly basic processes to decode and, with time and cognitive effort, learns to incorporate "deep reading processes" into the expert reading circuit.

31      The problem is that because there is no single reading brain template, the present reading brain never needs to develop. With far less effort, the reading brain can be "short-circuited" in its formation with little time and attention (either in milliseconds or years) to the deep reading processes that contribute to the individual reader's cognitive development.

32      The problem of a less potentiated reading brain becomes more urgent in the discussion about technology. The characteristics of each reading medium reinforce the use of some cognitive components and potentially reduce reliance on others. Whatever any medium favours (eg, slow, deep reading v rapid information-gathering) will influence how the reader's circuit develops over time. In essence, we human beings are not just the product of what we read, but how we read.

33      For me, the essential question has become: how well will we preserve the critical capacities of the present expert reading brain as we move to the digital reading brain of the next generation? Will the youngest members of our species develop their capacities for the deepest forms of thought while reading or will they become a culture of very different readers—with some children so inured to a surfeit

of information that they have neither the time nor the motivation to go beyond superficial decoding? In our rapid transition into a digital culture, we need to figure out how to provide a full repertoire of cognitive skills that can be used across every medium by our children and, indeed, by ourselves.

34     *Maryanne Wolf is the author of* Proust and the Squid: The Story and Science of the Reading Brain, *Icon Books, 2008*

## THINKING CRITICALLY

1. Why does Naughton refer to Nicholas Carr's article in *The Atlantic* as "an intellectual grenade"? Explain.

2. Naughton notes that just because people have fretted about the impact of each new piece of communication technology (including writing and printing), and life went on, it doesn't mean that their fears were not valid. What concerns are people expressing about the Internet and Google? What response do you think people a generation hence will have regarding these fears? Explain.

3. What view does writer Sarah Churchwell hold about the Internet and its influence (or non-influence) on our brain?

4. "No one today fully knows what is happening in the brains of children as they learn to read while immersed in digitally dominated mediums a minimum of six to seven hours a day." What impact does Dr. Maryanne Wolf fear the Internet could have on the developing brain?

5. How much time do you spend with digital media daily? Is it pretty much an all-day thing? Would you be able to go without access to any digital media for an extended period of time? A day? A week? A month? Explain.

## WRITING ASSIGNMENTS

1. Wolf wonders, "How well will we preserve the critical capacities of the present expert reading brain as we move to the digital reading brain of the next generation? Will the youngest members of our species develop their capacities for the deepest forms of thought while reading or will they become a culture of very different readers—with some children so inured to a surfeit of information that they have neither the time nor the motivation to go beyond superficial decoding?" If you have grown up in a digital world, try answering Wolf's questions. Consider the way you read, what you read, and how long you read. Do you think you have time to read long books or articles? Do you prefer information in shorter summaries? Finally, do you think your brain is any different than the brain of your parents or grandparents? Explain.

2. Question 5 in the Thinking Critically section above asks you hypothetically whether you could do without digital media for an extended period of time. Conduct an experiment in which you avoid digital media for a set period of time-a day, several days, or even a week if possible. This experiment means cell phone and handheld device use, Internet use (even for school), and video games. Keep a notebook with you at all times to record any concerns, frustrations, obstacles, or surprises you encounter during your experiment, and write about the experience. How did having no access to digital communication and media influence your daily life? The way you think and retrieve information? The way you communicate with others? Explain.

# Mind Over Mass Media
*Steven Pinker*

> Many of the articles and essays in this section have described the way technology is changing our brains, and not necessarily for the better. In the next article, an opinion editorial by Steven Pinker, the noted linguistic scientist explains why the hype is much ado about nothing. Yes, our brains may be influenced by new technology and new ways of seeking information, but that doesn't mean that these changes are bad. Rather, digital technology makes us more efficient, helps us think better and more efficiently, and allows us to approach research and promote discovery in ways never possible before.
>
> Steven Pinker is a psychology professor at Harvard University. He is internationally recognized for his research on language and cognition. In addition to being published in scholarly journals, his essays have appeared in popular media, including *The New York Times, Time,* and *Slate*. He is author of several books, including *The Language Instinct* (1994), *How the Mind Works* (1999), *Words and Rules* (2000), and *The Stuff of Thought* (2007). This opinion/editorial appeared in the June 10, 2010 issue of *The New York Times*.

1 New forms of media have always caused moral panics: the printing press, newspapers, paperbacks and television were all once denounced as threats to their consumers' brainpower and moral fiber.

2 So too with electronic technologies. PowerPoint, we're told, is reducing discourse to bullet points. Search engines lower our intelligence, encouraging us to skim on the surface of knowledge rather than dive to its depths. Twitter is shrinking our attention spans.

3 But such panics often fail basic reality checks. When comic books were accused of turning juveniles into delinquents in the 1950s, crime was falling to record lows, just as the denunciations of video games in the 1990s coincided with the great American crime decline. The decades of television, transistor radios and rock videos were also decades in which I.Q. scores rose continuously.

4 For a reality check today, take the state of science, which demands high levels of brainwork and is measured by clear benchmarks of discovery. These days scientists are never far from their e-mail, rarely touch paper and cannot lecture without PowerPoint. If electronic media were hazardous to intelligence, the quality of science would be plummeting. Yet discoveries are multiplying like fruit flies, and progress is dizzying. Other activities in the life of the mind, like philosophy, history and cultural criticism, are likewise flourishing, as anyone who has lost a morning of work to the Web site Arts & Letters Daily can attest.

5 Critics of new media sometimes use science itself to press their case, citing research that shows how "experience can change the brain." But cognitive neuroscientists roll their eyes at such talk. Yes, every time we learn a fact or skill the wiring of the brain changes; it's not as if the information is stored in the pancreas. But the existence of neural plasticity does not mean the brain is a blob of clay pounded into shape by experience.

6 Experience does not revamp the basic information-processing capacities of the brain. Speed-reading programs have long claimed to do just that, but the verdict

was rendered by Woody Allen after he read "War and Peace" in one sitting: "It was about Russia." Genuine multitasking, too, has been exposed as a myth, not just by laboratory studies but by the familiar sight of an S.U.V. undulating between lanes as the driver cuts deals on his cellphone.

7     Moreover, as the psychologists Christopher Chabris and Daniel Simons show in their new book "The Invisible Gorilla: And Other Ways Our Intuitions Deceive Us," the effects of experience are highly specific to the experiences themselves. If you train people to do one thing (recognize shapes, solve math puzzles, find hidden words), they get better at doing that thing, but almost nothing else. Music doesn't make you better at math, conjugating Latin doesn't make you more logical, brain-training games don't make you smarter. Accomplished people don't bulk up their brains with intellectual calisthenics; they immerse themselves in their fields. Novelists read lots of novels, scientists read lots of science.

8     The effects of consuming electronic media are also likely to be far more limited than the panic implies. Media critics write as if the brain takes on the qualities of whatever it consumes, the informational equivalent of "you are what you eat." As with primitive peoples who believe that eating fierce animals will make them fierce, they assume that watching quick cuts in rock videos turns your mental life into quick cuts or that reading bullet points and Twitter postings turns your thoughts into bullet points and Twitter postings.

9     Yes, the constant arrival of information packets can be distracting or addictive, especially to people with attention deficit disorder. But distraction is not a new phenomenon. The solution is not to bemoan technology but to develop strategies of self-control, as we do with every other temptation in life. Turn off e-mail or Twitter when you work, put away your Blackberry at dinner time, ask your spouse to call you to bed at a designated hour.

10    And to encourage intellectual depth, don't rail at PowerPoint or Google. It's not as if habits of deep reflection, thorough research and rigorous reasoning ever came naturally to people. They must be acquired in special institutions, which we call universities, and maintained with constant upkeep, which we call analysis, criticism and debate. They are not granted by propping a heavy encyclopedia on your lap, nor are they taken away by efficient access to information on the Internet.

11    The new media have caught on for a reason. Knowledge is increasing exponentially; human brainpower and waking hours are not. Fortunately, the Internet and information technologies are helping us manage, search and retrieve our collective intellectual output at different scales, from Twitter and previews to e-books and online encyclopedias. Far from making us stupid, these technologies are the only things that will keep us smart.

## THINKING CRITICALLY

1. What is Pinker's view of digital media? How does he support his position? Explain.

2. Why do cognitive neuroscientists "roll their eyes" when they hear concerns that new media is changing our brains? Explain.

3. Do you believe that email, Twitter, and other digital media distract you? Do they prevent you from focusing on tasks? Why or why not?

4. Pinker offers a solution to the concern that digital media can overwhelm us— turn it off. Is this solution feasible? Why or why not?

## WRITING ASSIGNMENTS

1. Review the book Pinker cites in his article, *The Invisible Gorilla: And Other Ways Our Intuitions Deceive Us* by Christopher Chabris and Daniel Simons. Connect the points made in their book to issues raised in this chapter about digital media.

2. Write your own opinion/editorial on the issue of digital media and its influence on our brain and use of language. You may refer to experts in this section or rely on your own experience as a "digital native" or "digital immigrant."

## MAKING CONNECTIONS

1. Try to imagine what your life would be like without digital media—email, Twitter, a cell phone. Would it be better? Worse? Write an exploratory essay describing what your life would be like without any digital media in it.

2. Critics such as Carr believe that the Internet is taking away our ability to be deeply involved with prose, which restricts our creative thinking skills. Yet Steven Pinker argues that the Internet encourages us to think creatively, efficiently, and rapidly. After reading these essays, explain why you believe one viewpoint is more valid than another, in whole or in part, and why.

3. Is there a connection between how you communicate using digital media and the way you feel about the people you communicate with? For example, do digital media eliminate the need for awkward social interactions? Does a good tweet or a bad email influence your view of the sender? Explain.

4. Research the work of one of the linguists mentioned in this chapter (Whorf, Chomsky, Lieberman, Lakoff, Slobin, Sapir, Pinker, Boroditsky, etc.). Write a paper summarizing his or her theories and contributions to the connections (or not) between language and thought.

5. Write about an experience with language in which you were able to think differently about something as a result of having new vocabulary to describe your world, thoughts, and interactions with others.

6. Write about a relationship you had with another person in which digital media played an important role in how you connected and felt about the other person.

7. Research how the Internet is influencing how we think and how it may or may not be changing our brains. Will the Internet be the next significant influence on our physical evolution? How might our bodies change?

# Credits

## Image Credits

**Page 28:** Printed by permission of the Norman Rockwell Family Agency. Copyright © 1943, the Norman Rockwell Entities. **Page 32:** Courtesy Toyota Motors North America, Dentsu America. **Page 36:** © Aliaksei Lasevich/Shutterstock. **Page 39:** © akg-images. **Page 40:** © Kavaler/Art Resource, NY. **Page 41:** © Snark/Art Resource, NY. **Page 55:** www.Cartoon-Stock.com. **Page 89:** © Thinkstock. **Page 115:** © George B. Abbott. **Page 125:** © Stock Connection Blue/Alamy. **Page 177:** © Minitrue.it. **Page 201:** © Julien Thomazo/Photolibrary. **Page 239:** From caglecartoons.com by Patrick Corrigan. Copyright © 2011 by Pat Corrigan. **Page 255:** © BananaStock/Thinkstock. **Page 282:** © Roz Chast, Conde Nast Publications/www.cartoonbank.com. **Page 309:** © Mike Russell/Alamy. **Page 351:** © Robert Mankoff, Conde Nast Publications/www.cartoonbank.com. **Page 355:** © America/Alamy. **Pages 389, 391, 393, 395:** Images courtesy of The Advertising Archives. **Page 397:** Used by permission of Deutsch Inc. as Agent for the National Fluid Milk Processor Promotion Board. **Page 420:** © John S. Pritchett. **Page 422:** © Jim Morin/Cartoonists & Writers Syndicate. **Page 423:** From caglecartoons.com by Jeff Parker. Copyright © 2011 by Jeff Parker. **Page 425:** © Susan Walsh/AP Images. **Page 451:** By permission of Mike Luckovich and Creators Syndicate, Inc. **Page 476:** © Sebastian Kaulitzki/Shutterstock. **Page 498:** CALVIN AND HOBBES © 1993 Watterson. Dist. By UNIVERSAL UCLICK. Reprinted with permission. All rights reserved.

## Text Credits

Michael C. Corballis. "From Hand to Mouth," from *From Hand to Mouth*. © 2002 Princeton University Press. Reprinted by permission of Princeton University Press.

Susanne K. Langer. "Language and Thought" from *Fortune* magazine, April 1944. Reprinted by permission.

Steven Pinker. "Horton Heared A Who!" from *TIME*, Nov. 1, 1999. © Time Inc. 1999. Reprinted by permission.

Ben Zimmer. "Chunking," from *The New York Times,* Sept. 16, 2010. Reprinted by permission of the author.

Margalit Fox. "Another Language for the Deaf" from *The New York Times*, April 14, 2002. © New York Times, Inc. 2002. Reprinted by permission.

Malcolm X. "Homemade Education" from *The Autobiography of Malcolm X*. © 1964 Alex Haley and Malcolm X. © 1965 Alex Haley and Betty Shabazz. Reprinted by permission of Random House, Inc.

Christine Rosen. "In the Beginning Was the Word," from *The Wilson Quarterly,* Autumn 2009. Reprinted by permission of the author.

Julia Keller. "Is PowerPoint the Devil?" (original title, "Killing Me Microsoftly"), from the *Chicago Tribune Magazine*, Jan. 5, 2003. Reprinted by permission.

Peter Norvig. "The Gettysburg PowerPoint Presentation" and "The Making of the *Gettysburg PowerPoint Presentation*," from www.norvig.com, July 2,2003. Reprinted by permission of the author.

Geoffrey Nunberg. "Blogging in the Global Lunchroom," from commentary broadcast on "Fresh Air," April 20, 2004. Reprinted by permission of the author.

David Crystal. "Texting," from *ELT Journal,* Jan. 2008. Reprinted by permission of Oxford University Press.

Kris Axtman. "'r u online?': Evolving Lexicon of Wired Teens," from *The Christian Science Monitor,* Dec. 12, 2002. Reprinted by permission.

Ammon Shea. "The Keypad Solution," from *The New York Times,* Jan. 22, 2010. Reprinted by permission.

Robert Kuttner. "The Other Side of E-Mail," from *The Boston Globe*, April 19, 1998. Reprinted by permission.

Tyler Cowen. "Three Tweets for the Web," from *The Wilson Quarterly,* Autumn 2009. Reprinted by permission.

Peggy Orenstein. "I Tweet, Therefore I Am," from *The New York Times,* July 30, 2010. Reprinted by permission.

Janet Holmes. "Women Talk Too Much." from *Language Myths*, Penguin Press, 1999. Reprinted by permission of the author.

Ronald Macaulay. "Sex Differences," from *The Social Art: Language and Its Uses*, © 1994, 1996 Ronald Macaulay. Reprinted by permission of Oxford University Press, Inc.

Deborah Cameron. "What Language Barrier?" from *The Guardian,* Oct. 1, 2007. Reprinted by permission.

Tony Kornheiser. "Women Have More to Say on Everything," from *The Los Angeles Times,* Aug. 2, 2000. Reprinted by permission of Creators Syndicate.

Deborah Tannen. "Oh, Mom. Oh, Honey," *The Washington Post Outlook Section,* Jan. 22, 2006, B1, B4, © Deborah Tannen. Reprinted by permission. Adapted from the book, *You're Wearing THAT?: Understanding Mothers and Daughters in Conversation.* New York: Random House, 2006; paperback: Ballantine.

Teri Kwal Gamble and Michael W. Gamble. "Nonverbal Behavior: Culture, Gender, and the Media," from *Contacts: Communicating Interpersonally. (*Boston: Allyn and Bacon, 1998) © 1997 Pearson Education. Reprinted by permission of the publisher.

Jennifer Akin. "Interpersonal/Small-Scale Communication," from Beyond Intractability.org. Reprinted by permission.

David Grambs. "The Like Virus." First published in *The Vocabula Review* (www.vocabula.com) August 2001, an online journal about the English language.

# Index of Titles and Authors